THE INNER SEA

THE INNER SEA

THE MEDITERRANEAN AND ITS PEOPLE

by

Robert Fox

SINCLAIR-STEVENSON

First published in Great Britain by
Sinclair-Stevenson Limited
7/8 Kendrick Mews
London sw7 3hg, England

British Library Cataloguing in Publication Data

A CIP catalogue record for this book is available from the British Library.

ISBN 1 85619 054 4

Typeset by Rowland Phototypesetting Limited
Bury St Edmunds, Suffolk
Printed and bound in Great Britain by
Clays Limited, St Ives plc

To Mediterranean Friends

Contents

A Note of Thanks

ONE of the best pieces of advice I ever received, was given me by my friend Rafael Atienza in the gloomy cavern of his office in old Seville. 'If you intend to traverse the whole of the Mediterranean, don't be too logical. Go backwards and forwards, retrace your steps so you can compare the experience of different peoples and lands, and enjoy the contrasts.' Rafael should know: he is the descendant and heir of one of Spain's greatest seventeenth-century explorers, the Marquess of Salvatierra.

At the time, in the autumn of 1984, I wondered if I would have the time or means to follow this recommendation. But in the years since I managed to follow the plan through accident rather than design, continuously crossing and recrossing the Inner Sea in body and mind. The experience has been as rewarding and stimulating as the current Marquess of Salvatierra suggested – but the perpetual mental and physical peregrination has made the account of the journey the more difficult to write. The book has been prepared episodically, compiled over four years between reporting assignments, many themselves in the Mediterranean. The experience is distilled from half a lifetime's wandering, reading and gossiping.

Another important piece of advice was offered by some old friends in Milan. 'You must give statistics where you can,' was the counsel of Roberto Menghi, one of his city's leading architects, 'otherwise your account will be superficial.' Now in Italy, in Naples especially, the charge of being 'superficiale' is a grave one. In Neapolitan dialect and in Italian it carries a more weighty indictment than the English epithet; it implies flightiness and vanity, carelessness and wilful ignorance.

I have not taken Roberto Menghi's advice literally, because statistics in the Mediterranean context can be dangerous things. They have a life of their own, and like Humpty Dumpty's words in *Through the Looking Glass* they often respond to the demands of their paymaster. Very few of the official tabulations and statistics I encountered in my Mediterranean voyages have proved entirely reliable. Frequently they simply do not add up, or flatly contradict each other. Italy has three main statistical institutes, sometimes coming to quite varying conclusions. Some figures from respected sources, such as the UNEP (United Nations Environmental Programme) projections on population growth in the area, are based on broad approximation. Many international compilations are flawed by the prejudices of the individual nations which are responsible for supplying the raw data. Thus the UN records that Albanian males have amongst the highest life expectancy in all Europe, largely on the say-so of the bureaucrats in Tirana. The strength in numbers of many of the minorities of the Mediterranean, ethnic and religious, tends to be underestimated in the records.

In the remoter parts of the Mediterranean and its fringes, truth becomes a scarce commodity, like water in the desert. It becomes flexible and stretches to meet local demand. It is leavened by rumour, gossip, myth, tales and romance.

A favourite phrase of medieval Italian chroniclers is 'si dice', 'they say that . . .' It drives the purist historians and scientific researchers of archives quite frantic. But it makes good journalism. The chronicler uses the formula to tell the reader what people thought and believed at the time; it signals what was in the air in the piazza, chancery and tavern. The fourteenth-century Florentine chronicler Giovanni Villani described the effects of torrential rain and storms over many months in lower Tuscany. The air was heavy with damp, the crops did not grow, and 'they say the earth itself was poisoned'. What they said was good reporting, a piece of acute observation. A contemporary of Villani in Siena, one Agnolo di Tura del Grasso, is usually written off as an infernal purveyor of rumour and nothing more. But when he talks about the devastation of the Black Death in Siena he describes how he himself buried his sons, and in such a way that he is obviously recording his own experiences; 'si dice' has become poignant first-hand reporting.

I have made liberal use of chronicler's licence in this account of my interpretation of the modern Mediterranean, and there is a fair amount of 'si dice' in it. What Mediterraneans old and new believe, hope and fear, interests me as much as what can be culled from cold records of the authorities and the state archives. After all, this is not an academic work, nor that otiose and overrated literary form, the finely written travelogue. It is a piece of journalism, a reporter's chronicle if you like.

Many of my researches and investigations took place in village piazzas and markets, the kafenion and Turkish tea house, with raki and mezzes, thick coffee and fine green tea to help the flow of gossip, dispute and rumour. Some of the conversations might be dialogues – real exchanges of views, with some unexpected conclusions – a pale shadow of the spirit of the symposium of the ancients or the *convivio* of Dante's time. I have spent hours wandering through Old Jerusalem with my friend George Hintlian, the Secretary of the Armenian Community there, pondering on such items as diaspora, exile and alienation, the movement of peoples and cultures round the Inner Sea, and the future of the minorities, the Kurds, the Palestinians and the Armenians themselves. Not surprisingly, we came to few definite answers.

Such things make the commerce of Mediterranean friendship, which has a radiant spontaneity and openness quite unlike any other. After working for six months in Italy on a leading newspaper in Milan, I was summoned by the former owner, one of the most formidable matriarchs in the city. 'I just wanted to say that we would like you to be friends of this family for life,' she stated simply with a directness and warmth most northern Europeans find impossible.

My journeys and activities about the Mediterranean have been sustained, shaped and supported by many good and generous friends of the Inner Sea. Preparing this volume has tested the friendship of not a few at home in England, not least my family. It is dedicated to them all, Mediterranean friends in body and spirit.

Prologue: The Sea and its People

THE early Arab and Jewish cartographers called the Mediterranean the Inner Sea. The label is apt, for its appeal is interior and abstract as much as external and physical. For most civilised people the Mediterranean today is a postcard in the mind, a souvenir of where their modes of thought and taste began.

For the ancient Egyptians it was 'the Great Green Sea', and for Homer's Greeks it was 'the wine-dark sea', a source of danger to be feared and propitiated as much as to be used and navigated. In the Roman mosaics displayed at Antioch the deity of the Sea (Thalassa) is shown as a raven-haired virago, with the muscles of a shot-put champion, ready to devour all who sail before her. Captains of Venetian argosies would lay offerings before the pearl-studded icon of the Madonna of the Deep in St Mark's to ensure a safe and prosperous voyage.

The Mediterranean is an untidy place with an untidy past – which makes it particularly difficult to write about. Manolis Andronicus, the archaeologist who recently discovered the tomb of Philip II of Macedon, Alexander the Great's father, says that, after a lifetime of living and working round its eastern shores, he finds the notion of the Mediterranean 'elusive'.

My first view of the Mediterranean was more than thirty years ago. Coming over the Sierra Nevada from Cordoba in Andalusia, we saw the flat, glittering lake beyond Malaga. As we stopped to survey the scene, two lorry drivers shoved my head into a horse trough fed by the ice-cold waters from the mountains. It was the baptism for the relationship of a lifetime. As traveller, student, journeyman reporter, I have worked in the Mediterranean more than anywhere else, including my native country. The first night on the shores of Andalusia we camped on the beach of Almuñécar – it was deserted save the donkeys carrying cane to the sugar factory, and a captain of the Civil Guard exercising his arab charger. Today that wild and lonely beach lies buried under the fortifications of a massive hotel complex.

In the years after the journey through Spain, before the hordes of mass tourism had ventured beyond their bridgehead in Majorca and the Costa

Brava, my interest in the Mediterranean switched to Italy, a country whose geography I know better than that of Britain. This relationship started unspectacularly with a spot of art – learning the language and studying paintings for a history degree at Oxford. In 1966 at the beginning of my final undergraduate year I was given a scholarship to look at Romanesque Art in Apulia. It was a rare chance, and I was as fascinated as much by Apulia in the 1960s as the twelfth-century Romanesque. The beggar children in Lecce were the toughest and wildest I had seen in all Europe.

As time and holidays permitted I continued with some gentle scholarship, researching the rural history of medieval Siena. In the morning one could spend a few pleasant hours flicking through the records of the State Archive in the Palazzo Tolomei, which had the best balcony view of the death corner of the *palio*, the horse race round the central square, the Piazza del Campo. In the afternoons, when the archive was in siesta, we could walk the lands of the *contado*, the subject territory of the medieval Commune of Siena. It is now a wonderful moonscape of rounded contours and bald hills, scraped and smoothed by the erosion of wind and rain. The story of the rural Mediterranean, the village and the land, have continued to fascinate me, as a son of the soil, as much as the charms of the great cities.

My affair with Italy took an unexpected twist when out of the blue I was offered a column as a guest writer on the leading Milan daily, *Corriere della Sera*, in the autumn of 1976. It enabled me to see from the inside a country that summarised many of the divisions of the Mediterranean, with its south sunk in almost Third World poverty, and the rich north desperately trying to scale the Alps and become part of northern Europe. The tensions were no abstract thing, either. A colleague at *Corriere* was killed by the Red Brigades' terrorists, one journalist friend was murdered by the Mafia in Catania and another driven by them out of Sicily altogether.

From Italy my work as an itinerant reporter took me in widening sweeps across the Mediterranean, to Spain, Yugoslavia, Greece and Cyprus, and on the southern and eastern shores to Algeria, Libya, Lebanon and Israel. Most of these journeys were brief tasters, to cover elections and earthquakes, natural and human upheavals, but they were enough to whet the appetite for further voyages.

The chance came in 1984 when I was asked if it was possible to write a book about the whole of the modern Mediterranean and its countries, *tutti quanti*. It was more of a challenge, a dare, than a serious and sober commercial proposition. Close friends in the journalistic trade said the mission was impossible, the subject too chaotic and incoherent. At a supper in my old college, Magdalen, where we had just celebrated the memory of our fellow history alumnus Edward Gibbon, an eminent historian of Renaissance Italy and the contemporary Arab world told me not even to try to make sense of the modern Mediterranean.

In an access of naivety or pure megalomania, I did not heed the advice of the historian and the journalists and took up the dare. It nearly cost me life and livelihood, but it rewarded me with a passion and education of a lifetime.

The best approach, I thought, was to look at the diversity of the Mediterranean, the parts rather than the sum. I tried to visit as many of the countries of the shore and the big islands as time and means would allow. This is the chronicle of that tour, a fragmented journey of several years. And I did succeed in reaching every Mediterranean country in the years from 1984 to 1987.

Since the Mediterranean is an untidy concept, any faithful account is bound to reflect its untidiness. Following the examples of a medieval chronicle or eighteenth- and nineteenth-century itinerary I have dwelt on the personalities, events and places, that happened to catch my eye and imagination. Gossip and rumour are the social cement and annals of the Mediterranean and the recording of anecdote as evidence began there with Herodotus, the father of history, lies, or modern journalism, according to taste.

Much of the incentive for the enterprise was a view that the modern Mediterranean was seriously underestimated by modern Europe and North America, and it will be an increasingly important part of their lives. This is one of the few convictions that was not seriously altered by the experience of my journeyings, and I hold it more firmly than ever now. Almost every other assumption I made as I set out for the Pyrenees in September 1984 I have had to discard. So fragmented is the human mosaic of the modern Mediterranean, that I thought it would be impossible to develop any overall themes. Facetiously I banned the word 'theme' from my mental vocabulary – except where it was used as the specific term of an administrative province of the Byzantine Empire, as in the 'theme' of Byzantine Apulia.

It was to take some months, years even, to realise I was wrong. From the *tesserae* of the mosaic of the modern Mediterranean, filed and worn by time and change, several clear themes and points of debate do emerge – and they affect us all. I was in for some surprises.

Even the physical outline of the sea, its architecture and proportion, today are deceptive. On the map it looks a neat package, a large lake, bounded by the shores of Asia, Africa and Europe. But the Mediterranean has come down in the world since prehistoric times. In history it lives in much reduced circumstances from former times. Before the Alps formed, it was part of the Tethys, the sea girdling the earth from west to east from some 6,000 miles – roughly the same length of Marco Polo's great land route, the Silk Road, from the shores of the Bosphorus to ancient China and the Pacific coast. As the new mountains formed, the Tethys dried up and the water returned to fill only the western portion, which was to become the Mediterranean.

The shoreline of the main basin of the Mediterranean makes a highly elastic, or porous, frame. It does not define the cultural and political limit of the Mediterranean world. It is a matter of debate whether this should embrace the Black Sea basin, and the river systems of the Tigris and Euphrates, the Gulf and the Nile Valley. Portugal does not share the Mediterranean seaboard, yet the Portuguese were among the foremost of modern colonisers of the Inner Sea, their culture and language pervades it from the dialect of Genoa to the ports of North Africa and the Levant.

The clearest definitions of the boundaries of the Mediterranean are held to be its flora and the light. It takes the sun roughly three hours to track from Jerusalem in the east the 2,250 miles to the Straits of Gibraltar and the Atlantic in the west. In the journey the sun hardly deviates from a straight line and the rare and consistent quality of the sun on blue or turquoise sea and white rocks is unique. On shore the boundaries of the Mediterranean world are set by the trees and plants, the olive, fig, pomegranate and the dense woodland, the maquis or macchie.

Like so much that has taken root in the Mediterranean in history, most of the plants are immigrants, and only a few are natives. The olive is believed to have come from Mesopotamia and Persia. One of the few natives is the holm oak, one of the ingredients of the maquis, which once mantled the shores of Anatolia and France and the islands of Corsica and Sardinia. Abraham is believed to have sheltered under the holm oak when he settled in Hebron. Another native is the carob, now being cultivated for homeopathic medicines. Its husks can yield a lactose which is a poor man's chewing gum, and it is said the Prodigal Son fed on them when he went absent without leave, and from the sustenance they gave as the 'locusts' of St John in the wilderness they are still known as 'Baptist's Bread'. On a visit to the Jewish ghetto on the island of Djerba in Tunisia one Saturday, I found groups of boys sitting outside their houses chewing carobs, their main diversion on the day of rest.

Teeth, lips, shirts were stained black, and the husks blew down the streets like swarms of locusts.

The story of botanical invasion of the Mediterranean matches the human tales of takeover and merger. Some of the most vigorous plant specimens are the most recent arrivals. The brilliant purple-flowered bougainvillea came from the Pacific in the eighteenth century. In the last century the eucalyptus or gum arrived from Australia and now covers the eastern shores from Libya to Lebanon like a rash. The miracle of horticultural production is the tomato, thanks to new low-cost frames of plastic sheeting, one of the biggest eyesores of the Mediterranean scene today. More than thirty million tons of tomatoes are grown for export each year – so lucrative is the industry in Naples and southern Italy that the local mafias have taken it over.

Like the plants almost none of the human tribes of the Inner Sea is a native of its present dwelling place – they almost all appear to have hailed from somewhere else, Dorian Greeks, Albanians, Arabs, Turks, Spaniards and Berbers. The metaphor of the Mediterranean mixture is Macedonia, a place where peoples mixed. The Italian and French words for a fruit salad are 'macedonia' and 'macédoine'. Most successful of early Mediterranean colonisers were the Phoenicians, who worked by absorption and merger as much as military conquest. They became so integrated with the Etruscans seven centuries before Christ that the art and craftsmanship of the two peoples of that era are all but indistinguishable.

More curious is the story of a people still with no real name who appeared in the thirteenth century before Christ and attacked the coasts of Phoenicia, Tyre, Sidon and Byblos, and the Nile Delta in about 1200. From the depiction of their eventual defeat by Ramesses III on his mausoleum at Madinet Habu near Luxor they are known simply as 'the Peoples of the Sea'. They are shown as tall men with feathered head bands, while others have helmets with horns. The 'Peoples of the Sea' are one of the great propaganda discoveries of the modern Mediterranean. Now popular myth describes them as coming from the islands of the Aegean, a race which raided as far as Corsica and Sardinia, and one of the early inhabitants of Crete. After defeat by the Egyptians they settled Gaza. Some modern Palestinians claim them as ancestors, the early Philistines, and the credential for their ancient title to the land of Palestine.

The Phoenician habit of migration and merger still persists round the Inner Sea. The boundaries and frontiers between peoples are not as neat and distinct as might be suggested by the lines on maps devised by the architects of peace conferences and congresses. As significant as the movement of peoples round the Mediterranean has been the sheer growth of its populations. In the past century this has been startling and it is one of the underlying themes of this book; it is becoming a motor of profound change throughout Europe.

Up until 1800 the population round the Mediterranean was relatively sparse and static. The Roman Empire ruled about 50 million people, and its former colonies round the sea did not change much over the centuries. The later Empire was 'grazed thin by death' according to St John Chrysostom. The population of the Ottoman Empire through disease and war went down in the first decade of this century, but with European colonisation came medicine and hygiene, and by the middle of this century the numbers started rising dramatically.

In 1986 the United Nations Environment Programme expressed the dilemma in crude diagrammatic form. In 1945, said its report on the Mediterranean Environment, two thirds of the coastal population of the Inner Sea lived on the European shore of the Mediterranean, which runs from Gibraltar to the Bosphorus. By 1985 half lived on the European shore and half on the southern and eastern coastline. By the end of the century the picture was set to reverse, a third living on the European side and two thirds at least in North Africa, Anatolia and the Levant.

While the populations of Europe, with the exceptions of Romania and Albania, remained static, elsewhere they are exploding. Half the Palestinian population of the West Bank and Gaza was under sixteen by 1990, and had hardly begun reproducing. By the year 2025, Egypt, Turkey and the three central Maghreb countries of Tunisia, Algeria and Morocco are expected to have a hundred million inhabitants. Cities of the coast like Istanbul and Cairo would have more than 20 million citizens each, many living in semi-rural slums on the outskirts.

The population of the Mediterranean countries is set to increase from about 350 million in 1985 to 550 million by 2025, quite a modest increase by comparison with what is likely to happen in parts of Asia, Africa and Latin America. But the impact on the fragile coastal environment will be huge, if not catastrophic. In the same period to 2025 UNEP calculated that the traffic of tourists was likely to go up from 80 million to 200 million.

One of the most curious landmarks I found on my journey was on the side of the vestry at Roncesvalles, the pass in the Pyrenees where according to the *Song of Roland* Roland and Oliver fought the infidel Saracens. In truth they were probably surprised by a band of marauding Basques. The plaque on the church records the height above sea level at Santander on the Atlantic and at Alicante on the Mediterranean. The surface of the Mediterranean is 87 centimetres lower – almost a yard. The Mediterranean is a low, shallow and relatively dead sea. Its harvests of fish are much thinner than off neighbouring coasts in the Atlantic. The waters move slowly, with only three narrow outlets at the Bosphorus, Gibraltar and the Suez Canal, and are replaced only every eighty years. More is lost by evaporation than can be replaced by rainfall, and the basin is topped up by the Atlantic and the great rivers descending into the Black Sea.

The main sources of pollution are from chemicals poured into rivers, the discharge from cargo ships and tankers, and human sewage. As the invading army of tourists grew, and the Mediterraneans themselves left the land for the cities of the coast, it was feared that the whole area faced ecological collapse. Though the strain has been severe, and the environment suffered grievously, it has not yet reached the scale of disaster predicted in the early 1970s.

Partly this is due to timely action by various agencies, among them the Cousteau foundation at Monte Carlo, Greenpeace and the United Nations Environmental Programme. UNEP succeeded in persuading nineteen countries of the Mediterranean, including Albania eventually, to sign up to a Mediterranean Pollution Programme and the Blue Plan for conservation of marine life. Some success was scored in restricting the discharge of chemical waste into rivers, cutting the levels of mercury, and prohibiting oil tankers flushing their holds in the open sea.

In my journey round the Inner Sea, it was possible to eat healthy, clean sea food in most parts of the coast – I found the most succulent crustaceans in industrialised ports like Izmir, Split and Palermo. But Mediterranean nature is not so easily mocked nor taken for granted. UNEP in its 1983 report said an adult of average body weight should not eat more than three fish meals a week – on some parts of the Tuscan coast they ate them seven days a week still – and such was the risk of mercury poisoning from swordfish that they should not be tasted more than once in six weeks. The appearance of swarms of jellyfish and a tidal wave of green sludge in the Adriatic in the summer seasons of 1989 and 1990 were early warnings that the ecology of the Inner Sea was out of joint.

Sadly, two of the Mediterranean's rarest species, the monk seal and the loggerhead turtle, have been victims of the monstrous tide of mass tourism. Of all living creatures the loggerhead, say experts, has the closest link in the evolutionary chain to the dinosaurs. They have been harried and driven from their nesting grounds on the Greek island of

Zakinthos and Dalyan on the Aegean coast of Turkey by speculators clearing space for new hotels.

The biggest single polluter is man himself, the new urban Mediterranean and his paying guests the tourists. As the end of the twentieth century approaches ninety per cent of the big cities and resorts of the coasts are dumping sewage into the sea untreated. Beaches in Italy have had to be closed on health grounds each summer. In the eastern basin of the Mediterranean the biggest single source of human pollution has been the megalopolis of Cairo, where the Nile is used directly as both drain and domestic tap.

Though many if not most of the new Mediterraneans are town dwellers, they have not abandoned their rural ways and habits altogether. In the large cities like Rome, Athens, Istanbul and Cairo, many of the outer districts and suburbs resemble small villages – the country has come to town. Income has to be spread thin through the extended family of the new arrivals in the city. The younger males make meagre pickings from casual work as shoe-shine boys, porters and carriers, bearers of messages, windscreen washers, and from indulgence in petty crime, hand-bag snatching, pickpocketing and dealing in drugs on the street. It has all the precariousness of the casual labour on the land, bringing in fruit and olives, scaring birds or picking stones from rough mountain pastures.

The Mediterraneans have never quite taken to the nation state nor to the centralised industrial city with the enthusiasm of their neighbours in Northern Europe or their cousins in North America. Even the most public activity seems to have a hidden aspect of private enterprise for most Mediterranean societies. Loyalty to the family, the clan and the community, comes above any abstract notion of public duty or service to the state – for good and for ill. Once a friend in Italy asked me to take an exam in English language proficiency on behalf of his girlfriend. When I protested, he said, 'But you are my friend; you have lived in my house – and it is yours whenever you wish,' as if this argument was irrefutable. The offer of friendship was not conditional – we were friends for life and so we should aid each other as best we could against a hostile world.

The family and the community are still powerful bonds in the Mediterranean, and appear to increase as the world becomes a more confusing and crowded place. The family is a private support system in a way that has been lost in northern Europe. In Naples they call it *L'arte d'arrangiarsi* – literally 'the art of arranging things' between members of the family and neighbourhood which becomes a private barter economy. But the clan-economy and family loyalty has its darker side. Often it can be downright criminal. In its most obvious and notorious form it becomes the Mafia, with its ruthless and violent codes of behaviour. In southern Italy, Sicily, and Sardinia at the end of the 1980s, the decade of the travels in this book, the code of *omertá* is as strong as ever. Literally it means 'manliness', but in practical terms it means the pledge to silence, which will be enforced by death, kidnapping or hostage-taking.

The model of the Mafia stems from the primitive societies of the old Mediterranean, and is now enjoying a fresh lease of life and energy in the new Mediterranean. Sociologists call this activity 'parallel power', where clans and syndicates endeavour to subvert public authority to their own private ends. The customs of the Druze in Lebanon and Syria are an exercise in parallel power, as much as the hidden rites of the old clans of the Sicilian and Calabrian Mafia. The extent and virulence of such customs and activities came as a considerable surprise. In my travels I found them – with national and cultural variations – in almost every land of the shores of the Inner Sea, from the tourist rackets of the Balearics and the Costa Brava, the underworlds of Marseille, Milan and Naples, the Turkish criminal mafias trading, through the Balkans, the offshore trading and smuggling of Tunisia, and the commerce of drugs and arms on which Lebanon now floats.

The darker forms of family life in the mafias, are one of the durable exports of the new Mediterranean. The Sicilian Mafia has been celebrated in novel and film as something quaint and antique. The patriarchies portrayed in films like the *Godfather* series and *Prizzi's Honour* have a folkloric sentimentality. The movies on the same theme made in the Mediterranean countries themselves are altogether more trenchant and realistic. The masterpiece of the mid-Seventies was Francesco Rosi's *Illustrious Corpses* (*Cadaveri Eccellenti*), based on a novella by Leonardo Sciascia, which prophetically showed how organised crime could subvert the political as well as the social order.

Today many of the mafias of the Mediterranean, from Turkey, Spain and France as well as Sicily and Italy, operate on a global scale with links to the drugs and arms dealing and money laundering of the syndicates of Latin America, and South-East Asia.

The influence of the Mediterranean in Europe beyond the mountains and North America is growing, and not only through the subversions of organised crime. The northern societies are becoming increasingly Mediterraneanised in manners and tastes. Self-respecting cities from Cologne to Calgary have trattorias and tavernas, and kebab and pasta are as common as steak and potatoes. Shopping streets the world over are decked with the banners of the new Mediterranean taste, the designer

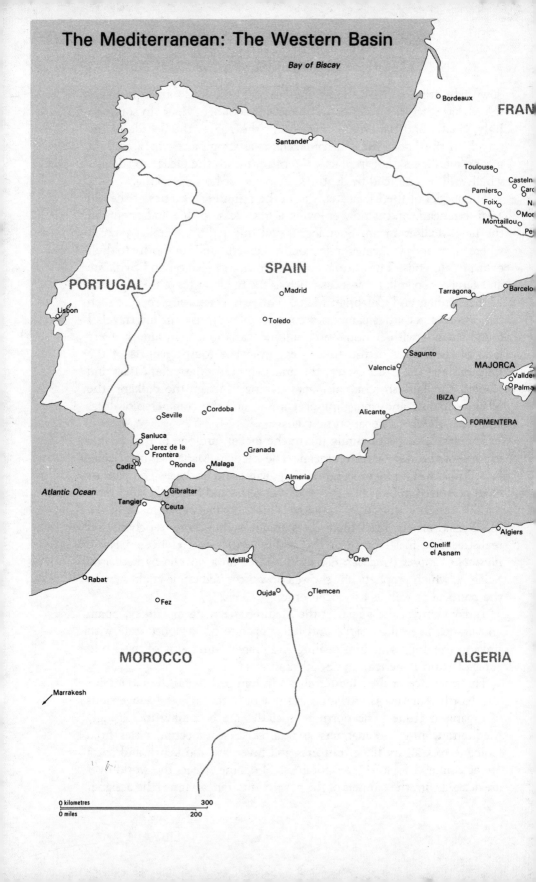

The Mediterranean: The Western Basin

Bay of Biscay

FRAN

○ Bordeaux

Santander ○

Toulouse ○

Casteln
○ Carc
○
Pamiers ○
Foix ○   N
○ Mor
Montaillou ○
Pe

SPAIN

Madrid ○

PORTUGAL

Lisbon ○

Toledo ○

Tarragona ○   ○ Barcelo

Sagunto ○

Valencia ○   MAJORCA
○ Valld
○ Palma

IBIZA

○ FORMENTERA

Seville ○   Cordoba ○   Alicante ○

Sanluca ○
Jerez de la ○
Frontera   Granada ○
Cadiz ○   Ronda ○   Malaga ○

Atlantic Ocean   Almeria ○

Gibraltar ○
Tangier ○ ○ Ceuta

○ Algiers

○ Cheliff
el Asnam

Melilla ○   Oran ○

Rabat ○

Oujda ○   Tlemcen ○

Fez ○

MOROCCO   ## ALGERIA

← Marrakesh

0 kilometres   300
0 miles   200

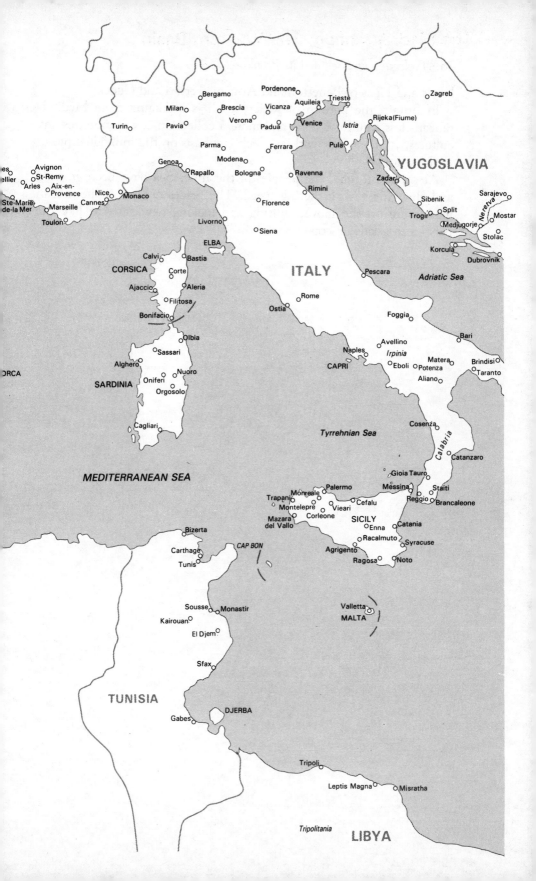

labels and logos of Benetton and Armani, Ferrari and Gucci.

In Britain the pattern of society itself is becoming more Mediterranean, less a cultural unity and more a collection of communities and cultures. It is a mosaic with as much emphasis on the individual pieces as the whole.

At the same time, the peoples of the Inner Sea have been growing and changing with gathering speed. The pieces of the Mediterranean mosaic are on the move, shifting and making new patterns like the pebbles in a kaleidescope.

One: Spain

i Andalusia: Mediterranean Overture

THE Romans, they say, planted the first vineyards along the Guadalquivir, and its landscape of rough meadow and tight terraces has altered little since. Modern Spain is turning back to the old world and discovering a new role in the Mediterranean. After forty years of isolation under General Franco, Spain is once again taking a leading voice in the councils of the Inner Sea.

Much of this renewal and rediscovery has taken place in Andalusia, which is bounded on the north and west by the valley of the Guadalquivir. It is one of the largest regions – the Spanish call it an *autonomia* – in the Mediterranean. It is also one of the most depressed and backward areas of the European Community – only Calabria and Basilicata in southern Italy are poorer. But the government in Madrid has set out to change all this. Timed to coincide with the 500th anniversary of the discovery of the New World, it launched a huge investment plan to change the face of Andalusia and its capital, Seville. Just about everything was to be redeveloped in the city except the cathedral containing the few mortal remains of Columbus himself.

A world exhibition devoted to the 'Age of Discovery', 'Expo '92', was to provide the excuse for opening up central Spain and the industrial north to the Mediterranean. The canal and the river, and their wharves, were to be altered and revamped; a huge motorway, the Mediterranean Highway, was to stretch as far as Valencia, and another to Madrid; a high-speed train link was to be built to Madrid, and the capacity of Malaga airport to be doubled and that at Seville quadrupled. The bill for the whole programme was to be nearly $100 billion.

The people of Seville were deeply divided about the prospect of the biggest change to their city since Columbus. 'I have pressed for this exhibition from the beginning,' Soledad Beceril told me. The first woman ever to serve in a Spanish cabinet, she believed that it would bring badly needed money and work to young Andalusians and establish Seville as one of the foremost cultural, and educational centres of Europe. But her husband, Rafael Atienza, whose ancestor had commanded the Spanish armada, viewed the prospect with foreboding. Like some gloomy character from Cervantes, he saw the old culture of Seville fading fast under the impact of 200,000 visitors a day.

Seville, like Andalusia itself, is a paradox. Though Spain was traditionally the most Roman Catholic monarchy in Europe, the underlying influences in Andalusia were Moorish and Islamic. Islamic Andalusia was a huge area straddling the Mediterranean at the Straits of Gibraltar, the greater part of which stretched into Africa. The bell tower of the Giralda by the cathedral in Seville was once a minaret, designed by the same architects as the Tour Hassan in Rabat and the tower of the Sultan Yacoub Mansour's mosque in Marrakesh. The Christians recaptured Seville in 1268, and the last of the Moorish kings in Spain was defeated in Granada in 1492. The year of Columbus was also the year in which the most Catholic King and Queen, Ferdinand and Isabella, stamped out the kaleidoscope of faiths and cultures which had made Andalusia one of the most varied and colourful civilisations of Europe; the Moors were defeated and the Jews expelled, forced to convert or martyred with hideous cruelty.

Although the capital of Spain's biggest Mediterranean region, through its river Seville opens onto the Atlantic. And the discovery of America made its fortunes. The key to this new wealth lay in the *fueros*, the royal monopolies in the commerce with the New World. The biggest gothic basilica in Europe, the cathedral, is a monument to the enterprise of empire in the Americas. Not far from Columbus's funerary box is a small statue of a madonna, blind and lost in thought – Our Lady of Antigua, from whom the Caribbean island takes its name. One of the most curious celebrations of Andalusia's past takes place in the choir, raised like a stage before the massive Flemish altar screen. Three times a year choirboys wearing breeches, jerkins and hats with ostrich plumes, perform with castanet and tambourine the dance of the *sexes* (from the number six), said to celebrate the city's deliverance from the Moors though the steps of the dance itself may be Moorish, or at least Mozarab (Moorish-Christian), in origin.

Even the massive fortified doors at the end of the nave can only be opened for kings and queens; there was great rejoicing when they were flung wide, after remaining firmly bolted for fifty years, to admit King Juan Carlos and Queen Sophia after their accession in 1975. The reign of Juan Carlos has been one of the great success stories of the Mediterranean in recent times – and one with particular relevance to Andalusia and Seville, for throughout the 1980s public life in Spain was dominated by the partnership of Juan Carlos and his socialist prime minister, Felipe Gonzalez, a native of Seville.

Given the tortured history of the house of Bourbon-Parma, his success came as a surprise to the old guard of the Franco dictatorship. The King had been brought up in exile, and spoke English, French and Italian better than Spanish, and had the disadvantage of having been nominated by Franco as his heir, but he played his cards with discretion and care. His style was one of studied self-effacement and informality; overnight he was to become the hero of his people and the saviour of their newly-won democracy.

In the early evening of 23 February 1981, a band of Civil Guards suddenly burst into the chamber of the Cortes or parliament, fired shots at the ceiling and shouted to the deputies to lie down. They were led by a moustachioed officer in a tricorn hat who looked like the demon king in a pantomime – Lieutenant-Colonel Antonio Tejero Molina, a compulsive *golpista* or coup-maker. When the outgoing Defence Minister, General Guttierez, told the Guards to put down their weapons and go away, he was knocked to the ground; the parliamentarians were then locked in their offices.

The conspirators' next move was made by the military commander in Valencia, Milans del Bosch, who ordered armoured units onto the streets. A few hours later, however, King Juan Carlos told the Spanish people over radio and television that he had ordered all military commanders to return to barracks, that he would not abdicate or go into exile, and that he would defend democracy and the constitution to the last. At dawn the round-up of conspirators began, among them the King's own military adviser, General Armada.

It is not clear how extensive the conspiracy was, though it was known that the older officers, nurtured under Franco, had been restive. Colonel Tejero's own performance included an element of high farce. While in jail, he wrote a self-justificatory article for a popular magazine. The piece was pure Don Quixote. The Colonel saw the glory of old Spain being betrayed. He wanted to preserve this wonderful land, he said, with its rolling plains and gentle hills, its lovely women with their sparkling eyes and lustrous thighs.

On the eve of the 1982 general election another plot was uncovered at a very early stage. General Milans and Colonel Tejero were again implicated, but it seemed like a dying whimper. That December Felipe Gonzalez Marquez and the Socialist Workers' Party (PSOE) won a clear majority, and it soon became evident that respect was mutual between the new prime minister and the king. Gonzalez was one of the youngest prime ministers in Europe, and a born politician. At Seville University he had been a student leader, and on graduating he had gone into exile to help establish the Socialist Party for the day democracy returned to Spain. In power he was to prove a pragmatist rather than an ideologue. He fought a successful referendum to stay in NATO, but not in its integrated military structure – though many of his party rank and file wanted Spain out altogether. He opened up the economy, and took Spain into the European Community, where he took an important role in steering it towards a single market and a single currency. He and his advisers had a clear view of how a European partnership should evolve, bearing in mind the Mediterranean dimension. His party adviser on foreign affairs, Señora Elinora Flores, believed that special arrangements would have to be made for trade, aid and investment with Mediterranean countries like Turkey, Morocco, Tunisia and Algeria, for fear that barriers erected by the European Community against them could be mutually damaging. In this Spain has been more coherent and far-sighted than its European partners in the Mediterranean, Greece and Italy.

Many of Gonzalez's team were from Andalusia, which remained his power base, though at the local level matters did not go so well. Like all parts of Europe's rural south, Andalusia has been affected by the need to change and to create new jobs, and by the demise of the old agricultural economy. But the centre of Seville retains its old charm. Its broad house-fronts painted in yellow and rose, their balconies and shady courtyards festooned with vines and geraniums, roses and marigolds, still look like a backdrop to Don Giovanni or The Marriage of Figaro, yet behind the façade much has changed. These small palaces, which once housed several families, have been converted into offices, schools or self-contained apartments for tourists; while the gypsies, who used to entertain with flamenco dancing the great families in town for the Easter procession of the penitents and the feria and horse sales of the following week, are gone. Once at the heart of Andalusia's culture of bullfighting and flamenco-dancing, they have now become a social and economic embarrassment and have been banished to unsightly suburbs on the edge of the city.

In the hot evenings of late summer people spill out of bars and cafés into the squares and streets of the old town. Most are drinking beer from a new form of hostelry – the cervezeria, or beer shop – that has replaced the wine shop or bodega. Many have no job, and little immediate prospect of one. Petty crime has become a way of life on the streets of Seville. Cars are broken into, handbags snatched, and premises burgled with depressing regularity.

The authorities have blamed much of the lawlessness on drug-trafficking from Morocco which has moved on from hashish grown in the Moroccan Rif to include heroin from south-west Asia and the Middle East. Despite rigorous surveillance of passengers at the ferry ports, the traffic is increasing, and has become the preserve of organised crime. Not that this is an entirely new development, for these parts have long been the preserve of smugglers. Smuggling encouraged the growth of clandestine societies, subversive clubs, and the forerunners of mafias that infest the shores of the Mediterranean from the Maghreb to the Middle East.

The smugglers and the gypsies of the bullfight and flamenco were the inspiration of Mérimée's tale, and Bizet's opera, of *Carmen*. In 1830 Mérimée heard in Seville of a young officer who had thrown away his career on a gypsy whom he then murdered. The enormous brick barracks of the cigarette factory where many real-life Carmens must have worked is now the home of the University of Seville. Today roughly 50,000 students are on the register, from the province of Seville's population of about two million. According to the vice-rector, Professor Rafael Sanchez Mantero, a historian of the contraband culture, nearly a quarter of all students drop out each year, but 'many are paid to stay here by their parents, as there are no jobs to go to'. The creation of the new universities at Malaga, Cordoba and Cadiz to supplement Seville and Granada had done little to alleviate unemployment in the region.

Underlying the economic crisis, Mantero believes, is the question of land – an issue since the attempt to break up the great monastic estates in the 1830s. The occupation of farms by peasants and workers has been the main platform of the anarcho-syndicalist movement, which waged several land wars in the countryside of Andalusia in the Twenties and Thirties, and sided with the Communists during the Civil War. Owner-occupation of land remains one of the principal demands of the Agricultural Workers' Union. The socialist regional authorities in Andalusia have reacted by offering small family holdings in six different areas set aside for reclamation of derelict land, but they may be too late, and the schemes may be killed by production quotas and price restrictions on Mediterranean produce imposed by the EC.

Jerez de la Frontera, the home of the sherry industry, is busy adapting to modern market requirements. Mentioned as 'sheris' in the Arabic map of the world produced by Al Idirisis for the Norman kings of Sicily in 1154, sherry's pedigree is jealously guarded by the producers of Jerez, and was the basis of a successful demand that the European Community should not accept products like Cyprus or South African sherry as being in anyway comparable to their own. Even so, the great sherry houses or *bodegas* have been facing a tough time, with labour disputes, falling markets, takeover bids and even the odd whiff of bankruptcy. Like the trades in malmsey, madeira, marsala and port, sherry has been promoted by a peculiar marriage of the sunny south with British mercantile phlegm.

'I am sorry I can't move more quickly,' said Manuel Gonzalez, getting up to greet me. 'I am a bit shaky on my pins – had a little accident with the motor, you know.' Don Manuel was one of the senior directors, with two cousins, of Gonzalez Byas, one of the few old *bodegas* with a largely family ownership – most of the others are part of multinationals or Spanish conglomerates. Gonzalez Byas beat off bids from both Guinness and Seagram in 1988, when they bought out their English partners for seven generations, the Byas family.

The cousins speak the highly polished English of P.G. Wodehouse of more than fifty years ago, and there is a hint of Blandings Castle about the manicured lawns and sprawling outhouses of the old Bodega Gonzalez.

'We had a spot of trouble with the tax inspector,' explained Don Manuel. 'Got up to a few dodges, overseas trading companies and so forth. It was useful to move offshore to the Bahamas, but the natives got a bit sticky, so we moved on to the Cayman Islands.'

Don Manuel confessed that 'we're rather a dull sort of family – not much to write home about'. But the Gonzalez had a raffish past. The founder of the *bodega* had been forced to leave the court in Madrid 'after a spot of bother'. The card of the family used to keep a barrel of 'something a bit special' in a little taproom where his chums could come for a quiet glass of *fino* as sherry is always known in Spain, and a smoke. 'So they just called it Uncle Pepe's sherry.' Thus was born the most famous *fino* of all, Tio Pepe.

The *bodega* itself is a series of huge storehouses for the barrels or butts of wine. One of the earliest is an elegant wrought-iron bandstand built for the visit of the formidable Queen Isabella in 1862; in the most modern shed, the vault is bigger than St Peter's. The butts are stacked one above each other, as part of the process called the *solera*, the key to sherry-making. Butts containing wines from different years are layered, so that the contents trickle down from one to another. The final product is a blend of the harvests of several years. The barrels in store are constantly sampled and tested, but this is done by nose, by bouquet rather than by taste. 'My father could do three hundred barrels in a morning if necessary, chalking each one with a number of strokes to mark the quality,' recalled Don Mauricio, Manuel's cousin, 'he used to say, the less chalk, the better the sherry.'

In the last store is the hall of fame, where celebrity visitors have chalked their names on the ends of the butts. Close to the signature of General Franco is that of Winston Churchill, while farther on is the monogram of the most famous voice in sherry advertising, Orson Welles. The Princes Edward and Albert (later Edward VIII and George VI) left their marks in distinctly shaky hands in 1927. According to Don Manuel 'the two princes made a day of it, and retired slightly the worse for wear.'

In those days eighty per cent of all sales were to England, and the main office was in London. For many years the managing director was a member of the Byas family, who had found it hard to adjust to office hours after distinguished service in the First World War. 'We used to keep important papers out of his way after lunch,' recalled Don Carlos, another of the Gonzalez cousins. 'Instead of managing director, we called him the damaging director.' Sales to Britain have fallen steadily – the Dutch are now the highest consumers of sherry per capita – with exports to Britain levelling off at about 100,000 butts a year. Each butt holds 500 litres, and total output is about 300,000 butts per annum.

Fino has never been widely drunk in Spain, and wine is less popular than it was. By the Eighties Spain had become a nation of beer drinkers. Gonzalez Byas took the hint and, having sold a packet of family shares to the Italian firm of Martini and Rossi, diversified into brandy, aniseed drinks and new sparkling wines which they produce with great success in Catalonia and Aragon.

But Spain's new prosperity in the mid-Eighties brought about a brief revival. The new rich of Madrid rediscovered sherry and the sherry cocktail as an after-hours tipple and an older clientele became interested; Don Carlos recalled a phone call from an old friend who had returned from a shooting holiday in Scotland. 'Did you know they drink sherry in Scotland, Carlos?' he said in astonishment. 'I mean they drink a lot of it – every day before lunch and sometimes before dinner. I didn't know it was so good. Could you let me have a case or two of the stuff?'

After my tour of the *bodega* and the grape-crushing plant, Don Mauricio took me to a lunch of fresh langoustines at a café on the coast road to Cadiz. He talked about the prospects for the land and the firm, and for the nature reserve of the Doñana. He had been helping to save the vast wetland and park from further encroachments – the last stretches of Andalusian beach on the Atlantic seemed doomed to suffer the same death from hotel and car park as those on the Mediterranean. Prime Minister Felipe Gonzalez, a namesake but no relation, had helped in a new tree protection project. Don Mauricio was worried about the recent strikes and militancy among the seasonal grape-pickers. It was a reflective meal in the windy weeks at the end of October, and we discussed the changes of rural Spain with some apprehension. Outside a gentle mist of rain was brushing the vines. 'Ah, just right for growth,' said Don Mauricio. 'Next year we should have a fine harvest.'

'Andalusia is divided into three parts – the valley of the Guadalquivir, the mountains of the Sierra Morena, and the old kingdom of Granada in the north-east, the Penevetica,' explained Rafael Atienza. His is the finest house in the mountain town of Ronda, its elaborate Renaissance portal, incorporating classical motifs and the family arms is its only touch of ostentation; inside is a maze of winding corridors and deep chambers. From the terrace one gets the same view across to the mountains that the Romans must have seen.

The town has Roman foundations, but the clusters of white houses that curl round the mountain like the shell of a mollusc have a Moorish appearance. The Moors remained here well after the re-conquest by the Spanish kings – in one house I was shown an elaborate wooden coffered ceiling made by Moorish carpenters in the sixteenth century. The fame of the town later rested on a family of bullfighters, the Romeros, who invented many of the moves involved in fighting bulls on foot, and the use of the cape and the *muleta*, the short stick-like sword. The eighteenth-century bullring at Ronda is the oldest, and one of the largest, in Spain. The museum includes photographs of its two most famous modern *aficionados*, Ernest Hemingway and Orson Welles.

In *For Whom the Bell Tolls* Hemingway recorded the most infamous episode in Ronda's recent history. The town is cut in half by a deep ravine, called the *tajo*. In the first months of the Civil War Republicans seized the town, rounded up Falange sympathisers, including priests, monks and schoolteachers, and hurled them down the canyon. A matter of weeks later the town was taken by Franco's Moroccan troops, whose bloody vengeance is still talked about.

A century ago Ronda was much favoured as a resort by the ladies of the Gibraltar garrison during the heat of summer. Its cool slopes lined with pine and rhododendron, the Sierra Ronda was the equivalent of the hill country bungalows of British India. A Lord Fullerton built the railway from the coast to Ronda, and the main hotel is still called the Reina Victoria.

But for Rafael Atienza tourism has been responsible for the destruction of much of what was good in old Andalusia. The bullfight, its deep symbolism going back to the ancient Mediterranean of the Hittites and the bull-worshippers of Crete, had now become the vulgar preserve of Japanese tourists; yet for him it evoked a time when meat was scarce and the bull a rare sacrifice. The old fortified farms, or *fincas* were being pulled down and replaced with modern ranch-house cafés and hotels.

'Spanish taste is dreadful,' he claimed. 'Nothing of value has been produced in the past fifty years. The emphasis is on the artificial, plastics and glass, with a conscious rejection of traditional architecture, crafts-manship and natural materials, for these are reminders of poverty. Anda-lusian culture is disappearing; flamenco and bullfighting are now things for busloads of tourists.'

In his fight against the pollution of mass tourism he had joined forces with the mayor of Ronda, a former malaria expert named Dr Julian de Zulueta. The mayor had campaigned in vain against a large, bilious pink building thoughtlessly located in front of the elegant eighteenth-century façade of the bullring – the headquarters of a savings bank, the Caja de Ahorros de Ronda, which had made several fortunes out of the tourist boom of the Fifties and Sixties when the Costa del Sol became the Blackpool of the Mediterranean. The bank had been firmly supported by most conservative politicians, said the mayor, who was a Gonzalez social-ist, as well as by the Church.

The mayor was a realist: he knew that Ronda needed to attract busi-ness, and had even recommended the siting of a state hotel or *parador* in an historic building. Two car assembly plants below the town could not offer enough employment, and a third of the houses in the old town were empty.

This, I realised later, is the tragedy of the package tour business throughout the Mediterranean: it brings employment in patches. Fifty years ago half Spain's population made their living from the land; now the proportion is about ten per cent of those in work. Catering for the planeloads of beach-worshippers does little for the economy away from the coast, while offering young people of the villages livelihoods which are often unstable and impermanent.

The Andalusian city least affected by the destructive fads of tourism is Cordoba. The line of the houses along the Guadalquivir cannot have altered much in centuries. Its agricultural provincialism contrasts with Granada, a university city which is an important administrative and industrial centre.

Cordoba was once the rival of Baghdad and Cairo, its skyline dotted with the domes, and minarets of more than a hundred synagogues, mosques and churches. In medieval times, under the Arabs, it boasted the greatest slave market in southern Europe, and it is still dominated by one of the most extraordinary pieces of Muslim architecture in Europe, the Mezquita, built and extended under successive caliphs and lords after the first Arab invasions across the Straits of Gibraltar in 711 AD. The succession of Arab dynasties began with the Ommayyids, who fled there from Syria in 756 AD and were succeeded by the Almoravides in 1031, and then – last and most cruel – by the Almohades, who ruled from 1149. Eventually Cordoba was captured by the Christian forces of Ferdinand III in 1236. For the Jews, especially, this was followed by a period of terrible intolerance. In 1371 the Christians carried out an organised massacre, of the kind that would later be called a pogrom. As a result, of the Almohades' persecutions, one of the most famous Jewish scholars, Rabbi Moses Maimonides, fled to Acre and then Cairo, where he became physician to the heirs of Saladin. His masterpiece, *The Guide to the Perplexed*, is still used as a commentary on Talmudic scripture and Aristotelian scholasticism.

The Mezquita stands in a grove of orange trees and palms, its elegant minaret soaring into the autumn mist. The forest of black and white striped horseshoe arches in the prayer hall has no equal anywhere. The *mihrab* or the prayer niche, lined with myriad tiles and chips of coloured glass, is the finest of all the mosque's embellishments by the Caliph El-Hakim II and it has been carefully conserved, despite the building's conversion to a Christian cathedral. Permission for this was given by the Emperor Charles V. When he saw the result, he made one of his few memorable utterances. 'You have built here what anyone might have built anywhere else,' he told the architects, 'but you have destroyed what was unique in the world.'

Not far from the square of the Mezquita, past the Hotel Maimonides and down a little alley, is the El Caballo Rojo restaurant. Its Mozarab menu provides a taste of Arab Cordoba, of the delicious herb soups and the lamb marinated with nuts and honey that the caliphs might have sampled as they listened to the *Tales of the Thousand and One Nights*.

East of Cordoba, along the banks of the Guadalquivir, Islam has returned to the village of Pedro Abad. Perched on the hills above the road are the twin minarets of a new mosque, the Mezquita Bisharat, which looks more appropriate to the landscape of India than of Iberia. It was built in 1982 by a Pakistani missionary movement, which originated in 1908 and, among other things, believes it guards the tomb of Christ in Kashmir, whither he had wandered after surviving the cross. The movement's new base is in London; it claims thousands of converts across the world, many in America.

It was certainly not short of funds for building new mosques. At Pedro Abad the building was presided over by a gentle Pakistani called Imam Mahmoud Ahmed Nasir. When I arrived, he was just ushering out a class of law students from the university of Cordoba. 'They had come to discuss the workings of Islamic law, the Sharia,' he explained. 'I think some might come to believe that the *Reconquista* [the Christian reconquest of Spain from the Muslims] might have been a mistake.'

Although the Imam was having difficulties learning Spanish, his daughters went to school in the village and had got to know the community. In 1919 and 1931 Pedro Abad had been the scene of serious disturbances by anarcho-syndicalists seeking to acquire land and half of it still forms part of the estate of the Duchess of Alba. Half the population had no work, according to the Imam. He was scathing about the performance of the Catholic Church: 'The three churches are badly attended. No serious person is interested in the church here, and one church has been converted into a technical school.'

This allowed him to launch into the message of his mission. Mosques, he said, had been built at Marbella for Gulf Arabs with houses there. At Pedro Abad he had small congregations of fifteen or twenty at most, but his purpose was not conversion. He wanted to preach the Islam of love and understanding, and not Khomeini's creed of war and vengeance. 'We believe in spreading the message of love and peace of Islam because we believe the whole future of humanity depends on it. Neither Christianity nor Communism can solve the basic problems. I am very sure Islam will come again, not only to Spain, but in the whole world according to the prophecies of God revealed to the Holy Prophet Mohammed. We are sure that Islam will be the prevalent religion of the next century, because only Islam can solve the problems of the world today.'

The gentle Imam dismissed me, saying he had a migraine. Down by the Guadalquivir a fierce sirocco was beating the olive trees and willows. For years afterwards the Imam pursued me with postcards, maintaining his duty in the vanguard of Islam's new advance across the Mediterranean.

ii Toledo: The Old Mediterranean Renaissance

Clouds pile high like columns of dark smoke over the green hillside, the grey buildings shrink into the valley. On the hill is the huge brutal block of the Alcázar, the citadel and then barracks for the army officers' training academy under Franco. The view of Toledo is still as El Greco painted it four hundred years ago.

Toledo was once the royal capital of Spain and the most Mediterranean of cities, in which Jews, Muslims and Christians rubbed shoulders, trading and exchanging thoughts on the nature of the world and the logic of Aristotle. All that came to an end when, in 1492, Ferdinand and Isabella passed their decree outlawing the Jews. Their fates were various: some fled, some converted, and many were put to death after horrible tortures by the Holy Office and the Inquisition. Some of the cruellest inquisitors, like Torquemada, were converted Jews.

The expulsion of the Jews and the defeat of the Moors at Granada left Spain culturally a much duller place. As riches began to flow from America, the countryside fell into decay and the kings and queens retreated into their new capital, Madrid, farther into the high plain of Castile.

Recently the Spaniards have been making tardy amends for their neglect of the brilliant medieval culture of Toledo. The most famous synagogue, the Sinagoga del Transito, has been restored, and a museum dedicated to the diaspora of the Sephardic Jews of Spain has been opened. When it joined the European Community, Spain established full diplomatic relations with Israel – the last of the major European countries to do so.

That something new was emerging from the discovery of the old Mediterranean culture was stated with some obviousness in an exhibition in Toledo in 1984, devoted to King Alfonso X of Castile. The contemporary of Henry III and Edward I of England, St Louis of France, and Frederick II Hohenstaufen, he was nicknamed Alfonso the Wise, not because he was clever but because he was an almost promiscuously cosmopolitan patron of all branches of art and knowledge, and his court one of the most brilliant and learned of the time.

The exhibition included collections of arms and armour, clerical vestments, manuscripts, lutes and instruments of all shapes, and mathematical tables prepared by Jewish scholars – and a copy of the Papal Bull excommunicating Frederick II Hohenstaufen, the only Holy Roman Emperor to have allegedly converted to Islam in order to learn the secrets of the necromancy and science of the Muslims.

The message of the whole show was made relentlessly clear in its publicity. Everything was due to the patronage of the new monarchs Juan Carlos and Sophia, who would preside over a new renaissance, placing Spain once more at the forefront of European civilisation.

The monarchy epitomised the breakout from the years of isolation under Franco, who for three generations gave Spain the politics of the sleepwalker. The Alcázar that El Greco depicted in his landscapes of Toledo was one of the most potent symbols of the cause of Franco and the Nationalists of the Falange movement. As the barracks for officer cadets, it came under siege from the Republicans in the opening weeks of the Civil War. Most of the cadets were on leave at the time. The commander of the academy, a fifty-eight-year-old colonel of infantry called Luis Moscardo, was called on to surrender. If he did not, the Republicans said they would shoot his son, an army captain, whom they had taken prisoner. 'If it be true,' telephoned the colonel to his son, 'commend your soul to God and shout "Viva España" and die like a hero.' Whatever the truth of the tale, the son was shot, and the Alcázar had to be relieved by troops from Morocco commanded by General Varela. They then went on a rampage of vengeance, killing wounded militiamen in their hospital beds.

The Civil War is the brutal fact that dominates Spain's development. It caused the deaths of at least a million people and it led to depression, misery and political isolation for generations. It put Franco firmly in the hands of his military, and security and repression became a substitute for any form of ideology. When the old man died in 1975, well advanced in years, he left no political legacy behind. Falangism melted away, as if bearing out Hitler's crude dismissal of it as 'the usual clerico-monarchical shit'.

Franco knew how to keep his distance from the disastrous schemes and foreign adventures of his fellow fascists, Mussolini and Hitler. But his isolationist policies left Spain deprived and cowed. The army was obsessed by its experience of the Civil War, and only in the mid-1980s was it commanded by generals who had not been young officers in the fighting. Most of its operational plans were directed at the defence of the two Spanish enclaves in Morocco, Ceuta and Melilla.

Towards the end, the isolation began to melt. An alliance of convenience was made with the Americans for naval and nuclear bomber bases. The coasts began to be laid waste by tourists in the first flush of industrialised travel, an easy way of acquiring foreign currency for Madrid.

Beside the army and the security police, the Guardia Civil, Franco had tried to rely on the Church to give strength to his regime. But it proved an unreliable ally. Toledo is the metropolitan diocese of the Catholic Church in Spain, rivalled in political importance only by Madrid. The huge gothic cathedral is a vivid testament of the development of the Church since medieval times. In one of the chapels priests still celebrate on special occasions the mass of the Mozarabs, the Arabs who stayed behind and were converted to Christianity at the time when Toledo was becoming the intersection of Christian, Muslim and Jewish cultures.

In 1969 Enrique Tarancon became Cardinal Archbishop of Toledo and later Roman Catholic Primate of Spain. He proved a subtle reformer, steadily prising the Church away from Franco when the dictator died, the Cardinal is said to have celebrated a Te Deum of deliverance. 'The conflicts are over at last,' he remarked, 'but now we begin the difficult times.' He backed the younger clergy against the conservative bishops. As a friend of Pope Paul VI, he supported the reforms of the Second Vatican Council. He condemned Basque terrorism, argued that Spain should be a secular state, and wanted to revise the Concordat, the constitutional treaty with Rome. Satisfied that his task was done, the monarchy and constitution secure, he retired to work as a parish priest in Castile in 1978.

Cardinal Tarancon's secretary was Monsignor Jose Maria Martin Patiño, a professor of theology with the Jesuit's habitual speed of thought and turn of phrase. A diminutive man, he appeared to have the energy of a rubber ball in his black soutane, punctuating his pithy comments with quick puffs on a ceaseless chain of cigarettes.

The monsignor was devoted to the memory of the old cardinal. In 1969 he and the cardinal sent a questionnaire on 260 different subjects to 15,000 parish priests – about half the number now practising in Spain. 'The results were quite surprising, as they showed the priests more worried than the hierarchy about human rights and workers' liberties,' said the monsignor, stubbing another cigarette into an obscene-looking brass gargoyle serving as an ashtray. 'Many priests were close to the socialists and communists. The conservatives accused them of meddling in politics. They were obsessed with dogma, doctrine, church-state relations and fighting Marxism. But this was 1969 and vital questions were now being posed by mass tourism, industrialisation, emigration and the ideas behind Vatican II.'

The new primate encouraged dialogue between the priests and the bishops, which the bishops hated. But their complaints were firmly slapped down by Pope Paul himself. The cardinal wanted a new and constructive partnership between Church and state, and he believed this had been achieved in the Spanish constitution drawn up between 1977 and 1978. 'The Church used to dictate morality,' explained the monsignor. 'Now we take a pluralistic approach to the moral code, with everyone responsible for his or her own behaviour.'

He thought the clergy was going through another bout of conservative reaction, good for neither the Church nor Spain. The number of clergy and new professions for the priesthood were declining rapidly; by 1980 Spain had 70,000 nuns, 20,000 monks, 30,000 priests for a population of about thirty-five million.

The problem, thought the elastic-minded monsignor, lay with the Vatican and Pope John Paul II, whom he saw as an arch-conservative. 'I don't think he's for the democratisation of the Church,' he concluded in his precise Gregorian university Italian, which he used as easily as his native Spanish.

But he and Cardinal Tarancon had bequeathed to Spanish politics a priceless gift. On the death of Franco they agreed that there should be no approved Roman Catholic Church party, nothing like the Italian Christian Democrats, who are heavily influenced in matters great and small by the Vatican. The cardinal stopped the Church meddling directly in the secular concerns of the state, which is one reason why Spain since 1975 has not been plagued by the fragmented loyalties and private feuds of coalition governments. Unusually for the Mediterranean, power has alternated between blocks of conservatives and socialists.

iii Barcelona: Heart of a Nation

Scratch Barcelona and you find the heart of a nation: Catalonia. The Catalans know they are marked out from the rest of Iberia by their language, culture, and tortuous history. They have lived and stayed alive by their wits, for they are the merchants and inventors and gossips of the western Mediterranean. They can also claim to be the makers and breakers of modern Spain, patrons and innovators in music, painting, architecture, commerce and industry. But it was also Catalonia's taste for radical politics that brought about the disaster of 1936, when Barcelona was the setting for the early rounds of the Spanish Civil War.

Under Franco anything Catalan was banned: the language, the politics and much of the culture besides. The Catalans felt themselves a people oppressed and under occupation. The Franco regime, in the manner of modern dictators, drove huge new roads and boulevards through Barcelona itself, as a means of keeping the natives down. But darkness and melancholy are not part of the Catalan character. As soon as the old dictator had gone, Catalonia exploded in a cultural firework display. Within a year or so Catalan was back as an official language of the region; within ten years more than 1200 new books were available in the language, and two daily and two weekly newspapers.

The revival was surprising, since only half of modern Catalonia's six million inhabitants are Catalans: the rest have migrated from Andalusia and Castile to work in the industrial plants of Barcelona and Tarragona. The Catalans are a people of Mediterranean light and the open sea, whose nonchalance and quicksilver touch annoy the heavier and more serious souls of Castile or Aragon. They are one of the few peoples round the shores of the Inner Sea who speak of themselves as Mediterraneans, and are proud of it. A favourite Catalan popular song begins, 'I am a man of the Mediterranean.'

To catch the essence of what it is to be a modern Catalan, one need only step a few hundred yards along the Ramblas, the central thoroughfare that was once a dried-up *wadi* running through the heart of medieval Barcelona. By the sea it offers the traditional maritime fare of rundown bar and sleazy hotel, but further inland the tone becomes more respectable where the trading houses – once the offices of companies trading in tobacco with Cuba or the Philippines – hide their grand façades behind the trees. In the open space between the buildings are stalls laden with books, magazines and published material of all kinds. Nearly half are in Catalan, and cater to hundreds of special interests. Catalans have a passion for associations and clubs, the *circolo* as it is called, and have more than the rest of Spain put together. They are compulsively social and gregarious people.

Barcelona rose to independent power as Charlemagne's empire in northern Europe fell apart in the ninth century AD. It was then that the Counts of Barcelona exploited the role of buffer state between the Franks to the north and the Muslims to the south, and from the first of the line, Wilfred the Hairy (Guifred el Pilos), they built their fortune on the sea. The city had featured in the maritime schemes of the Phoenicians and Romans, and had been a capital of the Visigoths, but by the thirteenth century it was the heart of an empire. A map of the Catalan empire at its height from the twelfth to the fifteenth centuries, shows it stretching as far south to Valencia, to the Balearic Islands, parts of Corsica, Sardinia and Sicily, and the Duchy of Athens in Greece.

It was a commercial as much as a military power. In Barcelona the Council of the Hundred issued a series of regulations called the Consuls of the

Sea – the most celebrated dated 1232, considered the first pieces of modern maritime legislation. The city fathers also introduced one of the first systems of shipping insurance. But the Black Death in the fourteenth century spelt disaster. Banks went bust, and manpower was unavailable for the famous fighting companies of Catalan soldiers. The population of Barcelona was to remain at about 35,000 for centuries; Catalonia itself became absorbed by Aragon, and then by the kingdom of Spain.

Barcelona's fortunes revived with the removal of the privileges in the Americas trade from royal ports like Seville. In the nineteenth century Spain's industrial revolution began in Catalonia, but again plague struck. The first industrial boom was all but crippled because of the ravaging of the vines of Spain and southern France by the phylloxera weevil. Catalonia escaped the first outbreaks in the 1860s, but could not avoid subsequent visitations.

During the nineteenth century the modern Barcelona began to emerge – a city that combined sound, traditional commercial sense with the patronage of wild and radical movements in the arts and politics. It became a home of revolution. Spain's first trade unions, the CNT and UGT, were set up in Barcelona; in 1909 a week's strike called by the socialists and radicals culminated in shootings and the burning of churches and religious houses.

This was the prelude. In 1931 the first Republic of Spain was declared in the city, and by the time the Civil War broke out Barcelona had become the pivot of the Republican cause. George Orwell was astonished and delighted to find it a city 'where the working class is firmly in the saddle,' as he recorded in *Homage to Catalonia*. 'Practically every building of every size had been seized by the workers and was draped with red flags or the thick red and black flag of the Anarchists; every wall was scrawled with the hammer and sickle and the initials of the revolutionary parties; almost every church had been gutted and its images burnt.' But with the fall of Barcelona two years later, in January 1939, the Civil War was effectively over. In a matter of weeks nearly half a million refugees, soldiers and 60,000 wounded had left for exile in France.

Franco immediately banned any manifestation of Catalan spirit and independence. The language was spoken only in backyards and kitchens; on paper it ceased to exist, and some feared it would disappear altogether.

One of those who kept Catalan studies alive in exile was Professor Joan Triadu, who became Reader in Romance Languages at Liverpool University, where he edited an elegant volume of Catalan poetry with parallel translations into English. He returned in triumph, if that is the right expression for such a mild-mannered person, to become Professor of Languages at Barcelona university. He also ran a centre, where up to 1200 people could learn Catalan on most evenings.

Catalan is a mainstream Romance language with origins similar to Italian and Provençal French. It is spoken today in a region from Lerida south to Valencia, and in a variation in the Balearics and parts of Sardinia. In France about a quarter of a million use Catalan in their daily speech, as do some expatriate communities in South America.

The earliest Catalan writer was the medieval monk Ramon Lull, the author of nearly a thousand works on different subjects, in several languages.

After Lull it emerged as a written language once more with the Romantic Revival, or Renaixanca, of the last century and in 1859 a bardic contest called the Floral Games was inaugurated. Catalonia has also produced a powerful revisionist school of historians, whose reassessments of Catalonia's past as well Spain's have been singularly hardheaded.

The banner of Catalan nationalism in politics is carried by the Convergence and Union Party, a coalition of several factions and forces. One section of the alliance was founded by Professor Ramon Trias Fargas, a renowned lawyer from a dynasty of lawyers and literati. Despite the savage reputation of Catalan soldiery, the Catalan nationalists had not chosen the path of violence to press their claims, he explained. In this they differ from the Basque nationalists – though few extremists may still nurture dreams of urban terrorism and guerrilla action to gain publicity.

The path to autonomy has not been easy, he told me. Before the First World War some form of independence was granted to the four provinces of Catalonia, but this was cancelled after ten years by the Spanish dictator Primo de Rivera. After the local elections of 1931, which led to the abdication of King Alfonso XIII (Juan Carlos' grandfather) a Catalan Generalitat was formed, using the name of the governing council in the Middle Ages. This was crushed by Franco after his victory, and the President of the Generalitat, Lluis Companys, was secretly executed.

It was to Companys' exiled successor, Josep Tarradellas, that Adolfo Suarez suggested an autonomous Catalonia under its own Generalitat. The 1977 statute seems to have satisfied very few in Catalonia. According to Trias Fargas, 'It doesn't give real autonomy, as Madrid always manages to take back with one hand what it has given with the other.'

He then castigated 'Spain', whose authority was bad for Catalonia in whatever form it appeared. 'The state had prestige in medieval times. But with the unification of Spain under the Catholic kings, it has been mistrusted. In many respects, Franco was hardly worse than the others, just more authoritarian and cruel.' The socialists wanted to be dictators, he claimed, while his party was for an open economy, minimum state control and a free rein to the Catalan spirit of enterprise.

The Catalan spirit, he said, was a bit of a paradox – romantic and hard-headed, flexible and realistic at the same time. 'We like to talk and we are romantic, but we are also more realistic than other Spaniards. When we were in exile in Colombia we loved to get together. We used to have lunch – Catalans always eat too much – and invite a good speaker. Listening to him the cigars would begin to tremble. We would cry a lot, and everyone would go home happy. Exile and migration are very much part of our story. We have a song, "Emigran", which goes, "Sweet Catalonia, those who leave you are sure to die of homesickness."'

This mixture of fantasy and realism is reflected in Catalan sculpture and architecture in particular. The gothic quarter, the Barrio Gotico, lacks the ponderousness of some other medieval cities. Inside the cathedral the scene is a Mediterranean marketplace. It is used as a short-cut by shoppers, who gossip in front of the confessional booths, their whispers amplified by the soaring fan vaulting. An agricultural note is lent by a gaggle of snow-white geese kept in the yard and ambulatory.

Not far from the cathedral, in an eighteenth-century townhouse built on Roman foundations, is a museum dedicated to Barcelona's most famous adopted son, Pablo Picasso, who came to Barcelona in 1896 from Galicia. The collection shows what Picasso gave to Barcelona and received from the city in its avant-garde heyday in the early years of the century. Sketches for the club Els Quatre Gats – the Four Cats – where he met fellow-artists like Braque, give the flavour of the roaring, radical Barcelona of the time.

The works of Picasso's greatest contemporary in Barcelona, Joan Miro, are housed on the hill of Montjuic, which looks out over the bay and the sprawl of the city with its discreet layout of halls and patios, the museum was designed by Miro's lifelong friend, Josep Lluis Sert, who has made it a combination of concert hall, library and hall for travelling exhibitions as well as the permanent home of Miro's own masterpieces.

Miro's dancing mobiles, rich tapestries and fantastic sculptures are the work of a true modern Mediterranean. He is Catalan to the depths of his creation – witty, oblique, carefully thought through to the last detail. In true Catalan style he could not stick to one thing, involving himself in dance, theatre and film as well as sculpting and painting.

The view of Barcelona's skyline from the hill of Montjuic is dominated by the four spires, giant masonry hollyhocks, of the cathedral of the Sagrada Familia, the unfinished masterpiece of Antoni Gaudi. Gaudi was an architect with the instincts of a sculptor and an engineer. In some respects he too epitomises Catalan genius. He had an intense and private spiritual life, and many of his wonderful designs are wildly impractical. But he was Catalan in his essence and upbringing – his grandfather had been a potter near Tarragona – and a professed man of the Mediterranean. 'We are brothers to the Italians, which makes us more able sculptors,' he declared. 'Catalans have a natural sense of plasticity which gives them a conception of things as a whole and of the relationship of things among themselves. The sea and the light of the Mediterranean countries generate this admirable clarity, and this is why the things of reality never mislead the Mediterranean people but instruct them instead.'

In 1883 Gaudi inherited from another architect the project of building a new cathedral on gothic lines. He was to change his conception of it continuously, and the project itself was to change his life. When he began he was a dandy, his politics fashionably socialist, but as the work went on he became an intensely devout Catholic.

Inside the cathedral he worked and reworked his fantasy of spiralling staircases, ceramic walls and palms and cypresses bursting from arch and pillar. He was killed by a tram in 1926 and his constant changes of plan have made trying to complete the project more than hundred years after it began something of a nightmare.

The best view of Gaudi's finished work is from the Paseo de Gracia, the broad street extending from the Ramblas beyond the Plaza de Catalunya. The Casa Batllo, at Number 43, is a relatively restrained effort compared to his later exuberance. At least it has the façade of a conventional house, though the window mouldings are sinewy and fungoid. The roof, on the other hand, twists and writhes under a spiked ridge like the razor back of a giant iguana. Number 92 shows no sign of any restraint: it is a long surging tide of balcony, roof and windows outside, while inside everything – doors, ceilings, corridors – on the curve. The astonished citizens of Barcelona, on catching the first full effect of this seething pile of masonry in 1906, immediately dubbed it 'la Pedrera' (the quarry). Those inhabiting the apartments are caught between pride at living in such a notable piece of sculpture and frustration at its practical shortcomings.

The view from Montjuic was due for another radical facelift in the closing years of the century; and this time its object was renovation as much as innovation. The occasion and, more importantly, the investment were provided by the choice of Barcelona to host the 1992 Olympic Games, forming part of the celebration of the five-hundredth anniversary of Columbus's voyage to America. It was in Barcelona's old city, in 1493, that the voyager reported his mission accomplished to the Catholic King and Queen, Ferdinald and Isabella.

To Catalans the Olympics had become a cheated birthright. The games were first awarded to Barcelona for 1936, but such were the disorders in the city that Hitler persuaded the Committee to transfer them to Berlin. The Generalitat decided to hold their own alternative international games, for they had already prepared a stadium, sports hall and swimming-pool in the parkland on Montjuic; but the festival was cut short after a week, when the Generalitat ordered the workers' militias to mobilise to defend the Republic. The Civil War had begun. Many of the visiting athletes decided to stay and fight, and began forming the International Brigades.

The team preparing the town plan for the 1992 Olympics was led by Professor Oriol Bohigas, the best known modern architect in Catalonia. In his comfortable English tweed jacket, the professor dispelled any impression of being another dreamy mystic or wild-eyed visionary. 'I don't believe in big town plans in the abstract. I am not a utopian. A city is not a system, more a collection of fragments and communities, particularly this one. I don't start with a general plan, but individual problems in the neighbourhood.'

Professor Bohigas had a lot to work on. The core of Barcelona is the port and the old walled city of Roman and medieval times. The walls themselves were finally removed in the last century when the new industrial city was laid out on a grid by a planner of genius, Ildefons Cerda. He was one of the patriarchs of modern urban planning, the father of the garden city concept and the radial town plan, and the inspiration of innovators like Ebenezer Howard who brought them to fruition in England. His scheme for Barcelona was no monstrous abstraction of lines and grids on a map; Cerda wanted his city to be harmonious, human and a pleasure to live in, bringing a whiff of the countryside into residential neighbourhoods. He arranged apartment blocks and houses round parks; each had access to a patio or courtyard. Balconies and roof terraces formed a Catalan version of the hanging gardens of Babylon. Nothing was left to chance, and everything blended down to the last detail and windows. Some of the original Cerda buildings still stand, rhythmic patterns of shapes and angles, of hexagons, octagons and diamonds in brick.

The harmony of Cerda's vision of nineteenth-century Barcelona suffered grievous damage, from growth of the new suburbs at the beginning of the century, and then from the new thoroughfares of the Franco era. Uncontrolled speculative building resulted in further defacement, and the older quarters between the port and Montjuic sank into melancholy decay.

'My plan is to rearrange the city, to make it more pleasant, without rearranging the population,' declared Professor Bohigas. He would open the older nineteenth-century quarters to the light and give them back the gardens of Cerda's original plan. The slaughterhouse and prison were to be demolished in the neighbourhood of Sants, one of the poorest in downtown Barcelona, to make way for two parks built round the disused railway tracks and station. The old port, once the destination of Columbus, was to be made into a centre for yachting and water sports, with promenades, cafés and housing for the elderly and retired. The commercial port has shifted further down the coast to the south, where its container terminal rivals those at Fos, Genoa, La Spezia and Livorno.

The Olympic development provided an opportunity to improve transport, hotels, and to build badly needed cheap accommodation for the growing student population. The village to house visiting athletes was designed with this end in mind, and the apartments were to be offered for subsidised rent or sale on the open market, the proceeds going to develop student halls nearer the university campus.

The campaign to get the Olympics to Barcelona had been directed with military precision by Pasqual Marigal, who was elected mayor in 1982. His dream of renovating the city was no idle piece of Catalan chauvinism. As a Catalan socialist he thought the policies of the conservative nationalists of 'Convergence and Union' irrelevant or obstructive.

'We have the highest density of population of any European city, except parts of Paris. Something had to be done,' said the mayor, looking decidedly young for his office behind his droopy moustache: like his fellow-socialist Felipe Gonzalez, he was barely forty when he attained office. His conversation was interrupted by bites from a huge bar of chocolate – the only form of sustenance he could fit in to his busy schedule.

With the decline of the old manufacturing methods, one in five of the working population was without job, and this had bred one of the most violent criminal cultures in European. It was a way of life that operated to its own rules, a common feature of Mediterranean ports like Marseille, Naples and Palermo, and based largely on the narcotics trade. The mayor believed he was facing a lost generation of youth in this underworld. 'Suppose each drug user consumes one gramme of heroin a day at 20,000 pesetas a gramme. That means a turnover of one billion pesetas a day. Half that comes from dealing, but half at least must come from crime.' Cure and rehabilitation would have to be within the community, which made the renovation of the older parts of the city all the more essential.

The foremost opera house in Iberia, the Liceu, was built with subscriptions from the Barcelona merchants enjoying the boom at the turn of the century. Inside, the theatre is a wonderful testimony to the city's artistic flowering in the era of *art nouveau*. In 1902 Ramon Casas, the great portraitist of the day, was invited to paint a series of scenes of Barcelona life for its patrons' club, the Circolo del Liceu. With their gleaming oak panelling, the rooms radiate the bourgeois comfort of the age, and Casas vividly evokes contemporary of musical and café life in Barcelona.

One of the best loved stars of the Liceu stage in recent times is the tenor Jose (or Josep to fellow-Catalans) Carreras. We had met a number of times in London, where he had shown himself an outstanding dramatic actor in roles like André Chenier. He had asked me to drop by at the Liceu if I was in town. 'It's more like a party than a rehearsal,' he warned, when I took up an invitation to watch him preparing for a performance of *La Gioconda*. He was right, for while the singing was fine, the Dance of the Hours owed something to the collision choreography of the Marx Brothers.

Jose is the epitome of the modern Catalan – quick-witted, generous spirited, and self-deprecating. His charm and ease of manner belied a difficult upbringing. He had grown up in the poor neighbourhood of Sants in the Franco years when to be Catalan was to be virtually a non-person.

'I was brought up in a lower-class home – you know nice lower-class – in Sants,' he told me. 'We were pretty poor because my father, who came from Figueras, had been a schoolteacher, but his licence had been removed because he had been a Republican in the Civil War. He had to work for twenty years as a municipal cop, guiding the traffic. My mother was Barcelona-born, and worked as a hairdresser. She was very keen on music, and together they pushed me to go to the Conservatory to study. 'Did we speak Catalan then? Of course, absolutely. All the time, in the home, among the family, and with the children playing in the neighbourhood.

'We have a privileged position, more open to Europe than any other part of Spain, and with direct access to the Mediterranean. We are more cosmopolitan than other Spaniards, and very idiosyncratic. The *piña* [the clan] is very important to us – in a positive way. We are entrepreneurs and hate being dependent. We're pretty self-confident, and that's why Catalans are a jokey people.'

Not long after we met at the Liceu, Josep Carreras was to need his Catalan strength of character to fight leukemia, which had cursed others in his family. In a display of sheer will he drove the disease into retreat and succeeded in returning to the concert platform, most often to raise funds for cancer research. He is, as the Catalan song says, a true 'man of the Mediterranean'.

iv The Moon Travellers of Majorca

The seaside resort of Magalluf is a piece of Majorca determined to remain forever England. The waterfront is festooned with English pub signs of a stridently royalist stripe – The Princess Diana, The Prince William and The Britannia. It is Blackpool on the Mediterranean, one of the great meccas of the package tour industry, where entertainment is provided with the rhythm of an industrial production line. One hostelry proudly proclaims 'Piper's Best Bitter flown in from Manchester today'. More black puddings and English fried breakfasts are probably consumed on this stretch of Balearic coast in one day than in the whole of industrial Lancashire.

The visitors take their pleasure seriously. Gangs of young men saunter up and down the promenade like off-duty Vikings, chanting the football supporters' anthem 'Here we go, here we go'; heat and drink lend them a vacancy of expression, as if they are unsure whether the home team has lost or won.

In forays of courtship the vanguard of the Manchester United and Liverpool football supporters' club become fainthearted conquistadors. Flirtation turns to tongue-tied simperings. Flowers of northern maidenhood sit on the long pub benches staring down into multi-coloured drinks, eyeing each other with the vigilance of vestals at the baths. New arrivals are undecided whether to lower their necklines or raise them to cover blistering results of the first day in the sun.

By the mid-1980s the Balearic Islands, Majorca principally, were playing host to more than five million tourists in a good year. More than two million came from the British Isles, and most of these headed for a few miles of coast either side of Majorca's capital, Palma. Where once a few fishing villages dotted the beaches, hotels, villas, clubs and pubs spawned like concrete fungus; within twenty years all but a fifth of the coastline of the island had been developed.

A yen for the sun brought Pauline Corrieri, her husband and another couple from Scotland to Papa JoJo's café, which they bought from a Welshman. 'It was a real hassle at first, getting through the paperwork. But we make a fair living now. You have to work really hard. We get good meat and produce from Bill the butcher in Palma Nova – he comes from Irvine originally. Two of us start at eight in the morning – the other two at nine-thirty and eleven-thirty. It's like that for four months. The only time off we get is when we close at four in the afternoon on Sunday. 'It varies from month to month. This month it's the Scots, and next it will be Liverpudlians.'

Behind her was the bill of fare. The Great British Breakfast of egg, bacon, sausage, beans, tomato, toast, marmalade, tea or coffee cost 385 pesetas. The bar list was almost blunt and to the point: 'Beer, Skol, San Miguel, bottles, 100 pesetas. Sangria, 200 pesetas. Pint of Lager, 100 pesetas.'

'No, we don't get much serious trouble. It's more rowdyism,' said Pauline. 'It is quite a place for drop-outs, but many of the visitors are abroad for the first time, and they don't really know where they are. We really have had enquiries about how to catch the bus to Gibraltar.'

Drugs, Pauline and her partners agreed, were more in evidence. A number of new clubs had opened on the beachfront, where touts enticed young people with tickets offering free drinks and 'cokina', which might be taken to mean Cola drinks but in reality was a signal that cocaine-based hard drugs were available. Few involved in the tourist business doubted that Mafia-related drug syndicates were active in the big beach resorts.

The ways of the tourists seem a world apart from the traditions and history of old Majorca. Mass travel is a relatively recent phenomenon, according to Antonio Munar, a former General Manager for Tourism for the Majorcan *autonomia*. 'I've grown up with this business since the early Sixties,' he declared. 'You might say that the travel industry has been my university, as it has taken me across the world.'

Majorca used to be a winter resort for dilettantes, intellectuals and the delicate in health from northern Europe. 'Then, twenty years ago, the omelette began to be fried the other way up. Between 1960 and 1973 more than thirteen hundred hotels were built and by the mid-Seventies its offer of nearly two hundred thousand beds was the most concentrated in the Mediterranean. The beginning of the boom was a big public relations exercise for Franco's dictatorship. There was no "planification" at all – a very big fault. We have now got to improve quality, take a more responsible attitude to the environment and forget about the numbers war.'

The numbers war meant that in under twenty-five years the annual tourist crop had come to out-number the residents by roughly ten to one. *Balearisé* had become a technical term coined by the French, so members of the sociology faculty at Palma university told me, to denote uncontrolled holiday development of the kind suffered by Majorca and its neighbours.

Many of the first generation manning the new hotels had come from the land. Because the islands had escaped the ravages of phylloxera, they received nearly a hundred thousand destitute peasant families from Andalusia and Extremadura within a few decades. The Majorca of their descendants came to have the highest average income in the entire Spanish kingdom.

Some of the sons of the peasants and immigrants had now joined the super-rich. The owner of the 4,000-bed Hotel Sor had begun life as a waiter when he was sixteen, while the proprietor of a neighbouring complex had started out as a bus driver in the Philippines. With the surge in wealth came rackets and organised crime, a feature of much of the holiday industry in the Mediterranean, in the larger islands especially. Local mafias began to emerge such as Union Mallorcina, strikingly similar to the Corsican underworld syndicate, L'Union Corse.

Now the emphasis is on to 'ecological management', on tourism based on quality rather than quantity, for which men like Antonio Munãr are the new visionaries and consultants. 'We have laid down new norms for development and building, and many of the older hotels are being brought up to higher standards. Greater areas of the islands are being put out of bounds to the speculators. It is not Utopia, but it is the best way forward.' So saying, the dynamic tourist consultant cut short our conversation to attend the opening of a nightspot on the other side of Majorca called 'Towards the Great Disaster of the Year 2000'.

Move a few hundred yards or metres inland, and one encounters an older, dignified and more serene Majorca, once the hub of the western Mediterranean. In 1229 the island was taken from the Saracens by Jaume I 'the Conqueror', and under his son, Jaume II, it became the centre of an empire in the fourteenth century whose influence stretched to Montpellier, the Pyrenees, Sardinia, Sicily, North Africa, and the Catalan Duchy of Athens. But the kingdom of Majorca lasted less than a century before being absorbed by Aragon in 1349, and ultimately by Spain itself. Though part of the Catalan family, Majorcans refer to their language and way of life as 'Majorcene' rather than mere 'Catalan'.

The most magnificent monument of the Majorcan kingdom – and a parable of the island's history since its loss of independence – is the cathedral, which dominates the old harbour-front of Palma. Its foundations were laid in 1239 on the site of a mosque at the behest of Jaume I, but its last section was not completed until 1601. The central nave is among the longest in Europe; the enormous structure has a surprising lightness, seeming to float like a biscuit-yellow ship.

Two features in its interior catch the eye – the weird suspended circlet of iron and glass, the *baldechino*, near the altar by Antoni Gaudi; and the delicate pale patterns of flowers thrown by more than eighty stained-glass rose windows, in the largest of which the stone of the supporting tracery has the weaving subtlety of Saracen craftsmanship, while the main struts seem to form a star of David.

In the basilica of San Francisco, airy and echoing as a barn, the effigy of Ramon Lull lies in alabaster repose. Lull was one of the most brilliant spirits of the kingdom of Majorca in its heyday under Jaume II, to whom he is said to have been tutor. He achieved so much that he deserves more than to be known merely as one of the first exponents of Catalan as a literary language. Part of the difficulty lay in his subsequent reputation as a master of necromacy and alchemy, because of his interest in Arabic sciences – a slur that has only recently been cleared. Following the fashion of the day, Ramon Lull led a dissolute life until the age of thirty in 1266. After that he virtually abandoned his wife and family, and his estates were put into the hands of guardians. 'He had no sense of pursuing art for art's sake – his was a frontier view of Science,' according to Anthony Bonner. One of the scholars responsible for re-examining Lull's life and works, Bonner studies in a house in the hills beyond Palma, a landscape Lull himself must have known well. He learnt Arabic from an Arab slave, who hanged himself following a dispute over a sword. Later he persuaded the king to establish a Franciscan foundation at Miramar in Majorca, where he taught Arabic and philosophy.

The most remarkable phase of his life began in 1290 in Genoa where he had a nervous breakdown, recorded meticulously in his writings. After this he undertook the first of his three missions to North Africa to preach the gospel in Arabic, as well as journeying to southern Italy and Cyprus to try to establish missionary schools.

Lull's great strength was his weakness: he was an infuriatingly reasonable man. He believed anything could be achieved by reason and faith, and had an elaborate system based on logic and the Aristotelian sciences. He represented his ideas by elaborate diagrams; one of which, made for the Doge of Venice, is still in existence, and shows his view of the universe as a pattern of wheels.

Between his travels he wrote poetry and philosophy, and on science and religion; his novel, *Blanquerna*, anticipates More's *Utopia*. On his third mission to North Africa he was stoned to death outside Bougie, in modern Tunisia; he was in his eightieth year, his ardour undiminished. A year later his body was returned to Palma.

'I suppose he was a fanatic, a one track-mind,' muses Anthony Bonner, 'You could say he was flawed, a bit cuckoo. But it's only now that scholars are beginning to see the man for himself to find out how the whole system worked. As a thinker his influence has been hidden but enormous, and he ranks only behind Aquinas among his contemporaries.'

Tourists have been leaving their traces in the interior of Majorca since before history was recorded. The first visitors to leave their marks were the Bronze Age people who built the *talayots* and *taulas* – megalithic circular forts and temples which dot the island and its neighbours. The Talaitoics were succeeded by raiders and traders – Phoenician, Punic Roman, Byzantine, Arab and Catalan. The biggest impression was left by the Arabs, who irrigated the plain with canals and ditches, introduced windmills, and terraced the hillsides.

In the east of the island, in open fields striped by irrigation ditches and flanked by four windmills built by the Dutch in the last century I came across an elderly couple picking tomatoes. They said that to make a living from the land was no longer as easy as it had been so many country people had been sucked into the holiday industry. Majorcans used to dominate the early season fruit market in the Languedoc and Paris, their early potatoes are still in demand at New Covent Garden in London. The land was still good, and the old drainage methods meant that no salt entered the soil from the sea. They could support their children and grandchildren from their twenty hectares, with a little profit from sales of potatoes, figs, almonds and apricots, when the middleman permitted. But the old couple were exceptions, for the number of Majorcan farmers has reduced to a quarter in forty years.

One winds past neat terraces and through lanes flanked by carob trees, whose fruits are now much prized by the homeopathic medicine industry, to reach the abandoned monastery of Valldemosa, the winter lodging of Frederic Chopin and George Sand, in the island's northern mountains. They arrived in Palma in the autumn of 1838. Chopin was in poor health and even worse temper. In early December he was writing to his friend Julien Fontana, 'I have been sick as a dog for two weeks . . . and have not been able to send the Preludes. . . . Three doctors (the best in the island) have examined me . . . but soon I will move to a monastery above Palma – sea, nature, by the cemetery. But still I lack a piano and have written to Pleyel about it.'

The Carthusians had been removed from the monastery only three years earlier, though a monk remained in the pharmacy, dispensing his favourite remedies of marsh-mallow and couch-grass root. The pharmacy is still there, laid out as a museum, as are the adjoining cells which were converted for Chopin and George Sand; contemporary furniture, prints and one or two manuscripts of compositions completed in Valldemosa are on display.

'Here I see the arcades, one of the most poetic cemeteries, in a word, there I would be well,' wrote Chopin. He was soon disappointed by his lodging. George Sand later claimed to have discovered Majorca as a winter resort for the refined and delicate, but her account of her sojourn, *A Winter in Majorca*, often descends into bad-tempered farce. She appears to have quarrelled with just about everyone. Her maids ate her food and that of her children; 'never have I known such a pious mouth so gluttonous,' she wrote of one of them.

In his loneliness Chopin composed three of his most famous Polonaises, and began or finished a number of other pieces – most of the Preludes, and the Mazurka, Opus 40, no. 2 in E Minor. His health got better. He only went for one walk in three months. The three doctors had to be called repeatedly, each arriving on a larger donkey, according to George Sand. The composer railed bitterly about 'the pitiful piano' he was forced to use. George Sand had to go down to Palma to wrangle with the customs officials for the release of the piano despatched by Pleyel from Paris months earlier. The instrument was hauled up to the Charter-house eventually at the end of January 1839, only a matter of weeks before the monastery's disgruntled guests departed.

Frederic Chopin and George Sand were trend-setters of 'winter break' tourism in their sojourn in Majorca. Their successors in the ensuing century and a half not only stayed for the long winter months, but put down roots and became permanent exiles. Despite the inebriated vulgarity of resorts like Magalluf, Majorca also became a holiday destination of quality – not least because it became a favourite sun spot for King Juan Carlos himself. Each year he was to stay at the elegant summer palace at Palma, where he would entertain his distant cousins the Prince and Princess of Wales, whose titles blazoned the pub signs a few miles down the coast.

Unlike the Spain of Franco, the Spain of King Juan Carlos and Felipe Gonzalez did not have to rely on industrialised tourism as a link to the outside world. Under their durable partnership Spain became Europe's steady voice in the Mediterranean. It was a bridge between northern European nations of the Economic Community and the Mediterranean, far more so than Italy or Greece, embroiled in their own domestic difficulties. As the Mediterranean world is steadily less European in complexion, with the rise of numbers on its southern shores, paradoxically it is becoming vital to the economy of the European neighbourhood to the north – a development of which Spaniards intend to be beneficiaries and not victims.

Two: France

i Languedoc: Cathars and Cultivators

Few towns conceal their past fame and prestige as well as Narbonne. It sits at the strategic crossroads of the main route from Toulouse to the Mediterranean, and the coast road which sweeps from the Rhône delta to Perpignan and the Catalan coast. The Emperor Augustus proclaimed it the capital of the second province of Gaul, to which it gave its name. Cicero called Gallia Narbonensis 'the corridor of Latin civilisation', while the poet Martial proclaimed it the fairest city beyond the Alps, and the most populous along with Lyon. The port of Narbonne exported meat, olive oil, wool, grain and aromatic plants to Rome. But the coastal corridor was also a route of continuous invasion – by Visigoths, who made their royal capital in the city, Saracens from the south, and the forces of Pepin the Short, Charlemagne's father, who retook the city in 759. The consuls of Narbonne had to provide levies for the Crusades of Louis IX, which departed from Aigues Mortes, a little farther up the coast. And the Narbonnais suffered their share in the march and counter-march of Napoleonic arms in the Peninsular War.

Today the little city basks in autumnal sunshine like a lazy, if elegant, dog. Hardly anything remains of the Roman settlement save the occasional broken column and funerary stone set into the medieval walls. The sandy texture of the stone give the buildings a particular lightness, with its huge scaffold of arches and flying buttresses, the cathedral of St Just – said to be the finest incomplete gothic building in France – seems almost to hover above the ground. As elegant as the cathedral and the bishops' palace is the Monoprix department store, with its delicate tracery and wrought-iron ballustrade. Narbonne has resisted the invaders well. In a survey of the regions of France in 1986, Le Monde found that the people of Languedoc-Roussillon, of which Narbonne and the département of Aude form part, were most contented with their way of life, a sentiment perhaps dimmed by the more recent recession.

The result of the opinion poll is the more surprising since a decade earlier the Languedoc was a byword for resentment and regional neglect.

The modern economy is based on the tourists that come in their hundreds of thousands to this part of the coast, and on agriculture, and in particular the wines of Roussillon and Corbières. Despite *Le Monde's* survey, a separatist movement has found fertile ground among students and some local politicians, based on the culture and language of the old region of Occitania, from which the name 'Languedoc' is derived. In the foothills of the Pyrenees a number of Occitanian dialect words are used, and villages quite far north still speak Catalan.

The 'Oc' is one of the vulgar Latin *patois* of early medieval Europe, a cousin of Provençal. How much Occitanian exists now as a separate language is hard to guess: one farmer confessed that he only spoke Occitanian 'when the people from the TV came round to interview him' – which they did quite frequently. One of the most extraordinary manifestations of medieval Occitania was the movement of Cathar or Albigensian heretics, a new enthusiasm for which has almost become a mania. It even forms the basis of a *tourisme de luxe* in the countryside west of Narbonne and south of Toulouse. American Express has promoted specialist tours to Cathar castles, while the 1986 Michelin Green Guide for the region was renamed 'Pyrénées Roussillon, *Albigeois'*. In a bookshop in Narbonne over half the local guidebooks on offer were devoted to the Cathars and their mysterious faith.

The Cathar castles provide a splendid introduction to the hinterland of the Languedoc; in some parts the traveller passes hardly a village which is not dominated by its castle or fortified church. Catharism was one of the great dualist heresies. Its priests or *parfaits*, either male or female, held that creation was a balance of light and dark; the heavens were made by God, and the earth and flesh by the devil. *Parfaits* rejected both the eating of meat and procreation, though the latter in particular was honoured more in the breach than in the observance. The heresy was related to Manichean cults in third century Asia Minor, and to the Bogomils who flourished in the Balkans in the tenth century. Mani was a prophet of the third century who grew up in Babylonia. He tried to combine the teachings of Christianity and Zoroastrianism, emphasising the divisions of creation into opposites of good and evil. The heresy arrived in Languedoc in the twelfth century from Lombardy and spread through an area which was long the setting for running conflict between local powers, such as the Count of Foix, the Church of Rome and the King of France. The Counts of Foix were to become the protectors of the Cathars in their refusal to pay taxes and tithes to the church.

The heresy was condemned in 1176, but the Albigenisan Crusade was not launched until 1209 by Pope Innocent III and headed by Simon de

Montfort, a byword for cruelty in the subsequent campaign until his death at the siege of Toulouse in 1218. The *casus belli* was the assassination of the papal legate, Pierre de Castelnau, at the door of the great abbey church of St Gilles.

The spiritual onslaught against the Cathars was led by St Dominic. He began by disputing with the Cathar bishop at Fanjeaux, an elegant little village whose fortified church overlooks the plain between Toulouse and Carcassonne. Inside are – supposedly – the ashes of the fire which refused to burn St Dominic's propositions of dogma, despite the Cathar missionary's thrusting the parchment into the flames thrice.

The Dominicans developed what was to become the most powerful single instrument in rooting out heresy which persists in modified form to this day – the Holy Inquisition. Set up in 1232 for the examination of Cathar heretics, it sanctified torture though seldom resorted to the death penalty. More common punishments were the confiscation of property, compulsory pilgrimages, and the enforced wearing of yellow crosses on cloaks.

The most poignant of the Cathar monuments is the castle of Montségur, perched on a huge volcanic pinnacle that rises from the surrounding hills like a gigantic pyramid. In 1243 a community of Cathars came to seek the protection of Pierre de Mirepoix and his garrison in Montségur. For nine months an army despatched by the Inquisition at Carcassonne and by the Archbishop of Narbonne laid seige to the castle until, in the snows of March 1244, the Count of Mirepoix agreed to surrender for the safe conduct of himself and his mercenaries. The Cathars refused to recant, and 207 of them, men women and children, were burned below the rocky citadel.

This act of peculiar savagery has made Montségur a place of pilgrimage ever since. It is a half-hour's straight, hard climb of seven to eight hundred feet from the road to the ramparts. From the walls of the modest courtyard of the castle I could see to the north across hillsides lightly dusted with new snow, to the south across slowly yellowing forests to the Pyrenees. It was hard to imagine that a hundred men-at-arms could cram into the small space of the fortress, let alone twice that number of peasant families and their *parfaits* – but in fact the castle I was standing in had been built on the remains of Pierre of Mirepoix's stronghold. On the way down I noticed a monument 'aux martires' of Montségur, erected in 1960; across it was daubed in thick paint 'Vive l'Occitanie libre'.

Several *parfaits* escaped before the end of Montségur. One myth suggests they took with them the legendary Cathar treasure – a tradition more honoured in fantasy than in fact, but now being successfully exploited by the tour companies.

Cathars hung on in other castles, such as Peyrepreteuse and Quéribus, which fell in 1255, eleven years after Montségur. Peyrepreteuse embraces a long, rocky ridge like the scales on a dragon's back. Beneath the castle lies the village of Duilhac, in the old olive mill of which Marise and Marc Maillol run a successful restaurant – wild boar the *plat du jour* on a cold November Saturday. Marc had helped build the electronics for the supersonic airliner Concorde at AeroSpatiale in Toulouse, but with the end of the project he came to Duilhac. A native of Bagnol, he spoke fluent Catalan; his wife, a daughter of the village, had a smattering of Occitan. The Cathars and their castle brought good business, they said. The economy of the village used to be based on olive oil, and the slopes of the castle were covered in olives. Now only three farms grew olives, though most produced wine for local sale. In the early Seventies the Corbières wines had acquired the *dénomination controlée* designation. Marc said he thought they compared favourably with many Bordeaux.

'The problem nowadays is over-production,' Marc explained. 'It would be fine if we didn't have so much from Bordeaux. I suppose we have the Rothschilds to thank for that. Now we have EC competition, all that muck made in factories in Italy and Spain. We can't go back to olives as it takes two generations to establish an orchard. It's made life really tough, especially for the young people. No I'm not a chauvinist [he pronounced 'chauvin' to sound like 'chauvang'] but my loyalties lie first to my family, then to my village and my region, Languedoc, then I suppose to France and to Europe.'

Well south of Montségur, just east of the main route through to Andorra and Spain from Toulouse and Foix, lies the village of Montaillou – a cluster of stone houses, plus a church, a school and a few modern chalets in open mountain pasture. It is surprising that Montaillou is not being covered with tourist signs, for it became a centre of Cathar practices half a century and more after the campaign against the heretics had ended at Quéribus. In 1308 all its villagers were rounded up by the Inquisition, with only the smallest children excepted. Between 1317 and 1324 the Bishop of Pamiers undertook a detailed interrogation of some twenty-five of Montaillou's inhabitants. Now deposited in the Vatican Library, the register of these proceedings formed the basis of Professor Emmanuel Le Roy Ladurie's historical masterpiece *Montaillou*, which provides an astonishingly clear portrait of life in a mountain village in Occitania, and of the mechanics and eschatology of the Cathar heresy.

The detail of the register prepared from the examination of the villagers was partly due to the persistence of the Bishop of Pamiers, Jacques Fournier, 'a sort of compulsive Maigret, immune to supplication and bribe', according to Ladurie. Fournier was a monk from the Cistercian foundation of Fontfroide which, though modified and restored, is still intact, couched in the hills south-west of Narbonne. He rose to be Bishop of Pamiers and then, briefly, of Mirepoix, before being elected Pope in 1334. As Pope Benedict XII he began the first phase of the Papal Palace at Avignon, summoning Simone Martini from Italy to work in fresco in the main chambers. In Montaillou he was best remembered for the support he gave the Inquisition, which then sat under Dominican control at Carcassonne.

With its enormous turrets and walls Carcassonne is one of the least satisfactory of all medieval monuments. It is so heavily restored that it seems to have the anal cleanliness of a Walt Disney costume movie, with very little left to the imagination. Altogether more colourful and three-dimensional are the deeds of the villagers as evoked by Le Roy Ladurie. Under the rules of the Inquisition, Bishop Fournier – who attended nearly every hearing over six years or so – provided a record of the cross-examination and a statement to be signed by the accused, before ending with an account of that individual's way of life. A community of some 250 people, Montaillou depended largely on the transhumance of sheep across the Pyrenees to the winter pastures of northern Spain round Lerida, and even as far south as Valencia. The two nominal authorities in the village were the Bishop's *vicaire*, and the Count of Foix's bailiff or chatelain. At a critical stage in the story these two who were brothers, Bernard and Pierre Clergue, were condemned for heresy. However Pierre Clergue, libertine and well-versed in the ways of the *parfaits*, proved a turncoat and betrayed the village to the Inquisition.

Béatrice de Planissoles was the widow of the châtelain, the *grande horizontale* of the village, whose greatest act of public intimacy with her lovers was to allow them to pluck lice from her hair. Most attractive of all is the shepherd Pierre Maury. A generous, solitary soul, he provides a graphic account of about the shepherds' lives. One worldly *parfait* duped the unfortunate Pierre into marrying his own mistress for three days in order to give his name to the child of their union, irregular by even the most liberal Cathar standards. But Pierre Maury was a free spirit: 'I earn my money and my fortune myself,' he tells one *parfait* 'and I mean to spend them as I like; I will not give them up for you or anyone else, because in that way I acquire many people's friendship.'

Through Pierre Maury's testimony the Inquisition learned of the beliefs of the *parfaits*. They were supposed to eschew the pleasures of the flesh and live off an austere diet of fish and vegetables. Their most important role was in offering the *consolamentum* ('consolation') whereby the dying become 'hereticated' and their souls were assured a clear passage into a new life, which might take the form of reincarnation in human or animal form – though some heretics suggested that the soul was 'made of blood and would die with the body'.

Bishop Fournier did his job well, his Inquisition called more than a hundred witnesses and examined ninety-odd cases but only one of the villagers he arraigned was burnt at the stake. The Clergues died in prison, while Pierre Maury disappears from the record. By the end of the fourteenth century the community of Montaillou had halved, though whether this was owing to the Inquisition or the Black Death is unclear. Professor Le Roy Ladurie concludes that Montaillou and its neighbouring hamlets saw the last gasp of Catharism, now 'no more than a dead star whose cold but fascinating light reaches us now after an eclipse of more than half a millenium.'

Arriving at Montaillou at dusk one Sunday evening, the place seemed deserted save for two dogs barking at the church walls. Fresh thin snow crunched underfoot as I trudged towards the remains the castle once commanded by Berenger de Roquefort, husband of the libidinous Béatrice de Planissoles. What of those whose names pour through Bishop Fournier's Register? Something of the spirit of Pierre Maury lived on in a shepherd whom I met a few leagues from the village. Henri Roi told me he had decided to give up his work near Paris to take up the 'full life' of driving two hundred sheep in Occitania. He had few regrets, save the poor price being offered for lamb. His sheep were protected by two enormous Pyrenean mountain dogs; their biggest threat came from birds of prey, hawks and buzzards, which carried off young lambs.

Is the Cathar heresy really 'no more than a dead star'? No one can deny that the idea of a Cathar church with its own priests and *parfaits* is long gone, while tourists with metal detectors hunt for Cathar treasure and the Holy Grail with a wondrous blend of commercialism and crankiness. But, as a wandering journalist, I can still see elements of Montaillou and the Cathars in many Mediterranean communities today.

Much of the heretics' protest was political. 'There are four great devils ruling over this world,' the *parfait* preacher Belibaste protested, 'the lord Pope, the major devil whom I call Satan; the Lord King of France is the second devil; the Bishop of Pamiers the third; and the Inquisition of Carcassonne, the fourth.' Much of the protest was about taxes and tithes, which helped to make the bishops and the clergy idle, rich and fat.

Resentment over tithes persisted, and contributed to the Protestant revolt in the Languedoc in the sixteenth century.

The authority of Church and crown seems to have been remote from much of life in Montaillou, where practical influence was exerted through a network of family alliances. The object of families like the Clergues was to suborn power for their own ends, but not to overturn the existing order. This is the essence of clan power, or *clanisme*, which still informs many Mediterranean communities, particularly in ports like Marseille, Naples, Palermo, and among the *cosche* of the Sicilian Mafia and the warring minorities of Lebanon.

Pierre Maury was one of the loners of Montaillou society, yet he maintained a network of important friendships through the *compères* and *commères* – the men and women with whom he had stood sponsor or godparent at numerous baptisms. The *parfait* Belibaste berated him for this: 'You spend all you have on this kind of festivity; and yet these baptisms and compaternities are good for nothing except to establish friendships between people.' To which the shepherd replied: 'If I try to acquire so many friends in this way, it is because I should do good to everyone; if someone is good [a heretic] I shall be rewarded; if someone is bad, at least he will try to return the good he receives at my hand.' The cementation of alliances through baptism (*comparaggio*) is still fundamental to the Sicilian and Calabrian Mafias, and their cousins in North and South America. Among the most important exhibits at the trial of 475 Mafia suspects which opened in Palermo in February 1986 were group photographs of *compari* gathered at a Sicilian clan wedding and at baptisms in New York and Caracas.

Finally, the Cathars' Manichean division between darkness and light, the realm of God and that of the devil, has persisted most vividly in the world of Islam. In his denunciation of the material might of the United States as 'the great Satan', the imagery of the Ayatollah Khomeini seems to owe more to the third-century Persian prophet, Mani, than to the teaching of the Prophet Mohhammed.

The people of Languedoc may no longer fight the tithes of Holy Church or the levies and taxes of the King of France, but the fiscal enemy lives on in the bureaucracies of Paris and, still more so, of Brussels. Resistance to the taxes and quotas imposed by the European Community burst into open violence in and around the port of Sète in 1975 and 1981.

Sète is one of the most elegant and tranquil spots on the coast of Languedoc, untouched by the ravages of tourism. Its warehouses and wharves, and its square houses with their shutters and wrought-iron railings belong to another century. The port was devised by Louis XIV's technologically-minded minister, Colbert, to serve the university city of Montpellier, thirty-five kilometers away, and to be the Mediterranean end of the canal 'des deux mers', which reaches the Atlantic at Bordeaux. The quiet atmosphere of the port and the little town on the slopes above it was summed up by its favourite literary son, the poet Paul Valéry, who could not imagine being born and brought up anywhere else. Sète, he said, was like a little island floating among the sand-banks. The town had retained its pleasantly self-contained quality. Its population has hardly grown in two centuries – at little more than 40,000, it has the same number of inhabitants as Narbonne.

As one approaches the port along the battered coast road the fumes of sulphur and gas from the Mobil refinery give way to the pungent whiff of grape pulp and of heavy southern wines in the early stages of fermentation. Behind the chipped wooden doors of the warehouses the wines of Sicily and Italy are stored by the metric tonne in aluminium silos like industrial gasoline tanks. A pontoon bridge opens to allow a grey-hulled coaster, the *Ampelos*, to chug through, homeward bound to Marsala. In August 1981 the decks of the *Ampelos* and the tanker waggons on the railway siding of the wharf became an open battlefield in the EC wine war. A party of local winegrowers, led by M. Jean Huillet boarded the ship and emptied drums of diesel oil into the hold, ruining 180,000 gallons of Sicilian wine. Roughly the same amount was emptied from the railway trucks. M. Huillet was the founder of the Herrault Action Committee, part of the Occitan Wine Intervention Movement. As the symbol of his cause, he wore round his neck the Occitan cross of the Cathars.

The winegrowers' grievance is directed at Article 30 of the Treaty of Rome, which forbids any restrictions or quotas on trade between members of the EC. The fortunes of Sète had for centuries been tied to the wine trade – initially as an exporter of French wines, then as an importer of heavy vintages from Tunisia, Algeria, Greece, Southern Italy and Sicily. As the EC's 'wine lake' grew, with production exceeding demand well before Spain and Portugal even applied for membership, local French growers became increasingly violent in their protests, claiming they could supply enough wine of their own. However, the argument is one of quality as well as quantity: on average Sicilian red wine contains five degrees more alcohol than its equivalent from the Languedoc. Shippers and bottlers like to use southern wines in their vats to make the final product more 'robust'.

My host in Sète was M. Claude Bonfils, President of the Chamber of

Commerce, which runs the old part of the port. M. Bonfils prides himself in being a 'man of the Mediterranean' or rather a man of the western Mediterranean. He was born in Tunisia, where his father was in the wine-shipping business. Their partner among the sizeable Italian community of growers was called Buonfiglio, and the Buonfiglio-Bonfils combination flourished until the defeat of the Fascists in Tunisia and the uprooting of most of the Italian farmers. The Buonfiglio family took up wine cultivation in southern Italy, and by the mid-1950s the old family alliance was back in business, this time between Italy and Sète. Sète was now part of an important union of ports of the north-west Mediterranean, encompassing an arc from La Spezia and Livorno in Italy to Barcelona and Tarragona. 'The Mediterranean is still for me the first sea of the world,' M. Bonfils proclaimed, 'though indeed its earlier glories are gone. Now all the fashionable theories point to the Pacific Basin as the hub of world trade. But I'm not too sure. I think the Mediterranean is gaining in significance rather than declining. Of course it will never reach the heights it did in classical times, but it is becoming an important link between the North Sea and the new trade with South-East Asia, particularly since the re-opening of the Suez Canal in 1975.'

Sète was no longer dependent on the shipping of wine, though he did not deny that the wine-shippers did form 'a little aristocracy' within the town. Only 300,000 thousand tonnes of wine had been moved the previous season – six per cent of all goods moving through the port. The refinery accounted for nearly seventy per cent of imports and exports; the balance was made up by importing manganese, phosphates and hard tropical woods, and by exporting cement. Apart from the cement and passenger services to Morocco, Algeria and to the Balearics, the pattern of commerce had become much as it was a century ago, when French imperial activity in North Africa and Asia was approaching its zenith.

In M. Bonfils' opinion, the community of Sète, was an 'anomaly' in the region, partly because it seemed only 'moored' to the coast. Its fishermen had originated elsewhere in the Mediterranean, from Liguria, Gaeta and Naples. The inland people were 'terrien', tied to the soil in their loyalties and fiercely xenophobic – 'a natural reaction, I suppose, to being the corridor for foreign armies from Hannibal onwards.' Great changes had taken place since the Second World War when the vineyards had been moved to higher ground, while the plain had been turned over to growing vegetables, fruits and cash crops like tomatoes.

For centuries Sète was isolated, moored to the sandbanks which stretch from the Rhône to Perpignan, the threat of malaria acting as a deterrent to potential settlers. But once the stagnant pools and basins behind the

coastal dunes had been drained, two hundred kilometers of sandy beach
became open to development – a project supported by De Gaulle himself.
The General had become alarmed at the drain of currency from French
visitors pouring into Spain for their summer holidays, and in the 1960s
beach establishments, nudist colonies and yacht marinas sprouted like
mushrooms. Most curious of all is the complex of holiday flats at La
Grande-Motte, a string of flat-topped concrete pyramids, which look like
the work of a design committee made up of Aztecs and ancient Egyptians:
it was designed in 1967 to house 40,000 holiday-makers, plus 1800 yachts
in its harbour. Following De Gaulle's instructions nearly 300,000 tourist
beds were to be provided along this part of the coast – which was receiving around two million visitors a year by the early 1980s creating some
20,000 new jobs along the coast of Languedoc.

The saddest victim of the tourist boom and marina mania is the little
fishing port of Les Saintes Maries de la Mer, at the tip of the Camargue
– a gathering place for gypsies, who hold a summer festival there at the
end of May. The church is nearly a thousand years old, heavily fortified
against Saracen pirates. On the outside wall the abbé has placed a brass
plaque requesting visitors not to enter indecently dressed in bikinis or
shorts, not to chew gum, not to make too much noise and not to smoke.
The warning seems wholly justified, for the port now resembles nothing
so much as some cheap seaside ice-cream booth, its flimsy chalets stretching into the open marshland of the Camargue, which is littered with
rickety shacks offering 'ranch-house' holidays and pony-trekking.

On the edge of the delta is one of the most curious of vineyards. The
Listel establishment should be billed as 'the vineyard that got away'. It
sits hard by the great molehills of gleaming white salt extracted from the
salines that run into the sea by St Louis' Crusader port of Aigues Mortes.
The salt pans and the vines were originally run by local monks, but now
both are managed with cool efficiency by a Franco-Swiss conglomerate.
The vines grow in a sandy soil reprieved from the sea and produce
wonderfully light white and rosé wines, and a quite singular 'gris de gris'.
The saltiness of the soil proved too much for the phylloxera weevil,
almost literally putting salt on their tails as they attempted to burrow
into the vine roots. In the great phylloxera plagues of 1873 and 1875,
Listel survived where other vineyards of the region perished. Survival
led to expansion, and today the vineyard and salt pans employ some
1800 people. Looking out through the dusk from the roof of the *caves* at
Listel I could see neat rows of vines being trimmed and pruned for winter.
The work was being done by a motley group of Moroccan and Portuguese
men and women. 'They're cheaper,' the young manager remarked tartly,

'but how long the Common Market will allow this is another matter.'

Nowhere in Provence do I find the past more embedded in the present than outside the rural market town of St-Rémy-de-Provence, where the St-Paul-de-Mausole monastery still serves as a hospital and asylum – exactly as it did a hundred years ago, when Vincent Van Gogh spent his last year here, pouring out his life in letters to his family and in paintings of an almost demonic energy. Even more than the Delft of Vermeer, the Toledo of El Greco or the San Sepolcro of Piero, the place is imbued with the spirit of the man. The patients and the nurses still drift silently through the courtyard, where the hedges and shrubs are exactly as he depicted them; the latches and the window frames are the same as those in his canvas of 'Vincent's Study in the Asylum'.

He had been drawn to the south by the brilliant provencal colours and the radiant Mediterranean light. Yet he remained ambivalent about such a fierce and direct assault by the elements: 'One never sees buckwheat or rape here, and perhaps there is in general less variety than with us (in the north),' he wrote to his mother.

In May 1889 he arrived at the hospital after a suicide attempt in Arles. 'As far as I can make out, the doctor here is inclined to consider I have had a sort of epileptic attack. But I did not ask him about it,' he explained to his brother Theo. Desperate about a recurrence of his illness, he became fascinated by the 'clearness of the air', by the peasants reaping in the fields and, above all, by the cypresses, which were 'always occupying my thoughts, I should like to make something of them like the canvasses of the sunflowers, because it astonishes me that they have not yet been done as I see them – as beautiful of line and proportion as an Egyptian obelisk.'

He left St-Rémy in May 1890 to return north, and killed himself at Auvers-sur-Oise that July.

I climbed the garden wall to see if the gnarled and pollarded trees and the old stone fountain were still as the artist had found them. I was caught in mid-trespass by the looming figure of a sister, her starched cap fluttering like an avenging bird in the wind. 'Monsieur, descendez immediatement!' she boomed: 'Monsieur, s'il vous plaît, c'est une terre sacrée.' My feeble explanations and protestations were in vain, and I left the grounds of the hospital like a naughty schoolboy.

As I headed away from the rocky spurs of Les Baux, the olive trees and the cypresses loomed black in the fading daylight. In the shapes of those trees and rocks the vision of the artist and nature itself have become inextricably interwoven. Somehow the obscene saleroom prices now fetched by Vincent's canvasses seem a vulgar irrelevance to the power and the accessibility of what he saw and painted. As if responding to such thoughts, the sky began to turn pink in the distance, and in an instant the sunset spread across the horizon like a flame, and the blue sky of which Vincent said he never could grow tired was consumed in a vast Heraclitean bonfire.

ii Marseille

Marseille has given the impression of hard times for nearly a century past – Victorian travellers were advised to hurry on, as there was little of interest to detain them in the port. In its physical decay, and in the activities of its underworld, it has a family resemblance to Naples and Palermo. France's third city is easily caricatured – by violent crime, racial discord, screaming fishwives and steaming *bouillabaisse*.

The grubby streets and buildings of the old centre, and its drifting, cosmopolitan population, are the direct creations of French Empire in the nineteenth century. The digging of the Suez Canal in 1869 gave the old port a commercial second wind, augmented by trade with North Africa. Strolling through the old Rue du Panier district – a wedge between the Cathedral and the Hôtel de la Ville by the Quai du Port – I saw not one European face. Most were Asian, Arab or sub-Saharan African; one tenth of Marseille's million residents come from North Africa, and its port and airport are the main entry points of migrant workers from Algeria into France.

The racial tensions in Marseille are the more acute as the city long enjoyed a reputation as a haven for political and religious refugees. In the past century its population has been leavened by Armenians, Greeks from Asia Minor, White Russians and Italians fleeing Fascism but as the African community spread from the old souk across La Canebière, the main artery leading to the Old Port, the voters of downtown Marseille registered their disquiet by giving Jean-Marie Le Pen's overtly racist National Front 35 per cent of the poll in the local elections of 1985.

In the Old Port itself some things seem never to change. On a crisp, bright Saturday in December I found the fishwives in full cry. Madame Luccienne tried to sell me some delicious-looking red mullet at thirty francs a kilo; beside them lay merlin, and something Madame called 'beaux yeux', but which escaped my piscine vocabulary. Two men dumped a huge octopus from a trolley and began thrashing the daylights out of the carcass, as if unconvinced that the creature was yet dead.

When I asked her whether she had had any difficulties with pollution, Madame Lucienne gave me short shrift. 'Pas de tout, Monsieur. Never had any trouble. Everything is fresh and everything is local!'

'Jamais de reproche,' chipped in her mate – 'my customers have never complained.'

'How's business?'

'Ah, that's another matter. It's not too good. Maybe it's the season, but more likely it's the terrible state of affairs in Marseille these days.'

On the quayside next to the fish stalls a large stone commemorates the foundation of the city by Phocian sailors, Greeks from Asia Minor, in the sixth century BC. The inscription grandiloquently proclaims this to have been the great moment when the eastern Mediterranean was linked with the west – a boast which the heirs of the Phoenicians in modern Tunisia would hotly dispute.

Now that the main freight port is now further up the coast, at what was until twenty-five years ago the fishing village of Fos, the Old Port has returned to its origins, its daily commerce largely reduced to local fishery and passenger ferry services, plus a forest of clanking aluminium masts in the yacht marina. At first the Fos-Marseille container terminal suffered from the same mismanagement and misplaced ambition that afflicted similar projects at Genoa and at Gioia Tauro and Sibari in Calabria; fears that it would prove a huge white elephant compounded despondency about the decline of traditional industries in Marseille itself. By the 1970s the marketing and production of its best-known product, soap, were in tatters – though recently a new *de luxe* trade has been established with such unlikely customers as Ireland and Turkey.

In spite of the setbacks, Fos-Marseille has become the fifth commercial port in the world, and the second in Europe after Rotterdam. Approaching the complex at night, the traffic becomes caught up in a maze of motorway interchanges, while the Provençal countryside is bathed in light from the lamps of container lorries disgorged down huge ramps onto quays and wharves gouged out of the sea shore.

One sector of Marseille life which has remained as buoyant as ever is organised crime. The Marseille underworld is linked to the southern European network of professional criminals including the Neapolitan Camorra and, more particularly, the Sicilian Mafia and their cousins in North and South America. For more than fifteen years past the bosses of the 'milieu' have been caught up in what is known as the 'limonade' war – 'limonadiers' being the proprietors of those cafés in the old town where the gangster barons go to be seen and receive homage. The 'lemonade war' is partly the result of the break-up, in 1971, of the notorious 'French Connection' racket, in which limousines were carefully fitted out with compartments containing heroin and then shipped to the United States; and partly an old-fashioned feud to decide who will be top dog in the traditional rackets associated with protection, prostitution, building, transport and corrupt local government. Immediately after the Second World War the biggest operators were the Guerini brothers, who took over from the Carbone and Spirito combination, which had survived by collaborating with the German occupying forces. The Guerinis came to an abrupt and sticky end in the late Sixties – one was shot in his car, while the other died of cancer after his release from a life sentence on compassionate grounds.

The battle for succession was joined by Gaetano 'Tany' Zampa, a footloose pimp from Naples, and the Hoareau clan. In the meantime tireless work by an investigating magistrate, Judge Pierre Michel, had established firm evidence for the ties between the drug refining and shipping operations of the Sicilian Mafia and the Marseille underworld; he and his team discovered no fewer than six heroin 'kitchens' for processing morphine base into narcotics for sale on the street.

Judge Michel was shot dead in Marseille in October 1981; three years later the 'lemonade war' reached its climax with the suicide of Tany Zampa in jail. In under nine months nearly fifty prominent Marseille gangsters had been murdered. In July 1985 'Monsieur Paul' Mandolini, thought to be one of the brains behind the French Connection, was shot, as were three of the 'chemists' responsible for processing drugs. 'Mimi' Ragazzi, who had designed the special containers that were sealed in the cars to be shipped to the American East Coast, was put in hospital after receiving a fusillade of bullets when his car stopped at a crossroads. From his sickbed he confessed to detectives that he would feel safer in gaol.

Despite sanguinary tales in the public prints, the 'lemonade war' was nothing like as violent or destructive as similar battles raging at much the same time between gangs in Naples and Palermo – in both cities the murder rate was running at almost two a day for over two years. In all three cities gangs were fighting to control the 'drugs bridge' from southwest Asia across Europe to the United States and the traffic in South American cocaine, as well as dealing in weapons for political militias and terrorist groups.

A raid on the Marseille Savings Bank in the Avenue Foch in February 1987 provided an almost theatrical footnote to the Marseille feuds. A gang of armed men held twenty-three hostages for much of the day, but towards evening the hostages were freed unharmed. There was no sign of the gang: they had disappeared through a tunnel they had spent at least three weeks preparing, down to carpeting the floors and laying in telephones. They made their getaway through the sewers in an inflatable raft powered by outboard motor.

A few weeks later police, recovered from their embarrassment, said the haul had amounted to about 20 million francs, and not the 200 million originally thought. When detectives had found the body of Gérard Vigier, the alleged heir of Tany Zampa, whom they suspected of being the leader of the raid, they assumed he had been shot by his own gang for not distributing the spoils.

Architecturally, Marseille is not in the first rank. Much of its waterfront consists of ugly post-war reconstruction, while the older buildings are weighty and austere Second Empire pseudo-palatial. The eighteenth-century Hôtel de Ville on the Quai du Port stands out in its charm and elegance – a remarkable survivor from the demolitions that followed the plagues of the 1740s and German reprisals against the Resistance in 1943 during which they ordered the destruction of nearly 1500 dwellings in a fourteen-hectare radius.

I was greeted at the Hôtel de Ville by the man who assumed power in the city when the Americans landed in August 1944. Gaston Defferre was one of the great city bosses of the century, a mayor in the mould of Drapeau of Montreal, La Guardia of New York and Daley of Chicago. A former Resistance leader, a millionaire and a life-long socialist, he ran Marseille as his personal fief, serving as mayor for four long terms from 1953. Under François Mitterrand he became Minister of the Interior, responsible for regional devolution in France in the early 1980s. Until the last moment he seemed indestructible, despite economic set-backs, the chaos of the Fos project, increasing gangland violence and one of his deputies being accused of being too friendly for comfort with the notorious Ventura brothers, Corsican racketeers in the Guerini mould. He died of a stroke just after he had been ousted from office by a coup in his own party in May 1986.

While relying on the traditional skills of an old-time city boss, Gaston Defferre had a clear vision for the future. A self-confessed 'enthusiast for the Mediterranean' – in our short conversation he regaled me with jokes about the Sicilian Mafia – he believed his corner of France was about to be transformed by high-technology industries, and cultural and educational centres for the computer age. The investment, however, was not forthcoming and development has been halting at best. Marseille continues to be a victim of geography and history, as its old quarters and suburbs become more a haven for North Africans. Not least of neighbourhood troubles is the continuing fatal attraction between the Marseille underworld and their cousins in Corsica.

iii Granite Exile: Corsica

The strip of water between Sardinia and Corsica can be wild and chilling, even in high summer. On the July afternoon when I took the ferry from Santa Margherita in Gallura the sea was lumpy, the drizzling clouds ragged hanks of dirty wool. The wind, the *tramontana* from beyond the Alps and Apennines, was throwing foam high above the heeling yachts brave enough to challenge the choppy narrows. Through those straits run the coldest and swiftest currents of the Mediterranean.

The little ferry was all but empty, save for a few hitch-hikers and one or two locals on a brief visit. Traffic across the straits is hardly brisk, though increasing numbers of Italians are taking holidays in Corsica; but most travel direct from the mainland. Though united in geography, Sardinia and Corsica have been divided by history.

Both are granite islands, with high rocky spines of mountains, and both conserve the dense scrub, the maquis, as no other region, save parts of the coast of Anatolia. Both received the attentions of Greeks and Romans, and their coasts were the haunts of Saracen raiders in the European Dark Ages. The kings of Aragon and the city states of Pisa and Genoa have left their mark to this day: both islands are dotted with fine churches in the Pisan style, striped in stone of different colours, decorated with men and beasts sculptured in stone pantomime.

Genoa retained its grip on Corsica until 1769, when, after the failure of a popular uprising led by Pasquale Paoli, the island was annexed by France. Sardinia went to Piedmont, so bringing a royal title to the House of Savoy; it was as King of Sardinia that Victor Emmanuel was to unite Italy under one crown in 1871.

Corsica has had no such nominal honour in modern France, despite being the birthplace of Napoleon Bonaparte. The French connection still implies to many Corsicans arrogance and intolerance towards their culture, their language, customs, and very particular ways of family and village life. In its rugged mountain interior Corsica seems an island exiled in its own landscape, wrapped by the deep woods and scrub of the maquis in a mantle of green melancholy.

The destination of the ferry that stormy July afternoon, Bonifacio, is protected by a huge rampart of sheer cliff in light biscuit brown and yellow. The little port itself is a creek cut deep through the rock. The lower town along the creek is French *touristique* in outward appearance, striped awnings, brasseries and crêperies. The upper town, with its austere façades and windswept squares, still bears the stamp of the Genoese, by whom it was privileged above other ports in the island.

The conflict of Italian and French influences is a paradox compounded by geography. Mainland Italy is roughly fifty miles away, whereas the shortest distance to the French coast is more than a hundred. On a fine day the northern finger of the island, the Cap de Corse, can be seen clearly from the island of Elba and the shore of the Maremma in Tuscany. Italian was the diplomatic language of the community until 1769, and today a foreigner travels more easily with Italian than French amongst Corsican nationalists.

In the old town stand the memorials of overseas adventure and commerce, both French and Genoese. The Place du Fondaco from the Arabic *fondouk* a warehouse or store – recalls Genoese trade with the Levant and North Africa. More explicit is the monument to the Foreign Legion in the Place Bir-Hakim, which was dedicated in 1963, when the Legion moved its training battalion to Bonifacio from the newly independent Algeria. The bronze statue of a legionnaire, dedicated to soldiers killed in the Sud-Oranais between 1897 and 1902, was itself removed from its original site in Algeria at Saida.

The Legion's base at Bonifacio is the only one remaining in the Mediterranean outside mainland France and it marks the end of France's colonial adventure in North Africa, in which it was born and won its reputation. For fiercer nationalist spirits it is a reminder of Corsica's past occupations by foreign armies.

Corsicans have had two natural defences against the invader: a hostile terrain and the nature of the people. *Clanisme* – or clannishness – can be an expression of pride, or fear and contempt, in Corsican society, much as the term 'mafia' is in Sicily. Community and family loyalty is still a strong social cement. Once it was the source of vendetta and banditry, a practice pursued by Corsicans over the centuries with peculiar virulence. The last great 'bandit of honour' to be executed was André Spada, guillotined at dawn on 21 June 1935 in the citadel quarter of Bastia. After years hiding in the maquis, he had been turned in by informers after he had ambushed a bus, killing two gendarmes and the driver and then burning their bodies. Spada manufactured his own legend, describing himself as the greatest tiger in the universe, and receiving foreign visitors in his mountain hideout. Like many of his kind, he was something of a mystic, declaring at his trial that he obeyed only the justice of God and Christ and not of men.

Last to hold out in the maquis was said to be a bandit called Muzarettu, who retired to a Franciscan monastery to die in 1952. By then banditry and *clanisme* had become infected by the ways of the professional criminal fraternity of mainland cities like Marseille, a process which began with the introduction of conscription to the island in the First World War.

At a day-to-day level Corsican clannishness works like any other system of patronage and recommendation in the Mediterranean. On the quay at Bonifacio I was a beneficiary of this at the hospitable hands of Monsieur José Gazano, consultant to the mayor, ship's chandler and proprietor of one of the main car rental concessions. He seemed to know everyone who counted, and sent me off to Ajaccio with a shoal of introductions. A genial mixture of general factotum and sorcerer's apprentice to the tourist trade, he seemed perpetually on the go. The problem, he explained, was the brevity of the holiday season from which he and so many fellow-Corsicans earned their living. In winter many small businesses close, and the town's population reverts to under 3000, whereas as opposed to nearly 20,000 from June to October.

With a permanent population of about a quarter of a million, Corsica was playing host to about 1,200,000 visitors a year by the mid-1980s. But national pride and the ruggedness of the interior have protected the island from the destruction and 'balearisation' by tourism which has afflicted neighbouring coasts in Sardinia, southern France and the Balearics. Corsica can claim to be the most unspoilt of all the large Mediterranean islands.

Halfway between Bonifacio and Ajaccio, where the river Taravo cuts through a gently wooded valley to the sea, lie a remarkable series of monuments to the island's earliest known invaders. Crowning a knoll overlooking open fields is a group of stone circles, a primitive system of fortified huts buttressed by natural formations of rock. These buildings and underground chambers were first uncovered by shepherds in the last century, but sustained scientific excavation began only after 1954. In the next few years experts led by the local archaeologist Roger Grosjean uncovered more than a dozen heavy stone pillars, some clearly in the shapes of men.

The stones were evidently part of a prehistoric megalithic culture. They were laid out to form a shrine, similar to stone circles of the same era found as far afield as Palestine, Cyprus and Avebury and Stonehenge in Britain. The worshippers were a peaceful shepherd people, who appeared in the coastal plains of Corsica as early as 6000 BC.

Some of the menhirs are powerful, phallic symbols of fertility. But the more recent statues have the features of faces while others shows vestiges of armour and weapons. These monuments, among the earliest to rep-resent human forms yet found in the western Mediterranean, are thought to be the shepherds' memorials to the fallen warriors of a strange people who came from the sea – probably the same people who eventually drove the pastoral tribes out of the southern part of the island and built rounded fortifications such as those on the hill at Filitosa. Similar to the rounded forts of Sardinia, the *nuraghi*, and the towers built at the same time by the Talyots in Majorca and Minorca, these structures earned them the name Torreans, or 'tower-builders'. But by the year 1000 BC, roughly four centuries after their first arrival, the Torreans seem to have departed Corsican shores.

A statue in the little museum at Filitosa provides an intriguing twist to the puzzle. It wears a helmet with a horn curling from the top – exactly the same shape as those worn by the warriors engaged in a ferocious sea battle on the temple of Ramesses III at Madinet Habu near Luxor. The accompanying inscription describes Egypt's attackers in year 5 of Ramesses' reign (1189 BC) as the 'people who came from the sea'. Today the upheaval in the central and eastern Mediterranean between the fourteenth and twelfth centuries BC is still called 'the invasion of the sea people', by scholars still puzzled by the exact identity of the warriors. It marked a cataclysmic change throughout the area, interrupt-ing Hittite civilisation and contributing to the rise of the early Phoeni-cian cities like Tyre and Sidon, yet no one knows exactly whence the invaders came, whether from Crete, the Aegean Islands, or even Sardinia as the statues at Filitosa might hint.

After their defeat by Ramesses, some of the invaders are believed to have settled round modern Gaza and to be the early Philistines, some of the forebears of the modern Palestinians.

The whole debate about the Sea Peoples, their origins and the devas-tating effects of their campaigns, has become a fascinating example of the way modern Mediterranean peoples are reinterpreting their origins. Propaganda aside, the Sea Peoples, to whom the Shardeans of Sardinia and the Torreans of Corsica almost certainly belonged, had a crucial role in the shaping of the Mediterranean world in its early history.

Filitosa seemed an enchantingly tranquil place, its meadows and mounds of stone bathed in sunlight broken by the umbrellas of shady trees. Cattle browsed among the rounded statues and sought the shade of a spreading chestnut, families wandered cheerfully over the hills. The only jarring note was provided by the visitors' clothing: why must the leisure-wear uniform of the *grande armée touristique* come in hues more appropriate to a sports arena or an ice cream sales campaign?

Turning to leave as the evening lowered its colours in a distant gleam of sunlight, fell in with a smart young Corsican woman, brought up in cultural exile in Paris. Michelle Marti had the fine, intelligent, dark looks typical of her people. She explained that she returned to her family home in the hills near Ajaccio as often as possible, but had gone to school and university in Paris. Many such exiles feel caught in a cultural twilight, belonging wholly neither to France nor Corsica, and frequently mistrusted or misunderstood in both countries.

Profound pride and deep love of Corsica shone out from her every remark – 'You see, we and our island have always been envied and coveted, and that is why we were never allowed to be independent for long' – while her view of Italians and her neighbours in Sardinia displayed the chauvinism of a true islander – 'The Sardinians are an untrustworthy bunch, and that goes for most Italians, too.'

Though nationalist by sentiment, Michelle had severe reservations about the wilder manifestations of Corsican separatism, particularly the bombings or *plasticages* by the outlawed FLNC, the Corsican National Liberation Front. She feared that such groups were becoming increasingly suborned by organised crime and the international drugs and arms trade.

In the 1970s France took steps to remedy the neglect of Corsica. In 1975 the island was divided into two *départements* instead of one; a year earlier Corsican had been recognised as an official language. And in 1982 Corsica became an autonomous region with its own elected assembly under the first and most radical statute in President Mitterrand's programme of decentralisation.

The capital of the region, and of the *département* of Corse Sud, is Ajaccio, a sprawling town with a touch of French provincial blandness about its squares and promenades opening to the western sea. Despite its heavy emphasis on its Napoleonic connection, the town is pleasantly unpompous. In recent years it has seen a fair amount of *plasticage* by the FLNC, who were unimpressed by the granting of regional status.

The offices of the *département* and the Regional Council were refreshingly candid about the stresses and strains in the Corsican economy and society. Jean-Baptiste Ferracci, *chef de cabinet* of the president of Corse Sud, explained that Corsica suffered by being the least populated of the large Mediterranean islands. Investment in new industry on the coast had been weak, and unemployment high. The biggest growth opportunity was in tourism, but great care was needed to protect the environment, particularly the coasts, from the boom in camping sites and cheap hotels.

'Our environment is our great opportunity,' he declared. 'No other island is so well protected and preserved as Corsica. We have little urbanisation, but our weakness is our low population – unlike Sardinia. We have a very special attitude to our maquis and mountains. The Corse is not a man of the earth who wants to cultivate his land. He's a *montagnard* who likes to travel, who prefers to reflect rather than till the soil.' Small wonder that Jean-Jacques Rousseau found his model of the noble savage in the Corsican *montagnard*.

'Corsica is really one huge mountain,' I was told by Jose Colombani, a senior adviser to the Regional Council. 'The mountain has more than three hundred and sixty *communes*, or local municipalities, which are very spread out and quite isolated.' Traditional farming in the highlands did not pay, and the most profitable agriculture was in the coastal plains, particularly in the east of the island. Much of the land there had been acquired for wine production by the *pied-noir* colonists who quit Algeria in the early Sixties. More than 17,000 came to Corsica, of whom nearly a quarter claimed some Corsican ancestry. Their presence became a running grievance for the separatists. But by the mid 1980s the farmers from Algeria were suffering. The bottom had dropped out of the wine and table grape market, and production had fallen to a third of ten years before. The only crop to enjoy an export boom in was the clementine.

Driving north across the island north from Ajaccio to the second city, the port of Bastia in the north-east, I came across a curious aspect of traditional agriculture. The road skirts round cliffs and ploughs through forests and gorges between sharp granite peaks. In the evening light the maquis surged across the hillside like ocean rollers, thin clouds of purple haze floating above. At the top of a steep pass I came across a clearing with a dozen trailers and cars parked in an impromptu market. Makeshift stalls sold wild honey, fruit, nuts, jam, butter, eggs and poultry live and dead.

The richest display was of *charcuterie*, based on the pigs of varying domesticity which roam the maquis. A bewildering variety of items were spread before us: black puddings, hams, trotters, bacon, salami sausages of all shapes, sizes and hues, infused with the smoky aroma of charcoal fires. Travellers were invited to sample these wares and eat their fill, and what was left over was seized by a snuffling, grunting rout of pigs, banging into customers and vendors and blissfully unaware that they too would soon be part of the *charcuterie*. Rarely can a food chain have been so brutally brief; the processes of production, distribution and consumption achieving a stark simplicity that a Chicago meat-canner would envy.

Towards sunset the road opened into an upland plateau flanked by hills suffused in evening mist, and I arrived in the small town of Corte, in the heart of the northern mountains of the island. With its wooden-beamed houses, and open square and street market, Corte still evokes its years of glory when it was the spiritual and political capital of Corsica's struggle for independence. The genius behind that struggle was Pasquale Paoli, General of the Corsicans from 1755 to 1769. He remains the symbol of Corsican nationalism, his lanky statue looking across the square a reminder that his spirit still hovers over Corte. Paoli was an extraordinary figure even by the standards of the European Enlightenment. Unlike most national heroes, the real man and his story are more interesting than the myth.

Like his contemporary, George Washington, Paoli was a great administrator in desperate conditions. But he was also something of a philosopher and a political visionary. Though born in Corsica, most of his upbringing was in Italy, where his father, the patriot Giacinto Paoli, was forced into exile in 1739 ten years after the struggle for independence had begun. He completed his education in the Royal Military Academy in Naples. Judging by his correspondence, Italian remained his preferred language, though he spoke French and English well. He could only manage a few words of his native Corsican dialect.

Paoli was summoned back to Corsica by the patriots in 1755. In July their assembly met in a remote monastery of the highlands to elect him as General of the Corsican People; his only predecessor, Jean-Pierre Gaffori, had been killed in an ambush outside Corte two years before, betrayed by his own brother.

Paoli's political and social experiments over the next fourteen years are a chapter of brilliant failure, but they gave the island the only semblance of independence it has enjoyed in over two thousand years. He drew up a constitution; a keen disciple of Montesquieu, he understood the division of powers as well as any of the founding fathers who were to frame the United States constitution more than thirty years later. He won the support of the Church and the clans, and he even had some success in suppressing the vendetta.

The crucial instruments in the Paoli constitution were the nine-man Council of State, and the Assembly, or General Diet, which met each year at Corte. Two-thirds of the deputies were elected by universal suffrage. Jean-Jacques Rousseau became a fervent admirer of Paoli, already having proposed in *Du Contrat Social* that 'there is still one country in Europe which is fit to receive laws, and that is the island of Corsica . . . I have a presentiment that this little island will one day astonish Europe.'

Rousseau was to introduce to him an even more ardent admirer, James Boswell, who journeyed to Corte in the autumn of 1765. But the General was away presiding over a circuit court, and Boswell had to traverse most of the island to catch up with his hero. 'My journey over the mountains,' he wrote in his *Account of Corsica*, was 'very entertaining [an epithet with an altogether more robust meaning then]. I passed some immense ridges and vast woods. I was in great health and spirits, and fully able to enter into the ideas of the brave rude men I found in all quarters.' At first Paoli thought Boswell a spy, but soon a firm friendship developed. The men were very different in temperament, with Paoli, a life-long celibate, constantly upbraiding the Scot for his libertine ways. For Boswell, Paoli was like a hero from the ancient world, a Cincinnatus, and he remained his steadfast champion even in defeat and exile.

Some of Paoli's most radical ideas concerned the island's economy. He established a free port at Ile-Rousse (Isola di Rossa), with a mercantile fleet under the Corsican flag of the blindfolded Moor. Fertile lands round the mountain villages were held as common property, and a number of feudal rights were suppressed. A programme of draining the coastal marshes and ambitious irrigation schemes were begun. Corsican ships were to open a new trade in timber, grain, wine, almonds, olive oil, and chestnuts with the southern ports of Italy. Jews came to Ile-Rousse from Livorno to supervise the commerce. But prosperity was to elude the new Corsica.

In the early 1760s the island was devastated by famine. Continuous rains poisoned the earth and destroyed crops; men and women starved to death while others survived in the wild on nuts, berries and herbs. The same famine struck Italy, killing thousands – possibly hundreds of thousands –in Emilia, Lombardy, and Istria, changing the human landscape more than any natural disaster since the Black Death. Poverty and destitution meant that Paoli and his administration could not stay in Corte the year round and moved about the island like a medieval court. Despite noble aspirations, much of his government was rough and ready, and had to adapt to the plight of the people.

The turning point came in 1768, when France virtually bought out the Genoa's interests in the island. Some 9000 French troops were sent to Corsica to help the beleaguered Genoese still clinging to their strongpoints on the coast. In the first engagements the French were beaten, but the following year fifteen battalions were despatched from France. Paoli had only six hundred regular troops, plus irregular militia, and was not a great field commander, unlike his eccentric and mystical brother

Clemente, who prayed for the enemy as he shot them. On 8 May 1769 a force of more than 30,000 under French command pushed back Paoli's army of 2000 to Ponte Nuovo, which guards the road to Corte from Bastia, where the Corsicans were trapped and cut down to a man.

The battle of Ponte Nuovo marked the end of Corsica's brief taste of independence, and the beginning of French domination of the island. Paoli went into exile, eventually reaching London where he was guest of Boswell and was fêted as a hero. The poet Thomas Gray told him he had been born two thousand years too late, and should have been a tribune of the Roman Republic.

After the Revolution in France he was allowed to return to Corsica as president of the *département* in 1790, but soon the Jacobins and Bonapartists turned against him. With the British seizure of the island in 1794, in which Nelson lost his eye in the siege of Calvi, the Anglo-Corsican kingdom was established, with Paoli agreeing to serve the viceroy Sir Gilbert Elliot, and once again producing a brilliant parliamentary constitution well ahead of its time. But inevitably the two men quarrelled, and in the summer of 1795 riots flared in the mountain villages of the Castagniccia against Sir Gilbert's rule. Fearing Corsica might otherwise suffer years of pointless civil war, Paoli agreed to return to London, where he lived on a government pension until his death in 1807. The Anglo-Corsican kingdom was over within a few months of his departure.

Paoli's enlightened views live on in the code known as the 'Legge Paolina,' still an element in customary law in the island. In Corte his greatest legacy is the university that bears his name. In 1763 a public university 'of all the sciences on the model of the best of the mainland' was established. According to the deed of foundation it was 'to dissipate the impression that Corsica is a barbarous place, an enemy of good studies and sciences, as the Genoese would wish the world believe'. By 1766 it had 150 students, but four years later the French forced it to close. Only in 1981 did the French see fit to re-open the university.

The campus is a collection of modest cement and orange stucco buildings. The morning I visited was taken up with a conference on the social and economic problems of Sardinia and Corsica between academics and local politicians from both islands. Delegates switched easily between Corsican and Sardinian dialects, Italian and French – the least preferred language of the four – the informal chatter and hubbub of the sessions was reminiscent of a Mediterranean fish market; appropriately enough, the most intriguing discussions concerned the revival of fishing after years of neglect.

A speaker from the University of Sassari said that in some fishing ports of northern Sardinia, such as Porto Torres, over half the fishermen were under thirty years of age. But old customs died hard. Although many of the fishermen now had degrees and diplomas, they were still unwilling to take women to sea – they talked too much, and were unlucky – and they were highly suspicious of such notions as cooperatives. At Porto Torres two families who shared a boat quarrelled so badly that when they put to sea they would take one end of the boat each and refuse to speak to the other the entire voyage. Both islands share the same fishing culture, she explained, and the fishermen have always migrated between the ports of both. She suggested that over the centuries the fishing communities have emanated from a handful of centres round the Mediterranean – which could explain why the names of the most common fish and the parts of a boat and were remarkably similar throughout the sea.

One day I made an expedition into the dense chestnut groves of the Castagniccia in the hills north of Corte. It was a particularly wet evening; the trees and woods seemed to crowd the way like a gloomy mob, and the road became little more than track in places. Mist and low cloud hung about the narrow coombs; the villages on the hillsides huddled under a curtain of fine rain. Until recently many of these communities must have been inaccessible to wheeled traffic, and only to man, mule and horse after a long upward slog. On one of the higher ledges sits the little town of La Porta with its magnificent baroque churchtower. Walking through the elegant square I saw the main door of the church was ajar, and a concert was in progress. The pure notes of a boy soprano suddenly cut through the damp and fragile air, the echo bouncing off the buildings opposite.

The Castagniccia is the heartland of Corsican independence and resistance, birthplace of the generals Paoli and Gaffori. Aleria down on the coast belongs to quite another tradition. It was the capital of the Roman colony of Corsica, and earlier the first Greek colonisers of Marseille had adopted it as a base: a fine archaeological site and museum mark the achievements of the classical occupiers. But in the late twentieth century, according to its mayor Vincenzo Carlotti, Aleria faces invasions and threats of a different order. Most of its income came from agriculture, but the three wine co-operatives were suffering from poor quality and overproduction, and farming offered little opportunity of new jobs for young people. But the mayor's biggest worry was the increase in organised serious crime, old and new. Banditry still persisted in Corsica and was linked with that in Sardinia. Lately a new form of mafia had began to show itself, taking over legitimate businesses, running hotels and nightclubs, dabbling in drugs, prostitution and bank robberies, and flourishing in the coastal communities which had switched from farming to mass tourism for their main source of income.

In the two years before our meeting no fewer than fifteen murders had been committed in Bastia, the second city of the island and the capital of Haute Corse. All, he suggested, were connected with the running of hotels and places of entertainment, and even of some of the boulevard cafés round the central square, the elegant Place St Nicholas.

Bastia has a less sunny aspect than Ajaccio, possibly because it faces east to the sea across its port. It was long the bastion of the Genoese and it still has a cool and reserved air behind its grey granite façades and ramparts. It is the principal port for the crossing to France – six hours away by sea, a critical factor in Corsica's economic isolation. Along with its own brand of patronage and *clanisme* it has absorbed some of the more dubious habits of the mainland, according to nationalist critics. The town hall was the biggest employer in the city, I was told, with more than 800 on its payroll – as many as the municipality of Bordeaux.

Michel Castellani is a member of the Corsican Assembly for the UPC, the Unione di U Populu Corsu – the 'autonomist' party which believes in achieving greater self-determination for Corsica by democratic means. He saw his party as the direct heir of Pasquale Paoli and his nationalist ideals. He was careful to point out the difference between the UPC and the more extreme nationalism of the MCA (Movimento Corso per l'Autodeterminazione) and the outlawed FLNC. The UPC had demonstrated aggressively against the wine companies of the Algerian *pieds noirs*, which they said had been favoured excessively by French subsidies. After one such protest in 1975, the UPC's charismatic founder, Dr Simeoni, had been imprisoned by the authorities.

In the following year the FLNC was formed and the *plasticages* and firebombings grew each year; in 1982 more than a thousand such incidents were recorded. In 1978 the radar at the air force base at Solenzara was blown up; in October 1980 the FLNC bombed seven banks in Marseille in one night. A bomb set off in a locker at Ajaccio airport before President Giscard d'Estaing's visit in April 1981 killed a Swiss woman tourist. In subsequent holiday seasons the extremists have detonated more than three hundred devices in the Ajaccio area alone. But, by the end of 1987, by careful intelligence work, the authorities had begun making inroads into the underground command of the FLNC.

The FLNC tactics were folly according to Michel Castellani. The most practical course was 'internal autonomy' or local self-government, with

France directing external security, monetary policy, and defence. The UPC programme made four simple demands: national rights for the Corsican people, official use of both French and Corsican, an economic development plan run from Corsica by Corsicans, and a recognition of political status for nationalist prisoners.

Corsica's biggest problem, he suggested, was summed up in Mussolini's phrase that the island 'was a cage without birds'. More than a quarter of a million Corsicans had emigrated over the past century, and over 30,000 had been killed in the First World War, somewhere between a sixth and a fifth of the population at the time. He feared the decline in the proportion of native Corsicans in the present population would continue unless something more was done to encourage young people to stay. 'With all our natural resources, it is ridiculous to think of the amount we are forced to import from France, anything from electricity to tomatoes and milk. Even the fruit businesses here last year lost more than five hundred million francs.'

Most worrying was the ageing of the population: by the mid-Eighties more than 60,000 Corsicans were over sixty years of age, more than a quarter of all residents in the island. 'In the last ten years a far more serious interest has been taken in the history of Corsica, but the pity is that I will have to send my son to Italy for higher schooling and university. Imagine! Corsica had the third highest population of all the great Mediterranean islands two centuries ago, but now we are fewer than the inhabitants of Malta. And they crowd into an area smaller than the Cap de Corse!'

The Cap de Corse is the finger of land to the north of Bastia, a slender peninsula dotted with villages, tourist hotels, granite hills of heather and maquis punctuated by small churches and sanctuaries in robust Pisan romanesque. Even under the noonday sun the Corsican scene never quite loses its natural and majestic melancholy. But in their love and defence of their land and their culture, the Corsicans exhibit a singular quality hardly matched by neighbouring islanders. In preserving their land from the worst excesses of industrial tourism and development, they may – to borrow Rousseau's phrase – come to astonish the rest of the Mediterranean world.

Three: Italy

i Order in Disorder

ITALIANS are the peacocks among modern Mediterraneans. Their sense of style and display rule the piazzas and galleries of the wealthy cities of the north of the peninsula with a tyranny of taste. Yet in the span of a mere generation the image of the country abroad has undergone a dramatic revolution. Once a chaos of chianti, sunshine and spaghetti, comic opera politics, corruption and crime, mandolins, mozzarella and Mafia, Italy today is the land of the designer label, the last word in style and fashion, from cookery to cars, from footwear to fedora.

The image revolution has been fed by the fastest economic growth of any European country. At the end of the Second World War Italy was largely an agricultural country, with half the population dependent on the land directly or indirectly. By the early 1980s the proportion had dropped to twelve per cent. 1986 was hailed as the year of the year of the 'sorpasso', when Italy overtook Britain in gross domestic production to become the third industrial power of Europe, and the fifth of the Western world.

Look closely, and the image fragments and shimmers like the reflection of a *palazzo* in a Venetian canal. Prince Metternich put his finger on it 1849, when he remarked that 'Italy is a geographical expression' – one which sits neatly at the crossroads of the Mediterranean, for Sicily is halfway between Jerusalem and Gibraltar, while part of the island is to the south of the northernmost African coast in Tunisia. Quite apart from the brawling residents – Latins, Etruscans and Romans – the invaders and colonisers who pillaged and pacified the land include Phoenicians, Greeks, Gauls, Carthaginians, Huns and Goths, Arabs, Byzantine Greeks, Normans, Germans, Spaniards, Ottoman Turks, Albanians, French, Austro-Hungarians, Nazi Germans and liberating Americans and British.

Understanding the culture of modern Italians can be unexpectedly difficult. Few peoples speak so eloquently of their predicament; from Neapolitan street urchins and Milanese bankers phrases pour like spun gold. I have travelled, worked and lived in the country for twenty-five years, and know its physical face, its landscape better than the country of my upbringing. Yet each time I return to Italy, some encounter or occurrence sets at nought my previous attempts at understanding – the place and its people are capable of constant surprises.

Public duty and loyalty to institutions still come low on the Italian list of virtues. One of Mussolini's few good quips was that governing Italians was not so much difficult, but impossible. Modern Italians have inherited from their Renaissance forebears the cult of the individual, the obligation to cut a dash whether up on the balcony or down in the piazza, to make *la bella figura*.

Much of the modern Italian distrust of public authority derives from the youthfulness of Italy's transformation from geographical expression to political fact, following the ultimate unification of the country under the House of Savoy in 1871. This is a cliché, but one easy to overlook and underestimate. In many respects the glue of Italian unity seems hardly dry. Despite the linguistic homogenisation of radio and television, more than fifty-five dialects are spoken, some – like Sicilian, Sardinian and the *patois* of Val d'Aosta and Friuli – are almost separate languages.

The years since unification have been riven by major upheavals, neutral disasters, economic depression, war and invasion. Italy's involvement in the First World War, as destructive of her manpower as that of any Western power, fuelled separatism, the rejection of unification, and the sense of deprivation which led to Fascism. In the Second World War the country's heavy industry was flattened by strategic aerial bombardment. After the surrender of Italian forces by Marshal Badoglio in 1943, the Allied campaign to drive out the Germans masked what became a civil war which opened rifts and wounds among Italians which persist to this day.

Both wars gave rise to regimes dominated by single parties, one dictatorial, the other democratic. Mussolini's Fascism lasted from 1922 to 1943. Already the Christian Democrats have doubled that record in the post-war era by participating in every government since the first emergency coalition formed by Alcide de Gasperi in 1946. One of the founders of the European Economic Community as well as of modern Italy, de Gasperi began his political career by representing the province of Trento, which belonged to Austria before the First World War, in the Imperial parliament in Vienna.

The most overtly Catholic of major European political parties, the Christian Democrats, have a remarkable record of durability, despite a regime initially beset by scandal and rumours of coups and subversion.

Ranged against them in what has seemed perpetual opposition since 1948 has been the Italian Communist Party (PCI), the biggest of its kind in a Western democracy. The fortunes, and misfortunes, of the Italian Communist Party are almost as big a mystery as those of the Christian Democrats. They have had three charismatic leaders – their founder, Antonio Gramsci, a highly original thinker who spent most of his political career in Mussolini's gaols; Palmiro Togliatti, the wartime resistance leader who supported the new Italian Republic but now stands accused of Stalinist practices; and the Sardinian minor aristocrat, Enrico Berlinguer, an architect of 'Eurocommunism' and a charming intellectual who became a highly popular figure throughout Italy, and under whom the Party gained in both local and national elections. The Communists' fortunes were based firmly in the trade union movement and in local government: their model regimes in the cities of Emilia-Romagna were renowned for decades. Berlinguer died of a stroke during elections for the European Parliament in 1984. More than a million people turned out to salute the cortège as it passed St John's Lateran in Rome. On polling day the Communists drew such a sympathy vote that their tally topped that of the Christian Democrats for the first and only time.

Since Berlinguer's death Communist support has slumped, at the polls, in membership, and especially among young people; control of key local authorities was lost amid accusations of corruption. Berlinguer's successor, Alessandro Natta, quickly became a legend of pedagogic dullness. No one talks of 'Eurocommunism' any more. As the winds of democracy began to blow through eastern Europe, the Italian Communists began to furl the red flag, and abandoned the gospel according to Lenin and Marx. In 1990, under a dynamic new secretary, Achille Occhetto, the party dropped the Communist label altogether and the party was rebaptised the Democratic Party of Italy.

The material success of post-war Italy has been won at some social cost, not least as the result of large-scale migration of workers and their families from the poor south, the Mezzogiorno, to the industrial cities of the north, and beyond the Alps to Switzerland, Germany, Belgium and Great Britain, as well as to Australia, Canada, and South America. Roughly four million left the fields and villages of the Mezzogiorno between 1945 and the early 1960s.

Whole areas of cities like Turin, Milan and Genoa changed their ways of life, leading to a form of cultural discrimination. Visiting the staff canteen of the main Turin daily, *La Stampa*, I found the tables segregated between groups of workers speaking local Piedmontese and those speaking Calabrian or Sicilian argot.

Recently, as industrial unemployment has grown, migrant families have begun returning to their roots in the south. For many the home-coming has been a shock. Despite enormous efforts by successive govern-ments – largely because so many national politicians are southerners and depend on local patronage – to encourage development in the Mezzo-giorno, the gap between rich north and poor south has been widening steadily over the past three decades. Few new large industrial enterprises have succeeded in the south; one of the most flourishing sectors has been organised crime, aided by the natural corruption of most southern local government, and fuelled by ill-controlled public development funds. Meanwhile the population in some parts of the Mezzogiorno is growing at a Third World rate, while that of much of the north remains static.

In the north the most serious symptom of social stress has been the wave of disorders caused by extremist groups of both right and left, most notoriously the Red Brigades. During the boom years of the Fifties and Sixties, rightists, driven principally by a romantic urge to revive the Fascist regime, were believed to have embarked on a 'strategy of tension', a programme of shootings and bombings which would lead to the instal-lation of an autocratic populist government. In December 1968 a bomb was detonated in the evening rush hour among shoppers queuing outside a bank in the Piazza Fontana in Milan. Sixteen people died and more than nineteen were injured. Ten years and a string of trials and arrests later, it was still unclear who was responsible, though evidence emerged of involvement of neo-fascist elements within the state secret services. On the biggest holiday weekend in August 1980, a bomb in a suitcase in the booking hall at Bologna railway station brought down the roof of an entire wing of the building, killing 84 people and wounding more than 200. Again no clear culprit was found, though neo-fascist groups in Italy and Latin America were uncovered by the subsequent inquiry.

More light was thrown on the criminal network behind the far right following another train bombing. Two days before Christmas 1984 a bomb hidden in a lavatory cistern exploded and derailed a night express between Florence and Bologna, killing at least sixteen people and injur-ing more than 150 other passengers. Assiduous work by magistrates in Florence led to charges being laid against members of the Sicilian mafias of Palermo, the Neapolitan Camorra, and Licio Gelli, the founder and director of the illegal P2 Freemasons' lodge.

Though no single operation by the Red Brigades caused slaughter on such a scale, it was they, more than the neo-fascists, that were to test the public nerve in the Seventies. The Red Brigades were no fashionable political import from the 1968 student movements of France and

Germany. They were an Italian phenomenon, spawned on disillusion-
ment and disgust at the ruling Christian Democrats and the Communist
Party in opposition. The founders of the movement emerged from two
distinct backgrounds – the new sociology faculties in the universities,
principally the one at Trento, launched with Christian Democrat money,
and militant workers' cells who had broken with the Communist-
controlled unions during wave of strikes which closed factories for
months in the 'hot autumn' of 1969.

Like the neo-fascists the original cohorts and sympathisers of the Red
Brigades had a curiously romantic streak, though nearly all their neo-
Trotskyite propaganda announcements were marked by a startling lack
of originality. Many of the founders came from strong Catholic backgrounds; their first philosopher-leader Renato Curcio, a student at
Trento, had belonged to a church youth group, while the lectures of
another ideologue, Professor Toni Negri of Padua, carried strong images
of blood and redemption reminiscent of the Catholic symbolism adopted
by the visionary of the Eastern Rising in Dublin in 1916, Patrick Pearse.
At Padua, home of one of Europe's oldest universities, a colleague of
Toni Negri dismissed his supporters among the student 'Autonomy' group
as children of the age motivated by 'Marx, Gramsci, the Black Panthers,
the Weathermen (a nihilistic band of bombers in America) and Bob
Dylan'.

At the height of their activity, in the late Seventies, the Red Brigades
and allied groups, which used more than a hundred different names, were
carrying out more than two and a half thousand bombings, shootings, and
hold-ups a year. Most significant was the kidnap and murder of the
President of the Christian Democrats and former Prime Minister, Aldo
Moro, in the spring of 1978.

Moro came from Puglia in the south-east, an area once ruled by the
emperors of Constantinople, and he played the political game with
Byzantine cunning. He had an almost oriental conservatism, a political
art based on Levantine inertia, but he understood power as no other in
Italy at the time. Fearing that thirty years unbroken rule could weaken
and possibly destroy the Christian Democrats, he arranged a parliamentary pact with the Communists which would compromise them with the
responsibilities of national office for the first time since the emergency
coalitions just after the war (though they were given no seats in the
cabinet), while allowing him the space in which to revive and reform
his own party. The plan was to cost him his life.

The Red Brigades understood that Moro was the most potent politician
of his day. So did others in the shadows and fringes of Italian

constitutional politics, for never did the establishment make so little effort to negotiate with the terrorists. The kidnap team grabbed the statesman from his car in the suburbs of Rome as he was driving to parliament for the confidence vote in the new government. All five bodyguards were shot dead in the ambush.

In fifty days of captivity Aldo Moro sent a series of agonised letters to his family and former political colleagues. Many contained pleas to negotiate with his captors, which were steadily refused; and they went on to produce devastating criticism of the weakness of the Italian state and the failings of individual ministers. Twenty thousand troops and police searched for the Red Brigades' hideout, but to no avail. On 9 May 1978 Aldo Moro's body was found in the boot of a car in the Via Caetani, midway between the headquarters of the Communist and Christian Democrat parties. He had been shot eleven times in the chest, his blood choking his lungs.

Moro's murder led to the downfall of the Red Brigades, cutting them off from support among the militant student population. Many of the hard-core Marxist left were shocked at the psychopathic brutality with which the statesman and his guards had been killed. Within a year or two the leaders of the operation had been rounded up, and by the mid-Eighties more than 1500 men and women accused or convicted of terrorist offences were behind bars.

The authorities got on top of the terrorist offensive by improved policing and tough anti-terrorist laws permitting long periods of arrest without charge or trial. More significant was a development with a distinctly Catholic flavour – a temporary law allowing former terrorists to renounce and repent their violent pasts in exchange for a reduction in charges and sentences. The law ran only for a year or two in the early 1980s, but it helped break the back of the Red Brigades and their allies. Throughout the Eighties sporadic killings continued to be carried out by small cells using the five-pointed star emblem and name of the Red Brigades, but such groups became increasingly enmeshed in the world of organised crime.

Several of those tried for the Moro murder confessed in court to the theatrical unreality of their actions. One woman said that, while seizing Aldo Moro from his car, 'I felt that I was acting in a play'. In the early days of the Moro kidnap I went with three colleagues from the French and Italian press to see a group of leftists running a magazine called Counter Information. For most of the night they subjected us to vapid debate and charades, punctuated by the most puerile jokes. Much later I discovered that the doors of the flat had been locked, and that we were to be held as 'witnesses' should the Caribinieri break in to make arrests.

A more profound drama was enacted at the memorial mass for Aldo Moro celebrated in St John's Lateran by Pope Paul VI, who had been a close friend of the dead man. The Pope had written a letter in his own hand asking the kidnappers in the name of humanity to spare the life of his friend, and was deeply shocked by what had happened. By now he was so frail that he had to be carried in the pontifical chair, a piece of pomp he had abolished as inappropriate to the modern Church. As he stood to give his homily and blessing, his arms were so wracked with arthritis that he could not raise them above his shoulders. 'Oh Lord, you did not hear our prayer to restore our friend Aldo to us safely, and we can only ask why,' he exclaimed. A tiny, sparrow-like figure clothed in brilliant crimson Paul VI for once struck the deep note of humanity which had eluded him through most of his difficult pontificate; three months later he too would be dead of a heart attack. At the end of the service the congregation of officials and politicians, which only half filled the huge basilica, shuffled out in embarrassment, all too aware of their own failure and inertia.

The era of the Moro kidnap and the worst of the Red Brigades attacks is now referred to as the 'years of lead' (anni di piombo). Yet recovery of confidence was swift, as the design revolution led a new boom in the Eighties. 'Made in Italy' became a new symbol of the new designer-label culture. In 1980 Fiat, the biggest private company in the country, was laying off 25,000 workers at its main Turin car works and putting as many on short-time, and Communist militants were threatening to occupy the plant, yet five years later the company was making huge profits and earning more than a billion dollars annually. Industrial leaders like Giovanni Agnelli, Fiat's president, Carlo de Benedetti, presiding over a huge conglomerate based on Olivetti, Raul Gardini, head of Feruzzi and Montedison, and the television magnate Silvio Berlusconi, earned far greater public acknowledgement than all but a few politicians. At the annual general meeting of his company Agnelli is like a Renaissance prince, answering questions in three languages on subjects as various as Fiat's balance sheet, East-West tensions, and whether pornographic film stars should be members of parliament.

During the 'years of lead', arguments of principle and conscience were rehearsed largely in print and in the cinema: writers and directors became the conscience of their country. Postwar Italy has enjoyed a flowering of literature and cinema, and the best of the political and social debate has been in books, journals, films and theatrical satires and revue. Directors like Francesco Rosi, the Taviani brothers, Bernardo Bertolucci, Ermanno

Olmi and Elio Petri have subjected the dark areas of Italian life to biting comment, with their films on the oppression of the Mafia, the poverty of the Mezzogiorno and political subversion. Elio Petri's *Todo Modo*, released two years before the Moro affair, told the story of a Catholic political leader whose party connived at his destruction and death, but it has not been reshown publicly in Italy since 1978. It was based on a novella by the Sicilian writer Leonardo Sciascia, who wrote a brilliant polemic after Aldo Moro's death, which had first to be published in France due to the sensitivity of most Italian publishers to its subject matter; and in the aftermath of the murder he debated the issues in the papers with Italo Calvino, one of the geniuses of postwar European literature.

Calvino's great stories are fantasies, full of wit and irony. I had met Calvino once in London, and we had strolled around the antique stalls and outré clothes shops of the King's Road, where he was enchanted by the hair-dos of the punks and the louche attire of their modish successors, the New Romantics. The wit and gaiety of his commentary exactly reflected the idiom of his books, and his simian features were lit up with pure delight and he told me he was determined to come to London to write a novel. Calvino was, above all, a storyteller, in the tradition of Homer and Herodotus, the chronicles of the Old Testament, the tales and itineraries of the great medieval Arabs. When I phoned him to ask if we would meet to talk about this aspect of Mediterranean culture for this book, he paused at the other end of the line, and then sniffed – he had the most humorous and eloquent sniff, a little snort which said everything. 'All right,' he said, 'but I need to think about it, let's meet in six months time.' Before we could fulfil the arrangement, he was felled by a stroke after a public lecture in Siena. A luminous figure, elusive to the last.

Just before he died Calvino had been preparing a series of lectures for Havard University entitled 'Memo for the Next Millenium'. In his argument, as indeed in his use of fantasy, he had much in common with one of the most flamboyant and intriguing masters of the Italian cinema, Federico Fellini. Both had severe misgivings about the polluting effect of the mass media on creative writing and speaking, both were concerned about broadcasting, and in particular about the wild, uncontrolled jungle of television in Italy.

Television is an overwhelming presence in Italian life. In the mid-1970s, when the state monopoly broadcasting was set aside by the courts, more than 600 'private' television stations started up in a single year, though barely more than a hundred were functional at any one time.

The developer Silvio Berlusconi quickly gained control of three national commercial stations. Italian television transmitted a higher proportion of advertising to programmes than anywhere in Europe, and more quiz shows than the major stations of the Continent put together. Most of the fare on offer from Italy's broadcasting companies is of a mind-numbing banality and mediocrity.

And yet the Italians' way of life exhibits an exuberance and a fantasy which save them from the zomboid purgatory induced by television. It is their taste for anarchy as an art form. Every public loyalty and pursuit has a private face: the family and the local community come first. This network of private factions and loyalties is both a strength and a weakness. It may well explain why an organisation like the illicit P2 Freemasons' lodge, one of the juicier political scandals of recent years, could not have been a plot to overthrow the state, but was more like a high-class trading ring of spivs, dealing in all kind of commodities – arms, hot money, political favours – and dodging in and out of the frontiers of legality, especially in finance. The P2 roll numbered some thousand politicians, journalists, police and military officers, civil servants, and its revelation brought down a government; not a very good government, it is true. Apart from the nasty hints of shadowy links between some lodge members and the mafia and right-wing terrorism, the whole affair had a faintly *buffo* aspect. One member described the induction ceremony conducted by the Venerable Master, Licio Gelli, in the Grand Hotel in Rome as 'like being initiated in the tribe of Big Chief White Feather'. The engaging journalist Maurizio Costanzo was moved to make a public confession on television: 'I have been a cretin,' he lamented.

No people deprecate themselves with such wit and style as Italians. But alongside the gentle art of anarchy runs the ruder skill of private survival. In Naples the expression is '*l'arte d'arrangiarsi,*' the art of arranging for ourselves, of getting by using community, faction and friend; in times of need we can always turn to cousins, sisters, brothers-in-law and their tribe of friends from school days, patrons and godfathers. It is a land of duality, discipline and indiscipline, fantasy and practicality – or, as they prefer to say themselves, '*ordine nel disordine*', order in disorder.

ii Cities of the North: Milan, Genoa, Venice

For much of the year Milan seems cut off from the rest of the world by a mantle of fog; by damp seasonal mists in autumn and winter conjured by nature, and in summer by a haze of industrial smog. In other respects, too, Milan is a city set apart from the rest of Italy. This may be due to the long occupation by the Spanish, the French and the Austrians. Only a few years ago a minor aristocrat lamented to me that Milanese society had been going steadily downhill since the departure of the Austrians after the bloody defeats at Solferino and Magenta in 1859.

The bustle and hectic commerce of Milan seem more in keeping with the cities of northern Europe than with the Mediterranean world. Milan has been responsible for many of the successes of postwar Italy. Today it is the country's capital for banking and finance, design technology, fashion, and mass communications. It has been a leader in political power and influence. It was the place where Fascism became a force in the early Twenties, and where Mussolini's public career ended with his corpse being hung upside down alongside that of his mistress Clara Patacci in the Piazzale Loreto in 1945.

Its physical aspect is not nearly so grim as the catalogue of commercial and industrial achievement might suggest. The gloomy streets lined with lugubrious nineteenth-century town houses and *palazzi* conceal remnants of every age since the Romans. The central station and the stock exchange are outstanding if contrasting examples of fascist monumental building. The façade of the station is an extravagance of motifs and ornaments recalling ancient Roman glories, while the stock exchange is austere and unadorned, a block of totalitarian severity. More gracious is the Pirelli tower, delicate as a razor blade set on end, the masterpiece of Pier Luigi Nervi.

In the heart of the city the cathedral with its forest of gothic pinnacles battles with atmospheric pollution and the vibration of the traffic. A piece of Milanese spiritual commerce by Duke Gian Galeazzo Visconti, a repayment by the populace to the Virgin Mary for deliverance from the plague in 1386, it took more than five hundred years to complete.

More evocative is the church of St Ambrose, with its shallow tiled roof, cloister, and square Lombard tower in red brick. It was on this site that Augustine of Hippo and his mother Monica must have heard St Ambrose preach and lead the choir. On the feast of Ambrose the city still takes a day off to honour their saint, and a week-long fair is held in the street leading to his church.

St Ambrose is also the patron of music and his *festa*, 7 December, marks the opening of the opera season at La Scala. Until very recently La Scala, Alfa Romeo racing cars and the *Corriere della Sera*, the country's leading paper for a century, were taken by many Milanese to be symbols of their city's superiority. Both Alfa and the *Corriere* have had troubled careers of late, but La Scala remains one of the great opera houses of the world, whose reputation rests on legend as much as fact. It was built in 1778 after its predecessor, the Teatro Ducale, had been burnt to the ground in the wild celebrations of carnival three days before Lent in 1776. Several times in its history La Scala itself was to be threatened with similar disaster. In 1898 it had to close during food riots brought on by a slump in the textile industry; dozens of Milanese died when troops put down the disturbances. During a carpet bombing raid by Allied aircraft on the night of 15 August 1943, the entire roof and most of the furnishings of the auditorium and backstage were wrecked, among them the fabled chandelier, which had been converted to electric light in 1883, so enabling the house lights to be dimmed – until then, in the Austrian court manner, the auditorium had remained lit, a distraction for performers and audience alike.

At times a symbol of the nation's political destiny, La Scala stands above all other Italian houses for the quality of its music and the lavishness – not to say excess – of its productions. Two figures dominated the theatre in the latter part of the last century and the first half of this: Giuseppe Verdi and Arturo Toscanini. Although only a handful of Verdi's operas received their first performance at La Scala, the most celebrated being *Nabucco* in 1842 and, after a twenty-year gap owing to a feud with the management, *Otello* in 1886 and *Falstaff* in 1893, he moved to Milan to be near the opera, and a famous early photograph shows the composer rushing through the piazza, instantly recognisable by his tall hat and his beard. Through his early operas, particularly *Nabucco* with its theme of the Hebrews' liberation from Babylonian captivity, he was seen as a prophet of the *risorgimento* and the new Italy; the letters VERDI were supposed to be an acronym for 'Vittorio Emmanuele *Re D'Italia*' (Victor Emmanuel King of Italy), though the legend has been gilded by hindsight. No other Italian composer has so consistently held the affection of the public.

Verdi died in 1901. The memorial concert was conducted by the young Arturo Toscanini who had made his debut at La Scala three years previously. He had started out as a cellist, but on tour with *Aida* in 1886, the conductor was booed off the podium during a performance in Rio de Janeiro, the young Arturo was prevailed to take up the baton, and his career was launched. His musical memory and iron discipline are legendary: no ornament or indulgence, he believed, should mar the composer's original intentions.

In 1921 he helped establish La Scala as an independent enterprise, an *ente autonomo*, but by the end of the decade he had chosen exile, refusing to Mussolini's face to accommodate the preposterous cultural dictates of Fascism. In America he became the principal conductor of the National Broadcasting Company, and after the bombing of La Scala he took his orchestra on a world tour to raise funds for the rebuilding of the theatre. At the concert for the reopening on 11 May 1946, the maestro was back on the podium with a programme full of old favourites – selections from Rossini's *Thieving Magpie* and *William Tell*, Puccini's *Manon Lascaut*, and from Verdi, the *Te Deum*, and the overture and slaves' chorus from *Nabucco*. When Toscanini died in January 1957, the theatre closed and thousands turned out to follow the funeral cortège. Piazza La Scala was a sea of black coats and hats.

Toscanini's bequest to La Scala was the guarantee of its independence: no politician would dare emulate Mussolini's interference. But with independence went extravagance. The bills for opening productions could be reckoned in millions, possibly billions, of lire, or hundreds of thousands of dollars. I was allowed backstage for the rehearsals of *Don Giovanni* which was to open the 1987 season in the opera's bicentennial year. The English bass-baritone Thomas Allen was taking the title role, and his dresser apologised for the unlaundered state of his long lace *jabot*. '*Tutto bello per Don Giovanni*,' she cried, '*tutto bello*' – nothing but the best for Don Giovanni! He was supposed to have freshly cleaned and laundered clothes for each day of rehearsal, of which there were thirty-five, most with a double cast and a fortnight with full orchestra – a luxury almost no other house in the world could afford, this being La Scala, in the final banquet scene, a genuine roasted pig had to be borne in, even in rehearsals.

Much the same aura of mystery and power that prevailed at La Scala pervaded the headquarters of the *Corriere della Sera*. The offices are in a rather plain building in via Solferino, about five hundred metres from the theatre. Most of the business was done on the first floor, which housed the editor, the main newsroom and the economics department. But it was the corridor that gave me an illuminating lesson in the finesse and sheer front that colours so much political intrigue in Italy, during a delightful sojourn as guest writer in the winter of 1976–77. After each meeting of the committee of journalists (the *comitato di redazione*) little knots of reporters and sub-editors would gather at different doors along the main passageway, each group representing a different political party or faction. The discussions and arguments were quite open and direct – socialists here, communists there, and extra-parliamentary left at the far end. In the Anglo-Saxon world such debates and plots would have been hatched behind closed doors, at *Corriere* they took place in the open thoroughfare of the principal corridor itself.

For nearly a century *Corriere* was Italy's leading daily, essentially a journal of regime. Until 1974 it was in the hands of one family, but then was bought up by the Rizzoli publishing group, behind which was the confusing web of duplicity and special interests of Roberto Calvi and the P2 Freemasons' lodge. When that scandal burst, Rizzoli was all but bankrupt and the prestige of *Corriere* severely dented.

In the mid-Seventies, before the Freemasons' grip had tightened, the paper took a radical turn under the editorship of Piero Ottone, a Genoese who had served as its correspondent in London, Moscow and the war in Algeria. Piero would have made his mark in papers anywhere; he is the best editor I have ever worked to, incisive, witty, brief on idle persiflage in editorial conferences. In his whole figure lurked something Byronic, a sly grin his most eloquent form of address. He set out to sharpen both the reporting and commentary of the paper and his own pieces were models of elegance and lucidity.

Above all he believed in debate. On succeeding days experts from different camps would unfold their views across the front page. Leading literary lights such as Alberto Moravia and Pier Paolo Pasolini spread themselves on topics such as abortion, human rights and, above all, what Italy was coming to – arguments whose fire contrasted sharply with the sterility of much of the proceedings of parliament in Rome. In one important respect Piero Ottone's sense of controversy helped change the face of Italian society. He was not a Roman Catholic and his political perspective was that of the liberal laity. In 1974 the Christian Democrats campaigned hard in a referendum to abrogate Italy's new-born divorce law. The *Corriere* under Ottone argued forcibly for divorce to be retained, and carried the day. The party of the establishment in Rome, the Christian Democrats, and – oddly – that of the local establishment in Milan, the Socialists, never forgave Ottone his open and free-spirited approach, and he left the paper after only five years at the helm.

For all the prestige and gloss of Milan's leading banks and manufacturers like Pirelli, Alfa Romeo and the chemical giant Montedison, the true wealth of the surrounding region of Lombardy has a more modest base. The backbone of the Italian industrial economy consists of thousands of small companies, employing between 50 and 150, usually family-owned with profits carefully concealed from public and official gaze. In Lombardy such enterprise is characterised by the expression '*il Lombardo in piccolo, piccolo*' – the little Lombard, a busy, rather conservative, but not ragingly Poujadist. Anecdotes about such figures are usually attributed to a family called Brambilla, the Lombard equivalent of Smith.

The Brambilla mentality and industry is not confined to Lombardy but spreads throughout the plain between the Alps and the northern spurs of the Apennines. Family firms making spun gold necklaces and jewellery round Vicenza are now world leaders, while Campagnolo is the leading manufacturer of racing bicycle gears and accessories. Along the Brenta Canal, between Padua and Venice, decorated with Palladian villas, small factories produce leather accessories and fashion shoes for Paris boutique and Moscow superstore, on sites where tanneries and workshops set the vogue for high-heeled shoes and other frivolities for the courtesans of Renaissance Venice.

To the west of Milan, among the misty tributaries of the River Po, the small firm of Gaggia has its factory. The name of Gaggia is synonymous with a minor revolution in taste and social habit. Fifty years ago Achille Gaggia was barman in a café near Porta Vittoria in Milan. He felt sure that his coffee could achieve a smoother, richer texture if steam was forced through the roasted beans at pressure – the basis for what later became known as 'espresso' coffee. The war intervened before he and an engineer friend could construct a machine to effect the espresso process. But since it was first produced in 1948 the Gaggia coffee-maker, with its pump handles and chronium bumpers, has become a popular icon along with the jukebox and the fruit-machine.

By the mid-1980s the taste for espresso was giving work to 180 employees at the Gaggia factories in Italy. Sales totalled more than $35 million in 1985 – the year in which the designs used in the first machines were finally abandoned. Achille Gaggia himself died in 1962 but the family maintained a generous stake in the firm, which diversified into ice-cream makers and machines for capuccino or espresso in the home, one appropriately named Il Fantastico.

For the Fantastico a new plant was opened at Motta Visconti. Expansion of the old factory at Abbiategrasso was forbidden as it lies in the National Park of the Ticino, a tributary of the Po running down from the Alps. The natural environment, particularly the countryside of northern Italy, has been one of the biggest victims of Italy's industrial expansion over the last forty years. The great rivers are polluted. The Po waters are dead to within twenty kilometers of their source in the mountains. The roads north from Milan to the lakes Como and Lugano are strewn with rusting cars, plastic, and ruined woodlands, as though the new town-dwellers, many originating from the south, wish to obliterate memories of their peasant pasts.

During Italy's post-war industrial boom regulating industrial development and protecting the environment were often left to the *comune*, the local town council. Greater Milan is composed of dozens of such *comunes*, so for years it was impossible to draw up and implement an adequate urban plan for the city and its burgeoning industrial hinterland.

The price of such lack of official vigilance was paid one July day in 1976. A safety valve blew at a chemical factory at Séveso, a *comune* midway between Milan and Como, showering nearby fields and gardens with dust. The dust was contaminated with a deadly poison, dioxin, which would continue to pollute the soil for up to thirty years. Animals and plants died; effects on humans were harder to detect, apart from an ugly rash called chloracne. The greatest risk was the development of cancer, particularly in the unborn; and on this the medical monitoring has been, at best, inadequate. Factory managers and health officers were arrested, but in time-honoured Italian fashion the scandal was hushed up, though the dioxin certainly remained in the fields. The company owning the Séveso factory, a subsidiary of the Swiss pharmaceutical giant Hoffman La Roche, made an out-of-court settlement of $120 million.

Séveso became the symbol of indequate government protection of the environment. However, private organisations have become increasingly active, from the cultural group Italia Nostra to Italy's own version of the British National Trust, the FAI, generously backed by Olivetti and its dynamic president, Carlo de Benedetti. Such initiatives have led to the restoration of many beautiful buildings and parklands for public enjoyment and use.

It was in this spirit that the nature reserve of the Ticino was established with backing from both local and national government. Within the park boundaries, factories like those of Gaggia are restricted in area and waste emissions carefully checked.

Milan today is the home of the designer label, of fashion for the street or the piazza rather than the salon or the showroom. The ground floor of the big department store Rinascente is a sea of trademarks, logos or *grif* in chic Italian argot. Trademarks and names famous for one product are borrowed or hired for a quite different line to inflate their value to the followers of fashion – the Ferrari label now sells pens and luggage as well as cars, and other famous racing names, such as Lamborghini, grace the latest in sports clothes and underwear.

One of the most prominent *grif*, shining above the counters and racks of perfumes of indeterminate gender orientation, is that of Armani. Giorgio Armani has become a highly effective one-man designer industry: the Armani style, if invited, can take over your life, from clothes and furniture to toilet water and soap. One year his sleek, flat telephone, *il notturno*, became the executive toy no Christmas tree could be without.

I met Giorgio Armani in his atelier after a gruelling day's work on his spring collection. He was a neat, lean figure, very fit-looking, with short-cropped hair and round-lensed spectacles. His bearing and discourse had the neatness and precision of a sculptor or engineer.

His own success, and that of Milan as a fashion centre, was the result of accident rather than calculation, he said. He had set out to be a doctor, but gave up his studies after three years. Eventually he found work in a design studio. At this point he says his mother-in-law became a decisive influence, lending moral and material support to his projects. He quickly found his ideas in demand from a number of different firms, and became 'style creator' (*creatore stilistico*) at the studio. 'Suddenly I found myself in the very marrow of the business. There it was – without searching for it, fashion was my life.'

That Milan ever became a fashion centre was a surprise to him and his colleagues. When he started in design, in the early Sixties, the capitals of high fashion were in Paris and Rome. 'The change came with the spectacular displays of new collections at the Pitti Palace in Florence, which brought labels like Valentino to the fore.' Gucci, whose base was in Florence, came to embody the style of the mid-Sixties as much as the Beatles and psychedelia. Whatever the fantastic creations at the Rome and Florence collections, says Armani, the product they were selling was made in Milan and the region round it.

'By the Seventies the years of the fat oxen were over,' he recalled, 'but Milan and the northern regions like Veneto and Piedmont had the advantage that the factories were here. The fashion business came to involve the community in Milan. Designers and their studios, as opposed to the fashion houses, became names in their own right. Fashion elsewhere had become exaggerated; here they wanted consistency and durability. The rich are a very stable but small market. Here it is a question of elegance with the minimum – how to be smart with very little, with thousands of different variations. With the kind of clientèle we have here, you cannot expect working people to change their wardrobes every six months.'

Armani credits his success, and that of his colleagues in Milan, to keeping in contact with the modern world, of designing for men and women in the street. 'But it is not enough for us to clap our hands and say we have beaten the French at their own game. Fashion has to renew itself, take risks, so in each collection we have some novelty. Though we in Milan may be less avant-garde, we have better public support than the other great centres. We have to show ourselves better entrepreneurs.'

Some of the best-known names on the Italian designer labels were associated first with the quality of their material, such as Missoni, or merchandising innovations, by which families like Benetton have planted their banners round the globe.

Despite the fame of his atelier, Giorgio Armani is ascetic to a degree of monkishness in the way he originates his ideas and concepts for a particular collection or look. 'I work from one simple, abstract idea, something worked out on a single sheet of paper. I always preferred drawing and mathematics to building with toys like Meccano. I may add things I see later which inspire me, the design of a lamp which I have seen at a play or in an old film, but such items are always adapted to go with the original concept.

'The time-scale and rhythm by which I develop each collection are regulated strictly. It is a dialogue between what people want, and what I wish them to try. The design has to have coherence or the public will not consider it.' The key to the Armani design vocabulary is self-discipline and minimalism. He says he is careful not to expose himself to too many visual sensations, even to the point of choosing carefully the same hideaways for his holidays.

'It would be too disrupting if I went to Istanbul to seek inspiration for a couple of days,' he ventured, concluding with a back-handed compliment to the journalist's way of life. 'It would be wonderful to roam the world as you do, to experience different cultures and communities. But if I were to do so, I could never come back to my real work.'

Genoa

The reputation of Genoa, like the character of its people, is one of the most difficult of the great Italian cities to appreciate. Cycles of success in maritime enterprise, commerce and banking, industry and political innovation, have been followed by bouts of almost spectacular failure. Not even the course of Genoese legends runs smooth. Christopher Columbus is acknowledged as one of the city's most famous sons, with rival claims by Catalans and Castillians finally demolished – yet no one can establish quite where in the old city he was born.

Usually swathed in sea mist and industrial smoke, the city crouches along its thin strip of Ligurian coast. Houses, wharves, factories, churches and palaces are squeezed against the shore line by the 'serpents' – the hills snaking down from the plateau of Piedmont and western Lombardy.

The cramped quarters seem to have affected the character and even the language of the people. The Genoese are the Scots of Italy – tough, careful and skilled in shipping, engineering and banking. The dialect reflects its trading past, with its scattering of words and terms borrowed from the Arabs and Portuguese, for whom the Genoese served as crews. In Italian a handkerchief is 'fazoletto,' whereas the Genoese 'mandorlo' comes straight from the Arabic.

Genoa's prowess in maritime enterprise, commerce, banking and insurance have proved far longer lived than that of its glamorous rival, Venice. Many Genoese trading colonies were established in the Black Sea and the Levant, in the eleventh and twelfth centuries, well before those of the Venetians. Genoa was the first Italian medieval city state to mint its own gold coinage; its financiers became the bankers to the Habsburg Empire, and until the middle of the nineteenth century the city was the centre of banking and insurance in northern Italy.

Until after the First World War, Genoa was Italy's most industrialised city, with the biggest concentration of steel and heavy engineering works as well as the largest commercial port. First in the field was the firm of Perrone, making locomotives for the railways, marine engines, heavy armaments and ordnance for the war – so much so that Genoa became virtually a company town. But many of the war contracts were not honoured, and the steel and engineering works had to be rescued by the state holding company, IRI. Today the only Perrone companies left are a modest but successful regional television station and a newspaper, *Secolo XIX*.

Until recently Genoa handled about a third of all Italian exports. But both the port and the engineering works have declined since the Seventies. To make matters worse, Genoa and its suburbs were the scenes of some of the most savage attacks by members of the Red Brigades and their allies. The 'movement' was virtually born on the city's doorstep. In the winter of 1970 remnants of groups involved in the 'hot autumn' industrial protests of the year before held a conference at a hotel in Chiavari on the riviera east of Genoa. A group led by Renato Curcio decided to go 'clandestine' and founded a militant underground faction which later borrowed the name of the Communist resistance groups in the war against the Axis, the Red Brigades.

Despite the dourness of the industrialised city, Genoa and its neighbouring towns of Portofino, Rapallo, Santa Margherita and Chiavari, became a playground of the rich. Banking and marine insurance brought the British, who promoted new fangled sports and aquatic pursuits. Dominating the exiles was the fabled Consul General Yeats Brown, who introduced the first motor yacht to the Gulf of Genoa. Twelve-metre yacht racing was almost invented in these waters and in 1926 a Swede took the championship, thanks largely to his use of a long jib sail drawn aft of the mast, henceforth known as the genoa. On a more arcadian note the British made their gardens in the steep wooded terraces up and down the Ligurian coast – most notably the sanctuary of tropical plants and trees laid out by the Hanbury family at Mortilla. To this day the city's soccer team maintains the English style 'Genoa' rather than the Italian 'Genova' – a gesture to Consul Brown and his friends, who first instituted 'The Genoa Association Football and Cricket Club'.

Today Genoa hardly features on tourist route. Yet squashed into the old quarters are several fine medieval churches, while the Via Garibaldi is one of the finest ensembles of sixteenth- and seventeenth-century town *palazzi* in Italy. But in many of the great buildings the accent is on the functional rather than the decorative, pointing up the contrast of both city and people between Genoa and Venice.

On the main waterfront, the Palazzo San Giorgio still serves as the office of the independent company of the Port of Genoa. The interior is surprisingly spacious and airy with its gothic window arches, grand staircases and vaulted ceilings. Littered about are trophies and memorabilia of the city's maritime conquests and commercial inventiveness. In the basement are traces of Marco Polo's prison. The staircase is guarded by stone lions seized in 1261 from the chruch of the Pantocrator, the principal landmark of the Venetian quarter of Constantinople. The upper floor opens into the tiled and gilded council chamber, where the deeds of the Vivaldo family are recalled – among them an attempt to sail the Cape route to India two hundred years before Vasco Da Gama, and the introduction of compound interest into banking practice.

The man appointed to revive the port's fortunes was Roberto d'Alessandro. The image of the modern Italian manager, he had worked for Pirelli, Fiat and the publisher Bompiani, and served as mayor of Portofino on what was fast becoming Italy's answer to the Côte d'Azur. D'Alessandro explained with beguiling frankness the source of the port's crisis. Modernisation had started promisingly, he said, and by 1969 it was the leading container port of the western Mediterranean basin, but within a few years it had been overtaken in efficiency and volume of traffic by Livorno and Marseille-Fos.

'Genoa will always be victim of its surroundings. It is trapped against the sea by the mountains, so space for developing onshore port facilities is limited. The petroleum crisis of 1973 struck hard, for much of the commerce was with north Africa, Libya especially. Traditional heavy industry, steel above all, was in sharp decline. Genoa simply could not match the rates and turn-round time of cargo of Rotterdam.'

An additional source of concern was a project to build the biggest floating dry dock in the Mediterranean, with Michele Sindona, sorcerer *par excellence* of semi-legal finance, as principal backer. The dream was to provide Europe's major facility for careening and repairing super-tankers of up to half a million tons. Costed initially at about $16 million the project, though much reduced, was still incomplete in the mid-Eighties though the bill had risen to almost $50 million, and it never was finished. In the meantime the Sicilian financier Sindona had been convicted of fraudulent bankruptcy in America and Italy, and complicity in the Mafia contract killing of an official receiver. Both spider and fly in the web of Mafia and P2 Freemason intrigues, he died in prison of arsenic imbibed in a cup of espresso coffee. His death bore the true Mafia stamp of double deception, a genuine suicide dressed up as murder, or vice versa; either way it was made to look bad for his associates.

The new team at the port, headed by Roberto d'Alessandro, embarked on radical reforms. They decided to cut the manpower, build a new container facility at Voltri and convert the old port to a marina, with berths for a thousand yachts. Faster handling and more competitive charges were to attract more freight from southern Europe bound for the Pacific and the Far East – freight which otherwise would have been shipped from Rotterdam and Antwerp via the Rhine.

The biggest obstacle to the reform was the organisation of dock labour, the Compania Unica. Heavily backed by the Communist trade union federation, this independent firm of stevedores resisted demands for reduced manning and greater productivity with a series of strikes and stoppages. But within a few years, the port's fortunes were visibly improving.

By the late Eighties employment in industry and the docks had gone down from just over 100,000 to about 90,000. The worst to suffer was the state steel company, Italsider. Many of the old mills on the waterfront were pulled down to make way for a trade fair and exhibition centre, and the extension of the city's airport. Apart from suffering from obsolete production methods, Italsider had been prey to some of the most brutal attacks by Red Brigades terrorists in the 1970s – so much so that the Carabinieri had checked attendance records to establish whether there was a cell of sympathisers or activitists at work in the furnace sector of the steel plant itself.

One October morning in 1978, Guido Rossa, a works foreman, was queueing for coffee at the main steel plant of Italsider. He noticed a Red

Brigades handbill stuck to the wall, which had not been there moments before. As an official of the Communist trade union, Guido Rossa reported to the works committee that he suspected the man in front of him in the queue of being a courier for the terrorists. The information, subsequently proved correct, was passed to the police. No special protection was given Rossa either by the works committee or the anti-terrorist squad and three months later, Rossa was shot dead as he left his flat for work.

Intended as a warning to would-be informers against the Red Brigades, the murder had quite the opposite effect. Genoa was outraged. Thousands, President Pertini among them, turned out to join the funeral procession. Within months suspected members of the Genoa 'column' of the Red Brigades had been arrested. Twelve months after he had left the leaflet by the coffee machine, Francesco Berardi, the Red Brigades' postman, hanged himself in jail in Cuneo.

'The reduction of labour has been very good for traditional industrial concerns like Ansaldo and Italsider, but it has been very bad for Genoa as a whole – unemployment is the biggest crisis the city faces today,' confessed the engineering director of Ansaldo. Ansaldo once led the market in heavy locomotives, marine turbines and electricity generating equipment, particularly in South America. But recently it has undergone a corporate earthquake to meet the technology of the nuclear age: personnel were made redundant or entirely retrained, product lines were terminated and workshops closed and sold. New products had to be developed for Italy's highly controversial nuclear energy programme. Large spaces on the old factory site were sold to small companies making components. 'Such companies might only last five or ten years, and others will replace them with different techniques and products. With such satellites revolving round the parent company, we have a far more flexible structure,' explained an Ansaldo executive.

Halfway across the city is Ansaldo's sister company of Elsag, which specialised in gunsights and guidance systems for naval weapons. The company recently developed a 'smart' rapid-fire gun to defend warships against incoming missiles, and the same technology has been adapted for an automated letter sorting-system in which an artificial intelligence 'reads' the addresses. In an unexpected sales coup this was bought by the Federal Post Office of the USA.

Faced with such rapidly changing technology, the management at Ansaldo radically altered their recruiting policy for engineers and executives. According to the director manager of engineering, 'we specifically asked for graduates not to be too specialised, a good foundation course at university would do. We told the recruit that he or she could expect to be retrained at least three times in their career with us in fields as diverse as mechanical engineering, electronics, computer technology, marketing and management.' From the window of the company's offices in Voltri, he pointed to a cluster of imposing buildings in the hills. Originally a Benedictine foundation dating from the twelfth century, it is now the Elsag training school where the company instructs novices and retrains its executives.

In the summer of 1990 I made a fleeting visit to Genoa, and found the place much changed. By the Palazzo San Giorgio I found the new citizens camped out, in shells of cars, empty freight containers and old stores. They were mostly Moroccans and Tunisians, and a few from West Africa. Each Saturday the ferry from Tunis brought two thousand new migrants from North Africa – and only in September 1990 was such travel subject to visa restrictions.

In the hours after dawn the new Genoese would leave their camping places round the piazzas of the old city to ply their trade. In summer they would sell trinkets, leather ware, belts and bracelets, and towels and gaily coloured scarves and towels on the beaches. In winter the pickings form such casual trade would be meagre to non existent.

In the Piazza delle Lavande high in the old medieval city I witnessed an exotic street market. On the ground were old clothes, bits of broken car, batteries, radios and the like. To the side rolls of bank notes and small envelopes were being exchanged, the most lucrative form of transaction in the market, evidently. An Italian woman approached me and shouted, 'Clear out! You have no reason to be here.' But a young Tunisian showed better manners. He wanted to explain why he was there.

Saleh told me in a strange mixture of French and Italian that he was 25 and had studied in Tunis and Damascus (of all places). He was an inveterate traveller. 'I leave Tunisia because, life, politics – very tough there. I get four months visa for Europe. I stay here – maybe go Svezia [Sweden]; I know a blonde there. I stay and travel Europe. Everyone look for drugs here, too many drugs, and it ruins it for rest of us. Too many Moroccans here in Genoa. They fight, make life difficult.'

In fact by the summer of 1990 the North Africans made up nearly a third of the population of the old city of Genoa, the most extensive medieval city centre that still exists in Italy. They accounted for some 13,000 out of 40,000 in the older apartment blocks. In the evening the older piazzas would be filled with the aroma of the cooking of dried fish and couscous, the cuisine of the Maghreb.

It was in 1990 that Italy discovered it was a target for immigration, the goal of the migrants of the exploding populations of Africa, after centuries as a culture and place of emigration. At the beginning of the year the government offered an amnesty for illegal immigrant workers, and by the deadline in June 1990 more than a quarter of a million had declared themselves. In all the authorities calculated that they had acquired one million new residents from North Africa in the space of five years.

Italians, who pride themselves on a hospitable nature, were shocked at their reaction. Racial conflicts broke out on the streets of Rome and Milan, and in the small industrial port of Piombino in Tuscany, which had become a haven for groups of Tunisians.

In the south the Africans have provided much-needed cheap seasonal labour on the land. Fruit and tomato production in the province of Naples would all but founder, according to charity workers for Caritas, the Roman Catholic relief agency, but for the Moroccans and Tunisians. Near Villa Laterno outside Caserta the workers live in large labour camps, believed to be operated by local crime bosses of the Naples Camorra. In the cities of the north North Africans have begun to get a toehold in the local economy. It is now calculated by town-hall officials in Milan that nearly every one of some 5000 employees in the city's bakeries will be Moroccan or Tunisian by the end of the century.

The flow of migrant workers from the southern shores of the Mediterranean brought a sharp response in local politics. The Lombard League (Lega Lombarda) has campaigned on a thinly disguised racist ticket. The leaguers want immigration to stop, and autonomy for Lombardy and its neighbouring regions of Italy's rich north. In the municipal elections of 1990, the League did surprisingly well, capturing fifty per cent of the vote in cities of the Lombard Plain, Brescia and Bergamo.

In Genoa Signora Rita Paglia and her friends began organising neighbourhood committees (*comitati di quartiere*) to stop the deterioration of the old city. Her husband worked in the Compania Unica in the port – in 1990 sadly declined to only 600 members. The harbour and docks offered little work for the new arrivals, she said. The giant dry-dock, begun on a promise of finance by the late Michele Sidona, had now been broken up to deal with small coasters and to service oil platforms. Signora Paglia, a lively, smartly dressed woman in her early forties, was worried about the deteriorating sanitation in the quarter where she was born and bred. 'They sleep up to a dozen to a room, and live in little more than sheds. There is no sewage disposal, and the streets are their toilets. We have all manner of disease, gastro-enteritis, hepatitis B, salmonella – a real burden on the hospitals now. But from the authorities it's the same old story: too many words, too few actions. Families that lived here for six or seven generations are leaving. It's a real exodus.'

She might have been writing a manifesto for the Lombard League. The biggest concern for her and her friends was the rise in crime in the squares and streets, and recently she claimed to have witnessed three gunfights between rival gangs of immigrants in the red light district behind the Piazza Garibaldi station. In the cafés round the Palazzo San Giorgio the more successful of the new arrivals would appear at midday to lounge at the bars and tables and display their sharp suits and expensive masculine jewellery. They had found a lucrative trade in drugs, according to the older residents. In one piazza I saw two of their customers at a trattoria table, a young man and his girlfriend so inebriated with narcotics that they could hardly sit up straight – the young man taking several minutes to raise his cigarette to his lips.

The wave of new migrants became visible with dramatic suddenness at the close of the decade of the Eighties. By 1990 the new travellers from Africa were changing the pattern of life from cities as far apart as Barcelona and Brussels, Athens and Amsterdam. The southern Mediterranean had come to the lands of the north and the movement is sure to swell. Those that had taken up residence in 1990 in Genoa and Milan, Rome, or Clermont-Ferrand in France, were the first wave – the better qualified maybe, who had taken the initiative to escape the growing demographic and economic troubles of Africa. Soon the wives and families and the second generation would follow.

Venice: Sinking Serenissima

'*Signori!* No masks in the Mass, please! *Niente maschere durante la Messa!*' pleaded the sacristan of St Mark's, with a cry which might have come from the libretto of *Don Giovanni*. Many were sporting masks with long beaks or grotesque devil features, periwigs and tricorns, chequer-board doublets, black and white pantaloons – the uniform of Harlequinade and the Commedia dell'Arte.

On that misty February Sunday, St Mark's Square was *en fête* for Carnival, a custom revived a dozen years earlier as a nostalgic fashion show. Roaming the piazza were dozens of would-be Casanovas and their coiffed and pomaded ladies in full eighteenth-century costume, self-consciously staring at their reflections in the windows of shops and cafés, and keeping a weather-eye for the pigeons.

The regenerated carnival grew spontaneously, an attempt to recall the last days of the Venetian Republic before the Napoleonic invasion. It was quickly captured by the spirit of Venetian merchant-venturing. It became a means for extending the winter tourist season as political salons of the Socialist Party promoted art and fashion shows, and the municipality drew up a programme of entertainments. Within a year or two of its rebirth in the 1970s, the leading couturiers and ateliers of Paris had offered to fund many of the displays, and *Carnevale* became an advertising clothes horse, much to the chagrin of many residents. '*Carnevale* is something you take part in,' one grumbled, 'it isn't a spectator sport. Everyone can join the dancing and the merry-making before the rigors of Lent.' Something of the wild libertarian ways of Casanova's times does enter the proceedings – despite the public regulation and the commercial exploitation.

Inside the cathedral that Sunday, I caught a glimpse of a much older Venice. By the altar rails in the chancel stood a row of priests and servers in white stoles, and green copes and chasubles embellished with dull gold embroidery, black tabs punctuating the collar yokes of their *pallia*. Both the colours and the vestments were exactly like those seen in the mosaics of the churches at Ravenna, built twelve hundred years ago when it was the most powerful see on the Adriatic coast. During the Mass the choir, stationed at four different points of the chancel, floated a delicate surge of polyphonic anthems, and sang responses in soft harmony to the harsh and cracked intonements of an ancient priest.

St Mark's is the most oriental cathedral in western Christendom, a monument to the city's involvement in the East over more than one thousand years. It was founded on the bones of its patron saint seized from Alexandria but the most extensive haul of booty, bric-à-brac and relics came from the sack of Constantinople in 1204, when the Venetian galleys were led by the blind Doge, Enrico Dandolo. In decoration and ritual St Mark's and the Venetian Patriachate of the Roman Catholic Church seem only a breath away from the churches of the East and Byzantium.

A Venetian friend once described the pivotal position of his city in the Mediterranean as '*cullo del' Occidente, bocca del' Oriente*' – backside of the West, mouth of the Orient.

Of the great international beauty spots, Venice has a peculiar position in the way it possesses the inner fantasies and imagination of so many

of its admirers. For countless visitors Venice signifies a special relationship: it has become *their* Venice.

'The fond spectator is perpetually looking at it from his window,' wrote
Henry James, 'when he is not floating about with that delightful sense
of being for the moment part of it, which any gentleman in a gondola
is free to entertain. Venetian windows and balconies are a dreadful lure,
and while you rest the elbows on these cushioned ledges the hours float
away.'

The pleasure is not merely aesthetic, the enjoyment of grand facades of
palaces, flower pot chimneys, pastel-coloured houses, the great distorting
mirror of perspective of the lagoon between St Mark's and the Giudecca.
For many suitors admiration for the beauty and historical glory of Venice
is tinged with pity for her present state of decline and physical decay.
Some are gratified in a belief that with their care and attention, petitions
and contributions to rescue funds, they may be able to do something to
reverse the trend.

Venice has been the object of admiration, and envy through most of
her history. That history has been one of almost seamless development
from the rise to success and glory as 'La Serenissima' – the Most Serene
Republic (a title which Genoa also adopted) – through long and calm
decline. The success was due to diplomatic cunning and commercial
acumen as much as feats of arms. Letters of credit were virtually invented
in the city, and the Rialto became synonymous with gossip and rumour
as Europe's first stock exchange. Venetians were political innovators from
the days of the first doges elected in the tenth century.

The elected dogeship and the extensive magistracies were all seen as
evidence of the 'balanced' constitution much admired by the supporters
of Oliver Cromwell and the parliamentary cause in seventeenth-century
England. Power was widely distributed throughout the merchant classes,
and well-organised charities looked after the poorer members of society.
Different races and creeds were tolerated, provided they contributed to
the city's wealth; the term 'ghetto' was first used for a Jewish quarter in
Venice, and Shakespeare created his Shylock from the tales of several
such merchants of the city recorded in the despatches of English and
Italian travellers of the day. Venice had achieved mercantile dominance
of the eastern Mediterranean from its defeat of Genoa in the thirteenth
and fourteenth centuries; by the cosmopolitan nature of its commerce
and culture, she managed to maintain a long reach into the Levant for
centuries after the rise of the Ottoman Empire.

The main topic of political debate and argument, tittle-tattle on the
Rialto and gossip in the cafés of St Mark's, is the salvation of Venice

from social decline and physical decay, principally through flooding, and the pollution of the atmosphere and waters. Two dates stand out in the present phase of the siege of Venice. On the night of 4 November 1966 autumn winds and tides conspired to inflict the worst flooding on the city in living memory. The *acqua alta*, as the high tide is termed, reached a depth of several metres in St Mark's Square. That same night a similar flood broke the banks of the Arno, wrecking precious paintings and manuscripts in the churches and palaces of Florence. But in terms of damage to the fabric and foundations of the buildings, the effect on Venice was far worse: some experts feared it might prove irreversible.

On the Easter weekend of 1987, more than 100,000 tourists poured into the city. The narrow passages between the Rialto and St Mark's became so jammed that a one-way system of pedestrian alleys had to be instituted. A barrier was erected at the head of the causeway from the mainland to stop more cars and buses entering. Residents feared that their city was being threatened by death from a thousand package tour operators.

Lamenting the plight of Venice is nothing new. For nearly two centuries it has filled the correspondence and journals of travelling aesthetes, ambassadors and their ladies. Its citizens suffered as well. Months of violence attended the attempts to rid themselves of alien rule by the Austrian Kingdom of Lombardy-Veneto, installed at the Congress of Vienna in 1815. Venice did not become part of the Italian kingdom until 1866, when 674,426 citizens of the province voted against 69 to join the new Italy and leave Austria, then about to be defeated by Prussia in the Six Weeks War. In the First World War Venice provided the base for Italian naval operations against the Austro-Hungarian navy, and was subjected to aerial bombardment as a consequence. In the Second World War the refineries and shipyards of the industrial zone were targets for Allied bombers, and eighteen hostages were shot by the German occupiers in reprisal for several successful ambushes by the Italian resistance.

Throughout the last century visitors wailed about the physical discomforts and threats of disease in the city. Only eleven of the palaces had been made into hotels, one correspondent complained. But the artists, composers and writers still came, wrote and composed, among them Henry James, Wagner, Joyce, Thomas Mann and Stravinsky.

Serious doubts about the city's survival began to be raised in the years following the Second World War. The city was sinking alarmingly, at the rate of several millimetres a year, and this was blamed on the digging of channels to the deepwater port and the construction of industrial zones, begun under Fascism in the Twenties and Thirties. To subsidence was added the pollution of the canals and the atmosphere by oil field and industrial chemical discharges.

A number of international bodies met to launch a rescue plan for Venice. Conservation funds such as Britain's 'Venice in Peril' were launched, and UNESCO was generous in money and advice. The Italian government voted funds for a special law for Venice, much of which disappeared in the mysterious byways of Italian bureaucracy.

The first priority was to build some form of barrier which could hold back the worst of the *acqua alta*, the high tide. Then it was suggested that the low water '*acqua bassa*' or low water was also a danger since the sinking of the canal levels in summer exposed wooden and brick foundations to the atmosphere. In 1873 a survey found that there were 5,339 wells in the city – 461 of which were deemed 'fetid,' potential sources of the dreaded cholera. By the 1970s the number of wells was a few hundred. A decision to seal all the wells in the old city was executed with surprising efficiency, and one of the immediate threats of subsidence was removed overnight.

On a sparkling sunny winter morning, I paid a call on Professor Francesco Valcanover, Superintendent of Fine Arts and Monuments, in his offices of modest splendour overlooking St Mark's Square. In a few minutes he managed to give me a vivid glimpse of the scale and complexity of the task of preserving and restoring the artistic and historical treasures of the city. His main preoccupation was money; despite the generosity of foreign funds, UNESCO, the Italian government, the Veneto Region, the Municipality itself, there could never be enough to go round – a lament I heard echoed on all sides.

The monuments he was trying to protect, he said, were under siege from several quarters – not merely flooding, but acid rain and chemical pollution of the atmosphere and waters. 'The process of chemical pollution never stops for a moment – a precipitation of acid rain over a few hours sets can start tremendous damage. We now face the accelerated deterioration of statues and sculpture. Marble just crumbles. With the carbonisation of chalk the pieces swell and burst.' He instanced the arches of St Mark's, while the principal gateway of the Doge's Palace, the Porta della Carta, had to be shrouded in wooden cladding to maintain a constant atmosphere while repairs continued.

Professor Valcanover claimed that Venice was the most heavily restored city centre in the world. Laboratories in the city itself and at Bologna and Rome had pioneered techniques of conserving and protecting marble, stone and fresco. Private companies had donated equipment such as the special infra-red spectroscope from Olivetti for examining the layers of paint on canvasses and wooden panels.

To survey the extent of the task, UNESCO paid for six survey teams to catalogue every major sculpture, picture, fresco and architectural orna-ment. Each team had an art historian, photographer, restorer and sten-ographer, who had to present on a single sheet of paper a brief description and history of the piece, its present condition, and a summary of repairs required, with what urgency and what cost. In six months, after which the money ran out, the teams had produced more than 40,000 schedules.

Over eighteen years Professor Valcanover's own staff had repaired and restored more than a thousand pictures. To show me the work a single item in the catalogue might entail, he invited me to the laboratory and workshops in the priory church of San Gregorio, which faces the Salute across a small canal. The church itself had been deconsecrated. One wall had been bulldozed and rebuilt in order to clear away rotting debris and concrete the floor.

Little remained to recall the church's original use; even the coat of arms of one of its more recent patrons, the Doge Pasquale Cicogna, who died in 1594, had been cancelled at his disgrace by order of the Senate. Resting on frames of pipes, and carefully placed against the walls, were the panels of Tintoretto's 'Paradiso', which usually graces the Hall of the Greater Council in the Doge's Palace and is by far the largest oil on canvas painting in the history of art.

The most casual and untutored glance could detect in a minute that there was much more to the 'Paradiso' in its disembodied state in the laboratory than would have met the eye in Tintoretto's day. The artist himself would have executed only the central figures, the angels, cheru-bim, seraphim and thrones being filled in by a platoon of assistants. Over the century the platoon had swelled to a small regiment, by the end of the eighteenth century fewer than a third of the hands and faces were faithful to the late sixteenth-century original. 'It was quite a shock to see to what extent the eighteenth-century restorers had changed the physiognomies, hands and feet,' recalls Francesco Valcanover.' In the end we decided to leave things as they are. It was too big a job to try to recover the original designs of Tintoretto's studio – many of which are lost – and too expensive.' Even so the bill for cleaning and retouching came to 190 million lire – about $100 million.

Francesco Valcanover, now retired from his post in Venice, is a man of mild, even timid disposition, but with vehement views on the politics of restoration. 'I do not love restoration for restoration's sake. I believe in restoration as part of creating a new culture, a new history based on the proper understanding of the old.' He thinks that Venice should present a modern image as a city of the future, 'the great museum city, the museum of men and not motor cars.'

Halfway along the Grand Canal between the Rialto and the baroque excess of Sta Maria della Salute is the Palazzo Papodopoli, a sixteenth-century palace with fine Tiepolo ceilings – not that they are generally available to the public, for the building is the local headquarters of the National Council for Scientific Research. The director of the research programme for many years was Dr Roberto Frassetto. During the Second World War he was involved in the midget submarine attacks which crippled Allied ships in Alexandria harbour. 'A foolish enterprise,' he confesses, 'but at least my capture led to my being taught English.' It also marked the beginning of his studies of the dynamics of oceans and seas, which led to him a lectureship at Yale University and world renown.

In Venice his expertise has focussed on two broad areas: the waters of the lagoon and the decaying fabric of the city itself. The threat of flooding could be reduced by building a barrier beyond the island of the Lido. In good weather ships would pass into the port through three entrances, which would be blocked by gates raised from the sea bed when foul weather threatened. This plan had emerged after more than twenty years of study, and many feared that it would take another twenty to execute.

'Meanwhile the problem of the flushing of the water through the canals gets worse,' declared Dr Frassetto. 'The waters have been getting steadily more sterile, mostly from detergents in the industrial zone, the Maghera, fertilisers, gases and solid waste. There used to be much better management of the canals. Only now are we beginning to understand the new chemical processes. One way we could encourage the circulation of water through the canals would be to open and shut the barrier gates regularly in the summer.'

Across the lakes of the lagoon, the spread of chemical pollution allowed micro-organisms to flourish in new blooms and clumps. In the city itself the most pernicious form of decay is eating at the material from which made up nearly 99 per cent of the great buildings, St Mark's Cathedral and the Doge's Palace among them are made – brick.

Recently an international competition was held in Venice to discover the cause and nature of brick cancer, and as yet little is understood about it. Early forms of treatment, such as injection with silicone and epoxy, may have done more harm than good, eventually causing the bricks to swell and shatter. New materials are being developed for the treatment of façades and structures without removing or replacing the brick. The success of this pioneering work is vital to other cities suffering from atmospheric pollution, Athens in particular.

Time is of the essence for Dr Frassetto's proposals for saving Venice. A group of his researchers have studied historical records from the fifteenth century for changes in the formation of the lagoon, climate and weather. The sea bed of this part of the Adriatic is highly unstable, and has been on the move for millions of years. In recent times the city's subsidence has accelerated to a rate of roughly 20 centimetres a century.

In his splendid sixteenth-century study, the lonely figure of Roberto Frassetto seemed the epitome of thwarted energy. Several ingenious solutions could be implemented immediately, he suggested, such as the use of mud-jacking to raise the flooded parts of the old city, in the way that parts of Long Island and the coasts of Holland had been raised above the sea. 'The main problem is political will,' he concluded. 'Public funds are distributed to too many projects, to too many political interests. If we had a co-ordinated effort we could really do something in five years to safeguard Venice for a century and more to come. A doge would have got it all done with no argument.'

The Countess Teresa Foscari Foscolo exudes the spirit of her ancestors the doges. Her apartment overlooks a courtyard and a shady garden, green with trees and shrubs throughout the year, not far from the Grand Canal. Her view was summed up by a headline from the London *Times* from the early Sixties: 'The Lagoon is a Spitoon.' A genial and welcoming host, she speaks her mind to friend and foe with good Venetian robustness. 'Venice is becoming much more difficult for Venetians. They don't have the money to buy houses and stay here. The danger is that the museum city could become a city without many true Venetian residents.'

On a medieval belltower on the corner of the Calle della Chiesa, between the Rialto and the railway station, some months after I first met Teresa Foscari Foscolo, I saw a poster which recalled her melancholy predictions. It was a manifesto against public housing policy, prepared by Urbanistica Democratica, the tenants' committee for housing rights. The committee claimed that by December 1986 only a tenth of the government's $10 million special fund for housing renewal in the old city had been spent, and of 250 dwellings refurbished, only 29 had been available for new leases and this, the committee claimed, had resulted in more 3000 evictions.

The population of old Venice by the end of the Eighties had reached about 80,000, though pessimists suggested that as few as 50,000 lived there the year round. In the Campo San Toma I was engaged by a man in his mid thirties on the trials of being a modern Venetian. 'See over there,' he said, 'that ugly penthouse – it's obviously for a foreigner. It'll sell for about a hundred and fifty milliards [about $150,000] – impossible for me – I could only raise about 20 million for a housing loan, maximum. I'm an administrator in the Magistracy of the Waters – not a bad job, but for my wife and two children it's hard. To go to the cinema, sport, the parks they have to go to Mestre, across the causeway. Mestre was once despised as an industrial dormitory, but now its the centre of social life for the young, with its cinema clubs, sporting associations and *trattorie* and restaurants we can afford. The biggest headache here in summer is the tourists. The authorities haven't planned adequately for them. Look over there, in that little nook. It's the only lavatory around – and it's for men only. God knows what the women do.'

In an alleyway just off the Piazza San Marco you can get a whiff of the more elegant days of Venice in the Thirties, in Harry's Bar. It is still presided over by *the* Harry, Arrigo Cipriani, though in the confusion of legend and fact it's sometimes hard to work out whether he was named after the bar or the bar after him. The truth is plain but romantic. Harry's father, Giuseppe Cipriani, was a barman and restauranteur of genius. In the late Twenties he met Harry Pickering, an American Rhodes Scholar at Oxford. In the winter of 1930, during the depths of the Depression, Pickering put up forty thousand lire to open a bar, which took his name – as did his new godson, Arrigo Cipriani.

Harry's is famed for its Bellinis, peach and champagne cocktails, for its Robespierre à la Cipriani, and above all for its atmosphere of homely glamour. It may have been the haunt of Maugham, Joyce, Noël Coward and Hemingway, but the peculiar genius of the Ciprianis is the ability to welcome a guest as a friend. However long the intervening years, Arrigo's greeting always seems to say, 'Where did we leave off? What were we talking about last time?'

Harry is only first-generation Venetian, since his father came from Verona. He told me once of the day he began his own career. 'I was studying law at the University of Padua. At about two in the afternoon I got my finals results. I telephoned my father: "I've passed, 19 out of 30." His immediate response was "My son, you'll never make a lawyer. Make sure you're behind the till here at Harry's by six this evening." I was.'

Harry is particularly concerned at the development of the old part of the city as a boutique, with stalls and shops for fresh vegetables and bakeries steadily disappearing. Very few businesses are created in the old city. Harry's itself has been made into a cooperative company, with employees taking shares.

In the afternoon we took a boat across the lagoon to the island of the Giudecca. The sky was trying to match the heavy grey of the water with a threat of snow. Beyond Palladio's masterpiece, the church of the Redentore, Harry guided me to a derelict factory building, the home of his latest brain-child, an international school for the preparation of pasta, and of his hugely successful ice cream and confectionery business, Harry's Dolci. 'It took ages to get planning permission to convert the factory,' he observed 'a real pity, since this is about the only new business to have opened up in this part of the city.'

Not far from the factory is Harry's Snack, a budget price restaurant and café aimed at a local clientele. As we stepped in from the cold a girl with a radiant face from a Bellini masterpiece came forward to take our hats and coats. 'You know what the boss always said at Maxim's?' Harry told her with a grin, 'the doorman is the most important person, you've got to make sure everyone feels welcome.'

A couple of days after our visit to the Giudecca, the sky fulfilled its promise and gently it began to snow. Before they were covered the buildings, the canal fronts, the Ca' d'Oro, the Turkish Customs House, shyly displayed their beauty unsullied and in pristine glory. Crossing the causeway back to Mestre and the *terra firma*, I saw the lagoon was fringed with ice.

iii Roman Politics

The year of nemesis for Rome in its newest political incarnation came in 1978. It had then been capital of the Italian Republic for barely thirty years – its previous republican status had been relinquished two thousand years before when the Roman Republic of antiquity was the heart of the greatest power the Mediterranean had yet seen.

1978 was a brutal coming of age for the Italian Republic, born of the chaotic collapse of Mussolini's Fascism and the confused campaign of liberation from Nazi occupation by the Allies. The year saw the reign of three Popes, the resignation of the Head of State in disgrace, and the kidnap and murder of Aldo Moro.

Less than three months later after he had conducted Aldo Moro's memorial service, Pope Paul VI, architect of the modern papacy, was dead. His unlikely successor was Albino Luciani, the charming homespun Patriarch of Venice. Of the earth of Alpine northern Italy, he liked to preach through parables based on the classics – anything from Dickens to Pinocchio. Allegedly, he was chosen because he was the only Italian behind whom the Italian cardinals could unite, and they were still just in the majority in the electoral conclave. But as Pope John Paul I he was ill-equipped and unprepared for the tortuous subtleties and conspiratorial complexity of the curia and the administration of an international church with the best part of a billion adherents. Never in the best of health, after a reign of little more than a month he died of a heart attack. Subsequently tales of dark plots and murder have abounded, nearly all a credit to the fictional powers of their progenitors.

At the October conclave, summoned to elect the third Pope for that year, the Italian cardinals were divided, and the choice went to a non-Italian for the first time in four and a half centuries – Karol Wojtila, Cardinal Archbishop of Crakow. The election of the new Pope, John Paul II, marked a further step in the internationalisation of the papacy, a process begun by John XXIII, and carried out by Paul VI and the Second Vatican Council, in which Cardinal Wojtila had played a prominent role. It is said that during the Vatican Council he came to the notice of a conservative group of cardinals led by Cardinal König of Vienna, and it was they who pressed for his election as a conservative as counterweight to the radicalism of the Latin American church, soon to be the largest in the Catholic congregation.

The Polish Pope has travelled more than all his predecessors put together. As an eminent world leader, he has distanced the papacy from the city of Rome. When he himself became the victim of an attempted assassination by the fanatic schizophrenic Turk, Mehmet Ali Agca, in May 1981, Roman reactions were more muted than to any of the events of 1978 – possibly because few at the time realised how badly the pontiff had been wounded. One aspect of the Agca conspiracy had much wider implications than the adolescent machinations of the Red Brigades.

During Agca's second trial, the judges endeavoured to discover exactly how the would-be assassin had survived nearly two years on the run from a Turkish jail where he had been sentenced to life for the murder of a prominent Istanbul newspaper editor. In jail he was almost certainly recruited to the neo-fascist Grey Wolves, largely responsible for the wave of terror which blighted Turkish life in the late Seventies. But in their concluding report to the trial the Italian judges suggested that Agca had fallen in with a group of Turkish Islamic fundamentalists living in the Rhineland, who supplied him with a weapon, money, documents and airline tickets. These may have had links with Palestinian terrorist groups and Libyan paymasters – suggesting that the Mediterranean has exported its own forms of extremist politics into the heart of Europe.

When the cardinals meet in conclave the Catholic Church reveals its parochial nature as the church of Rome. Each cardinal has a parish in the city where most of them celebrate Mass before sealing themselves into the Sistine Chapel to choose the successor of St Peter as Bishop of Rome. The formula 'To the City and the World', pronounced at the beginning of every papal blessing from the balcony of St Peter's on the great feasts, is the key to the Catholic church's structure, according to the Cardinal Archbishop of Westminster, Basil Hume. 'The church is now much more collegiate. We – the bishops and cardinals – go to Rome to advise the Pope and curia on the running of the church now. The papacy can still be pretty monarchical and anti-democratic, so there is bound to be some tension between the centre and the national churches – but it is a creative tension.

'Peter is the focus of unity, faith and charity, and the more I am involved in the church I realise the need for a central authority. I now look forward to my regular visits to Rome. Last time we prayed together from 11 in the morning to 3.30 in the afternoon with the Pope. I felt a tremendous sense of unity with Rome, Peter and the rest of the Church. And I came back with my faith strengthened.'

Cardinal Hume is the very model of a modern European Catholic churchman: lucid, humane, approachable, and with the inestimable advantage of looking like a medieval saint. As the century draws to an end, he claims that the Catholic Church is following the same path as its eastern counterparts of the Orthodox community, with young people turning to religious faith in search of 'deeper spirtuality' – a mystical rather than a rational approach.

Pope Wojtila, too, has become the epitome of a modern pontiff, an easy practitioner of all the modern skills of communication. At home in the Vatican he can attract crowds of visitors and pilgrims as none of his predecessors could. The midweek audiences in St Peter's Square have become the despair of the Rome traffic police. Around the walls of the Vatican, the Eternal City has become the eternal gridlock.

The first years of the reign of Pope Paul II were matched by a public performance of equal success by Italy's new head of state, Sandro Pertini, the most popular President of the Republic so far. Though very different in outlook – Pertini always declared himself a firm non-believer – both men displayed considerable theatrical flair and a sure touch with their public and they became firm friends in public and private.

Sandro Pertini emerged in 1978 as a last-minute compromise between the Communists and the Christian Democrats. By then in his seventies, he could have retired from public life ten years before. A lawyer with a heroic record in the resistance and a lifelong socialist, he had served on the margin of Italian public life. Yet more than any other public figure, he restored confidence and pride in the Italian Republic after the demoralising ordeals of the Moro plot and the resignation of President Lecre amid allegations of corruption. His great achievement was in being there, a wizened oak, the prop of the constitution and public decency. He refused to live in the elegant but pompous public residence of the President, the Quirinale Palace, built for Pope Gregory XIII as a summer residence for the papacy. He preferred his small flat close to the Trevi Fountain. His wife continued as an active campaigner for women's rights and rarely appeared on official occasions.

Above all Sandro Pertini made himself accessible to all Italians. Parties of schoolchildren used to flock to the Quirinale to hear him talk about the Italian Republic and how it worked, he was everyone's favourite great uncle. He loved to explain that 'it is not just a question of being old. I am ancient.' Going to visit him was like calling on Santa Claus.

When I met him he was in his mid-eighties and coming to the end of his seven-year term of office. With his thick snowy hair he cut a small but dapper figure against the surrounding pretension of Louis XV furnishings. Hearing him recall his early days in politics, as he dipped sugar lumps into a thick glass of grappa, was to touch almost half the history of the Italian state since unity and the Risorgimento.

As a lawyer in his native Savona in north-west Italy, he had fled Fascism and worked in Paris and Nice as a taxi-driver and bricklayer. Linking up with the resistance to Mussolini, he returned to Italy in 1927 only to be arrested, spending the first two years in solitary confinement – prison seems to have been his real political education – and he was held in custody until Mussolini's collapse.

No sooner was he released from prison than he was back inside again in Rome, condemned to death by the Germans for organising a resistance force. He and Giuseppe Saragat, also destined to be elected President, managed to escape from the gloomy fortress of the Regina Coeli jail. Pertini then headed north to organise socialist groups fighting the Germans and the rump of the Fascist regime in the Republic of Salo.

In the spring of 1945 he arrived late to join a meeting at the Archbishop's palace in Milan at which Mussolini offered to surrender in return for a guarantee of his life. 'I turned for a moment and saw a group of Black Shirts and among them I recognised Mussolini, wasted, thin, pallid and his eyes full of fear. He was going to the Prefecture to give a reply to the terms. I was introduced to Cardinal Schuster, Lombardi, Cadorna and other resistance leaders. They told me Mussolini had gone to consider a reply to their terms – if he agreed to give himself up his life would be spared.

'I told the Cardinal that the insurrection of Milan had already begun. Neither he nor anyone could stop it. Mussolini must put himself before a Tribunal of the Committee of National Liberation of Northern Italy and they must judge him. He could not dictate his own terms of surrender.'

Instead Mussolini fled, was caught near Como by Communist partisans and shot with his mistress, Clara Petacci. 'She could have flown off to Spain – Franco sent a plane. But she decided to stay with him. Her only crime was being his lover.'

Sandro Pertini embodied the highest standards of the Italian Republic. He insisted that public duty came before private and party interest, and he ensured that the prime minister's office was not to be the perpetual reserve of the ruling Christian Democrats. He appointed two non-Catholic prime ministers, and one, Bettino Craxi, ran one of the most successful of all post-war governments.

Some of Pertini's style of plain-speaking influenced other politicians. The political rhetoric of Moro had an almost Byzantine obscurity and he once talked of 'the converging parallels' of an argument. But in the late Seventies three politicians were outstanding for the clarity of their expression: Enrico Berlinguer; Bettino Craxi, the Socialist Prime Minister with whom Pertini argued as often as he agreed, who won considerable popular support because he spoke the language of the piazza; and Giulio Andreotti, the most Roman Roman of them all.

Andreotti is one of the most extraordinary survivors of modern European politics. In 1948, at the age of 26, he was chosen by Alcide de Gasperi, founder of the Christian Democrats and first prime minister of the Republic, to be his parliamentary under-secretary. He has hardly been away from office since, though he never led his party. Half his classmates at college became cardinals or bishops and there was always something of the seminarist in the stooped figure. For most of his career he was renowned for his Roman cunning. He beat off at least twenty-five attempts to investigate various alleged pecadillos of corruption and malpractice in office. Repudiating the charge that his party must be exhausted by perpetual office, he once said that 'Power only wearies those who do not have it.'

As Foreign Minister throughout the Eighties, he enhanced Italy's standing in the world, not least with the counties of the south and eastern Mediterranean, with eastern Europe, and with the Common Market, where he proved a master negotiator and more than a match for Margaret Thatcher. At the same time he managed to scribble a weekly column in a leading paper, wrote thrillers and published his diaries – all marked by a sparkling simplicity of language. In 1989, at the age of seventy, he was asked to be Prime Minister for the sixth time, leading Italy's fiftieth administration since the war.

The quality the Romans share with Signor Andreotti is shrewdness, a cynical wit and ability to look after their own. Rome wears its status as a modern capital more lightly than almost any other in Europe. The city still has the faint air of the theatrical about its piazzas and vistas, not quite taking itself seriously. It is still one of the best cities for walking about in the whole of the Mediterranean. Despite the hazards of modern traffic and pollution, the centre of Rome in early spring, the sunlight suffused through the umbrella pines and cypresses on the brick palaces and scrubbed columns in the forum, provides an effect of pure magic.

But the weight of traffic and the pollution from the exhaust fumes are taking their toll. The figure of Marcus Aurelius on his horse before the town hall in Michelangelo's Campidoglio was both victim and symbol of the disease – so eaten away was his gilded bronze form that he had to be removed. The stoic emperor made a forlorn sight as he was borne on the back of a lorry through hordes of belching cars. His form had been eaten by the cancer caused by their noxious fumes. In 1990 Marcus Aurelius returned to the Campidoglio, restored and protected with a layer of anti-pollutant paint. It was an act of faith as much as the triumph of technology for, in the ensuing years, the atmosphere of the city centre had become even more contaminated.

Part of the problem is that the modern city has never been completed to plan. It was to have been provided with a new administrative quarter for Mussolini's International Exhibition of 1941; but the plan was realised only in part – in the district known as the EUR, whose halls and palaces have stood the test of changing tastes and time remarkably well – while the accompanying road scheme was never fully put into effect. The peripheral motorway was finished only in the 1970s and much long-distance traffic passed through Rome rather than round it. Along the ancient routes, such as the Via Cassia to the north and the Appian Way, unplanned clutches of cheap housing and apartment blocks sprung up – human wastelands which give another clue to the identity of modern Rome.

For centuries Rome has devoured cheap labour from the poor surrounding provinces – fodder of the service industries and for the cumbersome administration of church and state. Labourers were needed by the thousand for the building of the Renaissance churches and palaces. Today the tiers of state bureaucracy has millions of posts – each a vital element on the client-patronage system which makes so much in private and public Italy go round. The Ministry of the Interior, located in the Viminale Palace on one of the seven hills of ancient Rome, is believed to have a pay roll of nearly a quarter of a million.

According to official statistics (always a negotiable commodity in Italy) the population of Rome is just under three million, but in fact it is closer to six million. The overcrowded suburbs of new migrants, some with the barest means of sanitation, and the army of poorly paid servants of the 'undergovernment' (*sotto governo*) are a reminder that Rome is part of Italy's poor south rather than the prosperous industrial north.

In the late Sixties a priest from northern Italy, Dom Mario Picchi, ran emergency soup kitchens and first aid for the young down-and-outs sheltering in their hundreds round the main railway terminus – an imposing monument of open stairways and cantilevered roof designed by Pier Luigi Nervi for the Olympics of 1960. Sensing that the level of drug addiction could only rise in his informal parish – drugs in Italy are now among the cheapest and plentiful in the entire Mediterranean – Dom Mario resolved to set up a permanent system of cure centres. The result was the 'Man Project' (*Progetto Uomo*) for curing young addicts in some two dozen cities throughout Italy. Remarkable though the project's success rate has been, the record highlights the sheer size of Italy's drug problem and the virtual impossibility of curing addicts in any great number.

I was taken to one of the project's centres at Castel Gandolfo in the Alban Hills close to the papal summer residence by a vivacious Catalan, Juan Corelli, who had worked with Dom Mario from the early days of the drug programme. Juan had the generosity of his countrymen, and has proved truly 'a man of the Mediterranean' with his many languages, lives and callings. He started as a ballet dancer, but deafness forced him to quit the stage to become a film editor in the 'nouvelle vague' era and an acclaimed choreographer of ballet for television. He seemed to know everyone in his milieu from the Royal Ballet and National Theatre in London to numerous patrons among the out-of-work royalty of southern Europe.

When his father, a wealthy architect, died Juan realised he had enough money not to need to work, and it was then that the link with Dom Mario was forged. By the mid-Seventies they had a team of twenty-five full-time staff who had studied schemes for alcoholics and long-term drug addicts in Scandinavia and northern Europe, America and Canada. By the late Seventies they were ready to start in a number of their own centres and in 1985 they had projects running in twenty-seven cities, with numerous day-care patients besides.

The Progetto Uomo is labour-intensive, long and exhausting for its directors and patrons. It has been fortunate in receiving money from big corporations like IBM and Olivetti and the personal patronage of the Pope, a frequent visitor to the San Carlo centre at Castel Gandolfo. 'With all this help, I still feel drained. And I feel like moving on to other problems before I get completely stale,' Juan confessed.

The statistics underline the intractable nature of the problem. Between 1980 and 1985 San Carlo had treated 547 patients, all but three successfully, and throughout Italy nearly 5000 young addicts had passed through the Project's hands in nearly seven years. In 1985 Italy had about 200,000 recognised drug addicts (a figure almost meaningless as many do not register with a medical practitioner). Most were victims of heroin – cheap cocaine and crack had not yet surfaced in Europe. A year later the authorities in Milan reported that they believed that two-thirds of the city's hard drug-users were HIV positive and infected with the AIDS virus.

iv A Civilisation Apart: Naples

Neapolitans often describe their city and themselves as 'difficult' and 'superficial'. The alarming physical and social decay of the old city makes Naples 'difficult', as does the fact that the metropolitan area has three times more cars than the roads can cope with. 'Superficial? I'll tell you what it means,' explained a Neapolitan friend. 'It's when someone who said he'll meet you early in the morning turns up after noon. This superficiality is killing Naples.'

In the way they describe their love-hate relationship with their city. Neapolitans are a civilisation apart. The place has been falling down for centuries, neglected by kings and viceroys, torn by revolutions, ignored by Rome once it became the capital of a united Italy. Yet few peoples on earth talk of their birthplace with such poetry and wit. Even the barefoot urchins by the port are natural philosophers, their view of the world based on managing the street jungle of the old city. Witticisms are coloured by the peculiar lilt, sprayed by the unmistakeable sibilance of the 's', which mark the local accent.

Parts of the city still betray a royal grandeur: for seven centuries it was ruled by kings and emperors and their viceroys, from the Normans to the Bourbons. In antiquity it was the greatest and most prosperous of the colonies of Greece in Italy, with a culture and commerce more diverse than Republican Rome until it was reduced to the status of a provincial municipality by the Lex Julia. At the time of the Black Death it was the largest city of the Mediterranean, possibly of the whole of Europe, with a population of about half a million. Decadence set in with a vengeance under the absentee Aragonese kings and then, until 1860, the more resident Bourbons. The Bourbons and their courtly hangers-on patronised wondrous palaces and gardens, but the Kingdom of the Two Sicilies (southern Italy and the islands of the south) was too poor to sustain such luxury and the demands of the court drained it of what substance it had.

Since then Naples has lived in a state of perpetual crisis. Life is seen as a lottery and Neopolitans are the most inveterate gamblers in Europe. When Queen Elizabeth II visited the city in 1980 practitioners of Lotto, the local game of chance, went crazy as the presence of royalty once more in the city was an omen of good luck. Naples is now the biggest centre of football pools, legal and illegal – hence the ability of the local soccer club, though at the time not even in the First Division of the Italian League, to buy the Argentine star, Diego Maradona, for $5,000,000 in 1984. Lotto has become the basis of the gambling rackets, the so-called 'numbers games', beloved of organised crime in America and Australia.

Even the decay of the city has an exotic gaudiness. On a sunny December day, the walls of the houses and the great palace at Capo di Monte glowing pink in the sunlight, I decided to stroll down the hill to the Via di Toledo, the main artery of the lower town. Blankets were hanging from balconies, and the peeling façades and cascades of rubbish in the street blossomed like a luxuriant fungus. 'Tuck everything inside your jacket, camera, notebook, everything,' said a woman from her balcony. 'Bad people live down there,' gesturing towards the port.

Theft allows full scope to Neapolitan fantasy. For some urchins it is almost an art form, and the staple of popular legend. During the war children used to leap on the tailgates of lorries in supply convoys and strip them of their cargo until sentries were hidden under the canvas to chop off the fingers of the miscreants as they tried to clamber aboard. An Italian naval officer told me his frigate was relieved of its main sea anchor, weighing several tons, when it docked in the harbour overnight. After a parley with a fruit vendor at the end of the wharf it was returned with an apology: 'I'm sorry, Signor Capitano, the boys didn't know it was one of ours, they mistook it for an American ship.' The following night they deprived an American destroyer of its anchor. The favourite, and probably apocryphal, legend is the coolness with which a gang posing as laundrymen entered Allied Headquarters near Caserta and drove out again in a jeep with the month's wages for the entire general staff in their laundry sacks.

For most citizens, *'l'arte d'arrangiarsi'* is the key to the survival game. The notorious areas of Vicaria and Sant' Antonio d'Abbate' have some of the poorest housing in Europe. The *bassi*, the tiny apartments, many dark, dank and subterranean, are rife with disease and misery, yet they are a hive of industry. The old city produces nearly half a million pairs of shoes a year, millions of pairs of gloves, hats and hand-made shirts. Naples is still one of the few cities on the Mediterranean to boast its own cholera isolation hospital and more than sixty victims died from the disease in the early 1970s after the local mussel beds had been contaminated by untreated sewage. Ten years later dozens of babies died in the old town after ominous black lumps had appeared under their flesh, followed by high fever – giving rise to suspicions of a variant of plague, though this was later discounted.

'Step out of the door, turn right, turn left and there before you lies the Via di Toledo, the most joyous thoroughfare in the entire universe,' Stendhal wrote in his journal for 9 February 1817. He had been drawn to Naples for exactly the same reason that I had arrived there in an unseasonably hot December in 1984: the opening of the newly-restored Teatro San Carlo – the most elegant opera house in the Mediterranean. Built in 1737 for Carlo of Bourbon, it has survived riot and civil commotion, revolution and heavy aerial bombing, to say nothing of the addition and subtraction of annexes, balconies and backstage areas by generations of meddling architects. The gentle horseshoe curve of its auditorium, the delicate and simple ornament of the balconies and the curving roof like a glorious pavilion, give it a light and airy sense missing in more sombre houses like La Scala.

I had been invited to a performance of Verdi's *Macbeth*, with which Riccardo Muti was opening the season. It was the first full opera he had conducted in his native city, where his spectacular musical career had unexpectedly begun – studying piano at the Conservatory, he stepped in at less than a day's notice to conduct the students' end-of-year concert, and a vocation was recognised instantly.

'I was born *Napolitanissimo*,' he declared when we met the day before the performance. 'My mother took a train through some of the heaviest air raids to return from Bari so that I should be born in her city.' He in turn had named his children after the saints of the three great churches of the old town: Chiara, Lucia and Francesco. He had spent the day walking round the old quarters and revisiting the haunts of his youth.

That evening there promised to be as much drama in the auditorium as on the stage. Little had changed since Stendhal had written: 'There were not a few fists flying, not a few rude elbowings to be endured or given. . . . Indeed, I was resolved to keep my temper, and in that I was successful; but my triumph cost me both tails off my coat.' Not a few elbows were at work when I arrived to take my place in the stalls. The restorers had forgotten to attach numbers to the individual seats and mine was occupied by a dowager weighed down by furs and clanking jewellery. An attendant, gargantuan, blue sweat shirt girthed by a cabin trunk strap, shoved the matron aside and lifted me to my seat like a human crane exclaiming 'Don't you realise, he's the guest of the maestro!'

The renovation of San Carlo is part of an energetic campaign which transformed much of the old city in the 1980s. Despite economic chaos, political upheavals and rampant crime, Naples has enjoyed a renaissance in almost every branch of the arts in the past ten years. The Baraco family have sponsored dozens of schemes to restore old houses and residences with their Fondazione Novanta. The Norman Tower, jewel of the Castel dell' Ovo, and the mightily fortified gate of the Hohenstaufen Castel Nuovo have been rebuilt and their ornaments re-embellished. The cloister in the old university has been completely rehabilitated and the massive structure of the Museo Nazionale, one of the great collections of classical antiquities, has been refurbished and extended. Archaeologists working at Cumae, where Aeneas consulted the Sybil before entering the underworld, have turned up some remarkable discoveries about the city's origins. They have found the shrines of at least six Sybils.

Presiding over the bay, Vesuvius rises like some natural weather cone – a faint banner of white cloud from the crater its only signal of activity. Its eruption, in a plume of smoke and ash like an umbrella pine, was witnessed by Pliny from his villa on the promontory opposite. Later, the same scene was viewed from Naples itself by Nelson and Emma Hamilton. In March 1944 an eruption was recorded by a young officer in the Allied Military Government trying to grapple with the rising anarchy of the liberated city, Norman Lewis. His *Naples '44* vividly evokes Naples at its most desolate: bombed, broken and with most of the population near starvation. 'The city of Naples of charred wood, with ruins everywhere, sometimes completely blocking the streets, bomb craters and abandoned trams. The main problem is water . . . German demolition squads have gone round blowing up anything of value to the city that still worked,' he records of his arrival in October 1943. Among the items destroyed by the Germans was the priceless archive containing the manuscripts of the great medieval emperor Frederick II, *Stupor Mundi* ('The Wonder of the World'), on science and statecraft, set on fire by an artillery captain in a fit of lunacy or ignorant vandalism.

In the city everything was for sale. The young and rather prurient Lewis calculates that of the 150,000 women in Naples, more than 40,000 earned a living from prostitution. Most of the surrounding countryside was in a state of near famine. In much of the old city the Allies' writ yielded to that of the Camorra, the Neopolitan criminal clans whose strength is, if anything, greater today. In 1944 they were abetted by such strange entrepreneurs attached to the Allied staff as Vito Genovese, a luminary of the American Cosa Nostra. The Camorra is compared to the Sicilian Mafia, but in important respects it differs. Like the clans of Palermo and western Sicily, its families rely on local control and a ruthless code of obedience and silence, *omertá*. Unlike Mafia organisations, its influence does not pervade all social and political classes. Initially at least the Camorra was based on protection rackets in the *bassi*, the old town and one or two villages in the Province of Naples. It had a monopoly of cigarette-smuggling, and later drug-trading in the city, and after the earthquake in Irpinia in 1980 it enhanced its earnings by several billion lire with rake-offs from aid to the victims pouring into the city. The very word 'Camorra' describes an activity – roughly equivalent to 'extortion' – rather than an organisation.

The pickings from the earthquake relief caused a crime war in the early Eighties. Among those killed were members of three firms of undertakers accused of over-charging in a racket which was termed '*il caro estinto*', named after Evelyn Waugh's *The Loved One* – a case of life imitating art.

The authorities arrested more than 1500 suspects and put nearly 300 on trial in the biggest criminal trial seen in the city. One round-up was carried out at a wedding party in a rustic restaurant. After the suspects had been led off an arsenal of hand-guns, machine-pistols and grenades was found in the ladies' handbags under the tables. The 'maxi-trial' of Naples was a messy affair, with many of the convictions being quashed as unsafe on appeal.

By the time of the trial it was evident that the Camorra had changed its nature, becoming more commercial and international, largely due to drugs. It has also benefited from the largesse distributed by the government – municipal, regional, provincial or national. By the early Eighties it had split into several large groups. The chieftain of Ottaviano, Rafaele Cutolo, the head of La nuova Camorra Organizzata, had acquired a national status far above that of any predecessor. Though serving a long sentence in the maximum security jail on the island of Asinara, 'the Professor', as he is universally known, still had a firm grip on his troops, holding regular clinics in prison for supplicants, known as 'board meetings'.

The Cutolo organisation is believed to have recruited directly in jails, and have made common cause with local elements of the Red Brigades. He was certainly involved in a curious episode in which Christian Democrat party bosses used the Camorra to obtain the release of a colleague, Ciro Cirillo, kidnapped by the Brigades.

One of the best publicised miracles in wartime Naples told of a flying monk in a suburb on the northern flanks of Vesuvius called Pomigliano. The holy man, who was graced with the stigmata, claimed to have flown to the rescue of an Italian pilot when his plane was destroyed in an aerial dogfight. Norman Lewis records that most Neapolitans believed him, and the monk later achieved fame as the faith-healer, Padre Pio.

The site of one of the biggest marshalling yards in Italy, Pomigliano d'Arco, was flattened by Allied bombers on 3 May 1943. The marshalling yards today are the setting for modern factories, the hope and despair of plans to bring industry to the south. One side are the works of AerItalia, building air frames and components for a range of aircraft. The company became a vehicle for one of the most lucrative stock market flotations of the early 1980s. With Alfavia, the aero-engine company, also returned to the private sector, more than 21,000 were employed in the aerospace industry in 1985; over half the workforce were highly skilled white collar workers, many locally recruited.

The complex on the other side of the old railway yards presented a more sombre picture. The production plant for Alfa Romeo Sud, Alfasud, it was the site of one of the most ambitious projects to introduce new industries to the Naples area in the early Seventies. In the early years, at least, it became a byword for absenteeism and sluggish productivity.

The chief engineer explained with brutal frankness the drawbacks of introducing modern technology too quickly to the south. By 1976 the new plant was producing just over half the planned target of 200,000 cars a year. On normal working days more than a third of the workforce might be absent, and the plant was often victim to wildcat strikes.

'It was very difficult to train people used to traditional work in the countryside,' explained one of the managers. 'On fine days some of the men on the assembly lines would head off into the open with their bread and flask of wine. One actually said "Why should we be expected to shut ourselves up in these noisy, dark sheds for hour after hour – I am used to the sky and sun."' As we spoke we were pronging up forkfuls of delicious pasta, shaped by the company chef in the form of the revolutionary door panellings of the new Alfa '33 model. First produced in 1983, the new line had virtually saved the company – and for the first time the plants in the south overtook those in the north in output and efficiency. But it was too late – the company was put up for sale by its parent, the state holding combine IRI. The management hoped Ford would buy, but Alfa eventually fell to Fiat, anxious to keep its grip on the domestic Italian market.

The production lines were indeed dark, if not satanic. At the time of my visit in 1986 it was evident that the plant was still working under capacity. Across the apron of tarmac used as a parking lot was another complex devoted to 'specialised' products – bullet-proofed cars for the police, ministries and private customers. A parable of modern Italian crime and violence.

With the demands on housing from the 60,000 earthquake refugees, some living in freight containers, pressures on local authorities have been unbearable. One year saw five mayors taking office in Naples in as many months. Yet the music of the streets goes on, the philosophising of the urchins, the lilting sibilant accents, the cultural renaissance, the boom in crime. The Neapolitans have an expression for the genius of their city and its way of life: 'Ours is the only Arab city without a European quarter.'

v The Mezzogiorno – the South

For those scratching a living in the barren countryside of the remoter parts of the Kingdom of the Two Sicilies, the capital Naples was a monster, the *testa grossa*, the engorged head sucking the life-blood from the shrivelled body of the realm. The kings and their courts, the absentee feudal lords, the army and navy, drew taxes and tribute which no one could afford. Not that the subjects got much in return: justice was corrupt or absent. In the wilder parts – Lucania, Calabria and the mountains of Sicily – brigandry was rife up to the demise of the Bourbon regime in 1860, and in some places survived well after the unification of Italy.

The richer citizens of northern Italy seem destined to rediscover the strange and bitter condition of the rural South once every generation. One such rediscovery was occasioned by the earthquake which struck the villages of the plateau of Irpinia, east of Avellino, and the Province of Naples, one Sunday evening in late November 1980. The tremor itself was not as great as the quakes of previous centuries, and had nothing like the effect of the Messina earthquake of December 1908, which killed 60,000 people and wrecked all but a tenth of the buildings in the city. But villages and farms were damaged or demolished over an area larger than Wales, and for many who lived there it tipped the balance between an adequate living and penury for years to come. Some of the tales of death and survival revived bitter folklore memories of neglectful absentee powers in Rome and Naples, and the abuse of local authority. In the parish of Balvano, on a spur running west of the regional capital Potenza, the quake demolished at a blow the back wall of the church, killing and injuring more than fifty – most elderly women – praying at vespers. Two days later the priest was driven from his living by angry villagers. They had discovered that he had been sent funds from migrant families in Australia to repair the church walls, but these funds had disappeared mysteriously and the work had not been done. Even the Pope fared little better – when he tried to dispense benedictions and sympathy two days later, he was greeted by catcalls and boos from the crowd. He decided to abandon his tour of the stricken area and sent money to the worst-hit parishes instead.

The evening after the main quake I arrived in the little town of Eboli, falsely believed to have been the epicentre of the tremor. Eboli marks the edge of the coastal plain of Naples and Salerno; the railway stops there, and the steep climb onto the southern central plateau of Italy begins. The central square was littered with bedding, rudimentary shelters and cooking fires. In the 'Pronto Socorso' first-aid station of the Red Cross I was told that much of the damage to houses had been slight, but more tremors and shocks were feared, so everybody had decided to camp out. The worst damage was higher up the mountain range, and one doctor had just heard that in a village called Laviano not a house was standing. Laviano hugs a spur of ground covered with olive groves and stunted vines from which most of the 2000 villagers derived their income. As I pulled up in a battered Fiat the village showed not a single light under the starlit sky. A few of the cheap apartment blocks were jagged stalagmites of gutted masonry. The only flicker of light was from a small bonfire on the edge of the houses. A lone and shrivelled man huddled beside it. He could not recall what had happened and could only repeat, 'I'm staying here, staying here till I die maybe, but I'm staying here until my son comes for me from Milano'.

In the valley below, like the twinkling of glow-worms, dozens of fires flickered and sparked between the olive trees, now the village centre. A donkey brayed at the moon, and from the makeshift hospital on the football pitch, a child ran from a tent screaming in panic at some sudden loss.

The newspapers and broadcasting stations of northern Italy wrote of the disaster as if some new continent had been discovered in the midst of their land. Good will became mingled with confusion and incompetence. Too much of the wrong material was sent south and too much got into the wrong hands. At the main Salerno intersection with the autostrada, I was offered blankets and clothes at a reduced rate by minor retailers of the Camorra commercial empire. Some northerners descended with trailers of supplies like Lady Bountiful, and met a characteristic southern reception. A good Samaritan from the north parked his car and caravan to ask the way, only to discover he was minus the trailer on his return. When he got back from reporting the loss at the police station, he found that the car had gone too.

Six weeks later, I revisited the area. The mountains were blanketed with snow and most of the roads laminated by sheets of ice. A student from the University of Bologna told me that she felt she was in a new country. 'Most here live by agriculture,' she explained, 'but they are simply incapable of working together to improve the farms and land. Look at these gloomy villages, the cafés and bars. I have never seen so many young men playing cards in all my life – that's all they do all day.' A medical team from Turin felt they had travelled backwards in time. 'In earthquakes you get a low incidence of injured to the number of dead – many die of shock,' said one doctor. 'But here we found a high number of people suffering from lung disorders, early stages of pneumonia and tuberculosis. We had a problem to persuade the older ones to go to hospital in Naples or Bari. We're back in the world of spells and charms. When we asked one family to move they cried, 'Ma dove sono i guaritori?' [where are the healers?] and insisted on taking the local spell-weaver with them to Bari.'

Such disasters were one small page in chapters of injury and neglect over the centuries. The question of the poor South, the Mezzogiorno, has proved an elastic-sided debate, particularly in the years since the Second World War – another crucial encounter between North and South – when serious attempts were made to introduce social and economic reforms. Estates were carved up, land redistributed, public works schemes started for roads and irrigation. Industry was encouraged to come south through subsidies from the new Cassa del Mezzogiorno, but at the same time the southern villagers moved away to the burgeoning factories of the north.

Despite the optimism of the early Eighties (not least in the EC Commision in Brussels) the most respected institute to study the Mezzogiorno in Rome, SVIMEZ, produced an ugly statistic in 1985 which told a very different story. It calculated that in the next ten to fifteen years the South would have to produce an extra 2.5 million jobs to maintain employment at its existing level – and in many places such as Cagliari, the capital of Sardinia, more than a fifth of the active population had no job. In the first year of the projection, only 65 new public posts had become available. The 2.5 million new jobs required made up nearly 60 per cent of all vacancies annually on offer throughout Italy. By 1985 the Southern Fund, the Cassa del Mezzogiorno, had dried up and been dissolved, to be relaunched a few years later in a different guise. Experts debated whether funds should only be offered for commercially viable enterprises or should be given as straight subsidies for public works and thinly disguised unemployment benefit. Industry had fared badly; it was increasingly apparent that the prime beneficiaries of public subsidies and grants were the organised crime syndicates. And the young unemployed of Palermo, Catana, Reggio di Calabria and Naples provided a rich recruiting ground for the foot soldiers or *picciotti* of local Mafia and Camorra bosses. To make matters worse, in the ten years from 1971 to 1981, the population of the Mezzogiorno as a whole rose 5.3 per cent from 18,874,000 to 19,881,000. This was after migration had been taken into account (a process which was beginning to slow to a trickle). The city populations of the South rose even faster over the same period at 8.4 per cent – with Palermo at nearly 10 per cent.

The most critical encounter between intellectuals of the North and the poverty of the South was generated by the Fascist regime's policy of sending political dissidents and opponents into internal exile. Academics, doctors, lawyers and students were sent south of Naples, many to Irpinia and the province of Matera – a region the Fascists, with typical hubris, reverted to its ancient Latin name, Lucania. A friend recalled being sent into exile forty years before with his father, a distinguished Turin art historian, to Potenza, the capital of the region now called Basilicata and destined to bear the brunt of the 1980 earthquake rescue operation. 'It was like arriving on the moon,' recalled my friend, 'the poverty and depression were indescribable.'

In 1935 a student doctor, painter and writer from Turin, Carlo Levi, was sent to exile in two small townships in the province of Matera – first Grassano, 'a little Jerusalem white upon a distant hill,' as he described it, and then the remoter and disease-ridden Aliano. His diary, *Christ Stopped at Eboli*, is one of the most famous evocations of the South. The lives of the peasants in Grassano and Aliano are riddled with superstition and fear of the supernatural; witches and spells are all about, and *incanto* (stronger than mere 'enchantment') is one of Levi's most common expressions for the villagers' spiritual and physical world. It was a world of abject poverty and disease. Malaria, strange cankers and growths, tuberculosis and a host of unidentified maladies, were rife. As if the wind, witchcraft and dulling disease were not enough there was the black farce of authority. In Aliano this took the human form in the strutting popinjay of the mayor, or *podestá*, as the Fascists renamed the post, Don Luigi Magalone and his pretentious sister Donna Caterina, a drunken pederastic priest, and offstage sundry absentee landlords, tax gatherers and sequestrators of property in lieu of payment.

Nearly fifty years after Levi's banishment I visited both his places of exile. Aliano was recognisably the village he had described so carefully, except for a few ugly concrete houses in the main street which proclaimed the new wealth of the villagers who had got away to the factories of Switzerland and Germany. At evening the older peasants still drove their goats, sheep and mules back to the village from the valley below – some sharing the ground floor rooms of their stone houses with them, along with a large television set. A few had light tractors for tilling the thick clay by the river.

In place of the pompous *podestá* was a woman mayor, and a Communist to boot. The wife of a pharmacist, Signora Santomassimo had been in office ten years when I called on her in 1983. She declared herself a Communist of a typically Italian stamp – 'a socialist in politics, sure, but also a Catholic, believing but not practising.'

'What has changed since Carlo Levi first came here? A lot and very little. The older peasants are much the same – their life is still hard. Donna Caterina the *podestá's* sister is still alive, over ninety – you can hear her shrieking at the moon on some nights, mad as a hatter. The roads have come, but they bring no relief to the young people. With school compulsory up to fourteen, the children are becoming over-qualified. They are after diplomas and don't want to work the long hours in the fields – a lot of the land by the river is becoming abandoned.'

In early January the rolling uplands of Puglia and Basilicata have become oceans of waving orange-gold wheat, a new granary for Italy. Here the public works projects for dams, reservoirs and irrigation systems have had dramatic effect, with the wide fields producing harvests three to four times larger than in the past, especially in the flatland of northern Puglia, where the territory between highland Basilicata and the spur of Mount Gargano known as Il Tavoliere di Puglia is the largest piece of agricultural land reclamation and improvement in the whole of the European Community.

Once this was a bread bin for ancient Republican Rome, said to provide most of the cereals required by the 1,200,000 inhabitants of the city in the first century before Christ. But in medieval times, the garrison city at the heart of the Tavoliere, Foggia, became the seat of the royal sheep stable, the Dogana delle Pecore. The plain of Foggia then provided winter pasture for some two million sheep, which migrated to the high mountains of the Abruzzo east of Rome in the summer.

Over the centuries the land fell into decay and as more reverted to marsh, malaria became ever more rampant. It was from such humid lowland places that the disease derived its name, though its victims thought it literally the effect of bad air, or 'mal aria.' Forty new villages sprung up in the mountains to escape the maladies of the plain, but it was not until this century that decline was reversed, largely as a result of the Fascist Law No 215, concerning 'Integral Land Reclamation' and promulgated in 1933.

This proved one of the lasting achievements of the Fascist era, a genuine reform which helped change the landscape of Italy. Under it the Pontine Marshes of Campania and Lazio were drained, Sardinia opened up as the fetid coastal lakes were cleared, and the process of drying and irrigating the Tavoliere began. Above all it meant turning the tide against malaria which had made millions of Italian lives a feverish hell.

After the war, the work was continued, helped by Marshall Plan funds and men like the engineer Guido Rotella, who headed the new Consortium for the Reclamation of the Tavoliere of Puglia in 1950. Dams were built, land was drained and farms were redistributed; by 1980 the harvests were of the same order of those that fed ancient Rome. New cash crops were rotated with the grain: sugarbeet, tomatoes, novel varieties of vines and olives.

'The really big change came after 1960,' Rotella reflected, when I met him a year before his death in 1987. 'The whole way of life of the *contadino* [cultivator] and peasant changed then. They earned high wages and were less tied to the soil.' A short journey outside Foggia bore this out. There was, hardly a house in sight, and only a few farm buildings. A member of the Consortium said that most of those who worked the land drove out from the town each day. They had adopted the habits of their formerly despised city cousins and become rural industrial workers.

The land was groaning with wheat, and production was going up each year despite the best efforts of the EC Commissioners to curb a surplus in cereals. The agronomist from the Consortium said that an old saying seemed more true than ever: 'Harvest by Saint Anthony's Day [13 June] and you'll have another by winter.' The second crop was the ubiquitous tomato, for the autumn markets of the North.

Most of the towns and cities on the rolling rich earth of Puglia are like fortresses. On the high ground of Calabria and Basilicata there are few villages as such, but communes of more than a thousand, in which the local populace once huddled against invaders from the sea.

Exile and invasion have been the lot of this tip of Mediterranean soil for as long as men can remember. Northerners embarking for the Levant on crusade brought their own legends and songs and left their marks in the sculptures and decoration of the romanesque cathedrals down the coast: the legend of Dives, the harrowing of hell, the dance of death and, above the door at San Nicola in Bari, the earliest depiction of King Arthur and his knights. The mosaic floor of the cathedral of Otranto, on Italy's east-ernmost promontory must contain every known medieval myth and legend, from Adam and Eve and the Passion to Charlemagne and the Song of Roland. The Ottoman Turks briefly took the place in 1480, the western-most thrust of their empire into Europe, but mercifully they did not have time to do much harm to the mosaic. Today radar scanners on the headland above the town sweep the sea to the east, vigilant against any new invasion.

Where the main thoroughfare of Castellaneta looks out over the plain of Puglia to the Gulf of Taranto stands a statue of an Arab, made from violent purple ceramic. This staggeringly vulgar piece represents the town's most famous, but forgotten, son in his most celebrated cinema role – the most incongruous monument to exile in all southern Italy. Rudloph Valentino was born here as Rodolfo Guglielmi in 1895; thirty years later, his fans erected the ceramic sheikh in his home town. It remains a bizarre memorial to the tens of millions who left Italy for ever in the past century and a quarter. Today there are no Guglielmis listed in the Castellaneta phone book, nor does even the most modest café, bar or gelateria bear the name of Valentino. And in the bank they found it hard even to offer an exchange rate for the dollar.

vi   South of the South: Calabria

'This is the south of the South,' said the old man sitting on the wall, 'the point where Italy finally crumbles into the sea.' The Aspromonte, the mountain plateau in the toe of the peninsula, is the part of Italy which seems nearest to Africa. The pace of life is drugged by the steady blast of the sirocco from Tunisia, or the lebice from Morocco. Faces are noticeably darker than in Adriatic Puglia and the women still carry their shopping and laundry on their heads with the steady, graceful gait of somnambulists.

Much of the highlands of the Sila plateau and the Aspromonte is deserted – the Sila still a place of thorns, exotic mushrooms and dark chestnut woods. Whole clusters of villages have simply moved out, so inaccessible were they and so inhospitable the terrain. Relatives overseas provide a lifeline for the communities that remain. 'In Rossano itself about 30,000 remain,' a priest once informed me, 'plus at least 15,000 more – they're the ones in Australia, but we still keep them on the parish records.' Between a quarter and a third of a million Calabresi left for Australia in the twenty years after the Second World War.

The coasts of Calabria have seen some of the most brilliant civilisations to take root in the Italian peninsula. The colonies of Magna Graecia at Crotone and Locri were large cities. On the fall of Rome the Byzantines ruled, spreading the gospel and building elaborate churches; at Stilo the chapel is a masterpiece of architectural symmetry to match the church or *catholikon* of any monastery on Athos. The Normans and Swabians came later. Deep in the olive groves by the lido of Catanzaro, the tiles of the Church of Santa Maria della Roccella radiate a rich red between the dappling shadows of the olive branches. It covers as much ground as Durham cathedral.

In the later centuries of neglect Calabria became a realm of bandits and rural warlords. The outlaws of today, the Mafiosi of the towns on the coast, still have a primeval quality. Renowned for its crudity and violence, the Calabrese Mafia is believed to have provided a disproportionate number of hired killers to other criminal organisations in Italy and southern France. Its name – 'ndrangheta – suggests a pagan order long ago. Its origins are subject of perpetual etymological and philological dispute, but the word is most probably a corruption of a Byzantine Greek phrase meaning 'our man's thing'; 'ndrangheta is closer to its rural roots than any other Italian criminal organisation. Today it is a chain of some two or three dozen clans, or *cosche* to use the local term, which means the clumping of leaves round a heart, like an artichoke.

Old, rugged, and resilient, the *cosche* of 'ndrangheta have not kept pace with the times and the flow of blood has been prodigious. Interventions by new authorities – local, national and international, in the form of the Common Market – have provoked campaigns of rural terror and gang warfare. One notorious cause of war was the decision to make a double track on the main railway down the toe of Italy to Reggio, while the plan to build one of Europe's main steel plants in the plain of Gioia Tauro (abandoned almost before it began production) led to a major offensive by local gangs to seize any agricultural land which might be developed and monopolise the local market for building contracts. Dozens of bodies were found near the site in a matter of a year or two, and the little town of Rosarno had a murder rate twice as high as greater New York, including Newark, New Jersey.

From Brancaleone on the coast, a few miles from the southern cape of the parting winds – Spartivento – it is a short journey into Aspromonte. My guide on one expedition was the headmaster of the local high school, Antonio Muti, a Tuscan who decided to settle there more than thirty years ago. He was a voluble and genial expert on the modern lore of the villages on the southern flank of the mountains, his own brand of optimism tempering the endemic melancholy of the locals.

Plunging through the shade of beech groves and bramble, we came to an early medieval church in brick, its walls capped with carved pyramids of stone. These strange devices gave the sanctuary its name, Santa Maria di Tridenti. The pyramid, said my companion, was a substitute for the cross, it also represented the trident of Neptune. The grove was reputed to have been a shrine for white magic cults long before the Christians arrived, and during the late Middle Ages it became the hideout of several famous robber bands.

Trudging up the hill, the schoolmaster pointed to a village to the north. 'Time moves very slowly here, you know,' he remarked. 'Over there they say two uncles exacted the seigneurial right of the first night – *ius primae noctis* – on a village girl as recently as 1929. They are a bit ashamed of the thing now as both families still live in these parts.' We seemed only a hand's breadth from *The Marriage of Figaro*.

The conversation in the little square before the parish church in the mountain redoubt of Staiti (pop. 6,000 – subject to seasonal migration, say the official statistics) epitomised Calabrian gloom. 'Times are bad, they are always bad,' said an ancient interlocutor, 'but they have got worse lately. I keep chickens, the odd goat if I am lucky. But anything bigger, a horse, a cow or a pig and *they* come to drive them off – anything substantial on four legs is just seized by *them*.' Everyone knew exactly who *they* were. They are the ones who still have herds of cows and flocks of sheep, guarded by fierce dogs and shepherds with sawn-off *lupara* shotguns, the choice weapon of Mafiosi. Their headquarters are in San Luca farther over the mountain, the only local community not bled by the haemorrhage of migration, where the population actually grows each year. Though none would be so foolish as to mouth the word out loud, 'they' are the local Mafia.

Six years later I returned on a sultry afternoon in July 1986 to look up my friend the Brancaleone schoolmaster, only to learn that he had died four years before. Retracing the walk we had taken, the mysterious tridentine church seemed in better repair than before. As I stood admiring its façade, an enormous figure in a baggy brown suit came crashing through the olives trees and asked me what on earth I was doing there. 'I am Bareco Giuseppe, ex-secretary of the Commune of Staiti,' he boomed. The epitome of the southern landlord in memoirs of fifty and more years ago, he immediately set about showing me that he was the all powerful local boss. After a brief discussion of my activities and his own history he eyed me up and down, before presenting me with a cheap edition in modern Italian of Caesar's *Gallic War*, copies of which were being given away at local petrol stations. The gift, complete with wobbly inscription, was a gesture of respect from a local baron.

The hillsides seemed if anything more abandoned than six years before. Brambles and scrub covered earth unploughed in recent seasons. And in the square at Staiti, even fewer old people were sitting about than on my last visit. They still complained that they could keep no large animals, and that *they* were as busy as ever with the rustling and highway robberies.

In the plain, scrubbed church the local priest had posted a request for the celebration of Saint Anna, patron saint of the parish, addressed to village families in exile overseas. 'We are less than a month from the feast of Sant' Anna and we all feel the duty and necessity to feel you close to us. We have remained few, but full of affection for you all. We need your help to celebrate your and our protectoress, Sant' Anna . . .' The letter asked the exiles to bear in mind that if they responded their names would be read out during the High Mass of the festival – 'that most beautiful moment when your names will bring some tears, some smiles and some sighs, the moment when we shall live together, united and full of love.' It was a poignant letter for spiritual and material help to sons and daughters overseas from a community that knew itself to be dying.

Three months later a Mafia war of exceptional ferocity broke out along the coast between Brancaleone, Reggio di Calabria. Three clans were involved in a conflict fuelled by family vendettas and the promise of funds to develop the transport infrastructure of the province. In 1986 and 1987 more than 150 people were murdered.

In the museum at Reggio, reminding Calabrians of more glorious times, stand two bronze statues, discovered by chance by an aqualung diver off Riace on the Ionian coast. Seeing a bronze arm waving at him from the sand, he called the local Carabinieri, who in turn called the fire service, the coastguard and the local archaeological authority. Everybody acted with impeccable efficiency, but it took nearly ten years for the figures to be cleaned and restored in laboratories in Florence. At first it was assumed that the two bronze men were warriors, but it is now believed that they are champions of the Olympic Games, possibly portraits of real heroes, from the Greek colony of Crotone farther up the coast. Dating from the fourth century BC, they are among the finest of all pieces of Greek classical sculpture – the rival and equal of the bronze charioteer of Delphi and the marble frieze of the Parthenon.

Italians greeted the appearance of the bronzes of Riace with the almost juvenile enthusiasm which they reserve for their heritage. In Florence queues circled the Palazzo Pitti, and when they were displayed in the Quirinale Palace in Rome, the queues stretched for miles. That summer on the beaches the young and the middle-aged strained to adopt their heroic postures. When the figures were sent back to Calabria, President Pertini and half the cabinet took the plane with them.

Two thousand years ago the bronzes might not have been considered that remarkable, given the civic wealth of the cities of the coast. 'This was once one of the richest places of the Mediterranean,' my friend the schoolteacher had once remarked. 'It still is a marvellous place of wide beaches, open sea and sun. Why does everyone think that Calabria is something out of the Wild West?'

vii Sicily: A Family Matter

For the time of day and the season the cathedral piazza in the little town was surprisingly full. Men and women – mostly men, for this was Sicily – stood about like the chorus in a silent public drama. Stoically they bore the afternoon heat of the June sun without comment as they awaited the signal.

'They're coming now,' yelled a youthful look-out from the church door. Slowly the coffin edged down the steps on the shoulders of the pall-bearers, with the grave momentum of a ship on a slipway. In an instant the square rang with the slamming of blinds and doors on bars, stalls and shops, their occupants standing before them in silent salute.

As the mourners made their way towards the cemetery, the road leading to the fields filled with a slow tide of humanity. First in customary precedence came the men, dark-suited and shiny shoed, or in shirt sleeves. Then followed the women in heavy black shawls, and young girl loosely linked by their finger tips.

The little town of Monterosso Almo perches on its rock above the great eastern plain of the island, a granite fortress with three churches as watchtowers. Its citizens had not come to the piazza to mourn some grand dignitary, powerful in office and local respect. The black-edged death notices at the street corners indicated that the dead man, one Luigi Scollo, had barely reached his twenty-first birthday. He had been killed on a construction site in Germany two months before. For the mourners following his coffin, the youth was a fallen soldier from the army of thousands who had left the upland villages year after year over the centuries to seek a future of work and hope abroad.

The procession approached the stone gateway of the cemetery along fields and lanes strewn with straw and husks of wheat – the last vestiges of the harvest. All afternoon the hills had crackled with burning stubble. In the distance plumes of heavy black smoke billowed skyward as if some battle fleet was steaming just below the horizon. The scene was a conflict of desolation and abundance – a desert of fertility, Goethe called it on his journey here two hundred years ago. The fields and orchards overflowed with harvested corn, peaches, pears, figs and vines – only humanity was scarce. This had once been one of the greatest store houses of the ancient world, yet it was the Romans who began the pattern of neglect with their *latifundia*, great estates tended principally by slaves. The *latifundia* continued until very recently – some would say they still persist in disguised form.

Though invaders came and went – Greeks, Romans, Byzantines, Arabs, Normans, Spaniards – few attempted settlement of Sicily's interior. Neglected by absentee landlords and largely ignored by the state, the communities established their own systems of power, protection and privilege. Those who could, left – by the million over the past century. In the 1860s – the decade of Garibaldi, the fall of the Bourbons, the emergence of the term 'Mafia', and much else that still affects the island for good or ill – its population was 2.4 million. By 1981 it had exactly doubled to 4.8 million – but had there not been the flow of migration, mostly to America North and South, the population by now should be at least 10 million.

The neglect and abuse of men has been compounded by the caprice of nature. Famine, pestilence and earthquake have been frequent visitors. In 1908 the earthquake of Messina destroyed nine out of ten buildings in the city and killed 60,000 people; and nearly the same number were to die of cholera in the ensuing months. In 1943 more than half the city was wrecked beyond repair by Allied bombers and 5000 people died – 900 on the night of 17 August, on the eve of the port's capture by the American army.

One of the best-kept cities in all Sicily is Ragusa, the capital of the southernmost province of the island. Much of the province is farther south than the northernmost tip of Africa, yet the old town is a splendour of eighteenth-century European architecture. The jewel is the cathedral of San Giorgio, its scrubbed white marble and stone façade the epitome of *baroca pulita* – 'clean baroque'. The cathedral rises from its steps like a stage-set facing the auditorium of the sloping piazza – perfect for *Cavalleria Rusticana*, the supreme melodrama of Sicilian blood, honour and revenge. Above the door of one of the palaces in the square are etched the words 'Circolo di Conversazione' – the conversation club where landlords and gentry met to indulge in chocolate and marsala, cards and political chatter.

But the town's architectural elegance cannot hide the fact that the community is dying. In the past thirty years the population has declined by two thirds to 4000, and in the old city on a Sunday only two of the thirty-three churches are open for worship. At the other end of the island, the port of Mazara del Vallo on Sicily's western tip, is the diametric opposite of Ragusa. Though well to the north of Ragusa, the waterfront at Mazarra looks distinctly African and its population is growing. It is now the home port of more than half the Tunisian fishing fleet. Along the quays barrowboys sell the produce of North Africa, mangoes, rainbow-coloured scarves and Berber blankets. The presence of the Tunisians has not pleased all the natives. In the past thirty years Italian and Tunisian fleets have come to blows – on occasion shots have been fired – over the rich prize of the waters between Sicily and North Africa, the harvest of tuna fish.

The old town of Ragusa, Iblea, has also seen change – a revolution even – which has affected the whole of contemporary western Europe. In the early Seventies a young engineer called Antonio Recca decided to challenge the monopoly of the Italian state broadcasting company, the RAI. The Constitutional Court in Rome eventually decided that this was legitimate, provided the broadcasts by other television stations were purely local. The floodgates of Italian television enterprise were opened in 1976. Not only was Tele Iblea born in Ragusa, but so too were some 600 other stations throughout Italy. It was the era of 'private TV', as local businessmen thirsty for fame and influence began to put out a potpourri of local news, sporting events, old films and, when audience interest flagged, home-grown striptease by housewives desperate for pin money.

Five or six years later fewer than a hundred of the private stations still existed, let alone broadcast regularly. Many had fallen into the hands of powerful companies, principally Canale 5 owned by the Milan entrepreneur Silvio Berlusconi, who had started to make huge profits. By the mid-Eighties Tele Iblea was in a curious state. It was run by two families, with wives, children and in-laws all helping to run the TV transmissions and the accompanying radio station. The standard fare consisted of programmes about local festivities, sport and, most importantly, the doings of the municipal and provincial authorities. The team had made an expensive documentary about the Knights of Malta, and they hoped to start broadcasting in Valletta and on community radio in Italian in London. Such stations seem to survive with little visible means of support, as local advertising revenue is meagre. 'We're not in it for the money,' I was told by one of Sicily's new TV moguls on another occasion. 'We're in it for the power – though it does not do for you to say so.'

The clans and families of the Sicilian Mafias have many code words, most of them euphemisms for a raw and often bloody struggle for daily existence. Mafia is one of the most enduring aspects of Sicilian character, as potent in its modern guise as ever, and the island's most durable export.

Mafiosi like to call themselves 'men of respect', belonging to an 'honoured society,' which is also referred to plainly as the 'mileu' or *ambiente*. They are bound to each other by *amicizia*, friendship, baptismal *comparaggio* or godparenthood. The strongest bond is *omertá*, the old Mediterranean notion of manliness – which in Mafia jargon has come to mean a vow of silence for which the forfeit is torture and death.

'I have breathed this phenomenon of Mafia from the first,' confessed Leonardo Sciascia, whose stories are the most vivid portraits of rural Sicily under the Mafia. 'It was always a criminal presence in our society – whatever the myths of Mafia nobility – and one based on exploitation.'

Seeking out Leonardo Sciascia in his home near Agrigento was to step into the atmosphere of one of his tales. At the bank below the castle in the town of Racalmuto a printed notice respectfully asks clients to leave all firearms at the door. On the edge of the town I asked the way of two men shovelling a pyramid of newly harvested wheat. The younger gave me a hard cold Sicilian stare. After weighing up my appearance and accent, and the hire car with its Roman numberplate, they decided my business with *lo scrittore* Sciascia could be nothing but literary. Their directions were elaborate and entirely accurate, though the house was three miles off.

Sciascia sat like a small Buddha puffing slowly on a pipe as he introduced his Sicily with the brevity and clarity for which the island's literature, and his works in particular, are renowned. 'The Mafia originated in the feudal world,' he explained, 'where the landlord was always absent in Palermo. The mafioso was the intermediary – trusted by his master, loyal, capable, intelligent – who at the same time exploited the peasants and robbed the boss.'

The mafiosi themselves were responsible for creating the myth of their own nobility – that they were Sicilian Robin Hoods. This was never true, says Sciascia, though with state justice almost completely absent in rural Sicily, the mafiosi became the arbiters in local disputes. Myth is larger than fact in Mafia folklore. Mystery is the essence of the power of the mafiosi, who like bogeymen terrify by fabricated reputation.

The term 'mafia' first occurs following the upheavals in Sicily of the 1860s after the fall of the Bourbon kingdom. Some pedants have argued that the Mafia did not exist before then, and that its power and influence are greatly exaggerated today. Others suggest that there is no such thing as *the* Mafia, a unified organisation under the command of a *capo di capi* in America and Sicily. And the term 'Mafia' describes a culture more than a single organisation.

Mafia (without the definite article) is a way of life of criminal association and rural banditry. Because it belongs to oral tradition, it is hardly surprising that there are no written references to it before the middle of the last century. It is a way of life, a centuries-old mentality from the neglected wastelands of the Mediterranean. The idea of its being a coordinated organisation owes much to the creative powers of professional crime writers.

Until a generation after the Second World War, the Mafia clans were largely rural in outlook and operation. They lived by protection rackets, smuggling, manipulating rents and dues, overseeing subtenancies from big landowners; its bosses were men of local power rather than great wealth. Mussolini had tried to suppress local gangs, and his special commissioner Cesare Mori had used the sledgehammer tactics of mass arrests; thousands were rounded up, the menfolk of whole villages at a time. The practice of *confino* or internal exile was used to send suspected bosses to the mainland, with the result that *la piovra* (the octopus) began to spread its tentacles throughout Italy. In Sicily the clans were battered but not beaten.

Relief came with the landings of the American forces on the island in 1943. Desperate to win the war cheaply and quickly, the US authorities released known Mafiosi from jail in the States – the most celebrated was Lucky Luciano – to convince their partners and cousins in the highland villages to throw out the Germans and the Fascists. The result was that within a year most of the mayors in Western Sicily were 'men of respect'.

But by the mid-Fifties mafia power was in decline – the old chiefs could not adapt to the new ways, and the villages were withered by migration. The first big change came with new layers of regional administration and Italy's membership of the EC. The Mafiosi became brokers and middlemen in the dispensation of public patronage, forging ever stronger links with

Rome. They massaged and manipulated funds for public works, the construction of railways and the autostrada network, and took their cut from grants from the regional and agricultural funds dispensed by Brussels – to the extent of inventing non-existent olive groves and reserves of olive oil to defraud the EC of billions of lire of subsidy.

The greatest change to the operation and appearance of Mafia organisations in Europe and America came in the mid-Seventies as they moved in on the burgeoning international narcotics trade – principally heroin. With the breaking of the 'French connection' through Marseille, the Sicilian and Italian clans ferried heroin between South-East Asia, Pakistan, Afghanistan and Iran to America. The clans became more anonymous and more international, linking up with organised crime operations across the world, including the drug baronies of Latin America and the Triads of South-East Asia and Hong Kong. The bosses became men of wealth more than local power, and some joined the ranks of the world's super-rich.

The effect in Sicily was a ferocious settling of accounts to decide who would be top dog in the drugs trade. In Palermo five hundred died in three years in the early 1980s, in shoot-outs, assassinations, kidnaps and disappearances – *lupare bianche* (literally 'white shotguns') in underworld jargon. Special laws were passed to get at the funds and bank accounts of alleged associates of the drug barons. The author of the legislation, the island's leading Communist, Pio La Torre, was murdered. The government in Rome reacted with the urgent despatch of General Carlo Alberto Dalla Chiesa of the Caribinieri, who had virtually dismantled the Red Brigades in two years, to be Prefect of Palermo and Anti-Mafia Commissioner. Within six months he and his young wife were shot dead as they drove from a restaurant in Palermo – with characteristic ceremony, his assailants closed the street to traffic before they staged the ambush.

Hundreds of suspects were rounded up for a series of mass trials. Leonardo Sciascia, who had been elected as a member of both the Rome and the European Parliament for the Radical Party, grew alarmed at the implications of the Mafia and terrorist trials. Judges were beginning to take the law into their hands, were becoming overmighty. 'Liberty in Italy is much reduced,' he lamented during our conversation in Racalmuto. His critics accused him of being too willing to defend Sicily's old ways.

High in the mountains of central Sicily is Corleone, the setting of Sciascia's masterpiece of rural conspiracy, *The Day of the Owl*, and the home of some of the most celebrated bosses of modern times – the Grecos, Luciano Liggio, and Dr Michele Navarro, who was accused of administering a lethal injection to a shepherd boy who had witnessed a murder. The town is less sinister than one might expect from Hollywood films, and the citizens take no notice of the tourists wandering round the broad windswept piazza. Standing on a rock above the town, I caught a sight of the old Sicily. Across the open hillside came hundreds of sheep, goats, mules and horses, escorted by yapping dogs whirling in the dust, and a cohort of mounted men armed with sawn-off shotguns. They might have been the retinue of some absentee landlord, or his cunning middleman and rentmaster, a *gabellotto* of traditional Mafia power.

Further east across the highland ridge Vicari broods behind its walls above the mountain road that bisects the island from Agrigento to Palermo. The place and its people seem turned in on themselves in a savage silence. Here the justiciar of the Angevin King of Sicily – Charles I – fled for his life from the capital in the popular uprising of the Sicilian Vespers in 1282 – much good did it do Giovanni di San Remigio, for he was dragged from his sanctuary and killed in short order. The place is a long blank, stare. A woman with her washing and a *contafino* leading a mule laden with straw seemed to gaze through me as if I, the outsider, did not exist.

I learned something of the inner life of Vicari a few days later when I was shown a testimony for the Mafia maxi-trial in Palermo by a former inhabitant of the town – an affidavit by a young lawyer, which was not admitted to the hearing as the volume of similar material was overwhelming. He claimed that his father was a self-confessed mafioso who, by explaining what this had meant, hoped to dissuade the son from becoming similarly involved. The story is a trail of petty delinquency and deceipt, of small disreputable deeds and favours for friends, particularly friends in power who could exact a tough penalty for their displeasure. The old man related his obtaining a driving licence illegally for a 'friend' on one occasion, taking bribes and gaining preferment for valuable patrons and allies on others. It revealed a pitiful and squalid spider's web of graft and peculation.

The most melancholy spot on the high crown of hills before Palermo is the green saddle of hillside called Portella della Ginestra – the Gate of Yellow Broom. Even in high summer it is a windswept desolate place, dotted with chunks of rock on which are carved the names of the men, women and children shot down during a May Day procession in 1948 by Salvatore Giuliano's gang; eleven people died and fifty-five were wounded. Giuliano was the most celebrated outlaw of his day, graduating in a couple of years from wartime black marketeer in corn and fruit to the robber king of Montelepre. Giuliano was a bandit rather than a

Mafioso, a law unto himself and above or against all other law. He revelled in his fame, even contriving to get himself pictured for the cover of *Life* magazine. As a believer in Sicilian separatism, which had real popular support immediately after the war, he became a tool of reactionary politicians. In much the same spirit, he became the ally of the Mafia bosses of Palermo and the west of the island, and it was in the crazy belief that he could staunch a Communist rising that he shot down the peasants at Portella della Ginestra.

As fears of a Communist-inspired revolt by the landless receded, the Mafiosi made common cause with the Christian Democrats. Giuliano was dispensable. After his gang had disintegrated he was murdered by his own lieutenant, Gaspare Pisciotta. At his own trial Pisciotta said he was put up to it by the police and the politicians. A year into his prison sentence he died from arsenic in a cup of espresso. Suicide made to look like murder, or murder made to look like suicide? In the ambiguity lies a classic Mafia ploy. The Sicilian banker Michele Sindona died by precisely the same device in a Milan prison nearly forty years later.

In Italian they do not hold trials but celebrate them, in much the same way that a religious rite is celebrated – though in the case of the 1986 Mafia trial in Palermo, the fortified court-room built into the city's main gaol was more reminiscent of a circus than a church. Round the edge of the underground arena, cast in a perpetual watery green for no daylight penetrated here, the accused stood in cages like wild animals about to devour some unsuspecting Christian in the Colosseum.

The king of the tribe of accused was Michele Greco, silver-haired and of patrician mien. Several of the hundred or so lawyers thronging the main hall formed a small court before him – always the defence lawyers of grand mafiosos are almost always called 'counsellor' (*consigliere*) rather than plain 'advocate' (*avvocato*). Michele Greco was arrested two weeks after the ritual opening of the great trial in February 1986 – he was found skulking in a farmhouse near Caccamo where the coast road leads into the mountains, and one of his counsellors assured me that his client was merely what the English would call a gentleman farmer.

The maxi-trial had taken years to prepare. There had been nothing of quite the same scale before, nor is there likely to be again. In all some 476 men and women were accused of a string of serious crimes embracing two continents over more than twenty years – murder, extortion, bribery and corruption, and running one of the biggest narcotics operations yet known to justice. Among the murders were those of several 'illustrious corpses', as the Mafia victims of power and rank are called after the display of cadavers of eighteenth- and nineteenth-century dignitaries in full fig – generals, admirals, abbots and bishops, great courtiers – in the catacomb of the Capuchin convent in Palermo. Some had been murdered in the course of the investigations leading to the trial – principal among them, General Carlo Alberto Dalla Chiesa.

Mounting the trial – the investigation, the preparation of the court in the Ugoccione Prison at a cost of nearly three million dollars – was a huge operation, particularly in the face of the vested interest of the Sicilian public in inertia. More than a thousand extra security police had to be drafted in for the hearing, which lasted nearly two years. An entire new barracks had to be built outside the western wall of the gaol.

The acts of indictment eventually ran to more than 8000 pages. 'I would put the whole of Italian justice out to tender, if I could have just three weeks of the speed and efficiency of English common law,' moaned Paolo Seminara, the acknowledged star of the defence *consiglieri*.

The aim of the acts of accusation was to spell out operations of Mafia networks in light of the drug wars in Palermo and New York of the late Seventies and early Eighties. In this the testimony of one group of witnesses would be crucial. Tommaso Buscetta was a minor mafioso who had fled to America, North and South, to escape the vengeance of his enemies and to make his fortune. Back home in Palermo his nephews and his son-in-law were to die in his feud with the Grecos. He was also involved in the 'pizza connection' operation in New York, where pizza parlours were used as a front for drugs trafficking.

After his arrest in Brazil, Buscetta decided to break the code of *omertá* and tell all. He was motivated by the terrible damage done to his family by men he claimed had betrayed the old values of the 'honoured society' for the huge financial profits to be made from drugs, violence, perversion and human misery. He claimed never to have dealt seriously in drugs. His testimony went further – and this is the most singular point of the whole saga of the Palermo maxi-trial – and suggested that the Mafia or, given his preference for the American term, the 'Cosa Nostra', was indeed one cohesive organisation in its major international dealings.

The Cosa Nostra, he said, was run by a commission which controlled the clans, their bosses, the *capi cosche* and their 'footsoldiers', the *picciotti*. The supreme command had influence over activities in Sicily and Europe, and among the seven Sicilian clans and their syndicates and satellites in America. The highest organ of control, he alleged, was called *la cupola* (the dome) and its head was Michele Greco, alias the Pope or the General, and the men of Corleone.

If the charge could be made to stick, it would change the traditional picture of the Mafia underworld as a loose grouping of clans and factions of Sicilian or Italian origin to a sharp-focussed portrait of the most powerful and coherent criminal conspiracy in the modern developed world. Moreover it would mean that a known mafioso grandee could now be charged with being the instigator or accessory to almost every major crime bearing the Mafia or Cosa Nostra label over the previous twenty years. Sweeping laws introduced in Italy since 1982 have made any association with mafiosi, however unwitting, liable to charges of criminal conspiracy and association in 'deeds of a Mafia stamp'.

The popular press and television leapt on Buscetta as the new breed of anti-hero, claiming that he was the first major Mafia 'godfather' to break the code of *omertá* and sing. Not true: it is doubtful quite how powerful Buscetta was in his criminal heyday, and he is far from the first, or the last, mafioso to turn state evidence. But how much could he be relied upon? The FBI used his evidence extensively following the pizza connection arrests, rewarding him with a reduced sentence, a safe house, and surgery to change his appearance. But could this be a desperate end-game of mafioso vengeance – the throw of a man who would do anything to bring down the enemy clans who had done so much to destroy his own world? Much about Buscetta and his tactics reeks of the blood and revenge of old Sicily, the tactics of a cornered mafioso against his own.

Three years before the trial opened I had paid a visit to the headquarters of the flying squad of the Palermo police in a solid building in front of the Norman Palace. Outside the palms drooped mournfully in the squalls of winter rain; inside I was ushered into the presence of a tall, youngish man, with a blue blazer, a trimmed moustache, and along cigarette-holder – Dr Antonino Cassara, doctor of law, Vice Questor and deputy head of the Flying Squad, a law-graduate from Calabria who had taken up his career as a vocation. He was evidently proud of his work and that of his squad of police officers and detectives. 'We have to enter the mentality of the criminals to be effective,' he explained.' But we are very few – only about seventy-five in all – and we expect one of our number to be killed every six or seven weeks.'

As he spoke a group of young men, unshaven, with heavy leather jackets, clutching short submachine-guns, passed through the bureau to pick up a car. The team had begun concentrating on the investigation of the Greco clan and the men of Corleone. 'Suddenly you get a clan like the Greco which has been dormant, and largely confined to the countryside, becoming very active and violent here in the capital,' the detective continued. 'You ask me how we work ? It's like archaeology, you start with the bones. When you find a body, you ask why was a man from one area dumped in another neighbourhood? What is the message being sent? It usually means the killers are from another quarter, and have a grudge against the clan of the dead man and the bosses of the sector where they left him. X plus Y equals Z – a strange algebra.'

In each branch of the investigation for the Palermo maxi-trial a leading law officer – policeman, carabiniere or magistrate – was to die. In the summer of 1985 Ninni Cassara travelled to England to interrogate associates of the Greco clan who had been arrested and charged with serious narcotics offences. Three days after his return from London Ninni Cassara was shot down as he entered the front door of his apartment block. In his cool approach, and his mental as well as physical courage, Cassara was exceptional, according to the leading magistrate in the investigation, Giovanni Falcone.

Falcone himself was the dynamo of the investigation. Six months into the trial, whose acts of instruction – the text to which the prosecution worked – he had largely framed himself, I managed to see him in the Judge Instructor's office in the Palermo Palace of Justice. The place was a fortress, with reinforced concrete walls, two-way mirrors, heavy metal grilles. Machine-guns on laps, guards lounged in armchairs with feigned nonchalance.

The judge was surprisingly athletic for a man of forty-seven constrained by security to live the twilight life of a mushroom. His brown eyes seemed constantly on the prowl, but the beard flecked with silver (since then removed) could not conceal a surprisingly jolly demeanour, given the circumstances.

'What's different about this trial?' he beamed, anticipating my first question. 'Well, in trials such as those involving the Spatoloa-Inzerillo-Gambino clans [in 1983], we only had a partial view of the organisations. Now we something completely new, a much more unified and vertical set-up, something far more articulated than we had imagined. The problem has been getting evidence. But given the hundreds of dead in the wars in Palermo and Catania in the early Eighties, *omertá* is not quite the force it once was.'

Falcone and his colleagues had been mapping the new world of Mafia, in which the clans had become super-capitalists and a global criminal force. The investigation had revealed three things: the Sicilians rather than American-Sicilians ran the narcotics trade, particularly in heroin; profits were being invested ever more widely in legitimate businesses such as real estate; and in the Middle East the traffic in drugs and arms were becoming intertwined, drawing the clans into the commerce of political instability and terrorism.

'Had the trial marked a leap forward in tackling Mafia crime?' I asked.

'A little jump ahead, yes, but there is always the possibility of a jump backwards. This thing is a serpent, a hydra – chop off one head and more will grow. How many Mafias are there? It will never finish.'

At one morning's hearing of the maxi-trial I discovered two distinct Mafia faces on display – one rooted in rural Sicily, the other in international banking and investment, and computer fraud.

First on the stand was Pippo Bono, putative 'boss' of Bolognetta, which guards the road from Agrigento where it descends to the coast towards Palermo. A large bulky figure, Bono was evidently a man of substance and wealth, with agricultural, commercial and industrial interests in Sicily, Milan, Caracas and Philadelphia.

To begin with, there was an awkward suggestion in the Buscetta testimony that Bono was one of the biggest drug distributors in America and Sicily. What were his dealings with Buscetta, enquired the president of the court?

In Bono's reply reality imitated art – at once we were in the realms of the Francis Ford Coppola movie *The Godfather*, (which on its first showing on state television a couple of years earlier had played to an audience of 25 million, such is the Italian penchant for Mafia mythology). The two pieces of evidence linking Bono and his accuser were a group photograph of the Sicilian community at a baptism in Caracas – truly a gathering of godfathers – and at a wedding in New York. 'We may well have been there together,' explained the accused, 'but there were hundreds of guests and I was never formally presented to Buscetta. Accusations that I am one of the biggest bosses and *spacciatori* (traffickers) of drugs are based purely on imagination. It is not for me to defend my innocence.'

He spoke in the accent of Sicily, with its distinctive click of the 'r' after the consonant, an attractive sound after the pretentious pseudo-aristocratic drawlings of northern Italy. But with the word 'droga' it had an ominous ring.

Courteously, the witness explained that his ability to conduct any business had been curtailed in recent years by the fact that he had been held on bail, had to report to the police and had his passport witheld. As was well known, he could have been seen any number of times at his favourite restaurant in Rome. 'Well I hope they give you plenty of discount, if you go back there, for all the good publicity you've given them,' quipped the judge.

The alleged *capo famiglia* of Bolognetta ('a little village I might have passed by once or twice' by his account) traced a bewildering web of business activities. In Sicily he had been involved in fruit and vegetable marketing. In Milan he had taken up the distribution and wholesaling of domestic appliances. Thence to Caracas, where he had bought up the biggest industrial development site, and traded in jewels. Finally to Philadelphia, where he became managing director of the Pronto Demolition Co.

Confessing bewilderment with this rags to riches story across two and a half continents, the judge asked for clarification about Pronto Demolition.

'Well, it builds large concrete containers, which are filled with spoil and then placed in the foundations of new highways.' The bench did not ask what extraneous materials might also go into the concrete coffins.

At the end of the testimony the prisoner on the stand offered a little homily to the court. Roughly it went: 'For those outside it is hard to understand our world, a world of respect and friendship, a milieu (*ambiente*) with its own sense of honour.' In the space of a couple of sentences the court was given the key code words of the alternative world of traditional Sicilian Mafia.

The next accused to take the microphone on the stand could not have been more different. A tall, thin, almost characterless figure in a sharp, tightly cut suit, he needed no lawyer to guide him. With machine-gun delivery he rattled off the articles, chapters and paragraphs of the Criminal Code under which he had been arrested, explaining in detail the technical flaws in the charge. After the defendant from the old culture of Sicily, we were hearing the voice of the hi-tech operative of the milieu, the yuppy of international law and banking, computer interfaces, global high and low finance.

The trial hearings ground on for more than a year and a half. The judges, both professionals and empanelled laymen, were locked in chambers within the prison for more than a month to deliberate their verdict. In December 1987, 364 of the accused, not all of them present – for some were still at large – were sentenced to a total of 2,700 years in prison, and 19 were handed down life sentences for murder.

No sooner was the trial over than the killing started. One of those acquitted was shot dead two days after his release as he was entering his house carrying a cake for a party to celebrate his liberty. A former mayor was murdered. In his papers was found a list of 'good' and 'dishonest' mayors and public officials in the Palermo city council over the previous decades.

The following summer the Palermo clans were feuding as before. The wife of a boss and her guards were shot down as she sat in the veranda of her villa taking morning coffee, her blue silk dress turning dark with gore – it was a *matanza*, as Sicilian fishermen term the tuna harvest that stains the sea red with blood.

The Palermo verdicts and sentences were sent to appeal. A few weeks earlier one of the appeal judges had been cut down as he was driving with his handicapped son down the mountain highway from Agrigento to the capital. On appeal many of the sentences were quashed or suspended. The appeal court was not prepared to accept Tommaso Buscetta's thesis that Cosa Nostra was under one unified command.

Further trials of political grandees, including several former mayors of Palermo and a former European parliament representative, were delayed. Serious squabbles broke out among the judiciary about the conduct of the cases. Judge Falcone was passed over for the post of senior investigating magistrate and judge of instruction. His new superior banned him and his colleagues from talking to journalists, and an attempt was made by senior judges to disband the anti-Mafia team of magistrates.

Italian judges are governed by their own autonomous elected body, the Higher Council of Magistracy, with the President of the Republic as its titular head. The Council controls the appointment and posting of judges and prosecutors throughout the Republic. The members of the Council, judges themselves, quarrelled bitterly and publicly about the role and powers of the investigating magistrates and Office of Instruction in Palermo. Two years after the maxi-trial the Council received a set of anonymous letters claiming that some of the anti-Mafia magistrates had shown irregular favour to one of the principal Mafia turncoats, Salvatore Contorno. It soon became evident, from fingerprints and other forensic evidence, that the letters came from a member of the Sicilian judiciary. Mafia tactics of suspicion, betrayal and mistrust were being used to destroy the Italian judiciary from within.

In Palermo the energetic young mayor, Leoluca Orlando, tried to clean up the public administration. He opened tenders for public contracts to international competition, launched arts festivals and encouraged Catholic and Communist student movements to reject the old ways of mafioso Sicily. He was backed by the Jesuits, a handful of his own Christian Democrats, and councillors from radical and environmentalist parties. But politicians in Rome, notably the leadership of the Socialist Party, denounced the mayor and his council as 'anomalous' and tried to remove him.

Mafia activity proliferated. In 1989 national police and intelligence services uncovered trade links between Mafia clans and Abu Nidal's Fatah Revolutionary Command – the most indiscriminately violent of Palestinian terrorist groups. In the autumn of the year before, the new anti-Mafia

Commissioner, Judge Domenico Sica, told the Rome parliament that 'there are now whole areas of Italian territory, Calabria, the Province of Naples and Campania, Sicily, that are beyond the control of the Italian state.'

In February 1991 the Appeal Court ordered that many of the sentences in the Palermo 'maxi-trial' be quashed. They had not been able to hear the appeal cases inside the time limit. One of those released was Michele Greco, once accused of being the Mafia 'Pope', the head of the clan from Corleone, who had been sentenced for conspiracy and multiple murder.

In name and local colouration, Mafia appears utterly Sicilian. It is also a pattern of life, a culture, which has pervaded the Mediterranean for centuries, and remains a potent aspect of Mediterranean behaviour today. Unlike traditional banditry and brigandage, and political revolution, mafia power aims to subvert the existing order to its own ends rather than overthrow it. It is reactionary and conservative, a parasite on established authority. It is a parallel and secret power with its own scale of inverted justice. This model of social conduct appears in the secretive Druze communities of Lebanon, the villages of Crete, the clans of Cyprus, Corsica, and the Ballearics. Public power, commerce and justice, are perverted for the private gain of the clan, and become a family business.

In a world of computers, fax machines, photocopiers and telex, where everything can be recorded, a mafia network which relies on blood-ties, sworn loyalties and verbal bonds, is peculiarly potent. Yet although the mafiosi have now entered the world of high finance, the symbols and the instruments of Mafia power come from the old Mediterranean. Professor Pino Arlacchi, a sociologist in Florence who has studied Mafia activity in Calabria first hand, believes that Mafia depends on the honour system of the ancient world – where virtue and honour are based not on moral goodness, but on power and blood. A mafioso can enforce his will, whether over a contract for shares, pizza, drugs, a construction deal or murder, because he has the physical might to make the defaulter pay with torture or death. The top mafioso is the man most powerful in blood. Arlacchi suggests that the first great mafioso of literature was Odysseus, and his destruction of Penelope's suitors in the palace at Ithaca is a classical Mafia settling of accounts. The very imagery of his appearance after the fight is that of the boss triumphant, the king of the beasts of the clan society: 'like a lion feeding on the farmer's bullock, with the blood dripping from his breast and jaws on either side, a fearsome spectacle.' The slain are described with what has become a familiar code word: 'they paid *respect* to no one who came near them – good men and bad were all alike to them.'

Over the last two centuries the writers of Sicily have developed a style peculiarly their own. Called *verismo*, it involves a seemingly simple and direct realism, though in the background lurks the mystery and ambiguity that infuses the island and its culture. Leonardo Sciascia shows himself to be an heir to the *verista* tradition through his elegant linear etching of the Sicilian landscape and its people in his novellas. Like so much in Sicilian art and literature, he claims the genre of *verismo* is a hybrid, owing much to French literary forms at the time of Stendhal. But he also suggests that one of its first and greatest manifestations occurred centuries before, in the pictures of the fifteenth-century master Antonello da Messina.

The best known and most loved of Antonello's paintings in his panel of the Virgin of the Annunciation – the prize of the newly restored Palermo National Gallery. The portrait reflects the fine detail and realism of the Flemish school, yet something about it is unmistakeably Sicilian.

The virgin is an oval-faced Sicilian girl with a firm mouth and a slight squint that gives her a distracted, distant air. A hand with tapering, forshortened fingers is held up in surprise; the other clasps a cowl, a dramatic triangle of ultra-marine framing the face. No photograph or reproduction can capture the subtlety of the tones and lights on the modelling of her features or the folds of her cloak.

But the most astonishing thing about her is the expression on her face. At first sight she seems submissive and accepting. But on second glance, her looks seem more ambiguous – the firmness of the mouth and the upraised fingers have an element of warning, of *minaccia* (threat) in Mafia lore. In her combination of submission and strength this Madonna is essentially Sicilian.

viii Cicero's Bitter Honey: Sardinia

When first the Phoenicians invaded Sardinia, they ordered the men of the island to turn out of their houses. Though vanquished, the islanders looked on their captors with a disdainful gaze – a sardonic smile.

So legend says. The alternative version of the myth is that when unsuspecting Romans were poisoned by the strangely sour herbs of the island, their faces seemed convulsed by laughter as they died. Writing to a friend, Cicero remarked 'In Sardinia even the honey is bitter.'

Bitterness and suffering are ingrained in the gnarled landscape, seemingly older and emptier even than that of Sicily, mitigated only by the mottled green scrub of the maquis. All year the hillsides are beaten by the winds, thinning the soil on the pastures, so the people who survive in the mountains are called *ferrigno* – made of iron.

Like Corsica, the island has been visited by a constant if irregular flow of invaders – and managed to reject many of them, or confine them to the coasts. The first may have built the huge funerary monuments in the north-east of the island in the second or third millenium before Christ, corresponding in time and scale to the stone circles of Stonehenge and Avebury in Britain. The tomb at Li Muri measures 27 metres, and may have a communal grave for sacrificial victims. The simple stone at its head is three times the height of the average Sard, with a clean line and stark shape that a Henry Moore or a Barbara Hepworth might have envied.

After these came the men who built the rounded forts or *nuraghi* of the northern and western plains in about 1000 BC, like huge conical beehives. Exactly who their builders were and where they came from is uncertain; probably they were akin to the Torreans of Corsica.

For all the impact on language and customs left by Romans, Phoenicians, Saracens, Pisans, Genoese, Aragonese and Bourbons, much of the interior remained untouched; and, although it was granted the status of an automonous region in 1948, Sardinia never had the prominence of Sicily in the affairs of Italy and the Mediterranean. Though only slightly smaller, it is less favoured by nature in the perpetual battle against drought; and whereas Sicily, despite migration, had a population of five million by the mid-1980s, that of Sardinia was just under one and a half million.

The men from Italy, the 'Continent' as it is always known, were kept out by a hidden line of natural defence – the malaria that flourished in stagnant pools and lakes along the eastern coasts of the island. The disease was eradicated much later than in continental Italy, and was not completely wiped out until the 1950s. The mosquitoes contributed to the remote and introspective nature of the island's interior and its pastoral communities. 'It is not that we Sardinians feel cut off from the Continent,' remarked a friend, 'for Sardinia is a continent in itself.'

No sooner had the mosquitoes succumbed and the malarial swamps round the lakes of the east coast been drained than a new invasion began. The newly sanitised parts of Sardinia became the playground of the rich. The trend was set by the young Aga Khan, who acquired 7,500 acres of the Costa Smeralada – the Emerald Coast – which soon became littered with the villas of the rich and famous. Twenty-five years later a modest abode with four bedrooms and servants' quarters would cost a round one million pounds sterling; a fifth of the sum paid by the former Saudi Arabian oil minister, Sheikh Yamani, to convert three villas into a summer palace in the late Seventies.

During the boom the Aga Khan acquired the local airline, Ali Sarda, which he emblazoned with his colours of bilious orange and yellow. It became one of the most expensive domestic air carriers of the entire Mediterranean – and with a virtual monopoly on flights from Rome and Milan to Olbia in the north of the island, it saw no need to offer concessionary or budget fares. Olbia became a magnet to the newly rich of Milan and northern Italy, unable to acquire to a toehold in the exclusive playground of the Costa Semralda itself. Soon whole tracts of the north and east coasts were given over to the development of holiday resorts. Woodlands mysteriously caught fire and peasants were bribed and bullied to leave their holdings to make way for production-line holiday villages and yacht marinas. The Milan property and television tycoon Silvio Berlusconi put his considerable economic muscle and political patronage into the development of a second resort at Olbia – unimaginitively christened Olbia Due.

Some Sardinians embraced the new holiday trade. It was easier and more profitable than fishing or farming, and the island is almost completely lacking in industry and mineral resources. In 1983 nearly a quarter of the working population had no jobs. The biggest single occupation was still farming, and that of the most medieval kind to be found anywhere in the European Mediterranean – the migratory pasturing of sheep.

The most enduring linguistic migration of the medieval Mediterranean took place in the port of Alghero, a pleasant and open town in the north-west. Today it is overrun by package tourists from Ireland and northern England, the townspeople of Alghero have fought hard to maintain its cultural singularity. Following the battle of Porto Conte (1353) the kings of Aragon planted the port with a colony of Catalans, and Catalan has remained the principal dialect to this day. Since the end of Franco's rule in 1975, Barcelona, Valencia, Palma in Majorca and Alghero have launched an ambitious revival of Catalan culture, music, theatre and poetry festivals as well as sponsoring a scholarly Catalan encyclopedia. The smallest community is that of the 10,000 citizens Alghero, though not the least in cultural self-esteem.

The very name of Sassari, the capital of the province of north-western Sardinia, evokes the rock and granite of its fabric – which gives its baroque cathedral and grander houses a closed and introspective air. Sassari has long been a centre of learning and liberty – it was one of the first parts of the island in which feudal obligations were abolished, and the university is an important centre for the study of Mediterranean societies. Its most famous son in the 1980s was Francesco Cossiga, elected President of Italy in 1985. His retiring and academic appearance seemed the personification of his native city. Although Cossiga was an ardent Catholic, his aristocratic second cousin was Enrico Berlinguer, while the Communist Party's greatest philosopher, Antonio Gramsci, was also a Sardinian, a native of Cagliari.

Gramsci spent the last 15 years of his short life in Fascist prisons – his most fertile years. Though his party's fortunes were to rise and fall, his mistreatment by the Fascists made him a martyr of the European Left. The humanity of his writing, and his endeavours to marry Marxism with the traditions of Catholic Italy, make him one of the most attractive radicals in modern Italian letters.

The name Sassari is a melancholy reminder that the Sassari Brigade – the infantry unit in which most Sards served in the First World War – suffered a higher rate of casualties than any other Italian units. The Italians – who joined the war in 1915, initially against the Austrians – suffered greater losses per head of population than any of the Allies, totalling 600,000 men. Of these 13,602 were Sardinians – 139 of every 1,000 men under arms were killed, as opposed to 104 from the rest of Italy. Nearly 2,500 officers and troops were killed from the two regiments of the Brigata Sassari alone, and more than 12,000 were posted 'mutilated, wounded or missing'. The population of the island then was just under half a million.

The Brigata Sassari was engaged in all the major campaigns on the northern front against the Austrian Imperial Army – the rocky ramparts of the Carso in 1915, the Isonzo, the Asiago salient and Monte Grappa, the rout at Caporetto, and the Piave in 1918. One soldier on the Carso reported 'mud up to the knees in the passageways [between trenches] – to get at all dry we had to hack caverns in the rock with our little picks.' The mud, lice, bad food and poor equipment compounded the misery, and after the battle 'the bodies were stretched out by companies.'

The disillusion and suffering of the troops, their disgust at the incompetence and arrogance of their command – only a handful of officers had seen battle, in Africa or, in the case of very few, as raw ensigns and subalterns in the Risorgimento – were to feed the political turbulence immediately after the war that led to Fascism. In Sardinia the effect was different. For most Sardinians the war meant involvement in the politics of the Continent, which they neither understood nor cared about, it was not business that should involve them or their island. Many of the young men who died in the Brigata Sassari were illiterate shepherds, little more than boys; many of those who survived determined on the separation of the island from continental Italy. On this platform the Action Party of Sardinia was founded. It has been a dominant feature of political life in the island ever since.

The cause has been pursued in Sardinia with varying degrees of vigour, though never with quite the concentrated bursts of violence of the separatists in Corsica and Sicily. Possibly this is owing to harsh and remote condition of the Sardinian shepherd communities, whose main aim is simply survival. Nowhere is the struggle harder than in the upland communities round Nuoro, in what the Romans called the Barbagia, the barbarous country where the wild things are. This is the land of bitter honey – in the woodlands reaching up to the high granite and limestone peaks grow thousands of plant species unique to the island. The villages and Nuoro itself rely on farming for their livelihood – and then mostly on itinerant shepherds, constantly on the move for the thin pickings of the highland pastures and elusive fresh water springs. Despite modern intensive husbandry and management, farming cooperatives have made grudging progress in the highlands, with their ancient systems of tenure and personal obligation. Markets are so poor that Sardinian lambs are killed at 4 kilos, whereas on the Continent they are kept until they weigh at least 22 kilos, when they can be sold at much greater profit. In spite of heavy state subsidies, light industry and tourism have brought to Nuoro little of the prosperity they have to the other provinces of Sardinia.

Shepherds of the Barbagia in search of wealth and honour indulge in a form of crime of a style uniquely their own – animal rustling and kidnapping, allegedly regulated since medieval times by a mythical 'code of the Barbagia', whereby a young man intent on a career of outlawry graduates through several stages, starting with sheep stealing, to rustling flocks, appropriating land and grazing rights, to kidnapping for profit. Until recently, in some parts of the high mountains of the Gennargentu, fathers refused their daughters' hands in marriage until the suitor could prove his skill in sheep stealing.

Only a tiny minority of the shepherds of the Barbagia are fully qualified kidnappers, but 95 per cent of all those convicted of it over the past forty years have been from the province of Nuoro. Between 1950 and 1971, eighty major kidnaps took place in the island, but in the following ten years the pace accelerated as the bandits turned to the newly rich holiday homes of the coast. In 1979, ten kidnaps took place at the same time, with nearly all the victims incarcerated in the mountains of the Nuorese.

From time to time the Continental power mounted large military operations to sweep the mountainsides of bandits, but with little success. Beside the kidnapping, there were bloody vendettas between the highland communities. Just before the unification of Italy, a deputy for Sardinia in the parliament of Turin wrote to the Minister of Agriculture, the young Count Cavour: 'They kill night and day, they kill in the piazza and the countryside, inside their houses and as they leave church.'

'*Andamus* – let's go!' said my friend. In its purest form the dialect of Sardinia is the closest to Latin of all those used in the Mediterranean. Ancient forms are given a local twist, often ending in 'u or 'au': Sards say 'mannu' instead of the Italian 'grande' for big or great, a derivation from the Latin 'magnus'.

I had been invited to the mountain community of Orgosolo, the home of the anti-heroes of the kidnap culture – the outlaws, the bandits on the run, or *latitanti* as the authorities always call them. With their dour granite houses, the streets of Orgosolo writhe round the mountain like serpents. Old women in black hobble down the steep slopes like limping crows scratching for food. The younger ones now wear bright head scarves and jeans, 'but underneath they still wear black – habits die hard here,' commented my friend.

Orgosolo's reputation for violence has endured since the war. In one year alone, 1951, the community of less than 5000 sustained no fewer than thirteen homicides, for which not a single culprit was brought to book. Twelve years later a holidaying English couple, Eva and Edward Townley, were killed as they picnicked in a field close to the town. The crime was exceptional, and with little apparent motive apart from the petty theft of personal trinkets. The bandit fraternity was dismayed by the attention it brought to Orgosolo from the authorities in Rome, and the murderers were probably dealt with by their own people.

Orgosolo now is prey to day-trippers from the coastal resorts enjoying the frisson of rustic food and wine in 'the unforgettable setting of traditional bandit country,' as the posters put it. The locals have a hard time living with their legend. Some twenty years ago an itinerant art teacher from Florence painted huge murals on the houses depicting the legends and fears of the mountain communities. Bandit chiefs are depicted, behind bars, before the justices and the Carabinieri, or being butchered in sanguinary ambushes. A scrawled legend proclaims 'Happy the people without need of heroes'.

Two square-framed men, their baggy moleskin trousers held up by heavy buckled belts, pulled us into a bar. Pouring thick oily red wine into tumblers, they discussed the woes of Orgosolo. 'Business is bad, the sheep don't sell, and there is no work,' grumbled one. 'The biggest payer here is the IMPS' – the state trust for pensions, a byword for malfunction and incompetence. As we turned to leave an eavesdropper at the bar beckoned me over and invited us to his house for a meal of roast wild pig. He had 'a problem' to discuss. His nineteen-year-old son was in gaol, sentenced for life for 'sequestrating persons' – condemned only on suspicion, mind you, he added quickly. The first year of his term had been served in solitary confinement. Could we do anything about it? And this at a time when the communities round Orgosolo had some dozen citizens on the run – *latitanti*, wanted for kidnapping or worse.

For all the lurid reputation of the bandits of the Barbagia, Nuoro's way of life has its champions – and first among them is Bishop Giovanni Melis, a keen student of the folklore and church history of Sardinia. 'Life has a more human dimension here,' he said in soft tones in his drafty palace. 'Here we have no excessive influence of television, drugs, and the muggings which plague other cities.' Nuoro had its poets and philosophers, a saint and two more beatified and now well on the path to canonisation.

'You could argue that this is one of the happiest cities in Italy,' agreed Emilio Pazzi, the *questore* or police chief of Nuoro. 'In some villages you can leave your keys in the car and it won't be touched – but that is only half the story.' After twenty years experience of kidnap investigations, he cautioned us against romanticising the shepherds and their bandit culture. The outlaws had brought misery to the highlands for five centuries, he explained, referring to the report on Sardinian banditry to the Rome parliament in 1971. The first traditional kidnap was recorded as far back as 1477 in Posada. By the decade of 1890 – 1899 the murder rate in Sardinia, Sicily and Calabria was 24.2 every 100,000 inhabitants, while the comparable figure for the rest of Italy was 14.2. This was surpassed in the decade of the 1940s when the upheavals war, occupation and their aftermath brought 1,544 civilian homicides and 5,166 kidnaps and hold-ups. The bandits respected age nor sex: in two incidents after the First World War, little girls of six and ten were seized and murdered – one the daughter of the Fascist mayor of Bono. The outlaws have recently exported their expertise to the Continent, and Sardinians are known to have been involved in some of the biggest kidnappings of industrialists in northern Italy. Some 150,000 Sardinians have migrated to the mainland since 1945. Many have achieved success and wealth as farmers, but among them must have been a good few hardened criminals.

Kidnapping is labour-intensive, Questore Pazzi explained, as a band needs at least twelve men to act at look-outs, messengers and negotiators, as well as seizing and guarding the victim. Unlike the Mafia families of Sicily and Calabria, the gang works together for one crime only, and then disperses.

The recent kidnapping craze was waning, he thought, though it would take long to die. Although it had been encouraged by the new wealth to be found in the tourist colonies of the coast, drugs trafficking was a more lucrative trade. Even so, in the winter of 1986 600 police and 1,500 Carabinieri were needed to patrol a province with just over a quarter of a million inhabitants.

The village of Oniferi crouches on its spine of rock like a wild beast sheltering from the wind beating up from the west. It was the setting for a family feud of Homeric brutality.

Late one hot July evening in 1986, its mayor and his family were getting out of their car after visiting the newly-born baby of a kinsman. Suddenly a volley of shots felled Giampiera Marceddu, his wife, who died where she lay in front of her husband and her two young daughters. She was the ninth victim in four years of the vendetta between four families.

Never before had a woman been killed in such fashion said the outraged authorities, stretching the truth somewhat. But as an experienced hand recorded laconically in the daily, *Nuova Sardegna*: 'Killing in the piazza in Oniferi and Orune is not so difficult – the silence of those who see or know is guaranteed.' After further threats had been scrawled on the church wall, the mayor resigned. No culprit was found, and the rest was silence – at least officially.

A year later, I found Oniferi a place of blank November desolation. In the bar I was greeted with courteous indifference and a polite invitation not to write ill of this deprived part of Sardinia. After all, 150 adults in a community of just over a thousand had no official employment.

The interlocutor between the old and new in Oniferi was a priest, Don Salvatore Melone. 'This is a place wedded to Old Testament hatred and revenge,' he claimed; his regular sermons on 'Three Aspects of Christian Love' had mostly fallen on stony ground, though he had persuaded two old mothers to shake hands in forgiveness over the coffin of a victim of the blood feud.

A more penetrating insight into the Oniferi feud was provided by Franca Poda, a lawyer in the Prefect's office in Nuoro, who had been sent as prefectural commissioner to the village following the killing of the mayor's wife and the resignation of the council. For more than a year she had administered the village, and took obvious comfort in being able to relate some of the nightmare to a foreigner.

'They say you should always look a Sardinian straight in the eyes,' she began, 'and if you look in the faces of Oniferi you see rage, hatred and envy. Everything I did or said was watched and transmitted like lightning on the bush telegraph. And the code of silence, of *omertà*, is as ferocious as any in Sicily.'

She was sure that the mayor's wife had been the intended victim of her killers. She was the strong character of the family, and had been investigating the murders of a brother, brother-in-law and cousin. All had been victims of the feud which began with the shooting of Antonio Sale, a shepherd, as he played *morra* – a game of spoof – outside the Carabinieri barracks one August evening in 1982.

Franca Poda's main task is prefectural commissioner was to get a new council elected to replace the one that had resigned after the murder – a process that provided her a rude introduction to the hidden powers that govern the minds of the mountain villagers. Four councillors were drafted, and the rest elected, but when the ballot boxes were emptied, she found that out of some 830 ballot papers, 119 had been spoiled deliberately, with black crosses, imprecations of magic, curses and threats of vengeance.

Before she quit her post, Signora Poda had to organise another poll – a referendum on whether a new tarmac road should replace the track across the ridge to the inappropriately named Benitutti ('all good'). Overnight Oniferi became ecologically-minded, protesting that 2000 trees would have to go for the new road. In the event only 30 voted for the road, which would have cut the journey and cost the village nothing, and more than 600 voted against. Franca Poda suspected that the vote was for a different form of wild life than the trees and birds: the old track had long been a haven for stolen livestock and illicit lovers, a place for aspirant outlaws to serve apprenticeship to the Code of the Barbagia.

But the wildlife enthusiasts had a point – the woodland and *macchia* of the Sardinia landscape has been scarred by fire more than that of any Mediterranean island. Since the 1950s hundreds of square miles of mountain and hill have gone up in flames, with more than 2000 major fires in most years. In one year alone – 1981 – 5,926 separate fires destroyed 120,000 hectares, while in the late summer of 1989 half the island seemed to be burning.

What lay behind the deliberate firing of this remote and dignified land has never been quite certain. Some may have been the work of arsonists, hired by developers hungry for tourist sites for the villas and palaces of tourism; some may have been a scorched earth tactic by the islanders against the commercial invaders from the Continent. Whatever the case, among the victims were the ancient colonies of herbs, flowers and bees, the constituents of Cicero's bitter honey.

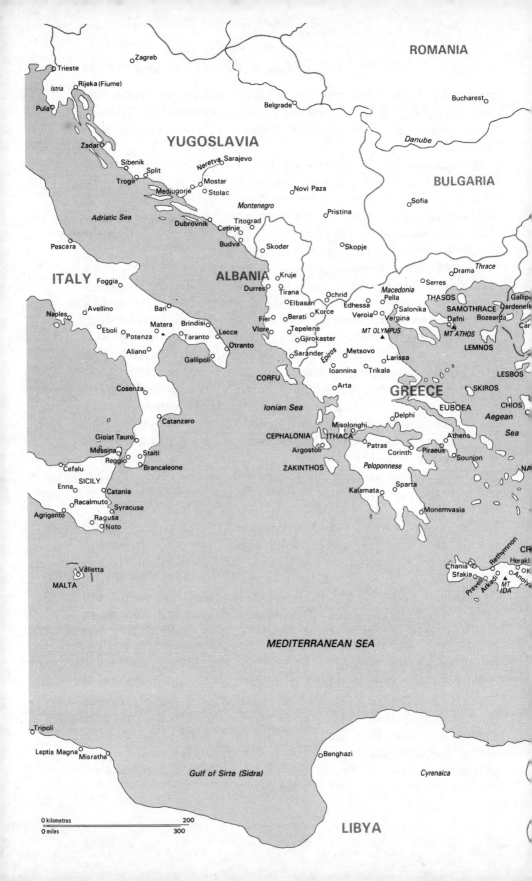

The Mediterranean: The Eastern Basin

Crimea

Black Sea

○ Batumi

○ Sinope

○ Trabzon(Trebizond)

○ Samsun

○ Erzurum

Istanbul

ea of
armara

Sakarya

○ Ankara

○ Diyarbakir

TURKEY

Euphrates

○ Urfa

rgama(Pergamon)

mir(Smyrna)

○ Konya

○ Adana   ○ Dortyol ○ Issus

Tarsus ○

○ Iskenderun(Alexandretta)
○ Syrian Gates

Ephesus

TAURUS   *MOUNTAINS*

Diocaesarea ○

Mersin ○

○ Bagras

○ Aleppo

Perge   Aspendos ○

○ Mut

Silifke ○

○ Antakya(Antioch)

Antalya ○

Side ○   Alanya ○

○ Apamee
○ Shaizar

Bodrum
(Halicarnassus) ○

Anamura ○

*KARPASSOS
PENINSULA*

Ugarit ○

○ Hama

SYRIA

RHODES

Kantara ○ ○ Kanakaria

Kyrenia ○   ○ Salamis
Nicosia ○ ○ Famagusta

Tartus ○

○ Homs

Attila Line

CYPRUS

Larnaca ○

Tripoli ○

Paphos ○   ○ Limassol

LEBANON

Beirut ○

○ Damascus

Haifa ○

ISRAEL

Tel Aviv ○   ○ Amman

Jerusalem ○

JORDAN

Gaza ○

Damietta ○   ○ Port Said

Alexandria ○

Suez ○   Aqaba ○

Cairo ○

EGYPT   ## SAUDI ARABIA

Four: The Arm of the Adriatic

i The Balkan Hinge: The Veneto and Trieste

As I left Venice for the Yugoslav border one chilly February afternoon, the east wind, the bora, was flicking clouds of snow from the Balkans. The undulating fields with their orange soil caked to mud seemed to belong to another and more northern Europe from beyond the mountains. In winter the light is alpine, rare and suffused, with little hint of Mediterranean sun. The plain marks a fold between Europe of the west, and that of the east beyond the mountains of the Carso and the Balkan chain – a fold hinged on the arm of the Mediterranean in the Adriatic.

The Veneto is a natural frontier zone, a buffer state made by geology and geography. Peoples and cultures have mingled here from before the time of the Etruscans and the Romans. Armies have marched and countermarched, invaded and pillaged, though few of the conquerors made good their occupation.

The farms and fields, the river valleys with broad gravel beds, are still criss-crossed by strategic military roads, broad highways seeming to go nowhere. In the winter sunlight the only things moving across the bare landscape seemed to be the vehicles and radars of the American missile silos and needle-nosed projectiles poking warily above the embrasures. On the chessboard of strategic confrontation between the land forces of NATO and the Warsaw Pact this was a key position.

Close to one of the strategic roads, the route from Pordenone to Udine, stands the Villa Manin, shining white in baroque splendour, set in its eighteenth-century formal parkland. Here Napoleon stayed at the end of his Italian campaign and he opened peace negotiations with the Austrians at Campoformido in 1797. The treaty he concluded there was to give much of the Veneto to the Austrians for a century to come, the cause of chronic conflict between Italian nationalism and Habsburg Imperial reaction, culminating in the terrible carnage and destruction of the campaigns of 1915–1918.

That war caused extensive damage to the Villa Manin itself, though now it is heavily restored. Flanked by long curving colonnades the grandiose edifice is more palace than villa, a miniature Veneto Versailles, with extensive farms and stables, and a rococo chapel. Inside the pews and pulpits are decked out like boxes at the opera. Even damnation had its theatrical aspect. Executed with the height of taste and virtuosity, an alabaster tableau in a side altar shows the well-heeled damned, clothed in the latest fashions, descending into a sea of flames.

Chapel, park and villa were once the property of Lodovico Manin, last Doge of the Venetian Republic. Venetian nobility and merchants turned to *terra firma* between Bergamo and Udine, both to flee the pestilence and foul conditions of their native city in summer and to seek more secure investment than the hazardous enterprises of the sea. And while they planted the landscape with their villas from the time of Palladio onwards, agriculture became more attractive commercially through the introduction of new crops like maize, adopted from their traditional enemy, the Turks; to this day the fields in spring and summer parade with the squares and columns of the Turkish Grain (*Gran Turco*), as it is still known. The Turks are also credited with another change to the look of the land as much of the medieval woodland was supposedly cut down to provide timber for Venetian arsenals to build hulls with which to combat the Turks in commerce and in war.

The fame and splendour of Venice in the region is rivalled by the older glories and achievements of Aquileia, today a modest village commanding the causeway that stretches into the lagoon of Grado. Its centre is dominated by the clean lines of the Romanesque bell tower, cloister and church, the achievement of the Patriarch Poppone in the eleventh century. They stand among cypresses and the ruins of a Roman city: columns, statues, inscriptions praising emperors and local worthies, large chunks of ornamental friezes, lie in the grass along the Via Sacra leading to the river port. Roman Aquileia had the same strategic importance as the American missile sites surrounding the village today. Founded as a military colony in 181 BC, it was to control the main roads north across the Alps and east to the Hungarian Plain and the Danube frontier, the Postumia, Giulia Augusta and Gemina ways. Through the river port came the merchandise of the eastern Mediterranean – glass, bronze vessels, marble, oil and cereals from Syria, Egypt, the Greek islands, Ravenna and southern Italy. In exchange Aquileia exported minerals and semi-precious stones from the Dolomites, cattle, barbarian slaves, the 'Pucinum' wine which so pleased the Empress Livia – the forerunner of the modern Prosecco.

Roman Aquileia was sacked by Alaric's Goths, Attila's Huns, and the Lombards, though it continued as one of the most important Christian centres of Italy, whose patriarch was considered second in rank only to the Bishop of Rome. The patriarchate disappeared as late as 1751, though it had been weakened by centuries of rivalry between Habsburg Austria and Venice.

In 381 the Patriarch held one of the most important Church Councils here, in order to combat the Arian heresy; one of those attending was St Augustine's master, St Ambrose of Milan. At about this time one of the greatest early Christian mosaics still extant in the Mediterranean was laid out in the nave of the basilica. To see this I needed to obtain the key from the priest, who seemed unconscionably detained in a pink house near the sacristy. Eventually Monsignor Magri emerged into the winter sunshine, baffled at being disturbed at such an unseasonable time and the aroma of garlic and heavy Veneto wine suggested he had been about more pleasant business.

As he opened the main door the floor undulated before us like the sea, pushed up by the damp foundations. Across it surged scenes in mosaic of the miracles, and the seasons, of fishing and the sea. In the centre lay the story of Jonah and the Whale, which looked like a benign Loch Ness monster with a curl in its tail. Surrounded by creatures of the deep, Jonah is spewed forth and comes to rest under a pergola of vines and courgettes, green and fresh as the morning though depicted seventeen centuries ago.

The monsignor began to lament the fate of his beloved parish: 'Imagine, this was once the greatest patriarchate of the West after Rome, more powerful than Venice, with huge lands. The patriarchs were princes and landowners, and because they took the wrong side with the Habsburgs their successor is me – a humble parish priest.' Moved by sorrow or enthusiasm, or the effects of his repast, he guided me to the edge of the excavations by the baptistry, and promptly fell in. As he struggled out, the foreman showed me some squares of polychrome tiling which he thought had come from a house of the earliest Roman colony of the second century BC.

The most moving monument at Aquileia is the cemetery to the dead of the First World War, half hidden behind the cathedral church, where the first victims of the fighting up to the plateau of the Carso and the River Isonzo in 1915 are buried. The front line passed through Aquileia, which had been part of Austria until 1915, and was reoccupied by the Astro-Hungarian Imperial Army and its allies after the rout of Caporetto in 1917. The tombs and graves give some indication of why the terrible campaigns of the Carso and Isonzo and Piave were such a shock to the soldiers and citizens of the new Italian kingdom, and why their trauma led to the chaos and confusion from which Fascism was to emerge. Many are of young Sardinians of the Sassari Brigade. The countryside around Aquileia contrasted strangely with the sanguinary story of the cemetery. Round Grado, where the Aquileians sought refuge from Attila, the lagoon was a frozen mirror, the beaches sprinkled with snow. To the east the villages began to change. The houses had shingled roofs and heavy gables to hold off mountain snow, the churches onion domes. The countryside seems to belong to Austria than a frontier region of Italy.

The claims of the Italians to this piece of land in the last century, provided the modern political vocabulary with a term of no small significance to the political and ethnic mosaic of the Mediterranean today – irredentism. The Irredentist Party was founded in Italy in 1878 to recover the lands of Italian-speaking peoples from foreign domination, principally those of the Austro-Hungarian Empire in the Veneto, including Aquileia and Trieste.

The term comes from the Italian 'irredento' – unredeemed – and carries an overtone of almost mystical nationalism, something more than staking a political claim to a piece of territory. Nationalist myths were a common strain in nineteenth-century national movements, and the Italian Irredentists sought to realise the dream of a unified Italy. In this century such dreams contributed to the more debased nationalism of the Fascist movements.

'Irredentism' deserves much wider currency as a political term than it enjoys today – it is not nearly as commonly used as 'balkanisation', to which it is complementary. Greek nationalists in Eoka have made irredentist claims on Cyprus, Yugoslavs of Macedonia on parts of Greece, Syria on the Hatay part of Turkey, Israelis on lands by the Jordan, Libya on parts of Chad, Berbers on Morocco and Kabyle on Algeria, and Palestinians, Sardinians, Basques, Catalans and even some Andalusians on their own homelands.

In the region where the concept was born, the longings of the Irredentists were fulfilled after the First World War, when the Veneto to Trieste and beyond, as far as Fiume (Rijeka in modern Yugoslavia), were given to Italy.

Trieste seems as much a victim as a victor of the processes of irredentism and balkanisation. Its culture is certainly Italian, as the ferment of Italian radical political movements of the last century bear witness. In 1907 James Joyce taught English there to one of Italy's greatest modern novelists, Italo Svevo, then toiling as a customs clerk under the name Ettore Schmitz. The long promenades and the cool, tall town houses and hotels of the esplanade are very much of that era, redolent of the dying days of Habsburg rule, when this was Austria's principal port on the Adriatic, through which nearly all the tea and coffee for the salons and cafés of fashionable Vienna were imported.

Today the city and old port sit lonely on a tongue of land jutting into northern Yugoslavia; for Trieste is now a buffer state in itself. During the Second World War it was occupied successively by the German Werhmacht, New Zealand troops and units of Tito's National Liberation Army – who bloodily repressed riots by Italian nationalists before making good their own withdrawal in July 1945.

Under the terms of the 1945 Treaty of Paris most of the port, the city and the hinterland, designated 'Zone A', were given to Italy, while the southern sector became a 'free port' or 'Zone B' which went to Yugoslavia in 1954. Despite the precariousness of its position, Trieste is the biggest commercial harbour and port facility in the Adriatic, and the centre of its marine insurance market. As I drove along the high road above the port the winter sun was turning ochre and deep purple through the haze of dust and smoke. Ships lay at anchor in the roads waiting to discharge. Every nook of coast, jetty and promontory seemed crammed with ships, men, containers and cranes.

With darkness gathering I came to a sprawling shanty town of shops and huts that passed for the frontier post of that extraordinary brew of races, nations, religions that is modern Yugoslavia.

ii Yugoslavia: Unstitching Tito's Empire

The tale of Yugoslavia's economic woes quickly unfolded. Round the frontier posts at the Italian border little shops ostensibly selling tobacco, sweets and coffee had posted hastily-scrawled notices of the rate of exchange for the dinar; usually these signs change daily – sometimes more often. Although technically such services are illegal, the Italians customs police don't seem to mind, however when a Yugoslav militiaman or policeman passes, the kiosks become unnaturally subdued.

The currency is offered in bundles of freshly-printed notes. Yugoslavia has been in the grip of hyperinflation and near currency collapse for almost ten years now – the price of rapid industrialisation over the past thirty years. When I crossed the frontier in February 1985 I got 270 dinars for my pound sterling, well ahead of the official rate. By December 1986 the official rate was posted as 677 dinars to the pound, and 457.18, to the dollar, and by mid-1988 tourists were being offered 4000 dinars to the pound. By 1988 inflation was running at a cool 130 per cent per annum, and external foreign debt at well over $20 billion. In 1990 a new 'heavy' dinar was introduced, worth 10,000 of the old. It did little to halt the hectic surge of inflation.

The currency and debt crisis are part of the stresses and strains of holding together the diverse collection of peoples that make up the Yugoslav Federation. Yugoslavia emerged from the First World War and the end of the Austro-Hungarian Empire as the Kingdom of Serbs, Croats and Slovenes, united under the crown of Serbia – 'great' Serbia as it was known for its expansionist ambitions – and was declared the Kingdom of Yugoslavia by King Alexander I in 1927. The union of the peoples was not a happy one, and growing resentment by Croats at Serbian domination led the King to assume dictatorial powers in 1929. In 1934 he was assassinated by a Croation nationalist during a visit to Paris. The regency of his brother, Prince Paul, bore many of the trappings of a fascist regime, and in March 1941 he signed a pact with the Axis powers.

This provoked civil war and the invasion of Nazi German and Italian Fascist forces, and a conflict which cost more than three million Yugoslav lives. The ultimate victor was the man who had become General Secretary of the illegal Yugoslav Communist Party in 1937, Josep Broz Tito. Half Croat and half Slovene, he had proved himself one of the greatest guerrilla generals of modern times while at the head of the partisans of the National Liberation Army, and he endeavoured to bind the disparate peoples of Yugoslavia together with his particular approach to Communism. In doing so, according to A. J. P. Taylor, he seemed to be fulfilling the role of the last of the Habsburg monarchs.

Tito embarked on a massive industrialisation programme, which embraced a singular notion known as socialist self-management, a concept copied only by the Algeria's Marxist regime. Since 1945 the proportion of Yugoslav workers employed on the land has fallen from just over three-quarters to under a third. But industrialisation brought uneven benefit to the peoples of the six republics and the two autonomous regions. By the mid-1980s, average earnings in Slovenia, the most advanced republic, were seven times those of the poorest part of Serbia, the largely Albanian-speaking province of Kosovo.

Throughout the 1980s Kosovo had become the major trouble spot of the Yugoslav Federation. The Muslim Albanians rioted, robbed and even murdered to win a fairer deal from Belgrade and the Serbs. After all, they argued, they were a population of more than a million and were denied status as a separate republic, a privilege enjoyed by neighbouring Montenegro with only half that number of inhabitants. In 1988 two journalists and an army sergeant in Slovenia were jailed by a military tribunal for disseminating reports of an imminent army coup there. Surprisingly, the Slovene Communist Party protested that the trial had been held by a military court *in camera*, against the tenets of Yugoslav democracy. With the debate about *glasnost* raging in the Soviet Union, the ripples were reaching Yugoslavia, and eight years after Tito's death the Federation he had fought for so ruthlessly was disintegrating. Slovenia was to be the first republic to engage the federal power in open hostilities after declaring independence, along with Croatia, in 1991.

The paradox of Yugoslav nationality is summed up in its languages and faiths. The principal language is Serbo-Croat, which Serbs depict in the Cyrillic alphabet and the Croats in the Latin. The other official languages are Slovenian and Macedonian. Minorities speak Albanian, Magyar, Italian, German and Turkish. One-third of the population, principally in Croatia and Slovenia, is Catholic, two-fifths Orthodox and a sizeable minority is Muslim. Religion is still a powerful emblem of regional and ethnic separatism and protest.

From the border post with its chaotic money market, I moved across the peninsula of Istria, the most Italian part of Yugoslavia. Between the world wars it was part of the Italian kingdom, briefly fulfilling of the dreams of the irredentists, but in 1947 Istria became part of Yugoslavia and a quarter of a million Italians went over the border into exile, causing bitter resentments to this day.

In pouring rain and pitch darkness I arrived at Pula, the main port of the Istrian peninsula, with its beautiful walled medieval citadel and old town. Nothing was stirring when I arrived – at least, nothing as welcoming as a café or hostelry. At the entrance to the huge arsenal, the Habsburg Empire's and now Communist Yugoslavia's biggest military shipyard, I had a desultory conversation in halting Italian with two security guards about prospects for a bed that night. They were quite baffled that anyone should be on so foolish an enterprise at that time of night, and in midwinter too. They said I might do better at the resort of Medulin up the coast, and so it proved. The Hotel Medulin was a huge barn of a place like a transit camp, all cracking ceilings and mildewed carpets. At the reception desk I asked if there was any chance of a meal, or at least a bowl of soup. The tall man behind the desk spoke a beautifully refined Italian; leaning towards me he said in a low voice, 'Of course you could get something here, though it's late. But take my advice, never eat anywhere run by the state if you can possibly avoid it. I know just the place for you back in the village. They'll look after you.'

My introduction to Yugoslav entrepreneur culture was as good as he'd promised. Private enterprise flourishes in thousands of such small family businesses in Yugoslavia. Bakeries, restaurants, hairdressing salons have run on such a basis for years, and their bright and cheerful atmosphere contrasts with the lugubrious air of the big state-run cafés, hotels and other places where recreation seems a duty to be endured rather than a pleasure.

By the late 1980s some three-quarters of a million of Yugoslavia's twenty-three million citizens were working abroad. Since Tito's later years they had been allowed to keep their earnings in foreign currency accounts – a means of acquiring foreign exchange for the banking authorities, and an encouragement for migrants to return to their families, for at least it meant their hard work in the car factories of Dusseldorf or the chemical factories of Switzerland would not be the victim of the diving dinar. Some modifications have been made to this generous allowance, and a ceiling has been put on the amount of foreign currency held by Yugoslavs in their own banks. Tito seemed to realise how deep was the urge to own property in what was until very recently a largely peasant society; well over 80 per cent of all farms in Yugoslavia are private, family holdings.

Daylight revealed the old part of Pula to be dignified but slightly down-at-heel. In the shops cheap electrical goods, mass-produced clothing – much of it second-hand – and plastic toys and utensils were the main fare. In the subdued consumerism of most Yugoslav towns I found something appealing – a respite from the oppressive vulgar commercialism of northern Italy, and wholly lacking in the humbug of neighbouring Albania where empty food shops, usually closed, sit cheek-by-jowl with window displays crammed with volumes of the most vapid propaganda. The shopping streets were reminiscent of towns in the south of Italy twenty years ago, with the emphasis on food and domestic fuel, cooking oil, and hand tools. Among such practical establishments I discovered one or two surprisingly good bookshops, with a courteous multi-lingual service and an extensive stock, including a good selection of maps and guide books. The amount and quality of such material permitted officially gave a good indiction of the broad-mindedness of a regime: on this scale communist Yugoslavia scored very high. The five geographical guides to the Dalmatian coast are amongst the very best of their kind in the entire Mediterranean.

The museum in the old quarter was dedicated to the Partisan struggle and Tito's victory: such shrines are virtually statutory in most cities of Dalmatia. The place was littered with the weaponry and detritus of war – posters proclaiming the heroism of the Partisans and celebrating the advance to Trieste, and documentation about the perfidy of the Allies Commission under Field Marshal Alexander.

Of far greater interest was the material devoted to Istria under the Austrians and the Italians. A panoramic photograph showed the Austro-Hungarian fleet, Dreadnoughts in the van, in full review before the port of Pola in 1913. Ten years later the Italians were in charge, but life was far from easy for the new authorities. No sooner had the dream of the Irredentists been fulfilled than it began to turn sour. A memorandum from the 'Civil Commissariat of Pola' to the general responsible for Civil Order in Trieste, dated 21 May 1921, describes the political situation as 'preoccupying beyond measure' following the *redemption*, as it calls the joining of Istria to Italy – the pure coin of irredentist rhetoric. Subsequent documents speak of the growing violence of Fascist thugs or *squadristi*, and a police file in 1931 reveals the dangerous subversion of a hundred women of one village who demonstrated on such various grievances as communal taxes, the reduction of school teachers, the abolition of the public laundry and the cancellation of subsidies to mothers of bastards. Despite such evident anti-Italian sentiments, when Istria was given finally to Yugoslavia in 1947 and Pola became Pula, some 29,000 people – three-quarters of its population – left for Italy.

I was given some clue to the historical complexity of the Istrian Peninsula by an official archivist living on the outskirts of Pula. He was a remarkably well-read man, but being dependent on a state salary he lived in considerable austerity, on the intellectual equivalent of iron rations. He could afford few new books, nor could he pursue his necessary researches in foreign archives.

Istria, he told me, had suffered massive depopulation over the centuries. The entire region had been almost stripped of humanity in the fifteenth and sixteenth centuries and those who remained were decimated by the terrible famines which pervaded northern Italy in the seventeenth and eighteenth centuries. During their brief rule the Ottomans tried to repopulate with Turks from Cyprus and Crete; under the Austrians the gaps were filled by immigrants from Croatia, Bosnia, Slovenia and Friuli. But the Austrian census figures were not to be relied upon, as they categorised peoples by language and not race, and in the nineteenth century anyone seeking work in the cities had to speak Italian.

When the tie with Italy was dramatically cut in 1947, and up to a third of a million Italians and Italian-speakers left, the void was filled by immigrants from all the six Yugoslav republics – excepting Serbia, but including Macedonia in the deep south and Albanians from Kosovo. Some of those of Italian origin stayed on – the archivist's own ancestors were from Friuli, non-Latin tribes of the northern Veneto and the mountains of Carnia. Yet, this sad and genial scholar gave a simple but devastating judgment on the state of modern Yugoslavia, the Yugoslavia of Tito's legacy. 'We are supposed to be brothers in our federation – but what is fraternity in these circumstances? It is nothing. It has all been destroyed by inflation and the disastrous economy.'

With such melancholy thoughts, I set off across the uplands of the Istrian Peninsula, across fields and farmlands strewn with rocks and sheets of snow and ice, through villages pillaged by hunger and bandits over the centuries. The southern part of the neck of the peninsula is guarded by Rijeka, and once the high tide mark and the Waterloo of Italian Irredentism. In 1920 the town was seized by a band of irregular 'legionaries' under the poet Gabriele D'Annunzio, whose ideas comprised a weird cocktail of Byronic Romanticism, Irredentism, and Mussolini's Fascism, and who declared the place the independent Italian Republic of Quaernaro. In 1924 the city became part of Italy. After liberation by Tito's partisans in the Second World War, the citizens were invited to choose between Yugoslavia and Italy. Although they chose Yugoslavia, irredentist sentiment lingers to this day. The 1963 Italian Touring Club red guide – the bible of the serious traveller in Italy – still refers to the city under its old name of Fiume (which means river in Italian, as does Rijeka in Serbo-Croat).

Climbing away from the town the road winds across the harbour, in which every space, natural and unnatural, has been put to use. Deep fjords cut into the cliffs of hard rock have been turned into loading wharves and dry docks. In the evening sun, I began my dash down the Dalmatian coast with its sparse heath and farm lands and glissades of rocky outcrop. The coastland was wild, rocky and desolate. In my hurry, I avoided familiar landmarks like Zadar and Sibenik as all cultural or historical reflection was subjected to a more pressing and banal preoccupation: how was I to get enough petrol to see me through to Split on a late Saturday afternoon?

In desperation I turned off the main road to a fishing village, beautifully arranged along a string of promontories. In a café where cars and football were the topics of conversation, I made myself sufficiently understood to get coffee and *grappa*, but when it came to *benzina* the light in the local Italian vocabulary inexplicably failed. No, they were not going to find anything remotely approaching *benzina*, not for dinars, lire, pounds sterling or US dollars, for they knew their precious litres were worth more than any of these. Courteously but firmly, they saw me on my way.

Several hours later the car, hot and bothered to the extent of blowing most of the lighting fuses, wheezed into Trogir, Romanesque jewel of the Adriatic – where I was to receive a wonderful tutorial on the mysteries of Yugoslavia's self-management economics, and take pleasure from the Emperor Diocletian in Split.

Twenty miles down the coast from Trogir, Split is today a sprawling industrial port. However a stroll by the old harbour reveals one of the most remarkable monuments of the late Roman Empire – the retirement palace of the Emperor Diocletian. Across the harbour the lines of the seaward wall, with more than forty columns still intact, are quite distinct. Galleys used to moor alongside, but now a broad boulevard with tall palms flanks the sea entrance.

Diocletian was born on the Dalmatian coast, and made his way up through the rough and tumble of army life during the upheavals of the empire of the third century AD. In 285 he became Emperor, earning a bloody reputation for the persecution of the Christians until his abdication in 305, an event celebrated in icons and frescoes throughout the Balkans, Greece and Southern Italy for more than a thousand years.

His palace has survived comprehensive sacking, pillage, fire-bombardment by Slavs, Avars, Turks, Venetians, Nazi Germans and Fascist Italians, while the socially ambitious and the well-to-do have pilfered its stones and ornamentation for their villas. Imperial apartments, store-houses, arsenals and the quarters of the imperial guard have been divided and subdivided by each generation to take up residence, lending it a particular charm and fascination. No mausoleum or empty museum, the palace is a Mediterranean village in itself, with its family houses and apartments, little shops and cafés and meeting places.

In the courtyards oleander and geraniums tumble over balconies, while laundry is hauled in great bundles to the pump and the wash-house. Under the sea wall, as thick as a town house is long, the cavernous cellars are used as a spring market, with bedding plants, seeds, bundles of pea and bean sticks, a few patent chemicals and fertilisers being traded in the green twilight of this underground bazaar. On the promenade outside a band of students, some wearing shaggy long-haired wool coats and masks of rams and bulls, paraded a strange totem, on top of which was an animal's head made out of cloth and adorned with antlers. They were celebrating Mardi Gras and the beginning of Lent with a rite much older than Christianity – a pagan salute to the approaching solstice. Perhaps they had decided to hedge their bets and were using an ancient formula to ensure a bountiful seed time rather than rely on the enlightened principles of Titoist socialism and the economic laws of self-management.

In an office on the sea wall I encountered Captain Aleksa Mekjavic, a merchant mariner who revelled in his status as honorary British consul. In this capacity, I consulted him about the feasibility of trying to take the mountain route through Serbia and Macedonia into Greece. 'Don't bother,' was his terse reply. 'They've had several metres of snow in the past two nights in the high mountains – you'll get to Sarajevo all right, but the roads south are pretty bad even in the height of summer.' The captain was a cheerful character who enjoyed life undeterred by inflation, self-management and the other preoccupations of his more intellectual compatriots. When I suggested that I should register with him in case I got lost in the mountains he waved my caution aside. 'It's not necessary. You can do what you like, say what you like in this country. Imagine. We have five daily newspapers, they write anything, and I really mean *anything*. It's a freer press than you get in many Western countries.'

Indeed the atmosphere was relaxed as students and schoolchildren crammed the cafés in the old quarter, drinking beer, soda pop and espresso coffee and wolfing hamburgers and hot dogs and other standard mid-Atlantic fare. Along one side of the Roman peristyle was the legend 'Sid Vicious Lives' in heavy spray paint – which did not seem to win the critical approval of a sleek granite sphinx guarding Diocletian's mausoleum, since the ninth century a Cathedral dedicated to the Virgin.

Much the same sentiment was expressed in an elaborate tableau just outside the walls of the palace, dedicated to Tito's birthday. Nearly every café and public office still carried a portrait of the former Life President, usually in his sparkling white Marshal's uniform. It was as though no one could replace the dead hero in his people's affection as the guide to their destiny – which is probably the way he would have wanted it.

Diocletian and Josep Broz have several qualities in common, superficially at least. Both achieved power in their countries through military prowess, both had a reputation for ruthlessness towards their enemies, and neither was above the cult of personality.

A decade after his death, Tito has remained an enigma. His achievement in defying Stalin's Russia, steering the middle way between the Nato-dominated West and the Soviet-dominated East, and founding the non-aligned movement, seems enormous. Yet mysteries and question marks persist. Hardline conservative revisionists in the West have portrayed him as a master conniver who was all along the tool of Stalinist and post-Stalinist Russia, a man who duped Churchill to pursue a ruthless and bloody civil war against the royalist Serbs as much as against the forces of Hitler and his allies. Such a view is quite clearly exaggerated, but it is certain that Tito pursued his aims with a single-minded ruthlessness, and at a great loss of life. He pursued and purged opponents inside the regime to the last, and however benign it may have seemed to some in the West at times, Titoist Yugoslavia continued to be an unreconstructed police state.

Like de Gasperi and Cavour, Tito grew up a subject of the Habsburg emperors. He served in the Imperial army in the First World War and was captured on the Russian Front, which led directly to his conversion to Bolshevism – indeed he probably witnessed many of the most dramatic events of the 1917 Revolution. In the late 1920s he returned to Yugoslavia, where he was imprisoned for his political activities, and in 1937 he became General Secretary of the Yugoslav Party in exile. Most of the Yugoslav leadership in exile in Russia was liquidated, yet somehow Tito survived.

After the German and Italian invasion of 1941, he used the Party structure to organise resistance. How he persuaded Churchill to supports his Partisans and not the Chetniks, the remnants of the royalist army under Colonel Mihailovich, is well known: the Chetniks were accused of collaborating with the Nazis, a judgment which was probably unjustifiably harsh as Milhailovich had tried to buy time in order to regroup, and was propagated by, among others, one Guy Burgess.

Belgrade was occupied by the Partisans with help of the Red Army. Enemies were pursued with the ferocity of a vendetta – particularly the supporters of the fascist puppet regime of Ante Pavelich and his Ustache movement in Croatia, and the royalist Serbs. Thousands of Croat prisoners-of-war were returned by train from Trieste by their allies, only to be murdered to a man. Controversy still rages over whether the Allied Command of Field Marshal Alexander and Harold Macmillan, the Minister Plenipotentiary for the Mediterranean, were aware of what might lie in store for these unfortunates.

In 1948 came the break with Stalin. Again the causes appear complex and the results were far-reaching. It is said that Moscow feared Tito's regional ambitions – that he might exploit the Greek civil war to grab the whole of Macedonia from Greece and Bulgaria in order to reach the Aegean, that he might swallow Albania or trap Hoxha's regime inextricably in his web. Though a Croat by blood, Tito was accused of ambitions similar to those atrributed to the expansionist and 'hegemonistic' 'Great Serb' over half a century before.

Out on his own, Tito steered the middle way with skill. The West – the Americans in particular, and old British pals who had worked with his Partisans – came to the rescue, providing materials and loans to industrialise Yugoslavia. But by the mid-1970s, no amount of soft credits and deferred repayments could conceal the inefficiency of many of the state industries and the horrendous level of debts accumulated.

Meanwhile Tito strode the international stage as the leader of the non-aligned group of nations – a grouping he invented with Nehru and, to a lesser extent, Nasser. To some he remained a hero, but towards the end of his life he became ludicrously vain, cocooned in an odious cult of personality. Some of his more innovative early supporters, like Milovan Djilas, had long before been imprisoned or purged – though Djilas managed to join his son in Britain, and remained one of the most pungent critics of Titoism long after the Marshal's death.

Titoism is a mish-mash of principles and personal pragmatism. At the centre remained the Party, but under the 1974 constitution each republic was theoretically autonomous and the leading officers of federal government are supposed to rotate on a regular basis. The economy was partly centralised, for it too was in the hands of the Party, but day-to-day responsibility devolved to the most local level through the self-management system, a Byzantine heresy of modern Marxist thought. By late 1990 the Party was dead in name and deed.

I was initiated into the mysteries of self-management at the Hotel Medena of Trogir, a monster barracks with more than 1,200 beds when the tourist season is in full swing. The night I arrived a Mardi Gras dance was going at maximum throttle, and the teen scene of lower Dalmatia was bopping to the strains of Elvis and his 'Blue Suede Shoes' under the crumbling plaster ceiling of the ballroom.

My contact was Ante Sabic, the reception manager and head of the front desk committee. He had worked for five years as a professional footballer in Italy and then for six more in the German League. His boss, or rather comrade colleague, was Ante Klaric, at thirty the youngest hotel manager in Yugoslavia. He had started as a hotel porter, then moved to the plastics factory in Trogir as a foreman and later a product analyst.

In high season the hotel had roughly 300 staff, plus 400 students helping out. Management was via a pyramid of committees, with the general committee meeting every Monday morning for more than an hour. The committees were elected, but every department still had a manager, and the Party could have the final say. The committees discussed practical day-to-day matters: 'We have self-determination,' said the Manager with sphinx-like lucidity, 'but we have to work within the guidelines of the five-year plan.' Despite the evident popularity of the place among Yugoslavs and foreigners, margins were tight and money for improvement scarce. This may have been due to the state of the Yugoslav economy and the slide in the dinar rather than the efficiency of the management. When I asked about maintenance and repairs, the two Antes were astonishingly frank. 'We try to do as much as possible of the routine work ourselves – decorating, plumbing and cleaning – with no outside help requiring extra wages. When it comes to obtaining materials, that's a big problem, but often we try to do deals with companies like the plastic tube factory here in Trogir. They give us some pipes and electrical bits and pieces, we give them concessions on holidays and our facilities here.'

Such a rule seems to prevail in much of Yugoslavia's state sector. Some industries have performed well and are comparable to competitors in the west – such as the 1st of May Textile Co of East Serbia and the engineering combine Energo-Invest – but others have become legendary in their inefficiency. The prime example is the nickel works at Feni in Macedonia, popularly supposed to have cost the public purse more than the repairs following the Skopje earthquake in 1963.

The solutions Ante Klaric attempted to apply would be familiar to any trader in downtown Naples – the art of barter and of arranging things between families and friends; the *arte d'arrangiarsi*, to which Yugoslav economic self-management in its practical form had become a blood relation.

As the coast of Dalmatia runs towards Dubrovnik, and the Republic of Croatia becomes a thin wedge, the River Neretva concludes its journey from the mountains, basking lazily in the sunshine of the Mediterranean as it filters through flat marshlands to the sea. The Neretva has been a frontier for centuries, dividing faiths, peoples and empires. It marked the boundary of the Habsburg and the Ottoman Empires until the Congress of Berlin in 1878, which gave Bosnia-Hercegovina to Austria-Hungary and brought the independent Republic of Montenegro into existence.

The road along the river reveals traces of its former occupiers. Slender minarets appear between clumps of poplar and birch. Many of the mosques are new, as the state authorities seem prepared to tolerate the religion of the small minority of Muslims of Turkish origin as a useful antidote to the fractious Christian domination of the region. In the uplands to the north of the Neretva the churches of the Roman Catholics of Croatia and Bosnia abound, while to the south those of the Serbian Orthodox appear with greater frequency.

Little villages mark the river bank at regular intervals, with rough pubs and transport cafés, repair shops and garages. The riches of the route in times past are hinted at by a wonderful Turkish *han* or caravanserai at Pocitelj, the main stopping point for the caravans coming down from Sarajevo and the mountains to the port of Dubrovnik. The covered courtyard has been wonderfully restored, as has the mosque, strategically placed on a bluff on the bend of the river.

Taking a turning to the north near the caravanserai, the traveller crosses a rocky escarpment before coming to a cluster of hamlets round the village of Medjugorje. In February 1985 Medjugorje seemed uncertain whether it had seen better days, or whether they were yet to come. Parts of cars and farm machinery lay in the ditches, alongside the unkempt road that led into the village bits of rusty fencing, while puddles spread across the open ground now serving as a car park in front of the white-washed parish church of St James. Since 1981 the church had been a centre of worship for pilgrims in their thousands, come to witness the miraculous manifestations of the Madonna in what has become, for believers in such phenomena, an apparition as significant as those reported at Lourdes and Fatima.

On 24 June 1981, the Feast of John the Baptist, a group of children walking on the hills of Podbrdo saw a brilliant light, which they later believed to be the Virgin Mary. A vision of the Gospa – as the Virgin is known in Croatia – then appeared regularly to a group of six young people, four girls and two boys, from the hamlet of Bijakovici, part of the Medjugorje parish. The favourite spots for these manifestations were the hillsides around Podbrdo and at a point nearby where a huge granite cross had been erected in 1933, on the 1900th anniversary of the death of Christ. It was also said that during some of the apparitions the cross actually rotated.

Messages were then given in the church of St James, and for several evenings a week some of the children assembled in a side chapel to hear, if not see, the Gospa, whose words were relayed to the faithful, assembled in the main church for evening mass.

The villagers were urged to be more pious, to heal their quarrels and draw closer to the Church and God. As at Fatima, 'secrets' of a more apocalyptic nature were vouchsafed to the original visionaries – proph-ecies of the second coming and the end of the world, nine in number for each of the chosen recipients. Strange portents in the heavens were reported by the thousands of pilgrims by now flocking to Medjugorje from neighbouring Catholic communities in Hungary, Italy and Austria. It was said that the sun had danced in the sky as if suspended on a string, that bright lights had appeared above the hillsides, and that shapes like

shrouded figures had shown up in photographs of the crowds of worshippers at the shrines.

The events of Medjugorje were soon enveloped in controversy. The
local Bishop of Mostar withheld wholehearted approval of the practices
in the village – at one time he is said to have called them part of a
'diabolical plot'. The Vatican has remained officially cool, refusing at
first to endorse Medjugorje and its hamlets as places of pilgrimage
(approval had been slow for Lourdes and Fatima as well). The state
authorities took a somewhat quixotic approach, at first expressing concern about the public order aspects of such a spontaneous confluence of
humanity. The parish priest and the small community of nuns who
lodged in the towers of the church were harried over petty infringements
of planning regulations when they tried to improve their premises to
cope with the flow of visitors. After four years the official powers relented
and helped to instal a much-needed public lavatory and washing facility.
By then hotels, hostels and stalls selling drinks, hot snacks and souvenirs
were burgeoning. The Madonna of Medjugorje was in business.

Vulgar commercialism had not yet taken hold when I was there in
February 1985, three and a half years after the visions were reported. On
that chill but clear winter day a certain suspicion of unheralded outsiders
hung in the air; the atmosphere was that of a community under siege.
The inside of the church was light and airy, the pews and furniture
gleaming and functional in local wood. By the altar stood a life-sized
statue of the Virgin in blue and white robes, looking just as described by
the children. The statue was similar to a figure in the same clothing
painted above the main door and depicted floating above the hillsides.
Years later I was surprised to learn that this picture had been executed
before the visions started – a fact I find disturbing and significant, as it
must have been a familiar image to the children before they reported
their communion with the Gospa.

On the plate glass or perspex partitioning the nave from the outer
porch I noticed three posters: one of the Black Madonna of Szestochowa
in Poland, about to celebrate its millenium as a place of pilgrimage, a
shrine dear to Pope John Paul II, and the other two containing messages
from the Right to Life anti-abortion movement of America. Both seemed
to give some hint of the kind of pilgrim prepared to make the long
journey to Medjugorje.

In the porch itself brief typewritten notes in Italian as well as Serbo-
Croat gave some of the more recent communications to the children at
the prayer gatherings in the side chapel. Some seemed almost Delphic.
'Dear children,' one began, 'today I wish to say that your hearts should

open to God as the flowers of spring seek the sun. I am your Mother and I wish always that you are closer to the Father. And that He may always offer many gifts to your hearts. Thank you for responding to my call.'

Further elucidation was provided by a lady called Anita from Dublin, who was guiding a group from Canada round the church. An unofficial helper in the parish for several months, she smiled seraphically, with an expression which seemed barely fixed on the matter in hand. She said the Madonna had told the parishioners to bring flowers for the crib at Christmas and to prepare specially 'otherwise it would be a day of suffering'. But all was well on the day: the Madonna appeared decked out in a robe of flowers, holding the infant Jesus in her arms, smiling but saying nothing.

Anita asked how long I would stay. Would I like to see the file or the video first – perhaps a time could be fixed for a viewing? The priests were not available but might be in a day or two, nor was access to the children permitted; one was unwell (Vicka, one of the oldest, later turned out to have an inoperable cyst on the brain, and was granted visitations in her bedroom). The mixture of piety and commerce would have been recognised by any of Chaucer's fellow travellers to Canterbury.

My replies were far from satisfactory to Anita, as I politely declined her offer of hostel vouchers, and said I would prefer to look at the written documentation of the manifestations. Moreover I wanted to absent myself briefly in the afternoon to see some medieval tombs nearby at Stolac. This marked me as an outsider, to be treated with caution if not suspicion. The distrust also marked discussions at the little shop under the presbytery where I bought a few postcards, and asked whether I could buy the book about the manifestations – preferably in Italian, though I would take the Serbo-Croat version as I had friends who could translate. I was told in no uncertain terms that this was forbidden to me, and that I should address all enquiries to Anita.

In the car park I was eyed equally suspiciously by a pair of Italian coach-drivers who had brought a party of thirty-three women and two children on pilgrimage from Milan. They were accompanied by a member of an order of irregular priests, a 'Comforting Brother' (*Frate Confertante*), for official pilgrimages to Madjugorje were then frowned on by many diocesan authorities in Italy. The drivers became visibly alarmed when I revealed I was a writer. 'Look,' one said, 'they don't like journalists nosing around here. I'd keep away if I were you. Strange things have been happening. That cross on the hill over there – they say it whirls round sometimes.'

At this point I have to declare my position. I am not a Catholic, nor

does a religious faith which relies on miracles and supernatural apparitions hold much appeal for me. On the contrary, I feel that reliance on
such goings-on detracts from the powerful ethical teachings of the Gos-
pels. Most of the literature about Medjugorje, in English and French at
least, has been written by out-and-out apologists for just such forms of
religion, for whom such irrational goings-on are central to their view of
Christianity. Among the thousands of pilgrims to the village, Pente-
costalists and Charismatics have been prominent. The sincerity and
urgency of many of the visitors is not to be doubted – literally hundreds
of miraculous healings have been reported – but in the accounts of some
of the devotions it is sometimes hard to distinguish between conviction
and superstition. I encountered one ferocious and wealthy matriarch
from near Venice who had collected a small sackful of stones from the
shrines on the hillside; on her return she would make it abundantly clear
which of her extensive family were in favour by bestowing or withholding
a gift of one of the precious lumps of rock.

Despite my position as a card-carrying outsider, I found, and still find,
the manifestations at Medjugorje profoundly fascinating. I saw there
something highly revealing about the nature of religion in the modern
world, the Mediterranean world especially, and about the complex politics of contemporary Yugoslavia.

Conflict over the parish of Medjugorje had erupted the year before the
visions, when the Bishop of Mostar had tried to reduce the role and
power of the Franciscan priests in his diocese. Bishop Pavao Zanic was
appointed specifically as a secular bishop, who did not belong to a
religious order. For centuries the Franciscan priests had played a powerful, and often highly political, role in the parishes of Croatia and Bosnia,
among them Medjugorje, and had been responsible for the survival of
the Catholic faith in the region; but during the Second World War many
openly supported the fascist puppet regime of Ante Pavelich and his
Ustache Movement in Croatia. The Ustache are blamed with atrocities
and massacres as bad as any of the occupiers of northern Yugoslavia of
the time, including the SS and Slovene White Guard. Nor did the leader
of the Croat Catholic community, Archbishop Stepinac, choose to
denounce them from the pulpit. Stepinac later was imprisoned by Tito
and today his tomb in Zagreb is strewn regularly with fresh flowers, as
becomes a Croatian hero. Roman Catholicism, often in the hands of
local Franciscans, has become one of the emblems of dissident Croatian
nationalism.

In 1980 – the year before the visions – Bishop Zanic attempted to
remove a number of his parishes from the Franciscans, and to appoint

secular priests like himself. Reactions were fierce: church doors were bricked and barred by parishioners against the new priests, who were abused and stoned. Two Franciscans said to be behind the protests were suspended by the Order in Rome, and pending appeal went to help in Medjugorje. Father Jozo Zovko, the priest in the village during the early days of the apparitions and a Franciscan, was subsequently imprisoned for preaching a sermon on Moses' forty years in the wilderness, said to be an allusion to the forty years of Communist rule in Yugoslavia. He was later released following a petition by 40,000 people from the diocese. Other Franciscans took his place in the parish and as guides to the visionaries: Father Tomislav Vlasic, who was officiating at the time of my visit, and Father Slavko Barbaric. Father Vlasic asked the children to question the Gospa at one of her manifestations about the suspension of his fellow-Franciscans, and the vision is alleged to have told the children that 'The two Franciscans are innocent – the Bishop has been hasty. He must act as a father and the Franciscans must show him their respect and love, and pray for him.' The Bishop is said to have replied that no vision would have sent a message like that to a bishop, and that the messages were the trite confections of the Franciscans, and of Fr Vlasic in particular. In this way the messages acquired political significance, not only for the internal squabbles of the Roman Catholic Church but also for relations between the nations of the Federation of Yugoslavia.

Taking with me an invitation from Father Michael Marr – a rather more accessible Irish priest – to return for the evening Mass, I set off for Mostar, the centre of which is one of the finest examples of Ottoman architecture in the Balkans. At its heart is an elegant single-span bridge across the Neretva, built during the reign of the Sultan Suleiman the Magnificent in 1557 and flanked by shops in the Turkish style. Mosques flank the river on either side, since nearly half the population is still Muslim.

On a wall I saw notices of necrology – deaths of loved ones – displaying a variety of symbols: green crescents for Muslims, crosses for the Catholics and Orthodox, and plain and undecorated for those wedded to the official atheism of the state. It was a nice comment on the make-up of Bosnia-Hercegovina, where Orthodox and Catholics are each outnumbered by Muslims who form more than forty per cent of the Republic's population.

Mostar was a Turkish provincial capital until just over a hundred years ago and the habits of the Ottomans still linger. Crossing the bridge I came to a café where I had delicious Turkish coffee, sticky sweets and cakes. The road opened into a market place, the stalls piled high with nuts and apples. 'Where you from? I once live Newark, New Jersey,' hailed a man introducing himself as Joseph. 'I come from Bitola south Macedonia. I used to live America but too dirty, pollution. I like mountain air at home.' Joseph was as optimistic as any in Yugoslavia with no cares save one – his apples – which he had shipped by train from the south. 'The snow – terrible, one metre last night in the mountains – roads blocked. Now no one buy the apples. Why? You buy the apples? Anyway you have some, my friend.'

His cheerfulness stayed with me as I took the road back down the course of the Neretva, and turned to the south in search of an open field near the town of Stolac, studded with huge granite blocks, some several tons in weight, etched with strange devices – the famous graveyard and mausoleum of the mysterious heretical sect of the Middle Ages known as the Bogomils. They took their name from their founder in the ninth century, a Bulgarian priest called 'Bogomil' or 'friend of God'. The teachings stem from attempts by the prophet Mani in Persia of the third century AD to combine elements of Christianity and Zoroastrianism, which nearly became the official religion of the Roman imperial army. The central theme of Manicheaism was that the heavens are God's creation whereas the world below and the flesh are works of the Devil. This dualism was to be central not only to Bogomilism but to its cousins in the West – the Cathar movement of Occitania in southern France; the Benandanti, the Happy Friars of Northern Italy in Dante's and Petrarch's days, and the Waldensians.

As in more recent movements, religious dissent was mixed with political subversion. At the beginning of the eleventh century the daughter of the Byzantine Emperor Alexius I, Anna Comnena, wrote of the 'cloud of heretics' and the Bogomil who 'inside is a ravening wolf', one of whom had tried to convert the Emperor against the church's view of the humanity and divinity of Christ. But like Lutheranism in sixteenth-century Germany, the new beliefs came to legitimate local power and authority, and in the twelfth century they were adopted by the kings of Bosnia. But centuries later the kings converted to Catholicism to win papal support against the Turks and the heresy was bloodily suppressed. Modern Medjugorje lies at the heart of the region associated with the Bogomil martyrs.

The story of the Bogomils is also relevant to the eastern Mediterranean today. Their doctrine was based on the division of the cosmos between realms of darkness and light, good and evil, damnation and salvation – a view devoid of ethical notions of rational behaviour towards one's fellows, the converted and the unconverted alike. In the past decade or so, the eastern Mediterranean has been infected by a similar message from modern-day Persia or Iran – a Manichean dualism of unquestioned damnation and salvation, based not on Mani's mixture of Zoroastrianism and Christianity, but on the teachings of Shi'ite Islam of Ayatollah Khomeini and his mullahs.

The tombstones themselves at Stolac bear devices of a strange dream world. Stick men jump with bows and arrows. In the state of grace on earth, stags and deer run, maidens dance, grapes and corn sheaves are harvested. Some of the messages are still indecipherable to experts, while others seem painfully obvious. A stick man on one, clearly martyred, points his symbolic bow and arrow at the sun, symbol of goodness and light, the Creator of the Book of Genesis and Mithra the light-force of Zoroastrianism. 'I have been pierced, I have been slashed, I have been skinned,' reads one inscription, possibly referring to the myth of the flaying of Appelles for challenging the art of Apollo, used to such powerful effect in Michelangelo's self-portrait on a flayed skin in the Last Judgment in the Sistine Chapel. Today the Bogomils and their tombs have found tranquillity, surrounded by cypresses in their beautifully trimmed field at Stolac.

I left the dancing maidens and running deer of the mausoleum to attend the Mass at Medjugorje, which starts with the Rosary at five every evening in winter. Brooding on the conflicts of the Bogomils and the Byzantines, the Turks at Mostar, and the upheavals at Medjugorje, my eye was caught by a flight of venerable-looking military jets skimming the horizon from the distant mountains.

As darkness fell I joined a queue of cars and farm trucks heading towards Medjugorje. A steady stream of worshippers was entering the church, among them entire families from the surrounding villages, grandparents included. From the four hamlets of the parish came a high proportion of young people in their teens and early twenties, kitted out in the functional fashional of the day – anoraks with woollen hoods, jeans and pointed shoes and boots.

Inside the Rosary had begun: a Franciscan priest knelt at the unpretentious altar, little more than a wooden table, and was leading the prayers and responses. Most of the pews were full quite early on – on that frosty February night more than 250 local people had turned out, and some fifty or sixty pilgrims from farther afield. Among the congregation sat the community of nuns. They were of all ages, some of them young, with corn-blond hair and handsome square faces with strong cheek bones. I imagined they hailed from Slovenia, northern Croatia and the Austrian communities to the north.

I slid into a pew at the side of the nave, and was joined by a group of teenage girls from the village, who buried their heads in their arms in prayer. The aisles were patrolled by young men in leather jackets and anoraks, athletic-looking youths of a slightly thuggish appearance. As the service began, the excitement became tangible. Late arrivals made obeisance by going down on their knees and kissing the ground. Several distracted worshippers wandered up and down the church, arms out-stretched, as if transported into ecstacy. One youngish man, crying aloud, kissed his hands and then stroked the statue of the Virgin – gestures he varied by producing dinar notes, which he kissed and then rubbed against the effigy. Out of the corner of my eye I thought I saw the girls in the pew beside me muffling a fit of giggles in their coat sleeves, looking closer, I saw that they were shaking with tears.

As the Mass went on, I felt like a sober late arrival at a feast where the company was already intoxicated. The host was elevated, the com-munion distributed to some hundreds of worshippers by a row of nearly a dozen priests with their servers – among them Father Michael Marr of Dublin.

Almost without warning, the children appeared from the side chapel. The pilgrims stood, craning to get a better view, and the murmur from the congregation rose to a roar. The children knelt above the altar and began to lead the responses in a flat, eerie, monotone, as if half their humanity had left them. After a few minutes of such prayer, they rose as abruptly as they had arrived and began to leave. Flash bulbs popped, cameras clicked and pilgrims stood on their seats to see them. I caught a glimpse of two girls, one with fur-hooded anorak, jeans and boots, and a boy who might well have been Jakov, youngest of the visionaries.

The service concluded with prayers for the sick and the pilgrims in Italian and German. Tersely a priest announced in the same languages that a message had been given by the Madonna that evening to the children in the side chapel, but this would only be given to foreigners the following morning at nine o'clock, and then only to the believers – the *credinti*. I wondered whether I had been spotted.

Moving into the cold night I met Michael Marr who was bubbling with joy and as welcoming as ever: 'Did you see that? Such simple faith, such simple adoration – I've never come across anything like it.' I asked him who was with the children during their vigil in the side chapel, the moment of their ecstasy in which they were said to receive the messages. Only a priest, he said – and, I learned later, a favourite nun from the local community. The public was not allowed in now – they used to bring video cameras and recorders, crowding in by the dozen. 'But the bishop soon put a stop to that', said Father Michael. 'It was becoming too much of a circus.'

We parted, exchanging good wishes and agreeing to meet in Dublin. As he climbed into his car, I'm sure I heard him say, 'Let's get going. I could do with a beer – after all this I've got a powerful thirst on me.'

On the road back to Dubrovnik I reflected on the experiences of this, one of the most vivid and extraordinary days I had spent on my Mediterranean journey. To some, like a scholarly friend on mine, experienced in mid-European matters, the whole phenomenon is little more than 'rampant Croatian nationalism'; to others it may seem nothing more than the skilful manipulation of the subconscious longings of a beleaguered community and the urgent needs of thousands of pilgrims. But for the majority of the faithful Medjugorje represents a geniune spiritual experience.

At the time I was particularly struck by the collective emotion generated by the community and the congregation in the parish. I have seen crowds explode in riots, stunned into silent grief at big funerals, and moved by great oratory, but the experience of Medjugorje was different, however one describes it – ecstacy, inspiration, mass hysteria and hallucination. Something of the same energy must have been generated by John Wesley as he preached to huge audiences in the open air. Rattray Taylor has called it the 'psychic masturbation of the masses' – a term used by E. P. Thompson in *The Making of the English Working Class*, to describe the powers of the great Methodist preachers in early industrial England. It was the phrase that came immediately to mind as I watched the sobbing girls and the exhibitionistic parades in the aisles of Medjugorje.

As for the children and the community of Medjugorje, they were now permanently affected by the visions and their reputation. Judging by reports, the Madonna was clearly Croatian and spoke the local language: did this account for the Vatican's official reluctance to pronounce on her utterances? The matter has been in the hands of the Vatican Congregation of the Doctrine of the Faith under Cardinal Josef Ratzinger, which has avoided taking sides on the issue. More surprising, perhaps, is the muted reaction of Pope John Paul II, whose devotion to shrines dedicated to the Virgin Mary, her miraculous appearances and ministrations, is well known.

Medjugorje lay on one of the great frontiers of the Christian Mediterranean, the line of Theodosius which divided the Latin-speaking world of the Roman church from the Greek Orthodox commonwealth of Byzantium. In the fourth century AD he had ordered that the churches of his empire should adhere to the Creed of the Council of Nicaea of 325 AD.

The Greeks and the Orthodox went one way, and the Latins the other. Centuries later the line of the Neretva valley formed the boundary of the Catholic world and the Habsburg influence and the Ottoman Empire. The officers of the sultans were to import the Muslim colonists from the East to the valley; and their descendants still worship in the mosques sheltered by the birch groves along the river.

The region had always been charged with the atmosphere of conflict, of Orthodox against Catholic, the persecution of the Bogomils, and the fight against the Ottomans. The clash between Catholic Croatia and Orthodox Serbia has threatened to sunder Tito's confection of a united Yugoslavia, within a decade of the dictator's death. The conflict is likely to be of greater consequence for the Balkan neighbourhood of the Mediterranean than the revolt of the Albanians of Kosovo. In this round of the conflict, the new spirit of Croatia appeared first at Medjugorje.

Dubrovnik has thrived on divisions and conflicts within the Adriatic. As the maritime Republic of Ragusa it was a centre of shipping insurance and the exchange and mart of intelligence, gossip, rumour and diplomacy between the Ottoman world and the powers of the West, principally Venice and later Habsburg Austria.

The Republic's constitution was modelled on Venice, which briefly controlled the city until the mid-fourteenth century and, like Venice, the modern city is adorned with smart shops and boutiques in elegant seventeenth-century surroundings. Dubrovnik is the centre of a well-run holiday trade, catering for the yachting harbours and beaches of the lower Adriatic and the mountain resorts of Montenegro. Its shops post their prices in dollars, to circumvent the perils of the plunging dinar, and many of the clothes and utensils on display carry the same labels as would be found in resorts on the other side shore of the Adriatic.

Dubrovnik – Ragusa – has survived, though only just. The seventeenth-century shape of the town is preserved, despite being almost totally destroyed by earthquake in 1667, in which nearly a sixth of the total population died. The old buildings and churches were faithfully rebuilt, among them the medieval Franciscan friary, the cloister of which houses a pharmacy, founded in 1319, where the sisters and brethren still dispense a wonderful array of powders and potions. Before the friary runs the main thoroughfare of the *placa* – from the Greek name for a town centre – under which the Ragusans laid a piped water supply in 1468. A further indication of their foresight are the huge grain silos, built to supply the city in times of famine and need. Granary wells are first mentioned in 1389, and government food reserves were established by the Senate in 1541. The grain was subsidised from the public coffers, and to be sold in times of hunger on the public market-place, the *fundik* – a word of similar Arabic derivation as the Fondaco at Bonifacio in Corsica.

The strength of Ragusa's ties with the Arabs and Berbers of North Africa was described to me by the director of the city archive, Dr Ilija Mitic. By the seventeenth century, he said, Ragusa's diplomatic network in the Mediterranean was second only to that of Venice. Ragusa, he suggested, was like Vienna after 1945 – an international city of espionage and intrigue between the east and the west. The city was represented abroad by eighty consuls, mostly in the Mediterranean, and five full ambassadors – all for a republic of some 35,000 citizens. Despite the discovery of the Americas, the number of merchantmen insuring at Ragusa actually increased – and prominent among them were the Dutch. The Ragusan governors often chose Dutchmen to be their consuls in North Africa – 'The Berbers liked the Dutch particularly because they knew they were against the Spanish,' Dr Mitic concluded.

The archive was run by the highly personable Dr Ivana Burdelez, who seemed thoroughly to enjoy the life, social and intellectual, of modern Dubrovnik. Our talk was interspersed with a truly Ragusan piece of bargaining for my Italian Borsellino hat, which she said would be a *pièce de résistance* at the event of the season, the Mardi Gras ball at the end of the week. I promised instead to send her a copy of George Steiner's *After Babel*, after she had revealed that her current studies in philology covered an area broadly related to its themes – and one which suddenly introduced a melancholy note to our conversation, a sad reflection on the steady impoverishment of the rich variety that until very recently existed in Mediterranean culture. She has been cataloguing the dialect of the Jewish community of Sarajevo, which stems from the language of the Jews of Toledo before they were expelled in 1492 or converted by the Inquisition. Many of its words are recognisably old Spanish – the Ladino of the Mediterranean Jewish communities, 'It is dying out now – those still speaking the language in Sarajevo are a handful in their seventies and eighties. I have to work fast,' she said.

Beyond Dubrovnik I travelled round the deep fjords and bays to the south, where prosperous ports grew and traded – Kotor (with its elegant Venetian customs house), Budva and Bar. Kotor lies in the foothills of the Black Mountain, Crna Gora – the mountain of Montenegro, that little monument of Balkan Ruritania bordering the Adriatic. The Montenegrans, like the Pathans of Afghanistan, were masters at seeing off invaders. For more than two hundred years this tiny principality – today the Republic of Montenegro with just over half a million population – was ruled by a dynasty of prince-bishops of the Petrovic-Njegos family: one briefly became king (Nikola I) from 1910–16, when he was driven out by the Austrians. Of all the family the most extraordinary was the Prince-Bishop Peter II Njegos, who ruled from 1830 to 1851, when he died at the age of thirty-eight. Ecclesiastic, man of action, scholar, expert on Shakespeare, he was the author of the most celebrated piece of romantic literature of the region, an epic poem called *The Wreath*. The mountain town of Cetinje, the old capital of the kingdom, with its elegant villas and palaces, is largely his creation. One of its finest buildings is that of the Austro-Hungarian embassy, all wrought-iron gates with huge double-headed eagles and ornate stucco faced in ghastly orange.

The Prince-Bishop was an expert pistol shot, and passionate billiards player – so much so that in 1840 he ordered a full-sized table, which had to be transported up the winding coast road from Kotor by a team of twenty-five men and mules. The splendid palace which housed the sacred table proudly bears the name of Biljarda.

I had taken the road of the billiard table in 1979, just after an earthquake had devastated Kotor and the coast as far as Dubrovnik to the north, and Bar and Budva to the south. The road was strewn with debris and the car inched its way along precipices that fell away for thousands of feet. I came across a cheery crew of disaster victims trying to reach their villages, all of whom conducted themselves with remarkable restraint and stoicism. Many lives had been spared because, following the devastation of Skopje, new houses on the coast were now being reinforced with steel rods against earthquake – precautions sadly lacking in similarly-vulnerable zones in Italy across the water.

I was heading for Titograd, the new capital of Montenegro, where I hoped to glimpse Tito himself visiting the afflicted zone. My last companion on that road was a man who had worked for several years in Germany. He invited me to a meal at his house in a mountain pass and we conversed in almost non-existent German and a bit of French on my part. Suddenly, as if harkening to some silent code of the mountain, he pulled out a pistol and slammed it on the table – a centuries-old gesture of hospitality in these parts, for it shows a man unarmed.

In my winter journey down the coast of Dalmatia in February 1985 I had hoped to cross or skirt the Black Mountain through Macedonia to Salonika on the Aegean, but the weather beat me, and I had to reach Greece by taking the ferry via Bari and Brindisi. I finally penetrated the heart of Montenegro a year later. The craziness of the pumpernickel principality, as enshrined in the palaces of Cetinje, seemed all the more glorious in brilliant July sunshine. But the extravagences and eccentricities of the Prince-Bishops of Petrovic-Njegos seemed positively routine and straightforward compared with the country I was on my way to, the regime of which worked with the logic of a clock whose hands move backwards.

iii Albania: A Law Unto Itself

Until very recently anyone travelling into Albania by land from Yugoslavia could not pretend to arrive unawares. In the waiting-room of the customs post, with its settees and armchairs covered in flower-patterned upholstery, a stern warning (in English) hung on the wall: 'Even if we have to go without bread, we Albanians do not violate principles, we do not betray Marxism-Leninism – Enver Hoxha'.

An ideological as well as a geographical frontier was crossed. To make the point the tourist was made to walk the hundred yards or so between the Yugoslav barrier and the Albanian sentry post bearing his or her own luggage, which was then duly searched. Arriving at this point on a boiling August Sunday in 1986 I had my first, highly courteous brush with the authority of the People's Socialist Republic of Albania. The customs official removed from my luggage a copy of the Rome daily *La Repubblica*, which indeed contained a hilarious report of the completion of the much-heralded single-track rail link between Albania and Yugoslavia: such was the animosity between Belgrade and Tirana that they boycotted each other's inauguration ceremonies and the date had yet to be fixed when rolling stock would rumble across the frontier – if it ever would.

The Albania I visited in 1986 could still claim to be the most isolated state in Europe, wrapped in its cocoon of ideological purity, by then the only true example of Marxism-Leninism at work thanks to the guidance of Enver Hoxha, the founder of the modern Albanian state and the Albanian Communist Party – or, to give it its correct title since 1948, the Party of Labour of Albania. Hoxha believed he was the only true follower of Stalin, and by the time he died in 1985 could boast of being one of the most absolute rulers in the world, with an unenviable reputation for cunning and cruelty. In the years after his death his name and image were everywhere in the country. The hills literally proclaimed his praises, for picked out in white stones along their crests and on huge hoardings on buildings and roadsides in remote countryside was the legend *Lavde Enver Hoxha* (Praise to Enver Hoxha). I later heard that recently grass had been allowed to grow over some of the inscriptions, a sign Albania too was being infected with the virus of *glasnost*.

Albania achieved much under Hoxha, though whether greater or less progress would have been made under different management is an open question. Independence came late to the country, in 1912, after four hundred years of Turkish occupation. From 1914 to 1920 it was dominated by the Italians, who again took up occupation from April 1939 to September 1943. In 1944 the new regime was founded by Hoxha's Partisan forces, who liberated Tirana with the help of their Yugoslav comrades.

The state of the country in 1945 was little better than when the Turks had left. Nearly nine-tenths of the people were illiterate, vendettas were rife, and a man could not expect to live beyond forty. There were no railways. Education, health care, and industrial and agricultural reforms were introduced via the most rigid centrally controlled system in Europe. Literacy rose, and average life expectancy reached seventy by the 1980s. Industrialisation began with the help of Stalin's Russia and then of Mao's China, leaving an inheritance of antiquated machinery in the factories and heavy wheezing tractors on the collective farms.

As the five-year programmes developed, so too did suspicion against outsiders from East and West. In 1948 came the break with Tito's Yugoslavia, accused of outlandish territorial ambitions in the Balkans. Seven years later it was Moscow's turn: Khruschev had betrayed the gospel and good works of Josef Stalin. In 1962 Albania formally withdrew from the Warsaw Pact, and soon after began the courtship of Mao's China. But with the collapse of the Cultural Revolution and Beijing's rapprochement with Washington, it was clear that China, too, was going the way of imperialist roaders. In 1976 a new constitution declared Albania's policy of self-reliance anew, and foreign credits or borrowing from abroad were outlawed. The People's Socialist Republic of Albania, in the eyes of critics, was becoming the Miller of Dee of Europe: 'I care for nobody, no not I, and nobody cares for me.'

A sad footnote to the policy of isolation was provided by a pathetic incident at the frontier the day I crossed. Albania has about three million people, but 1.2 million Albanians live immediately across the border in Yugoslavia, most in the province of Kosovo. A family had come to the barrier to bring relations gifts of furniture, mattresses and a cooker, which were loaded onto trolleys and trundled by customs officials over the no-man's-land between the two sentry posts. The families were not allowed to draw close enough to converse in normal tones, let alone embrace or shake hands. An old matriarch gave vent to her distress in an oriental display of weeping, breast-beating and wailing – many of the Kosovites are Muslim, and dress in the Turkish manner – but the guards in their heavy and ill-fitting Chinese comic opera uniforms were unrelenting, particularly with a party of tourists to shepherd through.

The tourists seemed an exception to the isolationist doctrine, though I suspect their role was important to Albania's convoluted foreign policy, providing a means of diplomacy and low-level intelligence on the cheap. Since 1970 Albtourist, the state tourist body, has brought in select parties of travellers from Western countries, who are given heavily guided bus tours of Albania for up to ten days. The travellers were often invited to sing the praises of the People's Republic on Radio Tirana and invited to join support groups such as Albanian friendship societies. Only four or five thousand foreigners were admitted to the country each year, but in 1983 all such tours were suddenly cancelled; rumours later reached the West of serious political upheavals and plots against Hoxha himself.

I had signed up on such a travel group from Britain, as the only way I reckoned I could get into Albania at all. Our party was made up principally of schoolteachers, plus one or two civil servants, a vociferous art historian and her daughter, a businessman and several others as determined as I to remain as vague as possible about the nature of their jobs and their intentions in travelling to Albania. Journalists are not welcomed on such enterprises, though nearly every tour seems to include a professional writer or reporter of some description. Every summer the English papers are full of feature articles about 'unknown Albania', the land hidden from journalists – which is simply not true, for Albtourist officials are well aware that, like sin, the fourth estate is always with them, and to their credit they turned a blind eye.

The company I found myself in proved a mixed blessing. Some were fellow-travellers, their lives at home so unsatisfactory that a radical alternative such as Hoxha's Albania was bound to be a good thing. Many of the tour couriers appear similarly orientated, as they return year after year seeing the same sights. But the biggest drawback was the lumpen lack of curiosity of most of the schoolteachers: they seemed oblivious or unwilling to question their surroundings or the conduct of the society in which they were paying guests.

The principal sources of information were our two guides – Edi, an old hand at the game, and Sali, a relative newcomer. Both were teachers of English and highly proficient speakers. Edi, tall, thickset and charming, was a born survivor. I guessed his family had been well-to-do before the revolution and that he still owned quite a bit of land. Once away from the didactic drone, the *de rigueur* patter of the Albtourist guide, he could be amusing and informative – to have to meet him regularly over several years would have provided an illuminating guide to changing attitudes in official Albania. If Edi was the smooth end of the Tweedle-dum and Tweedledee duo, Sali was the rough. He was a physical training instructor; as an ardent supporter of the regime, he was uncertain in his discussions with the tourists. When challenged, he could become quite aggressive – highly revealing, though in a very different way from his urbane colleague. The trio of officialdom was made up by the driver, Kope, who, I came to suspect, was much more than a *primus inter pares*.

From the frontier we headed through an open landscape populated with horses and carts, oxen and cows, rather than tractors and cars. We were moving through a time warp, into an Europe of fifty, sixty or even seventy years ago. The few cars roared past without care for man or beast – they are reserved for official business and for the use of senior Party dignitaries, rank being crudely displayed by the vintage of the model. Lately some new Peugeots and Volvos had been imported but only a few thousand cars were in working order in the entire country.

The most outstanding landmarks, conspicuous for quantity rather than quality, were the chains of dugouts and small gun-pits that followed the roads for mile after mile, punctuated by a sporadic line or two of concrete pillboxes and artillery emplacements. These symptoms of a siege men-tality occur on almost every main highway, and nearer the border break out in severe rashes. Hardly items of architectural beauty, they were equally unimpressive as defensive fortifications as many were broken down and collapsed like honeycombs, while others were so close together that an occupant would be as likely to shoot his comrades as the enemy.

Towards the afternoon we hauled into Shkodër, the principal indus-trial town of the north. It was a high day or holiday, for small crowds stood about the streets and squares of the old quarter in the finest tra-ditional costumes I saw in the northern Mediterranean – white baggy trousers and skirts gathered with broad sashes, worn with red and black tunics covered with elaborate embroidery of gold and yellow thread. The old town was very Turkish: squat, brown-fronted, whitewashed houses in the Ottoman style, with doors and shutters of light blue and green, and gently pitched roofs of biscuit-coloured tiles.

As I sauntered across the town during its Sunday afternoon siesta, I found myself being followed, though in not a very alarming way. Later I was to experience more bluntly the official surveillance and general busybodiness that seems such a fact of life in these parts. The contrasts between Shkodër old and new were stark. The Ottoman parts had great charm and grace, whereas most of the modern building was unrelentingly ugly in a functional way, unalleviated by the public statuary in parks and gardens – busts of Lenin and, more often, Stalin himself, as large as life, and frequently much larger.

The standard Sunday afternoon entertainment was the stroll, a *passagiata* similar to that of any southern Italian town, with, for variety a visit to a football match or a milk parlour for ice cream or yoghurt, a delight learnt to perfection from the Turks. The few restaurants seem reserved for the rarest of treats. That evening we saw a wedding party getting to a serious stage of inebriation in the main dining-room of one such hostelry, a slightly rundown wooden structure with a raffish and distinguished air. A small string band was squeezing out the mournful strains of a tango; at the centre table the bride's cheeks were beginning to match the scarlet of her blouse and clash with the carnation in her straw hat.

The organised visits at Shkodër established what was to become a familiar routine – to historical monuments, a copper-wire factory and the June 1st Infants' School. A climb to the fortress of Rozafat afforded a view of new housing developments on the edge of the city, built after the earthquake of 1979 – oblong caissons of red brick, held together by insubstantial bands of mortar.

The wire-factory took us into what was to become familiar territory: an enormous barn of a place, none too tidy, full of wonderfully heavy, clanking machinery still bearing the manufacturer's plates in Chinese. The spirit of Mao's China pervaded the establishment in other ways as well. Bureaucrats and managers had to complete at least one month's manual work there each year, and no manager earned more than twice the lowest wage of a worker. Seven hundred different cables were made at the plant, 80 per cent for export, according to the 'Comrade Engineer' – as Edi rather shyly called him, for he had quickly abandoned 'Comrade Visitors' when addressing us.

The establishment was quite literally a roaring success – such was the noise and activity that all attempts to wear safety gear, ear muffs, and to use protective shields had been cheerfully abandoned. In 1985 the factory had doubled the output target of 4000 tonnes set in 1980, while the workforce had increased in twenty years from 300 to more than a thousand. Albania is well-endowed with natural resources, including chrome and copper, and is a considerable exporter of energy in the form of hydro-generated electricity to countries such as Bulgaria and Hungary. But the message of the model copper wire factory of Shkodër was clear: according to Edi 'it shows that Albania is not just an exporter of raw materials but of important finished products as well.' For which an elaborate *lavde* above the factory gate with the legend *Lavdi Vepres se Ndritur e Te pavde Te Shokut, Enver Hoxha,* lest it slip the mind for a couple of seconds ('Glory to the lofty and immortal deeds of Enver Hoxha').

At the June 1st Infants' School, other uniquely Albanian products were being turned out. Teachers greeted us on the steps, their charges in long white smocks, in what seemed a well-practised routine. Workers had up to six months maternity leave, we were told, and crêches were plentiful and generous in the cities. At three and a half tots entered kindergartens like June 1st (named after the national children's day) to be 'brought up to love the party and leaders, and remember what the founder has done', according to the headmistress. Instruction quickly brought results: under a drawing of flowers one six-year-old had run off a few lines of verse which were translated as 'I saw the portrait of Enver Hoxha, I spoke to it. I went into the garden and picked the best flowers, and lay them before it.' A socialist hero in the making, no doubt.

Later in the afternoon we encountered a genuine historical hero of Albania. In the shell of a medieval church at Lezhë stands the shrine to George Castriotis, or Skanderbeg, who led resistance against the Turks from 1444, when he bound the feudal lords of the region into the League of Lezhë, until his death from malaria in 1468. Skanderbeg is an extraordinary and unlikely figure to be revered by modern Albanians. He was born a Greek Christian and was seized by the Turks to join their elite troops of janissaries. But after the victory of the Hungarian Crusaders at Nis in 1443 he defected and raised Albanian resistance against the Ottomans. His tactics are recorded in legend as much as fact. Once he tied torches to the horns of goats and sent them charging into the Turkish encampment, and he is frequently depicted in armour wearing a helmet adorned with goats' horns. At his death he was preparing to march against the Turks, backed by a crusade declared by the Pope. The two-headed eagle of his banner is the flag of the Socialist Republic of Albania. On the crusade, and on the traditional symbolism of the double eagle as the badge of the two Christian empires of Rome, East and West, official silence reigns.

Skanderbeg – derived from his Turkish title, Alexander, or Iskander Beg – and Enver Hoxha remain the only two Albanian super-heroes. The two eagles of the flag represent, according to the rough logic of the guide Sali, 'the two Albanias, of the mountain and the plain.' The fact that Albanians call their country Shqiperia was thought to stem from the word *shqiponje* or 'eagle' but more probably it comes from the word *shqip* meaning 'intelligible', later used as the name for the Albanian language as a whole.

Quite who the Albanians of Skanderbeg's bands were, where they came from and what language they spoke, remains something of a historical puzzle which my twelve-day-tour of high and low Albania did not solve entirely. During the sixth century BC the area was inhabited by Illyrians, whose language is said to provide much of the structure of modern Albanian. Early medieval missionaries are said to have influenced the spoken, if not the written word, though I could find little official mention inside Albania of the most famous of these, Cyril and Methodius, possibly since they are revered by such revisionist and back-sliding regimes as the Bulgarians and the Yugoslavs.

Today's language combines the dialects of the Gegs and Tosks, who live north and south of the Shkumbin River respectively, and achieved its full literary form in the last quarter of the nineteenth century. The language is said to be very formal and regular, characteristics it shares with Turkish. Despite the present emphasis on isolation and self-sufficiency, Albanians have for centuries been intimately involved in the cultures and destinies of its two powerful neighbours, Greece and Turkey. With their baggy trousers, rich bodices, fezzes and well-trimmed moustaches, many Albanians still look rather Turkish. Nine out of ten names on a war memorial at Durrës were of Turkish Islamic origin – Ismail, Ali and Mustafa. The ruling dynasty of Egypt, the family of ex-King Farouk, were the descendants of the Albanian Mehmet Ali, the catalyst of Greek independence.

The Albanians' role in the Greeks' struggle against the Turks was given brilliant publicity by Byron, who liked to be portrayed in the garb of the white-kilted Souliots, the Albanian tribesmen he took on his last expedition to Missolonghi. Sizeable waves of migration from the Albanian mountains as far as the Peloponnese took place in the fifteenth and eighteenth centuries. In modern Greece Albanians are called Chams: Chamaria is said to stretch over the Pindus mountains, the lands once ruled by Byron's patron, Ali Pasha, as far as the town of Arta – a slice of land which still generates irredentist longings amongst a few Albanians.

The mausoleum of Skanderbeg, in the remains of the basilica of Shen Koll (St Nicholas) at Lezhë, relies more on imagination than on historical artefacts. A plaque commemorates the grave of the warrior; modern replicas of weapons and the coats of arms of his supporters in bronze adorn the walls, with the obligatory helmet and goat's horns prominent in their midst. On the grassy mound above the church families picnicked under the trees, one clustering round a grandfather in baggy brown trousers and a white woollen fez. On the sandy track below, children in ragged shorts made mud pies.

At our next stop I had a fascinating assignation with the heirs of Skanderbeg and his feudal clans – quite by accident. Durrës or Durazzo is an austere port and industrial centre, which suffered heavy damage in the last war after the Italian Fascists arrived in April 1939. The old town boasts some remains, supposedly of the Illyrian era, and a fine Roman amphitheatre of the second century AD. For the Romans, Durrës held the road into the Balkans – the Via Egnatia, leading to Byzantium (Constantinople) itself. The Norman lord of Puglia, Bohemond the crusading conqueror of Antioch, made his last desperate expedition to take Durrës before becoming a Byzantine vassal – in 1097 the crusading armies had crossed from Italy to Durrës, and were escorted along the Via Egnatia by Pecheaneg cavalry serving the Emperor Alexius I Comnenus.

On the beach to the south of the harbour a colony of ramshackle huts and open-fronted chalets has sprung up – holiday homes for workers of outstanding character and achievement, allocated a fortnight's holiday by the sea at a subsidised price of 120 leks or roughly £60. Conditions in the Albtourist hotel were luxurious by comparison, and the menu fuller and more varied. Such establishments seem to be strictly for foreigners and Party and government officials.

Among our fellow-guests was a party of Italian schoolteachers from the Albanian- or Arberesch-speaking areas of their country. Arberesch is a medieval forebear of modern Albanian, the language of the armies, camp-followers and their kin who went into exile after the death of Skanderbeg. Their descendents still live in Sicily, in the Piano Albanese, in Calabria on the eastern fringes of the Sila plateau round the town of Spezzano Albanese (where Mass is still celebrated in an Albanian rite), and in Molise and northern Basilicata round Benevento and Campobasso. Arberesch language and customs are living traditions among nearly 200,000 Italian Albanians, who have their own journals and books in Calabria. The teachers were forthcoming about their community and culture, albeit with the formality and slight sense of reserve common to minorities in the Mediterranean – though they have suffered much less discrimination than most.

The Arberesch admitted that they were guinea pigs: this was the first time such a delegation had been invited to Albania from Italy with the official sanction of both governments. Just before they left, a sudden cooling of relations between the two countries had necessitated the party's being lodged for much of the stay at Durrës and away from the capital, Tirana. The row concerned rights of asylum and diplomatic immunity in the Italian embassy and although it cast a large shadow over the Arberesch teachers' tour, it almost put paid to my brief stay in the Shqiperia.

Later on I managed to catch up with the Italians we returned to Durrës; I was anxious to learn of their various encounters and cultural exchanges and, if possible, to talk to the professor who was their official host. But the isolation bug had bitten deep. The Italians told me, apologetically, that they had been warned not to talk to me – the authorities were suspicious about my knowledge of Italian and did not regard writing a book about the Mediterranean as a valid reason for my deeper inquiry. By now I was beginning to suspect that Albanians' policy of isolation and self-reliance contained a creeping paranoia.

Coastal towns and resorts like Durrës, Vlorë and Sarandë mark the point of entry for Italian influence into Albania in another sense. Pleasures for the holiday-maker by the sea are few and simple – swimming, the beach, volleyball, football and other sports. The shore and promenade at Sarandë was strung with groups of adults and children on stools and benches playing chess with large wooden sets. Beside them stood radios blaring out pop music from a variety of foreign stations; the favourites are the Yugoslavs, the Italians and the BBC World Service. The Voice of America did not feature in the cacophony by the shore. Recently, in an act of uncharacteristic relaxation towards consumer culture, Albanian factories had started turning out cheap radios in plastic casings of garish hues, sky-blue, canary-yellow and cardinal-red.

The radio brought one of the most revealing chance meetings of my travels in Albania. Swimming at one of the resorts I came across a group of boys who said they had learnt Italian from listening to the radio, and a little bit of RAI television which could be picked up in the summer months when atmospheric conditions were good. Over several days we managed to meet in the water and converse while swimming.

Two of the group were technical school graduates, two were unemployed. Their tale was one of unrelieved monotony, petty oppression and intellectual starvation. 'The world is so big for you,' one remarked when I explained a little of my travels, 'and so very small for us.' Another confessed he was seriously thinking of trying to seek asylum, of running to Italy, but a great deal of cunning and luck were needed. The Corfu Channel was practically impossible because of the security patrols.

The boys had formed a club to discuss the news and current events in Italian. They would not allow more than six or seven to join for fear of attracting informers. 'Informers are everywhere – such stupid people. They do it for only about 100 leks a month [£18] – it's more a way of life for them.' Talking to foreigners was expressly forbidden and they would get a severe beating from the authorities if they were caught talking to me, and worse on a second offence.

The boys gave some bare economic facts of their family life. One said his parents were amongst the best paid categories in the country, his mother earning 800 leks a month as a pharmacist with university qualifications, and his father, a mining engineer, earning 1,000 leks a month – a total income of £300 for the family, though giving dollar or sterling equivalents is virtually meaningless as it does not reflect the scarcity of goods and food or the Albanian price structure. One of the boys said meat had been scarce and over the past eighteen months had been restricted to a kilo per family, though whether this was for a week or month was unclear. A television set cost 5,000 leks or ten months' salary for the average earner. I never resolved fully the question of rationing – asking officials often met with hilarious evasions.

Albanians had no constitutional right to strike, and no religion. 'I have never seen a priest in a church. My grandmother worships alone, but we keep Easter among the family,' one told me. Another, of a technical turn of mind, remarked that 'the country as a whole is under-mechanised, and they like to rely on manual labour in the country where wages can be about 5 leks [80 pence] a day.' Attempts to strike may be punished with up to twenty-five years in prison and labour camps.

I was glad to haul myself out of the water after our long conversations, for most of the coastal water at Butrint, Sarandë and Durrës, is thick and glutinous with oil and pollution. At Durrës the water stung and a strong smell of DDT drifted from the main port. Later I was to see women dusting DDT powder over a field of cabbages, their hands unprotected by gloves.

Tirana, hub and capital of the Shqiperia, is a place of broad squares and tree-lined boulevards, nineteenth-century town housing contrasting with the starker lines of modern museum, congress hall and Albtourist Hotel. In the centre a bronze equestrian statue of Skanderbeg, goat horns *tous compris*, charges towards the square which bears his name (in a moment of official modesty and restraint, a move to rename it Hoxha Square after the great man's death was rejected). To the right of his line of attack is the beautiful nineteenth-century mosque of Haxhi Ethem-Bay, one of the best preserved Islamic buildings in the country.

Swinging to the left, Skanderbeg's charge would take him to the functional steps of the marble-faced national museum and the summation of all Comrade Enver's achievements. Across the broad cornice is a huge socialist-realist mural depicting the official version of the history of the Shqiperia. Illyrian foot-soldiers mingle with Skanderbeg's men-at-arms,

Souliot warriors parade in their kilts, and a flank attack is led to the right by a member of Hoxha's National Liberation Army with a cloth shako on his head and matching red flag in his left hand; while bursting through the middle, striding hand-in-hand, are the industrial worker in his dungarees, a young woman in a splendid striped traditional dress, and a militiaman in his No 1 dress – the new Albanians.

After a visit to a carpet factory, impeccably clean and light with high-quality production – a large proportion is exported – we plunged into a recitation of the Republic's successes in the Palace of Culture. In the Hall of Albanian Achievement, diagrams and products from bull-dozers to bath-tubs proclaimed how much had been done in forty years. In 1945, 89 per cent (always 89, not 90) were illiterate, whereas now nearly a third of the population is in the education system. But the Hall of Achievement might also be called the Hall of the Circular Argument. Average life expectancy is reported in one chart as seventy-one. Why? Because the United Nations World Health Organisation reports the figure as this. And why does WHO report this figure? Because the official statistics in Tirana say so; and so on and so on. Think of a number and send it spinning round the system. I found that nearly every official statistic in Albania had to be treated with caution in this way. Many were quite clearly intelligent approximations, while with others there was no way of finding out where they came from and how they were reached. This was particularly frustrating when it came to the ethnic and linguistic make-up of the population. The standard figure given for the number of Greeks and Greek-speakers fluctuated between 25,000 and 50,000 – though the authorities in Athens, worried about religious and racial discrimination against people of Greek descent in the south of Albania, put the number as high as 250,000. (It was said to be concern about Albanian Greeks, and some nasty incidents on the mountainous border with Greece, that caused the Athens government to press hard, and successfully, for an opening of the land crossing in the south after ministerial visits to Tirana in 1985.)

I found Edi, the more forthcoming of the guides, particularly poor on such matters. During our visit to Butrint and Sarandë in the south I asked him about various mountain peoples that lived on the borders with Ipiros in Greece, particularly the Vlachs, who speak a dialect with a Latin root. 'The Vlach?' he said, 'I don't know really what you mean – the Vlach is a Romanian, like a gypsy.' It was evident that for him the gypsy counted for little more than the lower orders of pond life. Albanians' grasp of their history before-Hoxha tended to be somewhat colourful and oblique. Disappointingly few of the artefacts in the historical section of the national museum in Tirana were original – most were copies and modern replicas.

Our tour group included four devout Muslims of Pakistani origin, whose leader, Haji Tashim Ali, was the minister of the East London Mosque in Fieldgate Street, near Aldgate. They formed part of a prayer group which travelled regularly to countries with Muslim populations, particularly in Eastern Europe. In Albania they visited the sites of mosques, whatever their state of repair, praying as they walked round the perimeter to ensure that the building remained consecrated. They drew a crowd of several hundred in Tirana when they went to pray at the Haxhi Ethem-Bey Mosque, under the gaze of the statue of Skander-beg and scores of policemen, security men and general busybodies. According to their leader, some of the crowd touched his robes and muttered a blessing, while others pushed their children forward for a laying on of hands, a greeting and a blessing. Such public demonstration was surprising in a country which had formally abolished religion in the 1960s and incorporated atheism in the constitution of 1976.

Haji Tashim Ali's observations on the Albanian journey were acute and wonderfully gentle. The follies of new Albania were matters of sorrow more than anger for him: 'It is all so childish,' was his refrain. He was a wonderful companion and I am not sure that he and his little group were not the sanest members of our tour by the time we reached the end.

That evening we received our heaviest and – sadly – only in-depth dis-course on the nature of the Albanian state and its system. This was given to us by Zvi Masi, an editor in the 8th November Publishing Committee, one of the most important publishers of historical and political matter (on 8 November 1941 the first clandestine Communist Congress was held in Tirana). Zvi's English was felicitous, fluent and almost without accent. He gave us first a run-down on the legislative structure, of which the highest organ is the 250-member People's Assembly which is chosen every four years, but meets for only a few days each year to rubber-stamp proposals emerging from the Party and the Politburo. The Members of the Demo-cratic Front of Albania – virtually the entire population over eighteen, except for 'antagonistic classes before the war, the most terrible collabor-ators and the mentally handicapped' – choose candidates for local People's Councils, who then choose the Assembly members.

The Democratic Front is a direct descendant of the wartime National Liberation Front, and from its ranks emerge the members of the Party, renamed the Party of Labour of Albania in 1948. The Party works through local committees and committees for specialised work sectors in industry, agriculture, education and so forth: it also monitors elections, the lists of candidates and the results. Its most important role is to set out the Five Year Plan. The Party is always present in one form or another, though the mechanism whereby its own members, are chosen and promoted seem somewhat obscure. In all there are about 200,000 Party members, about 6 per cent of the adult population. I later remarked to Sali that in the way they were looked to for guidance they were almost like a priesthood, a caste of clerics – a view with which he said he did not entirely disagree.

I asked Zvi about rationing, recalling the conservation of the Italian Club and observations of food shortages in shops in our perambulations up and down the country. 'I don't know what you mean,' he replied, after some whisperings and shufflings with the two guides. Shortages of meat, I countered, not enough to go round, restrictions to a kilo per family? Brief pause and then, showing rather too good command of English, 'I thought you said "Russianing" – I misunderstood your accent. No, of course no rationing. It was abolished in Albania years ago.' Like poverty, foreign debt and God, rationing was outlawed by the 1976 constitution.

The other question I managed to put was about the Albanian population in the neighbouring province of Kosovo in Yugoslavia. The Kosovites had been in a state of near rebellion since 1981, demanding greater automony, civil rights and eventually full status as a separate republic within or without the Yugoslav Federation and 1.2 million Albanians lived there, while Albania itself had a population of about three million. Pristina, in Kosovo, had been the old capital of Albania when it first achieved independence in 1912, and was the heart of a rich mining region. 'The Great Serb,' said Zvi, referring to the Belgrade government, 'had accused Albania of stirring up trouble in Kosovo, but this was not true. Albania supported the Kosovite claim to be a republic, but within Yugoslavia. We do not want a destabilised neighbour.' Albania would help with cultural exchanges and families could send food and clothes. When I asked if Tirana would agree to opening borders to allow in refugees, I received an emphatic no. Was it because the majority of Albanian Kosovites were Muslim, I suggested? 'Absolutely not. I've never heard of the suggestion before. Who told you that?'

The message Zvi sent us was that the heritage of Enver Hoxha was alive and well in the Shqiperia. No change could be expected at the Party Congress due in November, not a breath of *glasnost* and *perestroika* (though things have changed since then). As we trickled out to taste the nightlife in the lugubrious coffee bars of Tirana, Sali, the rough guide, who had been remarkably quick to prompt and hint in discussion sessions said, 'You forgot the obvious question. You should have asked if he was a member of the Party.' I suspect he was not, but worked so closely with Party propaganda that delivered its message in an even more undiluted form than a member secure in his position.

Before leaving Tirana we were taken to the war memorial and the grave of Enver Hoxha, a broad granite plaque watched over by two sentries. The cemetery was superbly set on a hillside overlooking the city. Only a handful of the 30,000 who died in the war against the Axis and the accompanying civil war were buried there – barely reflecting the terrible privations and pain incurred, especially in the mountains in winter. At the memorial to the Hoxha the Anglo-Californian courier stood at attention. His devotion to a leader and to a country he had never lived in, and whose language he hardly spoke, was hard to explain. The previous day he had been at Radio Tirana arranging a propaganda broadcast by some of the tour members for the English language service, a standard procedure for such groups.

Further clues to the life and times of Enver Hoxha – in the authorised version – were provided during our tour of the south in the town of Gjirokastër, his supposed birthplace.

Since leaving Durrës we had been criss-crossing a countryside for several days of brown mountains and river valleys, of newly irrigated fields of vetch and rye grass and yellowing wheat, in wonderfully varied colours. Sometimes fifty men and women would work a single field with hand tools, and in one a gang of half-a-dozen men in a line were scything long grass for hay. Tractors were the exception rather than the rule, and often dairy animals were harnessed to carts and harrows.

As one approached a town the roads were lined with files of men and women going to and fro, the optimists sitting under poplars and oaks, waiting for a bus or lift on a cart. In the little towns and villages an inordinate number of people seemed to spend their time standing about watching the world go by, as if their routine was one long shift break.

Occasionally one became aware that all was not as well lubricated as it might be in the great machine of the centrally planned economy. On the road to Tirana a herd of dairy Friesian cattle were being fed what looked like two tons of tomatoes – with what effect on their milk one hardly likes to guess. Elsewhere a dairy herd had been turned out on the driest of stubble with very little greenery to provide protein.

These rural scenes brought a touchy response from our official hosts. Requests to photograph the fields, the farms and the families were flatly ignored. Kope seemed to think the best means of defence is attack, and drove his bus full tilt down the roads like some demented charioteer, scattering cows, carts, people, chickens, dogs and cats. Even history was muscled aside in his headlong flight. Twice we passed without stopping the walls of Tepelenë, the fortress where Ali Pasha of Ioannina had entertained Byron in 1810, while Sali quoted fluently from the relevant pages of *Childe Harold*. For thirty-two years Ali Pasha – 'The lion of Albania' and a legend for his cruelty – was an independent feudatory, ruling his Pashalik from Tepelenë south to Ioannina and Trikkala. 'The vizier received me in a large room paved with marble,' wrote Byron in a celebrated letter to his mother: 'A fountain was playing in the centre; the apartment was surrounded by scarlet ottomans. He received me standing, a wonderful compliment from a Mussulman, and made me sit down on his right hand . . . He said he was certain I was a man of birth, because I had small ears, curling hair and little white hands, and expressed himself pleased with my appearance . . .' Perhaps because Ali Pasha's admiration for Byron was coloured by stronger emotions than the expedients of diplomacy he is not in the great pantheon of official Albanian heroes, though he was quite as tough and successful as Skanderbeg. He hardly gets any official mentions; Tepelenë is not on the official itinerary; and Byron is scarcely accorded a footnote, despite the publicity he gave to the Albanian Souliot warriors.

At Gjirokastër history caught up – and not all of it of the official, highly adjustable kind. The town sits on a spur of mountain overlooking the river valley, in the northern part of Ali's Pashalik. It is an imposing sight, and it looks as Greek as anywhere in northern Ipiros. The roofs are of grey slate over white walls and the lines of buildings are broken by green trees and flowering bushes. In the old town one of our company discovered a number of Greek-speakers – much to the guides' displeasure – and was invited in for tea, cakes and honey.

One of the more spacious houses had been spruced up as the official birthplace of Enver Hoxha, though it is now thought he was born in a village several miles away. The museum inside was devoted to the National Liberation struggle, including group photographs of Hoxha and his comrades during the Partisan war. A number of faces had been crudely scratched out – comrades no longer considered so comradely who had been obliterated from its record for ever. Among those was Hoxha's right-hand man, Mehmet Shehu, Chairman of the Council of Ministers from 1954 to 1981, when he was allegedly killed in a strange shooting incident – which prompted an intriguing definition of democracy from Sali: 'Many years ago we had a Prime Minister who woke up one morning and realised the will of the people was against him so he went out and shot himself. That is democracy.' Somebody quickly asked if he meant Mehmet Shehu. He hesitated for some time before admitting that it might be.

The versions of Shehu's death are illuminating. Sali's version is the most extreme; others say he was shot by a firing-squad after being convicted of treason, or that he had a monumental argument with Hoxha over economic planning, culminating in a duel. The most frequent rumour has it that there was a shoot-out at an official banquet, and that Shehu had tried to murder Hoxha as a signal to start a *coup d'etat*. All are indicative of the air of mystery and suspicion that surrounds Hoxha – an effect compounded by a man claiming to have been his secretary and interpreter, who fled to Greece in 1987 and alleged that Hoxha had been paranoid at the end and a rampant homosexual.

Some of his early life parallels that of Tito. He was an NCO who founded the Communist Partisan groups of the national Liberation Front, and through skill in the field against the Italians he managed to win Allied support, in preference to resistance groups of nationalist and royalist parties. But unlike Tito he engendered deep mistrust from some of the Allied liaison officers, such as Colonel David Smiley of SOE, who regarded him as devious and paranoid as he strutted about in his specially designed uniform, cannabalised from tunics and equipment despoiled from dead Italians.

Hoxha appears to have embarked on a scheme of liquidation and terror during the civil war that raged at the same time as the campaigns against Germany. But the war museum in the huge fortress of Gjirokastër suggests some hard evidence for his belief that Albania was encircled by enemies. Its exhibits include an American plane said to have been shot down on a photo-reconnaissance flight from Greece in 1957; the camera can no longer be seen, and it seems likely that the plane was on a training flight when the pilot got lost in the mountains. In 1946 the British withheld Albanian gold reserves after two corvettes had been sunk by mines in the Corfu Channel. Forty-six lives were lost and in a complicated judgment the international court held Albania responsible for not sweeping the Channel – though the mines may have been Yugoslav. Negotiations to return the gold reopened in 1991. In 1961, a group of Albanian exiles tried to land by air and sea, only to be picked up, betrayed by the British spy, Kim Philby. In the early 1980s a similar enterprise was mounted by exiles from the United States, and also failed.

In the first hall of the museum we had seen more of the fabled Illyrians, the first Albanians. But little indication was given of who they really were. They were said to have existed in these hills and mountains in the sixth and seventh centuries BC, but of their distinctive dress of speech little evidence remains. The Illyrian warrior drawn on the diagram looked like any other soldier or hoplite of Sparta or Athens, while the inscriptions on the splendid site of Apollonia – where there once stood a shrine to Artemis, and later a Roman theatre and a Byzantine cathedral – suggested a thoroughly hellenised culture.

This does not mean that the Illyrians did not exist as a separate people and culture. Much secondary evidence from the classical world suggest that they were a very vigorous people; in the first decade after Christ an Illyrian rising was reported near Apollonia.

The search for the Illyrians is all the more frustrating given the elastic official policy towards Albania's past. This was especially evident at the most beautiful and extensive of the archaeological sites, at Butrint (or Butrinto) in the very south – a fortified town in shady woodland, founded, according to Virgil, by families fleeing after the capture of Troy. A fine medieval church stands on one side, and the entrance is marked by a Turkish customs house, established at the ferry port on the orders of Ali Pasha himself. Facing the lake on the other side, where boatmen now paddle slowly among the nets of the state fish farms, is a fine Roman barbican, the Lion Gate, with a wonderful relief of an African lion above it.

Almost without reason the path is cut by a long, freshly-mortared wall with bits of inscribed stone scattered among the tiles and brick. The whole structure seems to have been thrown together, like a child's construction toy, and the crazy-paving impression of the wall's surface to typify Albanian attitudes to the past, involving little documentation and research and a lot of contemporary guesswork.

The more recent past intruded when we stopped at the museum on the site. There I met an American Albanian, Stefani, who was visiting relations along with a tribe of her extended family from Boston. Her parents had been supporters and helpers of the great Fan Noli, a bishop educated at Harvard, who had been the reforming prime minister of Albania in 1924 – too reforming, for he was quickly turned out by Ahmet Zogu, who declared himself King Zog in 1928.

In America Noli became a champion of the church in exile and one of the greatest Albanian literary figures, writing an epic poem about the life of Skanderbeg. He was bishop by virtue of election by his flock as much as by appointment from above in the hierarchy, a feature quite common in the Orthodox world. Stefani had known Noli as an old man – he died in 1961 – and he taught her Albanian. The link caused our guides both curiosity and discomfort.

Stefani said her visit to her family was exhausting, and raised delicate matters of etiquette and tact. Like other visiting exiles from Australia and America we met, she insisted, on the 'great achievements of modern Albania, considering the past' – all this with a fixed toothpaste advertisement smile. 'You really mustn't compare the two experiences of America and here,' she concluded. 'It would be a pity if the whole world were taken over by McDonald's hamburgers; but on a day like this I could sure do with a Coca-Cola.'

The little dramas of our tour reached a climax at Korcë, the main city of south-east Albania and one with a stormy political past. Wedged between the central highlands of Albania and the mountain barrier of the frontier with Greece where Macedonia runs into north-eastern Ipiros round Florina, it had the most Balkan feel of any major town we visited. It had first been settled by a Turkish bey in the fifteenth century, providing caravanserai and a mosque on a highly lucrative stopping-point on the caravan route across the central Balkans.

A more recent visitor was Ahmet Zogu, King Zog, fleeing the Italians in 1939. The mountainous area around Korcë was then governed by tribal law and the vendetta was rife. Korcë itself had achieved a brief moment of independent glory after its occupation by French troops from Greece in 1916: the population had risen and declared the Autonomous Republic of Korcë, which lasted until 1920, the year of Zog's first rise to power (he was displaced briefly in 1924 by Fan Noli's reformist regime before declaring himself King in 1928).

Korcë has a special place in the official annals of the People's Socialist Republic because it was there that the first Communist group was established in 1930. Six years later police shot and killed a number of peasants taking part in a demonstration in the main square. On the same spot in 1943 Italian Fascist troops shot seventy protesters. Today the Square of Demonstrations is all but deserted for much of the day, and is watched over by perhaps the most underemployed traffic policeman in all of Albania.

Well before Albania became independent Korcë had, in 1878, provided the first school to teach Albanian, as well as a printing press and publishing house for the literary works of the nation's nineteenth-century cultural renaissance. Today it has one of the best historical museums in the land, with a particularly fine collection of sixteenth- and seventeenth-century icons, beautifully displayed.

The museum is in the old part of town, where the houses are of the late Ottoman style, with broad white fronts, gently pitched roofs, and creeper and vines trailing from eaves and balconies and windows encased in wooden shutters – houses for a mountain climate, cool in summer, snug and fortified against the tempests and snows of the winter. The charm and elegance of these dwellings contrasts sharply with ugly anonymity of the brick apartment buildings at the opposite end of town, many of which are so badly built that the outer walls seem to lean crazily like a cardboard packing case about to collapse, and on closer inspection the bricks seemed thin and crumbling after a relatively brief exposure to the weather.

That summer, something was clearly wrong in Korcë. On our arrival we were told of a monumental argument only a fortnight before between the Albtourist authorities and a Dutch group similar to ours, which had left the town before the prescribed circuit of visits had been completed. There was a shortage of important foods – most of the shops were closed in the morning, their shelves were bare, and the butchers were only open for an hour or two each day. By contrast, we came across a bookshop generously endowed with the works of Enver Hoxha, a number of them English, French and German. Like Stalin, Hoxha was a difficult act to follow, for only one very slim volume attributed to his successor, Ramiz Alia, was on sale. Like Talleyrand, Ramiz Alia's greatest achievement had been to survive; after nearly two years in the saddle, he was proving less than charismatic by comparison with his predecessor and there were very few *Lavde Ramiz Alia* hoardings on the main roads.

On our way to Korcë, we stopped at the town of Pogradec on Lake Ohrid. It was a Sunday; the lake was full of bathers and was heavily patrolled by militia boats in case they tried to swim to Yugoslavia. More numerous were the families who had come to the shore to wash themselves and or do the laundry. One of my strongest memories of Albania is of groups of women washing their clothes in open ditches and irrigation channels, dams and public fountains – suggesting that domestic water supplies were limited. Their effect on Lake Ohrid, combined with industrial waste, can be easily imagined.

Declining an invitation to swim in the lake, two of us went for a walk away from the shore, where we came across a child carrying an open pan from the public oven. Inside was what we took to be the Sunday meal – a pie made of scraps of beans, tomato, aubergine, cheese, the skin of a pepper and little or no meat (an indeterminate lump may have been a piece of chicken). It was difficult to establish for how large a family it was intended, but the girl was surrounded by three or four brothers and sisters. Our suspicions about food supplies were not allayed by what we saw in Korcë itself, where the standard fare of spaghetti was thinner and blander than usual, with limited helpings of tomato.

Privations had produced a powerful stoicism among the townspeople, who usually proved friendly. On the evening of our arrival we were invited in to a wedding reception in a tavern, where we drank the health of the bride in throat-burning local *raki*.

By now I had been isolated in a room of my own in the hotel, with Sali and Edi accommodated on either side. I reckoned I might stand a chance of meeting people going to the fields if I got up early enough, while the guides were sleeping. I headed through the old quarter to the edge of town, where women and young girls were picking tobacco. Some of their clothes were very ragged and they looked as if they might be migrant workers. The pickers smiled and posed for photographs, though they were unwilling to come too close for fear of the gang leader.

As I walked away through a plot of rough parkland, a man began to wave and gesticulate furtively. I ignored him, thinking him to be another of those jack-in-the-box security men of the Sigurimi police who popped up from behind bushes and hedgerows at every step. He came nearer and pointed towards a café, where he insisted on sitting me down for breakfast. The language barrier made this a less fruitful encounter than that with the Italian Club, but the warmth of the welcome was unmistakeable. My host indicated that he drove a truck, but suffered perpetual mechanical failures and a shortage of spare parts. Suddenly, he had a brain wave, he thought the barman – who was serving thick coffee and hunks of bread and cheese wrapped in paper for the workers' lunches – spoke a little French.

By now we had a little symposium of three workers, including my host and the barman, who insisted I took bread, coffee and raki for breakfast. A lookout was posted among the trees to watch for the approach of officialdom. The breakfast party, like the Italian Club, confirmed that they were foridden to speak to foreigners, and that they longed to communicate with strangers. We spoke a Babel of French, German, Italian, English and Albanian – though on the subject of Albanian censorship and restrictions on movement (people are not allowed to move from town to town and district to district without prior directive from above), one of the party resorted to the most direct language of all. 'This government,' he implied, putting his finger to his temple and twisting it in a universally recognisable gesture, 'crazy!'

The element of craziness never quite disappeared that entire day. In the morning we visited a knitting factory. Photography was forbidden, so eliciting an immortal line from one of our company: 'What's the difficulty? Why no photographs? Are you knitting a tank in there?' Inside the women were working on old Chinese and modern Italian and East German machines. In many of the spinning halls the conditions were less than salubrious, with floor, walls and tables covered with fluff. We were assured that this was not normal, that the place was cleaned up once a month, and the end of the month was approaching. Each room held displays of the knitter or weaver of the month – though workers were not encouraged to exceed their norm by more than a quarter. 'We do not encourage work as an end in itself – a very bourgeois idea,' affirmed one of the guides. No Stakhanovite heroes for Albania.

Strolling back to the hotel I passed through a square in which a genuine Turkish *han* or caravanserai was being restored and converted into shops and apartments. A little farther on I saw a man climb down from his horse-drawn van, tie the horses to a tree, and retire to a café. Similar to dozens in Turkey and Greece, the café was remarkable for the appearance of the men inside. Like the driver, they all wore moustaches, not a straggly workaday apologetic kind, or prissy toothbrushes or exhibitionistic handlebars of the western variety, but thick gleaming dark Balkan moustaches. They were none too pleased at my appearance, and even less so when they saw my camera. Round the corner was a queue of some fifty people, women, boys and girls, with cans and tins of various dimensions waiting for supplies of domestic paraffin or cooking fuel. The queue had been there, we later established, for some two or three hours.

I passed to the end of the street, and back towards the hotel, not attempting to raise the camera in such a public place. Suddenly a sweaty man in a cheap suit, flanked by one of the Sigurimi lookouts and informers, headed straight towards me like an angry wasp. 'What are you doing here?' he yelled in Italian, waving his arms at the queue and the restored Ottoman buildings. 'Why do you strangers always want to look at the bad old Albania. These terrible old houses. Things are changing. We have a new Albania with modern housing, why don't you go there?' he said, pointing towards some leaning stack of brick, one of the newer apartment blocks or warehouses. In his lapel gleamed the red and gold badge of the Party of Labour of Albania.

All this was but an overture to the main event of the afternoon – a visit to the co-operative farm of Drenove. This had been on the menu for some time, and I had particularly asked if we could make such a visit.

Agriculture in Albania is organised into collectives, co-operatives and higher state co-operatives – super farms, of which there are said to be over fifty, where no property or land is held privately. In 1982 about three-quarters of agricultural production came from Albania's 421 co-operatives. Albania is self-sufficient in bread, cereals, maize and wheat, and its valuable cash crops include fruit, tobacco, sunflowers and cotton.

Drenove was one of seven villages making up a co-operative of 9,000 hectares and 9,700 people. It sits on a wooded tongue of land below the mountains and opens onto a broad, fertile plain. As the bus hauled into the village, several people waved, at which the guides said that 'The people of Denove welcome you, would like to greet you, and want you to see their village.' I am not sure if what happened afterwards was the result of officious oafishness or downright incompetence. It was quite clear that the guides' message of greeting was not meant to be taken literally; language – the English they spoke so well – had undergone the elastic treatment given to Albanian history.

Taking the guides at their word, however, I set off towards the main village. The brick houses were camouflaged by private plots and gardens groaning with fruits and vegetables of all kinds – private enterprise was allowed, this being an ordinary co-operative and not of the more utopian higher state co-operative variety. The abundance of the gardens and allotments contrasted sharply with the bareness of the fields and the unkempt nature of the farm's principal orchards. At one house the family came forward and shook me by the hand, proudly displaying the house cow and posing for photographs. We managed to communicate our good wishes and were promptly invited inside a spotlessly clean living-room, comfortably furnished with rugs and chairs and a few family mementos. As I left, the lady of the house came running up with a glass of raki on a tray. We laughed and raised the glasses in the brilliant sunlight. It was a strangely solemn moment of true Balkan hospitality, with something of the formality of the East, of the Levant, rather than the superficiality of many Western greetings.

We were called away to the community museum, which was intended to be the official and only means of 'seeing' the village. The female guide toiled over the exhibits and photographs, a recitation of workers' movements in the Korcë region, the National Liberation Movement and the agricultural collectives. On the statistics of Drenove itself she was somewhat vague.

Our schedule had been disrupted by our scattering through the village – one group had nosed through some granaries to find a gang of women and children winnowing grain by hand. We were told we could walk through the fields along the main road and pick up the bus by an orchard.

As we walked through deserted, fallow fields, past a tangled orchard and a complex of byres and stalls devoid of livestock, Sali, the rougher of the guides, began a tirade. 'What kind of manners do you have?' he shouted, surprisingly breathless for such a fit man. 'How would you like it if I came to your country and walked into your house in the way that you have here with these people? Do you normally behave like this?' This inexplicable torrent went on for several minutes, and became increasingly personal. It was time for the right of reply to be invoked. I pointed out that toursts often visited the part of London I lived in and some came into my house (a cheap piece of tit-for-tat, I agree). The people I had met in Drenove had invited me to see their gardens and houses and to take raki with them, hospitality I really appreciated. The official response to my request to visit a co-operative farm had been less generous. We had been shown a museum where the guide did not know the statistics of the community, badly tilled fields, unkempt orchards and animal stalls conspicuously devoid of cattle. When were we going to have a few questions answered by somebody in charge?

We caught up with the rest of the party in a peach orchard, and the chairman of the administration was summoned. With a red-faced Sali translating, this august personage responded to my barrage of questions. The Co-operative Bajgesore 'Ruga Raytiyaneve' Drenove had 6000 sheep, 750 cattle (now moved to another village), 800 goats and 450 sheep, and produced maize, corn, fruit and other cash crops. The farm was divided into seven villages and four sectors, each with a sector leader. The sectors subdivided into work brigades of forty to sixty people, depending on the size of the task, under a 'brigadier'. Production was for home consumption or for the state. Work was calculated on a work-day unit for a wage of between 14 and 17 leks (about £1). Work days were added up at the end of the year for bonuses and penalties, and a worker was allowed a number of days in the year to tend his own plot. Income from sales was deposited in an accumulation fund.

The interview failed to clear up suspicions that much of the country's cattle farming was mismanaged. Meat was scarce in several towns in which we had stopped, and undernourished dairy cattle were being used as draught animals. The state distribution of vegetables was hardly running smoothly for tomatoes and vegetables were in short supply or glut, depending on the region and the season.

Relations with Sali were never recovered. He muttered something about things being different had the vendetta been still in force, but never explained why the arrangements at the co-operative were so inadequate or why the warmth of the impromptu meeting with villagers had proved such an insult to the fair name of Socialist Albania.

Back at the hotel I ran into another group of American Albanians. They explained the fixed toothpaste smiles I had noticed most of their kind wearing in our presence. Unless they smiled and extoled Albania, they had been told, they might not be allowed to visit the country and their families again.

We turned north for the last time, across the central mountains. On the way we passed through an oil-producing district, with clanking well donkeys, old locomotives and engines awash in black oil and gasoline. We we passed the steel plant at Elbesan, Sali revealed that the original Chinese mills had been so inefficient that they had had to be discarded and new equipment bought from Austria, Sweden and Canada, resulting in one of the most modern production systems of its kind in the world.

As the bus continued in its headlong charge, we began to understand why Kope was playing the part of a demented charioteer. He could afford such anti-social behaviour because he was not as other mortals, such as Edi and Sali. As a Party member, a guardian of the Shqiperia, the other two had to defer to him. When we reached our destination, the beautiful hill town of Berati, with its shuttered wooden houses, Kope made quite clear his feelings towards me by throwing my bags across the car park at the hotel, while we exchanged oaths in our respective vernaculars.

That evening Edi submitted himself to his last and most illuminating session of grilling. Hitherto his partner had suggested there was no crime in the Western sense, but only 'antisocial elements who would see their errors'. This time we heard about the army, the police, the security service or Sigurimi, people's courts and elected judges, and the dominant position of the minister of the interior. Execution was the penalty for treason, and prison existed, said Edi, 'because the class struggle continues'. The dictatorship of the proletariat was still some way off, he added, because of 'the low level of consciousness of the people'.

Edi offered no response to the allegations of Amnesty International about large concentration camps of political prisoners near Tirana. Albania was not a military dictatorship, he claimed, but 'all people were armed for the defence of their country.' But he thought Albania would slowly become less isolated. Relations with East Germany, Sweden and Hungary were good and brought much technological exchange, he said, and while difficulties existed with Britain over such matters as the retention of King Zog's gold bullion pending a settlement of the Corfu Channel incident, 'matters could only improve – and the door is open.' No relations with either Moscow or Washington could be contemplated, however, for they were 'the enemies of peace'. Within five years the tune changed as Tirana sought recognition from Russia and the USA.

A piquant footnote to our journey was provided when we visited Skanderbeg's stronghold at Krujë on our last day. Strategically placed above the main route from Shkodër to Durrës, Krujë is defended by a chain of wooded hills. Its fortress was held against the Turks by Skanderbeg's supporters for ten years after his death, before it and fell in 1478. In the main hall of the castle keep the visitor can see two Skanderbegs – the official heroic version, and a more informal, historical version. The official hero consists of a huge bronze statue, at least twice life-size, armour, buckled goat's horns and all. Behind him is a large and brilliant mural of one of his battles – as imaginative, highly coloured and clean and tidy as a Walt Disney costume movie. At the opposite end of the hall, a room of books and writings about the hero, and a wall covered with reproductions of prints and drawings by near-contemporaries, display a Skanderbeg as he might have been. In only a handful of these does he appear as a warrior in armour, with hardly a goat horn in sight. Most show him as a man of affairs, brought up by sultans and capable of negotiating with cardinals and popes. He wears the loose drapes and doublet and soft hat of a gentleman, a *galantuomo* of the Italian Renaissance, a contemporary of Lorenzo di Medici. The real man must have been so much more fascinating than the cardboard cut-out of modern Albanian propaganda: a man of letters and diplomacy, conversant in several tongues and one of the greatest innovators of defensive tactics in the history of arms.

By now it was time to leave the Shqiperia and return to a more international milieu. After a rousing toast of raki in the tavern at Shkodër, we headed for the frontier post, and a strange parting ceremony like a school prize-giving. Those deemed helpful and well-disposed to the Shqiperia were asked to return. I was not. But as we shook hands Edi waid with a grin, 'Well, it has been an experience.' At least I got back my copy of *La Republicca*.

In my brief sojourn in Tirana in August 1986, I had tried to visit the residence of the Italian Ambassador, on the scent of a curious tale. The year before the two sisters and four brothers of a family called Popa had sought asylum from the Italians, because they said their father had worked for the Duce's forces during the war. The Albanian authorities had demanded that the Italian Ambassador hand back the fugitives immediately. He declined and so was refused permission to leave the country.

Strolling through the diplomatic quarter, I was waylaid by the ubiquitous Sigurimi police who popped out of a doorway. One tried to effect an arrest, but the language barrier proved insurmountable, and since the afternoon was very hot and tiring the policeman let me go.

The Popa affair rumbled on. So irked was Ambassador Carlo Gentile by the presence of the two Popa sisters in particular that he withdrew to his room, and eventually had to be sent back to Italy suffering from nervous exhaustion. In May 1990 the Popa family were allowed to leave Albania after the personal intervention by the UN Secretary General, Senor Javier Perez de Cuellar. This gesture was to have an electrifying effect – the lightning strike that was to set the house on fire.

From the previous winter with the breach of the Berlin Wall and the fall of the Ceauscescus in Romania, small stirrings of opposition had been heard in the land of the Shqiperia. In the Greek villages of the south of the country Sigurimi security police had gone into the squares to announce through loudhailers that, whatever was happening elsewhere in Europe and the Balkans, it would not be tolerated in Albania.

By the following summer the regime did not seem so sure, and Ramiz Alia himself began to hint at reform. With the release of the Popas the initiative was taken from him. Within a matter of two months thousands were invading the embassies in Tirana to demand asylum and a passage to Italy, Yugoslavia, Germany, or almost anywhere that the supplicant had heard of. In all some five thousand got away by train, coach and ferry. In February 1991 thousands descended on the port of Durrës, believing ferries would be provided to take them to Italy. Some fourteen thousand arrived in the port of Brindisi, much to the consternation of the Italians, who had nowhere to put them. Many fugitives had little more than the clothes they were wearing.

In March 1991 elections were held for the legislature in Tirana. Private businesses were licensed, Enver Hoxha's widow and her cronies were purged from the politburo. In the elections the communists won the countryside with ease, though they struggled in the towns – and even President Alia lost his seat. In the aftermath, ugly signs of the old Albanian method of settling disputes, the vendetta, reappeared. Three opposition candidates in the election were murdered.

The election left the communists in charge, but only just and with their grip on Albania slipping fast. The antiquated industry of the country was worse than that in Romania. And the population has been growing quicker than any other in Europe. By the end of the century it was expected to top five million. After the rigid certainties of Hoxha's regime of paranoia for nearly forty years, the republic of the eagles faces a future as unpredictable as any in the Balkan neighbourhood.

Five: Greece

i Who Are the Greeks?

SAILING south from Corfu – I had resumed my journey from Dubrovnik into Greece the roundabout way via Italy – the distant peaks of Ipiros gleamed under caps of snow. Part of that natural bastion shielded Dodona, the oldest amphitheatre in Greece today, where the Dorians worshipped Zeus among sacred groves of oaks three thousand years ago.

The Dorians later went on to conquer the entire Greek peninsula; they are said to have produced the blonde athletes who epitomised physical beauty in the classical world. Who were the Dorians and how exactly are they related to the modern Greeks?

Few people are more acutely aware of their identity and the differences between their culture and that of the world around them than the Greeks. But the story of the Greeks from ancient and medieval times to the present day is as strange and as fragmented as their land itself, a jumble of mountains and plains where the Balkan peninsula run out in a ragged fringe, and two thousand islands, scattered like the beads of a broken necklace across the eastern waters of the Mediterranean.

Some make their living from airing and discussing the great Greek paradox. Nikos Demou was a prosperous advertising executive in Athens with his own firm until runaway success with a series of books, essays and articles on the Greek identity crisis enabled him to earn a more than comfortable living as a journalist and belletrist.

Demou thinks the thread of continuity between ancient and modern Greeks lies in the language. It is claimed that no major language of the Mediterranean is as close to its classical forebear as modern Greek – though it must be said that intellectuals in the Independence struggle against the Turks in the last century tried to reinvent the classical tongue in the high formal language beloved of lawyers in Greece today and known as *katharevousa*. 'Take the word *thalassa* [the sea],' Demou argues: 'It's origins are older than classical Greek. It was used by the ancients, and modern Greeks use exactly the same word when they look at the same shores and waters.'

Many disagree with Demou and argue that the rise of the Byzantine Empire and of Constantinople as the centre and symbol of the Greek Orthodox faith, and the dramatic hiatus of four hundred years of occupation of mainland Greece by the Ottoman Empire, were more significant in shaping the modern nation. The process of assembling the modern national territory of Greece was completed only comparatively recently when the islands of the Dodecanese in the eastern Aegean, including Rhodes, were granted to Greece after the Second World War in 1947.

The struggle for liberation from the Turks, beginning with the War of Independence which Byron helped to advertise so effectively, is full of oddities and contradictions. A Greek friend whose ancestors fought in the war – 'mere bandits from the mountains,' he says with a chuckle – loves to remind me that most of the fighters for Greek freedom could hardly manage a word of Greek. He recounts that in one of the naval engagements – the Battle of Eli, in 1829 – the commander of the Greek forces gave the order to fire in Albanian: 'Vas'. A century later his grandson, a Greek admiral, repeated the same order when his ships engaged a German flotilla in order to give his fellow-Greeks a sense of historical continuity.

The birth places of two of the most prominent statesmen in the recent history of Turkey and Greece present a pleasing incongruity. Kemal Ataturk, the founder of the modern Turkish republic, was born in 1881 in Salonika, then part of the Ottoman domain and now the second city of the Greek Republic; while Constantine Karamanlis, who restored full parliamentary democracy after the collapse of the Colonels' dictatorship in 1974, was born in 1907 in Serres, about forty miles north-east of Salonika, when it was still part of the Turkish empire.

Even when all of mainland Greece had won its independence, the course of history did not run smooth for the Greeks. It was to be marked by upheavals, setbacks and disasters, all of which had profound effects on attitudes today.

Great cities like Athens and Salonika were particularly affected by the influx of refugees following the defeat in 1922 of Greek forces by the Turks in Asia Minor – still referred to as the Catastrophe – and by the turmoil in the countryside caused by the civil war from 1946 to 1949. The Catastrophe caused one and a half million Greeks to leave their homes in Asia Minor – the majority from Smyrna on the Aegean, which the Turks renamed Izmir after its capture by Ataturk. The minority of Turks in Crete were made to go to Turkey, many of them reluctantly, in the ensuing population exchange.

The blood-letting of the civil war followed the bitter experience of the war against the Axis, in which the Greeks had triumphed at first, over the Italians, though the occupation by the Germans brought terrible privations, the slaughter of the Jewish community of Salonika and star-vation to thousands in Athens. The defeat of the communist forces in the civil war inspired one of the most persistent myths of the Hellenic left. The communists of EAM-ELAS felt that they had not been defeated in a fair fight, but had been betrayed by unenthusiastic allies such as Tito and Stalin. More decisive was the intervention of the Americans on the side of the royalist right, following the enunciation of the Truman Doctrine in 1947. Truman won $400 million from Congress to fight communism in Greece and Turkey. The funds provided the royalists with an air force with which to strafe the *andartes*, the commu-nist fighters, in their last mountain strongholds.

The victory of the right led to a period of almost hysterical repression and the jailing of political dissidents. 'Reds were seen not under the bed but above it, on every street corner, and in the *kafenion*,' explained a friend who was disenfranchised in the process. The last fling of the right came with the military coup of 1967 and the vicious farce of the Colonels' dictatorship.

The formal process of reconciliation following the civil war has been completed only recently. When he returned from exile to re-establish parliamentary democracy, Constantine Karamanlis legalised the Com-munist Party. In 1983 Greece's first socialist government of the Pasok party, under Andreas Papandreou, introduced an amnesty allowing all communist combatants in the civil war and their supporters and families to return home after nearly a generation of exile.

For all the cruelty, conflict and bloodshed of their recent past, Greeks pride themselves on being essentially part of Western European civilis-ation. This in turn produces a paradox, which was summed up succinctly for me by a former Minister of Education, Antonis Tritsis, a man with wild hair and moustache reminiscent of the warriors who had first set Greece free, whose parliamentary seat embraced the islands of Cepha-lonia and Ithaca – the home of Odysseus. 'Greece,' he explained, 'is Balkan but not Slav, Levantine but not Muslim, Christian and European but not Catholic nor Protestant.'

Theodore Pangaloss, who was the witty deputy Foreign Minister responsible for relations between the Papandreou government and the EC, sees Greece as Europe's frontier in the eastern Mediterranean and firmly believes that Asia begins at the Bosphorus with Turkey. 'After all,' he argues, 'Europe has to end somewhere. If Turkey were to join the European Community [for which Ankara applied in April 1987] then we might say in the first years of the next century that between one in three and one in two "Western" Europeans will be a Turk!' He believes that Greece brings a much-needed element of Mediterranean civilisation to the Economic Community, which otherwise would be preoccupied with such mundane northern European obsessions as motor car or chemical production, and the dairy cow, on which Brussels Eurocrats have spent more than a third of the total Common Agricultural Policy budget.

Moving on to the question of population numbers, Theodore Pangaloss touches the tenderest point in the debate about the identity of the modern Greeks. In the mid 1980s the population of Greece stabilised at about ten million and now shows every indication of decline. In the days of the Ottoman period the great centres of Greek culture and commerce were outside the traditional homelands of Macedonia, Roumelia, Thessaly, the Peloponnese and the islands. The Greeks had been long established in Odessa, Alexandria, Cairo, Beirut, Byblos, Tyre, Sidon, Smyrna and Constantinople/Istanbul itself. Poetry and music came from these places. The bouzouki, which hailed from the highlands of Anatolia, or the mournful dirges of the rebetika, which originated in the hashish dens of Alexandria, Cairo and Smyrna, are what the tango is to Buenos Aires or the blues to New Orleans. The Greek populations of these great cities are now sadly diminished or gone altogether, leaving them much duller places. Today some of the greatest concentrations of Greeks are to be found in the new diaspora: New York and Melbourne are among the biggest Greek cities in the world.

While Greek numbers stabilise or decline, the population of Turkey is expected to top seventy million by the the turn of the century. When I mentioned this to a Greek friend during the visit by Turgut Ozal to Athens in June 1988 – the first by a Turkish Prime Minister to Greece in thirty-six years – she replied, almost absent-mindedly, 'Ah well, the barbarians were always many and we Greeks rather few.'

In raising such an ancient concept she had touched on the essence of Greekness in the eyes of most Greeks, which lies in their language and culture. For them the world is divided between Greek-speakers, and barbarians babbling in strange tongues.

The essential quality of language, the language of the ancients, transmitted to the moderns, in the Greek sense of onthology (as the philosophers termed the science of being) is the theme of The Passion, one of the greatest works of Odysseus Elytis, who won the Nobel Literature Prize in 1979:

Greek the language they gave me;
poor the house on Homer's shores.
My only care my language on Homer's shores.
There bream and perch
windbeaten verbs,
green sea currents in the blue,
all I saw light up my entrails,
sponges, jellyfish
with the first words of the Sirens,
rosy shells with the first black shivers.
My only care my care with the first black shivers . . .

ii Athens

If there is such a thing as the University of Life, then Kolonaki Square in Athens must be one of the most agreeable parts of the campus. Its architecture is unremarkable – bland façades of apartments and offices above gleaming boutiques. The serious business is conducted in the cafés, with their rows of padded seats like cinema stalls, sprawling under the trees and heavy awnings.

The commerce of the cafés is gossip, political and philosophical, speculation metaphysical and mundane, the price of the next drink and the meaning of life. Quizzed about the credentials of a rising star in the Greek diplomatic service, a friend once replied that he had been trained in the best of schools, had a good degree and had conducted an excellent course of postgraduate research in the cafés of Kolonaki.

The friend in question is Haris Bousbourelis, a remarkable chronicler of life in Athens since the Second World War. His French and English are as good as his Greek, and his observations of the Greek political scene have long graced the columns of the centre-left paper *Vima*, of which he was once editor.

Like many Athenians, Haris traces his origins elsewhere. He takes particular pride in the generations of his mother's family who lived in Constantinople. Much of his own life in Athens has been shaped by geographical accident and the turmoil of Greece's recent political past. His linguistic accomplishments he attributes largely to the necessity of reading in English and French political text books which the rightist regimes banned in Greek after the civil war.

One day as we strolled towards the Plaka, the medieval quarter now being gradually sanitised by the tourst industry, Haris suddenly exclaimed 'Look, during the civil war we lived in that quarter. Had we lived a few hundred metres away we would have been in the hands of the Communist forces of EAM-ELAS and my life would have been very different. When we played football in the streets here we could hear the gunfire in the distance beyond Kolonaki and we knew we had fifteen minutes to finish the game before the fighting reached our houses.'

The divisions and rancour of the civil war still shape Greek politics. As a minister in Churchill's War Cabinet, Harold Macmillan saw the first sparks of the conflict during a visit in Christmas 1944, when Communist ELAS partisans refused to hand over their arms and began to fire on British paratroopers. In the preface to his diaries of the period, he wrote, 'In Greece I found something that I hardly realised the existence of before: the bitter animosities, lasting for generations, which divided the political world.' To him the modern Greeks were tied to the cycle of tyranny, oligarchy and democracy as much as their ancient forebears described by Aristotle; above all, they had a taste for the politics of vengeance.

The vendetta of right against left following the civil war brought unsuspected benefits to some of its victims, as Haris suggests in a favourite anecdote. 'Look, I have a friend, a businessman whom you would call filthy rich, and he still votes communist. He used to be a civil servant, and could have expected to retire with the lowly pension of a Grade B principal officer. But they kicked him out because of his politics. He became a wealthy man, and has voted communist ever since in gratitude.'

According to Haris, Greece became a truly modern democracy only recently, after the fall of the military junta in 1974. Only since than has elected local government been extended to the whole country – after the civil war remote rural areas were firmly under the thumb of governors and villages under the eye of the gendarmes, who might even take it upon themselves to ensure that the votes went the right way in national elections.

Since 1974 the parliamentary scene has been dominated by two party blocs and their charismatic leaders, Constantine Karamanlis, whose conservative New Democracy party governed for seven years before giving way to Andreas Papandreou's Pan Hellenic Socialist Movement, Pasok. The smooth transition between the two might suggest that Greece is a parliamentary democracy, like any other in Europe but this would be to ignore the nature of Greek politics both inside parliament and out.

Both New Democracy and Pasok are portmanteau parties with many factions and compartments, whose fortunes have depended on the authority and popular appeal of their leaders. Beyond them are the two Communist parties – the Moscow-line KKE with around 10 per cent of the vote, and the smaller but more accessible Euro-Communist party, KKS. The Euro-Communists seem to have something of the intellectual grace of ancient Greece in their fond belief in debate and Socratic dialogue. They were founded by Leonidas Kirkos, a former partisan who had suffered years of detention and privation during the civil war and under the Colonels. He speaks of his experience without rancour, now firmly believing in open democracy rather than the Marxist route of armed struggle, and has taken a seat in the European as well as the Athens parliament – teaching himself good English and French at a late age to equip himself for the part.

The spirit of the Euro-Communists was summed up by a wonderful row during the elections of 1985 between Haris Bousbourelis and his friend Sofionos Chrisostimedes, editor of the Euro-party paper *Av Gi*. Brought up in Alexandria, where his family lived for generations, Sofionos has flawless French and a wonderful profile, his long aquiline nose and gentle mouth a caricature of Levantine Greek melancholy. The cause of the fracas was Haris suggesting that the Euro-Communists could have three or four seats in the new parliament as the other parties were campaigning so badly. 'Quite terrible,' exploded Sofionos, 'they would be utterly corrupted. Do they think they are in politics for power?'

The murkier side of politics is reflected in the growth of terrorism in Greece over the past decade, both from home-grown groups and gangs from the Middle East, principally Palestinian extremists. The November 17th movement takes its name from the day in 1973 when police bloodily put down a protest in the Athens Polytechnic. November 17th has been responsible for murdering prominent bankers, businessmen and security officers. Little headway was made by the police in identifying its leadership or curtailing its gang's operations.

The Administration of Ronald Reagan thought the Greeks almost wilfully slack on security measures. In a space of fifteen years a CIA station chief and a US military attaché were murdered in Athens, but even worse for the Americans were the actions of Middle Eastern groups, including the band of Shi'ite Lebanese who hijacked a TWA airliner from Athens to Beirut in 1985, and an indiscriminate attack in 1988 on passengers of a ferry returning from the island of Aegina to Piraeus in which eight were shot dead, many more injured and the vessel set on fire, which was almost certainly the work of the extremist Abu Nidal Palestinian group.

At one point the Americans suspected that the Greeks had arranged a secret 'sweetheart' deal with Abu Nidal whereby his men would be given safe passage provided no attacks were carried out on Greek soil – but this was never substantiated. Suspicion of American motives in spreading such suggestive rumours is part of the folk lore of the Greek left, who believe that the right won the civil war because of American intervention in 1947, and that elements of the CIA were behind the Colonels when they took over in 1967.

The home-grown brand of terrorism practised by November 17th seems to have developed from PAK, the resistance movement to the Colonels junta – from which Pasok was to emerge into legitimate parliamentary politics. Some members of PAK had strong ties with the Palestinian Liberation Organisation, to whom they turned for training.

The stark contrast between the very old and the very modern in Greek society is best displayed in the monster rallies which conclude election campaigns in cities like Patras, Salonika and, above all, Athens. Supporters of the different parties vie with each other in volume and noise; in the case of the two biggest parties, Pasok and New Democracy, they carry the colours of the circus factions, the Blues and the Greens, who fought running battles through the streets of old Byzantium. To the balcony and rostrum, the traditional forums of Mediterranean politics, have been added television and the motor vehicle. For the final rallies in Constitution Square each party tries to assemble the largest crowd, purely for the benefit of television rather than to its leader's words of wisdom. Such was the roar of fireworks and the blare of klaxons, the deluge of leaflets and streamers, that no one could have heard a single coherent phrase of Prime Minister Andreas Papandreou's concluding speech in 1985, for which thousands of people were hauled into Athens from the fringes of Attica and Thessaly in cars and coaches paid for by the party.

At the rally of the opposition New Democracy the new breed of young Athenian most clearly showed its colours. Many of its cheerleaders wore the same streaked blonde hair, designer jeans, jogging suits, blazers and cravats as their peers in Sloane Square in London, Parioli in Rome or the 16ième in Paris – these were the upwardly mobile descendants of Timon and Alcibiades, the Hellenist yuppies.

Modern Athens has much in common with most other European capitals – but it is also something of a monster, an adolescent grown beyond its strength and not quite in control of itself. Athens, the port of Piraeus and their suburbs house nearly four million people – almost 40 per cent of the total Greek population. Attempts to establish a coherent urban plan for Athens has proved politically impossible. When the radical architect Antonis Tritsis was the Pasok Minister for the Environment he ordered shanty towns on the outskirts of the city to be removed so as to establish a green belt of open parkland but such was the outcry from building contractors and developers that he was forced to resign from the cabinet. Times change. Tritsis became Mayor in 1991 on an environmentalist platform backed by the conservatives.

The sense of muddle is made worse by atmospheric pollution, which hangs like a dirty band of fog over the city on most summer days, trapped between the hills to the north and the sea. By 1987 the pollution from cars and factory exhausts was often double the danger limit set by the World Health Organisation of 200 micrograms of nitrogen dioxide per cubic metre. The first thing many Athenians do on rising in summer is to look at the state of the *nefos* or cloud. Governments have tried in vain to restrict traffic in the city, while attempts have been made to cut daytime emissions from factories, since more than half of Greece's industry is sited on the Attica basin.

The *nefos*, combined with ferocious heatwaves, puts hundreds of people in hospital with respiratory and heart difficulties. The most conspicuous inanimate victim is the Parthenon, bandaged in scaffolding against the mordant smog. Fears that the Elgin Marbles too could become victims are said to have discouraged the authorities from too energetic an insistence on their return from the British Museum.

Seen from the Plaka, the slopes leading up to the Acropolis still resemble that village, as it might have been painted by Edward Lear or David Roberts. With its crowds and charging traffic and filthy smog, Athens exhibits advanced symptoms of a malady afflicting other great cities of the Mediterranean and involving the relentless march of the motor vehicle and waves of immigrants from the countryside. But more than most other great cities, Athens has remained a collection of villages – which is both its virtue and vice.

One of the hangovers from the village are the kiosks, wood and iron buildings with green shutters which guard the pavements and squares like Kolonaki and Syntagma. Ostensibly they sell papers, sweets and tobacco. 'Look,' explains Haris Bousbourelis, 'they are the most wonderful examples of rural ingenuity. In that small space you can find a welfare service supplying biscuits, shoelaces, bandages and plasters, toothpaste, razor blades, aspirin, a telephone, a message service and all the latest rumours.'

Haris believes the Greeks are very tied to their rural past, though others with a vested interest in promoting the new Athenian might disagree. Evi Evangelidou is a jolly bustling woman, immensely proud of her origins in the Greek community of Bulgaria. Until it was closed down by the Colonels, she hosted Greece's first live television show about women's matters. She then started her own highly successful public relations agency, and sat for New Democracy on Athens City Council. Eli thinks many young Athenian couples are prepared to divide domestic chores like cooking, cleaning and child-rearing – 'But I don't imagine too much has changed out in the country,' she adds. Haris disagrees: Greeks still prize and spoil the eldest male child more than any other Mediterranean society, a relic from life in the country where a property of inheritance could be dissipated in dowries for girls. The male heir is still a prince, he explained one morning, after suffering from an outbreak at home. 'Look, I asked at breakfast if there were any croissants, but my mother-in-law said "No." So how about those on the shelf – six of them, if I'm not mistaken? The old lady immediately replied that they were for Paniotis, my son, her eldest grandson. "He was late last night and didn't have any – and the shops might not be open tomorrow, so none for you," she stated, firmly putting me in my place.'

Another anchor to the past is the Orthodox Church, still surprisingly important to the new Athenian. In the election campaign of 1985 a survey carried out for the New Democracy campaign by an American agency, Sawyer's of New York, suggested that by the 1990s religion would be one of four key factors determining which way the majority of Greeks cast their votes.

Anastasios, Bishop of Androussa and the head of the Theological School in Athens, is a brilliant interpreter of the Orthodox Church old and new. Unusually, for Orthodoxy can be as exclusive as some branches of Judaism, he is interested in comparative religion, speaks several languages, and has undertaken missions to other Balkan states and East Africa. I went to see him at the Theological School, but before I arrived he had prepared for me three short homilies.

The first dealt with the structure of the church and the role of the bishop, who beside being the representative of the church universal was the leader of the local community and responsive to its wishes – 'the Greek word *ecclesia*, which we use for the church, means a gathering of communities.' The church was also the body of Christ according to St Paul – who had spoken to Greeks in Greek, a fact of the utmost historical importance, the Bishop told me. For the church had given new life and vigour to decaying Greek culture and to the thought of the classical era. 'The platonic conception of good was provided with a new breadth and depth . . . The message of Paul in Athens was revolutionary in the new possibilities it offered to the evolution of Greek thought.' A novel emphasis was placed on freedom and love, through a personal relationship with God, and with Christ the redeemer. 'At first,' according to the bishop, 'the story of the resurrection scandalised our Athenians.'

Today the Orthodox churches are once again adapting old themes and breaking new ground in their approach to the sects of Islam in the Middle East, emphasising common historical and theological roots. The figures of the angels and devils depicted in the Koran, the Bishop suggested, were borrowed directly from Greek Orthodox teaching at the time of the Prophet Mohammed. In Palestine and Jordan Christian Orthodox communities had lived harmoniously with their Arab neighbours for centuries after the rise of Islam, providing advisers and administrators for the Ommayad Caliphs of Damascus.

In Greece itself the Orthodox Church is believed to have been trying to reconcile itself to its Marxist opponents through a movement called 'Neo-Orthodoxy'. To see this as a Greek version of the Liberation Theology of Latin America is a mistake, according to Bishop Anastasios. Neo-Orthodoxy, he says, is a label of convenience attached to a series of debates between churchmen and Marxist sociologists interested in the social ethic of Orthodoxy in the Greek community today.

The notion of a reconciliation with Marxists is a bitter paradox, for the Greek Orthodox Church has been viewed as both champion and villain in the struggle for political liberty over the centuries. Under Turkish rule it was seen as the leader of the intellectual underground, keeping Greek culture alive and promoting the struggle for national independence, yet its critics say the attitudes of the church during Ottoman oppression ensured that the Greek people were cut off from the intellectual revolution of the Renaissance in western Europe.

This view was given violent expression by the *andartes*, the guerrillas of the Communist EAM-ELAS in the civil war. They saw the parish priests as petty tyrants of the church and schoolroom. Their mark of superiority as the leading, and often only, lettered adult in the village was the long uncut nail on the little finger, indicating that the hand was for writing not digging – a badge of rank I have come across several times in my journeys in the Levant, most notably among the Shi-ite communities in Beirut. The long finger-nail was the mark of the enemy for the Communists in the civil war, inviting torture and death for dozens of priests.

Bishop Anastasios embodied the duality of Orthodox thought – a powerful feature of cultures throughout the eastern Mediterranean, embracing the universal and the local, the spiritual and the practical, the ethical and the metaphysical, the ethereal and the mundane. It is entirely different from the habits of mind of the Western churches and their cultures, Roman Catholicism especially. The Orthodox see the Roman church as rigidly hierarchical in its emphasis on obedience to the Pope and in its structure, and narrow and reductive in its view of the world – which they put down to the distortion of Aristotle's logic by the theologians of the Middle Ages such as Aquinas. In Western Catholicism the opposite of orthodox teaching is heresy, whereas in the Levant it is heterodoxy, a contrasting but not illegal opinion.

Though no great theologian, my friend Haris Bousbourelis, with his ancestry among the *fanariotes*, the Greek merchants with their grand houses along the Golden Horn, sees Constantinople as the capital in exile of Greek identity. To this day, when a male child is baptised in Greece, the words 'May he ride into the city' (*Asti poli cavalaris*) are pronounced; once the 'city' had fallen to the Turks, Greeks were forced to dismount on entering its walls.

Some of the flavours and aromas of old Constantinople have been preserved and pickled in a shambling building in the centre of Athens, the home of the Gerofinikas restaurant. Most of the staff come from three large families, exiles from the island of Imros, one of the two Aegean islands at the entrance to the Sea of Marmara granted in 1931 to the Turks, who changed its name to Gokceada. Much of its bomhomie and cosmopolitan hospitality is due to the personality of the *maitre d'hôtel*, who moves between the dining-room, the cellars and the kitchen with theatrical elegance, a Byzantine Maurice Chevalier. Bernard Ballini is a walking encyclopedia of the dining and cooking habits of the eastern Mediterranean, of Anatolia, Constantinople, the Aegean and the Balkans – all 'kitchens' (as he refers to cuisine and gastronomy) he has known intimately.

As his name implies, his family saga is also a rich and varied tale embracing much of the eastern sea: 'My great-great-grandfather left the island of Skiros to go to Egypt, his son went to Italy then his son left for Philippopoulis in Bulgaria, and my father and myself we were born in Constantinopole.' The family named Ballini was acquired when the islands were under the rule of the Venetians, and since that time the family have been baptised Catholics – hence the Christian name Bernard.

By the trays of fresh fish, vegetables and *hors d'oeuvres* Bernard Ballini took me on a gastronomic tour of the eastern Mediterranean, through the Aegean to Byzantium and Istanbul, the shores of Araby, the Balkans and the Russian steppes. The most truly Greek elements of his kitchen were the *hors d'oeuvres*, dolmades, taramasalata, and tzadziki. The Aegean was represented by swordfish, sea bass, crayfish, red snapper, and red mullet – the most delicate fish of all, whose name in Greek, *barbounia*, he rolled round his mouth with special affection.

With the meat dishes, heavily influenced by Turkish cuisine, we plunged almost inevitably into cultural controversy. While admitting the impact of Turkish taste on modern Greek cooking, Bernard Ballini hastened to suggest that the Turks had borrowed heavily from the Arabs in the use of hot spices, and from the Byzantines in the cooking of meat stews, though their Islamic faith forbade them pork, a favourite in old Constantinople. 'So you can see we get from the Turks too much spice, and too much lamb,' he concluded, damning with faint praise.

Greeks and Turks are united in a common approach to preparing kebab, dolmades and coffee, and divided in claiming and naming the process for their own. More surprising was the emphasis he placed on the Slav origins of the preparation of most Greek meat dishes – the use of the grill and the speared lumps of meat known as souvlaki. These originated in the mountain village communities of the north – in a world now largely disappeared.

In the summer of 1990 Papandreou lost the general election, which no party won outright. In all it was to take three elections over ten months before the conservative New Democracy party took power. Meanwhile serious charges of corruption and abuse of office were brought against Andreas Papandreou, and two of his former ministers were jailed. They had been involved in the spectacular fraudulent collapse of the Bank of Crete run by a young entrepreneur George Koskotas, who fled to America. Asked to explain the disappearance of some $130 million, the banker said he had been suborned by Pasok ministers. Policemen told of ferrying bundles of banknotes in baby's diaper boxes to ministerial homes. Papandreou himself seemed negligent or at best careless. His attentions, it was said, were too much taken up with his new dalliance with a pneumatic former air stewardess, Dimitra Liani, possessed of the improbable nickname of 'Mimi'. In failing health he married her after his election in the summer of 1989. At the age of eighty-four, Constantine Karamanlis became President of Greece for a second term in 1990 – though the powers of the office were greatly reduced from when he previously held it.

The indecisive election result in the summer of 1989 was to close the book on the bitterness and division of the civil war. For the brief autumn months of that year Greece was governed by a national government of the main parties, including the two communist groups. The grand coalition ordered the destruction of more than two million files on suspected subversives of the left from the civil war and the repressions of the right in its aftermath. So great was the documentation in the archives of the police, interior ministry and secret service, that a convoy of trucks had to be hired to shift the tonnage of paper to an industrial plant on the outskirts of Athens, which had the only furnace in Greece large enough to destroy the material.

iii   Mountains and the North: Metsovo, Salonika, Athos

My entry into Metsovo was less than triumphant, with the car tobogganing down through swirling mist and blizzard from the mountain highway above. The main road snaking through the high pass had been littered by lorries stuck in solid ice or drifts of snow – hazards ensnaring unwary winter travellers on what had long been the main route from Europe into Asia Minor.

The houses are typical of northern Greece, with heavy grey stone façades and roofs like cowls weighed down with snow, hugging winding alleys which become cobbled glissades in winter. Metsovo's people once made their living from guarding the road across the saddle of the mountain ridge that runs from Ipiros and the Albanian border to Thessaly in the south. In Roman, Byzantine and Ottoman times, horses and mules were changed and fed, their cargoes sheltered, and masters and drivers victualled and protected from marauding beasts and bandits.

In winter the migrant shepherds moved their flocks down from the mountains to the lowlands round Trikala. The women stayed behind to tend family and hearth when the village lay under siege from the snow – hence their nickname of 'white widows'. Today the movement of men and flocks, has slowed to a dribble, with only about 15,000 beasts making the annual pilgrimage to Trikkala – and usually by truck for at least part of the way.

Metsovo is one of the most prosperous communities in northern Greece with a growing population – highly unusual in a region where most villages are fading fast, and many have been abandoned altogether. Tradition here sits easily with the new. In the main square, the *plaka*, old men sit like bandit kings on the benches below the great plain trees, the symbols of Ipiros, while mules and donkeys park next to tractors and trucks outside the *kafenion*.

No sooner had I arrived on that frozen night than I was offered tradition mountain hospitality in the taverna in the form of a Metaxa brandy and a cappuccino (spelled out in Greek on a tariff board) on the house. Eventually I was collected by a friend, whose house was a splendid stone affair at the top of the town. The main rooms, with their wooden walls, glowed with warmth from stoves and fires, the chairs and benches were covered with rugs, like Ottoman divans. On my arrival my hostess said, 'We must sit down together for a few minutes, and have something to drink perhaps. You are a stranger, and we must get to know each other. It is the custom of the region.' Any demurral on my part would have offended an old and sacred code of hospitality. The last time I had been bidden to sit as part of a formal greeting had been in Palermo, more than twenty years before.

Some idea of what gracious living was like in Metsovo in Ottoman times can be gleaned from the house of the Tositsa family, who made their fortunes in cotton in Egypt. Together with the Averoffs, another powerful clan from the region, they established a foundation which is a principal source of wealth and patronage in the village. The mansion of Michael Tositsa is now a museum, and one of the finest examples of late Ottoman housing still in existence in Europe.

Outside the house is adorned with wooden ornaments, shutters and casements; within are divans and recesses, including a tiny minstrels' gallery for a gypsy band – well away from the bed, lest their presence prove too noisome. Exquisite miniatures, chests for dowries (still common in the village), accoutrements, ornaments, arms – among them an axe belonging to Ali Pasha of Ioannina – all tell the story of the shepherds and their martial lords. A naive painting chronicles the almost obligatory tale of romance and brigandage – the kidnap and ransom in 1884 of Evdokia or 'Doukou', beloved daughter of Nicholas Averoff.

The richly embroidered dowry shawls and rugs often recite a family tree or genealogical history. Many are not strictly Greek nor Turkish but come from the Vlachs, a Balkan shepherd people who make up a sizeable portion of the Metsovo populace. Many women still wear brightly-coloured bodices and heavily embroidered skirts as they herd their animals or steadily hack the earth or clomp slowly up the streets, as if bending into the wind or climbing a mountain path.

One morning I woke to hear an almost familiar clucking of voices beneath the window. A group of Vlach women were chewing over the week's events. I picked out the word 'semana', a cousin of the Latin 'septimana' or week: the Vlachs' dialect has a Latin base, as they are believed to have been one of the tribes deployed by the Romans to guard the Danube frontier. The Vlach patois is generally supposed to be entirely oral, but a literary form may have existed – suggesting it might have been a language related to modern Romanian. Traces of a large encampment, Beritoari, high in the Ipirot mountains was discovered several years ago by English scholars, who believe it shows the Vlachs had a substantial culture. But obtaining official permission to investigate further has been a slow business in such a sensitive frontier area.

The warm woollen skirts and exquisitely embroidered and braided bodices have become a craft industry promoted by the Tositsa-Averoff Foundation and one year the entire stock was bought for the Paris collections by Yves Saint Laurent. The Foundation also patronises a cheese-making co-operative, a dairy, vineyards (though the first vines from France produced a bitter brew and had to be replaced) and a public clinic. All this has encouraged the wood-working industry; the population of 3,500 supports nearly a hundred workshops, making beehives and cheese barrels for the whole of Greece.

Metsovo is no exception to the spirit of revenge in Greek politics. The main street marked the dividing line in the civil war, with the Communist *andartes* on the high ground above, and the artillery of the government commander Zervas across the valley below. Looking across the rooftops after the 1985 election, I saw half the village flying the colours of the conservatives and half those of the Pasok socialists: the blue and the green, the colours of the brawling factions of Byzantium.

The spirit of independence in Metsovo owes much to the astuteness of one Kirakos Flokas who gave succour to an Ottoman vizier forced to flee Istanbul in disgrace; restored in 1659, he gave Metsovo various privileges, including lower taxes, permission to herd large flocks, land rights and tolerance of Orthodox worship and education. As a result, Metsovo is less self-conscious about the Ottoman past than most parts of Greece, while the Flokan Liberties are acknowledged to this day in the red ribbons worn by the girls at wedding ceremonies. They are also commemorated in St Nicholas, the little monastery which guards the old road which shoots down a deep coomb from the mountain saddle.

After years of decline the monastic community closed in 1925 among scenes of clerical skulduggery. The abbot sent the two remaining monks to work the fields while he set off to sell the community's treasure – crucifixes, candlesticks and altar furnishings – in Ioannina. He never made it. At the monastery of Tourakane, where he stopped for the night, he was attacked in his sleep by robbers, who split his head open with an axe and escaped with the booty.

In the years that followed shepherds kept their sheep in the monastery buildings and lit fires in the chapel. And then, thirty years ago, the veteran politician and soldier Evangelos Averoff found himself scraping a particularly blackened part of the wall with his penknife, and from beneath the layers of soot deep reds, pastel blues, and burning orange colours began to emerge.

The process of uncovering and restoration was painfully slow, but the rewards dazzling. The interior of the church is covered with secular and religious scenes of saints, angels, apostles and patriarchs of the church, with the Emperor Diocletian, the great persecutor, depicted in his palace at Split. Some of the arrangements of the figures are quite unusual: each of the two domes carries the image of the Pantocrator, Christ the creator – a figure generally displayed only once in the roof of most Orthodox churches. The figure may have been repeated to give a clear view to the women, confined to the back by a heavy screen in true Levantine fashion.

Equally unusual is the lithe quality of the human faces and limbs, said to reflect the influence of Damaskenos, the Cretan master and companion of El Greco who journeyed to Venice with him but then returned to Greece. One clue to this is the fresco round the main door, in which the Madonna suckling her baby – a figure hardly ever seen in Byzantine paintings. The paintings seem to have caught a faint breath of Renaissance humanism, from Venice or Venetian Crete.

The monastery church is used again on feasts and festivals. At dusk one Lent evening I stood by the gate and watched the stooped silhouettes of the Vlach women swaying and clucking down the path from the village above. Each took a long tapering candle, the light making the frescoes dance in glory as the rumble of prayers and responses rose and fell.

Beyond the monastery walls a procession of women flickering lights climbed to a chapel on the hillside, moving up and down the narrow steps like the angels on Jacob's ladder in a medieval painting. The chapel held a miraculous icon of the virgin, which had flown up to its previous roost every time it had been taken to safety in the main buildings.

Down the valley I could see the lights of the construction gangs building a tunnel under the mountains for a new road down to Trikkala, which will bypass Metsovo and so preserve the idiosyncratic quality and colour of the community. Metsovo is exceptional among mountain villages of the northern Mediterranean in its cultural diversity and well-being, and freedom from the symptoms of neglect and abandon prevalent in such regions. Unlike the rocky survivors of Calabria and Sicily, wealth and longevity in Metsovo are not the gift of corrupt political patrons or the families of organised crime.

Already, however, the new road has brought change. According to my friend Apostoli the cheese-maker, who had learnt his craft in Parma, the engineering teams were Italian – which was why the taverna keeper had greeted me in Italian when I first tobogganed into town. In the clash of cultures of east and west the Italians had won the latest round – by a shrewd lunge to the belly.

Salonika

Salonika seems a city perpetually destined to take second place in the Greek world. Only Athens takes precedence in modern Greece; in the Byzantine Empire from the times of Justinian Salonika yielded in importance only to Constantinople itself. Today it has a heavy Balkan atmosphere, with its tall and dour buildings, dusty streets swept by the savage wind – the vardar – from the north in winter, and in summer they swelter in the sultry heat. The surrounding plain with its deep red soil is marked out by tall poplars, birches and plane trees – no hint of the Mediterranean in their stoic posture. Lorries churning up the mud on the roads crisscrossing the plain carry the number plates of distant capitals, Paris, Vienna, Budapest, Belgrade, Istanbul and Baghdad.

Over the centuries the city has been host to martyrdom and massacre, invasion and sack. The Emperor Theodosius had 7,000 spectators at the circus slaughtered following the lynching of one of his generals. The Emperor Justinian made Salonika the centre of operations to repel the invasions of the Slavs in the sixth century, and two scholars born in the city, St Methodius and St Cyril were to convert them to Christianity – St Cyril inventing a new script in the process. Another alphabetic pioneer, Ataturk, who introduced Latin script to Turkey (the form favoured by Methodius) was a native of the city in the last decades of Ottoman rule. One of the Turkish radical movements which was to set the state for Kemal Ataturk's national revolution in Turkey, the Turkish Committee of Union and Progress – the Young Turks – was born and grew up in Salonika.

Most of medieval Salonika was destroyed by fire in 1917 followed by a severe earthquake sixty years later. Worst hit were the Byzantine churches, which are the architectural glory of the city and date from the fifth century to the arrival of the Turks ten centuries later. Some have remained closed and shuttered behind cages of scaffolding, but an exception is the splendid basilica of Saint Demetrius, which houses the mortal remains of Salonika's patron saint, which were returned from Italy in 1978 – the year of the earthquake.

Saint Demetrius was martyred during the persecutions of the Emperor Galerius. He is said to have protected his city from pestilence and invasion, and his tomb is believed to exude a holy oil with wonderful powers of healing. Under the Turks the church became a palace and a mosque; the mosaics, equal in quality and dramatic power to those of Ravenna, were rediscovered almost intact after liberation in 1912, only for all but three or four to be destroyed in the fire of 1917.

Belief in the saint's miraculous powers is evident in the throngs that fill his church on his feast day at the end of October. At evening eucharist one dank autumn night I watched hundreds of people shuffling up the nave to the altar and the sarcophagus; so continuous was the flood of worshippers that the main doors were left open to the night. Raised on an easel by the iconostasis or the altar screen, was a miraculous icon brought especially for the occasion from Crete. The procession halted by the gilded and silver-encrusted tomb, as a girl shrieked in a fit of demented frenzy, while her parents prayed loudly for the saint to cure her her cries echoed to the roof while from the throats of the five man choir – evidently professionals all – rolled the most perfectly rounded Byzantine chant.

One of the richest elements of Salonika society has all but vanished half a century ago. In 1941 the city's Jewish community numbered some 60,000; at least 50,000 were deported and killed in the death camps, principally Auschwitz. This shameful episode is hardly mentioned in Salonika today, though the Jews keep a small museum to their community in a synagogue in a quiet side street – a feature overlooked by the guidebooks.

Most of the Jews came from Spain, expelled by the Catholic monarchs under the Edict of the Alhambra of 1492. With them they brought Ladino, the Jewish language of the Mediterranean in its purest form, which closely resembles old Castilian. The Spanish Jews linked up with Jews fleeing from Hungary, and by the end of the sixteenth century they were a community of 30,000, more than half the population of Salonika. The Jews were recognisable by their fur caps and huge overcoats trimmed with valuable pelts.

Until this century they continued to speak both Ladino and Greek – the beauty and subtlety of the former being reflected in the argot of Auschwitz, where only forty survived. In his journal of that dreadful ordeal, *If This Is A Man*, the Italian writer Primo Levi describes the quality of these extraordinary people:

> These few survivors from the Jewish colony of Salonica, with their two languages, Spanish and Greek, and their numerous activities, are the repositories of a concrete, mundane, conscious wisdom, in which the traditions of all the Mediterranean civilizations blend together. That this wisdom was transformed in the camp into the systematic and scientific practice of theft and seizure of possessions and the monopoly of the bargaining Market, should not let one forget that this aversion to gratuitous brutality, their amazing consciousness of the survival of at least a potential human dignity made of the Greeks the most coherent national nucleus in Lager, and in this respect, the most civilized.

The Jewish community used to produce two French-language daily newspapers, and in the nineteenth century Salonika was a more important emporium of international news, political gossip and cultural tittle-tattle than Athens. The railway, completed in 1888, established direct contact with Vienna. Journalists were specially assigned to collect the latest newspapers from Berlin and Vienna from the train, and to send on the most important items of news by telegraph for the afternoon editions in Athens. The influence of Vienna still lingers in the displays of rich cakes and chocolates on the confectionery counters of the cafés along Salonika's dusty boulevards.

Viennese taste continued to be the rage in Salonika well after the demise of the Habsburg empire, setting the fashion in furnishing and decor as well as in clothes and food. Families hastily setting up house after the peremptory expulsion from Asia Minor in 1922 and buying up second-hand Viennese furniture by the train-load are among the most vivid childhood memories of Manolis Andronicus, Professor of Archaeology at the University of Salonika, whose family had to leave his birthplace at Bursa close to the Sea of Marmara. That was not the end of his enforced travels round the eastern Mediterranean – his university studies in Salonika were interrupted by war service, in which he saw action in Benghazi and Tobruk with the Brigade of Immortals of the Greek army in exile.

His conversation is that of a man who has lived several lives and whose learning reaches beyond the lecture theatre and the library and he has been a successful newspaper columnist and essayist. The Mediterranean is for him an elusive and fragmented idea, yet he has provided a wonderful insight into an intriguing aspect of the Mediterranean world, ancient and modern, through his great achievements in archaeology which came to a dramatic climax on 8 November 1977, the Feast of Archangels Michael and Gabriel in the Orthodox calendar. Since the early summer he had been working on a huge tumulus in the little town of Vergina in western Macedonia, which ten years before Professor Nicholas Hammond of Cambridge – a wartime hero of the Greek resistance – had identified as the ancient Aigai, capital of the Macedonian kings, previously believed to be at Edlessa, some twenty kilometers to the north. After extending the digging season into the late autumn, Professor Andronicus had uncovered a large rectangular vault, which he believed might be a royal tomb.

Surrounded by colleagues, fellow-workers, dignitaries of the university, the local governor of Veroia and the Rector of Salonika University, he gave the word for the keystone to be removed from the building. It came away easily, and the archaeologists peered in before lowering a ladder. On the floor lay a jumble of vessels and equipment for the afterlife – bronze armour and weapons turned green by oxidisation, drinking vessels inlaid with silver, a Scythian quiver and a bowcase of gold, a rotting corselet, and everywhere twinkling leaves wrought in gold.

Professor Andronicus confesses he struggled with a confusion of thoughts and emotions in that supreme moment of his career; as he concluded his official report, 'The excavator felt a scientist's elation, a desecrator's guilt; of course, the first cancelled the other out.'

He knew at once that he had found the tomb of an important personage, and very likely a royal one, untouched since the day it had been sealed with funeral rites and sacrifices. This was a miracle in itself, since every comparable burial vault for miles around had been looted. Who had been laid to rest here with such hurried ceremony?

Inside the marble sarcophagus at one end of the chamber was a simple golden casket or larnax, embossed with a twelve-pointed star, the emblem of ancient Macedonian royalty. It bore, in the words of its discoverer, the stamp of 'simple luxury', a quality shared by nearly all the objects of the tomb. Wrapped in fine cloth inside it were the partially cremated bones of a man. The professor and his assistant gently removed the box, loaded it into their car and headed for Salonika and the vaults of the national museum.

The bones were those of Philip II of Macedon, the father of Alexander the Great, who was murdered in Vergina in 336 BC. 'We had touched history with our fingers,' says Manolis Andronicus, using the phrase which is almost the motto of archaeologists – though the only other finds associated with known figures from antiquity were the Phrygian cap of

Phidias and the helmet of Miltiades. Convincing proof was provided by
a trio of British experts in medicine and archaeology, Drs Musgrave,
Prague and Neave, in a brilliant piece of forensic art. After careful
examination and measurement of the bones of the skull, they managed
to reconstruct the head of the dead man along the lines of a waxworks
model. The results were startling. The face was that of a man whose
right eye had been gouged out, leaving a heavy scar down the cheek.
Philip II had lost his right eye during the siege of Methone in 355 BC.

I saw the reconstructed head in the laboratories at Vergina, a village
of one-storey houses, many hastily constructed by refugees from Asia
Minor in 1922. On one side lie open fields running into the Macedonian
Plain; on the other the foothills begin to rise towards the Pindus Mountains through sparse woodlands of stunted oak, their falling leaves a damp
gold in the autumn drizzle.

The tombs themselves are closed to the public, for fear of damage by
too much exposure to the open air. I was lucky enough to be guided
through the complex of three tombs in the Great Tumulus by George
Miltsakakis, Professor Andronicus' assistant, a genial walking encyclopedia devoted to his subject and his master. It was not difficult to appreciate why: the Vergina find fascinates on many levels, historical,
archaeological, political and aesthetic.

The most beautiful artefact on the site is in the small outer tomb,
which may well have deflected grave robbers from finding the tomb of
Philip himself. The chamber had been comprehensively looted, but on
the walls a series of frescoes are remarkably preserved, some of the colours
as fresh as when first daubed on the wet plaster. In one corner sits the
lone, cloaked figure of Demeter, hunched in a wonderfully natural posture of grief. On the opposite wall is a scene of frenetic drama – the rape
of Persephone by Pluto, a favourite theme of the time. The god drives
his chariot out from the wall, his half-naked prize struggling in his arms,
her auburn tresses streaming in the wind. The freshness of the figures,
the control of perspective and the balance of the composition match the
skill of any of the great Renaissance masters.

The painting is the only masterpiece of the Greek classical era yet
to be discovered virtually intact, according to Professor Andronicus.
Fragments and copies abound, but this is the only work by a great artist
of the time, possibly Nicomachus – though Professor Andronicus stresses
that this is mere conjecture on his part.

In much worse condition, yet historically as intriguing, is the hunting
scene over the lintel of Philip's tomb. The paint has been pock-marked
and scarred by damp and time. The subject is a royal hunt, with men

on horse and foot, accompanied by dogs, savaging a menagerie of wild beasts. One of the horseman is probably Philip himself, and a dashing youth in a pink tunic about to hurl a spear from his rearing steed could be his heir, Alexander the Great.

The hypothesis may be fanciful. It rests on the fact that the youth wears a laurel and that his gesture, appearance and pose are exactly those of the central figure in the mosaic known as the Battle of Alexander, made several centuries later, found in Pompeii and now in the National Museum of Naples. In the hunting scene at Vergina we may have the only likeness in the terms of his own Hellenistic culture of Alexander the Great – who did as much as any man to shape the politics and civilisation of the ancient Mediterranean – to be painted during his lifetime.

The events which brought Alexander to his throne were enacted about a kilometre away from the Great Tumulus and the royal tombs. On a piece of rising ground surrounded by thin woods lie the massive stones and foundations of the royal palace. Below them the team from Salonika have unearthed a small temple, vestiges of the town walls and a theatre – vital clues in a superb historical detective story, the physical corroboration of contemporary second- and third-hand accounts of how Philip met his end.

On the feast for the marriage of his daughter Cleopatra to Alexander, King of the Molossians, Philip and the wedding party, the future Alexander the Great among them, were walking from the main gate of the palace to a performance at the theatre when he was attacked and fatally stabbed by a former member of his guard, Pausanias, who ran off towards the city walls where accomplices had a horse for his escape. However he tripped on a vine and was immediately despatched by Philip's bodyguards. The layout of Vergina ties in exactly with later accounts by Arrian and Plutarch.

It was said that King Philip's court was riven with intrigue, a nest of treachery and bisexual debauchery according to his detractors. He had spent much of his treasure – hence, perhaps, the simple luxury in his tomb – in his wars to unite Greece and his plans to mount a campaign against the Persians, a scheme his son was to realise so brilliantly. As a Macedonian he was looked down upon by the more refined Athenians, but they shared the same Hellenistic culture.

How deep this went is evident in aesthetically the least spectacular, but politically the most explosive, of the finds at Vergina. In the Great Tumulus above Philip's tombs, which was raised by the invading Galatians in 274 BC, the archaeologists found fragments of no fewer than seventy-five funeral monuments, or *stelai*. The names on these were entirely Greek, save two which appeared to be Hellenised versions of

Thracian and Phoenician names. The implication is that Philip's Macedonia was thoroughly hellenised, an outpost of classical Greek culture;
and this touches the heart of what is known as the Macedonian Question,
very much a live feature of Mediterranean and Balkan politics today.

Professor Andronicus's conclusions were accepted by scholars throughout the world – with one exception. They were bitterly attacked in Skopje,
the capital of Yugoslavia's Republic of Makedonija, claiming that modern
Macedonians are a distinct people of Slavic culture who should be united
in their own state. Since the decline of Ottoman rule, the region of Macedonia has been the catspaw of partial or total political claims by Greece,
Bulgaria and later Yugoslavia. It is said to have been the basis of Stalin's
fears that Tito was aiming to extend Yugoslav territory to the Aegean on
the pretext of uniting all Macedonians.

Professor Andronicus says he is a scholar and not a politician. He
believes that the story of medieval and modern Greece is one of continuous infiltration with the Slavs arriving in the fifth century AD. The
implications of Vergina have not been lost on Greek politicians and
governments have continued to subsidise the excavations, while tighten-
ing the purse for other archaeological projects.

With regionalism and nationalism resurgent throughout the Mediterranean, the Macedonian Question is emerging again. In neighbouring
areas the nationalist and religious demands of Muslim Turks in Bulgaria
and Muslim or 'Ottoman' Greeks in Thrace have already smouldered into
life. The discoveries at Vergina are among the most potent pieces of
archaeology in the new political climate of the Mediterranean.

Athos

'When they cut my hair, they put some of it on the other side of the
icon of Christ – that was the first tonsure, which meant I had made my
vows to be a monk. Later, with the second tonsure, I promised to stay
with the community and to follow the orders of its abbot.' Such were
the simple terms in which Father Theologou of the community of Stavronikiti described the profession of his vows to become a monk on Mount
Athos – a formula unchanged in essence for more than a thousand years.

Ageless as the rule and regime of the monks may appear, the twenty
monasteries and two small villages of Athos have endured fluctuating
fortunes over the centuries – and not least in the past thirty years. Today
the mountain and its great houses are no mere reflection of a religious

world long gone, but the most powerful centre of Greek Orthodoxy and Christian monasticism in the Mediterranean. The new spirit of learning and contemplation now abroad on Athos deliberately promotes a view of Christianity sharply different from any available in the more material worlds of western Europe and America.

Thirty years ago the monasteries were dying. After the capture of Constantinople by the Turks in 1453 the community on Athos, swelled by refugees, reached 30,000, with more than a thousand in each of the larger houses. By the beginning of this century the numbers had fallen to 9000 and by 1971 only 1,145 professed monks remained. Suddenly the numbers began to rise, so that by the mid-1980s the total population, including lay and religious visitors on retreat, and lay brethren helping on the farms, was over 2000. Athos attracted those seeking the spiritual life not only from Greece, but from neighbouring Balkan countries, Western Europe, America, Australia and Canada. The average age of the monks, somewhere in the upper sixties twenty years ago, fell as younger men joined. Among those seeking the inner peace offered by the Holy Mountain were former doctors and dentists, social workers, military officers, a nuclear physicist and an oil prospector. But its full impact is unlikely to be felt in the rest of Greece and the Christian communities of the Levant for some years to come.

Like most monastic communities, those of Athos were not free from scandal in the years of decline. It was wildly rumoured that waifs and strays and idiots were seized from mountain villages to make up numbers and undertake menial tasks, and that young orphans were browbeaten into taking holy orders. In the late 1960s it was whispered that homosexual clubs in Germany were offering special hiking tours of the Athos peninsula.

Worse had happened in the not too distant past. Before the First World War a band of criminals on the run from the Czar's police took over the Russian Orthodox monastery of Panteleimon – a staggering arrangement of green onion domes piled on rich red brick – and the Greek government had to invite Russian help to dislodge them. The Czar sent a battle cruiser and the monastery was stormed by a regiment of marines.

Athos is the easternmost of three fingers of land jutting into the Aegean from the peninsula of Chalcidice, which lies to the south-east of Salonika. Access by land is cut off by a barrier of rocky hills and woodland, and the Holy Mountain can only be reached by ferry from the port of Ouranoupolis. According to legend, Mary the mother of Jesus and St John the Evangelist were on their way to visit St Lazarus in

Cyprus when their ship was blown off course and wrecked on the shores of Athos. So enchanted was Mary by the place that she prayed for it to be given her by Jesus. The first hermits dedicated the Mountain to the Virgin, so initiating the rigid rule whereby, according to the decree of 1060, no 'woman, female animal, child, eunuch or smooth-faced person' should be allowed there – though in recent centuries concessions have been made for hens, female cats, and products of the female domestic animal such as yoghurt, cheese, butter and eggs.

The monks enjoyed the privileges of Byzantine emperors and the toler-ance of Ottoman sultans. The first great monastery was founded by decree of the Emperor Nicephoras Phocas in 963. Catalans, Serbs and Turks raided the peninsula, but the community was hardest pressed at the outbreak of the Greek War of Independence in 1821. In 1912 Greek troops occupied the mountain as the liberation struggle extended into the two Balkan Wars. In 1926 the Mountain was given the status of a self-governing autonomous region with its own council of monks and a provincial officer, the Nomarch, to look after the interests of the Greek state. Under the Colonels the monks were suspected of being politically unsound and the regime attempted to force the younger ones into military service. Today the government in Athens has been generous in providing funds for the upkeep of monuments and the conservation of works of art and precious manuscripts.

My own journey to Athos had something in common with the legends of landfalls by saints, pirates and hermits – it nearly ended in shipwreck. The little diesel ferry was carrying a tractor with a trailer full of heavy stones and lurched alarmingly in the swell. Attempts to pull alongside the jetty at two of the monasteries had to be abandoned, much to the distress of some monks waiting to come on board. Behind them the outbuildings, turrets and walls of the monasteries rose in grey splendour, though many of the windows had a vacant stare and the roofs were caved in. Some hearty hymn-singing and praying by the pilgrims in our midst took effect, and the ferry made Daphni, the port of the Athos peninsula, without mishap. It was a wild early spring day, and the mist and fine rain made the trees and shrubs of the mountain a luminous green, while along the veranda of Daphni's only café the wisteria shone like purple neon. Taking to the wild grey sea from the other side of the landing stage was a caique or traditional sailing cargo boat, carrying a group of neophytes, their first growth of beard barely stubble on their chins.

They looked astonishingly young, not much more than fourteen or fifteen, and they wore their long black robes and stove hats with a swagger. Nowadays the treatment of minors on Athos is strictly regulated so as to counter any suggestions that they are there against their will. I was told that the bigger houses accept a small number of very poor boys and orphans to offer them education up to secondary school standard. They can then choose to leave the community and the Holy Mountain, or go on with the monastic life until they are adult, when they can consider taking full vows – in which case they are almost sure to leave Athos for a time to attend theology school in Salonika or Athens.

From Daphni the visitor takes a bus to Karyes, the administrative capital of the Athonite community, where an official issues an elaborate document, like a parchment scroll, allowing temporary residence for four days. In theory only visitors of serious cultural or religious purpose are admitted, and non-Greeks have to ask permission through their embassies or consulates.

Karyes is a theocratic ghost town, where long grass and weeds grow in the churches and houses and rusty corrugated iron sheets flap in the wind. Once it housed a community of five hundred, but now the regular inhabitants are fewer than fifty. Several times a year each monastery sends its elected representative to Karyes to sit on the Holy Council, the legislature of Athos, which in turn chooses four monks to serve for a year on the executive, the Epistasia.

Fortified by coffee and ouzo bartered from a curmudgeonly innkeeper in the ramshackle hostel which doubled up as the Karyes general store, I took the track towards the monasteries on the eastern shore. The path was covered by sweet-smelling pine needles, and a notice warned in English, 'Forest is a place of calm and God's smile. Keep fires out.'

It was raining and dusk was gathering when I reached the monastery of Pantocratoros. With its solid square fortified tower and gate, and the sea crashing over the stone quay of the harbour, it looked like some forgotten cousin of Childe Roland's Dark Tower. I signed on for a straw mattress in a draughty guest room, and a meal of lentils, coarse and wholesome bread, and rough wine and ouzo.

The convents of Athos fall into two broad categories, the coenobitic, where the monks form a regulated community, and the idiorhythmic, a much looser regime with the brothers choosing their own paths on most matters. Pantocratoros was very idiorhythmic, with its sixteen monks gathering only for worship in the chapel and a few communal meals. The abbot, who kept a jeep to drive to Karyes, was in charge of the upkeep of the buildings and the workforce of laymen in the fields. A monk I met on the stairs by the upper tier of cells told me he had worked in the merchant marine on boats to England and America. 'After sundown, when you are lost in life, there is only one way forward – and

I am old enough to know right from wrong,' was how he explained his reasons for becoming a monk. His companion said he once had his own restaurant in Canada, adding 'I don't like money. I believe in Jesus, God and Mary.'

With its brisk and neat appearance, the monastery of Stavronikita is quite different from the sleepy, ramshackle Pantocratoros. One of the smallest houses, it is in the forefront of the Athonite revival. Its fortified gatehouse is flanked by neat terraced gardens, overflowing irrigation troughs, and shady bowers for meditative perambulations. Always at the ready, it seems, is the *simandro*, the wooden plank which is struck repeatedly with a mallet to sound the call to worship – the same instrument with which Noah is believed to have summoned the animals to the ark. The woodpecker rattle of the *simandro* is the quintessential sound of the Orthodox Church in rural Greece.

In the 1960s, when Father Vasileus arrived, the community at Stavronikiti consisted of some seven aged monks. He brought with him a band of young monks from Philotheou – which with the convents of Grigoriou, Simona Petra, and Stavronikiti itself have led the spiritual revival of the Holy Mountain – and in 1968 he reorganised the community on coenobitic lines, the first of the Athos monasteries to do so in the modern era. The term and the idea derive from the word 'konovium', a community first given Christian expression by St Paul. A konovium on Athos means that the monks agree to worship, work and eat together, their lives regulated by the abbot and the weekly council meetings or *synax*. The reputation of Father Vasileus has travelled far beyond the Holy Mountain. Two of his books, *Mount Athos and the Education of the Nation* and *The Hymn of Entry* became bestsellers, and he made frequent pastoral visits to America, Australia and northern Europe.

For all its recent changes, Stravronikiti gives a very good idea of the pattern and ritual of Orthodox monastic life. Time is still measured by the Byzantine clock and the Julian calendar, and the hours set by sunrise and sunset. Monks worship for eight hours and work on most days for about six. In winter vespers and matins are celebrated in almost total darkness, and monks rising from cells and dormitories to shuffle along balconies into the sweet incense-filled dark of the chapel is my abiding memory of Athos.

I arrived on a blazing spring day, the downward path from Pantocratoros choked with thorn bushes, the lilacs and chestnuts in full flower. A school of dolphins bounced and raced in the gleaming sea. Two monks escorted me to a guest-room, well provided with books and tracts in English.

In the late afternoon I went for a walk among the vines along the terraces overlooking the sea with Father Theologou, a young monk from Edhessa in northern Greece who was the convent librarian. He explained the natural progression from his first tonsure to taking full vows to remain with the monastery, which meant he adopted the *megali schema*. He said he had come to Athos in a personal search for God, and not as a result of his learning.

He insisted that Orthodoxy represented a unique focus of Christianity in the eastern Mediterranean, 'embracing many races, and linking the Balkans and the Middle East,' as he put it in his careful and deliberate English. Athos for him was an antidote to Western materialism, and what he saw as the poverty of Western scholasticism (a view common to most Orthodox thinkers). His preferred reading was of the Church Fathers – St Gregory and Theologian, St Basil the Great, St John Chrystostom, and the Anthologies of the Mysteries.

Father Theologou combined utter self-confidence and a powerful intellect, with not a trace of vanity. His colleague, who took over my instruction on Orthodox monasticism, seemed an altogether more troubled soul. Father Ieremias had been born into a Greek family in Australia and had been a social worker in Sydney. A craving for the spiritual life, and a belief that human nature and the evil in humanity could not be changed by men alone, had drawn him to the monastic life. 'Western spiritual life is so dead, so theoretical and abstract,' he told me in his quiet Australian twang. 'You have to live the spiritual life, and it has to be lived from the inside.'

Time and again his conversation returned to St John Chrysostom's saying that 'Nothing can hurt a person who does not hurt himself.' As the monk's conversation ebbed and flowed between earthly failings and eternal rewards, its rhythm seemed to match the lowering and hauling of nets by two monks and the gliding of their little boat back and forth across the bay in the gathering dusk.

During the night the librarian fetched me for the service of vespers, which starts at about three or four in the morning in the summer months. The *catholikon*, the chapel which is the core of the monastery, is one of the smallest on Athos, and a jewel. As the sun rises its first rays touch the frescoes of the Creator, archangels, apostles, saints, martyrs and prophets ranged in order of rank down the walls of the central dome. The Pantocrator, the Creator of All, comes first, because he is before all creation, even before light.

The most precious icon at Stavronikiti is a thirteenth-century mosaic portrait of St Nicholas. In the sixteenth century it was stolen by pirates, only to be found years later washed ashore. An oyster had become embedded in it, and when it was removed blood gushed from the scar it left. Half of the oyster was kept, and the other half was sent as a gift from the Abbot to the first Patriarch of Moscow.

Next day I came across the site of another miraculous legend, the shrine of the Holy Spring near the fortified convent of Iveron. Hermitages or *sketes* abound on Athos, and the Holy Spring must be the best appointed of them. Its custodian was Brother Alexander, an Austrian by birth, and he hallooed me to ask if I was English or German. A short distance from the spring are the main chapel, the barns and the house, which Brother Alexander had kitted out like a Tyrolean guest house.

With his breathless conversation and squeaky giggle, Brother Alexander must be the polar opposite of a Trappist monk. He insisted I stayed the night, and showed me his guest chamber with its Austrian bedcovers. 'The only way is the straight way' was embroidered over the door, in English. Somehow the straight way seemed to have eluded Brother Alexander's spirit, adrift on a raft of chatter in a sea of unfathomable loneliness.

Halfway up the mountain, with a splendid gatehouse and extensive courtyards, Philotheou had the toughest regime of any of the convents I visited. With more than sixty monks, it is in the vanguard of the Athonite revival, sending monks out to reform houses on the Mountain and throughout the Orthodox world. Guests are kept apart; they are not allowed to dine with the monks, and are asked to keep to the back of the chapel during worship.

It was my good luck to meet Brother Serafim, a young monk from Chicago, who turned out to be a wonderfully droll and down-to-earth guide to the physical and spiritual life of the house. I met him hanging out of an upper window chatting to a Canadian brother. 'You'd better whisper,' he said out of the side of his mouth, 'we're not supposed to speak to guests or speak English.'

Serafim said he had converted from Catholicism, and had been drawn to Athos by the Jesus prayer, which is repeated endlessly by the monks like a Buddhist mantra. He had taken his name from the miraculous icon of St Serafim at the Russian monastery of Panteleimon, the first icon he had learnt to venerate. The cult of uninterrupted silent prayer, and the Jesus prayer itself that had so mesmerised Serafim, had been promoted by the sect of the Hesychasts in the late Middle Ages. The Hesychasts were to be one of the most powerful orders of late medieval Byzantium, but they had their share of enemies. In the fourteenth century Barlaam the Calabrian condemned them as 'omphalopsychoi' – the men with souls in their navel.

As we walked across the grass in front of the *catholikon* I could hear the monks rehearsing their splendid unembroidered Byzantine chant, punctuated by the hooting of owls among the basket work of the wooden balconies.

Before I went to sleep, I read the tracts beside my bed. They were emphatic about the differences between Orthodoxy and Catholicism, rejecting the supremacy of the Pope, and the Western belief that the Trinity was made of Father, Son *and* Holy Ghost. This formula is taken by the Orthodox as implying that the Spirit flows from the Father and Son, and comes from them. It is known from the Latin as the dispute of *filioque* or procession of the spirit and led to the split between the Eastern and Western churches in 1054; four hundred years later it thwarted the desperate attempts to reunite the churches and save Constantinople from the Turks. The debate is still far from dead.

I was woken for early morning worship by Serafim, carrying a glass of steaming Nescafé. 'Off the record,' he vouchsafed, 'you're going to need it – it can get pretty tough on your feet and rear these cold dark mornings.'

On the battered old coach from Karyes to Daphni later that morning I was joined by an American with a rusty beard – Father Elias, a charming soul from the idiorythmic community of Xeropotamou. 'I came here first during the time of the Colonels,' he explained. 'It was really run-down and monks were being hauled off to the military. Now it's changing – we've gone up from six to twenty brothers.' His own story summed up the appeal of Athos in the modern world: 'I was in the US army and then a geologist for an oil company. I hated the questionable ethics of the business, and I'd always wanted to be a teacher. My parents were Greek and I had kept some of the language. I decided to get myself sorted out, so I came here first.'

iv Islands: Cephalonia and Crete

The island of Cephalonia has been famed for its wild and wandering seafarers since the days of Homer. A jagged crag of clay, rock and pine forest in the Ionian Sea, west of the Greek mainland, it lies next to Odysseus's kingdom of Ithaca.

In the best traditions of Mediterranean individualism and non-conformity, each group of Greek islands is quite distinctive in character. Both Ithaca and Cephalonia escaped Ottoman rule, and were far more influenced by Venice than most of the Aegean islands.

In the early nineteenth century the islands were seized from Napoleon's short-lived Peninsula Republic by the British. At the time British rule was best known for the mayhem caused among the youths of the fishing communities by the homoerotic tendencies of the Consul, Sir Charles Napier. But the British had a more lasting influence, building roads and establishing a fully regulated merchant marine, complete with modern maritime insurance. As a result, men from the islands, and in particular those from the Ionians, have had a predominant role in the establishment of Greece's mercantile fleet – the single most successful commercial endeavour since Greece achieved full independence. Starting with the judicious buying-up of cheap Allied freighters after the Second World War, Greek magnates built up one of the biggest merchant fleets in the world, and men of the islands such as Aristotle Onassis and Stavros Niarchos achieved Midas-like status in modern folklore.

Towards the end of the lives of these homeric figures, the fortunes of shipping throughout the world took a heavy downturn. The causes were both particular and general. Some Greek owners were caught by the collapse of the whaling industry; others were affected by the upset in oil shipping from the Gulf and Saudi Arabia, first by the closing of the Suez Canal by the Arab-Israeli conflicts of 1956 and 1967, and then its re-opening in 1974, which obviated the use of the deepest draught supertankers in the Mediterranean. The monument to these maritime misfortunes lies strewn across the Bay of Salamis, a dinosuars' graveyard of rusting hulks, peeling supertankers, flaking freighters, coasters and ageing container-ships of all sizes.

Today Greek shipowners are again amongst the most powerful players in the business and political world, though their trade is a more finely calculated affair than a generation ago. The operators of passenger services, of cruise liners and ferries, have suffered most from the psychological as well as the physical impact of terrorist attacks like the PLO's seizure of the cruise ship *Achille Lauro* in 1985 and the suicide attack on the ferry *City of Poros* in 1988. The impact of such attacks shows up starkly in the official statistics: in 1984 the number of cruise passengers rose to just over half a million for the first time, only to fall to 465,000 the following year, while over the same period the registered cargo fleet of Greece fell from a total of 18,796,073 tons to 16,097,464.

The lure of the sea, dreams of achieving fame and fortune in America, Australia or Canada, the destruction and upheavals of world war and civil war have resulted in Cephalonia's population, like that of most Greek islands, dwindling to a fraction of what it was at the turn of the century.

The relentless exodus is a misfortune common to the island communities of the Mediterranean, akin to the shortage of fresh water through the long slow roast of summer. By the mid-Eighties the winter population of Cephalonia was little over 23,000, whereas fifty years previously it had been about 80,000, and a scheme of special subsidies was being mooted to keep indigenous families in the island. Looking after the islanders' interests is the responsibility of their deputy in the national parliament in Athens. Once the island returned four members, but now the constituency is shared with Ithaca. With his sharp aquiline features, bushy bandit moustache a mountain *klepht* might envy, and flowing silvered locks, Antonis Tritsis, its deputy in the Eighties, looked the wild Ionian personified. A trained architect, he insisted that new houses and apartments in Cephalonia should have proper roofs, preferably of tile, and should not be left incomplete with thickets of rusty steel rods sprouting from concrete struts and pillars – a notorious way of dodging local taxes throughout much of the Mediterranean, by claiming the dwelling had yet to be finished. In the capital, Agostoli, he lent his support to a proposal to restrict houses to two storeys, so preserving the character of the charming central square.

It was in this little square, blown with oleander blossom and bright red Communist Party posters, that I set out one May morning on a day's electioneering with the sitting member. He had already opened his campaign in New York, for more Cephalonians live in America than in the islands, and would end with big rallies in the sports stadiums in Piraeus and Patras – which, he suspected, would deliver more votes than the meetings in the constituency itself. As if to make the point, a Pasok supporter who was to be my host for the day added, 'I am the only male of my family left here. We were twelve and the rest are in the United States. My wife is the only one left in the islands of her family, too. I stay because I like it here. They work too hard in the US, and most of them are dead by sixty.'

As we chatted in front of the café in the square, we were given an extraordinary prologue in mime to the day's politicking by a gypsy boy who could only speak in grunts and growls. Taking the stage in front of a row of parked cars, he began to play the politician on the stump. First he surveyed his crowd, chest puffed out, thumbs in lapels. Looking up, he began to strut. An arm shot forward in admonition. He bounced on his heels, turned, looked down, and the other arm began proffering silent advice, finger wagging. Suddenly he reached into a pocket for a piece of paper, smoothed it importantly on the bonnet of a car, and held it up for declamation. The paper was upside down, and the small crowd roared and clapped, threw coins and sent the dusty outcast on his way. The timing and economy of each movement and gesture had exposed the humbug of the hustings with surgical precision and the brutal dismissal betrayed the embarrassment of the onlookers at the boy's art.

The first campaign stop was in a little village, outside Agostoli. The church bell was rung, a green Pasok banner was waved, and a bouquet of wild flowers was presented to the deputy as he began to address a small gathering of supporters. He explained his belief in democracy in action, which meant that he would hold public meetings in the island every time a tough decision had to be taken by the party in parliament or by the government itself. His whole outlook, he said later, had been formed by the recent history of Cephalonia. In 1943 it had been occupied by German forces and the 9000-strong Italian 'Acqui' Division. Rather than surrender to the Germans when Marshal Badoglio pulled Italy out of the war in September 1943, the Italians on the island fought on. After seven days of battle the 3000 survivors surrendered, only to be slaughtered, it was later alleged, at Hitler's express order. Only thirty-four Italians survived.

Antonis Tritsis's most vivid memory of the ensuing civil war was of government soldiers returning to town with the severed heads of their enemies hung from their saddles. Eventually he became a founder-member of PAK, the underground resistance movement under the Colonels, which in turn became the Pan Hellenic Socialist Movement, Pasok. He was to become Mayor of Athens as an independent.

The highlight of the day's electioneering was to be a triumphal motorcade from Agostoli to Sami, the port facing Ithaca on the northern shore. In the late afternoon an exotic caravan of cars, trucks, heavy lorries, tractors and buses, several miles long, set out across the mountains to the trumpeting of klaxons, hooters and air-horns blowing off short bursts of 'Yankee Doodle Dandy'. Blazoned on the radiator of the largest articulated tanker was the unlikely icon of a twice life-sized portrait of the former professor of economic theory at the University of California, now prime minister and philosopher-founder of Pasok, Dr Andreas Papendreou. As the convoy chugged up a pass garlanded by pink and white oleander and yellow gorse it was greeted by friends and supporters standing on rocky outcrops brandishing flags in self-conscious poses – histrionic gestures more associated with a national liberation movement than a Western European socialist party.

By the time we reached Samis, with its open square of white walled houses, dark thunder clouds were gathering over Ithaca. The candidate was to give a speech from the broad balcony of the town hall – as potent an instrument of propaganda and persuasion in these parts as the printing press or the microphone.

As the young mayor began his speech of welcome, the skies grew ever darker over the harbour where Don John of Austria had anchored his ships before defeating the galleys of the Ottoman fleet at Lepanto. Five decisive sea battles had been decided in an arc of barely two hundred miles around these coasts: Salamis; Actium, where Cleopatra lost her kingdom; Lepanto; Navarino Bay, which set the War of Independence on course; and Matapan, at the tip of the Peloponnese, where Mussolini's battle squadron was nudged by the British into largely sinking itself.

My reverie on such matters was interrupted by the candidate stepping forward forth to address the crowd. Hardly had he opened his mouth before Zeus replied: the first bolt of thunder boomed and rattled round the hills and across the bay the lightning cropped the peaks of Ithaca Tritsis's speech became a heroic dialogue as the bursts of lightning cut the loudspeaker system time and again. Undeterred, he outlined his plans for wine co-operatives, improved animal husbandry, subsidies for tourism and the happier world of Pasok socialism before retiring soaked and triumphant. The downpour had long since emptied the square; while the king of the gods retreated towards Ithaca in peals of thunderous mirth.

Crete

'Rose before four, having slept very tolerably, thanks to lots of flea powder,' runs the entry in Edward Lear's *Cretan Journal* for 20 May 1864. 'Up and dressed 4.50. Coffee: see church – oldish (leave 24 piastres) – then draw on the outside. Ida *would* be lovely, and the whole scene delightful, but clouds stopped all.'

The 'oldish' church is at the monastery of Arkadi, which in summer basks on a plateau of rocky meadow dotted with lazy umbrella pines – in spirit and detail exactly the scene Lear depicted in watercolour in his journey across Crete. This comes as something of a shock, for two years after Lear's visit, Arkadi was the setting of an extraordinary gesture of courage and self-sacrifice in the 1866 uprising against the Turks, which has made it the national monument to Cretan independence.

That November a small garrison force, a band of monks and refugees from surrounding villages were besieged in the monastery by a superior force of Turks, who threatened to destroy the place with artillery. After three days the Turks broke into the yard – at which Abbot Gabriel Marinakis gave the signal to set a match to the gunpowder magazine in a storeroom in which hundreds of women and children had taken refuge from the slaughter outside. Over eight hundred people died in the explosion, and the outrage at last brought Crete's struggle against the Turks to the notice of the European powers.

On holidays Cretans come to the monastery to see the museum to the holocaust and to read the names of the families who died with Abbot Gabriel. They visit the fine collection of icons and the gunpowder store, where the roof is still a ragged hole.

The monastery now has a community of fewer than a dozen monks and lay brothers, inhabiting the cells opposite the fine neo-classical façade with its tall belfry, which has more than a hint of Venetian influence having been built at the height of their dominion in the seventeenth century. One crystalline summer evening I watched the brothers assemble for compline. The bell had been rung, and the chant began to echo through the opening door. It was then that I witnessed an episode which seemed to sum up the dilemma of modern Crete. A party of overweight Belgians came clattering through the yard, and a particularly hefty specimen in ballooning pants grabbed the bell-rope fastened by the door and tried to toll it again, quite unconcerned that the worship had started. She joined her raucous colleagues inside the chapel, where they proceeded to flick ash from their cigarettes while the priest read the prayers. Boredom soon set in, minutes later the party swooped out like a flock of starlings to climb into their luxury coach, complete with air conditioning, video and chemical toilets. The monks had done their best to preserve their dignity, but the young Greek courier had done nothing to restrain her charges.

Tourism on the island expanded rapidly after the collapse of the military dictatorship in 1974. New roads along the northern coast, subsidised hotels, and beach complexes have brought shoals of holiday-makers, so that the population doubles in the summer months to well over a million. The impact has been greatest on the eastern end of the island, and the remoter villages and ports of the west have retained much of their rugged charm. To offset over-dependence on tourism, the European Community has begun providing funds under a scheme known as the Integrated Mediterranean Programmes (IMPS) to improve the husbandry of the shepherds and the produce and marketing of the olive- and fruit-growers. Most needed are modern reservoirs and aqueducts, for as in the other great islands of the Mediterranean many of the mountain villages of the interior are parched all year round.

Despite the changes to the landscape wrought by conveyor-belt tourism and industrialised agriculture, many parts of the island, particularly in the wilder uplands, evoke the spirit of an older Crete, its rich and complicated past and its proud, fiercely combative independence. It remains quite distinct from the rest of Greece. In early times it was one

of the centres of the Minoans, who built the palace at Knossos and
its labyrinth, the legendary home of the Minotaur and the creation of
Daedalus; but more significant to the mythology of the modern Mediterranean is the possibility that Crete may have been the home or temporary lodging place of the mysterious Sea People of antiquity, which
could explain the tall and powerful build of many Cretans, in contrast
to the smaller stature of most other Greek islanders.

After the capture of Constantinople in the Fourth Crusade in 1204,
Crete was ruled by Venice until the Turks took over in 1669 – with the
result that, more than any other part of the Levant, Crete was exposed in
visual terms at least to the humanist world of Renaissance Italy. In Chania,
for example – once the capital of the island of Candia – Venetian influences are unmistakeable: the coloured façades of the houses ranged round
the port, the broad quays, and the square windows are reminiscent of one
of the islands of the Venetian lagoon, like Torcello or Iesolo.

The Ottoman Turks soon became powerful landowners, as well as
being merchant and soldiers. After more than a century of resistance
and revolt, Turkey relinquished control in 1898. Crete then became a
regency under Prince George, and was not joined to Greece until 1913.
The union was promoted by Eleftherios Venezelos, a native of the island,
a leader of the anti-monarchist cause and the greatest Greek statesman
of this century.

The Cretans have displayed their independent streak to this day. In
the 1930s opponents of the Metaxa dictatorship contemplated offering
the protection of the island to the Duke of Kent, on account of his
marriage to Princess Marina. Even so, the loyalty of Cretan regiments
to the colours of Greece in the Second World War was such that they
were fighting in the northern mountains on the mainland when the
Germans overran their island.

In May 1941 the Germans seized Crete in what some consider the
most successful operation by parachute forces in military history. In ten
days of fighting British and Commonwealth forces, aided by Cretan
irregulars, managed to inflict more than 6000 casualties on the invading
forces, before being killed, captured, or rescued by submarine from the
south of the island.

The campaign of resistance in the island has become the stuff of
romance and legend, and it was to yield an important legacy. The success
of operations depended on the shepherds in the mountains as an effective
guerrilla force. The British, who had a monopoly of arms supply, forced
the leaders of the rival royalist and communist factions to work together
– with the result that there was hardly any fighting in the island during

the Greek civil war. On the other hand, when the Colonels took over in 1967, Crete was one of the few areas to mount some form of resistance.

For an outsider, especially from Britain or America, to speculate on the distinctive nature of Crete and its people can be dangerous in the presence of modish radicals of the Pasok mould. I was once berated by a professor at Rethimnon University for inquiring into the unique aspects of the island's political history and archaeology – for him it was redolent of the CIA's plotting during the Colonels' dictatorship to separate Crete from Greece to preserve US bases at Souda and Heraklion. Why else, he demanded, as providing final proof, did the Israeli tourist offices issue separate maps for the island and for the rest of Greece? The professor was not a native of Crete, but had been born in Cyprus and studied at the Sorbonne, of which he was enormously proud. His line of argument was not uncommon among the fashionable left of Crete's university campuses.

Moving inland to the upland plateaux and mountain villages, an older and highly individualistic way of life manifests itself. Many of the men still wear the baggy breeches, high boots and a vestigial turban, the *mandili*, perched on the crown of their heads.

The approach to the Sphakia region is advertised by gunshot holes in the signs along the road as it climbs into the mountains from the main highway between Chania and Rethimnon. One wet April day in the village of Askyfou I called with a Greek friend at the café of Manolis, whose state of lubrication was matched by the deep olive oil fry of his cooking. Having dealt with his regular Sunday clientele with several rounds of ouzo, he approached our table and ordered several more rounds, thumping the table with his glass as he took another swig.

On the wall Manolis displayed a pantheon of Cretan heroes. Eleftherios Venezelos, then a member of the Athens parliament, posed with his son and grandson. A newspaper clipping showed the triumphal entry of King George II into Gjirokastër in Albania during the winter campaign of 1940, in which Cretans played a prominent part; nearby hung a painting, in rustic realist style, of heroic defeat, the German airborne invasion of Maleme and Souda in 1941. Below this was a map in which all the Greek-speaking areas of the Balkans, the islands and Asia Minor were coloured red: the *Megali Idea*, the 'Great Idea' dreamed of by nineteenth-century nationalists, whereby all Greek-speaking regions including parts of Anatolia and Pontus on the Black Sea would be incorporated into the new nation of Greece. Such sentiment came to the fore when the Greeks, with Lloyd George's connivance, mounted their disastrous campaign against the

Turks in Asia Minor, culminating in the Catastrophe. In the subsequent transfer of populations of 1923, 30,000 Turks were sent to Anatolia from Crete, while about 10,000 Greeks left Turkey for the island.

A framed engraving showed the handsome, turbanned head of the shepherd singer, Nikos Xylouris, who became a modern legend through his rendering of traditional Cretan songs in a pure natural high tenor, accompanied on the lyra, the ancient stringed instrument known to ancient Greeks. His fame took him to Athens, where he was adulated like a pop star, before dying at a pathetically early age. His recordings are still played throughout Greece; in the back-street tavernas of Rethimnon you can still hear musicians playing the lyra with his kind of natural grace.

On many of the farms in the foothills outside Chania the past sits uneasily with the present. At Gerani, Ilana Isihakis runs the farm she inherited from her father, which he bought from a wealthy Turkish landowner. It is a sizeable property of 200 stremata (the ancient measure of the area one ox team can plough in a day) with 2000 olive and 1000 orange trees, the olives a sea of silvery green up to the slopes of Mount Ida. Some of the trees, with their black and buckled trunks, were planted by the Venetians. The oranges arrived less than a generation back, some of them new varieties to catch the winter trade – one a hybrid whose sweet taste Mrs Isihakis detests.

The olives are harvested by day labourers who receive one third of the crop as their wages. Such methods are frowned upon by the farmers who have joined the socialist co-operatives, the pride and joy of the Pasok agricultural policy, and live in the new concrete houses of the village across the ravine. An uneasy truce seems to exist between the new farms and the old.

Mrs Isihakis says she can always gauge the state of neighbourly relations by the number of visitors on the feast of St John the Baptist. The eucharist is celebrated in the little Venetian chapel dedicated to the saint, which stands in the old farmyard. Afterwards she gives a picnic for the entire village – a turnout of more than fifty guests promises a harmonious year to come.

The Isihakis family home, on the other side of Chania from the farm, overlooks the deep natural harbour of Souda Bay and the shady lawns of the Commonwealth War Cemetery. Among the regular lines of granite headstones one stands, startling in its simplicity – that of Captain J. D. S. Pendlebury, General List.

John Pendlebury belonged to the heroic era of archaeology, working with Sir Arthur Evans on the Palace of Knossos, where he was curator for a short period. With the approach of war, he was given a post as supernumerary British vice-consul – cover for his preparing a resistance network among the shepherd communities. As an archaeologist he had tramped the mountain tracks, and in the weeks immediately before the German attack he criss-crossed the island several times and in all weathers, in superhuman feats of walking. When the Germans arrived at Heraklion, he went down to reconnoitre their strength and positions. He was ambushed and killed when German soldiers found him in a farmhouse, where the family was trying to dress his wound, and was buried in an unmarked grave nearby.

Such were the outlines of the story put together six years later by the writer and critic Dilys Powell, whose husband Humfry Payne – who had died tragically young as Director of the British School in Athens – had been a colleague of Pendlebury. Pendlebury, she told me, was one of the muscular school of Oxbridge archaeologists working in Greece at the time. Though he knew Crete and its people well, he was never intimate with them – a trait he may have inherited from the autocratic Evans, whom she remembered vividly. Other archaeologists, such as the Tasmanian Thomas Dunbabin, who also played a heroic part in the resistance, had a far more warm and egalitarian approach to the islanders.

When Evans first came to Crete, archaeology tended to be a matter of monstrous egos and vain intellects. A man of means, Sir Arthur first saw the Knossos site in 1894, bought it from its Turkish owner, and began digging in earnest in 1900. The palaces he uncovered at Knossos, and the volumes he dedicated to them, are his monument.

Evans claimed, with justification, to have revealed the artefacts of a hitherto unknown Bronze Age civilisation, that of the Minoans. He estimated that some 80,000 people may have inhabited the city Minoan civilisation was its height. But their story, like that of classical and modern Crete, was one of sudden breaks and cataclysmic disruption, by earthquake, volcanoes and invasion. In about 1450 BC not only Knossos but every other major centre on the island seems to have suffered both natural disasters and attack from over the sea, possibly by the Myceneans from the Peloponnese. Some seventy years later, the throne room, the centrepiece of the most elaborate palace Evans excavated, was destroyed by fire.

Once he had laid bare the sites of the palaces, Evans tried to restore some impression of what the original structures were like, with their grand stairs, gloriously fresh wall paintings, and gaudy brick-red pillars and capitals. Some say he overdid it, and the colourful reconstructions owe more to invention than history; but the staggering quality of the art and civilisation of prehistoric and ancient Crete becomes evident after a visit to the

National Museum at Heraklion. It is one of the greatest collections of ancient artefacts in the Mediterranean – rivalled only by the National Museum in Athens, the Cairo Museum and the Bardo in Tunis. Walking through its plate glass doors is like falling through cultural and historical space. Two overwhelming sensations strike one immediately: the exquisite beauty of many of the pieces, the more ancient in particular, and the presence of cults and mysteries common throughout the Mediterranean. The dominant figure is that of the bull, the symbol of the Palace of Minos, and the head of its most potent mythical creature, the Minotaur. More delicate are the small figures of acrobats jumping the horns of bulls, who re-appear in the red and ochre fresco at Knossos.

The bull, the disguise Zeus took when he raped Persephone, is a constant theme for veneration and sacrifice throughout the Mediterranean, and finds its last echoes in bullfighting in Spain and France, and the sacrifices of bulls on the summer solstice by the Berbers of the Rif. For the ancients the bull embodied power and strength and majesty and fertility – and meat in a world in which food was meagre and scarce. The rituals and taboos associated with them are apparent among the artefacts of the ancient Hittites, contemporaries of the Minoans of Crete, on display in the Anatolian Museum in Ankara – great masks carved and etched as totems for tribal worship. Perhaps the most eloquent celebration of the bull in all mythology is the injunction to the followers of Odysseus against slaying and eating the fat Oxen of the Sun as they graze in the lush plains of Pyla – an injunction which they disobey, so displaying the frailty of mortal flesh.

Quite as wonderful as the bulls and the acrobats are the images and effigies of fertility deities – including the elfin figure of a goddess whose flower-pot hat is adorned with poppy seeds, for opium was doubtless part of her enchantment – and a ceramic statuette of the bare-breasted goddess of the snakes, also found at Knossos.

Most intriguing are various inscriptions, including the fragments found by Evans in the throne room at Knossos in which appears the script known as Linear B. John Chadwick's account of how Linear B's code was cracked is one of the most thrilling of all archaeological detective stories. Its hero was Michael Ventris, an architect and a brilliant amateur archaeologist since his school-days. He was also a mathematical genius. In the face of hostile professional criticism he evolved the notion that the symbols of Linear B did not represent individual words or letters but the syllables of an early form of Greek. By comparing it with other ancient languages the secret was broken. Soon after Ventris was killed in a car crash in England in 1956 at the age of thirty-four. The script known as Linear A still defies interpretation.

Sir Arthur Evans and the British should not be allowed to hog all the limelight. Schliemann, the excavator of Troy and the discoverer of Mycenae and its lost civilisation, was the first to suspect that a palace existed at Knossos. Major work has been done by the Germans, the Americans, and the French, while the Italians have excavated the palace at Phaistos and uncovered the fabulous deposit of arms and armour in the Cave of Mount Ida. But Evans was remarkable for the independent and autocratic way in which he conducted his grand projects. Like many British proconsuls of his day, he almost behaved like a soveriegn power. His workers and collaborators were his subjects. Dilys Powell recalls how, at the end of a digging season in the 1920s, he summoned the workers and foremen to be paid. A table was set up with a bowl of water, a pile of drachma bills of various denominations and a pair of scissors upon it. First he cut the bank notes in two – a perfectly legitimate practice in those days of high inflation – and then, as he handed each worker his wages he dipped his hands in the bowl and dried them, as if freeing himself of such vulgar contamination.

Sir Arthur and his entourage made their headquarters at the Villa Ariadne, a rambling house among the trees on a slope to the north of the main site. When he retired he gave the villa to the Greek government, and it is still used by itinerant archaeologists and their students working at Knossos. During the war it was taken over by the Germans as the residence of the occupying general, and so became involved in one of the most bizarre and celebrated incidents of the Cretan resistance.

A few kilometres beyond Knossos the road forks east and west. It was here that a band of partisans chose to ambush and kidnap the German commander as he drove back to the Villa Ariadne late one evening in the spring of 1944. Disguised as German soldiers, two British officers, Patrick Leigh Fermor and W. Stanley Moss, flagged down the staff car and the general was grabbed, eventually to be spirited across the mountains and away to Egypt by submarine. The operational success of the escapade was blunted by the fact that the original target, General Muller, the garrison commander since the invasion, had been replaced by General Kreipe, veteran of the Russian campaigns, whose knowledge and intelligence of German plans and deployment in Crete was limited.

Leigh Fermor has refrained from writing about the episode and his service with the Cretan resistance, though he is the most accomplished of writers on the culture and history of modern Greece. He loves to repeat the comment of a member of the German High Command –

'They've kidnapped a general? Thank God they didn't take anyone really important, like Corporal Schmidt!'

The Kreipe kidnap triggered off fierce reprisals by the Germans, who had probably already planned a scorched earth campaign for that summer before withdrawing from Crete. Villages, churches, houses were gutted by fire, their inhabitants rounded up and many suspected supporters of the resistance shot. One of the first villages to be devastated was Anoyia, on the slopes of Mount Ida. Nearly all the houses were razed, the charred frames of icons and the blackened scar of the only wall left standing still recall the day when the Germans put the little church to the torch. Anoyia had contributed one member to the kidnap band, though its most celebrated post-war figure, Mayor Giorgos Klados, had worked with Leight Fermor on other operations in the mountains.

Giorgos Klados told me that he had been a convinced communist all his life. We met in the mayor's parlour, looking out across a windy mountain ridge towards Ida. He was an extremely fit sixty-four-year-old, with the bright blue eyes, long moustache and flowing locks of the true montagnard. His personal prestige overcame political barriers and most of those who voted for him were not communists. The fact that he was mayor of the 3000 strong community was something of a personal tribute since a municipality should have more than 10,000 inhabitants in order to quality for its own mayor and council.

He had brought many improvements to the village – better roads, help for the farmers and shepherds, water reservoirs, and amenities for skiing and mountain-climbing, in the hope of attracting a 'tourism of quality'. His pride and joy was the new observatory, which he had persuaded the university at Heraklion and the Max Planck Institute in Munich to build in the clear air of the slopes above the village.

As I left the town hall, I noticed that a fresh set of murals had been daubed on the walls by supporters of the Communist Party of Greece, KKE. Using bold colours and solid, realistic figures, they pleaded for peace in Crete and an end to NATO and American bases in the island. In one a woman in a long black skirt and shawl was throwing a bomb marked USA into the sea, beside her was an islander in the traditional finery of waistcoat, turban, bandolier and dagger, a green map of Crete at his feet. 'One day my Crete will be free of all these foreign pests,' she was crying.

A fierce swirling wind was battering the houses with such force that one felt it would split one's head – the livas, the wind from the Libyan Sea. A few days later planes from the American Air Force and Navy bombed Tripoli and Benghazi.

Six: Turkey–Crossroads to Asia

i Istanbul and the New Turkey

In the glaring light of an Istanbul summer day it is easy to overlook an ornate gateway, layered with dust and soot from the traffic that lurches down the hill from the Topkapi Palace and Hagia Sophia to the Golden Horn and the Galata Bridge. Now the entrance to the offices of the provincial administration, the very name of the gate, the Sublime Porte, once conveyed an aura of power comparable with the Kremlin, or the Pentagon today. For the last two hundred years of the Ottoman Empire, the Sublime Porte was the office of the Sultan's most powerful minister, the Grand Vizir. Today, caught between its past grandeur and the more prosaic present, it epitomises the paradox of modern Istanbul and modern Turkey.

Istanbul, and its older incarnations of Christian Constantinople and ancient Byzantium, was an imperial capital for a millenium and a half, from the times of Constantine the Great to the day in November 1922 when the Sultan Mehmet VI renounced his throne and was conveyed from the Bosphorus into exile aboard a British warship. It was also the centre of religious orthodoxy, both Christian and Muslim and it remains so for the Greek Orthodox world. The Ottoman Sultans were the Caliphs of the Sunni Islam world, an office which was stripped from Mehmet VI's cousin Abdulmecit II in March 1924. Four days earlier the Caliph had held the last great *selamlik*, the public procession and audience for Friday prayers.

The caliphate was abolished by a decree of the Grand National Assembly, which had declared Ankara to be the capital of the new Turkey – a cornerstone of Ataturk's secular political revolution, which turned his country from a cosmopolitan empire in to a unified nation state in which 'the Turkish people would feel at home in Anatolia.'

It would be easy to depict Istanbul as the emblem of the old Ottoman Turkey and Ankara as that of the new secular nation founded by Ataturk in 1923, but the description doesn't quite fit. As more immigrants pour in from the countryside, in particular from the poorer provinces of eastern

Turkey, Istanbul's citizenry is becoming more Anatolian and more Turkish, and less the rich cosmopolitan mixture it was in Ottoman times. The minority communities of Greeks, Jews, Armenians and Albanians, who provided the empire's traders, bankers and administrators, are sadly diminished. Together they number under 100,000 today. In 1886 the Greek population alone in Istanbul was 152,741, the Armenians 149,590, the Jews 22,394, and 'foreigners', as the census put it, were 129,243; while the Muslims – predominantly Turkish and Arab, presumably – numbered 384,836.

Istanbul displays the conflicting claims on modern Turkey of the heritage of Islam and the Ottoman empire, and the ethos of the secular Kemalist nation state. Despite Kemal's reforming success, religious observance is high in Turkey today, and long coats, yashmaks and headscarves – the uniform of the new fundamentalist believer – are common sights.

The image of the empire in the dying years of the sultanate was one of decadence – bloated, cruel and venal, summed up in Gladstone's phrase as 'the sick man of Europe'. At the turn of the century the Sultan's eunuchs still guarded his harem; and were not the Turks behind the massacres of Bulgarians, Kurds and Armenians luridly reported by Protestant missionaries? Istanbul was the pleasure capital of the Mediterranean, rivalled only by Cairo in the last century and the match of Monte Carlo, Beirut and Alexandria in this. For playboys and princes, and the early tourists, it was a place of Turkish delight and fleshly indulgence. So well organised was this traffic, that at soirées and receptions social entrepreneurs in full evening dress used to present visiting cards inscribed with the title 'conseiller de plaisir' – counsellor of pleasure.

The gaudy myth camouflaged the influence and power of Ottoman rule and concealed genuine attempts to reform of their creaking regime by Ottoman Sultans and their suzerains, the Khedives of Egypt. The Tanzimat reforms introduced in 1839 introduced a measure of parliamentary rule and some constitutional rights for the minority peoples; and as the Sultans retreated into their palaces along the Bosphorus, their public and private lives became more austere.

The achievement of the Ottoman Empire was to weld together many nationalities under a rule which was above nationality. At different times it reached as far as Vienna, Persia, the Gulf, the Red Sea, Otranto in southern Italy and the coast of Barbary in North Africa. Algiers itself was ruled by a Bey who presided over one of the most famous slave markets of the Maghreb, and the descendants of his human merchandise can be seen in Ankara or Istanbul, conspicuous for the rich ebony complexions of their African ancestors, yet as much citizens of modern Turkey as the president himself. The Empire embraced what are now twenty-four states of the Mediterranean, the Balkans and the Middle East, and the peoples of some twenty tongues.

The genius of the system was that it was open to the talents – on a slave basis. Greeks, Albanians, Kurds, Persians, Turkomen, Tartars, Armenians, Arabs, Jews and Vlachs were sucked into the administration of the Grand Vizir; and all of them could rise to be amongst the powerful at court or in the army, while remaining the servants of the Sultan, the 'shadow of Allah'. Promising candidates for service in the harem, the administration of the Porte or the army, were often seized as children, and if Christians forcibly converted. These Christians formed the elite corps of janissary guards, whose martial music, strutting marches and clashing cymbals enchanted Europe in the eighteenth century. Satirised and mimicked by Mozart and Rossini in the *alla turca* style, it influenced to the development tradition of western military music, not least the marches of Sousa. At the same time European trade in fabrics, furnishing and architecture fell under the Ottoman influence.

Ottoman rule differed from western imperialism by governing at one remove. There was little sense of direct colonial administration or occupation, and minorities and tribes were often given considerable latitude provided they paid tribute in manpower and money; taxes were put out to farmers for collection. The provincial lords, the Beys, held large estates with feudal rights, but they were few and far between. Ottoman terms and methods are still used throughout the Levant and the Maghreb – in land measurements like the *dunum*, and administrative officers like the *mukhtar*, the village governor.

Such a loose structure could not withstand the rising nationalism of the nineteenth century, beginning with the Greeks, and then their Balkan neighbours – Serbs, Bulgars, Montenegrans and Albanians – and the peoples of the Caucasus – Armenians, Kurds and Tartars – and finally the Arabs. Faced with such internal upheavals the Sublime Porte was hardly a match for the aggressive new empires, fuelled by industrialised wealth, of Britain, France and Czarist Russia. The Empire was replaced by a mosaic of states, protectorates and tribes aspiring to be states, and a legacy of nationalism which is now at the heart of the crisis in the Middle East.

From the opening days of the Greek War of Independence in 1821, the Empire's boundaries begun to shrink. Egypt became virtually a British fiefdom. By 1913 most of the Balkans and North Africa were lost, with

Tripolitania (modern Libya) and the Dodecanese going to Italy. Involvement in the First World War brought an end of all the Levantine and Arab provinces. The Turks retreated into Antolia, and Constantinople was put under the control of the victorious Allies.

An Empire with a total population of 39,000,000 in 1897 was reduced to a nation of 13,270,000. About two and half million Turks and Ottoman subjects had died in the Great War and the War of Independence from 1920 to 1923.

The scenes of disruption in the capital as war came and the empire was destroyed are vividly depicted in one of the most fascinating and eccentric memoirs of the time, Irfan Orga's *Portrait of a Turkish Family*. The author had been born into a well-to-do merchant family, but their old wooden town house was burned in one of the great fires, allegedly started by spies. His father died of disease on the way to defend the Dardanelles, and an uncle was blinded in the Syrian campaign and perished on the trek home. Orga himself became one of the first pilots and commanders of Ataturk's air force, but when he eloped with a British officer's wife while the air attaché in London in 1940 he was stripped of his Turkish citizenship and had to live in impoverished exile.

The main protagonist of the story is his mother, who was ultimately driven mad by the disasters that beset the family. Married at thirteen, she had never expected to go to work, but with the death of all the adult males in the family she took a job in a factory making army uniforms. Years before Ataturk's reforms she removed her veil and took the wooden shutters from the windows of her apartment in the Galata district, and was stoned as a prostitute for doing so.

Each episode of the grand drama of the end of empire is told in metaphors of tiny details, like a bright miniature from the Topkapi Museum. When the fez was abolished, the military cadets were issued with pillbox caps, which they found laughable:

> We had always worn a fez with the Turkish moon and stars woven into the front and we were now very much ashamed to be seen with our new headgear, which was really, we thought, too much like the hat the Christians wore. So we carried the offensive hat in our hands as often as we dared and the few boys who were brave enough to keep it on were called 'Gavur' – an epithet relating to a Christian in an unsavoury way.

The harshness and discipline of the military class as described by Irfan Orga was common to the Ottoman order and to Ataturk's regime. Ataturk relied on his army as the guarantor of the new constitution – which it still is. In the past forty years the army has taken over the reins from civilian governments no fewer than three times – in 1960, 1971 and 1981. Generals like to say that Turkey is not a dictatorship because the army is always prepared to march back to the barracks once the political stable has been cleaned. But the army remains a constant source of power, and though burdened with obsolete equipment it is acknowledged to be one of the best trained in NATO, as well as being the largest apart from the United States. In 1987 it numbered 522,000 men, 497,000 of them conscripts. A military career provides a young officer with the best technical and university education available, and marks him one of the élite in modern Turkish society. Turks are constantly reminded of the importance of the army by the barracks which are strategically – and unavoidably – placed on the outskirts of major towns and cities.

Turkey's reputation has undergone an astonishing transformation since 1918 as the sick man of Europe has become a regional strong man. Some commentators expect Turkey to become a regional superpower, linking Europe, Asia and the Middle East. Turks like to boast that their country is 'Europe's promontory into Asia, Asia's bridge into Europe' – the ideological basis of the Turkish government's application in the spring of 1987 to become a full member of the European Community.

Turkey's application brought strong objections from most of the existing members of the Common Market. The reaction of Western European politicians may well owe something to Turkey's Ottoman past. Turkey has also been playing a larger role in Mediterranean and Middle Eastern affairs, as a leading light in the Organisation of the Islamic Conference and an increasingly powerful figure in western and central Asia as honest broker between Iraq and Iran, born of a common border with both and claims of Turkic kindred with 40 per cent of the population of modern Iran. And the adolescent nation which sang 'Now we are fifteen million' sixty years ago had a population of 50,664 458 by 1985.

The exact figure is important, because the government had expected just to tip the fifty million mark. Instead of a growth rate of around 2.0 per cent the census revealed an annual increase of 2.3 per cent, one of the highest in the Mediterranean. This could mean a Turkish nation of 100 million people by the year 2020 – the same number projected for Egypt and the three central countries of the Maghreb. For Europe the dilemma is obvious. Already Germany has difficulties in coping with its two million Turkish 'guest-workers' and their families. Turkish membership of the EC promises a steady wave of men and women from Anatolia seeking work in Europe's capitals, and the relative poverty of their homeland could be a heavy burden on Community funds. In 1987, when

Turkey applied to join, the average per capita income was little over $1000 a year, roughly one fifth of the average in the Common Market – which includes Greece and Portugal, which are poor by the standards of northern Europe.

Some misgivings about Turkey becoming part of the EC are downright racist, based on religious intolerance and fears of a large Muslim country becoming part of Europe; others, however, concern the doubtful record of successive governments on human rights, torture, the suspension of civil liberties and the administration of justice and prisons. Democracy has been an intermittent phenomenon in modern Turkey. Prison is a degrading experience, and many children are left in penal institutions characterised by violence and sexual abuse. Amnesty International has raised hundreds of cases of mistreatment, which it claims have continued despite the Ankara government's signing both the European and UN conventions on the banning of torture. But the international human rights organisations have not been able to quantify their allegations, many of which have the lurid colouring of travellers' tales.

Between 1983 and 1989 (when he was elected president) the civilian governments of Turgut Ozal made some improvements to the record. But shortly before the general elections of November 1987, the leaders of the outlawed Communist Party (TKP) and the Marxist Turkish Workers' Party (TIP), Haydar Kutlu and Dr Nihat Sargin, returned to Turkey for what they knew would be a test case. They were arrested, stripped, deprived of sleep, and suspended from the ceiling during interrogation, according to testimony to Amnesty International. When they came to trial the following summer, hundreds of lawyers came from Europe and America to support them and witness the hearings – so many that not all of them could squeeze into the courtroom, and the police had to disperse the crowds waiting outside in the street.

Striking a balance between preserving the past and meeting the needs of the present-day city with its ever swelling population proved a fervent personal mission for Bedrettin Dalan, Istanbul's popular and hightly publicised mayor during the mid-1980s. A neat figure with blue eyes, moustache and a slightly rumpled dark suit, he appeared very much a product of the new Turkey when we met in 1985 in his glass-showcase parlour somewhere between the Sublime Porte and the barbican walls built by the heirs of Constantine the Great.

He had started life in an upland village in northern Anatolia, had trained as a civil engineer, and entered politics as a founder member of Turgut Ozal's Motherland Party (ANAP), which came to power after the military authorities had begun to return Turkey to civilian rule in 1983.

The Motherland Party and its leading lights, such as the Ozal family and Mayor Dalan (who later founded his own party), combined a dash of technocracy with a seasoning of old-fashioned Muslim piety, generously garnished with free enterprise economics, the Anatolian version of the policies of Reagan and Thatcher.

The mayor explained that his biggest ambition was to restore its past glory to his city in the most practical way, by cleaning and tidying the shores and channel of the Golden Horn, the channel into the Bosphorus, whose polluted waters and decaying wharves had outraged travellers for the past two centuries. 'My plan is to make these waters as blue as my eyes,' he boasted Mayor Dalan at our first encounter. 'My critics say we won't succeed, but I assure you we will.' By our second meeting in the summer of 1987 the work was all but done. But inevitably there were casualties in the tidying process: seventeenth- and eighteenth-century wooden merchants' houses were destroyed, some once belonging to the wealthy Greeks, the Phanariots, who had taken their name from this quarter; a fifteenth-century church was threatened with the bulldozer.

The new water circulation system, which cost a cool half billion dollars, did not destroy the sewage and filth polluting the Golden Horn but merely pushed it farther up the Bosphorus towards the Black Sea – already contaminated enough by all accounts. Modern Istanbul cannot be cleaned up in so short a time and on the Marmara shore of the old city the leather works and tanneries, now enjoying a new lease of life as suppliers to Italian fashion houses, belch their noxious fumes and waste into the air and sea. The municipality has few means with which to tidy them up.

But under Mayor Dalan much has been done to preserve old Constantinople, which has dozens, possibly hundreds of monuments of the Byzantine era. He has rebuilt the fortified walls of the Emperor Theodosius II, which expanded the perimeters of the city, which Constantine had established as the capital of the Empire of the East a century before. The enormous underground cisterns, said to be the biggest Roman water supply system still in use, have also been the subject of constant repairs.

One of the great hidden treasures of the city was its collection of mosaics; some were said to have originated in Constantine's great palace, while others were of the fifth and sixth centuries AD. Until recently they were stacked and mounted on great slabs of granite in the narthex, at the rear of the cathedral of Hagia Sophia, but now they have been carefully laid out in a small museum beyond the Blue Mosque – a marvellous menagerie of snarling lions, menacing bears, gazelles savaged in the hunt, and grinning donkeys, all in subdued hues of dark luxuriant green, rich orange and thick chocolate brown, with hardly a hint of Mediterranean brilliance.

Outside a little souk of shops, cafés and carpet stores by the mosaic museum sat groups of men and women trying to eke out a living from bits of ornament and fabric, cheap kilims and rugs. These were the human faces of the biggest dilemma facing Mayor Dalan in Istanbul, and Turkey as a whole, for many, if not all, were recent migrants from the villages of eastern Anatolia. They are the poor cousins of the established traders in finery, carpets, trinkets, spices, jewels and precious metals in the Grand Bazaar, where in these tourist-rich days a lease on a comparatively modest stall can cost more than $50,000. According to the mayor, the city's population was expanding by more than 350,000 a year by the mid-1980s, and over half were migrants from the countryside. Between four and five hundred new citizens were arriving each working day – requiring roughly one new primary school to be built a week, houses in the grey and dusty suburbs, and, above all, work. The same pressures are visible in the great cities of the non-European Mediterranean – in Tangiers, Algiers, Tunis, Alexandria, Cairo and even in the chaotic Shi'ite suburbs of south Beirut.

The problem was spelt out more clearly by Mrs Mubiccel Keray, the Professor of Sociology at Marmara University, one of five universities of Istanbul. On first meeting she appears everybody's favourite intellectual aunt, whose warm, almost motherly personality conceals her radical but commonsense approach to social issues, and not least the plight of women. She has concentrated on the rapid changes in Turkish society since Ottoman times, and the shift of populations from the country to the town which has accelerated so sharply in the past ten years. In Ottoman times, she told me, about 90 per cent of the population was tied to the land; 7.5 per cent were urban craftsmen and artisans, while about 2 per cent were administrators and soldiers. Since 1923 there have been land reforms, most recently in the 1980s, when a further redistribution to those who farmed it took place. By then the tractor had arrived, with each machine replacing roughly ten pairs of hands on the land. In 1945 Turkey had roughly 400 tractors, which forty years later had reached over half a million. In the same period the most common agricultural holding increased from 20 acres to about 50 acres as the more successful rural entrepreneurs swallowed up their weaker neighbours. All this meant an end to life on the land for nearly two-thirds of the country's peasants in the span of a generation.

Most of the dispossessed peasants headed for town, where they tried to carry on as before, maintaining a rural approach to life in an urban setting. More than half the working population is self-employed; many become part of what Mrs Keray calls the 'informal economy' – fringe service jobs, portering, carrying messages, shoe-shine and cheap repairs, washing the windscreens of cars stuck in traffic jams.

The informal economy is one of the most pervasive features of urban society throughout the developing Mediterranean, and is different from the 'black' or 'hidden' economy. The black economy merely involves work or transactions done for cash, which are not accounted for to the taxman or official statistician. The informal economy is based on the ways of earning and spending of a village community. One worker can have several dependants in his immediate or extended family; frequently the paltry wages from odd jobs do not go round; many of the bread-winners are children as young as seven.

The strains of scratching a living as new arrivals in the cities fall heavily on women. According to Mrs Keray, 'The status of women in Turkey is what you call an age-specific affair. At first everyone is very affectionate. From the ages of 8 to 10 the little girl starts helping her mother, to whom by 15 she is confidant and friend. The whole social process prepares her to become a member of a hostile environment in marriage. On the other hand, boys are raised to be independent and dominant – in other words spoilt – a highly Mediterranean quality in males!'

To escape the hostile environment of marriage and drudgery in the home women tend to persevere more at getting regular work outside of the home. Paradoxically Turkey has a higher percentage of women lawyers, judges, doctors and university teachers than France or Germany.

Two other striking details from Mrs Keray's graphic map of Turkish society today are the comparatively low life expectancy of adult Turks, and the role of religion in the cities. Most terms of service in the public sector are for only twenty years; life expectancy for the average male Turk in the 1960s and 1970s was 54, though today it is put officially, and rather optimistically, at 64. The steady improvement in public health care and the decline in infant mortality will further encourage an already surging population growth. Despite an alleged improvement in literacy – according to the 1980 census, one-third of those over the age of eleven were illiterate – birth control remains a hit and miss pursuit.

More obvious and intense observance of Islam was to become an outstanding feature of Turkey in the 1980s. Mrs Keray has had some direct experience of the new religious fervour, with members of the Sufi cults and brotherhoods – the *tariqat*, disrupting her lectures and classes and demanding a curriculum respectful to their view of the world.

Islamic fundamentalism seems an almost misleading description of these groups, too suggestive of sectarian warfare among the Shi'ite clans and factions of Lebanon and Iran. Turkish Muslims are mainly Sunni, and some of the cults of Sufi saints and teachers have been established for centuries. The most famous of these Sufi orders are the whirling dervishes from Konya, whose spiralling dance is part of a ritual for attaining a higher spiritual experience. Under Ataturk's new order, even the dervishes were banned from public activity. The modern constitution proclaims that although most Turks are Moslems, and should be allowed the liberty of conscience to be so, the state is secular.

The crux of the debate over the Islamic cults is whether they aim to overturn the present political order to introduce a regime rooted in Islamic principles. Some claim to be little more than prayer meetings and discussion groups. Mrs Keray is not sure, and thinks that some of them aim to overthrow the constitution and introduce an Islamic regime.

The biggest of the cults are the Naqshibendi, which took root in Syria and now has followers in America and Holland and a religious school or *medressa* in Birmingham. Mrs Keray claims that the cults are a distinctly urban phenomenon. Religion in the countryside is more concerned with anecdote and legend than with the mysticism and philosophy of the *sheikhs*, the prayer leaders and teachers of the cults.

One of Mrs Keray's teaching assistants has researched the cults for a doctoral thesis. Some of the *tariqat* are very old, she explained; some, like the Suleimanci, have a nationalist or regional flavour as others are connected with the rising middle class, the financiers and international entrepreneurs of the boom years of the 1980s. The best example of this is a powerful Naqshibendi offshoot, the Jerai, with contacts in the business circles associated with Turgut Ozal's family – though he himself has been careful to avoid endorsing such groups in public. My guide to the cults suggested that the *tariqat* may have filled the vacuum after the abolition of the established political parties following the military coup of 1981 like the sectarian groups of Cromwell's day or the revivalist movements associated with the Wesleys. Outwardly the cults have been coloured by fervour and mysticism, while their cohesion makes them a veiled network of power and influence.

The search for identity and spiritual comfort provided by the cults for many young Turks in the 1980s came after a decade of mounting social chaos and violence. In the late 1970s twenty-five people died on average every night in Turkish cities at the hands of politically motivated extremists – ultra-left Marxists, neo-fascist Grey Wolves and Kurdish secessionists. Behind these groups were criminal organisations, the Turkish mafias, dealing in weapons and drugs, dirty money coming from south-west Asia into Europe via such arteries as the international trucking TIR network.

Memories of those bad years are particularly vivid for Mehmet Barlas, one of Turkey's leading journalists, and a genial bear with a refreshingly pragmatic view of the world. In February 1979 he succeeded to the editorial chair of Istanbul's leading newspaper, Milliyet, after his predecessor, Abdi Ipecki, had been shot in the street by an illiterate gunman named Mehmet Ali Agca – later to achieve fame for attempting to murder Pope John Paul II. Agca was almost certainly in the pay of the Grey Wolves of Colonel Alparslan Turkes's National Action Party. Ipecki had steered his paper's editorial policy on a sensitive and reasoned middle course, criticising the excesses of right and left. Mehmet Barlas was stunned to learn of his friend's death. Within hours later he was trying to get the then Prime Minister, Bulent Ecevit, to agree emergency measures with his main opposition rival, Suleiman Demirel, to stem the rising swell of terrorist violence. The two rivals, whose perpetual bickering emphasised the impotence of parliament, could not bring themselves to work together, nor even to be seen shaking hands in public. The extension of martial law to province after province, leading to full intervention by the armed forces in 1981, seemed the only practical way out.

Barlas thought that Turkey was still riding the crisis. It was one of the few democracies in the eastern Mediterranean, he pointed out and a powerful voice in the Organisation of the Islamic Conference (OIC). But he thought Turkey had been dangerously isolated by the invasion in Cyprus in 1974 'for it mortgaged the foreign policy of this country for the rest of the century.' Though he felt thousands of Turkish Cypriots had to be protected, the operation had been a mistake.

Despite the huge changes of recent years, Istanbul remains the home and heart of the Greek Orthodox world. Some sense of the extraordinary artistic and material wealth of the capital of the empire of the Greeks, Byzantium, gleams through the battered and frayed mosaics of great monuments such as Hagia Sophia; those that remain in the basilica today, including the Virgin Mary in the apse and the portraits of the Empress Zoe and Emperor John II Comnenus, are still wonderfully fresh and direct in their appeal. How such art looked in its heyday, when mosaics and frescoes covered the walls of the churches and convents of the city, is best seen in the Kariye Museum, once the church of St Saviour in Chora. Near it the holiest icon of the city, the image of the Mother of God, was paraded before the defenders on the city walls during the last days of the great siege by the Turks in May 1453 – only to vanish for ever from the people and empire it was supposed to protect.

The entrance porch, narthex and cloister possess the most complete cycles of Byzantine frescoes and mosaics in existence, presenting a continuous drama of the life of Christ and the Apostles, the Holy Family, the prophets, the church fathers, the great councils and the empire. The church was damaged several times, so the present decoration is almost entirely restoration work carried out in the early fourteenth century by Theodore Metichetes, chief minister to the Emperor Andronicos III.

The patriarachate, the home of the Greek Orthodox community in the city today, looks almost drab by comparison – judging by its exterior at least. It stands not far from the Chora, where the Golden Horn meets the Bosphorus. Its massive walls and huge dark gate give the air of a church under siege, and the gate commemorates the hanging there of the Patriarch Gregory V by the Ottoman authorities, expressing their displeasure at the outbreak of the War of Independence in Greece.

Nothing has so marked the change from the cosmopolitan atmosphere to old Constantinople to the plainer, more exclusively Turkish texture of modern Istanbul than the steady erosion of the Greek community. Until forty years ago some 150,000 Greeks still lived in the city. During the crisis over Cyprus in 1955 the populist prime minister, Adnan Menderes, deliberately fomented riots against the Greeks. Greek property rights were restricted, and after a further bout of disorder over Cyprus at Christmas 1963 all Greek citizens were expelled from Turkey. A community of 12,000 in 1964 had fallen to roughly 5,000 by the time of the Cyprus upheaval of 1974, when Greek and Turkish armed forces mobilised against each other.

I was received by the Patriarch's assistant, Bishop Bartolomeus, a man of overwhelming if quiet generosity. He told me that times had been very tough for the Greeks in the city. They were seriously concerned about finding enough priests for the parishes, and whether there would be enough candidates to provide a future patriarch – who has to be chosen from the community of Constantinople itself.

Constantinople is still the senior of the great ancient patriarchates, the first among its equals of Antioch, Alexandria and Jerusalem. As things stood, explained the genial bishop, the patriarchate had some hundred priests who looked after fifty churches in the city. The real question now was whether the Turkish government would allow the reopening of the theological school attached to the Monastery of St George on the Prince's islands, or Kalki Hebdel Adadi, in the Sea of Marmora. If they did, and pupils could be admitted from abroad, the future of the Patriarchate of Constantinople would be assured. Nor were the present community of priests intellectually starved – they were free to attend the theology schools of Athens and Salonika.

The Bishop was careful to give full credit to Mayor Dalan of Istanbul and the then Prime Minister, Turgut Ozal, for providing funds for the restoration of the patriarchate. Displaying wonderful Byzantine intellectual dexterity, he referred to Turgut Ozal as 'our prime minister', for he and his clergy are all citizens of the secular Turkish state.

Shortly after our meeting a small step was taken to ensure that Constantinople would remain the physical home of the Patriarch of the Greek Orthodox Church, with jurisdiction over Asia Minor, Greece, the Islands, Western Europe and North and South America. At their meeting in Athens in June 1988 the Greek and Turkish prime ministers proposed the restoration of full property rights to Greeks in Istanbul, and the possible return of some Greeks expelled in the upheavals of the 1960s and 1970s. Time seems to be working for the spiritual heirs of the church of Constantine and the patriarchs.

ii Ataturk's Citadel, and the March to the Sea: Ankara, Izmir and the Coast

'Soldiers, your goal is the Mediterranean!' was the order of the day posted by Mustafa Kemal to his armies on the night of 25 August 1922, as they prepared for the final push against the Greeks, who had begun their offensive in Turkey three years before. It took just three weeks before Ataturk could announce to the parliament in Anakara that the Greek armies in Anatolia had been destroyed and that the coast had been won.

Kemal knew that for his armies advance to the Mediterranean would set the seal on his revolution and guarantee the independence of the new Turkish nation, which he had forged from the wreck of the Ottoman sultanate. A rugged fastness locked in by the rocky hills of Anatolia and smothered in Asian dust by the hot, dry winds of summer and chilly blasts from the steppes in winter, his new capital has little of the Mediterranean about it, yet Ankara has been an important outpost for the traffic to and from it for nearly two thousand years. It is at a junction of the land route across Asia with the Silk Road; the Romans built a fortress here, and the inscriptions of their garrisons can still be read on the walls of the old citadel. Not far from these ramparts, in 63 AD, Pompey the Great, the partner and then the rival of Julius Caesar, defeated Mirthadates King of Pontus, the biggest threat to the Roman eastern provinces of his day. A later marauder from the east, Tamburlaine seized the city with his Mongol armies, from the Sultan Beyazit the Thunderbolt in 1402 AD, and thus postponed the fall of Constantinople and the Byzantine Empire for fifty years. Tamburlaine, descended from Genghis Khan on his mother's side, showed little interest in crossing the waters of the Bosphorus, and retreated to his capital of Samarkand, where he died in 1405.

Ankara is bound to seem a drab, modern inland city after Istanbul. But it has its quiet attractions. Behind the walls of the citadel, the old quarter has the air of a Turkish village before the arrival of the car and the tractor. Artisans work metal and copper on open braziers and gouge leather for shoes and harnesses, while beneath yellow cascades of laburnum families sort bundles of cotton and winnow grain and heaps of brilliant saffron. A short way down the hill stands the Arslanhane Camii or Lion-House Mosque, one of the three great mosques of the Seljuk era, in which a forest of polished wooden columns, each with a roman capital, sprouts in the green shade of the carpets and wall hangings.

Near the mosque is one of the finest and most suggestive archaeological museums in the entire Mediterranean hinterland. Particularly impressive are the displays devoted to the Hittites and the Assyrians, the civilisations which first left their marks on eastern Anatolia. Sculptures in bronze and stone and huge reliefs show processions of kings and queens with their armies, driving forth in chariots, throwing spears, plunging swords, drinking and dancing in celebration. Reliefs tell the Babylonian story of the Flood, the Epic of Gilgamesh, and include sacred bulls, winged men, and stone lions, long ago relieved from sentry duty at the magnificent Water Gate of Karkamis, overlooking the Euphrates. Some more intimate scenes suggest that domestic life has not altered much. A warrior takes his dog for a walk on a lead; rituals of cooking and washing involve pots and ewers familiar to modern Anatolians; a minstrel strums a *saz*, a favoured instrument of the rhythm section of bands in the cafés and village squares of Turkey to this day.

Crowning another hill, like a modern citadel, is the mausoleum dedicated to Kemal Ataturk. It is a windy rampart in the monumental Thirties style, anonymous and rather forbidding in its isolation in a broad parkland. Soldiers in the white belts and 'snowdrop' steel helmets favoured by American military police stand guard by the eternal flame and the huge slabs of marble and stone inscribed with extracts of the Ghazi's (the leader's) most celebrated speeches. More revealing is a small museum of his personal belongings – clothes, photographs and memorabilia. Turkey's first president is revealed as a bit of a dandy, with more civilian clothes on display than military uniforms – astrakhan coats, silver-topped canes, a Jaeger British 'warm' overcoat from London. These are surrounded by sets of silver-backed hairbrushes and toilet articles, and smoking equipment – he even had brands of cigarettes named after him. Recently these articles have been removed as a part of the government's campaign against smoking in public places.

The personal articles, luxurious though they are, suggest the well-ordered essentials of a commander in the field, always ready to strike camp and move at a rush. The overriding impression is of a man of driving energy and iron purpose; and the dominant image is that of Ataturk himself, with his aquiline features, clear blue eyes and blonde hair, betraying his vaunted ancestry on his mother's side among the Yuruk, the migrant Turkish peoples from beyond the Caucusus.

He was the son of a government clerk in Salonika, and besides his Yuruk ancestry he also had Albanian blood. His difficulties with the Muslim *hoja* (preacher) at the local school turned him against religion in the secular and political life. A brilliant graduate of the War School in Istanbul, he was famed above all as a soldier, outstanding at rallying poorly-armed irregulars against superior odds. In 1916 it was Colonel Mustafa Kemal who organised the defences at what came to be known as Anzac Bay near Gallipoli; later he organised the lines of retreat before Allenby's armies in Syria. Sent by the Sultan as inspector-general of the armies in eastern Anatolia, he realised the empire was lost and raised the standard of nationalist revolt. Within three years he had defeated the superior armies of the Greeks, who landed with the connivance of the French and British at Smyrna in 1919.

But his battle honours are less than half his achievement. More extraordinary was his political insight, a combination of vision and masterly tactical skills – particularly in late-night sessions in committee rooms, which were literally smoke-filled whenever he was present.

As a young man, Kemal was involved in the Committee of Union and Progress – better known as the Young Turk movement – which originated in his native Salonika. But the most important experience of his early political education was his appointment as military attaché to Sofia in 1913, regularly viewing sessions of the new Bulgarian parliament from the stranger's gallery. He also fell in love with Dimitrina, daughter of the Bulgarian Minister of War, General Kovatchev. The liaison ended abruptly when the general said he would rather cut off his own head than have his daughter marry a Turk. The rebuff seems to have had a permanent effect, for no liaison was to last thereafter.

His skill at manipulating representative assemblies was evident from the early days of the war of independence. Following his 'declaration of independence' at Amasya in June 1919, he summoned a congress at Sivas, which led two years later to the Grand National Assembly at Angora, as Ankara was then called. The Assembly conferred on him the titles of marshal and 'Ghazi', or warrior leader.

Within a month of victory over the Greeks Ataturk began the reform programme by which he shaped modern Turkey to this day. In October 1923 Ankara was declared the capital and the new republic proclaimed; in 1924 the caliphate and religious institutions and schools were swept away; in 1925 the fez, religious brotherhoods and cults were abolished, and a new civil code proclaimed. In 1928 came the great reform which was to boost literacy and strike a blow at the obscurantism of religion: the introduction of the Latin alphabet. The printing press had come late to the Ottoman empire during the eighteenth century and even then it was difficult to mass produce Arabic script, so that the Koran and other religious texts had remained, almost exclusively, the preserve of the sheikhs and teachers. Turks were also told to find surnames – Kemal choosing Ataturk, or Father Turk.

Legislative and social reforms, such as the emancipation and enfranchisement of women, were complemented by programmes of economic development. In these his ministers evolved a system of 'étatism' or 'autarchy' – state direction of capitalist enterprise – was evolved. It remains a feature of the Turkish economy, though increasingly criticised and modified under Turgut Ozal's policies of *laissez faire*.

Ataturk was a dynamo of reform, continuously touring the country to meet his people. The most valuable gift he had given them was himself, a living legend of the new Turkey. But the pace at which he worked and an increasingly irregular and dissolute private life, with long nights given over to carousing with cronies in such haunts as the Pera Palace Hotel in Istanbul, and an over-fondness for *raki*, laid him low. In September 1938 he died of cirrhosis of the liver at the relatively young age of fifty-seven.

The living monument to Ataturk in Ankara is the Cankay, the presidential palace specially designed for him. Its incumbent in the 1980s was a man in the Ghazi's own image, General Kenan Evren, who had led the military intervention in September 1981, becoming the civilian president a year later. When I met him in the summer of 1988 he seemed the epitome of the soldier-statesman with a ram-rod back – very much in the style of his nation's founder. He began with a short lecture on the Kemalist heritage, the secular state, the national flag, and the observance of the law. He said leftists who challenged the prohibition of Marxist parties and unions would have to take the consequences of their actions, as they knew they were transgressing the law. Not that he believed in military rule. 'The army does not make coups in Turkey as in other countries,' he observed, 'each time it has invervened to restore order it has soon returned to barracks.'

He was particularly interesting on the public revival of religion. The year before he had warned a group of students that the head scarf – the symbol of religious observance by women – 'was a bigger threat to the stability of Turkey than communism', but since then his line had moderated. Most Turks were Muslims, he said, and their faith should be respected. Turkey played an active role in the Organisation of the Islamic Conference but it did not participate in its legal committees, with their emphasis on extending the public influence of Islamic law, the sharia.

A rather different perspective on the Kemalist tradition was provided by the man Kenan Evren removed from office in 1981, the socialist prime minister Bulent Ecevit. When we met in his flat overlooking the burnt hills on the capital's outskirts, he was still under house arrest, for he had been banned from political activity for ten years under the new constitution. Bulent Ecevit speaks with the clarity of a philosopher rather than the pragmatism of a politician, and is one of his country's leading poets. Fluent in English and German, he also has a great taste for art – his mother was a celebrated painter. With his neat dark-suited figure, aquiline features, moustache and jet black hair, he sat bolt upright in a simple chair – his silhouette oddly reminiscent of Whistler's portrait of his mother.

Ecevit was also a direct political heir of Ataturk. He had been the last secretary-general of Ataturk's Republican People's Party, and like Ataturk he had tried to make politics for the people rather than for a narrow coterie of professional practitioners. His short-lived premierships in the 1970s had been dominated by the landing of Turkish forces in Cyprus in 1974, which he himself had ordered, and the increasing public disorders and terrorist violence, which led first to the imposition of martial law in province after province and ultimately to his own removal from office.

Like President Evren, Bulent Ecevit was concerned at the increasing role of religion in public affairs, pointing out the new phenomenon of mesheets or little chapels in ministries and offices. The real test, he suggested, would be whether the army would be tempted to play the religious card to maintain its authority against a Marxist threat, real or imaginary. In 1986 a year after our meeting, ninety officer cadets were dismissed from the military academy for espousing fundamentalist Islamic cults.

But he was most graphic when describing the Cyprus crisis of 1974. He had taken the decision to order troops to land on the island during a visit to the city of Afion. He had gone there to dissuade farmers from growing opium poppies as part of the drive against narcotics production co-ordinated with the United States' Drug Enforcement Agency. At the airport he learned of attacks on Turkish villages in Cyprus, and gave the generals the order to go.

He described vividly his failure to persuade the Americans or the British to act together to restrain the Greeks. His most poignant recollection was a dinner with Harold Wilson in Downing Street. 'Wilson kept saying he had to go to the "loo". He did so five times, but I knew he was phoning Joseph Sisco, the American Assistant Secretary of State. By the end of the dinner I knew the British and Americans would do nothing.'

The Aegean Coast

From the ramparts of the Genoese fort at Cesme the island of Chios lies grey and lumpy in the Aegean like a sea monster about to wake. It is only two or three miles from the Turkish coast, and this proximity lies at the heart of the Aegean dispute. Technically the argument between Greece and Turkey is over rights to the continental shelf and territorial waters, the exploitation of the sea-bed and the control of air space. But to leave it at that would be to glance at the price rather than read the book.

The Aegean dispute is one of the most complex and revealing of any between neighbours in the Mediterranean; and it reflects how both Greeks and Turks define their identity in terms of their relationship, past and present, with the sea. For Bulent Ecevit some of the more extreme Greek claims smack of 'irredentism'; whereas Greek politicians describe Turkish claims to exploitation and navigation rights as a form of *lebensraum*. For Greeks the Aegean is their home, the centre of the world of Hellenism; for Turks it it an outlet to the Mediterranean, a passage from Asia into Europe.

Islands like Chios became Greek as result of the Balkan Wars of 1912 to 1913; a position confirmed at the Treaty of Sèvres in 1920 at the end of the First World War. Essentially the Aegean dispute rests on three treaties: Lausanne in 1923, at the end of Ataturk's war of independence; Montreux in 1936, which regulates access to the Bosphorus; and the Treaty of Paris, implemented in 1947, whereby the islands of the Dodecanese, among them Rhodes, Patmos, Syme and Cos – once Italian possessions – became Greek. A huge and additional complicating factor has been the quarrel over Cyprus.

For many Turks the Greek claim to the islands is part of the 'Great Idea', the scheme to gather into Greece all the Greek communities of the Turkish Aegean coast, along with the Sea of Marmara and Pontus on the Black Sea – a dream which evaporated with the crushing defeat of the Greek armies in Anatolia by Ataturk in his march to the sea in 1922. Reconciliation between Venizelos and Ataturk led to the Treaty of Montreux, which restricted the passage of warships through the Bosphorus – and addressed the status of military garrisons on the eastern islands. It also confirmed the status of the only two Turkish islands in the eastern Aegean, Gokceada and Bozcaada (formerly Imros and Tenedos), which guard the entrance to the Sea of Marmara.

Old antagonisms and suspicions were rekindled as the Cyprus dispute boiled over in the mid-1970s, which coincided with a flurry of enthusiasm for the fossil fuel and mineral potential of the Aegean sea bed. When, in 1974, a Turkish survey ship sailed from Canakkale at the mouth of the Sea of Marmara to prosecute exploration licences in the Eastern Aegean issued to the Turkish state petroleum company, she had to be escorted by thirty-two warships. In 1976 another survey vessel was fitted out to prospect round the island of Thasos, so adding tensions and leading to lengthy and inconclusive talks. When in 1987, its successor the Sismik II prepared to survey round Chios, the armed forces of both countries had to be fully mobilised and Greek air force pilots were ordered to sink her and her escort if they pushed into the Aegean. So frightened were the two governments of conflict that they began talks in 1988. War had come ever closer after the Greeks had placed defensive garrisons in the eastern Aegean islands following the landing of Turkish forces in northen Cyprus in the summer of 1974.

Equally vexed is the question of air traffic control and navigation of the skies above the Aegean. The Aegean belongs under international convention to the Flight Information Region (FIR) of Athens airport, on the practical grounds that otherwise domestic flights to many Greek islands would have to go through international or Turkish air space. As the armies of both countries were mobilised over Cyprus in August 1974, the Turkish authorities ordered international pilots to report to them when entering Aegean air space. The Greeks replied in similar vein, claiming that the Aegean was now unsafe because of the conflict in air control authority. International flights were then suspended.

The bones of dispute have to be rehearsed in some detail for two reasons: the argument is potentially lethal, and the explosion could be triggered by any number of issues. The technicalities are infinitely complex and could take the jurists of the International Court at the Hague years to unravel. Part of the problem is that different distances are proposed for the limits of the continental shelf, the sea bed and the waters around and the air above the islands, with a limit of two to five miles in some cases and up to twelve or twenty in others.

Some sense of the depth of emotion stirred by the dispute was given by the publication entitled 'Threat in the Aegean', which I was given in the Greek embassy in Ankara a few days before the Turkish prime minister was due to visit Greece in June 1988. Under the title runs the motto, 'There are no differences between Greece and Turkey. There are only Turkish designs on Greece.' Subsequent pages bear such statements as 'The Aegean is the cradle of Hellenism. The Greek nation has lived here from the dawn of history. We do not negotiate our sovereign rights.' On Turkish claims the booklet declares that 'The Turks appeared on the scene very late' and that 'Turkey does not claim legitimate rights in the Aegean because it simply has none.'

It would be rash and impertinent to offer judgment in so complex a dispute here, but any traveller round the Aegean is sure to be struck by a paradox. Whatever their differences in history, religion and ethnic make-up, Turks and Greeks share common habits and tastes for coffee, kebabs, dolmades, grilled crayfish. The matter for debate is to whom they belonged first, and to whom they speak most directly of their origin, identity and soul.

The signs of Greek culture and habits, representing more than 2500 years of habitation on the Turkish coasts of the Aegean, are vivid and unmistakeable. Pergamon and Ephesus are among the finest and grandest monuments to Hellenistic civilisation. Until the Catastrophe, Smyrna was a Greek port to rival Piraeus and Salonika. Little of the old Greek city has survived. As the Turkish troops approached in September 1922 a huge fire swept the main part of town. The Turks blamed panic-stricken Greek soldiers fleeing to their warships in the harbour. A witness to the destruction was a former mayor of Izmir, Dr Behcet Uz, who in 1931 erected a statue in the town to his hero, Kemal Ataturk. 'The fire was started when a powder magazine exploded in a church in the Armenian quarter,' he recalled. 'It quickly jumped across the narrow streets and the wooden balconies of the houses, and soon one-third of the town along the promenade was gone. It took eight years to clear away the mess.' In the old quarters only a few narrow streets and small mosques remain. Dr Uz had been responsible for much of the rebuilding. Some of the new projects were inspired by Ataturk himself, he claimed, such as the Luna Park, a permanent site for trade fairs and recreation proposed by the Ghazi after his visit to the Moscow Fair in 1926.

With its bright lights, pop music, stalls of sticky sweets, soft drinks and glutinous coffee, the Luna Park still draws the crowds at weekends. By contrast the ancient Greek sites are havens of repose, even at the height of the tourist migration season. Ephesus and Halicarnassus are becoming as familiar in the iconography of postcards as Delphi or St Marks in Venice, but no reproduction can capture their proportions or grandeur.

One burning September afternoon I stood at the top of the amphi-theatre where St Paul once preached in Ephesus. The umbrella pines flickered like flames in the haze off the distant sea. I was struck by the size of the city, an impression enhanced by the best preserved façade still standing, the library of Celsus. This beautifully proportioned porticoed edifice, with its elegant statuary, stands at an oblique angle to the main street, which suggests that it was a latecomer, squeezed between palaces and edifices at least as imposing.

Towards the harbour, now well away from the sea due to continuous silting, I came across the huge outline of the Basilica of Mary the Virgin. It was here that the third of the great councils of the Church was held in 431 AD. Appropriately enough the Council declared Mary to be *theotokos*, the Mother of God, and it continued the process begun at the first council at Nicaea of defining the doctrine of the Trinity and the nature of Christ. Twenty years later, at the Council of Chalcedon, it was declared that Christ was one person, but of two natures, God and man. These debates and dissensions still occasion conflict among the Christian communities of the Levant and Middle East today.

In essence they represented a clash between the two great schools of theology of Alexandria and Antioch. In the fourth century AD Arius of Alexandria had maintained that Christ, as subordinate to God, was essentially human; the Arian heresy was condemned roundly at the Council at Nicaea in 325 AD. The opposite position was propounded by Nestorius of Constantinople, who said that Christ was of two persons, human and divine, and therefore it followed that Mary could not be *theotokos*. This too was denounced as heresy, by the council which assembled in the huge church of the *theotokos* at Ephesus. Nestorius was stripped of his office and banished to Petra, and later died in exile in Egypt. His teachings persist in the Nestorian churches of the Middle East.

Another heresy was that of Monophysitism, held most notably today by the Coptic Churches, according to which Christ is one nature indivisable, both divine and human. This was discarded and condemned at Chalcedon in 451, when the council of five hundred bishops gathered in the Church of St Euphemia acclaimed the *tome* (papal epistle) of Pope Leo the Great which proclaimed faith 'in one and the same Son, perfect in Godhead and perfect in manhood, truly God and truly man, acknowledged in two natures, unconfusedly, unchangeably, indivisibly, inseparably . . .' The Maronites say they subscribe to this belief in its purest form, and that it is their sacred duty to safeguard this doctrine on Mount Lebanon. It is a faith for which some Maronites say they are still prepared to die.

The Council of Ephesus was dominated by the figure of Mary Mother of God. Mary was supposed to have come to Ephesus with St John; the site of her death, in a leafy glade above the ancient city, is now a place of pilgrimage, and nothing in the whole region arouses the awe and interest of the Turks as the Maryama shrine.

Until 1923, Greeks celebrated here each 15th of August the Feast of the Virgin, a ritual which was a thinly disguised continuation of the fertility rite of the mother-goddess Artemis. Not far away across the fields lies the site of one of the greatest temples to the goddess ever known, the Artemesion – one of the Seven Wonders of the World, according to Philo the Byzantine. The great temple was buried and lost for centuries, before being discovered once again about a hundred years ago. All I could see of it was a pool of thin grey mud, the playground of some joyously honking geese. Two farmers were watering their vegetables between the low foundation walls, their goats and a donkey tethered to some fragmentary and forlorn columns. But the finest monuments to the goddess are the glorious effigies and statues now in the museum in Ephesus, covered in cascades of sculptured breasts – vivid witnesses to the potency of the fertility cult.

The flourishing of Greek genius along these coasts in antiquity is quite striking. Here Homer, or one bearing that name, is believed to have composed and recited. Herodotus – the father of history, and certainly the first great reporter – was born at Halicarnassus. Near Pergamom lie the extensive ruins of the Askleipion, the hospital of Galen, one of the founders of medical science.

Unfortunately the view from the Asklepeion to the hill of Pergamom, where the Altar of Zeus once stood, is obstructed by an extensive army training camp and tank park – so emphasising the curiously semi-detached attitude of the Turks to most of the great classical monuments. They protect them, and keep them scrupulously tidy, but are not over-concerned about their restoration and excavation – as if to say that they respect these artefacts but feel they belong to a different culture from their own.

Not far from Pergamom is the village of Candarli, whose Genoese castle overlooks a fishing harbour entirely absorbed in the pleasures of the present. Trays of tea were being carried out to the tables under the Judas trees beside the white-walled cafés; rowdy arguments were punctuated by the slamming of backgammon pieces in games of 'tric-trac', while families swayed back along the road in stately promenade. The tea, the men's moustaches, the crack and crash of tric-trac were distinctly Turkish, but the setting, the evening light and the careless pleasure of the community were essentially Aegean.

The Turquoise Coast

From Antalya you can take the low road from the edge of the Aegean into Asia – as I did in the deep glowing days of autumn. The path is not easy, and the road rears and writhes round the rocky mass of the Anti-Taurus mountains where they tumble into the Mediterranean. Faced with the immovable barrier of the range, crusading armies used to travel by sea. An exception was the Emperor Frederick Barbarossa, who chose to cross the mountains, mindful of a prophecy that he would meet his death by water.

Even so, the Emperor drowned. He had tried to ford in full armour the Goksu River, which slices through the rocky massif to the sea at Silifke. Caution was thrown to the winds, apparently, when Frederick was bitten by that peculiar desire of martial dictators, from Caesar and Charlemagne to Chairman Mao, to show of their prowess at swimming to their armies. The spot is now marked by a panoramic car park on the edge of the river gorge, complete with commemorative plaque.

The modern caravans that take the coast road consist of tourist buses and huge articulated trucks heading up the two-lane highways, the modern if more prosaic version of the golden road to Samarkand, into the heart of Asia, to Afghanistan, Uzbekistan and the western borders of China. The lorries and trailers groaning under bales of cotton and bundles of tobacco are interspersed with the gentler rhythms of more traditional traffic – raucous flocks of sheep, the odd string of lumbering camels and gangs of mangey and noisome goats. Beneath the road is one of the splendours of the Mediterranean: the sea, no longer Homer's wine-dark deep, is a radiant turquoise. This is the Turquoise Coast.

The move into Asia is marked by subtle clues and hints. Beyond the coastal mountains open up plains that stretch to the Caucasus and the outer defences of the Hindu Kush. Faces broaden, eyes narrow, and at some indefinable point on the coast road the fashionable tight blue jeans of tourist-driven western Turkey are discarded for the more commodious and becoming baggy trousers and kaftans of the east.

Antalya itself is a brutally ugly commercial town of modern shops and apartment blocks, with factories and food-processing plants on the outskirts. Its mitigating factors are the curling bay below the old city, and the fading gentility of the wooden-fronted Ottoman houses within it, which huddle for protection under the outstanding monument of Seljuk architecture – the exquisite, brick-red Yivli Minare or fluted minaret, built by Sultan Alaeddin Kekyubad in 1219.

Still limpid green in high autumn, the plain round Antalya benefits by its proximity to the Mediterranean and is protected by the mountains to the north against the harsher elements of the central Anatolian climate. For four months the slopes have sufficient snow for skiing, while the coast enjoys more sunshine throughout the year than almost anywhere else on the northern shore of the Mediterranean. The flatlands grow more than 250 floral species, some unique to the plain, and over a third of the fruit, vegetables and cereals produced commercially in Turkey. Colonies of tomato beds under tattered and glinting plastic blot the landscape, mercifully interrupted by rolling fields of wheat and dignified cotton plants, their fruit like clumps of snow.

The natural wealth of the land must have attracted the first Greek settlers after the sack of Troy for some of the grandest and most elaborate remains of ancient Greek cities can be found here, including Perge, Aspendos, Sillyon and Side. A clue to the size of ancient Perge is provided by its theatre, which lies some way outside its southern gate. Much of what remains is of a Roman design, with a seating capacity of 15,000, suggesting a total population of between 100,000 and 150,000 – in its day, the greatest city of the Roman Empire of the east.

Inside the walls are paved streets, deeply rutted by chariot wheels, stall-holders' pitches in the fish market marked out by mosaic symbols and names, and the largest and among the finest baths of any classical site – that unique gift of antiquity to the modern Mediterranean. The three chambers of *tepidarium*, *caldarium* and *frigidarium* are clearly defined; their white stone and marble floors and wall facings in a veiny light green marble were shamelessly plundered from the islands of the Aegean. The same system of warm, hot and cold chambers formed the basis for the bath-houses that the Ottoman Turks transmitted to more than half the Mediterranean, from Marrakesh to the coasts of Marmara.

We were climbing the steep auditorium of the perfectly preserved Roman theatre at Aspendos. My trousers were suddenly grabbed by a small hand through the grill by one of the entrances – the suggestively named *vomitaria* – through which actors poured onto the stage. 'Psst, you buy coins?' whined the owner of the hand. 'My father find with tractor – mister, you look Alexandros – the face of Alexandros, cost you twenty dollars.' In the grubby paw were a few gleaming discs bearing the unmistakeable leonine head of Alexander of Macedon – the most emotive figure of the old Mediterranean in myth and reality.

Coins and heads of Alexander were to pursue me halfway round the Mediterranean, into Syria, Lebanon, Israel and Egypt; a chance meeting in Antioch was later to explain their abundance.

By its very name – it means 'pomegranate' – Side epitomises Mediterranean abundance and fertility. Its site was virtually undisturbed until forty years ago, when excavations by British and Turkish scholars from Istanbul began to reveal the most extensive Roman town plans in Asia Minor. Unlike the first colonisers of Greek Perge, the early Sideans came from the Aegean coast round Ephesus, and not from Troy. The deity of Perge is another of the many-breasted figures of Artemis, cousin to that almost indecent embodiment of fecundity, Artemis Polymastros of Ephesus. The Sideans seem to have had a sense of martial inferiority about their origins, since the Trojan experience was missing from their pedigree. To compensate, their coins bear the image of Athene Nike, goddess of Victory – though the obverse bears the ubiquitous pomegranate, in recognition of the real source of their wealth and strength.

The journey east took us well into the hours of darkness. Although it was well into the autumn, most of the barracklike-hotels round Alanya were full intimations of invasions and ruinations to come.

We stopped by the great castle of Anamura. With its curtain walls and more than thirty turrets intact, it is Armenian in origin, though a small mosque in the main court claims it for the Ottomans. Here Ali, our guide, revealed his great preoccupation: his forthcoming arranged marriage, and the necessary exchange of gifts and endowments between bride and groom. As with more than half the Turkish population, his bride had been selected by a relation – in this case an uncle. Ali had seen her three times, he had been received by her parents, and the union approved. She was in her early twenties while he, I guessed, was at least ten years older. He already had a regular companion, a doctor whom he had known from his university days – 'more like a sister than a friend', as he put it. His fiancée, an agriculturalist engaged in research, met with his approval.

Money and endowment of worldly goods in the wedding contract had begun to haunt Ali like an obsession. 'I am expected to give her jewellery, but I told her I couldn't give her great wealth,' he protested. 'I'll give her about £1000 worth of jewellery – but in the villages they ask for three metres of gold chains or ten gold bracelets, just like prizes in a beauty contest. Some weddings can cost eight years' income – a big strain on the family. I have bought some of the furniture, and my brother helped find the apartment. In my father's day a family was a guarantee of security. Now we are supposed to have pensions.' Since Ali's monthly income was just over £100, juggling his finances in order to get married seemed more a matter for a migraine than a mere headache.

After Ali had finished telling us about the perils of Turkish matrimony, we escaped into the hills beyond the Goksu gorge. As it climbs up to the Anatolian plateau the road is overlooked by Roman tombs, stark in the sandy bluff, inscrutable sentinels guarding the southern access to ancient Diocaesarea. Startling though the tombs are, they give little hint of the wonder to come. Beyond a village a Roman arch opens on to the temple of Zeus Olbius, a parade of Corinthian columns marking out its grand, regular plan. As I walked through the village down a Roman road, I entered a scene of tranquillity and harmony of the old Mediterranean and remote from the discordant images of the new. On a flat roof a woman slowly winnowed her corn, occasionally raising the sieve, a disc of dull gold to match the sun. Old olives and oaks formed a canopy of broken shadows across the shrine of Zeus, their leaves a green mantle fit for his daughter, bright-eyed Athene. By the smaller temple of Tyche a shepherd prodded two recalcitrant donkeys from their grazing.

Along the coast, east of Silifke and the mouth of the Goksu, lie the remains of the Byzantine city of Corycius, huge chunks of anonymous masonry and neglected sculptures strewn across a lunar landscape. By contrast, the twin castles of the Maiden, the Kiz Kalesi, are compact and light, the one on its promontory nodding to its companion, which seems to float above the sea at sunset. Once linked by a causeway, they are memorials to the medieval Armenian kings of the Rubenid dynasty. According to an inscription in Armenian the castle in the sea was founded in 1151 AD. The Armenian origins of these monuments is pointedly passed over in the tourist literature.

The Armenians established their kingdom along the Cilician coast after they had been pushed from their northern homeland round Van and Mount Ararat by the first Turkish invasions. The royal dynasty eventually married into successive generations of Frankish crusading families – so much so that some Turks today will tell you that the Rubenid kingdom was little more than a Latin Crusader fiefdom. But the rich array of illuminated manuscripts, embroidery and regalia from mediaeval Cilicia now in the Armenian Convent in Jerusalem reveal a quite distinct culture and style.

The further pressure of invasions, this time from the Mongols in the early fourteenth century, proved too much for the kingdom, though the *coup de grace* was administered by the Lusignan king of Cyprus, Peter I, who captured the Kiz Kalesi in 1361; the capital fell to the Mamluks of Baybars in 1375.

Armenians lived in Cilicia until the early part of this century, but by then their very name and culture had become the stuff of murderous controversy. The Armenian problem still cuts deep into the psyche of modern Turkey. For an outsider to write or say anything about the matter is likely to cause offence on both sides, so strong is the sense of hurt and injured pride. Its historical truth is often buried beneath layers of myth and propaganda.

The Armenians believe that the Ottomans carried out a series of massacres in a deliberate policy of expelling the Armenians of eastern Anatolia during the First World War, between 1915 and 1916. They claim that a million and a quarter Armenians were killed or deliberately uprooted from their lands, so as to snuff out their dreams of becoming a separate nation. According to Armenian nationalists, they were promised their own state at the Treaty of Sèvres in 1920 – peace terms which the Allies tried to force on the Ottoman Sultan, but which merely swelled support for Ataturk's nationalists – but any prospect of an independent Armenia was cancelled in the Treaty of Lausanne in 1923.

In March 1921, an Armenian shot dead in a Berlin street the man most Armenian nationalists hold responsible for what they see as a calculated policy of extermination against their people, Talat Pasha. He was former Grand Vizier and Minister of the Interior, and one of Enver Bey's closest allies in the Young Turk movement and the revolution of 1908.

The murder of Talat still antagonises Turkish officers of the old school, who see the assassination presaging the spate of attacks since the early 1970s against Turkish diplomats carried out in the name of the shadowy Armenian Secret Liberation Army (ASALA). One former Turkish ambassador told me that many of the allegations against Talat, and the very notion that Armenians had been deliberately massacred, had largely been got up by the British Foreign Office and the so-called fact-finding commission headed by Lord Bryce and Arnold Toynbee in the First World War; while any believe in the distinct ethnic and cultural identity of the Armenians was merely a wilful and mischievous display of ignorance.

But other, more scholarly voices, speak in moderate tones. The historian Mim Kemal Oke of the Bosphorous University, who has studied the issue both in Turkey and in Britain at Cambridge and Sussex universities, says the debate is riven by a fundamental difference of outlook and perspective between the Turks and the British and Europeans on the issue. 'Undoubtedly a lot of killing went on in the chaos of retreat and the collapse of the Empire,' he once told me, 'but other minorities beside the Armenians, such as the Kurds, were afflicted as well.'

Early in 1989 the Turkish government said it would open the state archives to re-examine the entire question of the Armenian massacres – a possible move to boost Turkey's candidature for full membership of the European Community. It is likely to prove a lengthy process as the archives were badly damaged and disrupted, and some in Istanbul were burned down in the last days of the Sultanate. The bulk of the material is likely to be in old Turkish in Arabic script, which only a handful of scholars can decipher.

Armenians claim that they were one of the first peoples in the Roman Empire to embrace Christianity. Some centuries before Christ they had settled round Mount Ararat – the resting place of Noah's Ark, in the frontier land between Turkey and Soviet Armenia. They gave their name to one of the buffer provinces guarding the eastern flanks of the empire of Augustus and Tiberius. Further evidence of their singularity is provided by their language, their strange script – all hooks and curls, their architecture and their churches, now in sad decay in north-east Anatolia.

The Armenians are one of the most singular peoples to be without a homeland, and some of the most expert exiles of the modern Mediterranean. They are natural entrepreneurs in religion – characteristically they are divided into Catholic and Orthodox churches – as well as in arts and commerce. The folk memory of the massacres is potent nourishment to their sense of being a nation in exile. Later in my Mediterranean journey I was to be given a vivid illustration of how their culture and identity are maintained.

The cities of the Cilician plain, the crease of low land between the Anti-Taurus and the highland barrier before the Syrian desert, are monuments to modern Turkey, with few memorials of times past. Mersin is the principal naval base of the coast, whence the fleet departed for the landings in northern Cyprus in July 1974. It is a place of high-rise offices and hotels, their lobbies bustling with long-robed Arabs from the Gulf, trading oil for textiles, clothes and jewellery and seeking a touch of low life in the port's night clubs whose reputation is as lurid as their lighting.

The huge sprawl at Adana proclaims a city on the make: it is the centre of trade in tobacco, cotton, textiles and ceramics. Of nobler and more ancient pedigree is the Adana kebab, made of delicately ground meat, marinated in oil and covered with sesame and nuts and cooked inside the oven rather than on a charcoal grill, as with the kebab of the Aegean. It is served with freshly baked bread, unleavened and crusty and warmed in the oven with the kebab. A good Adana kebab can be the length of the table, but the meat is remarkably light and fragrant – its slightly sharp, spicey flavour giving a hint of the East and India.

In Tarsus, midway between Adana and Mersin, the past seems to have been forgotten among the modern urban developments. A plain house in a quiet sidestreet is supposedly St Paul's birthplace – its authenticity owing more to tourist hokum than to history. The one monument of any size, a Roman gate, known variously as St Paul's Gate, Cleopatra's Gate or the Gate of the Bitch, stands alone in a whirling frenzy of traffic; it was to this gate that Cleopatra sailed in 41 BC for her first date with Mark Antony.

On the quays at Mersin, I came across a scene of enchantment and entertainment, though of a more modest variety than that staged by Antony and Cleopatra. The open-air cafés were thronged with sailors and townspeople, eating mezes and drinking raki, beer, or colas. A group of Yuruk nomads were cooking their meals over charcoal fires and selling their embroidery and cloth. The cafés reverberated to the swoop and wail of arabesque love ballads of singers, whose accompaniment was partly traditional, partly raucously electronic – among them a white-suited youth of about fourteen or fifteen, Mehmet Ali Kurt, singing of some long lost love. His voice, pure and seamless, with that sob peculiar to the Arab world and the East, was of the kind that could mesmerise an audience in a second. His casual grace gave some hint as to why singers and dancers are adored above ordinary mortals in the Levant, and in Egypt and Turkey in particular, with crowds weeping and fainting in their presence. Mehmet Ali's audience were ecstatic – shouting, whistling, waving and banging their beer glasses. Suddenly a military policeman, white-belted, with a night-stick and white 'snowdrop' helmet, strode through the tables. It looked like trouble. Were Mehmet Ali's papers in order? Had he failed to respond to his military draft? A hush fell among the tables near the stage. And then the soldier presented a bunch of red roses to the boy, embraced him in a bear-hug, and smothered his cheeks with kisses before being restrained by a comrade-in-arms.

East of Adana the open and rugged plain offers a distant prospect of Asia. Trucks heading east to Mosul and Baghdad take the southern route; to the north lie the Soviet borders, Tehran and Isfahan, Afghanistan and the lands beyond the Oxus. Standing above the roads into Asia, dark silhouettes wrapped in clouds of lime smoke from the quarries and red dust from the fields, a string of castles and fortress villages watch balefully over this furthest corner of the Mediterranean coastland – among them the Yilan Kalesi, the castle of a mythical Armenian king of Sankes. Slightly more hospitable are the grassy ramparts of Toprakkale, first built by the Emperor Nicephoras Phocas II in the tenth century as a strong-point against the Arabs before being sacked and occupied over the next three centuries by Armenians, crusading Franks, and Mamluks, who brought it to its present state of abandon. The towers that remain afford a magnificent view across the Ceyhan river and its unexpectedly bounteous plain.

For all the exhilaration and promise of the open road to Turkestan and China and the dark magic of the brooding castles and sabre-toothed mountains, the landscape is not yet as barren and uncompromising as the wild places of Turkey farther east, beyond Erzurum and Van. The fields are aglow with the radiant green of winter crops and deep red-brown of soil well husbanded and tilled. Across the open prairie move whole families, men, women and young children, picking and packing all manner of crops. Only a few are Yuruk nomads, in tent encampments, who used to be the main work-force for such seasonal tasks before the shift of population from country to town and the mechanisation of traditional farming.

Gaudily decorated tractors are as common here as the horse and the mule – and serve not just as an instrument of cultivation and harvest, but a means of transport and, above all, a potent status symbol. But despite the benefits that they have brought, the daily round on the land remains harsh. In a field near Toprakkale I met Halime Celo, who was harvesting peanuts with some thirty of her relations. She had an almond face with a broad smile, a filling in a front tooth glinting gold. With one hand on her heavily pregnant belly she told me she had married at seventeen and was expecting her seventh child. She was twenty-seven, but from the lines on her face she looked much older. Her family worked about 23 hectares – cotton, sesame and wheat, though 'this year we find peanuts are more profitable.' The family came out from the village and set up camp in the fields until the picking was done. She said it was hard to estimate the total income of her extended family, but with peanuts expected to fetch about 270 lire a kilo their earnings for the year might be anything between two and three million lire – between two and three times the average per capita income in Turkey in 1985.

From the castellated plains of Ceyhan we turned south to Dortyol, a terminal of the oil piped from the Kirkuk fields in Iraq and the site of the Battle of Issus in 333 BC, at which Alexander the Great defeated Darius of Persia, so opening the way to Syria and central Asia. Alexander made clever use of the seashore and the river when deploying his army, but it was his own presence of at the head of his cavalry that seems to have been decisive; the moment at which he gained the initiative is caught in the heroic Alexander mosaic in the National Museum of Naples – which in turn may have been inspired by the hunting scene on the frieze of the royal tomb in Vergina.

One fruit of his victory can be seen along the curve of the coast to the south – the port of Iskenderun, once known as Alexandretta, which lies under a haze of smoke from the factories onshore and from the freighters and tankers crowded at anchor in the roads. Following Alexander's line of march east from Alexandretta, through the Hill of Belen, one comes – quite unexpectedly – upon one of the most dramatic and spectatular pieces of scenery anywhere in the Mediterranean – the Gates of Syria, plunging chasms of chalky rock caught in low cloud and mist, and opening onto the rich green plain running south to Antioch. As we descended into the valley beyond, cohorts of troops were strung across the foothills, their tanks and vehicles gleaming like green insects in the evening sun – a reminder of the continuing strategic importance of the pass. The tanks and field-pieces seemed old but well kept; the soldiers themselves were the fittest and most businesslike I have seen in the region.

To the south of the pass the strategically placed castle of Bagras sits on a remote pinnacle of rock, its history is displayed like the layers of a cake. The original fortifications were probably Hellenistic and Roman, some of the walls that are still visible are Byzantine. In 1097 it was seized by Count Bohemond to guard his march on Antioch during the First Crusade. Later it was taken by Arabs, Armenians, the Mamluks of Baybars and, in the sixteenth century, by Ottoman Turks, who abandoned it, its tactical value receding as their empire expanded.

The village below the castle was enchanting, with its grey stone houses between which tall women with oval faces walked with a graceful, swaying gait, chains of children holding their hands, baskets and bundles on their heads. But Ali our driver said he felt threatened and claimed it was a nest of Shi'ites. The villages were obviously not Turks, and were most probably Halevis from the Syrian Plain. The valley to Antioch is known as the Hatay; formerly part of the French mandate in Syria, it awarded to Turkey in 1939, largely as a means of securing Turkish neutrality in the coming war against the Axis powers.

Antioch, modern Antakya, is disappointingly oblivious of its past – as if it wanted to forget the riotous erotic cults of the shrine of Daphne, the marriage of Antony and Cleopatra, the preaching of St Peter and St Paul, and the lascivious practices of Byzantine heretics. Straddling the Orontes river as it branches south to Syria and Lebanon, it is a solid, modern provincial town.

While looking for the soap for which the old Dionysian shrine at Daphne was renowned, we were shown into the workshop of Ibrahim Ozalp and his family. Ibrahim said he was a 'copier' – a profession pursued by his father, who had sold souvenirs and replicas to French soldiers in Syria. The benches and tables were covered with books and art calendars from New York, London and Paris. Ibrahim said that, given time, could copy almost anything – in stone, marble, soapstone, bronze, copper and lead. As he spoke the sun momentarily glinted on a silvery disc on the corner of a bench – and there, once again, was the leonine head of Alexander the Great. Had I traced to its source the merchandise held out by that grubby hand, thrust through the grill in the theatre at Aspendos? Not that Ibrahim would ever admit to counterfeiting coins. Manufacturing tourist souvenirs and reproductions for museums provided him and his brother with a healthy income of about a million lire each – on top of which they owned their own orchard, and were self-sufficient in fruit and vegetables.

The inspiration for Ibrahim's art can be found in the Hatay Museum, which houses one of the two most resplendent collection of late Roman mosaics in the Mediterranean. The finest pieces are devoted to the cult of Dionysus at the shrine of Daphne, and the harvest of the sea. A heavy Poseidon drifts on waves of briney blue and green, thronging with fish, squid and nameless monsters of the deep; the glowering form of Thalassa, the divine epitome of the deep, her thick tresses flaring from her horned head like flames, suggests that to the Romans the Mediterranean was to be feared as much as loved.

Little else remains of Roman Antioch, which in the times of the Caesars was famed for its covered markets, the original of the souks of the Levant – hence its name the Kayseri. The market today is a maze of streets, stalls, kiosks and shops, a mosaic of different races and peoples. Bedouin women, scarved and shawled, sift through sacks of grain and pepper and saffron; Kurds – 'mountain Turks', in the official euphemism – load up with kettles and tools before returning to their villages; the keen-eyed Armenians gravitate to the gold and jewellery kiosks round an inner courtyard. At noon a sheikh, in neat trousers and a short-sleeved shirt, climbs to a wooden minaret perched like a rickety dovecot above the shops and unhooks an electric megaphone. Pure as fresh water, the *muezzin* for a moment silences the clucking and chatter of women, children, chickens, dogs and donkeys.

In the slumbering courtyard of an Orthodox church I managed to catch a faint echo of the old Christian world of Antioch. It belonged to the Syriac Orthodox, whose adherents in Crusader times were a byword for ferocity and skill in archery. I was beckoned into a side-room by a man who introduced himself in halting French as Samir Boulos Sabagil, the brother to the priest, who was away visiting the patriarch in Damascus. He told me sadly, in tones that matched the soporific late autumn afternoon, that the Christian community was now reduced to some three hundred families – about a thousand people. Typically for these parts, the Christians were divided between Syriac and Greek Orthodox, Greek Catholics and Armenians, who are both Catholic and Orthodox. The Orthodox of his church and the Catholics usually celebrated Christmas together, but Easter for the Orthodox was quite a different matter, and each community observed the festival in its own manner.

As we hurtled across the plains of Ceyhan back towards Adana, convoys of tractors and trailers loaded with families returning from the day's labours kicked up screens of fine red dust in the sunset. By the roadside I caught a glimpse of a young woman in baggy trousers and a magnificently embroidered bodice, gaudy as a boulevardier's waistcoat; round her head she wore the vestiges of a turban, barely more than a scarf. Her profile was that of a Kurdish princess who might have witnessed but a moment before the hordes of Genghis or of Tamburlaine.

Seven: Cyprus

i Turkish Cypriots

ON the frontier between the Greek and Turkish communities in Nicosia, you can read the tale of two Cypruses at a glance. To the south the skyline is crowded with new buildings – symbols of the recent wealth of the Greek Cypriot community. In the Turkish part to the north the pace is much slower; more old buildings have survived, some of them remarkably well preserved. The covered market selling fruit and vegetables seems to belong to a world at least thirty years behind that of the bustling supermarkets and restaurants of Greek-speaking Nicosia beyond the barricades, policed by UN peace-keepers in their blue berets.

Both communities look across the divide with a twinge of envy – Turkish Cypriots longing for some of the Greeks' new-found wealth, Greek Cypriots casting nostalgic glances at the old-world charm and languid ways of the Turkish part of the capital.

Cyprus has had its divisions since antiquity – though none so obvious as the barbed barrier of the 'Attila Line', which sliced off two-fifths of the island after its occupation by Turkish troops in 1974. The Selimiye Mosque, the grandest monument in the Turkish part of the capital, reflects the presence of diverse races and faiths. Though adorned without by tapering minarets, and within by *mimbar* and *mihrab* – the Islamic pulpit and the shrine pointing to Mecca – it still has the pointed arches and columns of the original building, the gothic cathedral of Santa Sophia, begun by French craftsmen in 1209.

When the cathedral was built, Cyprus was enjoying autonomy and independence under the crusading dynasty of the Lusignans. The island had been handed to Guy de Lusignan by Richard Coeur de Lion after he seized it in 1191 and it became a forward base for the Crusaders after the fall of Acre in 1291 and the extinction of the Christian presence in Palestine. The last of the Lusignan dynasty, Caterina Cornaro, was forced to cede the island to the Venetian empire in 1489, and Cyprus did not regain its independence until 1960, under Archbishop Makarios. Venice gave up the island to the Ottomans in 1571, and in 1878 the

Ottomans surrendered it to British tutelage at the Congress of Berlin.

It was about this time that the notion of *enosis* or union with Greece began to germinate among nationalists of the Greek Cypriot community. Enosis was an extension of the *Megali Idea* – the Great Idea – whereby all the Greek-speaking parts of the Ottoman Empire would be united under the flag of Greek independence. In 1931 it became the battle cry of a full-blooded revolt against the British, who imposed severe restrictions on both communities, curbing local assemblies and censoring the press until 1945. 'In a way this was a golden era,' a Turkish Cypriot remarked ruefully, 'because the communities could not threaten each other.'

The British presence left its mark in the legal system still used in both parts of the island. For generations Greek and Turkish Cypriot lawyers trained for the Bar at the Inns of Court in London, giving a slight British seasoning to the politics of the island – a feature of public life shared only by Malta in the Mediterranean. The generous proportions of the building which houses the parliament and the higher courts of the self-styled Turkish Republic of Northern Cyprus epitomise the old British colonial order, its roof like an awning against the midday sun, its wide veranda and its broad wooden balcony are evocative of some proconsular outpost in the tropics.

Not far from the Parliament House is a white-walled residence built in a similar style – the home of the president of the Turkish Republic of Northern Cyprus. Though it was not fully declared until 1985, eleven years after Turkey's military intervention, the Republic – known by the acronym TRNC – had no takers in the international market, and was given formal recognition solely by its Turkish patron.

The first president to occupy the white-walled was Rauf Denktash, a London-trained lawyer who was to personify the cause of Turkish Cyprus. For opponents, particularly in Greek Cyprus and Greece, he became the most serious human obstacle to a long-term settlement. For all the largeness of his frame, Denktash could never have been described as forbidding. His voluble, expansive and witty manner of speaking suggested a breadth of mind too large for the stage on which he walked. Comfortably overflowing his armchair, he seemed a man of surplus energy, who longed to perform in a grander court than a Mediterranean sitting-room with English suburban decor.

He has been involved in every crisis to affect Cyprus since 1945. As a schoolboy he became known for his newspaper articles demanding full community rights for the Turks and insisting that they should not be fobbed off with minority status; and this remained his firm resolve ever since. He believes that, if necessary, the island may have to remain divided in order to maintain the status and full political rights of both communities.

Mutual suspicion dominated Greek and Turkish relations, officially, at least. A legacy of Ottoman rule, it scarcely diminished under British suzerainty, which became a fully colonial administration from 1925. The Turks feared that the Greeks would never abandon their desire for *enosis* – after all, the head of the Greek Cypriot community, Archbishop Makarios III, had promised to realise the dream when he was sworn in as Ethnarch and head of the Cypriot Orthodox Church in 1950.

Turkish fears deepened with the outbreak of Colonel George Grivas's EOKA terrorist campaign in 1955. After this had been crushed, Makarios was sent into exile, returning within two years to agree to the British plan for independence, and become the new republic's first president. For a time it seemed as though the Turks would be given full community rights under the new constitution. By now Denktash was the Turks' leading political activist, the right-hand man to Dr Fazil Kucuk, their revered leader and vice-president to Makarios.

But a wave of communal violence in the 'Christmas Crisis' of 1963 led to United Nations intervention and the establishment of a permanent peace-keeping force. Denktash himself was banned from the island by Makarios, who called him 'an instigator of rebellion against the state of Cyprus'. Arrested after trying to land clandestinely from Turkey, Denktash eventually opened talks on community rights with the veteran Greek Cypriot politician, Glafkos Clerides, who had also trained at the English Bar. The two men not only respected but liked each other; over the years they continued to send each other greetings on anniversaries, on one occasion Clerides crossed the green line in Nicosia for a Denktash family funeral.

Makarios set off the chain reaction which was to lead to the arrival of Turkish forces in 1974, thousands of Greek and Turk refugees, the division of the island and a garrison of 29,000 Turkish soldiers in the north. By now he had abandoned *enosis* as a practical policy, largely in reaction to the crude nationalism of the Greek military dictatorship, who were fomenting trouble through Greek officers in the Cypriot national guard and a new terrorist group, EOKA-B. When Makarios asked the Athens regime to withdraw the officers, they staged a coup appointing as president Nicos Samson, a pschopathic ex-EOKA gunman.

The arrival of the Turkish troops were heady days for Turkish Cypriots, such as they had not seen since Ottoman times. Turkish Cypriots regale visitors with the story of the landings near Kyrenia in July 1974, in waters so deep that the first assault troops nearly drowned. First to fall was the heroic Captain Fahmi Ercan, who gave his name to the north's only civil airport, hastily resurrected from an old RAF base. An all-out battle later developed with artillery, tanks and aircraft. The Greek regulars fought bravely, say the Turks, but lacked logistical support.

The result was a stalemate, with little prospect of a settlement for at least a generation. Turks believe the Greeks will never quite abandon *enosis*, while the Greeks suspect the Turks want to keep the island permanently partitioned. Talks through the UN have been labyrinthine and inconclusive. In 1983 Denktash became the first president of the TRNC – a move which enraged the Greeks, annoyed their allies, and left the rest of the world indifferent.

Critics, even among the Turkish community, suggest that Denktash's diplomatic style was too abrasive to achieve a lasting settlement, and that he was too dependent on the settlers from Anatolia brought in after 1974 to boost the Turkish community – between 40,000 and 60,000, according to most estimates. His apparent intransigence has been guided by his determination that Turkish Cypriots should not suffer the same fate as the Turks who were expelled from Crete under the Treaty of Lausanne of 1923.

Turkish Cypriots are acutely aware of being fewer and poorer than the Greeks. The tension between the communities from the mid-1950s led to a steady flow of refugees from both sides – Turks from the south and west, and Greeks from the Morphou and Karpassos districts in the north in particular. Many Turks had to abandon their farms and vineyards to move to more difficult land in the north, which suffers long months of drought in the summer. A plan to pipe fresh water from Turkey had to be abandoned as it would traverse some of the deepest parts of the Mediterranean. Farmers and fruit producers have also suffered from what amounted to a virtual boycott by the European Community at Greek and Greek Cypriot behest. Much of their produce is sold in Turkey and some in Britain; new markets in Canada and Scandinavia incurred high transport costs.

Financial ties with Turkey have brought inflation and the steady decline of the Turkish lire. A waiter in Kyrenia told me that in ten years his standard of living had halved. Although more than 100,000 visitors came from Turkey every year, they stay only a few days, often visiting relations in the Turkish garrison. In 1987 Turkish Cyprus received about 37,000 foreign tourists, as opposed to nearly a million in the south, although the wild landscape, the castles and mountains, and the sandy beaches of the north are among the most beautiful parts of the island.

Despite the Anatolian immigrants, the population has remained below 200,000; whereas that of the Greeks was over 650,000 by the mid-1980s, sustaining thriving clothing and construction industries and, with the collapse of Beirut, a lively offshore banking sector serving the Gulf and much of the Middle East. Through Greece and Britain, Greek Cypriots have enjoyed ready access to the markets of Europe through the Economic Community.

Before the troubles, some Turkish Cypriots were renowned for the wine they produced in the south. A farmer told me of the day in Christmas 1963 when trouble broke out in his village – Asporia, in the mountains above Paphos – and the Turks were forced to flee. 'In the villages we had rural constables or *mukhtars* [an Ottoman title] to look after the crops and vines and keep the animals out,' he told me. 'In our village we had two *mukhtars*, as we were a mixed community, and two coffee shops side by side, one Greek, one Turkish.

'Because of the troubles, the Greeks and Turks had not gone to their fields. At about ten o'clock that morning a flock belonging to a Greek shepherd entered the fenced vineyard of a Turk close to the village, and the goats started grazing among the grapes. The owner jumped up in the coffee shop and shouted to the two *mukhtars* to do something. The Turkish constable turned to his colleague: "Mr Vasilis, get your men to take the goats out of the vineyard." But the officer replied "Mr Ali, it is a time of tension and I cannot do anything." The tension grew and grew, and eventually we had to leave that village.'

A few days later, we came across another victim of the tension, Raif 'Ozie' Ozal, merchant extraordinary of Famagusta, in a café in a mountain glade close to the castle of Kantara, perched like an eyrie above the plain of Famagusta. The huge cisterns dug deep beneath the ramparts suggested that water shortages were as troublesome for crusader forces as for any Cypriot farmer today. A government spokesman, my escort on this occasion, was extolling the rosy prospect for the north, but Ozie knew different.

Ozie had served for 21 years in the Royal Ordnance Corps – in Aden, Belfast, the Rhine Army, Brunei and Nepal. Like many Turkish Cypriots he had joined the British Army during the first EOKA crisis of 1955, as it offered a secure career.

After leaving the Army, he returned home to set up shipping offices in Istanbul and Famagusta – but business, he claimed, was lousy. 'They're mad here, you know, they show you how to run a deflationary economy. Look at the rates of Famagusta, which should be a free port – 75 per cent of Rotterdam's, but in Rotterdam you can unload 25,000 tonnes in

23 hours, whereas here it takes 25 days! Whisky here is taxed to the sky. So what happens? More brandy smuggling from the south. I've had it with the Mediterranean routes – the Gulf's the place to make money.'

Together with the evocatively named Buffavento and St Hilarion, the castle of Kantara forms part of a chain of fortifications which look across the blue-green waters to the Turkish coast. All three were captured and then altered by Richard Coeur de Lion in 1191, and provide some of the most marvellous crusader castles to be seen anywhere.

Between St Hilarion and the port of Kyrenia, with its sea wall and bleached white crusading citadel, the abbey of Bellapais basks on a low line of hills. In keeping with its name, it is a place of wondrous tranquillity, despite turbulent history of the surrounding countryside. Originally the seat of an Orthodox bishop, the site was given by Aimery de Lusignan to Augustinian monks, who, laid out the abbey on its present generous lines. It was a favourite spot of Lawrence Durrell, who composed his essay on Cyprus, *Bitter Lemons* under the celebrated tree of idleness, which shades the taverna by the western wall.

The most evocative of all crusader churches is the cathedral at Famagusta – a city which has been cut off from its natural hinterland to the south, and has lost thousands of its Greek citizens as refugees. The cathedral of St Nicholas, now the Lala Pasha Mosque, is its outstanding landmark – no modern development obscures its lines, and the conversion to Islam has left the principal towers and the ornamented triple-arched porch intact. For Greek Cypriots, it is associated with one event above all – the abdication of the Lusignan Queen of Cyprus, Caterina Cornaro, to the Venetians in 1489.

When little more than a child Caterina was married by proxy in St Mark's in Venice to James II of Lusignan, the last member of a Frankish dynasty ruling over a predominantly Greek people. Only seven months after Caterina had joined him, James died, and his posthumous heir was to die in infancy. Caterina ruled alone, but had to rely increasingly on her native Venice to repel her enemies, who included the Mamluks of Egypt. In time the Venetian Council of Ten decided they had had enough and demanded that she surrender the sovereignty of the island. In a splendid ceremony in the cathedral of St Nicholas Caterina was handed the banner of St Mark, which she then returned to the Captain-General of Venice, Francisco Priuli, so sealing her abdication. On the castle walls the emblem of the Lusignans was lowered for the last time, and as the device of the Serenissima was hoisted the Venetian sailors aboard the galleys in the harbour sent up a cheer. Caterina left aboard a galley belonging to a kinsman, her former subjects wading out to sea to bid her farewell. According to the chroniclers her tears did not cease until Cyprus dipped below the horizon. She was the last independent ruler of the island until Archbishop Makarios.

No fewer than five operas were to be devoted to Caterina's story, so vividly did she capture the imagination of European romantics. In exile at Asolo in the Veneto, she became one of the great patronesses of the Italian Renaissance, numbering among her beneficiaries Titian, Gentile and Giovanni Bellini. Venetian rule in Cyprus lasted less than a century; in 1571, the year of Lepanto, they surrendered it to the Ottoman Turks.

One Venetian administrator was more honoured in myth than in fact, though a prominent piece of Famagusta's fortifications, Othellos's Tower, bears his name. Shakespeare's Othello was based on a composite of historical characters, including Cristoforo Moro, the lieutenant-governor in 1506, and a mercenary captain, Francesco de Sessa, nicknamed 'il capitano moro' on account of his swarthy complexion. The story is given a completely different twist in Shakespeare's play and in the Mediterranean folklore of the day. Shakespeare's tale of a noble figure flawed by jealousy and mistrust has the sentimentality of northern Europe; the Mediterranean account is altogether more brutal and realistic. Popular legend says that the real Othello was an epileptic; the Council of Ten in Venice had lost confidence in him, and ordered him to be murdered. This at least gives a motive to Iago, whose blind malevolence is otherwise almost completely inexplicable.

It was St Barnabas, a native Cypriot, who brought Christianity to the island in the first century AD and became its patron saint; today many of the shrines and churches of the heirs of St Barnabas in northern Cyprus are abandoned or converted to other uses. One autumnal Sunday morning I made a melancholy journey through the villages of the Karpassos, which had a large Greek community until 1974. Some churches were empty barns, occasionally visited by itinerant pigeons or sheep; others had been hastily converted to mosques – in one the bell-tower had been made into minaret, crowned with an aluminium cone like the nose on a child's toy rocket. In the denuded white church at Ayios Thyrsos the iconostasis had been stripped of its images of the saints and left a skeleton of flapping wood. In cemeteries undisturbed for centuries, the soil glistened in freshly tilled vegetable gardens.

The authorities allow some Greek villagers to make a pilgrimage to the monastery of Apostolos Andreas in the northern-east tip of the island on 15 August, the saint's feast day. Less formal visits are not so welcome. I had just been visiting a mosque in a village called Derince when I was approached by an angry group of villagers – some of whom had a smattering of French, which suggested that they may have been settlers from eastern Anatolia, near the former French mandate in Syria. The reason for their hostility soon became clear: behind an old church I had found fragments of marble inscribed in Greek – the casually destroyed headstones of the village graveyard.

Much controversy surrounds the alleged destruction, smuggling and looting of Christian and classical artefacts from northern Cyprus. Turkish Cypriots claim that many Greek refugees carted off their own treasures to hide or sell, and accuse priests of trading in smuggled icons; the Greeks have catalogued for UNESCO the considerable destruction of churches and monuments by Turkish forces in 1974, and claim that soldiers and settlers have been involved in the wrecking or smuggling of antiquities. Some items have appeared in the salerooms of Germany and Britain; the director of the National Museum in Nicosia had to pay what amounted to a ransom for a classical bronze urn and tripod on auction in London.

The doors and windows of the solid church at Kanakaria – said to contain some of the finest of all Byzantine mosaics – I found barred and wired up. Climbing onto a window ledge, I tried to make out in the apse the mosaic of the Virgin with the archangels Michael and Gabriel. Created in the sixth century, it had survived a fire lit by Arab raiders and the destructive frenzy of the Iconoclasts in the eighth and ninth centuries. I could see nothing, but this may have been due to poor light. Jumping down from the window ledge my feet crunched on pieces of glass and stone in the gravel: the *tesserae* of a broken mosaic.

In the summer of 1989 a district court in Indianapolis in America charged a Mrs Peg Goldberg, a local art dealer, with 'trafficking in stolen and plundered religious treasures'. For the sum of $1.2 million she admitted buying from a Turkish dealer in Switzerland four pieces of mosaic showing a Madonna and Child, apostles and an archangel. They were the badly damaged remains of the mosaics of Kanakaria.

She had offered the treasures to the Getty Museum at Malibu for many times the sum she had paid for them. The Getty Foundation alerted the Embassy of Cyprus in Washington, and the Greek Cypriot Church and Greek Cypriot Department of Antiquities began the laborious legal process of recovering their property.

Scholars were united in their appraisal of the importance of the works, which they agreed were from the sixth century AD. One was the first known portrayal of Christ with a halo.

ii Greek Cypriots

Close to the airport of Larnaca on the southern coast lies the village of Kiti. Just beyond gardens of long grass and brash orange geraniums, its masonry garlanded in spring by the pink and white blossom of cherry and almond, stands the church of Panayia Angeloktistos. A cruciform Byzantine church of about the tenth century, it has a central drum and tiled cone roof, and a pug-nosed belfry of Latin style, with three crusader coats of arms emblazoned on the masonry beneath.

The glory of the church is its interior. In the apse the Virgin stands on a large stool, a golden robed infant Christ in her arms, while the archangels Michael and Gabriel, resplendent with wings of peacock feathers, bow on either side. Possibly from as early as the sixth century, and no later than the ninth, the mosaic is probably now the finest piece of its kind in Cyprus, and is rivalled only by those of Ravenna and Salonika. In style, quality and subject matter, it suggests what the mosaic of the Virgin at Kanakaria might have been like.

Like an icon of history, the church built by angels embodies the essence of the community to whom Barnabas brought Christianity – the Greek Cypriots. Greeks have lived for some three thousand years in Cyprus, known in antiquity as the island of Aphrodite, the goddess of love. The Turkish intervention and the partition of Cyprus are regarded by most Greek Cypriots as an unwarranted lesion in their land, involving the loss of more than one third of the island, and properties the Greeks held for centuries. The Greeks left behind them 80 per cent of all citrus fruit groves, 30 per cent of all factories, and 60 per cent of all tourist installations. However, recovery was rapid, and by the mid-1980s the economy was growing by a steady seven per cent, though internal and external debts remained high – the cost of reconstruction after the shattering experience of 1974.

Great efforts have been made to diversify the economy. Agriculture is less prominent, though the climate has favoured new varieties of early vegetables, such as carrots and potatoes, which reach the markets of northern Europe nearly a month before similar produce from the western Mediterranean. New manufacturing industries have grown up, including clothing for the new middle class of the Gulf States and over seven million pairs of shoes a year for the Arab world alone. Upheavals in Lebanon have created a lucrative offshore finance sector, with more than 3500 banks and companies registered, though only about a quarter of these are trading actively. The troubles of the Middle East have brought problems as well, in the form of terrorist organisations and the criminal syndicates which supply them with arms and money.

The biggest earner of foreign exchange is tourism, though its mushroom growth alarms many Greek Cypriots, who have seen whole tracts of the coastline devoured by beach camps and retirement homes. The hotel and tourist industry was all but destroyed by the 1974 crisis but within fifteen years 950,000 tourists were visiting southern resorts, bringing a revenue of nearly $600 million. The prospect of more than a million visitors each year causes serious misgiving. 'We want quality rather than quantity,' a government administrator confided. 'We are already having trouble with some of the visitors from Europe who want everything on the cheap. They foul the beaches, and have some pretty filthy habits – the young Scandanavians especially.'

Glafkos Clerides has been witness, as almost no other, to tribulations of Greek Cypriots since the Second World War. In the Seventies and Eighties he founded and then led the largest political party, Democratic Rally. He never quite made it to the presidency, but if this was cause for bitterness, it has been camouflaged well beneath his natural courtesy.

In many respects his career paralleled that of his old sparring partner on the Turkish side of the green line, Rauf Denktash. He too had begun his political career at school where his refusal to retract newspaper articles criticising the restriction of civil rights by the British led to his summary expulsion. He went on to fly in the RAF in the Battle of Britain; after switching to Bomber Command, he was shot down over Hamburg in 1942, and spent the rest of the war as a prisoner, despite two attempts to escape.

Returning to Cyprus as a qualified barrister, he was appalled at British policies and practices as the demand for independence grew and the EOKA campaign began, and dismayed at the rough methods used by interrogators who had been dealing with the Mau Mau in Kenya. 'It was only when judges were sent from the United Kingdom that my faith was restored in British justice.'

By then Clerides was working closely with Makarios. They had met at school; the future archbishop, five years his senior, was a dazzling speaker and vied with the elder Clerides sister for scholastic honours. On graduating the young Mihail Cristodoulou Mouskos, as he then was, continued his studies in the monastery of Kykko in the Troodos Mountains – a favourite retreat to the end of his life, and now his burial place. In 1946 he was ordained priest, and two years later he was consecrated Bishop of Kition at the age of thirty-five. He organised the opposition campaign in the referendum on British plans for constitutional reform, and under his guidance 95.7 per cent of Greek Cypriots voted for *enosis*. Those voting against union with Greece were threatened with excommunication.

Two years later, with his elevation to Ethnarch and head of the Orthodox Church of Cyprus, the name of Makarios became synonymous with the cause of *enosis*. Since the early days of resistance to Ottoman rule, *enosis* had been the preserve of the church, and the symbol of Hellenism as well as Orthodoxy.

As the first president, of the new republic Makarios was a political paradox, and a terrible disappointment to the most virulent Greek nationalists. As Ethnarch he was head of the Greek community, but as president of he was head of a republic that included Turks as well as Greeks. Some Greeks said he should have dropped one of his two supreme offices, and chosen either the life spiritual or the life temporal. Makarios now saw independence as the realistic course for Cyprus, with *enosis* becoming a matter of history for Greek Cypriots.

Nationalists who identified with the military regime in Athens were also enraged by Makarios' leftist politics, his prominence in the non-aligned movement, and his friendly overtures to Moscow. Matters came to a head in 1974, with the activities of EOKA-B and the agitation of nationalist officers of the Greek army attached to the Cypriot National Guard. Makarios was determined to call the bluff of the right-wing nationalists and the military dictators in Athens. According to Glafkos Clerides he then made a near-fatal tactical mistake: he decided to publish a letter insisting that the Greek junta withdrew their officers from the island, thus triggering the abortive coup by the EOKA-B supporters of Nicos Samson, the attempt on the Archbishop's life, and the subsequent Turkish invasion.

Glafkos Clerides had maintained his admiration for the diminutive cleric with the soft brown eyes and slow levantine smile. A beguiling talker and an excellent listener, Makarios was hard to best in argument, he recalled; yet Dr Clerides has shown himself hardly the Archbishop's inferior in political and intellectual agility. He has been more flexible in his approach to the problems of Cyprus since 1974 than almost any other Greek political leader. Only the Communist Party, AKEL, has taken a more conciliatory line towards the Turkish Cypriots. Dr Clerides had been prepared to do a deal on the division of territory, the share of office, and community rights between the two groups of Cypriots. But when we met in the spring of 1986 he did not regard the future with optimism. 'When I grew up the two communities at least knew each other, though there was suspicion between us,' he told me. 'The new generations do not know each other, and suspicion has been replaced by fear. Time is not on the side of either Greeks or Turks. Those to come may see the gun as their only means of negotiation.'

Such forebodings about different communities in the same land are not unique to Cyprus. I have heard precisely the same lament from Jews who lived alongside Arabs in Palestine before the advent of the state of Israel.

The archbishop's palace in Nicosia is one of the most curious buildings in Cyprus. A hybrid of Venetian palatial and English semi-detached suburban – the design is said to have been Makarios' personal choice – its eccentric lines are set off by the brilliance of its brickwork. I had come to visit the Archbishop of Nova Justinia and All Cyprus, Chrysostomos, a pupil of Makarios and his successor as Ethnarch.

The Church of Cyprus is proud of its independence. It became self-governing at the Council of Chalcedon in 451 AD, since when it has been the spiritual, cultural and political shield of the Greek Cypriots – the repository of their Greekness as well as their Christianity.

'Because the members of the church are Greeks, the church considers it its duty to struggle for these people when they are in danger,' he told me. 'We have tried to find a way to give people freedom and justice – and to survive as Greeks in this island. But *enosis* is not possible now, and our people understand they have to live as an independent country.'

The vehemence of his words was belied by the genial demeanour of his large figure, adorned by crosses and chains, the badges of his office. On the chances of a lasting settlement for the island, he was surprisingly optimistic: 'Turkish Cypriots feel much closer to us than they do to Turks on the mainland. Cyprus is too small to be divided, confidence can be restored between the communities as soon as the Turkish troops withdraw. Everyone can enjoy equal rights before the law.'

His biggest practical concern was the four hundred churches, chapels and shrines in the northern part of the island. Some of the icons had been brought south, but many of the best had been left behind and have disappeared. The rescue and restoration of these artefacts, and of the treasures from antiquity, has been undertaken by the Director of the National Museum in Nicosia, Dr Vasili Karageorghou, whose sense of mission is equal to that of the Archbishop. He had led the treasure hunt through the salerooms of Europe, searching out objects pilfered and smuggled from northern Cyprus. The hours spent combing through the catalogues of auctioneers like Sotheby's and Christie's, sometimes buying back pieces at inflated prices, were eased by funding from the Leventis Foundation, a cultural charity set up by one of the island's wealthiest merchant dynasties.

According to Dr Karageorghou, 'Frescoes and mosaics have been ripped from walls and cut up and sold. At Antiphonitis [part of a Coptic and Armenian monastery site destroyed by Turks in 1975] they stripped the head of a fresco from the church, leaving the painted background in place.' He had summoned UNESCO to the rescue. The organisation had listed twelve of the most precious Byzantine frescoes in the World Heritage list of treasures, and given generous assistance in conserving Greek and Roman mosaics at Paphos – one of which, dedicated to Dionysus or Bacchus, demonstrated the techniques of wine-making in antiquity with the precision of a modern recipe book.

The National Museum has embarked on an ambitious reorganisation, with a new building in Nicosia and a medieval collection displayed in the citadel at Limassol, plus sections for Islamic arms and artefacts. Cyprus is unusual for the continuity of its treasures and monuments from Neolithic times through the Bronze Age and antiquity to the Middle Ages. Quite apart from the damage done by the Turks and by amateur archaeologists, jealous Orthodox priests obsessed with their Byzantine heritage had destroyed classical statues by smashing their heads.

The aim is to preserve a series of sites for 'cultural tourism', a vogue term in the Mediterranean. In Cyprus the test case is likely to be at Kourion, the Roman Curium, between Limassol and Paphos, a large settlement of houses, theatre, baths and market place looking over green cliff tops to the sea and complemented by the extensive shrine to Apollo a mile away, where public works contractors have rebuilt several columns of the temple.

Kourion itself is graced by some of the most vivid classical mosaics still in place, one showing two gladiators helmeted like motorcyclists and about to do their brutal worst with short, stumpy swords. By the baths a mosaic panel displays the female figure of Ktisis, the symbol of creation, holding up a measuring rod, the length of the standard Roman foot. She appears to be a female forerunner of the Pantocratoros of Byzantine icons, while the ornaments on the surrounding panels, pomegranates and fishes, are the coded symbols of the early Christian church.

A flavour of old Cyprus lingers in the village of Pyla, north of the British Base area at Dhekelia in the east of the island. In Pyla Greeks and Turks still live side by side, more or less in harmony.

The old square is distinguished neither by beauty nor history, a cluster of homely, low buildings, *kafenions* and tavernas for the Greeks, shops and tea houses for the Turks. The Turkish army watches warily from the sandy hill above, advertising themselves with the crescent flag and a lowering silhouette of Ataturk. Opposite the Greek *kafenion*, which dominates the centre of the square, Swedish soldiers of the UN lounge in a tin lookout tower, perched uncertainly above a greengrocer's.

Next to the big Greek café is their *mukhtar*'s office, where his committee made me welcome and told me how the seven hundred Greeks and three hundred Turks have managed to keep on terms. There was no fighting here in 1974. 'We have our committee and *mukhtar*, and they have theirs, and then there is the UN,' volunteered Christophorous, a former *mukhtar*. 'When we want anything we go to the Turkish tea house and coffee shop. They can come to our shops – they always come to our co-operative supermarket. We can live together.'

Beneath pictures of Christ, Makarios and his successor, Kyprianou, he explained that the Turks could always take their complaints to higher authorities in Larnaca. 'They can go down there, but of course we cannot go to the north,' he reflected, with only a touch of bitterness.

In the drafty barn which served as the Turkish tea house, the *mukhtar*'s committee painted a less rosy picture than the Greeks. Relations were not always agreeable, he claimed. Greek police had a nasty habit of dissuading tourists from shopping in the Turkish stalls. In the Fifties and Sixties shooting had broken out round the village, though not in it, and in 1974 hundreds from both communities had left, some seeking refuge in the British base – 'but when the Greeks came back, they found not one shop or house disturbed or looted.'

I began to get a glimmering of what lay behind the subtle arrangements between the two communities of Pyla in the shop belonging to Nejar Ti Enver. By then I was replete with strong Greek coffee and Turkish green tea, with ouzo and raki on the side. Nejar explained that, like many of the villagers, he carried a British passport. On it he had travelled to Australia and Britain 'but too many Cypriots on green lines,' he nodded sadly.

Surely, I thought, it was only natural that Cypriots should live round the green line dividing north from south Nicosia? But 'not green line,' he emphasised in a fruity accent that combined east Mediterranean and east London: 'I mean green lines, North London, you know, in England. My cousin still has tobacco and newspaper shop in Hackney.' He wrote the address – Green Lane, London N7 a mile or two from where I live.

According to Nejar the harmony and understanding between the Turks and Greeks of Pyla, was founded on commerce and trade. By now

I was sitting on a chair in the shop shaking hands with his large family. The restaurants and tavernas of the village, I was told, boasted the finest fish menus in all Cyprus – especially the Black Sea caviar and sturgeon and other delights brought from Turkey and smuggled across the Attila Line dividing the island. The peaceful relations between the Greeks and the Turks of Pyla were based on that familiar lubricant of Mediterranean life – a common taste for smuggling.

Recently the village has been closed to all outside visitors.

The Mediterranean

FRANCE

SWITZ

AUSTR

Bordeaux

Santander

Toulouse

Marseille

Milan

Venice

Tr

Turin

Parma

Genoa

Florence

ITALY

PORTUGAL

Madrid

SPAIN

Toledo

Barcelona

CORSICA

Bastia

Ajaccio

Rome

Lisbon

Sassari

Naple

Valencia

SARDINIA

Palma

MAJORCA

Seville

Cordoba

Alicante

Cagliari

Granada

Cadiz

Gibraltar

Palermo

Tangier

SIC

Rabat

Oran

Algiers

Agrigento

Tunis

MAL

Fez

Kairouan

Marrakesh

MOROCCO

ALGERIA

Sfax

TUNISIA

DJERBA

Trip

0 miles 300

0 kilometres 500

AYSI

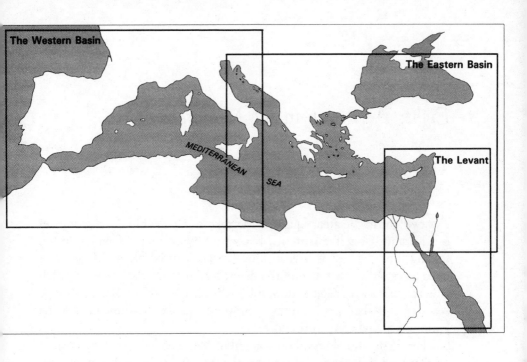

Eight: A Month in the Maghreb

i Morocco

AT twilight in the great square of Marrakesh, Djama El Fna, the oranges
on the stalls glow like lanterns. Except for a last gash of flame from the
setting sun, the rest is a deepening harmony of purple and blue. The
dyed faces of the blue men of the desert fade into the dark as they watch
the magicians with their performing scorpions and owls, and the intricate
steps of a Berber dance troupe performing to the rhythms of a string
band, an ancient *saz* to the fore.

Marrakesh, the old southern capital of Morocco, is a strategic outpost
of the Mediterranean, a picket on the barrier of the Atlas mountains
between the Sahara and the coastal lands of grape, grain and olive. The
sea of faces in the souks and markets – black African, Arab, Berber
and European – proclaim this as one of the great junctions of human
commerce.

Despite the desert's reputation as one of nature's greatest barriers, the
navigation of the Sahara has been as vital to the peoples of North Africa
as that of the Mediterranean. Since late antiquity the caravans from the
south have brought with them commodities beyond price. Most prized
was gold – the legendary 'Muslim gold', as it was known throughout
medieval Christendom.

'Those who live by agriculture or animal husbandry cannot avoid the
call of the desert,' wrote Ibn Khaldun, the great fourteenth- century
historian of the Maghreb. 'It alone offers wide fields, pastures for animals,
and the other things the settled areas do not offer.' The fringes of the
desert must have been more fertile six centuries ago, and the tribes were
much thinner on the ground. But his descriptions still catch the spirit
of the peoples of the Maghreb, whom he divides between the sedentary,
the Berbers in their towns and villages, and the migratory, principally
the Arabs, whom he puts under the label of the Bedouin.

The Berbers are the barbarians of the ancient Greeks, the babblers in
strange tongues. The Bedouins, or Arabs, came later with the upsurge
of Islam, which took them from Medina and Mecca to the Atlantic,

across the Straits of Gibraltar and over the Pyrenees by 717 AD – less than a century after the death of the Prophet.

At dusk Marrakesh recovers some of its old splendour. The dark inoculates the city against the vulgarities of processed tourism. The outlines of mosques, minarets and palaces recall the Moorish civilisation which dominated this region and southern Spain for several centuries. This is the world of Al Andalus, the light of the south, more potently preserved in Marrakesh, Fez and Rabat than the vacant sadness of the monuments of Moorish Spain.

The dynasties and tribal confederations that held sway in the golden days of Al Andalus are bewildering – only an Ibn Khaldun could unravel their complexity. The old city of Marrakesh was founded by the Almoravides in the eleventh century, and in the following century it became the centre of the Berber kingdom of the Almohades. The outstanding member of the dynasty, Yacoub al Mansour, a contemporary of Richard Coeur de Lion, ordered the minaret of the Koutoubia to be built. With its intricate tracery and pointed windows, it is the finest monument of the southern capital, though infidels have to admire it from a distance as they are forbidden to enter the courts and gardens of its surrounding mosque. The same architects were ordered by Yacoub al Mansour to build the Tour Hassan in Rabat and the Giralda in Seville. In their sober strength they are the masterpieces of the Hispano-Moorish style.

In the sixteenth century another dynasty of builders left their stamp on Marrakesh – the Saadians, whose tombs and mausoleum recall the Generalife and the Al Hambra in Granada, though in more austere and restrained fashion. Cool and silent, their gardens, courts and the magnificently columned chambers contain the remains not only of kings, but of their servants, their women, and their courtiers, all apportioned their resting places according to rank, category and status.

The Saadians were Sharifians, direct descendants of the Prophet – a distinction shared with the present Moroccan ruling house – giving them a unique position in the Arab and Islamic world. King Hassan II's father, Mohammed V, who won his country's independence of the French in 1956, was the thirty-fifth heir of Mohammed.

By one of the most silent and imposing of the palaces of Marrakesh stands a painted bronze 77-mm Krupp cannon. In its day one of the most modern pieces of ordnance in Morocco, it symbolised the power and authority of the El Glaoui clan, the last great lords of the Atlas, who could command armies of thousands of horsemen from the mountain villages. During the French protectorate, between 1912 and 1956, they were equal in strength to the Sultans themselves, like the barons of medieval Europe.

The Krupp cannon was the gift of the Sultan Moulay Hassan, who had mounted an expedition or *harka* to gather feudal dues from recalcitrant tribes of the southern Atlas in 1893. The expedition was cut to bits, not least by disease and the onset of winter in the High Atlas; for the Sultan himself it proved fatal and he died within a year from the disease contracted in the campaign. The El Glaoui could have compounded the misery of the Sultan and his ragged army as they retreated north by ambushing them in the passes and holding the Sultan to ransom, only the Sultan had no immediate heirs to organise its payment, so the young chieftain, Madani El Glaoui, decided to play a different game. He opened his kasbah at Telouet to the royal army, feeding them for weeks on thousands of sheep specially cooked for them by his tribesmen. His reward was the title of *khalifa*, or royal representative throughout the region, and the pride of the royal artillery, the 77-mm Krupp bronze cannon.

In 1912 Madani's younger brother, T'hami, became the chosen ally of the French, and was appointed Pasha of Marrakesh. For four decades he ruled as the potentate of the southern capital and the southern Atlas in spectacular if somewhat anachronistic style, keeping his harem, dozens of concubines and retainers in the traditional dress of the Berber warrior, with curved daggers slung across their bodies like badges of office. The salt repository was ostentatiously maintained. The salt trade was directed by the Jews, and salt was the vital ingredient for preserving the heads of decapitated enemies, displayed as a public reminder of the authority of the *caid* or feudal lord.

At the Casablanca Conference in January 1943, following the arrival of the Allied armies in North Africa the previous year, T'hami El Glaoui struck up a friendship with Winston Churchill, who later invited him as his personal guest to Queen Elizabeth's coronation. That same year he made the major error of his political career. He had underestimated the power and significance of the independence movement led by the Istiqlal Party, with its demands for a free Morocco under a constitutional government led by Sultan Mohammed Ibn Yousuf. In August 1953 T'hami and several other *caids* ordered an army of southern tribesmen to march on Rabat and, with the connivance of the French, to demand the removal of the Sultan. Mohammed agreed to go into exile but refused to abdicate. An elderly uncle, Moulay Mohammed Ben Arafa, was made Sultan in his place.

The demands for independence, accompanied by riots, massacres and murders, did not stop. The French changed tack completely, and invited Mohammed to return and guide his country to independence. In an hotel suite in Paris, T'hami El Glaoui, the Eagle of Telouet and Pasha of Marrakesh, had to kneel and beg for forgiveness before the newly restored Sultan. According to the established ritual of the court, a retainer forced his shoulders down with both hands to make sure he made the job properly.

Within a year T'hami had died of cancer. His body was exhumed and trampled on by his enemies. His palace is now a slumbering echo of history. The Eagle's Nest, the kasbah at Telouet, is host to bats and mountain creatures, and the occasional ancient retainer shuffling to the postern. The remaining inheritance of the last Lord of the Atlas is little more than a footnote.

Its foreshores pounded by the steamroller surge of the ocean, bedraggled palms lashed with spray, Rabat in winter seems an unlikely capital of an African or Arab kingdom. Of all the capitals of the countries touching the Mediterranean, it is the only one on the Atlantic coast. The tides of the ocean have done their best to erase the imprints of previous conquerors and traders – Phoenician, Roman, Portuguese, Spanish and French. What remains suggests a country and peoples with a past and future of equal mystery.

Traces of Roman settlement can still be seen in the ruins of an ancient necropolis beyond the medieval walls. In spring its gardens are a profusion of gaudy flowers and shrubs, dominated by the strident purple of the ubiquitous bougainvillea. The legacy of the Romans was taken up by the Portuguese and then by the Spanish as they built up their seaborne empires in the fifteenth and sixteenth centuries. They established their own enclaves at Ceuta and Melilla on the Mediterranean and Ifni on the Atlantic coast – the latter was only relinquished by Spain in 1969. Both Spaniards and Portuguese have left their marks in the grand merchants' houses near the sea, with their networks of cool rooms and terraces, ornamented gates and doors, sculptured mouldings, bronze hands of Fatima and iron knockers with heavy phallic motifs.

By the mid-nineteenth century France had become the most prominent colonial power in the Maghreb. The subjugation of Algeria in 1844 meant that Morocco would become increasingly entangled in the French African empire, though not without some spirited counterclaims by Spain. But it was the threat of German colonial ambitions which brought Morocco under direct French influence. The crisis provoked by the arrival of the German battlecruiser *Panther* in the port of Agadir in 1911 led to Berlin recognising Morocco as a French sphere of influence, as Britain had seven years before. The following year the French declared Morocco a protectorate, and it remained as such until 1956.

The most potent symbol of French rule is the breakwater constructed by the first and greatest of the Residents-General, Marshal Louis Lyautey. It was supposed to be the first stage of a grand project to construct a commercial harbour at Rabat – something that had been dreamed of since Phoenician times. The strength of the coastal currents and tides thwarted the French engineers, just as they had the Portuguese.

French is still an accepted *lingua franca* throughout North Africa, but in Morocco the process of linguistic colonisation went further than elsewhere, and the argot of the streets and souks is infested with French – and Spanish – words and usages. Arab nations of the east scarcely regard Moroccan as Arabic at all, but some strange mongrel dialect from the shores of the Atlantic.

For all the veneer of French culture, Arabic Morocco can still be savoured in the old quarters of Rabat and Sale, the fortress settlement across the river built by Spanish mercenaries of the Sultan. In Rabat itself the ramparts of the kasbah plunge directly into the ocean; in its alleys water-carriers in crazy multi-coloured hats and coats, kings of shreds and patches, ply their trade from urns and metal beakers polished by years of wear. In the upper town at Sale a small square is festooned with cobwebs of brilliantly coloured yarn. In the wool market a traditional auction is in full cry. The items for sale are paraded by the vendors round the middle of the square – metal trays, caskets, cloth, children's shoes and, bringing up the rear, an old man proudly holding aloft a pair of long-john underdrawers like a battle standard. The audience shout their bids, and provide a voluble commentary on the artistic and commercial merits of the parade.

Beyond the markets in Sale, on the slopes towards the sea, stand grand houses with open courts and the beautifully beamed and pannelled halls of the Islamic school, the *madresa* – the woodwork and marquetry of which is in the same style as in the large houses of the hill towns and villages round Ronda in Spanish Andalusia. The school is a smaller version of its contemporary in Fez, the Madresa of Bou Inania – in its day one of the most venerable and famous seats of learning in Islam. Outside its walls, the open ground leading to the shore is dotted with *marabouts* – the domed mausolea of saints, and an important feature of Muslim observance in the Maghreb. The size of the *marabout* depends on the fame of the dead saint and on his powers of healing and intercession; some are small mosque complexes in themselves.

One of the most difficult buildings to find in Rabat is the synagogue, hidden behind its unprepossessing facade. The Jews for long played a prominent and vital part in the commerce of the cities and courts, as bankers, dealers in commodities and monopolisers of the salt trade. Until recently the Jewish population of Rabat was some 20,000, but tensions led to a increasing emigration to Israel. In Jerusalem the worlds of entertainment, cuisine and popular culture have been galvanised by a brilliant and dynamic new generation of Moroccan Jews.

Concern for those who stayed behind led King Hassan II and Shimon Peres, the then prime minister of Israel, to make a bold diplomatic gesture in 1986. The King entertained the Prime Minister during his short visit, which passed off with almost none of the recriminations that were heaped on President Sadat after his rapprochement with Menachem Begin nine years before.

The move was typical of Hassan's combination of self-will and adroit manouevring. For Hassan (who succeeded to the throne in 1961), survival has been a feat of physical courage: in the early Seventies he survived no fewer than three abortive coups. His closest shave was in 1972, when the royal plane was shot up in mid-air by fighters piloted by disgruntled air force officers.

Yet that same year he became one of the founder members of the Organisation of the Islamic Conference, which was established in Rabat. His Islamic credentials are a key attribute to Hassan the international statesman, in keeping with his pedigree as a direct descendant of the Prophet.

The first cause to be taken up by the Islamic Conference was Jerusalem, and in particular the safeguarding of the Al Aqsa Mosque; and over the years it has grown in voice and influence. In the Middle East it has come to parallel the Arab League; it also acts as a bridge between the Arab and non-Arab nations of Islam, a forum in which Iran, Indonesia, Turkey and Pakistan can deal directly with the Arab states. By the end of the 1980s it had forty-eight members; Egypt was expelled in 1981 but readmitted in 1984, the Afghanistan was excluded after the Soviet occupation of 1979. Its influence in the affairs of the Mediterranean is sure to increase.

Bound in by the great seas of the Atlantic, Mediterranean and Sahara, Morocco is itself a commonwealth of nations. Its desert frontier was the cause of King Hassan's most serious dispute with his neighbours – about Spanish Sahara, which Spain had agreed to relinquish.

Its attraction lay in its phosphate deposits, and before long it was learned that Mauritania and Morocco had made a secret deal to divide the former colony. The UN and the International Court said it should be independent, and three liberation groups – of which the Polisario Front is the best-known – claimed the right to rule the new nation. Hassan organised an invasion by 350,000 civilians – the Green March – which the Spanish authorities halted just inside its frontiers in November 1975.

The following January the last Spanish troops left, at which Morocco seized mineral-rich areas in the north, while Mauritania appropriated chunks of land in the south. As the Polisario's campaign gathered pace, Morocco cut off diplomatic relations with Algeria, which provided bases for the guerrillas, and closed the frontier.

Polisario hit-and-run raids against Moroccan garrisons proved highly effective. Counter-measures were elaborate and costly, and in 1982 the Moroccan forces began to build a 'wall' of sand, equipped with electronic sensors, along the boundary of the contested area, now called Western Sahara.

By the mid-1980s the Sahara War had raised Morocco's defence expenditure to at least a million dollars a day. Despite the cost, the military build-up was another example of the king's diplomatic dexterity. It ensured he had a powerful military – and one which would be supported and equipped by the West, for the guerrillas' main supporters were Algeria and Libya.

The war petered out after the reconciliation of King Hassan and President Chadli in 1987 – the frontier was re-opened, and the dispute over the Sahara referred to the UN – but not before the King had taken measures against left-wing activists accused of being in the pay of the Polisario; while the year before more than fifty people accused of belonging to the fundamentalist Islamic Youth and Moujhadine movements had been similarly charged. The King's attitude to his political opponents is significantly different to that of his neighbours in the Maghreb. Though a partial democracy – the King and his council of ministers remain firmly in control – it is also a multi-party state. The King has worked by a process of divide and rule, switching between parties to form his governments.

Like its neighbours in the Maghreb, Morocco is undergoing a spectacular population explosion. In one decade the population of Morocco went up by more than one third, from 15,300,000 in 1971 to 20,400,000 in 1981 – excluding the families of migrant workers in Europe, by now well over one million. By a conservative estimate Morocco should have around thirty-five million inhabitants by the turn of the century. By the year 2025 the three Maghreb countries together will boast some 100 million inhabitants.

In the souks and markets of North Africa children swoop and flock like small birds. Below the citadel and the Roman necropolis in Rabat lies a sprawling maze of insubstantial shelters, some little more than makeshift ensembles of packing-cases and mud, bursting at the seams with new Moroccans. Thirty or forty years ago between half or a third of a young family in Morocco or Algeria (usually up to eight or nine members) could hope to see their fifth birthday. Today fewer than ten per cent of infants die from disease and malnutrition. The number of births has not diminished – extended families become even more extended.

'The Mediterranean is part of our civilisation, and geopolitically Morocco is a Mediterranean country,' the jovial Muhammad Benaissa, Minister of Culture, stated as if the proposition was irrefutable.

Modern trends and styles in the fine arts, design, decoration and, above all, architecture showed Moroccan taste belonged to the Mediterranean, he claimed – though a brochure for the latest international arts festival seemed to suggest that most Mediterranean architects, apart from a weakness for garish ceramic ornament, thought they should be in Finland.

Other ministers worry that the European Common Market could put up barriers to the countries of North Africa. In 1983 Morocco formally applied to join the Economic Community. Northern Europe treated this as a joke – which the Moroccan government took as an insult and as a sign of Europe's lack of understanding of the tensions in the area.

The minister responsible for dealing with Brussels at the time was Azeddin Ghessous, a sauve, softly-spoken intellectual. His biggest concern, he told me, was that Moroccan trade with the EC would diminish following the admission of Spain and Portugal. Quotas of citrus fruit and some craft products, he explained, were being cut to favour Spain; by 1985 Morocco had chalked up a $600 million trade deficit with the Community.

In a sense Morocco has long had a presence in the EC in that more than a million Moroccans now work in France, Belgium, Holland and Germany. But for Azeddin Ghessous the employment of Moroccans, Algerians and Tunisians as the helots of the Common Market was not good enough. The attitude of European governments could lead to growing instability in the Mediterranean. After all, the struggle between the north and the south for scarce resources – the granary of Sicily in particular – was, according to Polybius, responsible for the war between Carthage and Rome.

'How can Europe not include Morocco? Spain is only fourteen kilometers away. The southern standard of living in the Mediterranean cannot suffer because of the north. In classical terms this is a setting for war. How can you make one of the great corridors of commerce of history into a barrier, a fortification? This could result in conflict.'

The thin slice of plain trapped between the mountains and the sea, and between Tangier and the Algerian frontier, is home to the Berbers of the Rif. They have the reputation of being the most Mediterranean of Mediterraneans – mettlesome, argumentative, factious, fractious and jolly. Many have fair skins and hair reddened with henna, and their brightly striped cloaks and djebellas, voluminous as tents, reflect their origins of among their tribes and villages.

I had no time, alas, to travel through the Rif during my winter month in the Maghreb. Navigating through the mountains can be difficult in the best of weathers, and this is not tourist country. Travel agents and car hire firms are put off by travellers' tales of the brigandish ways of the Rifians, and in particular of the smugglers and traders in hashish. This is a highly rewarding cash crop throughout the Rif, smuggled in large quantities across the Straits from Tangier to Algeciras and Cadiz. The Spanish police believe that this is also a conduit for hard drugs from the eastern Mediterranean, and Tangier and the Rif now loom large on the global map of the narcotics trade.

Two small bites of the North African coast, remain – for the time being, at least – firmly Spanish. The ports of Ceuta and Melilla have Spanish police, Spanish garrisons, Spanish post offices and even Spanish bullrings. Both are sovereign Spanish territory, not colonies.

Ceuta, which sits on a promontory opposite Gibraltar, was seized by the Portuguese in 1415 – the banner of Prince Henry the Navigator was the first to enter the captured citadel, marking the beginning of the era of Europe's seaborne empires. In 1580 Portugal yielded the city to Spain, and it has remained Spanish ever since, apart from a brief occupation by the British in 1810. In 1936 Ceuta was the headquarters where General Francisco Franco issued orders for his legions in North Africa to cross to Spain to ignite the civil war there.

Melilla, nearly 150 miles to the east, was captured in 1470. In the early years of this century it was the Spanish base of operations for suppressing revolt in the Rif. Today the two enclaves – Ceuta has just over 70,000 citizens, Melilla just under 60,000 – are a source of continuous niggling between Rabat and Madrid. The Spanish army spends a good deal of time thinking about, and training for, the defence of the enclaves. When, in 1984, one of Spain's leading generals suggested that the army's preoccupation with Ceuta and Melilla was anchronistic, not to say absurd, he was invited to hang up his sword at once.

The lump of dirty white Jurassic limestone called Gibraltar, which sticks into the sea from the Andalusian coast opposite Ceuta, might seem similar in status and historical circumstance to the Spanish enclaves in North Africa. Not so, says Spanish officialdom: Ceuta and Melilla are sovereign Spanish territory, exactly like Castile and Aragon, whereas Gibraltar is a British Crown Colony whose divorce from Spain is illegal. For most Spaniards Gibraltar is as much part of Andalusia as flamenco and gaspacho. The socialist Prime Minister Felipe Gonzalez, an Andalus himself, described the Gibraltar question as 'a pebble in my sandal'.

Gibraltar has remained British because the Gibraltarians wish it to be so. They cleave to their citizenship as the Barbary apes cling to their homes in the upper parts of the rock and in repeated referendums they have voted to stay with Westminster. In outlook they are not dissimilar to the inhabitants of that other anomaly of the British Empire, the Falklands – which is hardly surprising since several families from Gibraltar went with the first substantial band of Falklands settlers.

With its garrison and its military bands, Gibraltar seems like a last toot on the trumpets of the British imperial retreat. Not that it was ever much of a jewel in the crown of empire; to some – like Pitt the Elder, who offered it to Spain – it was more of a carbuncle.

In 1704 the rock and its fortress were seized in less than a day's desultory fighting by English and Dutch marines commanded by Admiral Rooke, then used as a bargaining chip in resolving the War of the Spanish Succession. In 1713 the British were given possession of Gibraltar in perpetuity at the Treaty of Utrecht, the basis of all the claims and counterclaims between Madrid and London.

London took little interest in the colony in the early years; Gibraltar only grew in importance with the need to protect the sea route to India and the East – and even more so after the opening of the Suez Canal in the 1870s.

During the two world wars the naval base came into its own. Between 1939 and 1945 it sheltered and equipped Mediterranean convoys and their submarine and aircraft carrier escorts.

In the post-war years the yards and docks declined; Gibraltar's prime military importance to NATO was in signals communication and surveillance. In 1969 Franco, anxious to break away from Spanish isolation and win friends in the Third World, closed the land frontier with Spain. Local Andalus lost their jobs, and the naval repair yards were manned by Moroccans.

The row grumbled on, until in February 1985 the frontier was reopened as one of the conditions of Spanish accession to the European Community. Tourism may well heal the rift: Gibraltarians, British and Spaniards have a shared interest in developing the airport on the spit of land between the Rock and the mainland so as to bring in tourists for the resorts of south-western Andalusia. The Treaty of Utrecht seems conveniently ambiguous about this strip of land, and the airport has been laid out in such a way that some of the runway is on treaty territory while the main terminal and access road is in Spanish Andalusia.

The Gibraltarians, now some 28,700, welcomed the opening of the frontier in 1985, as did the Spanish on the other side, who enjoy shopping expeditions to the colony. The governments in London and Madrid seemed to hope that the argument might be resolved, doubtless later rather than sooner, in the bonhomie of EC partnership and mutual commercial advantage.

A curious sidelight was thrown on the relationship when, in March 1988, three IRA members suspected of planting a bomb were shot dead at close range by members of the British Special Air Service Regiment who had been flown in specially from England and discharged the operation with clinical precision. Numerous journalistic investigations that summer and the inquest into the deaths questioned both their motives and the tactics used. It was discovered that the two Irishmen and the young woman had not planted a bomb, though they may have been reconnoitering the site for future action. A singular aspect of the whole affair was the lengths to which Spanish police and security forces had gone to assist the British operation. They had tracked the suspects for days, if not months, and followed them on the last journey from a hotel in Malaga to the colony.

The Spanish authorities said very little publicly about their role in the episode, even when the British defended their actions by suggesting that their Spanish colleagues had slipped up and lost the suspects during the last phases of their surveillance. Although no official comment or reply was made by Madrid, most of the officers involved won promotion and commendations for their work.

Less than a year later the British garrison was reduced to less than one resident battalion. The bands parading in the squares and narrow streets seemed destined to fade away on a valedictory bugle call.

ii *Agony and Introversion: Algeria*

A great quarry of chalk was how a French engineer described the port of Algiers on the eve of the French colonial invasion. A natural anchorage protected by an arc of low hills, it has long been one of the richest centres of commerce on the North African coast. The port of Roman Numidia, and the great slave market of the Ottoman world, it was the base of the most successful freelance maritime enterprise of the eighteenth-century Mediterranean – the Barbary corsairs. It was to combat their freebooting that the US Navy was constituted. 'You would call them pirates,' an Algerian professor remarked, 'but they were our first freedom-fighters.'

Above the port, the most prominent feature on the skyline today is a gargantuan piece of granite and iron. A huge and heroic sculpture of warriors brandishing machine-guns and flaming torches, it seems more in keeping with eastern Europe than with North Africa – though in fact it was designed by a Canadian. It is a memorial to the one million Algerians who died in fighting for independence from the French between 1954 and 1962; a figure that is hard to visualise, and seems even more stark when set against Algeria's total population in 1960 of 9,569,568.

The Algeria that emerged in 1962 is one of the enigmas of the modern Mediterranean – the most influential power of the Maghreb and a powerful mediator in the Arab and Islamic worlds. Through its Marxist ideology the new state was linked to Eastern Europe, though it was careful not to get too close to Moscow, preferring to identify with Tito's Yugoslavia, even to the point of embracing the same creed of economic self-management, with equally disastrous results. But language and culture involve direct ties with the Arab world, though one-fifth of the population is Kabyle or Berber – who, like their cousins in Morocco, have become increasingly insistent on rights for their own culture.

The pivotal role of Algeria as a broker between the West and the new powers of Islam was reinforced in 1981, when it negotiated for the release of the American diplomats held hostage in Iran. In 1988 government officials ended the hijack of an airliner carrying members of Kuwait's ruling family. This time Washington's thanks were less than effusive after the hijackers, believed to be pro-Iranian extremists from Beirut, had been allowed to go free.

Algeria is by far the largest country on the Mediterranean, and the second in all Africa – only just surpassed by Sudan. In the early morning at Algiers airport, Arab families huddle in shawls and blankets waiting for the flight to Tamanrasset in the Sahara to the south – a longer journey than to Amsterdam. The huge expanse of desert and the remoteness of the coastal highlands of the Kabyle make Algeria a southward-looking, almost introverted, nation. Despite the Barbary pirates, Algeria seems to turn its back to the sea. Even in the coastal ports the character of its people is one of rugged and distant courtesy bordering on indifference – a merciful contrast to the continuous pestering and importuning in the bazaars of Morocco and Tunisia. Though the coast has hundreds of miles of sandy beach, Algeria has showed little interest in mass tourism.

Another ingredient in the enigma of Algeria is its fatal intimacy with France. Unlike Morocco and Tunisia, which remained protectorates, Algeria became a part of metropolitan France after 1871.

With its long boulevards and promenades above the port, Algiers itself still has an astonishingly French appearance. The tall white buildings, with their broad windows and balconies with wrought-iron scrolls and grilles, suggest an elegant provincial capital of southern France. The focal point of all this Frenchness is the huge post office in the lower town – though the black market money-traders lurking in alcoves betray that this is North Africa and not Provence.

This part of town was built and maintained by the French. Its casual state of disrepair and the persistent whiff of drainage reflect the absence of skilled workmen, who left when the colony ended. In offices and hotels clanking iron lifts, magnificent sculptures in iron, move slowly or not at all. In one hotel the lift never gets beyond the first floor – much like the creaking economy of post-colonial Algeria.

If the streets above the port seem like provincial France, the Kasbah, the old quarter, is entirely North African. The streets that climb like intersecting ladders and the overhanging houses shutting out the light are the heart of old Algiers, and a living monument to the fight against the French.

Most of the killing in the war of liberation from 1954 to 1962 took place in the villages and countryside. It was there that one of the most hideous weapons of modern war, napalm, was used systematically for the first time, by the French. Algiers itself was to see the first examples of modern urban guerrilla warfare, well before such methods became commonplace in Latin America, brought anarchy to Turkey and tore the heart from Beirut. Nationalist rebels would carry out assassinations and bomb bars, cafés and cinemas in the European quarters, before dashing for cover in the warren of the Kasbah, where the French army, paratroopers and para-military police would try to winkle them out.

Today a European outsider is greeted in the Kasbah with distant civility. With two Algerian companions I was invited into one of its houses, a network of corridors and rooms. In the last century, the dark spaciousness of these houses excited fear and wonder in curious foreigners. The English traveller J. R. Morell wrote in 1854: 'The narrowness and obscurity of these lanes at first shock the European, but the coolness resulting from the same cause speedily reconciles him to these drawbacks. The only thing wanting in the Moorish houses are exterior openings to ventilate them. They are in other respects more picturesque and better adapted to the climate than our architecture.'

A gap in the buildings marks the most famous shrine of the Kasbah – the last refuge of the guerrilla hero Ali la Pointe, the deputy chief of the FLN (National Liberation Front). An urchin of almost no education, Ali graduated from street-peddling to gambling and pimping, and joined the rebellion at an early stage. He shot and killed the mayor of Algiers. Just before the funeral a bomb exploded in the cemetery. The settler community of the capital went wild: young thugs beat up and killed innocent Muslims, smashing veiled women on the head with iron bars.

Three years later, in 1957, at the height of the Battle of Algiers, the FLN ringleader in the Kasbah was betrayed and captured, but Ali managed to escape to the house at Rue des Abdarmes. French police and paras called on him and his companions to surrender three times. There was no reply. The soldiers laid plastic charges, allegedly to remove the wall behind which the three were hiding. The explosion was heard all over town. The body of Ali was discovered in the rubble, recognisable by his tattoos. With him were the corpses of his two companions, and an Arab family with four children, one a girl of eight.

This episode signalled the end of the Battle of Algiers. Over the next few years the French army and police gained control, and acts of violence and terrorism declined. But the colonial forces were losing the publicity war. A few hundred yards above Ali's last hideout stands an old French fort, the base for French paratroopers and police in the Kasbah. It soon acquired an ugly reputation for the methods of interrogation and torture used there.

The systematic use of torture has been explained away, in part, as the work of an army bitter at its recent humiliation in Indo-China, or as an overreaction to the hideous methods of Ali La Pointe and his commander. The Battle of Algiers had begun in September 1956, when a band of girls from the Kasbah, made-up to look like colonial or *pied noir* girls returning from the beach, left bombs concealed in shopping baskets in a milk-bar on one of the main boulevards. Three people died in the explosion and more than fifty were injured.

The torture and brutality employed by the French attracted the attention of the world's press. Amnesty International made its name by publicising the plight of Algerian prisoners who had been tortured or detained without trial, or had simply disappeared. Public opinion in France was aroused. The Algerian troubles had already caused enough political traumas. Following an attempt by the Algerian colonists to take the law into their own hands in the colony, the Fourth Republic had collapsed in 1958 and de Gaulle had returned to power as President of the Fifth Republic. But the general did not turn out to be the colonists' friend, and the Evian Agreements of 1961 laid the foundation for Algeria's independence. Disaffected soldiers and settlers joined General Salan's secret army, the OAS, and were responsible for a rearguard campaign of sabotage and terror, at one time briefly seizing Algiers itself. In a 1962 referendum 91 per cent of the Algerian electorate voted for independence, which was proclaimed two nights later by the president. Almost overnight more than half the million *pieds noirs* left, principally for Corsica and the south of France. Their abrupt diaspora was to have lasting consequences for both Algeria and also their new homelands – not least in the rise of right-wing nationalist parties such as Jean-Marie Le Pen's National Front.

Though the knot of colonial domination had been severed, other ties with France remained. In 1954 more than 400,000 Algerians were working in France. Roughly double that number would have jobs in northern Europe by the late 1980s, leaving Algeria as economically dependent as ever on metropolitan France. By 1991 more than four million legal and illegal migrants were living in France.

The troubled relationship began in 1827 when, publicly and deliberately, the Ottoman Dey of Algiers struck the French consul in the face with his ceremonial fan – or, more accurately, he brushed the diplomat's face with the tips of the fan's peacock feathers. The gesture was a calculated rebuff; he was furious at the consistent refusal of France and her merchants to pay for Algerian wheat, procured for the armies of Napoleon's wars. It was the excuse Paris had been looking for. Invoking a treaty of 1535 with the Sublime Porte granting France nominal privileges in

Algeria, the French navy began a blockade of Algerian ports. Three years later a full-scale colonial occupation began, and in 1830 Algiers fell to French troops.

The war was to drag on for forty years, and Algeria was only finally subdued in 1871. As in the war against the nationalists of the FLN a hundred years later, special forces had to be raised. The best known of these was the Foreign Legion. Founded in 1831, it consisted of six battalions by 1841, four German, one Polish and one Italian. 'Well born and well bred, but wild dogs, and the reprobates of all Europe, having saved courage from the waste of their folly, they come and ask protection from themselves under the French flag and a feigned name,' according to a contemporary observer.

The bloodshed and destruction were as copious as the war was long. 'From Africa,' noted the historian Alexis de Tocqueville in 1841, 'the afflicting notice that at the moment we are making war in a manner more barbaric than the Arabs themselves.' Atrocities were frequent – in 1845 French troops under Colonel Petissier burned to death a thousand people, men, women and children in the caves at Dalera. Altogether one million may have died – roughly the same number as in the liberation struggle and from a population in 1886 of 3,287,000.

One major obstacle to the French conquest was the nature of Kabyle society. The Kabyles (relatives of the Berbers of North Africa) were in North Africa in Herodotus' day, before the sun rose on the Roman Empire. Their egalitarian ways baffled the young Marx on his short visit to Algiers: village councils were simple democracies, and inheritances were often divided equally between all the heirs.

J. R. Morell found the contrast between the Arabs and Kabyles of Algeria startling – the one were tent-dwellers, the others preferred houses; the Arabs were dark and the Kabyles fair, often with red hair. And 'while the Arabs speak with southern imaginations, personifying material forms – the Kabyles have a northern precision of thought and expression, confining themselves to a precise and critical statement of facts. Patriarchalism is the dominant principle with the Arabs, communism with the Berbers or Kabyles.'

In time Algeria was harnessed to the needs of France, providing fruit, wine, minerals, energy and labour. During the First World War 170,000 Algerians were under arms by 1917. The experience of the Second World War laid the foundations of the struggle for national freedom. The presence of Allied forces, particularly the Americans, offered the promise of democracy and liberty, while service with the Allied armies provided the techniques and organisation for the campaign to come. The first President of independent Algeria, Ahmed Ben Bella, was decorated for gallantry at Monte Cassino while serving as an adjutant in the French army. He went on to lead the political umbrella organisation of the FLN, which was backed by the military force of the ANL (Army of National Liberation). Much of his campaign was spent in captivity after his plane had been seized by the French on a flight from Morocco to Tunis.

Ben Bella proved too quixotic, too much a man of his own idiosyncratic vision, and was thrown out after three years by Colonel Houari Boumedienne, who had commanded the liberation fight from Tunisia and Morocco. Boumedienne tried to put the country back on its feet using traditional Marxist methods. He died of a rare blood disease in 1978, and was succeeded by the relatively unknown commander of Oran, Colonel Chadli Benjedid. He managed to survive by skilful manipulation of the army, the party and the administration. But after ten years he began to seem less the master of events than their victim.

The fabric of the country was in ruins in 1962. Bridges, wells and aqueducts had been destroyed, and whole settlements had been razed in the murderous play of terror and counter-terror. Entire areas of carefully cultivated orchard, field and vineyard, and their farmsteads, were abandoned as the *pieds noirs* departed. Nearly thirty years later these rural ruins are still a common sight.

By the end of 1962 some 90 per cent of the European settler population had gone. This merely added to the chaos. During the war nearly half a million Algerians had fled as refugees to Morocco and Tunisia and two million had been rounded up as detainees. The resulting disruption brought native unemployment of about 80 per cent. During the war the FLN and the ALN had divided the country into six *waliya* or autonomous districts, harking back to Berber and Arab traditions before the Spanish and French conquerors. This method of division was ditched by the autocratic Ben Bella in favour of rule by the Party, the FLN, with workers' committees below practising *autogestion*.

Much of the new order was wildly utopian. During the conflict it had been decided to develop 1,000 model socialist villages. Only some 300 were built, and the project withered away. Theory had outstripped reality; although the buildings were beautifully designed, the means of support and of employment proved inadequate.

The aspirations of Boumedienne's Algeria were enshrined in the National Charter of 1976, which stated the obvious – that the country was to be socialist and run by the FLN. The new Charter adopted in

1986 marked a change; for the first time the state openly acknowledged the importance and value of private enterprise.

By the mid-1980s the economy was already showing signs of crisis. Despite the fertility of the coastal lands – which, as ancient Numidia, had been a food store for imperial Rome – and the creation of model farms and dairy centres, Algeria still had difficulties in feeding its own people. More than 80 per cent of dairy produce, principally milk in powdered form, had to be imported from Europe.

Algeria's principal exports are oil and gas. In 1978 daily oil production was 1.2 million barrels; nine years later the figure was about 670,000 barrels. In 1986 it was reckoned that the country had reserves for another twenty-two years. The post-petroleum era – the *après petrol* referred to constantly in the press – was looming. More and more it seemed that the economy was like the hotel lift – stuck at the first floor.

Algerians have a natural stoic dignity, a dogged and almost Prussian efficiency in the way they organise their lives in adversity. Some of these qualities were noted in the Berbers of the Kabyle by nineteenth-century travellers and scholars. Young Algerians are proud of their country's independence, but privately acknowledge that the economy is grinding to a halt.

One afternoon I was accosted by a group of young men in the Hydra district, where the new ministries are housed in concrete boxes – though tendencies to East European monumentalism have been tempered by more homely Maghrebian touches. They were students, and some of them were still doing military service. They were nothing less than polite, but they insisted on making me aware that their country was the strong man of North Africa, with the most powerful army and air force.

As I emerged from a café a day or two later, one of the same group grabbed my shoulder. He was as polite as ever, but any elements of swagger and bluff had vanished. He said he was in desperate straits: his studies had been disrupted, and he needed money and a job – above all, a job abroad. He would like to go to Paris, but London was his real desire, so that he could start learning English. It was a cry for help, and for contact with the outside world. Such demands are not uncommon in the Mediterranean, but the incident was remarkable because of the dignity and insistence of the supplicant, and because I was to receive more than a dozen similar requests in only a few days in Algiers.

Algeria's population is a source of both strength and weakness. In 1986 it was estimated to have reached 22.5 million – as opposed to a mere 13.75 million in 1970. Throughout the 1980s it had been growing at about 3.2 per cent annually – one of the fastest growth rates in the entire Mediterranean. Morocco, with the same number of inhabitants, is not far behind; with Tunisia, the Maghreb could have more than 100 million people by 2025. This could prove the most disruptive force in the western Mediterranean over the next century: and its ever-expanding migrant communities will cause increasing problems within western Europe itself.

I was taken on a tour of the outskirts of Algiers by an old companion-in-arms of Ahmed Ben Bella. Ouassini Yadi had been a teacher in Morocco, but had moved to the border town of Oujdah when the struggle against the French began, and was put in charge of policing and security for the FLN operating from Morocco. He had broken with the Ben Bella, but had been allowed back on sufferance.

As we walked through the ramshackle suburbs, he explained how the Marxist dreams of Boumedienne had gone sour. Boumedienne had tried to bulldoze all illegal housing, causing serious riots and disorder. There were enormous queues for petrol and domestic fuel, even though they were home-produced. It had taken Yadi six months to get water supplies connected to his own house; most of Algiers received water for only half the day.

We were on our way to visit a friend whom Ouassini Yadi described as 'truly a man of the Mediterranean'. He lived in scholarly squalor, surrounded by books and papers, in what looked like a half-built house. A Tartar from the Crimea, he had served as an interpreter with Italian troops in Albania in 1941 and 1942. He had then – or so he said – studied in France and at Harvard; his conversation was peppered with the names of exiled royalty now sheltering in Rome. Marriage had brought him to Algeria and although his children had long fled, he found Algeria as congenial as anywhere in the Mediterranean today.

His fractured reminiscences were those of a good old-fashioned snob, but outside his house were signs of the Algeria to come. From a cage of scaffolding sounded the wail of the *muezzin*. Each street seemed to sprout a new mosque, nearly all half-built. In a derelict field near the sea front, no fewer than three different mosques were under construction, including an ambitious affair in pre-cast concrete, with two domes and four minarets.

My guide explained that funding such establishments was a complex matter. Sometimes a mosque or a religious school was built to save the field and its temporary shacks from developers. Most of the money came from Saudi Arabia and – in theory – from Libya, though he thought

Colonel Qadaffi was more generous with rhetoric than cash.

My companion suggested that the real counterweight to the regime would come from Islam. But he did not see this as necessarily a bad thing – Islam was a flexible, egalitarian and tolerant religion, exactly suited to the difficult times Algeria was going through. It was often misunderstood by narrow, over-rational northern Europeans and Americans.

The growing importance of religious cults and observances had been acknowledged by the allocation of an hour for prayer and spiritual debate on state television each evening. Similar tolerance had not been extended to my gentle and civilised host, Ouassani Yadi. A year or so after our meeting, the authorities insisted on taking him to an 'unknown destination' in the desert, and detaining him there for several months.

A rather different view of the new Algeria was provided by another acquaintance in Algiers. Mohammed had a degree in engineering from a British university – though he preferred to talk French, reflecting the indelible stamp of France on his life. He worked in a government department, and spent some time training other builders and architects. But the system was so disorganised that he and his workmates spent most of their energy helping their own communities and villages in the countryside.

None of this brought much in the way of material rewards, and Mohammed lived frugally – though what he had, he shared generously. He was from the Kabylia, and was very proud of his Berber origins. He had been thrilled when it was announced that state television would be giving more time to Kabyle culture, particularly music and poetry. One of Mohammed's carousing companions, a Kabyle poet and playwright who had spent much of his life in Eastern Europe, detested the heavy-handed Arabisation of the regime since independence: 'I am not an Arab, but I am Algerian. Why should I have to submit to one form of cultural imperialism when we've only just got rid of another?'

In October 1988, price rises and shortages brought serious rioting to the poor districts of Algiers. Officially 176 people died and nearly 4000 were arrested, but in the streets and the Kasbah it was said nearly 500 had been killed. It was the beginning of the end for the old order. A year later President Chadli, taking his cue from Eastern Europe, announced that Algeria would become a mixed market economy and a multi-party state, though his old guard in the FLN and the army were reluctant to change their ways and seemed fossilised in indecision. In the vacuum the Muslim activists of the FIS (Front Islamique de Salvation) became more outspoken and active, smashing shops and houses, and beating and stoning women who opposed their demands for adoption of the Sharia, the code of Islamic law.

The summer of 1990 saw further demonstrations and counter-demonstrations in Algiers between Islamic supporters of the FIS and backers of the regime. Early in the year 50,000 Berbers took to the streets to demand official recognition of their language, which they claimed was spoken by at least a third of Algeria's 24 million inhabitants.

The hour of victory was at hand for the Islamic militants of the FIS. On 12 July in the first administrative elections since 1962 they captured more than half the seats in Algeria's local and administrative councils and committees. With some trepidation, and numerous conditions and escape clauses, President Chadli offered full multi-party elections for the national legislature for the following year.

In September 1990, looking hale for a mid-septuagenarian, ex-President Ben Bella returned from exile. He announced he would contest the forthcoming elections. He seemed, however, more a reminder of struggles past in Algeria than a leader for those to come. The arrest of the two leaders of the FIS in the summer of 1991 lead to further weeks of bloodshed and the declaration of a state of emergency by President Chadli.

El Asnam, formerly Orléansville, was a provincial capital some five hours' drive to the west of Algiers. In September 1980, after a violent earthquake, the town died.

The earthquake struck at midday. Schools were coming out, meals were being cooked and Friday prayers recited. Hundreds of tons of heavy prefabricated concrete slabs, the material of nearly every public building, broke like pack-ice in the spring. About 20,000 people were killed.

Twenty-four hours later the pandemonium of rescue was in full force. French medical teams worked with dogs to find the living under the stones. Fires flickered across the ruins, pariah dogs bayed from broken parapets. An old man sat by a broken wall trying to remember his name. The French military doctors raised mangled people from cellars and stair-wells, hacking and amputating limbs at an alarming rate, the only way, they said to prevent gangrene.

In the dawn the collapsed floors of the provincial hospital seemed like a surreal sandwich from another world, with bodies sticking out at either end. On a lawn hundreds of bodies lay rolled in blankets, as if they had been wrapped up for the night at a caravanserai. The trees, metallic blue in the growing light, bloomed ghostly white clouds of roosting storks.

In the morning convoys of trucks with grain and water arrived. No

panic nor frenzy followed them, but jostling queues displaying gritty
Algerian fortitude. The path of devastation continued across the fields,
where a locomotive and its trucks had been ripped from the tracks and
hurled aside as if by some giant child in a tantrum.

For all the courage and strength in adversity, El Asnam was condemned to disappear. The ruined town was bulldozed, and even the
name was erased. The district officially became the *wilaya* of ech-Chelift
– but true to the spirit of Algerian resistance the locals still call it
El Asnam.

Just as the smarter part of Algiers seems French, the houses round the
port of Oran have a mildly Spanish air. The second city of Algeria is a
gentler, more introverted place than the capital.

The Spanish came here long ago – the first Andalusian community
was established in 919, when the Arabs had already built a fort to guard
the harbour. The attraction for traders and raiders were the riches of the
lands round about – corn, wine and oranges, the promise in the city's
very name. More than Algiers, it was a destination for caravans from
across the desert, bringing dyes, salt and slaves from as far as the Congo,
and ivory, ostrich feathers and gold from Sudan. Overland routes reached
across the mountains to the Atlantic and the ports of Tangiers, Sele and
Rabat.

The Spanish came again in the sixteenth century – but preoccupied
with the riches of the Americas, they yielded to the Ottoman Turks,
and in 1586 the king of Spain made over rights to the port to the Turkish
Dey. Local historians that say the Spanish presence was a 'restrained
domination' – contact with Madrid was difficult, and the Spanish garrison was under continuous threat of eradication by corsairs from Algiers.

The last Dey bequeathed Oran to the British, hoping to keep out the
French after Napoleon's forays into Egypt. Landing sites for the French
invasion were prepared with scientific precision by a Captain Boudin,
who had served with Napoleon's forces at the Battle of the Pyramids.
The British consul-general negotiated its surrender to the French in
1830. Ten years later Abd el Kadir raised his flag in the Oran district.
He fought the French for nearly seventeen years; when captured he was
transported to Paris, where he was treated like a prince in exile.

Captain Boudin suggested to the bourgeois monarch Louis Phillippe
that the kasbah at Oran contained a fabulous treasure, for which noble
slaves from beyond the desert had been ransomed. The treasure of Oran
probably had as much foundation in fact as the gold of Prester John in
Ethiopia, but its lure proved irresistible. French troops comprehensively

sacked the kasbah but found nothing. The process is only now being completed, for the kasbah, said to be one of the most beautiful in North Africa, has been torn down to make room for apartment blocks.

Oran was once the great wine port of Algeria. Though the wine still flows somewhat unsteadily into tankers bound for Europe, the fortunes of Oran have switched to another liquid – petroleum, particularly in the form of gas. The port of Arzew is one of the world's biggest installations for the liquification of gas, with terminals for three main petrol and gas lines from the desert. The twisted frames of tanks and tubes and a forest of flares smother the landscape. My attempt to visit the complex, the citadel of Algeria's economic salvation and an omen of impending crisis, proved to be a tale of bureaucratic confusion.

A pass authorised by the ministry in Algiers was meant to be waiting for me at the gatehouse. Lengthy deliberations revealed that it was not there, though it might be in another building. Could I go there? No: I had no permission to move beyond the gate. Could we phone to Algiers? No. There was no authorisation to use the telephone. 'Ah, but you should have *insisted*,' said the lady at the Ministry of Energy, 'it is the only way to deal with this dreadful bureaucracy!' Such confusion would have delighted a functionary in the Bourbon court of Naples.

Along the coast the countryside seems derelict. Farmsteads lie abandoned, their roofs broken, the fields have lain untilled for decades, their vineyards are tangled clumps. In a grove a thick-leafed rhododendron embraces a pair of palm trees, a cherry flowering shyly in between – the emblems of Europe and North Africa, colonist and colonised, side by side. In the villages the men sit in rows, squatting by their houses, with no work and no destiny to go to.

'Unemployment? It hardly figures – *pas significatif*,' said a statistician at the offices of the *waliya* in Oran. But somehow it didn't add up. The land was not being worked as it had been under the French, the city was bursting with over a million inhabitants, and the post-petrol crisis, the dreaded *après petrol*, was looming. The people of Oran looked on the uncertainties of the future with calm, as though something in their Spanish temperament said it could all be left to tomorrow, to *manyana*.

The more langurous Oran had always yielded in importance and urgency to Algiers, which had the major Ottoman customs post in North Africa as well as the market in fish and Christian slaves. There was no comparable tradition of violence, even at the height of the fight against the French.

During the fight for independence Oran saw nothing like the Battle of Algiers, nor the insurrection of the settlers against de Gaulle in 1961. The stiffest fighting it saw was a last skirmish by General Salan's OAS in the spring of 1962. The heavy pock-marks left by cannon and machine-gun fire can still be seen in the walls of office buildings.

The corniche has a bland and perversely unexotic look to it. Its buildings are modern in the main, and those with an interesting past do their best to conceal it. The grand National Theatre, pompously French to the last column and capital, is firmly closed. The main cathedral, formerly a mosque, has been deconsecrated and turned into a cavernous municipal library, with few of its shelves occupied by books.

Beyond lies the Porte de la Caravanserai, the entrance to the kasbah. Its name suggests Maghrebian mysteries and Arabian delights, but the old houses of the kasbah have all but gone, tidied up or replaced because of the persistent threat of disease. More than by war, the population of Oran has been afflicted over the centuries by cholera and plague.

Plague is the metaphor for the city's most famous literary monument – the novel *The Plague* by Albert Camus. Of French and Spanish settler parentage, Camus grew up in poverty in Oran. He was a brilliant student at the university, and also played goal for the national soccer team. His streak of melancholy was reinforced by a long convalescence from tuberculosis in which he evolved his brand of existentialist philosophy. Later he became one of the principal propagandists of the French Resistance as well as being a playwright, novelist and polemicist, winning the Nobel Prize for Literature in 1957. Four years later he died in mysterious circumstances, possibly connected with the war in Algeria.

Much of his thought is based on the sense of alienation of the poor colonist, caught between the culture of the land in which he dwells, or is forced to dwell, and that of the country of his parentage. The dilemma of the rejected colonialist was described by another Algerian, though of African origin, Franz Fanon. In *Colon et Colonisé* he described in neo-Marxist terms how settler and settled could become each other's victim.

Although set in Oran, *The Plague* was a parable about resistance to the alienation and brutalisation of a Europe occupied by the Nazis. Camus's writing is the most eloquent evocation of the crisis of the European colonist in North Africa, betrayed by the experience of colonisation and abandoned by the mother culture. His exploration of this hidden corner of colonial experience in the Mediterranean is unique.

The opening paragraph of *The Plague* provides modern Oran with its epitaph: 'The town itself, let us admit, is ugly. It has a smug placid air . . . a town without pigeons, without any trees or gardens, where you never hear the beat of wings or the rustle of leaves – a thoroughly negative place in short.'

iii   In the Shadow of Hannibal: Tunisia

Cato the Elder must qualify as the great bore of ancient history with his exhortation that 'Carthage must be destroyed' – the inevitable conclusion of all his speeches to the Roman Senate. In the modern parliamentary jargon in Rome, he would be called an old trombone. His experience of Carthaginian military might during the Second Punic War against the fierce and crafty Hannibal, the greatest Carthaginian of them all, had convinced him that Rome would not be safe until Hannibal's heirs and their city had been wiped out entirely.

Cato could hardly have imagined how thoroughly the job would be done. In 150 BC the Roman army took Carthage, sending its remaining inhabitants into exile and slavery, and destroying its port and acqueducts, its palaces and fountains. If one visits its site today, on a splendid promontory at the northernmost point of the African coast in Tunisia, not a foundation wall, street paving or statue of the city that Hannibal knew remains among the rubble and ruin. 'All that you see are the outlines of houses and streets of the settlement built later by the Romans, which became the second city of the Empire,' laments the director of the archaeological museum at Carthage, Abdelmejit Ennabli, mourning the glories of Punic civilisation.

Yet the idea of Carthage is as potent as ever in Tunisia today. Modern Tunisians believe they are the new Carthaginians, inheritors of the world of Hannibal and his Phoenician forebears, who founded the city in the ninth century BC. The Phoenician streak shows up in their cosmopolitan outlook, combining the European traditions of their former colonisers, the French, Spanish and Italians, and those of the native Berber and Arab peoples. They are encouraged to see Tunisia as the meeting-point between southern Europe and north Africa, the pivot of the Mediterranean east and west.

The first president of modern Tunisia, Habib Bourguiba, was explicit in claiming his credentials from ancient Carthage. He thought of himself as the first independent ruler since the destruction of the city by Cato's Roman friends, as the new Jugurtha, the King of Numidia who resisted Rome only to be betrayed and murdered by the consul Marius – though this time he would succeed – and another Hannibal. For his return from

France to lead Tunisia to independence in 1956, he commissioned a special landing-craft from which to splash ashore on a gleaming white Arab steed; and he built his presidential palace in the village at Carthage itself.

The significance of ancient Carthage to the Mediterranean today goes well beyond the propaganda requirements of the regime in Tunisia. The city and its civilisation represented the supreme achievement of the Phoenicians, of those navigators from Byblos, Sidon, Tyre and Acco. Largely unsung compared to the Israelites, the Greeks and the Romans, their world is only now emerging from the archaeological shadows. The Phoenicians, and particularly their Punic cousins, the Carthaginians, were not only vanquished in the field, but in the written word as well.

Like most Mediterranean peoples today, the Phoenicians had a genius for living on the brink of chaos and barely controlled anarchy. They mingled and traded with friend and foe alike; they were traders as much as raiders, even when they set out on their long voyages to the western Mediterranean and beyond, always lending and borrowing, absorbing skills and habits from other peoples and being absorbed by them. Their alliance with the Etruscans in Italy led to a complete merging of styles in artefacts, utensils and jewellery. The elasticity of their outlook has made the epithet 'Phoenician' mildly abusive to this day, suggesting a Levantine shiftiness, the perpetual spiv of the Mediterranean – that unruly, unreliable streak of the Mediterranean character which so upsets the tidier teutonic minds of northern Europe and North America. They were the great link men of Mediterranean history, their maritime technology enabling them to join the western Mediterranean to the east for the first time, and to navigate accurately out of sight of land.

Mohammed Fantar, the Superintendent of Antiquities in Tunisia, has no doubts about the identity of the Phoenicians and their role in the early history in the Mediterranean. 'The story of Carthage is at the heart of our history,' he explained to me in his cool, tranquil office in a palace built for Turkish Beys. 'The Phoenicians enabled the cultures of the East, of Persia and Mesopotamia, to influence the west. They discovered how to build keeled ships made from overlapping planks held together by nails which could take to the open waters, where the sailors learnt to navigate by the stars.' An expedition under Hanno sailed round the west coast of Africa in the fifth century BC. Herodotus said he had heard that Phoenicians had sailed all the way round Africa, though he showed a characteristic Greek sniffiness about their claims. However he does credit the Phoenicians with an invention for which the Greeks, and the whole Mediterranean, were forever in their debt – the alphabet, which they had taken from centres in Assyria and refined in their cities on the Lebanese coast. Only fragments of their own extensive literature have survived. The constitutions of Carthage were admired by Aristotle, who said they led neither to tyranny nor to popular revolt, while Mago the Carthaginian's manual on agriculture became a standard text for Roman farmers.

The Phoenicians were early practitioners of lateral thinking, ingenious craftsmen and inventors who, confronted with a problem, would side-step it rather than attack it head on. They liked to build their ports on islands or promontories, like Tyre and Carthage, which were hard for an enemy to surround, and easy to escape from. Their city designs were elaborate, as the foundations now being uncovered at Kerkouane on Cape Bon reveal; Carthage itself had the first urban plan in the history of North Africa. They were artists in ceramic, stone and precious metals – and may have invented the first modern mirrors. They took their name from their passion for purple dye or *phonikia*, establishing that purple, their purple, would be the colour of royalty.

Their skills made them the natural choice of King Solomon – doubtless clad in purple raiment – to build his temple. 'And King Solomon sent and fetched Hiram out of Tyre,' records the Book of Kings. 'He was widow's son of the tribe of Naphtali, and his father was a man of Tyre, a worker in brass: and he was filled with wisdom, and understanding, and cunning to work all works in brass.'

But praise was mixed with warnings about Phoenician deceit and cunning. In the *Odyssey* we learn how

> One day there came some Phoenicians, famous navigators,
> Rascals, with a host of knick-knacks in their dark ships.
> Then, in my father's palace there was a Phoenician woman,
> Tall, beautiful, and skilled at splendid needlework . . .

On the Greek and Roman stage the Phoenician became a figure of fun – a confidence trickster and Levantine artful dodger. 'This fellow knows every language, but cunningly pretends not to – he is a true Carthaginian' Plautus wrote in *Poenulus*, while a fragment of a comedy attributed to Aristophanes declares, 'I am becoming a true Phoenician: with one hand I give, with the other I take away.'

Such heavy-handed contempt was tinged with envy and fear. The Phoenicians were disliked because they tended to be there first. They dwelt in the promised land as the Canaanites before the children of Israel got there from Egypt; they sailed across the Mediterranean to found colonies in Africa, Sicily and Sardinia before the Greeks and the Romans. They were reviled for their exotic religious cults. Above all they were the great idolators of the Old Testament, worshippers of El, a supreme deity whose image and influence affected Judaic culture and spawned a host of gods, and Baal in particular. When Solomon turned to idolatory, he embraced the deities of the Phoenicians. Ahaziah, son of Ahab, 'made Israel to sin. For he served Baal, and worshipped him and provoked to anger the Lord of Israel.' Baals spread themselves in many forms, at Tyre and Sidon, at Palmyra, at Baalbek and in the new North African colonies. They were busy deities, like that mocked by Elijah, either talking, or hunting, or travelling, or sleeping.

Even today it is believed that the Phoenicians and the Carthaginians indulged in widespread child sacrifice. A stele or funeral monument shows a priest of Baal with a knife poised above a baby, which could suggest that infants were sacrificed in moments of extreme crisis and danger. Large numbers of children's bones and even the remains of foetuses, have been found near the sanctuaries called *tophets* in several cities, including Carthage itself; it is now thought that these are not the remains of sacrifices, but children and babies who died prematurely and were buried on hallowed ground to ensure a smooth voyage to the hereafter.

On the figure of Hannibal was focussed all Rome's hatred of Carthage and its works. Hannibal gave the Romans the fright of their lives, inflicting the worst military defeat in the history of the Republic, and threatening to capture the city itself. Unlike Alexander the Great and Julius Caesar, no likeness of him has survived on coins, engravings or monuments; yet he was their equal, and in some respects their superior, as a soldier and tactician. His story reads like a parable of the contemporary Mediterranean.

He was the son of the great general Hamilcar, who sent him at the age of twelve to finish his education with the army in Spain. By the age of twenty-five he was in full charge of that army, quickly proving one of the best of all commanders in the field. A major war over possession of the central Mediterranean, and Sicily and Sardinia in particular, was all but unavoidable. Hannibal realised that his strategic options had been crippled by the failure of the oligarchs who ruled Carthage to properly equip a navy – strange for a people whose reputation had been built on sea power. (The Phoenicians had invented the trireme and the quinquereme, the most efficient and lethal warships of antiquity.) He felt he had no choice but to mount a land invasion from Spain to catch the Romans unprepared.

The campaign opened with the siege of Saguntum in Spain in 219BC. The following year he made his epic journey with a cohort of elephants and 40,000 men across the Alps. Much has been made of the struggle through the early winter snows, and the use of elephant power in the battles of Ticino and Trebia and the ambush at Lake Trasimene. In 216BC he won his most surprising victory at Cannae in Apulia, on a rocky field about the size of a municipal sports field. It demonstrated his military genius at its height. He had come south because he knew he could not hope to take and hold Rome itself; despite his victories, few Italian cities would join him. At Cannae he relied on his infantry, welding disparate peoples into a coherent and disciplined force. He persuaded his Libyan auxiliaries to abandon the long spear in favour of the short sword, and he made the phalanx, a wall of infantry sixteen deep, an instrument of a hitherto undreamt of flexibility, bending and stretching like a piece of chain mail rather than a solid wall of steel. It could yield in the centre without breaking, so allowing the cavalry on the wings to sweep round and attack the enemy's rear – the classic encirclement manoeuvres of Alexander the Great and Philip of Macedonia brought to perfection. This is the essence of 'enveloping' tactics in modern manoeuvre warfare

The Romans were cut to pieces. One of the two consuls, Aemilus Paulus, was killed; nearly 48,000 men died with him, 20,000 were taken prisoner, and fewer than 15,000 escaped. But Hannibal knew he could not last long in Italy, enduring years of sieges and the treachery of unreliable allies. In 203 he returned to Africa, and the following year he was defeated by the mighty Scipio Africanus at Zama – which, like Waterloo, was a damn near run thing. He employed the same tactics as at Cannae, but at the crucial moment he was betrayed by his cavalry on the left flank, who refused the order to encircle the enemy.

Following the harsh peace terms imposed by Rome, Hannibal became a reforming governor of his city, trying to reduce the influence of the corrupt oligarchs who had monopolised power till then. He and his family planted and irrigated extensive lands in what is now the Sahel province of Tunisia – an area is now suffering some of the worst encroachment from the desert in North Africa, a vital battleground in Tunisia's struggle to feed its young and rapidly growing population. Eventually he was forced into exile in Syria and Bithynia on the Aegean coast of modern Turkey, where he committed suicide in 182 rather than surrender to a Roman extradition order. Like Alexander the Great, he had become fascinated by the new learning and mysticism from Persia, Mesopotamia and beyond. In this may have been influenced by the mystic teachings of the early Phoenician religions, according to which the cosmos was originally an egg which broke into two, dividing our world into a heaven of light and earth of darkness – the basis of Manichean philosophy, which is being reborn in new forms in the Mediterranean today.

Hannibal's defeat at Zama was curiously prophetic for the future of the Mediterranean world. The triumph of Scipio Africanus laid the foundations of an empire that would rule the entire coastline of the Inner Sea – the only power in history to do so. But Hannibal's genius contained the seeds of the Roman Empire's destruction, and that of any other empire that attempted to dominate the region. His genius of command had brought together disparate tribes and peoples from Africa, Spain and Italy, and made from them cohesive forces. He could obtain absolute loyalty from fickle and inconstant mercenaries in the midst of battle – the great exception was Zama. His ability to bring together different nations and people is a powerful metaphor for the Mediterranean today, as numbers and expectations rise on its southern shore while the nations of the north smugly retreat behind the barriers of their own material wealth.

What traces of the Carthaginian linger on in the everyday habits of the Mediterranean? 'You can find a lot in small things,' Professor Fantar suggested. 'For example, in most Tunisian houses you will find bread baked in clay ovens, and stoves with open earthenware pots for the dough – those are entirely Phoenician.' And harbours from Tarragona to Tyre, from Valletta to Venice bob with small fishing-boats with raked bows and high stern-posts, the distinctive lines of which would be recognised at once by a Phoenician or a Carthaginian, the structure of their planking to the painted eye in the prow, a warning and protection against the aquatic cousins of the great god Baal.

In recent years, thanks to the patronage of President Bourguiba, Carthage has become the most desirable residential area of metropolitan Tunis, the prey of speculators and developers, building pretentious ranch-house villas close to the island where the triremes of the Carthaginian navy had been launched, and encroaching on the sacred ground where hundreds of children had been buried. As we paced the mausoleum and picked our way through the two Punic naval slipways which had already been uncovered, Abdelmadjit Ennabli spoke about the uphill struggle to preserve what he could; once again, he reflected, Carthage faced a losing battle.

Just over a year later, in November 1987, Habib Bourguiba – the man who dreamed of being a second Hannibal – was removed from his office as life president when a panel of doctors had pronounced him too senile to continue. He was replaced by General Zine Al-Abidine Ben Ali, a former police chief and the first military officer to assume cabinet rank. He was a practising Muslim, and his elevation had the wholehearted approval of Washington and its agencies, including the CIA.

The souks round the Bey's Palace and the Great Mosque of old Tunis must be the most mild-mannered and gentlemanly in all North Africa. They shy away from the fierce sun, seeking instead the shade of the covered alleys and the canopies of the palace roofs, spreading like huge umbrellas. Trade is conducted in casual badinage. It is a most unbazaar-like bazaar.

The quiet confidence of the traders may be an echo of their Phoenician ancestry. The merchants of Tunis have learned to manipulate invaders and foreign overlords in much the same way as the southern Italians – the European neighbours they most resemble, and with whom they main-tain the closest links.

A leather merchant offers me two Moroccan belts. I can only use one and there's no need to buy anything. We have a rambling conversation about belts, the beauties of Tunis in spring, tourism and its problems and other bits of persiflage which float like the first almond blossom on the air of that bright February morning. Well content with our chat, the twinkling merchant says, 'Pay for one, and take the second as a present.'

The Tunisians have become accustomed to the sudden shocks and upheavals that litter their history. After Carthage fell Romans came to rebuild; the Vandals invaded, only to be driven out and reconquest by the Byzantine army of Count Belisarius in the sixth century; and then, in 647, the Arabs arrived from the east. With them they brought a new religion, the Word of God, as given to the Prophet Mohammed, brought by Arab horsemen and their followers barely a generation after it had first been taught and recorded by Mohammed in Medina and Mecca. The pattern for the future was set. Whatever conquerors came and went, this part of North Africa was culturally and politically part of the Arab world, and Islam the religion of most of its people.

The late Roman civilisation and the medieval Arab culture of this part of North Africa produced two thinkers and writers, giants out of proportion to their circumstances and their times – St Augustine of Hippo and Ibn Khaldun. Augustine studied at the university in Carthage, a pagan enjoying the pleasures of the flesh – his prayer 'Give me chastity and constancy, but not just yet,' suggest that such temptations were with him long after his conversion. He was finally brought to baptism by his mother, St Monica, who was of Berber stock (his father had been a

Roman magistrate). Though he studied in Italy at Rome and with St Ambrose in Milan, he spent most of his life teaching, converting and writing in North Africa at Hippo Regis (now just inside Algeria) where he was bishop for thirty-four years, a selfless guardian of his flock and a formidable scourge of heresy. On hearing that Rome had been captured by Alaric the Goth in 410, he began his monumental work *De Civitate Dei* – 'The City of God'. One of the great meeting-points of Mediterranean culture, it fuses the thought of classical antiquity, the world of neo-Platonism, Cicero and Roman Law, with the teachings of St Paul and early Christianity. The notion of the Eternal City, the new Jerusalem to be realised in heaven or on earth, is one of the most powerful emblems of all political aspiration.

Nearly a thousand years after St Augustine, Ibn Khaldun served in the Arab courts of Tunis, where he had been born. The politics and the intrigues between the various tribes and dynasties of North Africa were so bewildering as to beggar description. However, Ibn Khaldun set out to explain how they came about, why powers and tribes flourish and decline, how they associate and fall apart and, above all, how human societies are affected by their physical environment, and in particular by the desert and the rugged mountains and uplands of North Africa. The introduction to his universal history, the *Muqaddimah*, has a peculiarly modern ring; he is one of the first true sociologists and historiographers. He was a restless spirit, moving as councillor and teacher from Tunis to Fez in Morocco before being appointed Professor and later Supreme Justice of Malakite Law in Cairo in 1384 – the pinnacle of academic achievement in the Arab world at the time. On a journey to Syria in 1400 he interviewed Tamburlaine the Great as he left Baalbek to attack Damascus – though the brief account given in Ibn Khaldun's *Journey in the Orient and Occident* is less than scintillating, with the Mongol confining himself to tedious small talk.

Like Hannibal, both Augustine and Ibn Khaldun are celebrated today as heroes and forerunners of modern Tunisia.

The domes and cool courtyards, the shaded balconies and shuttered casemates of old Tunis reflect the influence of the overlords who displaced the Arab dynasties in the sixteenth century – the Ottoman Turks. The Turks came at the invitation of the chieftain of the Barbary Corsairs, Khair El Din 'Barbarossa', and after forty years of bloody tussles with the Spaniards they established an Ottoman regency in 1574. The Ottomans have left a shadowy but strangely durable mark. In the best imperial tradition the civil administrators, the Beys, and the military commanders, the Deys, went native, becoming so North African as in outlook and loyalty that under them Tunisia became virtually independent. But, as St Augustine could have warned them, the temptations of fleshly decadence proved too much. By the mid-nineteenth century the Ottoman overlords were mere cyphers and other colonial powers, principally Britain and France, were on the march. The last of the line, a Bey in name and nothing else, died in 1957.

A few miles outside Tunis on the road to Carthage, hidden behind trees and flowing vines and shrubs, stands the most elegant memorial to the Beys – one of their summer palaces, now the residence of the British ambassador. It is a masterpiece of late Ottoman architectural extravagance, a Palladian villa of the Levant. The great room on the first floor, the piano nobile, provides a vista through huge windows and is cooled by a thousand pieces of blue, white and green Ottoman tiles – though the British brutishly added an annexe to the piano nobile and a heavy external staircase from the drive outside, unbalancing the whole visual effect. This was the work of Sir Richard Wood, the British Representative from 1855 to 1879, who acquired the residence in lieu of debt from the Bey. Sir Richard treated British foreign policy as his private property. He had been educated in the British mission in Istanbul, and may have been of Armenian stock. His entire consular life was spent in the Levant and North Africa, where he developed a natural flair for manipulating the financial weaknesses of the Bey and his circle.

Wood was the proconsular godfather of his era. As in Egypt, the British practiced the colonialism of indebtedness, vying with French bankers to fund with massive loans new building works, railways, roads, telegraphs and ports. Tunisian debts grew ever greater, until an International Finance Commission was imposed in 1869. The last shreds of independence vanished when Britain and France carved up North Africa at the Congress of Berlin in 1878, with Egypt and North Africa going to the British and the Maghreb to the French. On the pretext that a Berber revolt in Tunisia threatened their colony of Algeria, the French poured 30,000 troops over the border in 1881; and under the terms of the Treaty of the Bardo the Bey surrendered all real authority to the new French Protectorate, keeping only his ceremonial posts and titles.

Under the French Tunisia retained and even enhanced its cosmopolitan character. By the turn of the century nearly a fifth of the population was European: the Italians numbered over 75,000 and the French 35,000, while a large migrant workforce from Malta gave the British a claim to interfere in the colony. French domination was more easygoing than in neighbouring Algeria, and opposition was slow to develop. The first serious independence movement, the Destour Party, emerged in 1920;

in 1934 the more vigorous and radical Neo-Destour Party took the field under Habib Bourguiba, a French-educated lawyer who had been born into poverty in Monastir thirty years before.

The new party lasted only four years, before being banned. Bourguiba's real opportunity came after the Second World War. Democracy and self-determination were in the air, but it was some time – ten years to be precise (in 1956) – before they were realised. After some riotings and disturbances, the French granted elections and Habib Bourguiba – who had spent much of the intervening years since the war on the run – emerged triumphant. He declared Tunisia free of foreign rule for the first time since Carthage was crushed by Scipio Africanus.

Not that the French went away entirely peaceably. In 1958, during the war in Algeria, French air force planes bombed the Tunisian border village of Sakiet Sidi Youssef, claiming it was used by Algerian rebels. The Tunisian army tried to force the French out of their naval base at Bizerta, losing 1200 dead in the process, though the French agreed to leave by 1963.

Unfortunately the excesses of his later life have obscured Bourguiba's position as one of the great leaders and thinkers of the Arab independence movement in North Africa, a figure comparable to Nasser, Ben Bella, and Mohamed V of Morocco. Like them he was part nationalist and part socialist, but unlike them he had a peculiar streak of cultural cosmopolitanism. He nationalised foreign property, he downgraded the Islamic University in Tunis, and he aimed – briefly – at wholesale collectivisation of the land. But, deeply affected by his education in France, he urged Tunisians to respect the French traditions which had shaped their country. He liked to refer to the culture of *romanité*, as he put it. He was friendly to Europe, and aped its secular culture, though sometimes his governments drew the line. In the mid 1980s it was decided that too many American television programmes might damage the social fabric, and popular soap-operas like *Dallas* and *Dynasty* were banned from national television. But it proved an empty gesture, for at the same time the cabinet had approved the relaying throughout most of Tunisia of Italian television, which showed more of *Dallas* and *Dynasty* than any other.

On the other hand, Bourguiba never forgot Tunisia was part of the Arab world, albeit one of its most moderate voices in it and an early advocate of negotiations with Israel over the Palestinians. In 1979 the headquarters of the Arab League were moved from Cairo to Tunis after Egypt had been expelled for signing the Camp David Accords in 1978; but in 1990 the League returned to Cairo after Egypt's readmission, much to Tunisia's chagrin. In the 1980s Tunis became the headquarters of the PLO. This had its price. In October 1985, after three Israelis had been killed in Cyprus, Israeli planes swept in from the sea to bomb the PLO settlement, in the hope of murdering the movement's head, Yassir Arafat. They did not, but seventy-two people died in the attack, twelve of them Tunisians. Two years later Israeli raiding parties landed from the sea at the village of Sidi Bou Said, the Saint Tropez of Tunis, to murder a senior PLO figure, Khalil al-Wazir, whose nomme de guerre was Abu Jihad, in his bungalow; the Israeli government believed, erroneously, that he had organised the Intifada in the Occupied Territories.

Bourguiba's rule was a tricky balancing act. His country had fragile resources – a bit of oil, minerals such as phosphates, a fertile coastland and tourism. But the oil and the minerals were plainly running out by the late 1980s. Agricultural production was faltering, but the population was increasing fast. Bourguiba's rivals were expelled or jailed with almost routine regularity, and by the end of the 1970s Tunisia was a one party-state in all but name; and Bourguiba himself, in far from good physical and mental health, was made president for life.

Serious trouble was stirring. In January 1978 the General Union of Tunisian Workers (UGTT) demanded reforms and called a general strike. Fifty-one people died in riots in Tunis, and the UGTT leaders were rounded up. In January 1984 the storm really broke when the government ordered a 115 per cent increase in the price of bread. In the ensuing rioting eighty-one people died and nearly 1,000 were severely injured.

The undoing of the President was to come from a different quarter. For years the regime had feared underground Islamic movements and parties, particularly the Islamic Tendency Movement (MTI) of the charismatic Rached Ghanouchi, who was arrested in early 1987. Later that year thirteen tourists were injured when bombs exploded in hotels in Monastir and Sfax. At the time responsibility was claimed by a group calling itself Islamic Jihad, but later a group of suspects 'confessed' on television that it was the work of Islamic Tendency, who wanted to destroy Tunisia's dependence on tourism. Sixty-nine members of the Tendency were given long jail sentences, including Ghanouchi, and seven were condemned to death, four in their absence.

Bourguiba flew into a paroxysm of senile rage and demanded a retrial to condemn all ninety of the accused to death. Doctors declared him mentally unfit to govern and sent him into retirement at his birthplace of Monastir. The prime minister, General Zine Al-Abidine Ben Ali, who had been a powerful interior minister, stepped in. He reduced the sentences on the Muslim leaders, and began to open up Tunisian political life. He quickly mended his fences with those neighbours in the Maghreb with whom Bourguiba had quarrelled, joining a five-power Greater Arab Maghreb which included Libya and Mauritania. He held a summit with Colonel Qaddafi on the island of Djerba to patch up the rift caused by the expulsion in 1985 of 35,000 Tunisian workers from Libya. President Ben Ali had begun his own delicate balancing act auspiciously.

With its simple message there is one God, and Mohammed is His Prophet, Islam has the most universal appeal of any religion. As with the other great religions, its observance is shaped by the culture and geography of its adherents. Its outward face changes by region, tribe and nation – not least in the Maghreb, where Islam is shaped by the peculiar civilisation and traditions of the Arabs and Berbers of North Africa.

As Islam has revived in more radical and politically vehement forms, the West has tried to attach to it the crude convenience label of Islamic fundamentalism – a term which conceals as much as it reveals, and has become virtually meaningless through hackneyed abuse. The notion of Islamic fundamentalism is flawed by its excessively Western and Christian perspective, as though Islamic fundamentalists were the Middle Eastern equivalents of Protestants or Catholics in the seventeenth century.

No part of Islamic life has been left untouched by the mood of spiritual, political and social revival and the Maghreb is no exception. My guide to the Arab civilisation of the Maghreb, and to the new manifestations of Islam, was a senior figure in the Arab League, a professional diplomat who later distinguished himself through his efforts to find a settlement in the Lebanon. He asked me not to quote him – thinking his conversation and observations of little importance – so I have tried to preserve his anonymity.

In the early evening dark his house seemed a honeycomb of airy courtyards and terraces. Away in the distance, beyond Carthage, the sea lay hiding from the moon; inside the house the tables were spread with sweetmeats and small dishes, jars of tea and cups of Turkish coffee. My guide's conversation was that of a man of the Maghreb, a philosopher in the tradition of Ibn Khaldun.

'From the early days the majority of Arabs lived in Africa and on the Mediterranean coast,' he began, 'and they have become a Mediterranean people in outlook and culture, contributing as much or more to what is essentially Arab than the people round Medina, Mecca and even Damascus. Even today the Maghreb is as vital to the Arab world as the Mashlek – the Arab cultures of the east.'

The Arab and Islamic culture of the Mediterranean grew as a result of its contact with Christianity – 'Mostly in conflict, sometimes in co-op-eration but never ignoring each other.' An important feature of the Maghreb was its attitude to Ottoman rule: whereas in the east the Arab peoples regarded themselves as being liberated from Turkish colonisation when the Ottoman Empire collapsed, the Arabs of the west had seen themselves as partners in a Muslim empire which happened to be based in Istanbul. 'In North Africa we are very much aware that we are part of the Mediterranean – an essential element of our vision today' – which, he argued, was why the newly independent Algeria, despite the help it had received from the Soviet Union, refused to sign a formal pact with Moscow, unlike Syria and Egypt. The Maghreb would continue to look to western Europe for security.

Any discussion on the politics and people of the Maghreb was bound sooner or later to turn to Islam and its new manifestations. It was hard to find one satisfying explanation for the revival of Islam in so many forms and 'in so many different countries – revolutionary Algeria, conservative Saudi Arabia, feudal Morocco and liberal Tunisia'. Under the French, he suggested, Islam had been a refuge, a shield behind which to hide until better days came; but that was not the simplistic kind of faith that had been adopted even by highly intelligent Arab students, particularly in the engineering and science faculties of universities in Egypt and the Maghreb. This new kind of observance claims to identify all the ills and injustices of modern society, and to provide a simple truth as a perfect antidote. It also fuels a violent reaction against the values of the former colonisers. Clear instructions on every aspect of life can be found in the Koran – including how to produce enough wheat to feed Egypt, for instance. 'This is a very unhealthy approach – a kind of sickness,' he concluded.

Arabs, he suggested, were out of touch with the great achievements of the golden age of learning, more than five hundred years ago – 'Most do not know Ibn Khaldun at all' – yet driven by a feeling of tremendous disappointment in their own times, Islamic radicals were trying to find a magical way back to their own version of a Golden Age. Faith had become the enemy of reason and philosophy. The secular philosophies of the new Arab nations, the revolution in Algeria, the vision of Nasser in Egypt, the nationalism of Feisal in Saudi Arabia, the Ba'ath Move-ment in Syria and Iraq, had all 'run out of steam', and mystical and fanatical religion filled the vacuum.

Behind the renewal of political Islam, either as catalyst or cause, was a population explosion throughout the Middle East and North Africa. The confluence of the Tigris and Euphrates, the Mediterranean coast, the Fertile Crescent, the Nile Valley, the Sahel and the uplands of Kabylia, Rif and Atlas could become like rafts with too many passengers on board. Expectations and outlooks have altered at the same time. In Rabat I had met a banker from Tripoli who said his grandfather still lived in a tent; his father had opened a small shop in the village, and one of his cousins was doing a PhD in Massachusetts. 'Saudi Arabia now has more than 90,000 university and college students,' my anonymous interlocuter in Tunis observed. 'You cannot rule such a country in the same way as a nomadic people running round the desert.'

The growth of, and the changes among the people of the Mediterranean will be critical to relations with the rest of the world. In Tunisia the balance between an expanding population and the resources with which to feed them is at its most fragile. When the French took over in 1881 the population was about 1.5 million; at independence in 1956 just under four million; and in 1985 about seven million. It is expected to rise to at least 11 million by the end of the century and at the time of my visit in 1986 half the population was reckoned to be under the age of seventeen.

'More than a third of all the cars in the country are jammed in to this one square kilometre or so of Tunis,' exclaimed Mohsen Boujbel, a young government official who became my constant companion during my week in the capital. 'Just think what will happen in five years, if the number of cars continues to increase at this rate.' We were stuck fast in a Friday evening traffic jam.

Mohsen spent week days as a senior technocrat in the Ministry of Agriculture, attending to the most urgent problems of Tunisia's growing population. At weekends he returned to his village about an hour from Tunis, where he was the mayor, and its most distinguished citizen. That rainy Friday he had taken me to visit his constituents and his family.

The village streets were a criss-cross of puddles and cart tracks. A dash of colour of the piles of vegetables in the market – onions, fennel, radishes, carrots, cabbage and cauliflower. Opposite the market, behind the steamed-up windows of a rickety shed, men and boys bent over glasses of tea and slapped backgammon pieces on the boards – the recreation of half the Ottoman world.

Mohsen's family home was an outsized suburban bungalow. The main rooms gave onto a small open courtyard, a half peristyle in the Roman fashion. The furniture was mass-produced in the main and chairs seemed optional, younger members of the family clearly preferred to sit on the floor. The women kept to themselves until presented, and there was much clanging offstage from a very modern-looking kitchen. Bread was cooked in a clay oven in the courtyard, such as Hannibal's mother would have recognised.

Women have been given special status in modern Tunisia. Habib Bourguiba introduced secular divorce and legislated against polygamy. Women were the focus of health education and birth control policies, and in many categories of employment were given equal rights with men. The first Minister for Women and Family Matters was Madame Fathia Mzali, who took office in 1983; she was also the wife of Mohammed Mzali, who happened to Prime Minister and briefly heir-apparent to Habib Bourguiba in the mid 1980s. She was a generous, jolly, young-looking figure, liberally decorated with jangling jewellery.

She was immensely proud to have been one of the first Tunisian women to have studied at university in France. As a lawyer she was involved in implementing the new laws on polygamy, the right to work, divorce and, above all, the government's birth control programme – which, she admitted, had been 'introduced in a totally anarchic manner'.

The government was trying to limit families to a maximum of four children. The most delicate issue was polygamy. The Koran said a man might have four wives, but 'You have to remember that the Prophet was born into a polygamous society and in a polygamous city. The emphasis must be on the equitable treatment of the wives. It is a question of education and independence.' On the matter of dress, she produced the classic Islamic argument for women covering their hair and limbs: 'It makes them more independent as they do not have to suffer the indignities and invasions of the stares of men.' Madame Mzali herself was dressed in smart modern European clothes.

Alas, Madame Mzali was not to see her ministerial dreams fulfilled. Later that year her husband fell victim to Bourguiba's uncertain temper, and was accused of embezzlement and treason. He was stripped of his property and fled into exile. The fall of Bourguiba restored their fortune, but not their former rank and status.

For Tunisians, Kairouan is the fourth most venerated city in Islam after Mecca, Medina and Jerusalem. On its plateau of baking dust it heats like a clay oven in summer. In the spring it is awash with the aroma of jasmine and orange blossom.

On my first visit to this most Arab-looking of North African cities I fell into a spider's web. At a crossroads, a tall thin young man ran towards me, waving his arms about, and asked me if I could give him a lift into the city centre since his car had broken down – pointing to a dusty vehicle in the ditch for confirmation.

He proved a pleasant companion, enquiring if this was my first visit to Kairouan, and how long I had been in Tunisia. Did I know, he went on, that Kairouan was the most famous centre of carpet-making outside Persia and Turkey? It just so happened that his family was engaged in the rug trade, and he would like to show me some. 'It's a fascinating business. Come and look. You don't have to buy anything. But come and take a glass of tea with us. I insist on thanking you for giving me a lift. No, no it wasn't a trick, I promise you.'

In an instant we were inside. Trays were rattling, pale, refreshing mint tea was being poured and sweets handed round. Soon the carpets were being unrolled, twisted and turned in the glaring sun that streamed through the windows. The art of gentle persuasion began.

Kairouan was chosen as a holy site in 670 AD by the first Arab invader, Oqba Ibn Nafi. The old city still has a strong classical Arab flavour to it, and the designs of the carpets that are made there reflect the shapes of the city's battlements and of the great mosque and its massive minaret. A favourite theme consists of infinite variations on patterns inspired by the lamp hanging inside the prayer hall of the mosque. The carpets are knotted, ranging from between 40,000 and 120,000 knots per square metre.

The woven Berber carpets go in for wilder, more exuberant colours, while their subject matters may include camels, fortresses and mosques. The Berber rug is an all-purpose piece of equipment, serving as a mat, a windbreak, a saddle-cloth, a curtain and even a roof for a tent.

Inside the workshop, groups of women were knotting and weaving. An apprenticeship takes up to five years, at the end of which a girl presents her first carpet as an offering to the Mosque of the Barber in the old city. The work was hard; they wanted more money, and were threatening to go on strike. Within weeks of my visit many of the hundreds of carpet shops in Kairouan were closed by strikes for several months. The demands for higher wages reflected the impact of tourism, raising both the cost of living and expectations.

By the end of my tour I knew I had been hooked, and I chose an unlikely-looking Berber rug in turquoise, green and blue with two ferocious lozenge shapes in white and red. I was told it somehow represented the all-seeing eye of good and evil, one of the oldest motifs in the Mediterranean.

Making good my escape, I made my way to the Great Mosque, one of the splendours of Islam and one of the great buildings of the Mediterranean. Its lines are austere, and nothing fussy interrupts the huge space of its open court and above a wall of baked biscuit-coloured mud stands the minaret, a solid but perfectly poised lantern. Children and pilgrims swept across the court like small birds in search of crumbs. Inside the cool, cavernous prayer-hall a group of girls, their heads covered by white scarves and veils, sat in a circle, their dress proclaiming their vows to an order of Islamic sisters.

Above them, obscure in the twilight of the ceiling, hung an enormous and elaborate lamp, an intricate affair of glass and metal – and to either side of them were more than a hundred polished columns, each crowned with a Roman capital – glorious pieces of antique plunder, some decorated with common acanthus leaves, some florid and busy, some plain and squat. Traces of Roman Africa dotted the great building like clues to the city's ancient past. On one outer wall an entire lintel and door-post consisted of marble egg-and-dart and bead-and-reel decorations, untouched by time.

Across the souks of the old quarter is a mosque of homelier dimensions. The Mosque of the Barber has the flickering arches and domes of the Andalusia, and basks in the gentle shade of shrubs and orange trees. It is the mausoleum of Abu Zama El Balaoui, a companion of the Prophet. He was known as 'the barber' because he kept three hairs of his master's beard about his person – under his tongue, his arm and next to his heart.

The entrance was a scene of domestic chaos, as mothers fed their children surrounded by pots of tea and coffee and dishes piled with rice, all casually strewn across carpets of rich crimson. At the shrine itself the hall was thick with rugs of all shapes and sizes, green and dark with age – the first fruits of Kairouan's apprentices in centuries past. Peering into a gloom lit by dozens of flickering lanterns, I wondered if I should enter – customs vary from mosque to mosque and from country to country. In Morocco the authorities are fairly strict about excluding unbelievers from the most revered shrines.

Eventually a large figure in white, the *sheikh* in charge of the mosque, came to my help. Of course I could come in, he beamed. 'Islam believes in tolerance and hospitality – and peace,' he added in efficient French. Before we went into the shrine – its Ottoman tiles reflecting the greens and golds of the carpets – the priest said he would like to offer me a blessing for my journey. After holding my hand he sprayed me with water perfumed with orange blossom, his benediction a typically casual piece of Tunisian generosity.

In the dry and dusty fields of the plains round Kairouan I came across a lone camel plodding a weary furrow through crumbling soil that was hardly more than thick sand, jerking behind him a single tine of wood that was his plough. These lands form the Sahel Province – a sea of fine dust in summer, but once a byword of fertility, an arcadian paradise of rich vegetation and exotic animals. Pliny must have had such a place of wonders in mind when he wrote 'Out of Africa there is always something new.'

Some idea of the novelties of nature offered to the Romans by Africa can be derived from the mosaics in the Museum of the Bardo in Tunis. It is an archaeological jungle, too rich to penetrate or digest in one visit, the greatest display of Roman mosaics on the southern coast of the Mediterranean, matched but not surpassed by those in Antakya in Turkey. Other antiquities include a fine engraving on a funeral monument of what appears to be a Carthaginian priest about to slay a baby, one of the earliest pieces from the Punic era, it doubtless contributed greatly to the canard about the Carthaginians' penchant for child sacrifice. The building itself is a sixteenth-century Bey's palace, the size and massiveness of which is disguised by delicate wrought-iron balconies and kiosk casemates. In spring curling vines of wisteria provide extra camouflage, wafting clouds of perfume and purple flowers across the courtyards.

Most striking of all are the rich colours of the mosaics, deeper and more varied than any to be found in Roman Europe. Whereas in the north, it is said, the Romans favoured strongly coloured wall paintings, but preferred plainer hues for floor mosaics, the mosaics of Africa were a garden of delight: the seas groan with fish and candy-striped lobsters and crabs; tigers, joyously striped like a child's toy, bounce through vivid green jungles. The Eden which inspired these scenes is now more threatened by shifts in climate and population than any other part of North Africa.

Beyond the sandy fields the greatest monument of Imperial Rome sits on the horizon like a broken crown of sandstone. The Roman arena at El Djem is the greatest amphitheatre on the southern coast of the Mediterranean, and equal in size to the Colosseum in Rome. It must once have served a community of 50,000 locals but today it adorns a small town of low and unremarkable Arab houses. It is festooned with beggars and self-appointed guides. An old man with a mangy camel offers to capture the unwary through an even more ancient camera, the bellows of which are as moth-eaten as his beast. Although the arena has been plundered by local builders, and a large chunk of wall was destroyed when an Ottoman powder magazine blew up a couple of centuries ago, it is far better preserved than the Colosseum, giving one a vivid sense of the scale of operations in the entertainment industry during the last days of Roman rule.

The landscape round El Djem is more vulnerable than most to quirks and sudden shifts of climate and to global warming now upon us. The Mediterranean lands as a whole seem particularly vulnerable to the raising of the sea level, which would have the effect of flooding lakes, rivers and reservoirs with salt water. Coastal lands are particularly at risk. Analysts working for UN Environmental Programmes (UNEP) suspect that the sea level could rise 20 centimetres in the next century, and that the annual mean temperature could rise up to three degrees centigrade. Farmers in the deltas of rivers like the Nile, the Po and the Ebro would have to take drastic measures to preserve their livelihood – provided they could prevent their land from being drowned in salt water. Wetlands would be liable to higher rates of evaporation than ever before. Since 10,000 BC, when civilisation first appeared in the Mediterranean, the mean annual temperature has not changed by more than 1°C even during the Little Ice Age. UNEP experts now expect a rise in annual average temperatures of up to 1.5°C between 1990 and 2025.

In Tunisia its effects are marked by the return of the soil to desert at an alarmingly visible pace. A study of an area of 106,000 square kilometres in the south of the country showed that between 1965 and 1977 some 12,500 square kilometres reverted to desert. The government and international agencies have now established several protected areas for study and conservation, the biggest being the wetlands round Ichkeul, Tunisia's biggest lake. But particular attention is being given to expanding fishing and fish farming, and to protecting the coastlands – for it is there that the battle to feed the growing number of new Tunisians has to be fought and won.

One of the most curious settlements on the edge of the Tunisian desert is the island of Djerba, deep in the Gulf of Sidra or Sirte. Linked to the mainland by a narrow causeway, it is a mixture of ancient myth and modern fact. The myth is that this was the Land of the Lotus Eaters in the *Odyssey* – a distinction shared with many other Mediterranean islands, for which not a shred of factual evidence exists.

Today it is a haven for a new breed of lotus-eaters, who inhabit the lawns and pools of its huge hotels like basking sharks. They are tended by the new wanderers of the Mediterranean, poor migrants from worlds beyond the Sahara – most of the reception staff in the echoing glass palace I visited were from Sierra Leone.

Djerba has been a port and a centre of trade for three thousand years. Having learned the tricks of the trade from the old Punic enemy, the Romans made Djerba the centre of the purple dye industry, and carefully nurtured the murex (the mollusc which produces it) along the surrounding coasts. Today Djerbans, like the ancient Phoenicians, are noted for their entrepreneurial bent, forming clannish communities throughout Tunisia and abroad.

The Aragonese tyrant of Sicily, Roger de Loria, set up a naval base on the island in 1289, and in 1507 Barbarossa's corsairs began to operate from the island in alliance with Ottoman Turkey against Imperial Spain; when the Spaniards counter-attacked the corsairs retreated to their castle, only to be massacred by their putative Turkish allies. The incident was commemorated by a cairn of hundreds of skulls.

Though the Turkish fort is the main landmark of the little harbour of Houmt Souk, the villages and markets in most of the island are Arab in style but with some highly individual touches of their own. Houmt Souk lives up to its name, with two large covered markets selling fine spun silk for scarves and handkerchiefs, and blankets and coats of fine wool – the staple goods of Djerban merchants for thousands of years.

Protected by the desert on one side and the sea on the other, Djerba has long been a place of refuge. Clues as to the identity of some of those who sought refuge can be found in the heavy rounded white walls, stubby minarets and squat domes of the mosques, some of which are like small fortresses, their whitewashed walls gleaming in the balding desert lands. Some of them were founded by the Kharijites, one of the great sects of early Islam. Like the Shi'ites and the Ismailis, they were originally followers of Ali, the son-in-law of the Prophet. But they then broke with the followers of Ali to found a separate community, first in Mesopotamia before spreading across North Africa. At one point they had their own state, which stretched from the mouth of the Nile to the Kabylean plateau in northern Algeria. But when their power waned and their communities were divided and defeated, Djerba was their refuge. The Kharijites take an austere, almost puritanical, view of Islam's teaching, particularly in sexual matters, often refusing burial rites to transgressors of their laws. They are an old and important sect of Islam, often overlooked by non-Muslim writers. Their communities still have a significant voice in the Arab world, not least in Yemen, the Gulf, and parts of Lebanon and Iraq.

The Mosque of the Stranger is far from puritanical in appearance. It sits in the shade next to the Turkish bath, the *hamman*, and some of the exuberance of bath-house design has rubbed off on it – Ottoman tiles abound, with a band of them circling the minaret like a garland. Even more exotic still is the Mosque of the Turks with its strangely rounded minaret; its builders were followers of the eighteenth-century Arabian reformer, Ibn Abdul Wahhab, regarded in their day as wild revolutionaries. Today the royal house of Saudi Arabia are the principal champions of Wahhabism, for which they are considered heretics by many Muslims, particularly the Shi'ite clergy of Iran.

Saddest and most ancient of the human jetsam of Djerba are the Jews, huddling in small hamlets like El Hara El Kebira outside Houmt Souk. In 1956 Tunisia had a population of 105,000 Jews, more than half living in Tunis itself. In the early 1960s most left for Israel, and by 1985 the total population could have been little more than five or six thousand, most of them in Tunis, Sousse, Sfax and Djerba.

I took a cautious walk through the streets of the village early one afternoon. A few characters of ancient Hebrew were daubed on the concrete walls. It was the Sabbath, few people were about. Small boys with skull caps scattered as I rounded a corner; another, bolder group sat on an old cart, casually chewing sunflower seeds and carob pods. They affected to know no French or English, and little Arabic. Suddenly one asked, in a good French accent, 'Your are a writer, a journalist?' His companions, feigned lack of interest, went on cracking the seeds and spitting the husks from their blackened lips. The boy said he did not like journalists, or foreigners for that matter, but he would not say why as he spoke little French, only Hebrew which he learnt at the synagogue.

His response was not adolescent surliness, but a carefully tuned sense of self-preservation. A year or so earlier two Djerba Jews had been murdered in an act of folly encouraged by Qaddafi's Libya. Broadcasts from across the Libyan border, only a hundred miles or so away, had urged the 'killing of all Jews', and some fanatic had taken them at their word. The Jews, I learned later from an Arab merchant in the market at Houmt Souk, are skilful craftsmen and traders in jewellery. They are versed in languages – most speak perfect French, but prefer to speak Moroccan Arabic. Very few have any Hebrew beyond the teaching of the synagogue.

The blight upon the Jews of Djerba seemed all the heavier by contrast with the gentle sense of dialogue and compromise which seems to colour so much of Tunisian culture and society today. Tunisia seems one of the most truly Mediterranean of all countries. Most Tunisians are Arab, deeply committed to the evolution of the Arab world and Islam, but they are aware of the movements of the past that have affected their country, in fact as much as in myth. Tunisians are as attuned to the currents and conflicts of the Mediterranean world as any, and more so than most. Unlike, say, the Lebanese, most Tunisians by nature appear given to tolerance and debate. This gives Tunisia a unique charm and allure – but will it last?

Visitors to the Synagogue of the Miracle 'El Griba' in Djerba itself are told about the foundations of the Jewish community there. Some say that the first Jews were refugees from the first diaspora in 566 BC; while others believe the settlement really began after the second diaspora of 71 AD that followed the destruction of the Temple of Herod. The Jews themselves say they settled here after Jerusalem had been taken by Nebuchadnezzar and after the destruction of the Temple of Solomon.

Inside and out the mosque, completed in 1920, is unexciting to look at. The stained glass in the windows matches the tiling of the arches and walls. The furnishings are simple and sombre, with railings and stalls of heavy dark wood. On the walls is written a simple prayer in French. It asks 'he who gives victory to kings and authority to chiefs . . . to bless, protect, assist, elevate, glorify and render sublime the Supreme Combattant Habib Bourguiba, President of the Tunisian Republic' – an eloquent vote of thanks to the old president for his protection.

Nine: Libya – Qadaffi's Mixed Metaphor

'At first we thought it was thunder. Then I heard the rat-tat of the guns, and I knew it wasn't.

'We all went downstairs and I shouted to my father, "Babi, come down. Come down." Then the planes approached – you know that terrible feeling when they come towards you.

'Suddenly there was a blinding white light, really blinding so you had to close your eyes. Then a huge ball of orange flame. The whole house shook, plaster fell everywhere, and glass shattered. My mother had a splinter cutting the white of her eye and blood was everywhere. She had a nerve cut in her leg. I looked at her and there was a glass bowl stuck on her leg.

'A friend next door had been looking out of the window, and a flying splinter cut her neck, cut her throat. Killed her just like that.'

The images of the American bombing of Tripoli were to remain violent and vivid in the mind of Huda Khalil long after the event. Her home was among the villas and apartments of Bin Asshur, which passes for one of the Libyan capital's smarter and leafier suburbs. It was wrecked when the American planes attempted to hit a nearby radar installation.

Huda's family had been pillars of the establishment of the old Libya – her father was Chief Justice under King Idris. But it was a very different Libya that the Americans had in their sights on the night of 15 April 1986, the new Libya of the Socialist People's Libyan Arab Jamahiriya, a regime stamped in the image of its Revolutionary Leader, Colonel Muammar Al-Qadaffi. For the Americans Qadaffi had become the most prominent sponsor of international terrorism in Europe and the Middle East. And the aim of the April raids on Tripoli and Benghazi was to get Qadaffi. They wanted to show that he too was mortal.

The Reagan Administration believed they had incontrovertible evidence that Qadaffi had been a backer, if not the direct instigator, of a series of terrorist attacks over the previous six months. Libyan involvement was suspected in the hijacking by PLO dissidents of the Italian cruise liner *Achille Lauro*, during which an elderly American Jew making a holiday pilgrimage to Israel, Larry Klinghoffer, was beaten and thrown overboard in his wheelchair. Two days after Christmas that same year, gunmen belonging to the Abu Nidal Al-Fatah Revolutionary Council attacked with grenades and submachine-guns the counters of Israel's national airline El Al at Rome and Vienna airports. Seventeen people died, several of them children.

On 5 April 1986 a bomb exploded in the La Belle Club, a recognised nightspot for American servicemen in Berlin. An American soldier and a Turkish woman died in the blast. The Americans believed intercepts of radio traffic to the Libyan People's Bureau – the Libyan embassy – showed that Qadaffi's men were involved in supplying the explosives and detonators. Probably they were not the only instigators, as subsequent information has suggested that the main inspiration came from radical Palestinian groups in Damascus.

But President Reagan's advisers believed they had their *casus belli*, the justification for attacking Qadaffi in his home, said to be an elaborate Bedouin tent in the compound of the Aziziya Barracks in the outskirts of Tripoli. The raid was signalled well in advance. Reinforcements of the heavy F-111 bombers had to be moved from their home bases in America to Britain. Preparations had to be laid for long flights to the Mediterranean via the Bay of Biscay, with several relays of in-flight refuelling from tanker aircraft as France refused the Americans right to fly over its territory.

By the night of the 14–15 April a small army of pressmen were in Tripoli. Some had taken balcony seats, their cameras already set up, hours before the raid began, while others had opened telephone lines to their offices and bureaux, who had warned them that operations were about to start.

At about one o'clock in the morning, the planes swept over the corniche in Tripoli, the elegant curving seaside promenade fashioned by the engineers of Fascist Italy. The lights were ablaze in the streets, and were only doused after the bombers had gone. The anti-aircraft defences were quite unprepared, and began firing in earnest after the skies were empty of all aircraft.

The American planes struck at Tripoli airport, at radar installations and at military barracks. Despite using laser guidance systems in combat for the first time, some missed or mistook their targets altogether. Bombs fell on orange groves in Benghazi, the villas and spacious apartments of Bin Asshur, and the French embassy in the capital. The Americans lost the two-man crew of an F-111 which plunged into the Mediterranean – the Qadaffi publicity machine made much of this, claiming they had been eaten by the sharks in almost Biblical retribution. The Americans claimed that thirty-seven civilians had died, though journalists on the spot said the figure must have been more than a hundred. Among them was a little girl of fifteen months, Hanna, adopted recently by Qadaffi's wife.

As for the Libyan leader, he was not in his tent when the bombers came, but underground in his bunker command-post. He appeared to have suffered little more than a sprained arm, which he held in a sling, and a very bruised ego.

What was intended to be the moment of truth for Qadaffi turned to be more a moment of propaganda. In a way, Qadaffi and President Reagan were made for each other's highly individual brand of rhetoric. For Reagan, the Libyan leader, with his almost girlish good looks, was the 'mad dog' of the Middle East, a 'flake' and, in line with his weakness for Hollywood-speak, a 'loony toon'. Qadaffi's own posturings were reminiscent of Rodolfo Valentino as the Sheikh, and indeed he had been born in a Bedouin tent, and as a child had followed the nomadic life of his family and tribe.

The cultures of Ronald Reagan's America and Qadaffi's Libya were so far apart that the two nations and governments had hardly the remotest chance of understanding each other. American accusations about Qadaffi's complicity in international terrorism had considerable justification. He had messed with extremist groups in Lebanon, Egypt and Yemen, and with the IRA, to name but a few of his favourite causes. He had backed the psychopathic Idi Amin in Uganda just as his dictatorship was tottering. Qadaffi's own version of the cultural revolution, the declaration of the Jamahiriya in 1977 and the establishment of People's Committees at home and People's Bureaux abroad, set off a chain of vendettas against Libyan dissidents in exile. Members of the People's Bureau in London fired on a demonstration by Qadaffi opponents and killed a young British policewoman, Yvonne Fletcher, in 1984; this led to the siege of the embassy, the expulsion of all its occupants, and the severing of diplomatic relations between Tripoli and London.

Qadaffi's support for extremists and terrorists, like so much of his foreign policy, was inconsistent and chaotic. Nor was he as generous with his money as might have been expected, given Libya's oil wealth. Much of the materiel he distributed was second-hand, dumped on Libya by his supporters in the Soviet bloc and included huge quantities of grenade-launchers and Kalashnikov AK-47 assault rifles. After the fall of the Communists in Prague, Vaclav Havel revealed that the old regime had shipped hundreds of tons of Semtex explosive to Tripoli – 'enough to keep the terrorists going for 150 years,' as he put it – and that Qadaffi, surprisingly, paid a steep price for the almost undetectable plastic explosive.

The Libyan leader was liable to fall out with even his most favoured chums in the terrorist playpen. A few months after the American raid it became clear that he had broken with the Al-Fatah Revolutionary council and its mercurial leader, Sabri al Banna, better known as Abu Nidal, who had taken up residence in a Tripoli suburb; yet it was his relationship with Abu Nidal as much as anything that had brought the American bombers. As an Israeli military analyst later explained to me, 'It was necessary to restrict Abu Nidal's area of operations, so the obvious thing was to get the most vulnerable point, where the network was weakest. If they couldn't strike the really big centres of Middle East terrorism like Damascus or Baghdad, they could at least try to close down the branch office, Tripoli.' But many Americans disagreed with the thinking behind the raids. American ambassadors in the Mediterranean region were not informed about them in advance, and were furious at being kept in the dark. The ambassador to Greece, Bob Keilly, about to visit the US 6th Fleet Headquarters at Naples, was told of the raid by a member of his staff some ten hours before it took place. He was stunned by the news, he told me later, and believed the display of military muscle had tainted Washington's diplomatic standing in the region.

In the short term the raids achieved something. Qadaffi went ominously quiet, and the threats of revenge were muted – apart from two Scud missiles launched at the Italian island of Lampedusa, which missed by nearly fifteen miles. Serious retribution occurred elsewhere. A Jordanian, Nazir Hindawi, tried to smuggle a bomb aboard an Israeli El-Al jumbo jet at Heathrow airport, but was caught in time. His connections with Syria led to the breaking of diplomatic ties between London and Damascus. In Lebanon two British university teachers were murdered, and the journalist John McCarthy was kidnapped on his way to Beirut airport.

Within a year Qadaffi had resumed his activities. In 1987 a coaster, the *Eksund*, was intercepted off the west coast of France on her fourth run with guns, ammunition, rocket launchers and Semtex for the IRA in Ireland. A year later it was clear that the Libyans had been building something suspiciously like a chemical weapons plant at Rabta in the desert south of the capital, though with reports of a series of fires in 1990 it began to be doubted whether it had ever achieved full production, or was likely to do so. Qadaffi in the meantime was making it up with his Arab neighbours of the Maghreb. In one thing he was consistent: to enemy and ally alike he remains an enigma.

The enigma lies in the origins and nature of the revolution led by Qadaffi and his group of Free Officers against the ancient King Idris in 1969. Qadaffi was an army captain of twenty-seven, astute and self-taught but surprisingly naive about the world beyond North Africa. He was to provide Libya with a revolutionary programme and philosophy of its own, specially tailored to its own circumstances and enshrined in the message of the Green Book.

Libya was young both as a unified nation and in terms of the age of its population. Though one of the larger African countries, its population was little over two million in 1969 the year of his coup; twenty years later it was still under four million, but growing fast. By then half the population were under the age of fifteen. Qadaffi's Green Revolution had been a children's crusade.

The new regime benefited from one enormous stroke of fortune – the discovery of oil under the Libyan desert. Exploitation had begun in the 1950s under King Idris, but much of the management was in the hands of neo-colonial multinational companies like BP, Exxon and Mobil. Under Qadaffi oil revenues swelled, not least with the tripling of oil prices by OPEC after the 1973 Arab-Israeli war – making Libya the richest country of North Africa, indeed of the non-European Mediterranean. In 1986 Libya had an oil income per head of population of some $8,400 a year, though this was reduced to some $7,600 by 1989 because of the unsteadiness of the oil market. The average income per head on the southern shore of the Mediterranean was $1,200 a year in 1986 and as low as $600 in the poorer parts of Morocco.

Oil dollars allowed Qadaffi to indulge in the theories set out in the Green Book, which had been gestating since his school days at Sebha. Its central message is embodied in Qadaffi's Third Universal Law – 'third' in the sense of being a third way between the capitalist West and the communist East. Its simple slogan was 'Power to the People' – Qadaffi's people, the children of the Green Book. The people would not be represented by parties but by People's Committees. The book spins a web of jargon and rhetoric, a dose of Nasserite Arab socialism here, Iraqi Ba'athism there, a bit of Marx, a bit of the Koran – though Qadaffi subsequently was to react violently to Muslim radicalism in Libya.

To the Western eye the four volumes of the Green Book might appear a disparate jungle of half-baked notions and borrowed slogans. But according to experts on Bedouin culture and history, like John Davis of Kent University, the Green Book makes sense from a Libyan perspective. The thoughts of Qadaffi reflect the egalitarian customs and lore of the Bedouin tribes, struggling to survive on the hoof in a challenging and hostile world. But Libyan society is no longer nomadic, and is now urban in the main – with the result that Qadaffi's Green Revolution has become the biggest political mixed metaphor of the Mediterranean and the Middle East.

On the first anniversary of the American bombing, Qadaffi threw a party – by now the American attack had become a great Libyan victory. The Libyan leader had a penchant for festivities, organising them for every conceivable occasion. Dignitaries and fellow-travellers from round the world would turn up, some paid for by the Libyans, while for journalists they guaranteed a precious visa, otherwise granted only after a weary game of diplomatic chance.

The clientele for the first post-bombing party was mixed, to put it politely. A few serious journalists were surrounded by groups which could best be described as the Great Sixties Hangover – Red Indians and Eskimos demanding ethnic rights, scions of the Old Left from Britain and France, a survivor of the Chicago Seven from 1968. In their enthusiasm for anything parading the banner of national protest, the organisers managed to confuse their left with their right and invited a hard-right group of Canadian neo-fascists along with the Marxists and the Inuit and the Red Indians. A freelance journalist on his first trip abroad thought he had a scoop when he revealed the thugs' real identity. Next evening he fell to his death from the flat roof of the apartment block in which the Canadians had been billeted; the circumstances were never explained.

Journalists, activists and fellow-travellers were sealed and bound together in a Grand Programme of events. The Programme, honoured more in myth than reality, proved a remarkably flexible instrument for coercion. Just as one was about to sneak out of the El Khebir Hotel – a beach view and a listening bug in every room – for some clandestine sight-seeing or a visit to one of the few local cafés, a functionary would spring out reproachfully waving his arms: 'Where are you going? Programme! New visit. Now we prepare questions for the Leader. Programme! We hear Peoples Committee debate on Americans bombing. Programme! This way, mister. We must keep to Programme!'

The first big attraction on the Programme was a grand parade on the race track to the east of the city. Children and adolescents in the uniforms of scouts and young pioneers marched behind large and vivid icons proclaiming victory over Uncle Sam and everlasting devotion to the Leader; sharks with a mischievous twinkle leaped from the waves, their scissor jaws snapping up American pilots; Reagan's America was evoked by a huge leering octopus, its bulbous head emblazoned with the Stars and Stripes. In more reverential vein, a beautiful young Bedouin girl was portrayed holding aloft the Green Book towards a sun rising over the desert. 'The American Fleet must leave the Mediterranean,' read a slogan in English – in tones remarkably restrained given the occasion. Some hundreds of paintings – evidently the main endeavour of the fine art syllabus for the previous academic year – were halted in line for inspection. Apart from vivid renditions of the Defeat of the Evil Capitalist Imperialist Armada, the favourite topic was the Leader himself in a bewildering variety of garbs and guises – as a Bedouin Sheikh, a liberating general in tiger-stripe camouflage fatigues, and a yachtsman in a peaked cap, worn with the aplomb of Noël Coward at his most nautically jaunty.

The display of the icons was followed by a march-past of tribesmen, functionaries, youth volunteers and service personnel in designer fatigues. A ragged band attempted a couple of martial airs before settling on a home-grown version of 'Old MacDonald Had a Farm'. Finally, scampering through the dust, came a band of tall, lean young men in a particularly cool line of desert camouflage – Qadaffi's elite special forces, the equivalent of the British SAS or the American Green Berets and Delta Force. They whirled, whooped, pranced and shouted – everything short of thumping their chests. And then, like some collective conjurer's art, they suddenly produced a flutter of scrawny chickens, and a rabbit from their midst, which they then killed and dismembered, apparently devouring hunks of the raw meat. Quite how this reflected on the martial prowess of Qadaffi's chosen cohorts was not quite clear, but the whirling commandos closed the parade in a thunder of official applause.

Much of the Programme was given over to gestures of solidarity, and debates about the barbarous deeds inflicted on the oppressed peoples of the world. Without warning, the assembly hall and the stadium erupted into marathon displays of denunciation. Wrongs were paraded by speaker after speaker with all the self-absorption of an adolescent in the throws of teenage rebellion. The bombing of Tripoli and Benghazi was denounced as 'one of the most barbaric acts of all time'. Vernon Bellacourt, of the American Indian Movement, spoke of the 500-year stand of the Red Indians 'against the state terrorism of the United States, beginning with the colonial pirate Christopher Columbus'. Elizabeth Tarrant, of the British Women's Movement, denounced Mrs Thatcher for allowing the American bombers to use British bases for the raids. The speeches merged into a long drone of condemnation, with positive proposals in short supply. The Great Peace Conference did remarkably little conferring. If the message of the Green Book and the Third Universal Law was, as it claimed, a blueprint for mankind, it never got much further than the tent flaps of its creators' minds.

The high point of the Programme was the visit to the Qadaffi dwelling in the Azaziya Barracks, which had been kept in the state of ruin wrought by the American planes a year before. The apartments were in a spacious but not over-ostentatious building to one side of the parade ground. The upper floors were a gaping hole of flapping fabrics, shattered mirrors and sagging ceilings. Some of the rubble had been tidied away for easier access, and pathways taped off for the steady flow of visitors. The furnishings were garish but not lavish. On the floor lay a woman's shoe, some toys and a child's exercise book. The message was plain: the bombers' main target had been a slice of Libyan domestic life – which happened to belong to the Jamahiriya's first family.

Outside the apartment, a barbecue of lamb was sizzling, in the fragrant smoke of which the Red Indian Peace Party danced and howled at the moon. More speeches were made. One woman began hers with the word 'Shalom', hardly the thing at the court of the self-styled greatest friend of Palestinian liberation.

Of the Leader himself there was little sign. Suddenly a band of guards, male and female, machine-guns swinging at their waists, hove into view, followed by a whirling flash of grey, the shade of designer jump-suit favoured by the Leader and his more intimate guards, the women in particular. The grey flash shoved a youth onto the platform, and was gone. That was all we saw of the Leader or his shadow. The youth was the fourteen-year-old heir apparent, Sahedi Qadaffi, who then delivered the ritual denunciation of imperialist oppressors, which was relayed in a ponderous and approximate translation.

Next morning the pilgrimage to the barracks was repeated in daylight. The roads were filled with youths in uniforms of every shade and colour. An informal bagpipe band, flanked by Bedouin dancers, tried to be heard above motor horns and klaxons. We shuffled round the apartment shrine once again, this time between girl guides and pioneers. Many of the girls wore the headscarf of Islamic Sisterhoods, while others wore military fatigues; their handsome oval faces were pleasantly unwarlike, and none carried a weapon.

In the throng of thousands, almost nobody seemed older than twenty-five, reflecting the accent on youth which has always pervaded the Qadaffi culture and only the most senior officers and functionaries are over forty. The emphasis on youth is appropriate propaganda, for the notion of Libya as a unified nation state is only a few generations old. To Herodotus Libya meant the whole of Africa, but until very recent times it has been little more than a geographical expression, politically less than the sum of its tribal parts. Only on the eve of the Second World War did the Italians bring administrative unity to the country. Since independence – not least under Qadaffi – the scale and pace of social and material development has been dramatic compared with its immediate neighbours.

Although Herodotus admired the red soil of the coast, he recognised that for the most part Libya was a wild, empty, desert place. It has always been one of the least populated parts of all Africa – in 1875 the population numbered only one million. And despite its Mediterranean coastline, its people have shown little interest in the sea. The son of a prominent Libyan political exile told me that Libyan proverbs still speak of the sea as a source of evil, menace and danger. 'We have always turned out backs to the sea, if we possibly can. It's only use has been for a certain amount of trade.'

Like Gaul, Roman Libya was split into three parts – though the southernmost desert region was of little significance. Trade and farming were concentrated in Cyrenaica to the east and in Tripolitania – divisions that continued under the Ottomans and in Mussolini's Fascist colony. Like most of North Africa the Libyan coast was invaded, occupied and infested by Arabs, Ottomans, Spaniards rulers and Barbary pirates. In 1711 a janissary captain, Ahmad Qaramanli, made himself Dey and the virtually independent lord of the coast. But the Barbary pirates made the life of his heirs a misery and whittled their inheritance to a shred, so that in 1835 the Ottomans once more imposed direct administration from Istanbul.

The ports, Tripoli and Misratha to the west, Benghazi and Darnah to the east, were the outlets of the great trade routes of the Sahara to the Niger and the Gulf of Guinea, Lake Chad and the distant branches of the White Nile. The north-south caravan trails met the great east-west artery in the desert region of Libya, the Fezzan. This was the exotic path from Cairo and the Nile Delta to Timbuktu and the Atlantic beyond, hinting at gold, rare dyes, salt and the most steady source of profit – slaves. Commercial raiding for slaves began well before the era of European colonisation of North Africa, and in remote and isolated pockets was to outlast it. Slave auctions may have been held well into the 1940s in the more secluded oases of the Fezzan, and as late as the mid-1950s the United Nations was passing resolutions and sending fact-finding missions in an effort to stamp out slaving in Saharan Africa.

Expeditions to the Fezzan would net up to 1500 slaves a year for sale in the markets of Tripoli and Ghadames, where they accounted for more than a third of the total value of all imports. Prices fluctuated greatly. The favoured few, beautiful Abyssinian girls especially, might never be sold in public. Most prized were the eunuchs for guarding the women of the household and bossing the domestic staff, who might fetch up to 700 Spanish piastres on the open market in the 1820s. Castration was carried out in the most savage and casual manner on the journey north; the commonest method was to squeeze the testacles between red-hot coins.

But at the same time that Numidian eunuchs and Abyssinian children were being haggled over in the oases of the Fezzan, a new spirit of Islam was abroad in the Libyan deserts. The Sanusids were destined to become one of the most powerful Muslim Brotherhoods of North Africa, one of the great *tariqa* or cults which are such a potent feature in the revival of Islam today. The movement took its name from its charismatic founder, Muhammad ibn Ali al-Sanusi, the 'Grand Sanusi'. He was born in Algeria in 1787 of a Sharifian family, claiming to be a descendant of the Prophet.

He studied at the great Islamic school of Qarawiyyin in Fez in Morocco and at the Al-Azhar University of Cairo, where he quarrelled with civil and a spiritual leaders alike, including the Mufti himself. The Grand Sanusi was a Sufi scholar, a mystic and an intellectual, who refused to accept the Koran at face value. Eventually his vision and teaching brought him to the Libyan coast where he set up his first school or *zawiya*; later he established his base at Jaghbub, a hundred miles inland and close to the Egyptian border. Jaghbub was both a school and a political directorate where, in the classical tradition of the *tariqa*, men would come from the tribes to be educated and receive instructions on all aspects of public and private conduct from the leader or *sheikh*. The brightest students might be sent to Mecca to complete their education. The Grand Sanusi was the founder of modern Libyan nationalism; there is also an element of what was to become Arab socialism in his political teaching.

The Sanusids did not resist the Turks, and supported neither the rebellion of Arabi Pasha against the British in Egypt nor the revolt of Muhammad Ahmad, who proclaimed himself the *mahdi* or saviour in the Sudan, and whose Dervish supporters were finally defeated at Omdurman in 1896. The son of the Great Sanusi, Sayyid al-Mahdi said his aim was 'to reform Islam through peaceful means, and not bloodshed'. But with the invasion of the Italians in 1911, the Sanusids became the focus of armed resistance, and this was to continue under Mussolini's rule of the Fascists. By then the spiritual leader of the movement was Amir Sayyid Muhammad Idris, the grandson of the Grand Sanusi. When Libya became fully independent in 1951 he assumed the title of King Idris I. Eighteen years later the king was overthrown in the coup led by Qadaffi. He died in exile in 1983, at the age of ninety-four.

The pervading influence of the Sanusids in the making of modern Libya has always affected Qadaffi's attitude to Libyan nationalism and Islam. In the early stages of his revolution, at least, it made him favour the more secular vision of Nasser's pan-Arab socialism and nurture a deep suspicion of anything that smacked of Islamic revivalism or fundamentalism.

Sanusi militancy ran parallel with the Italian conquest and occupation of Libya. Italian involvement in Libya is a bizarre and fractured tale – and one that took a long time to complete. In 1911 the Italians opened hostilities against the Ottomans in Cyrenaica and Tripolitania on the thinnest of pretexts – that Italian 'vital interests' were being threatened by the Turks, and Italy anyway was due for a prize in the great colonial race of the European powers in Africa. The war did not go well. The Turks despatched Ali Fethi Bey and Enver Pasha to command their forces, which were assisted by Libyan levies organised by the Sanusids; but defeat in the Balkan Wars of 1912 led the Sublime Porte to surrender its claims to Libya to the Italians. But the fighting continued, and by the outbreak of the First World War virtually the only secure parts of the new Italian colony were the coastal cities of Benghazi, Tobruk, Darnah and Tripoli.

The next real push from Rome came with the advent of Fascism. Some of Fascism's biggest names were sent to Libya. Generals Graziani and Badoglio (who was to surrender Italy to the Allies in 1943) finished Sanusid resistance in the Fezzan, herding prisoners and refugees into concentration camps. A barbed wire fence was erected along the frontier with Egypt.

But there was another side to Italian rule. The Italians dug wells, irrigated the coastlands and laid out the best husbanded orange and olive groves of North Africa. From the air the coastal farms of Libya are a haven of orderly green and red soil compared with the neglected wastelands round Algiers and Oran. The Italians also built a modern road network. Aside from the misery and disgrace of the detention camps and the sporadic wars of conquest, there was almost a sense of innocence about the Italian attempt to be colonists. In his memoir, *A Cure for Serpents* a young colonial doctor, later granted the grandiose title of Duke of Stajano, recalled working among the Berber and Bedouin tribes of Cyrenaica. It is a tale of endless intrigues, tribal chiefs with many wives, soothsayers whose prophecies are blurred in fumes of alcohol and bare-breasted slave girls whose beauty had a strange knack of monopolising the good doctor's attentions. Spells, witches and weird imprecations were common fare, for many of his patients had no single God, but many. The animists' world of many-spirited nature had not yet surrendered to the embrace of Islam.

The destruction of Fascism was long foretold in its preference for empty martial rhetoric. Once Mussolini decided to go to war in 1940 the Libyan colony was done for. Graziani attempted a surprise attack on the British in Egypt; among its victims was Italo Balbo, Fascism's leading air ace, and one of Mussolini's closest henchmen who was shot down over Tobruk in 1941, probably by Italian anti-aircraft batteries. But the war in the desert provided Libya with one useful by-product. The Allied and Axis armies left behind thousands of tons of mangled ironmongery, the debris of the battlefield. What Abyssinian slaves were in nineteenth-century Tripoli, army surplus scrap metal was in the mid-twentieth. Until oil came on stream, it was Libya's major export.

Libya under King Idris was slow to move from the European shadow, and showed every sign of reluctance to do so. The British and Americans maintained large military bases. The Italian influence was strong, and traces of it remain. Older Libyans speak Italian perfectly. The Italian touch is still reflected in the cathedral, an extravagant sand-stained basilica, and the former casino. Tripoli was a gambler's paradise in the 1950s and the casino a haunt of professional players and rich tourists from Italy.

But other forces were at work. The youth of Libya was being slowly ignited by the new gospel of Nasser's Arab socialism and the Ba'ath movement of Syria and Iraq – among them Muammar Qadaffi, who asked his teacher in his secondary school at Sadeh for private tuition on how to make a pyramid structure of revolutionary command, and about the message of Arab socialism. Later, in the army, he found kindred spirits, frustrated at the corruption and inertia of King Idris's regime and its thrall to the foreigners. On 1 September 1969 the coup began in scenes of silent movie confusion – the officer sent to seize the radio station in Tripoli circled the area several times in his jeep, not knowing where his objective was and without a map.

Later that day, over the radio, Qadaffi assured the people of Libya that their gallant army had toppled 'the reactionary and corrupt regime, the stench of which was sickened and horrified us all'. But Qadaffi had only just made it and now he had won the revolution he had to make it work, and the extraordinary process of do-it-yourself radical politics had to be set in train. It was to become the Greening of Libya.

Despite the sinister reputation of the Libyan regime, Tripoli is a remarkably tranquil and friendly place. The spacious Italian villas along the corniche look as if they have seen better days, but the numbers of cars prowling along the palm-lined boulevard hint at good times and better to come. Greetings to foreigners are polite but distant. The attitude is one of you mind your own business and I'll mind mine – the code of survival, given the Leader's unpredictable swings of mood.

Tripoli works on parallel systems of information – the official version, and the more truthful if approximate commerce of gossip and rumour. State television dutifully pumps out the propaganda of the day, leavened by interminable Egyptian dramas and serials, replete with rolling eyes, tongue-clicking prudery and cardboard staginess. Italian television can be picked up with relative ease – a few years ago some ingenious Sicilians tried a bit of freelance destabilisation of the Libyan regime by broadcasting pornography from a powerful transmitter in the south of their island.

The plain diet of official information provided through television and newspapers allows the bacilli of rumour to breed wild and free. The whole city seems to live on a grapevine of news, whether speculation about Qadaffi's quarrels with old supporters or rivals, or where to buy the best second-hand furniture. Some of the stories can be quite extravagant. 'Under the surface Libyans are intensely political, and politics form a main ingredient of gossip,' a Libyan public servant once told me. 'You'd be amazed how quickly stories fly around the capital – because there is no other real information.'

One of the main services provided by the rumour news agency is an unofficial shopping guide. About half a family's energy seems to be spent on queuing and shopping – the tall, rather sullen buildings of the commercial quarter are swathed in coils of veiled figures waiting for fresh supplies. 'A lorry-load of shoes which turned up after two or three months of bare shelves blocked a street for almost an hour and nearly caused a riot the other day,' a diplomat told me.

A peculiar form of cabin fever afflicts better-off Libyans. Many have money, but are allowed to travel only once a year and then with heavy restrictions on how much currency they can take with them. Those with money have very little to spend it on. Pleasures tend to be private, shared behind closed doors.

Foreign workers, often hugely rewarded for a few months in the oil-fields, also take their pleasure behind closed doors. The riskiest venture is 'flash', the near-lethal home-distilled alcohol with which professional petroleum bachelors seek their solace. Even when relations between the

White House and the Jamahiriya were at their worst, several thousand Americans continued to work the oilfields, while expatriates from Britain and the Commonwealth have manned a string of projects, from building hospitals to operating radars at the civil airport. Foreigners provide both the know-how and muscle-power and on many development projects the Libyans themselves are conspicuously absent.

The first twenty years of Qadaffi's rule have seen huge gains in hygiene, hospitals, housing and education. Three-quarters of Libya's children now get schooling to a secondary stage. Tripoli now has over a million people – more than the entire country a century ago. More children now survive infancy, and Libyan families of ten or twelve are not uncommon. The population will almost double in the next twenty years, though at five or six million it will still be small compared with its neighbours in Egypt and the Maghreb.

The hard work on the big projects is now done by labourers from Pakistan, Korea and the Philippines. One of the largest, stamped with the visionary touch of the Leader himself, is for a 'great man-made river', bringing millions of gallons of water by huge concrete ducts from deep natural wells under the Sahara to irrigate the farms and market gardens of the coast. The scheme has suffered many delays, the total bill has risen to over $25 billion – and now it may well be that the river will flow in the wrong destination, as the need for fresh water is more urgent in the cities than on the coast.

I first visited Tripoli in October 1981. The morning after my arrival I found the streets round the hotel awash with blood. Thousands of sheep were being slaughtered in back-yards and on roof tops for the Haj, the great festival of the pilgrimage to Mecca. The sense of abundance on such occasions can be deceptive, for Libya's distribution systems are startlingly unreliable. Hospitals equipped with the lastest surgical theatres and wards may lack the simplest items. One medical supplier who had waited for nearly a year for confirmation of a $3-million contract for hospital equipment was astonished to be given a rush order for more than half a million insulin syringes, since neither of Tripoli's two big hospitals had one left.

My second visit coincided with another great religious festival – the beginning of Ramadan, the month of fasting. Riding at anchor in the Bay of Tripoli were a dozen freighters with sheep from Romania, Turkey, New Zealand and Australia, destined for slaughter in courtyards and on roofs but the congestion in the port made it unlikely they would could all be unloaded in time.

The Ramadan celebrations that spring of 1987 were marred by a sense of fear and foreboding, particularly among families with sons of military age. For some weeks it had been rumoured that young men were being drafted on the spot for military service. The army was greedy for recruits because, according to increasingly reliable intelligence through the rumour telegraph, it had suffered a major reverse in the desert war in Chad. Of all Quadaffi's foreign adventures, the entanglement in Chad – originating as a dispute over frontiers – has had the greatest impact on his own people. The sporadic campaigns beyond the borders to the south absorbed tens of thousands of young Libyans. Some had been posted south and disappeared without trace. Others have returned hideously wounded in body and spirit, with tales of bitter and chaotic fighting in the heat of the Sahara. Later that same year the Libyans called an uneasy truce and offered to go before an international tribunal for a decision on the border.

The Qadaffi years have been through three distinct phases: the first runs from the coup to the completion of the cultural revolution and the declaration of the Jamahiriya in 1977; the second covers the years when Qudaffi saw himself as an international agent for liberation, and ended with the American raid in 1986; and the third is that of the revolutionary realist.

The first phase was one of nation-building and of socialism, of new hospitals and schools and the nationalisation of foreign oil companies. Nationalism came first, certainly before militant Islam. In 1971 Qadaffi condemned the Muslim Brotherhood, then re-emerging in Egypt. 'The Muslim Brothers in the Arab countries work against unity, against socialism, against Arab nationalism, because they consider all these to be inconsistent with religion,' he said, accusing the Brothers of fulfilling the divisive role in the Arab world, once pursued by the European colonial powers.

This was followed, from 1975 by the period of the Green Book and the People's Committees – and the hunting and murder of opponents at home and abroad. Foreign adventures grew more bold; to neighbours like Egypt and poor relations of the Arab world like North Yemen were offered alliances, and terrorist groups were sponsored. At least nine Palestinian factions became his clients, with headquarters and sanctuaries in Tripoli and Benghazi – the most favoured being Abu Nidal's Fatah Revolutionary Council. In the early Seventies the professional killer Ramon Sanchez, alias 'Carlos the Jackal', appears to have used Libya as his base.

But Qadaffi was often careful about where and by whom his funds were spent. In the early Seventies Amal, the Shi'ite movement in Lebanon, was a favourite cause, but he became impatient at rumours of profligate spending by its brilliant and magnetic founder, the Imam Mousa Sadr, whose open, freewheeling approach to life belied his mullah's cloak and turban. When the Imam visited Libya in search of more funds in 1978, he disappeared without trace. The mystery was never explained and Qadaffi forfeited the support of Lebanese Shi'ites at a stroke.

Even before the American air raids, it was clear that something was going badly wrong with Libya's foreign relations. Despite some initial billing and cooing about external friendship and political union, the Leader's compulsively quarrelsome nature provoked long-running disputes with his neighbours, and with Egypt and Tunisia in particular. In 1985 Egyptian and Ethiopian workers were sent home, and when some 30,000 Tunisians were unceremoniously dumped back across the border President Bourguiba immediately cut diplomatic ties. Qadaffi responded that the Tunisians had been taking valuable jobs from Libyans, who had to learn to stand on their own feet. In fact Tripoli's economy virtually ground to a halt in a matter of weeks, and the Tunisians were back within the year.

To make matters worse, the Jamahiriya was strapped for cash, due to a simple error. The plans for the economy had been based on the assumption that Libyan oil would sell at $18.65 on the European markets, but by the spring of 1987 the price for a barrel of Libyan finest crude was about $16.50, and several favoured clients in the Soviet bloc were demanding heavy discounting. The upshot was a Libyan budget deficit of around $7 billion, and cancellations and delays in major state contracts.

Qadaffi reacted with one of his quiet spells. His public appearances became less flamboyant, apart from a gathering of non-aligned nations in Belgrade, at which he appeared with Bedouin tents, female bodyguards, and a string of camels to provide him with his daily pint of fresh milk and yoghurt. Qadaffi the idealogue has moved aside for Qadaffi the diplomat and even Qadaffi the mystic. He tried to forge a reconciliation between Palestinian splinter groups backed by Damascus and Yasser Arafat's mainstream PLO; he went to Damascus to beg President Assad to attend the emergency Arab League summit in Baghdad in the spring of 1990; once again he embraced union with his North African neighbours in a scheme for the Great Arab Maghreb.

His speeches began to take a prophetic turn. He warned that he might not always be with his people, and they would have to learn to do without him. Libyans should go back to their villages, and learn to be less dependent on oil – a smokescreen under which to encourage a revival of family businesses. But old enemies still stalked the Jamahiriya. In early 1987 nine Muslim Brothers were arrested for plotting to poison Benghazi's water supplies. The three soldiers in the group went before a firing squad, while the six civilians, among them a mullah, were hanged in a brutal and bungled ceremony in a public arena. They had accused Qadaffi of leading 'an ungodly Russian-dominated dictatorship'.

The old strategy of terrorism by proxy continued as before – guns and Semtex to the IRA, training weapons and funds to extremist Palestinians. In May 1990 Libya was the base for a series of raids on Israel's beach resorts in small boats manned by the Abu Mousa group – so scuppering the Bush Administration's dialogue with the PLO. A few weeks later Qadaffi claimed that Libya was developing nuclear weapons, which it would not hesitate to use in support of the Palestinians in the Occupied Territories. Given the difficulties experienced by Pakistan and Iraq in obtaining the technology and qualified personnel for their nuclear programmes, Qadaffi's boast seemed short of evidence – at least on first appearances. More substantial was the claim by the CIA that Qadaffi's 'pharmaceutical plant' at Rabta was for making chemical weapons.

For all his dabbling in subversion, mayhem, murder and terror, Qadaffi was beginning to look tired, a yesterday's man. He was, after all, a son of the Sixties. More powerful figures were making the running in support of the Palestinians; President Saddam Hussein had emerged victorious from a bruising eight-year war with Iran, and he had at his back an army of a million men, more than 5,500 tanks and medium-range missiles, and would take on the Americans in the West. As the century moved into its last decade, Qadaffi could no longer claim to be the Dennis the Menace of the Arab world.

From the roadside it looks like a municipal parking lot behind its high wire fence. Trucks and old French cars slump under the eucalyptus trees like basking water buffalo; beyond them the carpets of flowers unroll, the marigolds a sheet of blazing orange. This is the unprepossessing entrance to Leptis Magna, the best preserved Roman city of North Africa.

Leptis was a port from Phoenician times, trading in the grain, fruits and oil raised on Libya's red soil and so admired by Herodotus. What you see today is essentially the creation of one man – Septimius Severus. A son of Leptis, he became Emperor at the end of the second century AD. Soldier, builder, lawgiver and astute financier, he raised his native city to the highest imperial status, equal in rank to the leading Italian cities under the *ius italica*, and his capital in Africa.

Beyond the marigold carpet are the baths, half the size of a Victorian railway terminus. Their grandeur and space, bigger than any other Roman baths now visible in Africa or Asia Minor, suggest that Leptis had a very large population, or that Septimius was a fanatic for hygiene and cleanliness. The latter may be nearer the truth: Septimius ordered the free dispensation of medicines to the poor of Rome, and his son, the Emperor Caracalla, gave his name to the most famous Roman baths of all.

The best preserved are the *tepidarium* and the *frigidarium* – the luke-warm pool and the cold-house. Faced with green marble, the walls are punctuated by windows set at an oblique angle, offering bathers a glimpse of what was happening in the room next door. The underfloor heating, the hypercaust, must have taken half a forest to fuel.

The piles of stone, bricks, column and shattered statuary in the forum suggest a quarry in which a chain-gang of giants have been breaking rocks. Along one side in rows are sculptured heads of Medusa, five times human size, some in almost perfect condition; casually dropped on the ground before them is a cracked but exquisitely ruffled and folded Corin-thian capital hollowed to serve as a stoop or font for a Byzantine church. The wonder lies in the sheer sense of scale and Roman order, despite the damage done by scavengers and gerry-builders – and this is only a part of what remains, for three-quarters is still to be uncovered and revealed.

Across the eastern end, about the size of a small football field, is a paved yard enclosed by massive brick walls. 'It was the judicial palace,' said a portly man in a brown jacket – 'il Palazzo Giudiziario' were his precise words in flawless, unaccented Italian. Be that as it may, this part of the forum became a basilica in Byzantine times. I asked the guide, or *custode* as he called himself, how he managed to keep his Italian in such good repair. With a snappy answer he closed the conversation and made off – any more disclosures of his Italian connections might jeopardise his status as the Janus of Leptis today. But before then he had pointed out the lintels and pilasters on the doorways at either end of the building – finely tooled marble figures of the Labours of Hercules and of Bacchus, both groping through a jungle of sculptured foliage and fruit, and entirely untouched by any trace of atmospheric pollution.

The grapes of Bacchus symbolised the natural wealth of Leptis, which must have been celebrated daily in its market place. Stone tables still bear marks for measuring grain, olives, grapes and other fruits and vegetables. Between them its Roman builders and nature have conspired to produce an overwhelming sense of abundance, embodied in a huge fig which drapes itself over the walls near the market – a dense cascade of green foliage and heavy fruit, the mightiest Roman fruit tree of them all.

Sated with the wines of Bacchus, market-goers must have been easily lured into the well-preserved amphitheatre next door, which is as strategically placed by the sea as a bandstand on the promenade in Blackpool or Brighton. The clientele that day seemed less than charmed by the setting. It was Friday, a day of rest, and apart from some school parties in pioneer uniforms, the seats were occupied by rows of bored Korean and Pakistani workers. From time to time an elderly Berber burst onto the stage from a rickety shelter in the wings, to wave a stick at the shrieking children and glum Asians.

The exit from Leptis is suitably monumental and theatrical – the Arch of Septimius, a piece of martial sculpture as much in keeping with the age of the Duce or the Leader as its own. A few miles down the road to Tripoli I came across an informal, modern version of the market at Leptis. Cars, wagons, small trucks and tractors seemed to have parked in a hurry under the eucalyptus trees, spilling their wares onto the ground. Turkeys protested from their baskets, vermilion cabbages jostled with clumps of radish, spinach and beans, peanuts and Brazils slumped in sacks, oranges and tomatoes glowed between jars of oil and mimosa honey. This form of trading was only just becoming legal again in Libya as part of the Leader's plan to get the nation back to work – hence the market's informal appearance. Sales were brisk – surprising in view of the prices, which would have been high in a market in Milan or Manchester.

A thriving port in ancient times, Misratha, east of Leptis, is a city fashioned in the image of Libya's new Septimius and Qadaffi's alternative capital. With the overcrowding of Tripoli, several ministries have been shifted there, and three new harbours constructed.

In April 1986, as part of the Great Victory anniversary celebrations, Misratha was host to the Conference of the Revolutionary Progressive Forces and Peace Movements in the Pacific Region, which took place in the brand-new Alkhaliji Hotel, a sparkling railway station of a place complete with miniature golf and swimming-pool – provided somebody had remembered to fill it up.

'Muammar Qadaffi is a leader of the revolution for all the world' proclaimed a banner above a triumphal arch of gaudy electric light bulbs. For a time it was hard to make out the precise focus of the gathering, but after an hour I was put out of my misery by Mohamed Abdel-Salam, one of the organising committee and a secondary school history teacher in his spare time.

He did not have much time for teaching, he stressed, because of his various People's Committee activities. 'But that doesn't matter, we don't believe in oppressive and coercive teaching methods in the classroom. When I'm away my friends come in and help out in school. We believe in open education – you don't need a classroom to teach or learn. In his new theory of education, set out in his speech on 7 April, the Leader said you should not be limited by time or place, but always have the freedom to choose what you study.'

Slowly the conversation lumbered round to the conference. 'We have released the role of the Jamahiriya to the revolutionary forces in the Pacific, where previously we have been blockaded by the imperialists. We have gathered as one body to challenge the imperialists.'

Exactly how would Libya's revolutionary message be transmitted to the peoples of the Pacific, I asked. Would it mean subsidising liberation movements? Which countries and nations were to be its main recipients? A long pause concealed a piece of mental throat-clearing. 'Actually, we offer political more than material support. Previously no money was offered. The main nation we're interested in – well, I think it is Vanuatu.' And indeed it turned out that Libya had given generous backing in arms and money to nationalist rebels in Vanuatu, the former British and French colony in the New Hebrides. Australia became so concerned about Libyan activity in the region that it closed the People's Bureau and broke diplomatic relations with Tripoli.

After the promising topic of solidarity with Vanuatu, the conversation drove abruptly into a *cul de sac*. My asking why the Leader himself was not at the conference, and why he had been so shy about showing himself throughout the April celebrations brought about a controlled explosion. 'That is not true. He has been at the parades. Anyway it doesn't matter if he doesn't come here to Misratha. You don't understand. Al Caid – the Leader – is always with us!' At this our interpreter, a gentle soul of cosmopolitan disposition, rolled his eyes skywards, groaned and cut short the interview. He, for one, had had enough.

The new administrative centre of Misratha was like a townscape in a surrealist painting, an empty building site in which the palaces of the new ministries were cubes of glaring ochre in the afternoon sun. In the centre was a grotesque iron clock made in Sheffield, though the Italian designers of the whole piazza so disliked its lines that they were trying to get it shifted. The marble facings of the fountains and steps had been shipped from Turkey, the granite from Italy. Most of the workforce in the new capital were Turks, living in makeshift camps on the edge of town. Their supervising engineer, Mugla Bilicek, said they worked from seven in the morning to nearly six in the evening, all day and almost every day – they just wanted to do the job, collect the money and go back home.

Their Libyan supervisors might appear from between eight in the morning and two of the afternoon, but more often than not they did not bother to turn up. It was largely a townscape without Libyans. Except one. By the grandest ministerial palace stood a pedestal carrying four portraits – of a Bedouin sheikh, a functionary in a suit, an admiral and a soldier. Each of the four images of the Leader was in the best pop art style of Ray Lichtenstein – or even more appropriate – the great comic strip draftsman Frank Hampson, creator of Dan Dare, Pilot of the Future.

Though a law unto itself, much of the rhetoric and posture of Qadaffi's Libya relies on borrowed styles and labels. On the way back to the hotel I came across a friendly doctor talking to two boys under the most effusive bougainvillea I had ever seen. He explained in a mixture of French and English how he would like to go back to Egypt, where he had trained, to get some medicines and other supplies which he needed desperately for his practice. The two boys then introduced themselves, eager to show off their new jogging suits in fashionable Libyan green and, even better, their trainers, which were made in England but specially 'processed' in Libya. The processing, one of them explained, consisted of dyeing the shoes the colour of sand, removing the British label. Neatly sewed in its place another, more appropriate to Libya's home-grown designer revolution, one that read 'Jamahiriya'.

Ten: Maltese Crossroads

Like a point in mathematics, Malta has position but no size. The dimensions of the island and its smaller neighbours are paltry – a few square miles of thinning soil and flaking rock. But its position has a stragetic significance unparallelled in the Mediterranean. The rocky inlets and deep channels make it the perfect base from which men may ply the arts of maritime warfare. History has cast Malta in the role of garrison and citadel, set in a sea of sieges. The landscape, natural and man-made, has the look of a fortress, from the banks and stone walls that dice and segment the dusty fields to the medieval ramparts of Rabat and Medina, and the bastion of the Grand Harbour and Valletta itself.

It is the last piece of Europe before North Africa, and the last hint of the Arab world before Sicily and the European shore. More vital, though, is its position on the sea lanes running the length of the Mediterranean, the trade route which follows the path of the sun and links the Atlantic with the Levant, Arabia and the Gulf. History and geography have conspired to smother the identity of the Maltese themselves in a continuous process of invasion, settlement and migration, though they have never quite succeeded.

Invaders have left their marks on the landscape and culture with varying degrees of success. Among the first to arrive from the east were the Phoenicians. They left little behind except, according to folklore, for one vivid legacy, the Maltese fishing-boat. With its high prow and stern post, and its brilliantly coloured planking dotted with two eyes, obligatory charms against the evils of the deep, it is said to have originated with the first voyagers from Phoenicia, the men of Tyre and Sidon. The Romans left more solid reminders of their presence, and their villas and settlements are still under excavation. The Arabs also appear to have been great builders – but more curious, perhaps, was their effect on the language. Maltese is more than a dialect, largely due to the Arab influence. Arabic words litter its vocabulary, and are responsible for the Maltese weakness for names and words that include the letters 'x' and 'z' – like Naxxar, Tarxien, Marsomxett, Zebbug and Zebbien.

After the Arabs had been driven out, the armies of the Normans and

Germans from Sicily endowed the island with their flag of red and white
– it was said the knights had snipped the last two stripes off the flag of
Norman Sicily. The last two great foreign powers to rule the island both
embellished its flag with a cross. The cross of the Knights of St John is
now the Maltese Cross, and the alternative emblem of the island; the
George Cross, the highest award for civilian gallantry in the gift of the
British Crown, was awarded to the Maltese people by George VI during
the Second World War. Despite the end of British rule and Malta's
becoming a republic, it still adorns the top left-hand corner of the
national flag.

The era of the Knights and that of the British began and ended with
a siege. One of the great martial orders of the Crusades, the Knights
Hospitallers of St John, began by guarding the hostels for pilgrims on
the road to Jerusalem. With the loss of Jerusalem to Saladin, they
embarked on a slow retreat across the Mediterranean, from Acre to
Cyprus to Rhodes. In 1530 they fetched up in Malta. The island was
not a natural choice since it was suffering from drought and disease and
under continuous threat from Barbary pirates and the Turks. The Knights
had estates and influence throughout the lands of Europe, but under the
terms of the lease for Malta they had only to pay the Emperor Charles
V one falcon a year. In exchange they were to provide a military barrier
against the Turks from Tripoli to Syracuse.

The arrangement was put to the test in 1565 when the Turks and
their allies attacked in strength. The Siege of Malta helped to ensure
that the Ottoman Turks no longer threatened to dominate of the western
Mediterranean. It also made the fortifications and arsenal of the Grand
Harbour as they are today. The siege lasted all through the heat of the
summer. A fleet of some 200 Turkish vessels was reinforced by the corsair
Dragut Reis, whose fiery and quarrelsome temperament was later blamed
for the failure of the Sultan's forces. In all the Turks had some 20,000
men, and the Knights only 9,000 men at arms, more than half of them
Maltese militia. In the Grand Master, De La Vallette, the Knights had
one of the great strategists of siege warfare. He knew that his positions
were not as well prepared as they should be – he was to remedy this later
in the fortified harbour city which now bears his name – but he understood how and where to place his artillery and defences so as to achieve
a maximum field of fire, and how to force the enemy to attack on a
narrow front. He also led by example, convincing his men that he would
die in the breach with them.

At first things went badly for the Knights. The Fort of St Elmo,
recently built to the latest Italian design to guard the mouth of the Grand

Harbour, fell after a month of attacks. Some 1500 Maltese soldiers died, including 130 Knights – but the Turks lost four times as many men.

The forts inside the harbour were defended with the utmost skill and cunning. Batteries were repositioned so as to ambush galleys approaching the main defences at French Creek, Birgu and Fort St Michael, while at Birgu walls were secretly built within walls. Once through the outer fortifications the Turks were trapped below torrents of burning pitch and crushed by their own reinforcements. The attackers should have won outright when they blew a mining charge under the forts at Birgu and entered the town, but Vallette himself led a counterattack and threw the Turks out; and with the arrival of the imperial relief force under Don Garcia de Toledo, the Turks withdrew.

The victory of the Knights meant that Malta was to be shaped by their version of enlightened despotism for nearly two and a half centuries. They built palaces and fortifications, farms and villas; the capital was fashioned by them in the same 'clean baroque' style as the towns of southern Sicily, giving it a gleaming unity of eighteenth-century grace. Under them Italian became the official court language, and was only dropped by the British in 1902. Under the Knights the Maltese prospered and multiplied five-fold.

After a brief Napoleonic interlude, the British took over from the Knights in 1802. Malta had been a vital part of Napoleon's expedition to Egypt in 1798, the ideal staging and fuelling port for fleets coming from Toulon. It was equally vital to Nelson's Mediterranean strategy to thwart the French. In 1805, the year of Trafalgar, Admiral Keith provided a lyrical assessment of the facilities Malta afforded.

> The whole harbour is covered by its wonderful fortifications . . . in the hands of Great Britain no enemy would presume to land upon it, because the number of men required to besiege it could not be maintained by the island, and on the appearance of a superior fleet, that besieging army would be forced to surrender . . . or starve. At Malta all the arsenals, hospitals, storehouses etc. are on a great scale.

Grand Harbour Malta was to be the home and fuelling base of the Royal Navy's Mediterranean Fleet, from which it could patrol the route to India via Alexandria and the Suez Canal. In the Second World War it became the pivot of naval strategy in the Mediterranean. The day after Mussolini had declared war against the Allies in June 1940 Malta's second great siege began. At 6.49 in the morning of 11 June ten Savoia-Marchetti SM-79 bombers attacked Valletta, and the Axis bombing was to continue for more than two and a half years. For more than a year only a handful of ships managed to bring in bulk supplies, and the population nearly starved. The island became a huge aerodrome set in a hostile sea. The docks and stores, arsenals and wharves, were pounded and pummelled by hundreds of bombers at a time. Ships took shelter in bays and creeks round the islands, and inside the Grand Harbour itself. After a year the Navy had to withdraw its capital ships and submarine flotilla from Valletta to Alexandria, so hazardous had their moorings become.

To begin with the RAF's only air defence consisted of three sedate Gloster Gladiator biplanes, inevitably named Faith, Hope and Charity. They held out for weeks until Hurricane and Spitfire reinforcements arrived. Like their Ottoman and corsair predecessors, the Axis generals dithered and changed their minds, which allowed Malta to elude them. The Italians carried out daring raids, using one-man assault boats to penetrate the Grand Harbour booms and blow up any shipping in their path; but twice, in the summers of 1941 and 1942, the German Command switched bombers stationed in Sicily to operations on other fronts, principally Russia, and Malta was let off the hook. With the Allied victory over Rommel at El Alamein, the siege was virtually at an end; and once the British and Americans had landed in Sicily in the summer of 1943, Malta was out of the front line for the rest of the war.

The siege had cost the lives of 1,490 Maltese; more than 50,000 people had lived through the hottest months of the year and the bombing in caves and underground shelters. Some 35,000 houses were destroyed. Most Maltese lived through 1942 in a state of near-starvation. It was for their suffering and endurance, as well as their gallantry, that the people of the 'Island Fortress of Malta' were awarded the George Cross. Of more practical use was the grant of a £30 million war damage fund by London to start rebuilding and reconstruction.

Although it was that clear Britain's power in the Mediterranean was on the wane, the Maltese found it hard to let go. The Royal Navy and the White Ensign had become an inextricable part of the Grand Harbour. Maltese politicians had the confused emotions of adolescents growing to adult independence. In the 1950s Dom Mintoff, an Oxford Rhodes scholar who became the spirited and brilliant leader of the Labour Party and later Prime Minister, actually proposed that Malta should be integrated with the United Kingdom in order to keep the naval dockyards going.

Many older Maltese look back at the days of the British Empire when the Royal Navy seemed a permanent fixture in the Grand Harbour, with a mixture of nostalgia, resentment and affection. One evening while strolling round the upper ramparts above the main entrance to the harbour, I was accosted by a small round man in his early fifties. Without warning, and almost without pause or punctuation, he delivered an extraordinary soliloquy, a statement of his being and that of his nation.

'You from England?' began this strange interlocutor, who spoke like a Mediterranean creation of Samuel Beckett, with a touch of Chico Marx in the lilt of his delivery. 'My Grandfather from England too – from Cheshire. You see over there? The new port – great thing for Malta now. With the big silo cost millions. No longer fleet here – all changed now from warships to civil ships – no longer the £11 million from British and for NATO base. What was it spent on anyway? No, no, now we spend on other things, new port, new houses for the workers.'

After the briefest of pauses for a wheeze and a check on the audience reaction, his refrain resumed. 'Along that wharf used to be the destroyers – stay for ten days, maybe a fortnight – now things change, new businesses, new press. You know we print history books about countries all over the world? We print multi-colour newspapers.'

A further pause before a coda, in more plangent mode. 'Good thing no longer warships, HMS *Bulwark*, *Albion*, *Eagle* – the carriers used to be over there, *Eagle* along here. Today no real inflation – things not bad. Good thing no *Eagle*, *Bulwark*, used to come in right here. *Eagle*, yes, *Bulwark*, all the big carriers . . .'

I left him reciting the names of the last of the British Mediterranean squadron like some strange incantation – a small round figure tossed on the linguistic high seas between Maltese and English.

The trappings of Britain's legacy have been slow to disappear. Maltese drivers still keep to the left of the road, and have long had a penchant for old Ford Escorts and Morris Minors – models that now might sell for a fortune in the motherland of their manufacture.

Many of the lowlier institutions that catered for British tastes give the appearance of having seen better days. For years part of Strait Street, known affectionately as 'the Gut', was the nearest thing to a garden of delights for Jack Tars on a quick run ashore. Now the number of red-light bars has shrunk to a handful. I was ambushed in one such bar by a generously-proportioned madame. 'You want a nice girl? You want to come inside, have a nice time – a bit of a party? Go on, ducks, give it a go!' Under its awning the bar seemed like a cavern in which any sense of excitement was soon dampened by the melancholy of its faded surroundings.

The self-appointed navigator of Malta's course from a British maritime colony to an independent Mediterranean nation was Dom Mintoff. Malta became an independent member of the Commonwealth in 1964. In 1971 Mintoff became Prime Minister, and his reign was to last some thirteen years. In 1974 he declared Malta an independent presidential republic, and served notice to quit by 1979 on the British and on NATO, which had its Southern Command headquarters in Valletta.

Mintoff wanted Malta to seek friends – and funds – from wherever it could. His vision was of Malta as the focal point of a Mediterranean that had become a 'sea of neutrality and peace'. Even as NATO and the Royal Navy were hauling down their flags and ensigns, the Soviets were invited to use the port for bunkering their Mediterranean squadrons. Soviet funding was sought for a new ship-building facility to run alongside the maintenance yards and dry docks. New alliances and friendships were sought with Libya, Syria and the PLO. China offered to refurbish a dock for supertankers and to subsidise seven new factory plants. Within a few years only half a dozen supertankers had been near the dock, and all but one of the plants, a chocolate factory, had been forced to close. The economy of the new Malta did not rise like the sun on funds from the East as Mintoff had intended.

Mintoff's attitude to the British seemed at times to border on phobia. The British were less worried by his courting of the Russians than by his overtures to his more immediate neighbours – and Qadaffi's Libya in particular. Libyan investment mounted steadily, in anything from real estate to industry and tourism. Relations cooled in 1981 when shots were exchanged round an oil rig planted by the Maltese in disputed waters south of the island, but by 1984 relations were so cordial that a full economic and defence treaty was signed by Mintoff and Qadaffi.

At the same time a treaty of security and friendship was in force with the Italians, involving generous aid from Rome. The Italians were quietly insistent that the two agreements were inconsistent – Malta could not trade defence secrets shared with a NATO power – and one that was in the alliance's highest councils on nuclear strategy – and with Qadaffi's Libya. By now Mintoff's own phobia was becoming official paranoia, and almost all foreign newspapers and broadcasting services were banned under a new Non-Interference Act. This meant among other things that the measured tones of the BBC's World Service were no longer rebroadcast in Valletta – after serving as the backbone of Maltese broadcasting for a generation.

Dom Mintoff's foreign policy of mixed bedfellows received a severe set-back in November 1985, after he had handed over as Prime Minister. Earlier that month an Egypt Air passenger aircraft was hijacked by Palestinian extremists as it left Cairo. The plane traversed the Mediterranean before eventually landing in Malta. President Mubarak of Egypt demanded action, and the Maltese government were ill placed to resist. A squad of Egypt's 'thunderbolt' commandos stormed the plane, firing as they went. Sixty-one people died in one of the bloodiest hijack rescues in the history of Middle East terrorism.

'Polarisation between right and left has always been bad, but it's got worse since the last election,' said J. G. Vassallo of the Chamber of Commerce when I called on his offices in the summer of 1986. 'Polarisation' is the watchword of Maltese politics, which marks them truly as part of the modern Mediterranean.

He argued that the Mintoff 'sea of neutrality' foreign policy, and his version of a socialist economy at home, had mortgaged Malta up to the hilt. 'Malta had to replace the money it got from the bases, and Mintoff never really managed that.' More than eighty state enterprises had been started, with limited success; the Soviet-designed shipyard had orders for only eight timber carriers for Russia – and 'we're not allowed to know the price or terms, as they are official secrets.' Unemployment was rising, and the social services budget was disastrously overspent.

The magisterial editor of the *Sunday Times of Malta*, Anthony Montanaro, was more cautious about criticising Labour's legacy. 'If Mediterranean politics means irresponsibility, I resent the term. Malta has always been involved in what's going on in the Mediterranean and in Europe, and now it has realised that the two cannot be separated. Mintoff tried to get money wherever he could and to keep his options open but now even he realises that this was a mistake. Deals with the East have scared off Western investment.

'Who are the Maltese? Look at our language – semitic, with strong Italian and English overtones. We feel Europeans, and we have a certain prejudice against the Arabs. In the end we get out of it by saying we are Mediterraneans. And we take some pride in being Maltese while realising that we cannot live here in isolation.'

Almost every serious political discussion in Malta inevitably comes back to the same question: who are the Maltese, the people at the heart of the Mediterranean compass? A particularly lucid answer was given me by the man who succeeded Mintoff as Labour Prime Minister, Carmin Mifsud Bonnici. More like a schoolmaster than a tub-thumping socialist politician, he had risen to prominence as the highly effective lawyer of the General Workers' Union, the backbone of the Labour Movement.

'Various peoples have chequered our history,' the Prime Minister explained. 'We have assimilated a lot, but they have been grafted onto a basic Maltese stock. There is nothing physically that ties us to the Arabs, but many of the basic words of our vocabulary are Arabic – *allah* (god), *hops* (bread), *laba* (meat) – and we use Arabic numerals. But the fundamental fact of Malta is strategic and not linguistic, in that the nearest country to us is in North Africa.'

The themes of neutrality and peace continued to be the vital ingredients in governmental policy. 'Throughout history Malta was always a naval base, and warfare its staple industry, but we have decided to break completely with the notion of warfare, and to work in peace, live in peace and bring peace to the region. It may take a long time to permeate other countries, but at least we have made a conscious start. Between 70 and 80 per cent of all work here used to be directly or indirectly related to the military. This has gone now – a real indication of change.'

He pointed to the £165 million Maltese pounds the government had put into industry in the mid-1980s and the 600,000 or so tourists who arrived each year. But Labour's dream had cost heavily in terms of polarisation, and most prominently in a running battle with the Church.

The image of battle is not excessive, for in the autumn before we met the Prime Minister had been accused of being directly involved in the storming of the Archbishop's offices by a mob of demonstrators, who were said to have smashed up furnishings and pictures with iron bars. Labour's relations with the hierarchy were especially complicated because although the clergy had threatened anyone voting Labour with excommunication, Archbishop Gonzi, the primate of Malta for some forty years, had been a founder of the party.

The Church was long the guardian of morals, manners and learning in Malta, a position which repeatedly brought it into conflict with the British and then the Maltese governments. The biggest issue was education. The Labour governments of the 1980s tried to marginalise church education by demanding higher taxes and fees. Church school scholarships, an important means of improvement for the poor, were curtailed. The rich sent their children abroad for their education – the nationalisation of Maltese banks had already encouraged them to send their money abroad, resulting in a sizeable drain on the nation's capital resources.

'Like the Church in Ireland, the Maltese Church has not caught up with the times,' the Prime Minister told me firmly. 'The issue is socialism and not Marxism. The state cannot go on paying for church schools as before. There is also the question of religious tolerance. We should not accept a denial of civil liberties and freedom of conscience,' he went on, referring to Church opposition to civil marriage.

Playing opposite Mifsud Bonnici was the trim and vigorous figure of

Eddie Fenech Adami, leader of the Nationalist opposition. Brisk to the limits of good manners, he gave me a short sharp interview, as though he was in a hurry to organise his party's return to power, which did in fact take place some months after our meeting in 1986.

Mr Fenech Adami regarded polarisation as the major problem of Maltese politics. 'Too much polarisation has brought about a crisis of democracy. Now we have almost a failure of the rule of law.'

Eddie Fenech Adami describes the Nationalists as a 'modern Christian Democrat party'; he has close links with Italy, and speaks excellent Italian. He told me that he would uphold human rights and 'give social issues a more human face'. His programme was simple: liberate the economy from its dominance by the government, encourage foreign investment, open up the harbour as a free port and run down the shipbuilding yard, which he described as 'the biggest mistake of all'.

The Church-state row was largely 'a reflection of Dom Mintoff's personality'. More grave, he thought, were the implications of the neutrality policy and the treaty with Libya. 'What suits Switzerland does not suit us. The adoption of the whole concept of legal neutrality is probably a mistake. On the other hand Malta does not have to be tied to the superpowers; the bases are gone and won't come back.'

If Malta had to choose, Eddie Fenech Adami left no doubt that it would choose Europe. His simple and unsurprising programme is interesting if only because the brisk and brusque Eddie actually stuck to it and carried it out. In 1988 the special arrangements with Libya were ended; the government was opened up to include distinguished members of the opposition; the economy was deregulated; and formal application was made to become a full member of the European Economic Community.

The economy remains the outstanding problem facing governments of whatever stripe. Since independence, the biggest single source of foreign earnings has been income from overseas visitors, tourism, and remittances from Britain. Once Malta was a tax haven for retired servants of the Empire – old soldiers of the Indian Army or District Officers from East Africa who found neither the political nor the physical climate of the Old Country any longer to their tastes. They became known as the 'sixpenny settlers', on the grounds that they only had to pay sixpence in the pound income tax. The colony of 'Ancient Brits' once numbered well over 10,000, but by the mid-1980s age and Dom Mintoff's xenophobia had reduced this to a quarter.

Even after British rule had ended, the Maltese themselves garnered something over a third of their incomes from dockyard pensions, war allowances and pensions and other subsidies from Whitehall. Former

British servicemen and their families came back to the new beach hotels on package tours. For them it was home from home. There were no language problems – everyone officially spoke English – life was cheap, and old memories were included free of charge.

By 1985 Malta was host to over half a million tourists, just under half of them from Britain, and government planners aimed to double that figure by 1990 – an ambition that was not to be realised. By the mid-1980s things had begun to change. The entertainment provided for the tourists was often on the sleazy side; casinos owned by mysterious foreign interests opened and closed. It was feared that Valletta could become a parking lot for laundered Mafia money. The advertisements for luxurious five-star hotels seemed like the hard sales talk of croupiers and gigolos.

The possible influx of up to a million tourists in the main summer season posed a greater threat to Malta than to any other island resort in the Mediterranean. With a resident population of about 350,000, the Maltese islands are the most densely populated of any in the Mediterranean. Although there are nearly 100,000 more Maltese than Corsicans, they live in an area no larger than the slender finger in the north of Corsica, the Cap de Corse.

By the mid-1980s the Maltese were having to provide space for nearly double their own number of visitors, and the effects were beginning to show. Beach hotels and camps looked overcrowded and worn out. Planning regulations for the waterfronts began to go by the board. In Sliema once a fishing village beyond the walls of the capital, houses could not be built above two storeys.

Although some mention was made of 'cultural tourism', the policy-makers of the Maltese tourist industry did not seem interested in pursuing quality rather than one of quantity – in the interests of both residents and visitors. Instead I was given some snide cracks at the most faithful and lucrative part of the clientele – the British.

A modest clump of huts and jetties on the natural wharf of Manuel Island, at Sliema Bay, might at first be mistaken for yet another instant yacht hire station, waiting to turn a fast Maltese pound from the fleeting tourist; but those who work there have as precise idea as any in the Mediterranean of the lasting effects on the environment of an expanding population of residents and visitors. The huts are the headquarters of the United Nation's Regional Centre for Oil Pollution in the Mediterranean, which answers directly to the Mediterranean Programme run by the United Nations Environmental Programme (UNEP) in Athens. Though primarily charged with preventing industrial pollution from oil, chemical and petroleum spillages and discharges into the sea, the centre has also investigated other, and more pernicious, sources of human pollution.

In 1986 the team was led by Michel Varin, a retired rear-admiral of the French Navy and a trained engineer. His chief scientist was a Yugoslav, Darco Domovic.

On the threat from oil pollution, the admiral was cautiously optimistic. 'The illegal discharging and cleaning of tankers in the Gulf of Genoa and off Marseille has improved considerably.' He added . . . with only a hint of gallic chauvinism – that the French had achieved a great deal in treating sewage discharge into the sea.

The Mediterranean has seen mercifully few oil spillages resulting from collisions and shipwrecks. One of the worst involved a Greek tanker, the *Patmos*, carrying 70,000 tonnes of crude, which collided and caught fire in the Straits of Messina in March 1985, spilling 5000 tonnes of oil into the sea as far south as the tourist beaches of Taormina in Sicily. 'Aircraft with sprays to disperse the slick were only launched after forty-eight hours – too late,' the admiral explained. 'We learnt a lot from our mistakes, and this has gone into the training programme.'

But there has been little cause for complacency, as one delegate pointed out at a meeting of the UN Convention for the Protection of the Mediterranean Sea in 1989. 'The optimists say the Mediterranean has been spared a major oil spill. It does not need one; every year 650,000 tons of crude oil – the equivalent of twelve spills the size of the *Exxon Valdes* – are spilled here intentionally or unintentionally.'

He went on to say that traffic in harmful cargos, chemicals especially, was increasing and that more than 600 ships, one-sixth of the world total, were to be found in the Mediterranean on any one day.

Though the admiral and his staff of nine were primarily concerned with the analysis and prevention of contamination from oil and chemical spillages, he and his Yugoslav assistant emphasised that the major long-term danger to the Mediterranean was likely to be more directly human in origin – sewage. As the population increased, more pressure would be put on the already inadequate – and in many places non-existent – facilities for treating human waste. One statistic they gave I found particularly startling, and an omen for the future perhaps. The biggest single source of human pollution in the Mediterranean, they calculated, was the city of Cairo, where most of the 14 million citizens conducted their ablutions with the Nile.

The booming population and birthrate of the native Maltese can be ascribed – in part at least – to the teachings of the Church. Malta is one of the most Roman Catholic of Mediterranean countries, and the Maltese Church is among the most conservative of all those under the authority of Rome. In 1985 the population was ministered to by 800 priests with parish duties, while seminaries received some 800 applications for 150 places. The Church had social and political prestige, as well as spiritual authority.

In 1735 the Pope gave special permission for every parish priest in Malta to be allowed to wear a mitre, but it was hard to imagine Father Peter Serracino Inglott doing so. Once a leading radical – his enemies accused him of being a Marxist, which he always denied – he was respected by both ends of the political spectrum as a university teacher and writer, one of Malta's leading historians and sociologists, a genuine intellectual without side or snobbery.

The two biggest causes of friction between Church and state, he suggested, were the absence of a new concordat or constitutional treaty between the civil authority and the Church, and the legacy of the Second Vatican Council. The absence of a concordat was largely due to Mintoff – 'without his dominating presence much that has happened would not have taken place. Now as things drift we will get increasing pressure for divorce and abortion here.' On the other hand, he felt the clergy had been too conservative and too domineering: 'There is now a general feeling that the Church leaders dictated too much, socially and spiritually.'

As far as birth control was concerned, 'In Catholic doctrine the individual's conscience is supreme. A person might see contraception as a lesser and not an absolute evil. A confessor must make clear the view of the Church, but if a man is firm in his conscience, he must follow it.'

Father Peter then gave me a quick account of the clash between priests and the politicians over the past century or so. To begin with the Church had a close and protective relationship with the people, who had few other spokesmen, but as representative politics developed the sparks began to fly. After the war the hierarchy quarrelled with both political parties, Nationalist as well as Labour, particularly over the question of education.

The image and prestige of the Church militant in Malta were long the property of the Knights of St John, and the Cathedral of St John in the heart of Valletta is their shrine. Its floor is a mosaic of memorial tablets to more than 400 knights, their achievements and pedigrees recorded in scrupulous detail in baroque Latin. To the side are the chapels of the eight 'langues', the national divisions of the order – Auvergene, Provence, France, Castile, Aragon, England, Germany and Italy. With their engravings of mitres, swords, and palms of martyrdom the chipped flagstones radiate a vanished distant pomp.

The monuments of the cathedral embody what was, for practical purposes, the last flowering of Christian chivalry. The names of the old royal and aristocratic families of Mediterranean Christendom are strewn across the pavement like autumn leaves – Lascaris, Piccolomini, Pinto, the Counts of Brandenburg from Germany. Many of the monuments refer to a profession of vows and to military service 'from puberty' or 'from adolescence', and many are reported to have served in the triremes of the Order in the wars against the Turks in the Peleponnese.

The presence of the Knights in Malta today is little more than symbolic amounting to little more than an embassy. Since they were forced to leave by Napoleon's army in 1798, their headquarters have been in Rome, where they still enjoy some prominence and some influence. The Knights retain an aura of secrecy, a sense of Roman Catholic free-masonry.

New versions of the order sprang up to fill the vacuum they left in Malta itself, the most prominent of which is a peculiarly anglicised organisation known as the Venerable Order which runs the St John's Ambulance Brigade and an opthalmic hospital in Old Jerusalem, and offers training courses in first aid and nursing. Just as the old, or Sovereign, Order is responsible to the Pope, so the Venerable Order owes its allegiance to the British Crown. And 'apart from us,' explained one of the organisers of the Venerable Order, 'there are at least 176 pseudo-orders of the Knights of Malta.'

Connections with the British and with the Knights still carry enormous social cachet and prestige in Maltese society. The two strands have become curiously interwoven over the years. In 1989 an English schoolmaster with impeccable Maltese links was elected Grand Master of the Order. Fra Andrew Bertie had been a master at the Worth Priory school in Sussex, when he was well known for his habit of waking boys in the morning with his imitation of a *muezzin* and for driving a Rolls-Royce. Only one Englishman had been elected Grand Master before Andrew Bertie, and he died in battle at Tiberias, a defeat which opened the way for Saladin's armies to capture Jerusalem in 1189.

The worlds of the Knights and of the British come together most vividly behind the high walls and hedges of the Villa Bologna, one of the most intriguing buildings in all the islands. Its name is misleading, for it was once the summer residence of Pinto de Fonseca, a Portuguese nobleman who ruled the Order from 1741 to 1773. The house is part eighteenth-century Mediterranean villa, and part English country house. In recent times it has been the seat of Sir Gerald (later Lord) Strickland, the prime minister from 1927 to 1932, whose fight against Church privilege led to the suspension of the constitution. His wife, Lady Mabel Strickland, became a legendary figure of Malta folklore, and she created a garden to match. Over slices of bread and homemade jam and mugs of tea, the de Trafford family – the Strickland heirs – bemoaned the difficulties of maintaining the style to which Lady Strickland was accustomed. They had to hire out the house for parties and wedding receptions – brides and bridegrooms finding the great classical portico with its pennants of vines and wisteria the perfect frame for a nuptial photograph.

Beyond the house lies the huge kitchen garden. It has almost nothing of the Mediterranean about it, apart from a few shrubs and avocado plants. The high wall, the greenhouses, the twisted dwarf apple and crab-apple trees, the cold frames (now sadly broken), and the iron pergolas were as English as Mr Macgregor's garden in *Peter Rabbit*. This was Mabel Strickland's kingdom, and its air of genteel neglect was the most poignant symbol of vanished English glory in Malta. 'Mabel employed sixteen gardeners,' her heir told me. 'Now we can barely afford two.'

The wealthy Maltese of Valletta tend to look west, to the island of Gozo, for their out-of-town retreats. Five miles from Malta, and once fit only for goats and fishermen, it is the place to buy and be seen buying for those Maltese who have made it home or abroad. It is also the place in which to watch the Maltese indulging in their traditional pastimes, including firework displays, the nearest they have to an indigenous outdoor sport.

The island has suffered its privations – the Turks and Barbary raiders are said to have taken the entire population into slavery in 1551. The capital, Victoria, changed its name from the Arabic, Rabat, in the year of Queen Victoria's Jubilee and some would now like to change it back.

The cathedral in Victoria is a riot of Mediterranean baroque, complete with a wonderful *trompe l'oeil* painting on the dome which makes the whole giddy structure, laden with angels and cherubs, seem as though it is about to crash down on the beholder's head. Saints and their legends flourish in surprising abundance for such an infertile land, providing the excuse for fireworks, petards and the cacophany of band clubs. On a rocky spur stands a modest shrine to the Greek saint, Demetrius. According to a legend, his icon once took horse to rescue a child from the clutches of a marauding Turk, leaving his footsteps across the cliff tops as evidence. To this day the icon is said to be of a restless disposition, frequently taking flight to survey the wild and rocky shore of the island.

The buildings that lie beyond the citadel of Victoria embody Malta past and present. The streets round Gharb are filled with eighteenth-century lodges and stables that once belonged to the Knights and their followers, and with pleasant villas, their balconies are weighted down with vines and fruits and the gaudy shrubs of the Mediterranean. Most of them seem shabby and run-down behind their high walls and arched gateways. Nearer the coast these venerable piles give way to modern houses belonging to Maltese who have made it abroad, and have returned to build and show off. This is 'Happy Valley', a place of distinctly antipo-dean flavour. It is said that half a million people of Maltese extraction now live in Australia and New Zealand – though this is almost certainly an exaggeration. One brass-ornamented bungalow proudly proclaims itself 'God Bless Australia House', while its neighbour goes under the name of 'Joy Dar Pascal'.

Over dinner in one of these residences I confronted some of the last of the Ancient Brits. At the top of the guest list was the widow of a celebrated popular novelist, whose fame goes before her in such circles. The garb was casual British tennis party, but the talk conversation combined Home Country nostalgia with an almost ferocious Maltese chauvinism. A gentleman in flannels and gingham shirt and choker berated me for not persisting in trying to interview Dom Mintoff, now retired and something of a prickly recluse. 'He did great things, you know, and was the first to really understand the Palestinian problem, which he did a lot for.'

The contrast between the gentleman's demeanour and his xenophobic waspishness took me aback. Quite clearly the Mintoff magic was still potent, and would be for some time to come, and I suppressed some uncharitable thoughts about how much the Palestinians in the refugee camps of Lebanon might feel they owed to Malta's former prime minister. This piece of Maltese bombast was a vivid reminder of Malta's predicament as a point of great strategic significance but of negligible dimensions.

The following morning, a Sunday, rival batteries of band clubs were turning up for their weekly symphonic combat. Two clubs in Victoria were on the brink of fisticuffs – both were trying to hire the same opera touring company from Italy. Old Mediterranean habits never die. Along-side the bugles and the glockenspiels, the pyrotechnicians were tuning up as well. Rockets and firecrackers burst into the bright blue sky, releasing cascades of stars in redundant splendour.

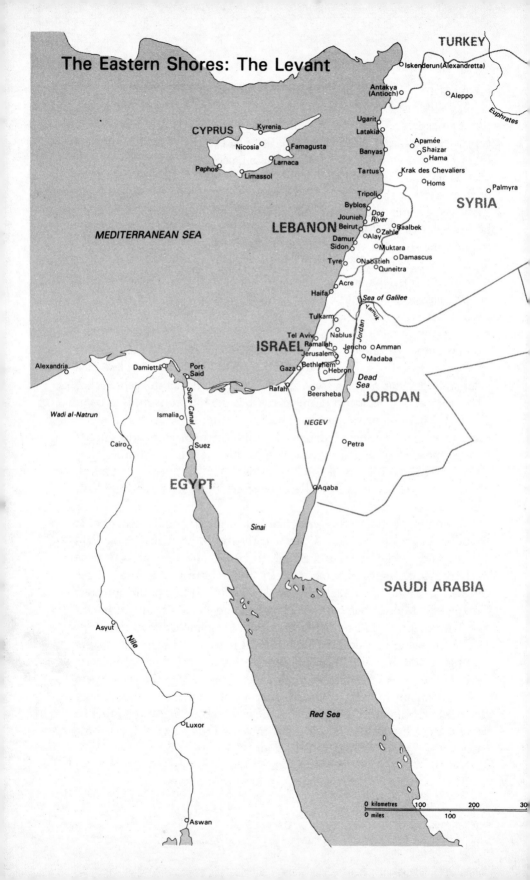

The Eastern Shores: The Levant

TURKEY

Iskenderun (Alexandretta)

Antakya (Antioch)

Aleppo

Euphrates

CYPRUS

Kyrenia

Ugarit

Latakia

Apamée

Shaizar

Hama

Nicosia

Famagusta

Banyas

Larnaca

Krak des Chevaliers

Paphos

Limassol

Tartus

Homs

Palmyra

SYRIA

Tripoli

Byblos

Jounieh

Dog River

Baalbek

MEDITERRANEAN SEA

LEBANON

Beirut

Zahle

Damur

Alay

Sidon

Muktara

Damascus

Tyre

Nabatieh

Quneitra

Acre

Haifa

Sea of Galilee

Yarmuk

Tulkarm

Jordan

Tel Aviv

Nablus

Amman

ISRAEL

Ramallah

Jericho

Jerusalem

Madaba

Alexandria

Damietta

Port Said

Gaza

Bethlehem

Hebron

Rafah

Dead Sea

JORDAN

Beersheba

Wadi al-Natrun

Ismalia

NEGEV

Cairo

Suez

Petra

Suez Canal

EGYPT

Aqaba

Sinai

SAUDI ARABIA

Asyut

Nile

Red Sea

Luxor

0 kilometres 100   200   30

0 miles   100

Aswan

Eleven: Egyptian Complex

i Scratching the Hieroglyph

IN the fresh light of early morning, the river was half asleep, wrapped in its own thoughts. It had none of the powerful generosity ascribed by Herodotus when he claimed it was the donor and creator of the land of Egypt. At Luxor the Nile is a few hundred yards across, a lazy flood flowing rust-red from the soil of Upper Egypt.

To fix the time and place of the birth of a civilisation is a hard enough task. In legend ancient Egypt emerged from primal mud much farther up – at the isle of Elephantine by the First Cataract, now the site of the Aswan High Dam. The first capital of a unified Egypt was farther down – at Memphis, where King Menes of the First Dynasty fused Upper and Lower Egypt, the lands of the river and the delta.

Luxor, the ancient capital of Thebes, saw the Pharoahs at their height. Four thousand years before Christ, the king-gods built a way of life and thought which still astonishes. They established the first political and military empire of the Mediterranean, stretching from Syria and Turkey to Sudan. They shaped forms of religion which still inform theological thought – notions of the trinity, the transcendance of the soul, the immaculate conception and even a version of monotheism. The sophistication of the Egyptians dazzled the Greeks and the Romans, and through them was to be a profound influence across the Mediterranean – the Great Green Sea, as pharaonic chroniclers called it. The ancient soothsayers of the temples that flanked the Nile were the forefathers of modern astrology; freemasons use the figures and symbols of the priests of Egypt, the omnipresent sun (the god Re or Amun-Re) and the all-seeing eye of Horus, god of Egypt and son of Osiris, lord of the Dead and of Judgment, and Isis, spirit of life and renewal and of the Nile itself in its flood.

By the time Herodotus arrived in Egypt in about 460 BC much of the learning of the courts of the great Pharaohs had been lost. Priests could hardly read the hieroglyphs, and Herodotus is accused of listening to tittle-tattle and old wives' tales. He wrongly believed the miraculous flooding of the Nile each summer – the real life-giver for Egyptians, turning their narrow land into some of the most fertile in the world – to be the work of a freak tide, making the river reverse its direction.

But despite his journalistic approach, Herodotus was right about the importance of the Nile to Egypt. The adage of the ancient Greeks – 'The Nile is Egypt, and Egypt the Nile' – still holds good. And to some extent our whole sense of history is the gift of the Nile. Herodotus recorded how climate and geography influenced the development of an entire civilisation; and when Bishop William of Tyre, visiting the Nile Delta from the Crusading Kingdom of Jerusalem in the twelfth century, his writing approaches something like a modern history rather than the flat recitation of events of a medieval chronicle. Enthralled by the artefacts they found, Napoleon's officers and academicians from his expedition of 1798 became the founder members of modern Egyptology, the catalyst of so much modern archaeology.

Egyptians have always been governed by the narrow strip of the Nile and the desert beyond. Today the Nile is parallelled by the human artefact of the Suez Canal. But the strategic boundaries of Egypt are still set by the waterways and the desert – in the uplands of Sinai to the east and the Sahara to the west.

The other fundamental of Egyptian life is the balancing act involved in supporting so many people on such a narrow strip of fertile land. Nowhere in the modern Mediterranean is farmed so intensively and so inundated with the humanity; and no part of the shoreline is so vulnerable to climatic change from the greenhouse effect.

The Pharaohs have given modern Egyptians an intense pride, a belief in the age and complexity of their pedigree and their past. With this comes an acute sensitivity about the poverty and squalor of life in the cities and the overcrowded villages. Cynics say that, on a land of scarce commodities, truth is among the scarcest; and the fact that, since the Pharaohs, most of Egypt's rulers were colonisers from outside has made Egyptians defend themselves by saying one thing to foreigners and another to themselves.

The fact that Egyptian society is the most complex in the eastern Mediterranean, with deep and mysterious roots, is a deterrent to swift and simple analysis. I felt I needed to spend twice as long there as anywhere else to begin to understand it.

Egyptians today differ from the Pharaohs and their subjects in one crucial respect – modern Egypt is essentially Arab. It is not certain exactly where the ancient Egyptians came from, some say from Nubia, in the upper reaches of the Nile, modern Sudan or even the heart of Africa. They gave way in turn to Assyrians, Persians, Macedonians and Romans, but the biggest break occurred the invasion of the Arabs in the seventh century. They established new dynasties, built a new capital at Cairo, and introduced new religion, Islam; and most Egyptians today are Arabs. Egypt is the most numerous Arab nation, and is likely to remain so for the next century. The weight of numbers and its position as the link between North Africa and Arabia, Palestine and the Levant make Egypt paramount in the councils of the Arab world. In 1985 its population was over 50 million, and is set to double within forty years. In terms of demography Egypt will be a regional superpower, rivalled only by Turkey.

The ancient buildings and monuments of Luxor were high on the intinerary of the first modern tourists to the Levant – the intrepid travellers who made the early fortune of Thomas Cook, who personally conducted his first party of tourists up the Nile in 1869. Baedeker's *Guide to Egypt* of 1929 extolled in lyrical vein the setting of Luxor – or Thebes, the name given it by the ancient Greeks, which Baedeker persisted in using:

> 'The verdant crops and palms which everywhere cheer the traveller as soon as he has quitted the desert, the splendid hues that tinge the valley every morning and evening, the brilliant unclouded sunshine that bathes every object even in the winter season, lend to the site of ancient Thebes the appearance of a wonderland, richly endowed with the gifts of never-failing fertility.'

I must admit I was bowled over by the unexpected limpid beauty of the scene a few hours after dawn. I had always disdained the expression, and even the idea of, 'culture shock'. After crossing the Nile by river boat we passed a small creek on the way to the Valley of the Kings. Under the shade of some bushes and trees buffalo were slowly grazing and drinking, their drivers stacking thick reedy grass in a cart – a scene that must have taken place here for thousands of years. Time appeared to have imploded, the centuries seemed nothing – and, yes, it was a shock.

I was wrong, of course, for something had changed. This creek would have been covered each year in the great inundation, the flooding of the Nile which so fascinated Herodotus, the waters lapping round the feet of the two huge colossi of Memnon which mark the beginning of the tombs and memorials. The last such flood occurred in 1966, since when the flow of the river has been regulated by the Aswan High Dam, which after many false starts was completed, largely with Soviet finance, in 1970, the greatest change to the Nile and the economy of its people in Upper Egypt since history began.

Quite apart from the 'culture shock', I was quite unprepared for the fresh and vivid impact of the hieroglyphs, reliefs and huge mortuary statues, and the daring design of the temples and mausoleums. Each part of the complex comprising Luxor, Karnak and the Valleys of the Kings and Queens has a direct appeal greater than almost any of the sites of classical antiquity, including the Parthenon.

Journeying west from the Nile is to enter the land of the dead, Duat, the kingdom of Osiris where the boat of the sun-god Re sinks into night. No civilisation has devoted more energy, mental and physical, to the rites and needs of the dead as the ancient Egyptians. The tombs abound with the images of the great embalmer and divine undertaker, Anubis, with his jackal head. Usually he is accompanied by the recorder of the passage, Thoth, with bird mask and long secretarial beak, flanked by his emblems of the sacred ibis and gangs of chattering baboons. Life itself is the body of a young woman arching through heaven, alternatively a great cow or the river under the earth which carries the raft of Re (or Ra) back to the east each night to begin the promise of a new day at dawn. For the journey to the next world the Pharaohs would be provided with all means of comfort and survival, food, furniture, arms and votive ornaments – fashioned and depicted in the finest and most varied detail.

In the Valley of the Kings and the Valley of the Queens of the west lands of the Nile at Luxor lie the living records of some of the first recognisable personalities of Mediterranean history. The Pharaohs celebrated here are no longer the stylised images of myth, but in their deeds and traits shown upon their monuments they assume the quirks and oddities of real human likenesses; though they strove to be seen as gods, they are portrayed here as only too mortal.

Best publicised of the early Pharaohs is Ramasses II (who ruled from 1304 to 1237 BC in the 19th Dynasty, the New Kingdom), though his funerary temple, the Ramasseum, is in poor repair. With his soubriquet of 'Ramasses the Great' subsequent generations have hailed him as the first of the martial emperors, a hero of his nation, either a Mediterranean imperialist or a colonising dictator, a fascist even, the forerunner of Napoleon or Mussolini. Like most of his military breed he had a megalomaniac desire to advertise, and his stylised portrait is one of the most familiar in ancient Egyptian statuary. It graces another of his temples at Abu Simbel farther up the Nile. When the valley was flooded as part of President Nasser's scheme for the Aswan High Dam, the statues and temples of Abu Simbel were raised to the heights above in a rescue operation organised by UNESCO at a cost of $35 million. The sculpted portrait appears again in the colonnades of the temple on the east bank of the Nile at Luxor and Thebes. But best preserved is the basalt statue of the Pharaoh discovered a hundred years ago at Memphis and now displayed in the museum there.

The most celebrated of the Ramasses portraits is the most ruined. It was discovered by the scholars and engineers of Napoleon's expedition inside the crumbling funeral temple of the Ramasseum at Thebes, and their reports were the inspiration of Shelley's *Ozymandias*. In the court-yards rest 'the two vast and trunkless legs of stone' and 'shattered visage' that so fired the poet's imagination. The colossus is calculated to have weighed a thousand tons, and the height of one ear was four feet. The epitaph, 'My name is Ozymandias, King of Kings: look on my works ye mighty and despair', is a loose translation of the inscription on the pedestal.

Contrary to the romantic spirit of the poem, the statue and the temple were designed to inspire awe more than pity. Much of the outer structure, the pylon or gateway support, is all but gone, but what has survived of the scenes etched on the inside walls is flagrantly triumphal. One shows the Pharaoh trouncing the Hittites at the Battle of Kadesh (circa 1285 BC) on the northern marches of the Egyptian Empire in Syria. A panel shows the great Ramasses himself in his chariot being propelled into the thick of the fray, loosing off arrows by the shoal at his retreating enemy. His prowess as empire-builder is enhanced by the display alongside the text of the subsequent peace treaty with the Hittites, one of the first in recorded history, and the beholder is left in no doubt that this settlement was entirely due to the famous victory at Kadesh. Unfortunately archae-ologists digging recently at the ancient Hittite capital of Boghazky (in modern Turkey) have discovered a different interpretation of the same campaign, which the Hittites claimed they won. It seems that war and propaganda began their uneasy partnership very early in the Mediter-ranean.

More intriguing in the puzzle of identity of the early peoples of the Mediterranean are the battle scenes on the walls of the funerary temple of Ramasses III at Madinet Habu at Thebes. Ramasses III (who ruled in the 20th Dynasty, the New Kingdom, from 1198 to 1166 BC) was a slavish admirer of his namesake the Great Ramasses. His temple gives us the same diet of martial prowess as the Ramasseum, but this time by sea as well as land. In what is thought to be the earliest depiction of a sea battle we witness the invasion of the dreaded 'Peoples of the Sea', wild men with horned helmets and feathered headdresses who brought fire and pillage to the very coasts and rivers of Egypt herself. The invaders, who burst on the coasts of Egypt and Syria some time before

1150 BC (the date of the construction of the Madinet Habu temple), were probably the prototype Mediterraneans of the islands, the cousins of the builders of the Nuraghi forts in Sardinia and the warriors sculpted in the stone circles of Filitosa in Corsica, the Philistine ancestors claimed by some modern Palestinians.

The battle with the Sea People may have stretched over many campaigning seasons, recorded in chronicles by scribes as well as in sculpted reliefs at Madinet Habu. Working on clues left by ancient Greek travellers, modern historians surmise that the archives of the two great temples of Ramasses II and Ramasses III may have been the inspiration of the library at Alexandria established by the successors of Alexander the Great, the richest repository of knowledge of the ancient world.

Near the mouth of the Valley of the Queens, to the north of the line of the temples of the two Ramasses, is a low flat building with colonnade and ramp locking into the jagged hills beyond, a perfect blend of artefact and nature, and stunning in the modernity of its line. This is the Temple of Hatshepsut (who ruled in the 18th Dynasty, New Kingdom, from 1503 BC to 1482 BC), the first Queen to become Pharaoh in her own right and one of the most remarkable women in history. She pushed aside her heir and co-regent the Pharaoh Tuthmosis III to seize sole command. To justify the move, the propaganda paintings on the temple wall show her divine birth – an early representation of immaculate conception. The god Amen-Re (Amun-Ra) enters the body of the Queen's father, the Pharaoh Tuthmosis II, in order to impregnate his sleeping wife Queen Ahmes. Further scenes disguise the feminity of the Pharaoh Hatshepsut as she goes about her imperial tasks. One episode shows the peaceful embassy to the land of Punt – rich in forests, laden with fowls of the air and beasts of the sea – probably Tigre in modern Eritrea.

Her successor got his revenge. Tuthmosis III was to be a great empire-building Pharaoh. At his order all the images of Queen Hatshepsut, his step-mother, aunt and predecessor, were erased. In all but a few places on the walls of her temple, nothing of her name and face remains but a rough scar.

The best witness of the cares and joys of daily life and death in ancient Thebes is given in the tombs of the servants and officers – the Pharaohs themselves were doubtless too preoccupied with regal matters of war and peace and disposing of family rivals to worry about such mundane matters. Some buried in the Valley of the Nobles had immense authority; Senenmut, Queen Hatshepsut's steward, had more than eighty titles and more than twice the offices of an entire modern cabinet of ministers. Some of the walls show an almost domestic preoccupation with the preparations to quit life and embrace death. In the tomb of Usherat, a royal scribe and tutor, we see the noble having a last haircut under a tree; in the fields harvesters cut the corn and hunters catch wildfowl for a last meal and offering to the Pharaoh. The preparations radiate the abundance of the earth and the harmony of nature's round.

Least spectacular of all the tombs, but eloquent in its emptiness, is the small set of chambers close to the entrance of the much grander burial suite of Ramasses VI in the Valley of the Kings itself. It was here on 4 November 1922 that the freelance archaeologist Howard Carter uttered one of the most celebrated remarks in the story of archaeology. To the anxious inquiry of his patron Lord Carnarvon as to whether there was anything to see in the newly breached tomb, Carter replied, 'Yes. Many wonderful things!' (A canard has it that Carter entered the tomb secretly the previous night, and removed some small ornaments.)

The chamber shows every sign of hasty preparation. After all, King Tutankhamun was a boy in his teens when he died. His tomb is as plain as the collection of the treasures found within are sumptuous and diverse. No piece of Egyptological lore has gripped the imagination as much as the unearthing of the boy-Pharaoh, not even the unearthing of the Sphinx at Giza and the Rosetta Stone with the key to the code of the hieroglyphs by the scholars and officers of Napoleon's expedition.

Howard Carter's bungalow is preserved as a rest house for weary travellers to take cool drinks and chew kebabs; local entrepreneurs offer minature soapstone busts of the boy Pharoah, Ramasses, Nefertiti and the Sphinx. A whiskered old man recalls how as a lad he had been a guide to Carter, and how he and his mates pointed the way to the opening of Tutankhamun's burial chamber – a well-worn patter, that has earned him over the years a few dozen crates of soft drinks.

Egyptology seems to have roused more passion, jealousy and enmity than any other branch of archaeology – a notoriously quarrelsome pursuit at the best of times. The guides at Luxor embellish the story of the great Egyptologists with an entire sub-text of gossip about artefacts robbed, records falsified and rivals ruined. Given the undertones of suspicion, the resentment at neo-colonial scholars and expeditions, and the national pride involved, the wonder is that so much productive work continues to be done. Major discoveries are still being made at Karnak and near Memphis. In February 1986 Dr Geoffrey Martin of London University and Dutch colleagues from Leiden uncovered at Saqqara the tomb of Maya, Tutankhamun's treasurer. Though comprehensively robbed of its ornaments and artefacts in antiquity, its walls yielded an incomparable treasure – life-sized portraits of the deceased and his wife, and details of the kings they served, including Tutankhamun.

Managing the sites at Thebes for both experts and tourists is an increasingly difficult operation. Tourists have been an important part of the scene for more than a hundred years, and have helped to fund discoveries and restoration work directly and indirectly. Surprisingly, very little gratuitous vandalism has been recorded over the years.

The responsibility of protecting the sites lies with the Chief Inspector and Director of the Egyptian Antiquities Service, who has a small office at Luxor, not far from the colossi of Memnon – the two crumbling sandstone giants that Greeks imagined to represent heroes of ancient Troy. On a roasting hot day in late May 1986 I called on Dr Mohammed Nasr, who had a team of seven inspectors, a civil engineer, an architect, an electrician and thirty workmen at his command.

His biggest worry was tourists. 'On a day like this, when the temperature is already over 40 degrees centigrade, we have more than a thousand visitors on the site. In the cooler months we may have 3000 on some days.' The tourists caused the walls of the tombs to humidify, and their steps to crumble. He had to keep an eye on more than 440 burial monuments and chambers, maintaining a constant catalogue of repairs needed and a record of each excavation by the ten national teams now working at Luxor. 'The big headache is the presence of numbers seeing any one tomb – we've had to put some of the wall-paintings under glass. We also measure the humidity daily, so we can open and close the tombs to visitors by rotation.

For all their dedication, Dr Nasr and his colleagues face an uphill task. The monuments of Egypt – one-third of the world's archaeological sites – appear to have deteriorated more in the past thirty years than in the previous thousands. At Giza sewage threatens to undermine the Sphinx, while chemical polution in the air is eroding the Pyramids. At Luxor polluted waters of the Nile have made an ugly stain on the foundations of the temple. Chunks of limestone have been breaking from the hills round the temple of Queen Hatshepsut, and the walls of Tutankhamun's tomb have sprouted a strange fungus. The rescue mission will need more funds than can be raised from the gate money paid by tourists visiting Valleys of the Kings and Queens and the *son et lumiere* in the temple at Karnak.

Returning to the land of the living on the other side of the Nile was an unexpectedly theatrical experience. The locals easily outnumbered the tourists and were brimming with chat and bonhommie – evidently relieved to have finished toiling the fields in the heat of the day. Carts loaded with hay, vegetables and fruit jammed the causeway to the ferry as we swept along like conscripted extras in a Hollywood costume epic. The rust-bucket ferries with their canopies and crazy funnels belching black smoke seemed like left-overs from the movie of *The African Queen*.

From a distance the temple of Karnak looks like a movie set. It inspired several early epics in the style of Cecil B. De Mille, while its huge columns and spreading capitals influenced the design of Art Deco cinemas in the 1920s and 1930s as architects in Britain and America caught the Egyptology bug following the discovery of Tutankhamun's treasure. The taste for theatrical excess continues at Karnak. In the late 1980s performances of *Aida* were staged there for tourists, with casts including Placido Domingo. The shades of the Pharaohs must have laughed, the weather was less than clement and the acoustics reportedly dreadful.

Karnak is a temple to the all-powerful Amun, and it celebrates the almost megolomaniac delight in war and conquest Ramasses the Great and the other martial Pharaohs of the New Kingdom (1567 – 1085 BC). The great squares and colonnades, the ranks of stone rams, the sacred lake provide a perpetual glorification of Amun and his princely heirs, the Pharaohs. It is the largest sacred monument known to man.

The dominant decorative theme at Karnak symbolises the relationship between Egypt and the Mediterranean. Most of the capitals are shaped like the closed head or the full bloom of the lotus and the papyrus, the symbols of Upper and Lower Egypt. Several columns display the two together – a fusion of the Mediterranean world of the Delta, and the world of mystery and magic beyond the cataracts in Africa.

The Temple of Karnak has been enhanced and embellished many times; discreet and careful restorations were added by the Ptolemys, the heirs of Alexander the Great who ruled Egypt as Pharaohs. The soldiers of Napoleon, another would-be Pharaoh, carved their names and initials at the gates.

Karnak spreads to the north of the modern town on the east bank of the Nile, while the smaller more compact Temple of Luxor lies at its heart. The clumps of columns and statues sit easily with the gently rambling collection of mosques, low-roofed houses and casually decaying hotels. The temple walls trumpet forth once more the victory of Ramasses II at Kadesh, and the central court celebrates the campaigns of his predecessor, Amenhotep III. More recent conquerors, too, have left their mark, by subtraction as much as by addition and adornment. One of the pair of obelisks of the first courtyard was looted by the French in 1831, and now adorns the Place de la Concorde in Paris.

On the west wall of the sanctuary at Luxor a young Pharaoh in full fig offers a libation to the god Amun. It is a stylised portrait of an Egyptian king-god wearing the ceremonial double-crown, the Red Crown of Lower Egypt combined with the White of Upper Egypt. The Pharaoh is Alexander the Great as he wished to be depicted as the ruler of his new subjects of the Nile, after their conquest in 332 BC.

The fusion of east and west in Alexander's adventures, the marriage between the mysticism of the orient from Egypt and beyond with the reason and logic of the occident is one of the most potent legends of the Inner Sea. Alexander is a myth conjured from history, as evocative of the restless Mediterranean spirit as the wandering of Odysseus, a myth conjured from art.

ii   Losing Alexandria

Alexander the Great made his Egyptian capital on the Mediterranean coast, and the city that bears his name has been associated with Greeks ever since. Just under a century ago, 100,000 Greeks lived in Alexandria, with their own schools and hospitals, churches and clubs, and more than ten regular newspapers. In the Second World War it became the home of the Greek government in exile, the base of the Royal Greek Navy and the garrison of the army – where the Brigade of Immortals mutinied against the heavy-handed management of their English allies.

Alexandria can still conjure up a glow of literary enchantment for cosmopolitan aesthetes. Much of their delight was physical rather than spiritual, according to an eminent Copt academic whom I met in Cairo. 'Frankly the great attraction for Alexandria for most of the literary set – especially the British – was that they could let their erotic fantasies run wild. It became a haven for homosexuals.' It was also a resort for gambling and sport – the Le Touquet of the East Mediterranean – when, in the hey-day of British suzerainty, the capital moved to Alexandria for the summer months.

For centuries Alexandria maintained its Greekness. Its Greeks had a peculiar refinement not found in the other cities of their diaspora, Odessa, Beirut or Cairo itself. In Athens I have been beguiled by the melodious French, precise arguments of the exiles of Alexandria. Waiting once in a hotel lobby in Libya with a Greek journalist, we began to talk of her Alexandrian childhood. Why did the city cast such a nostalgic glow, I wondered. 'It was wonderful, it was a paradise,' she replied simply and burst into tears.

Cosmopolitan Alexandria is now a golden glimmer in the memory. Lovers of history tend to indulge in references and metaphors, real and imaginary, from the past, yet modern Alexandria seems to have made an almost clean break with its past. Alexandria today is a modern commercial port, coping with the problems of modern Egypt. Little of the old style remains. At the Hotel Cecil, pride of the sea-front hotels of seventy years ago, they were hard put to rustle up a hard boiled egg on the morning I arrived.

In 1800, before Mohammed Ali, the Greek-Albanian Viceroy imposed by the Ottomans, began his programme of break-neck modernisation, Alexandria's population was said to number about 5000. Now it numbers over three million and is the second city of Egypt. As a commercial harbour its shares the same problems as Fos and Marseille, Barcelona, Genoa or La Spezia.

Rear-Admiral Anwar Hegazy, one of the leading commanders of the Egyptian Navy, is in charge of its transformation into a modern container terminal. 'Alexandria is one of the oldest harbours in the Mediterranean, it was first developed by the Pharoahs in 1900 BC,' he boasted. The Admiral had a team of 3000 at his command – pilots, tug crews, safety officers, firemen, engineers and workshop crews, computer operators and administrators, plus more than 7000 stevedores.

His aim was to handle 60 million tons by the end of the century – twice as much as at present, and equivalent in size to the terminals at Fos and Marseille. The more traditional passenger services had held up remarkably well, the Admiral claimed, despite changed patterns of travel.

But Alexandria's position in the commerce of Egypt had changed dramatically over the past thirty years. 'Because of air travel, Cairo has become the base for all business. In the past, people used to come up from Cairo to visit banks and brokers here. Now we have to go down to Cairo.' And the revival of the Suez Canal had shifted some traffic from Alexandria to Port Said.

Modern Alexandria is as plain and sober as the plans for its new industrialised port. The opera house, where the first performance of *Aida* was given for the inauguration of the Suez canal, was closed. A few bookshops gave enticing hints of Greek poets, but the main thoroughfares were dominated by advertisements for Coca-Cola, Ford and Gaz stoves. But in one window front I caught a glimpse of the old city. Water pipes, hubble-bubbles, of all sizes hung on the far wall – and it was clear they were not for decoration. Inside the café the murmur of gossip was punctuated by the clatter of backgammon players. Play and talk were interrupted only for a slow inhalation of the pipe or a suck from glasses of clear green tea. The commerce of the teahouse was the common currency of the old Ottoman world.

This was part of Old Alexandria as celebrated by E. M. Forster and Lawrence Durrell, the city which titillated the Anglo-Saxon imagination with its hint of Levantine exoticism. Forster made Alexandria his private resort from the early 1920s and wrote an extraordinary guidebook to the city past and present – a work based as much on imagination as on fact.

The British had shaped Alexandria in their own image in the years when Egypt came under their rule, the most substantial undeclared piece of Empire. In 1882 the fleet bombarded the port during the campaign to put down Arabi Pasha, after which Alexandria became their summer capital in the Mediterranean.

What the bungalows of Simla were to the rulers of British India, Alexandria was to the British in Egypt. It was a watering hole, a place to desport and idle away the heat of the summer. The British built the Sporting Club with its racecourse, the railway terminus and esplanade hotels like the Cecil. British rule in Egypt, almost more than anywhere else in the world, was marked by almost breathtaking condescension. Tourists were encouraged to adopt the same airs as the administrators. As Cook's *Handbook* observed in 1906, 'One of the greatest enjoyments of many classes of the modern Egyptian is to do nothing, especially if he has sufficient means to provide himself with coffee, and with some narcotic in the form of tobacco, opium, hashish . . .'

'Few cities have made so magnificent an entry into history as Alexandria. She was founded by Alexander the Great,' states E. M. Forster. But although Alexander's architect, Dinocrates, built new fortifications and laid out a new street plan, he was working on well-established foundations, according to Professor Fawzi el Fakharani of the History Faculty and Institute of Mediterranean Studies of Alexandria University and an expert on the Phoenician settlements of the Mediterranean and the activities of the Sea Peoples. The Professor said he thought the geographer Strabo, who visited Egypt in 25 BC, was responsible for giving so much credit to Alexander in shaping the city. 'Strabo was given most of his information by Greeks who would not have said anything to belittle Greek achievement. I think one of his main purposes was to deny the harbour to the Persians, as well as exploit the opportunities for commerce.' His message was clear: Alexandria was founded first and foremost by Egyptians – a view that reflects the preoccupations of modern Egyptian nationalism.

Alexander is said to have been buried near the crossing of the two main thoroughfares of the city. On this subject the professor seemed to glow, a slave to the legend of the Greek Pharaoh. He was determined to find the tomb, and was sure he was on the right track. The search for Alexander's tomb has all the fabulous qualities of the hunt for Tutankhamun and claims have been made as far apart as Turkestan, Istanbul and even Sumatra; but according to Professor el Fakharani, Pausonias and other sources are convinced that, after being embalmed in gold leaf and laid in a sumptuous coffin, he was brought to the crossing of the ways in his city, where thousands made pilgrimage. Although both coffin and tomb were soon stripped of their gold ornaments, successive Greek and Roman authors refer to the tomb as a major attraction of the city. But in the fourth-century AD St John Chrysostom wailed, 'Tell me where is the tomb of Alexander the Great?' By then it had clearly been lost.

The professor and his team were computing the classical sources and accounts by Arab travellers in the Middle Ages. He was convinced that some archaeological detectives had come pretty close already. The most promising find was a mystery block of alabaster one metre thick from in the Latin cemetery – approximately the old royal quarter.

Of the great monuments of Alexander's capital, almost nothing remains except the artefacts in the museum. The remnants of the lighthouse, one of the Wonders of the World according to Philo, were destroyed by earthquakes in the fourteenth century; the library founded by the Ptolomies was burnt by the legions of Caesar. The library was one of the most attractive items of the Alexander legend. Under the last Ptolomies it held more than 650,000 papyrus scrolls and was to be the universal storehouse of knowledge in its day. Aristophanes, Euclid and Archimedes studied there. Most importantly, it gathered together the works of both the ancient Greeks and the Jewish law-givers – the basis of patristic literature and the fusion from which history, philosophy and theology as we know them are derived.

The idea of the library greatly appeals to Egyptians today, so much so that in 1990 their government launched an appeal for $150 million to build a new library and international institute. Foreign governments, including the Greeks, have pledged generous support, raising nearly a quarter of the sum in a few months.

Just as important as the legacy of ancient Greece is that of Christianity. According to legend Alexandria was converted by St Mark. In the fourth century it was the scene of theological battles, which led to riot and bloodshed and still reverberate through the churches of the Eastern Mediterranean. Here the Arian Heresy was first propagated, only to be condemned by Athanius at the Council of Nicaea. Arius's views on the human nature of Christ persisted among the Monophysites and are held still by the Coptic church in Egypt.

Like Alexander the Great, the Greeks of modern Alexandria seem to have been extremely cosmopolitan. In the Second World War the British insisted on sending a Royal Navy liaison officer to take notes of every council of war held by the admirals of the Greek Navy. On one occasion, according to the young lieutenant commander, a fluent Greek speaker, 'the Greeks started speaking a strange tongue of a Balkan nature, which I didn't understand.' They were in fact speaking Albanian, the mother tongue of many Greek naval officers since the early days of Greek Independence – and the language of the founder of the last line of Egyptian kings, still nominally ruling in the 1940s.

The great celebrant of Greek Alexandria was the poet Constantine Cavafy, who was taken up by E. M. Forster, Lawrence Durrell and others. A self-proclaimed homosexual who for thirty years worked as an assistant in the Ministry of Public Works, he derived as much pleasure from the presence of the beloved as from anything more strenuous. Late one afternoon I was shown down an unprepossessing alley to the Pension El-Amir. On the second floor was a dingy room. The curtains were drawn and the air was fetid with sleep – three night workers, possibly Sudanese, were taking their rest. This had been Cavafy's home.

Though lionised immediately before his death from cancer in 1933, Cavafy was indifferent. He sensed the decline of his community and city and since then all the great cosmopolitan centres of the Mediterranean – Constantinople, Beirut and Alexandria – have nearly gone.

Cavafy summed up the mood of Alexandrian decay in one of his early mature poems *The God Forsakes Antony*. This masterpiece of 1911 reads like an epitaph for his city.

> When suddenly at midnight you hear
> an invisible procession going by
> with exquisite music, voices,
> don't mourn your luck that's failing now,
> work gone wrong, your plans
> all proving deceptive – don't mourn them uselessly:
> as one long prepared, and full of courage,
> say goodbye to her, the Alexandria that is leaving.
>
> Above all, don't fool yourself, don't say
> it was a dream, your ears deceived you:
> don't degrade yourself with empty hopes like these.

As one long prepared, and full of courage,
as is right for you who were given this kind of city,
go firmly to the window
and listen with deep emotion,
but not with the whining, the pleas of a coward;
listen – your final pleasure – to the voices,
to the exquisite music of that strange procession,
and say goodbye to her, the Alexandria you are losing.

iii   Ismailia and the Canal

At Ismailia the bungalows hide from the port behind screens of jacaranda and flame trees, which loose a desultory rain of purple and orange blossom onto the parched lawns. These are the domestic arrangements of empire. The verandas and porches suggest distant frontiers, while the sensible lines of roof and window hint of Surrey suburbs and Home Counties villages. Originally designed for British pilots of the Suez Canal Company, the bungalows are now the homes of the Egyptian managers of the waterway.

The Suez Canal has featured in the history of modern Egypt almost as prominently as the Nile in the annals of the Pharaohs. For the British it served first as a means of dominance, and ultimately as the source of defeat. The purchase of the Canal shares from the impoverished monarchy in Cairo paved the way for Britain's undeclared imperial rule; in 1956 the word Suez acquired much the same meaning for Anthony Eden as Waterloo had for Napoleon.

Until 1956 the Canal and its hinterland had largely been a British- or French-run affair. Three hundred British pilots ran the waterway from Port Said in the Mediterranean to Suez at the neck of the Red Sea, though the Suez Port Company itself was a French creation. Now the Canal is entirely Egyptian, and a considerable success story at that. Though closed for eight years by wars after Nasser nationalised it in 1956, it is now one of the most efficient enterprises in Egypt, netting the government more than one billion dollars in overseas earnings in 1985. Its smooth running is a miracle of modern maritime management.

Its headquarters are in a tall building with a glass cage on top like an airport control tower. It overlooks the quays at Ismailia, strategically halfway between Port Said to Suez, where Lake Timsah provides a natural basin for repair yards, pilot boats and fire vessels. To the south lie the Bitter Lakes, and to the north the longest single reach of the man-made waterway.

Inside the building I was engaged in bubbling conversation by one of the chief pilots, Captain Aly Nasr. He was piloting a freighter of the Glen Line in the Bitter Lakes when hostilities began in 1956. Captain Ali had trained as an officer with the Royal Navy in England, and that autumn British servicemen commandeered his apartment in Port Said. His ship was trapped with fourteen others in the Bitter Lakes for the duration of the hostilities. He managed to return.

The main channels were cleared in 1957, but ten years later the Canal was bombarded and blocked by another war with Israel. In 1967 Ismailia once more came under siege, and remained festooned with fortifications until 1975. In the meantime Captain Ali Nasr had moved to Tobruk in Libya, whence he was asked to return with ten volunteers to restart the Canal Pilot Service.

Since his return in 1975 he had been battling with 'the changes in the tonnages', as he put it. The aim was for the Canal to carry super-tankers of up to 400,000 tonnes capacity, and freighters of up to 60,000 tonnes. By 1980 the banks had been raised and the channel dredged to over fifty feet so as to take 250,000-tonne tankers partially loaded. A second phase of expansion had been postponed as the super-tanker was going out of fashion. 'Much is going to depend on the outcome of the Gulf War between Iran and Iraq,' Captain Ali mused. For the time being all was going well. The pilots in his command were drawing some of the best public salaries in Egypt, and the service enjoyed high international esteem.

His words about the Gulf, uttered in May 1986, proved prophetic. In the crisis over Saddam Hussein's invasion of Kuwait, the American nuclear-powered aircraft-carrier *Eisenhower* made a stately passage from the Mediterranean to take up station blockading Iraqi tankers in the Red Sea – vivid proof of the increasingly intimate connection between the commerce and politics of the Gulf and the Eastern Mediterranean.

On the May morning of our meeting, Captain Ali had narrower pre-occupations than global politics. He said he had 59 ships under his care in transit through the Canal. In future he expected a regular flow of 85 vessels – which would require meticulous regulation of the timetable whereby convoys going north and south are alternated every day or half day.

The Pharaohs dreamed of cutting a channel to the sea. According to Herodotus – employing characteristic journalistic exaggeration – 120,000 Egyptians died in an attempt to divert the course of the Nile. Darius, the Emperor of the Persians, built a forerunner of the Fresh Water Canal (which provided drinking water to villages along the Suez Canal during its construction). This ancient channel – in which two triremes could pass each other – was restored and embellished by the Emperor Trajan.

Linking the Mediterranean and the Red Sea with a waterway is said to have been commended to Louis XIV of France by the philosopher Leibnitz. Napoleon's engineers began digging, but soon gave up. The Napoleonic plan was taken up by a French consular official, Ferdinand De Lesseps, whose biggest difficulty was finance rather than the work itself. The digging and building took ten years, much of it using heavy machinery and skilled labour from Europe, and the grand opening took place on 17 November 1869. It had cost £19 million, two-thirds of which had been raised by the shareholders of the Suez Canal Company.

The profligacy of the principal shareholder, Khedive Ismail of Egypt, gave the British their opportunity. Like his ancestor Mohammed Ali he was an ardent moderniser, and his indulgence in new-fangled projects like railways and the telegraph brought him to the brink of bankruptcy. In 1875 the British Prime Minister, Benjamin Disraeli, bought 176,602 of the Khedive's shares for 4,080,000 Egyptian pounds. The British were now virtually in charge.

But not without resistance. Arabi Pasha led a revolt of Egyptian officers against the rule of Ismail's successor, Tawfiq. A French and English fleet arrived at Alexandria and bombarded the city 'to clear the air', as the English commander put it; and that same year, 1882, Arabi Pasha's force were overrun at Tel-el-Kebir by a British expeditionary army under Sir Garnet Wolseley. Arabi and his brother officers were sent into exile in the Seychelles.

The guiding hand of the new order was Evelyn Baring, of the banking family, who was appointed Consul-General and Agent. Later ennobled as Lord Cromer, and known earlier in India as 'over-Baring', he seems now a caricature of British colonial condescension.

Lord Cromer believed that 'subject races' were incapable of governing themselves. Under him began the undeclared British occupation, the 'veiled protectorate' whereby the Egyptians under the Khedive were allowed to rule themselves provided it fulfilled British requirements and conformed to the wishes of the British government.

Cromer balanced the books and maintained British strategic interests in the Canal, in Egypt itself and in Sudan to the south. He encouraged the growth of cotton as a raw material for English mills and discouraged any local industrialisation; only one per cent of the budget was spent on public education.

His reign came to an end with an incident which is still commemorated by nationalists. In 1906 a group of British Army officers went pigeon-shooting near the village of Dinshwai in the Delta. The previous year they had been warned off as the locals reared the pigeons for a living. This time the farmers, the *fellahin*, were prepared and ambushed the soldiers. One of the officers went for help but died of sunstroke as he reached the nearest detachment. He showed signs of having been beaten by the peasants and in a show trial ordered by Cromer, four of the locals were hanged in sight of their village, while others were flogged and given prison sentences. These were later commuted but the damage was done. Dinshwai was celebrated in ode and song, and within a year Cromer had resigned.

In 1914 a British Protectorate was at last declared formally, and with it martial law. Egypt became a garrison for the British armed forces – as it was again in the Second World War. In 1922 it was declared officially independent, but under the new treaty Britain maintained four reserve powers: control of all external defence policy, protection of the Suez Canal, protection of foreign nationals, and defence of Sudan. It was the veiled protectorate rewritten.

A delegation of Egyptians had insisted in attending the Versailles Peace conference, and formed themselves into a political party called the Delegation (Wafd), which was to be the main vehicle of nationalist political expression for a generation to come. Its imposing leader, Saad Zaghlul, became prime minister after elections in 1924. He had been a friend of Cromer, but he was the first Egyptian prime minister not to be of Circassian or Turkish stock. As one of them, he could speak the language of the *fellahin* of the Nile.

By now the *fellahin* were in poor case. Wages and farming prices had been eroded, the population had risen from 10 million in 1897 to 14 million in 1927 (just under one million of whom were foreigners). Violence was on the increase in the cities and banditry in the villages.

Political opposition began to take a new direction, the significance of which goes far beyond Egypt. In 1928 in Ismailia, a secondary school teacher, Hasan al-Banna, began to preach a new way of life based on helping one another and conforming more strictly to Islam. His followers became the Muslim Brethren, and al-Banna their supreme guide. The Muslim Brethren are potent throughout the Arab world today, credited with a fanaticism that matches their puritanism. The very term Muslim

Brotherhood has become a generic for the expression of radical Sunni piety in politics. The Brothers are a force of increasing power from the Maghreb to central Asia, and at times have shown a fanaticism to rival the most militant Shi'ites.

Their influence has been seen in terrorist attacks in Lebanon, in the uprising against the Assad regime in Syria in Hamas in 1982, and in the group that murdered President Anwar Sadat in Cairo in 1981. The Brethren were behind the murder of Nuqrashi, the Egyptian Prime Minister, in the debacle of the first Arab-Israeli War of 1948, and in a revenge murder Hasan al-Banna himself was killed in turn.

The rise of the Muslim Brotherhood of Hasan al-Banna in Egypt was matched by the growth of other puritan movements within the Sunni Muslim community. In 1912 Ibn Saud, the Lord of Nejd in Arabia, had embraced the sect of the Wahhabites, founded by a religious reformer Mohammed Abdual al Wahhab in 1745. The Wahhabi movement in this century took the simple name *Ikhwan*, the Brotherhood – the same name that al-Banna's followers adopted for themselves.

In 1936 the British negotiated the final term of their military lease of Egypt. The treaty permitted British troops to remain in the Canal Zone until 1956, when it might be re-negotiated. The outbreak of war meant another build-up of garrison forces. More pious Egyptians disliked the boom in bars and brothels to amuse the troops in Alexandria; and in 1942 they came to see the British command in a less flattering light when as the guns of Rommel's Afrika Korps came to within seventy-five miles of Alexandria, and the RAF base at Heliopolis was bombed nightly. The British prepared to retreat. 'I can remember them burning the files in the embassy garden in Cairo – the lorries went out from Cairo all night long, night after night,' a distinguished Copt academic, recalls, 'they were preparing to do a bunk and leave us to it.'

The war over, the denouement was not long in coming. Once again, Ismailia played a crucial role. In January 1952 British military units surrounded an Egyptian police station in the middle of the town in the belief that the local police had abetted guerrilla attacks against British troops in the Canal Zone. The soldiers called on the police to give up, but they refused on orders from the Interior Ministry. The British replied with tanks and artillery, killing forty and wounding seventy more before the remaining police surrendered. Next day British shops and offices in Cairo were put to the torch in a massive protest.

In under six months it was all over. On 23 July 1952 a group of 'Free Officers' of the Egyptian Army under Colonel Gamal Abdul Nasser took charge in a virtually bloodless coup. King Farouk, the descendant of

Mohammed Ali, was forced to leave. A year later a popular general, Mohammed Neguib, was made president and Egypt declared an independent republic. For the first time since the last of the Pharaohs, Egypt was ruled by an Egyptian.

In 1954 negotiations were concluded for British forces to quit the Canal Zone. By now Nasser was firmly in control and seeking new friends and defence suppliers, particularly from the Soviet Union and its satellites. This annoyed the arch-conservative American Secretary of State John Foster Dulles, who hit back by withdrawing US funding of the Aswan High Dam project – a pet scheme of Nasser's. Nasser had to find alternative finance for the dam, and so he turned to the biggest currency-earner in Egypt – the Suez Canal, which he nationalised in July 1956.

The British Prime Minister, Anthony Eden, believed Nasser had broken the treaty of 1954, and described him as a new Hitler, not to be appeased at any cost. The expedition of Anglo-French forces was hopelessly bungled from the first, and doubly damned in Arab eyes by its collusion in an attack by Israel. By the time the French and British landed in November 1956, 'the Suez Canal was flowing through Number 10 Downing Street,' in the immortal phrase of one political commentator. The Prime Minister had become half-crazed, and soon resigned on grounds of health.

It was the end of more than the British in Egypt. Eden was succeeded by Harold Macmillan, who foresaw 'a wind of change' blowing through Britain's colonies. Under him the glue of Empire began to melt as never before. In the 1960s Harold Wilson ended the British military presence East of Suez and the Canal ceased to be a British strategic frontier.

iv Fellahin: Farming and Fertility

The reaches of the Nile along the road from Ismailia to Cairo groan with human settlements – villages of low-walled dwellings, with thatched and mud-bricked roofs, which hang over the banks like heavy fruit. These are the dwellings of the *fellahin*, the backbone of Egyptian rural life and some of the most ingenious cultivators on earth.

By 1990 Egypt had more than 55 million mouths to feed – give or take the two and a half to three million working abroad. Only one-thirtieth of its entire territory is cultivable – the rest is desert. With numbers increasing by nearly 3 per cent per annum, demand has outstripped supply, and in the mid-1970s Egypt became a net importer of wheat for the first time.

The *fellahin* have had their share of exploitation too, and under the British the imbalance of landholding became something of a scandal. In the 1930s 12,000 landowners held nearly half the land, the rest being farmed by 2.2 million *fellahin*. Greediest of all was the royal house. By the time King Farouk abdicated in 1952, he owned farms of more than 100,000 *faddan* – a *faddan* being 1.038 acres. Breaking up the great estates was central to Nasser's revolutionary programme, and he limited holdings to 200 faddan, and later to only 50 faddan, per family.

One of the families to suffer from the reforms was that of Ahmat 'Butch' Baghat, a freelance agricultural engineer of genius. His father had been one of King Farouk's estate managers, with quite a bit of land of his own. 'We managed to hang on to some farms near Alexandria,' he confessed with an enigmatic smile. He spoke of the past without rancour, and addressed the problems of Egypt's growing population with intense practicality.

Butch dreamt of perfecting a multi-cropper reaping machine that could transform the lives of the farmers of the Nile in the Delta and Upper Egypt. He had begged and borrowed funds from home and abroad, and already some 600 prototypes were up and running in Egypt and through-out the Middle East. The machine had to be serviceable at low cost and be capable of cutting and threshing nearly a dozen diverse crops as well as pumping water. It should also winnow in an hour the amount of corn that would take a man nine days to do by hand. 'The trouble is so much gets lost on the granary floor – even at the best of times. Farmers regularly lose a fifth of their wheat after it has ripened. I have had to find the tool to thresh and winnow at the same time – and I think I've got it.'

Mechanisation had come slowly to the *fellahin*. Farmers in the Delta have very different needs from those of Upper Egypt. In the Delta the main crops are wheat, clover, maize and rice; straw was at a premium and almost as valuable as the grain. Farther south they grew legumes, pulse and sorgums, and needed different machines for harvesting.

The farmers of the Nile needed machines because labour was becoming less easy to find. As educational standards rose, sons and daughters were reluctant to tie themselves to the land. In 1975 Egypt had 16,000 trac-tors, of which only 10,000 were in working condition. In 1985 the average farming family earned about $600 a year – exactly half the average per capita income given by the UN for North Africa. Given rising prices and inflation the *fellahin* have not been overgenerously rewarded for their labours.

Butch was putting his faith in what he called 'the greenhouse revolution' and in schemes to irrigate the desert. Three thousand greenhouse plots would be put up by the government in a year alone, but it would have to be more energetic in regulating prices for new produce like strawberries and tomatoes. However, making the desert burgeon with tomatoes creates its own problems. Some projects have proved very costly, and there is a very real prospect of climatic changes resulting from the Greenhouse Effect causing serious erosion and inundation in the Nile Delta. The *fellahin*'s grip on the narrow strips of fertile river plain could become still more precarious.

For a settlement of 20,000 inhabitants, the village of Tant el-Gezira appears remarkably compact. Every square millimeter of land crammed between the irrigation ditches and the river seems to sprout wheat, maize or patches of alfalfa grass, clumps of bananas burst from the banks in vulgar profusion. Along the road-side oranges, peppers, tomatoes and apricots are laid out for sale. Donkeys, horses, oxen, a rare camel, an occasional tractor and the ubiquitous small pick-up trucks kick up the dust. A woman in a black veil passed by on a donkey, her head garlanded with tomatoes. At the government store the door is open for distribution of the sugar allowance – one of the main commodities subsidised and dispensed by the public authorities. The wait has been irksome and the queue has become somewhat informal. Voices are raised at the front and the good-natured pushing and shoving is punctuated by fisticuffs near the door. A man is forcefully ejected, the door slams shut, and business for the day ends prematurely as a running fight goes pouring down the road.

We had come to the village to see Abdul Azim Al-Shazli. As the local Omdah, he was the lynchpin of local government; his mandate would have to be renewed every ten years. Village complaints go first to the Omdah, who then prepares the case for judgment by the four Sheikhs, each of whom is chosen for life.

The Omdah was in his mid-sixties, his eyes twinkling with shrewd calculation. He told me that he had decided to go to school at the age of twelve to learn to read and write. 'Life as a farmer was very hard, so I learnt my trade as a weaver.'

The Omdah's family consisted of two sons, four daughters and six grandchildren, and was representative of many of its kind. One son-in-law was a weaver, assisted by his wife. 'The rest are not interested in the weaving business,' he said. Only two of his daughters had gone on from elementary to secondary school. One of the boys was in the army; the other was an accountant in Cairo, but had worked two years in Iraq to earn some foreign currency. More than 500 villagers had gone abroad, most to the Gulf and neighbouring Arab countries. Many exiles were teachers – so many in fact that the Education Ministry had forbidden teachers to go abroad for five years after their training.

By the end of the century Egypt will be a nation of approaching 70 million, by which time Tant el-Gezira could well have been swallowed up in the greatest rural city of the Mediterranean world – Cairo – by then the dwelling place of more than 20 million people.

v Cairo

I saw Nefertiti in a taxi in Old Cairo, with the same proud profile as her bust in the Berlin Museum. A young woman strides across the street gripping two live ducks at the bases of their wings – exactly as her wooden forebear in the Cairo Museum. The greatest Arab capital calls to mind a string of dazzling images from the past as well as a hint of what life may be like in the future for much of the Eastern Mediterranean.

At night the roads are alive as the old city exhales humanity to the new suburbs. A long queue at the bus terminus suddenly kneels as one for prayers at noon. In the outskirts women scramble for water to wash pots, pans and children. Turn the corner and one gets a sudden vista of the Nile, the tall rigged, white sailed feluccas drifting like swans. At rush hour the flyovers are jammed with dusty cars and trucks. Everywhere hospitality begins with the offering of a Kleenex, in coffee shop, taxi or office, as a sandstorm from the desert perpetually threatens. At Ramadan the squares and cafés explode into parties with the setting of the sun.

Cairo's fame and power is as an Arab capital. It was settled in 641 AD by the Arab conqueror of Egypt, Amr, who was told by the Caliph Omar, second successor to the Prophet, to build a mosque at Fustat. This would be the new capital and not Alexandria, which was deemed too remote and cut off from reinforcements. In 969 AD Cairo was conquered by the Fatimids and a Shi'ite caliphate was established – making it one of the great spiritual as well as political centres of the Arab world. This in time was demolished by Saladin, the half-Kurdish ruler who united much of the Arab world. Cairo became the capital of his short-lived Ayyubid dynasty, and the mighty walls of his citadel are the most prominent medieval monument in the city.

Saladin's heirs could not live up to his achievement, and the branches of the Arab nation began to diverge. The Mamluks, Turkish soldiery, rose to power in Egypt, and Ottoman rule was established in the sixteenth century. Much later Mohammed Ali, the Greek-Albanian viceroy of the Ottomans, massacred the Mamluks on his way to supreme power. His heirs fell prey to the French creditors and British overseers; only in 1952 did Cairo become a capital city once again.

The city had always had a cosmopolitan feeling to it. The Copts, who claim to be the link with the Ptolomies and ancient Egypt, revere it as a Christian shrine, the destination of the Holy Family in the Flight into Egypt from Herod's massacres. In medieval times there was a sizeable community of Jews – though not as large as that of Alexandria, which was reported to have 40,000 Jews at the time of the Arab conquest in 641.

The city became renowned as a centre of Islamic learning – a reputation it still maintains. The Al-Azhar has been the home of the oldest and most famous Islamic university since the foundation of the mosque there in 970. It is a paramount voice in the teaching of theology and Islamic law. It was here that Ibn Khaldun studied law and the Great Sanusi, founder of Libyan nationalism, was instructed in theology. Of all the great Islamic schools Al-Azhar alone continued to teach both theology and Arabic letters throughout the Ottoman period.

The Al-Azhar is a potent expression of Cairo's central position in the Arabs' destiny. Egypt is central to the Arab world not only because of the material strength of its population and economy, but because of the texture and depth of its culture – and the role of its schools in the promotion of Islam.

Tugged between the old and the new, Cairo is a place of perpetual experiment. Like the ancient Egyptians, modern Cairenes seem to be dominated by death and the Nile – so much so that the sprawling cemetery district of the City of the Dead is now host to the living as thousands of Cairenes have made their homes among the tombs.

Throughout the city death is a frequent visitor. Infant mortality remains high, often caused by poor sanitation. As a woman in a poor suburb once explained, 'Come and see the sewage in the street – I lost three of my children because of it.'

The supply of water for drinking and washing is critical for most of the new suburbs, as well as for the older and poorer ones. Eighty per cent of the capital's water is taken from the Nile, and a good deal is drained back into the river. Problems of water supply provoke reactions of pride and shame – foreign interest sometimes been taken as a calculated insult to Egyptian dignity and self-respect. Providing a supply of clean water and disposing of waste and sewage is bound to be a major problem for any great city.

A survey carried by an Egyptian and American team for the American University Cairo in 1980 showed the scale of the problem. Nearly twenty per cent of those surveyed had no drinking water piped into their homes; six per cent had no access to running water or any toilet facilities. Very often water was supplied in much the same way as in the villages of the Nile Delta. Importing the ways of the rural communites into new towns is the essence of the informal economy, common to nearly all the major cities of the Mediterranean.

The central feature of the public supply was the communal tap, which often has its own public tap guard. The tap is the meeting-point of women – almost exclusively so. One old man, a widower, said he had been warned away from the taps as this was women's work – one dowager of the fountain had told him to get married again so that his partner could fetch water for him. The tap was often the scene of violence and fighting, two women reported being heavily bruised from blows delivered by their rivals' water containers, while some men who had recently arrived from rural Upper Egypt refused to let their women go to the taps until after midnight for fear of their being beaten and maltreated. Water-carrying is time-consuming – in some families the women might spend four hours each day hauling water. Access to public toilets was equally problematic. In some quarters they were almost non-existent; one neighbourhood allowed a family to make their home in one after as their house had collapsed.

Since medieval times water supply, bathing and toilet amenities have been the responsibility of the local mosque. Bathing and toilet facilities inside the mosque were restricted to men, though taps are often set up outside in the street. Since the Middle Ages a common figure of the water business has been the *sakka* or the water vendor, who carries his water in huge goatskins or *kirbah*, and tends to operate on the fringes of the law. Nowadays poor women, *malaya*, may be hired by the better-off to haul water from the taps.

One in ten of those surveyed suffered from bilharzia, caused by water-born parasites penetrating the skin. Contaminated water also carried typhoid, malaria, and kidney troubles. Considerable ingenuity is now being devoted to using as much of the waste water as possible, and the Italians have developed simple methods of treating the drainage channels so that they can be used for arable irrigation. Communal fountains are becoming increasingly efficient, and less likely to cause fetid swamps in the streets.

The water problem is symptomatic of the virtually uncontrolled growth of the outer suburbs. Between 1960 and 1976 the population of Greater

Cairo grew from 4,350,000 to over 8,000,000. The most spectacular growth was in Giza City, which more than doubled to a million and a quarter. By the late 1980s it had merged into Cairo itself, which had grown from just over a quarter of a million in 1900 to about 15 million.

According to Dr Tim Sullivan, who teaches sociology at the American University, about four-fifths of the new building has been technically illegal; planning regulations and the law have been unable to keep up with the pace of development. The great influx had begun after the 1967 Arab-Israeli war, and now whole villages were being swallowed up on the periphery. Some ten new cities are planned by President Mubarak, new desert developments to absorb the rising population and migrants returning from abroad.

Did all this contribute to the growth of the informal economy? It did indeed – 'You have to throw away your text books and look for yourself. You see it everywhere, from water-carrying to illegal hospitals and hostels. Just about every sector has its informal aspect, I think we're seeing an entirely new Egypt emerging – soon virtually the whole country will be semi-urbanised. This is where I think the Islamic revival is significant – Jamiat Islami councils among the students and the young are particularly important in giving them a sense of direction.'

One of the most vivid manifestations of the informal economy are the garbage-collectors, the *zebellin*. Although sophisticated Cairenes hate mentioning them, they have almost become a tourist attraction for itinerant sociologists and journalists. The *zebellin* are Christians, Copts from Asyut, and they are responsible for about 60 per cent of the garbage collection in Cairo and Alexandria. The British introduced them to pigs, against which they have no religious prohibition, and the pigs thrive on the garbage. They lie in it, sleep in it, and eat it.

The *zebellin* bid for garbage concessions through a middleman, the Wahi Zariba, who shares his profits with the collectors themselves. Different concessions vary in value from area to area; in the zone round the Sheraton hotel 30,000 Egyptian pounds has been paid for a pitch.

The garbage is collected in small high-sided wooden carts, invariably towed by donkeys. The trundle of the carts as they heave into view, spilling the overflow of their loads, are familiar sounds and sights in the Old City. President Mubarak told the *zebellin* to clean up their act, banning the donkeys and carts and providing tractors instead – but the tractors broke down, the scavengers protested, and half Cairo's daily 4,000 tonnes of waste went uncollected.

The *zebellin* excited the tenderest maternal instincts of the professional aid world. The Common Market, Oxfam, Ford Fountation, Catholic

Relief and Mother Theresa's nuns have all offered funds and advice. In one camp toilets and taps for 20,000 were provided, but hardly used. Their biggest settlement is at Moqqattam, not far from Saladin's citadel, where half Cairo's 15,000 *zebellin* are encamped. The place is a small mountain range of debris, cloth and rags, glass, tins, paper and rotting food. Intermittently a house is squeezed between these slag heaps of deteritus, where snuffling pigs, goats, dogs, rabbits, poultry and children root and play without a care. The occasional cart bursts through the gate like a covered wagon bolting from Red Indians in a western, ragged children whooping alongside.

At Moqqattam the community lives by its own rules; official enquiries are told that birth certificates and other documents have been 'eaten by the goats'. They may not live by bread alone, but they certainly look to rubbish as a means of sustenance. The community appears to have adapted astonishingly to its eccentric economy, but disease is never far away, for man and beast. The place is like a virologist's laboratory. Dogs, man, woman and child, carry hydatids which can cause severe viruses in humans; taperworms, tetanus, meningitis, bilharzia are rife.

Life at Moqqattam was 'a bit overwhelming' according to Teresa, a mother of four children, eleven rabbits, goats, chickens and a cat. But the vets, nurses and teachers from the aid organisations have made some headway. More than seventy workshops have been started; diet has been tested and practices such as the feeding of raw meat to children stopped; proper animal husbandry has been introduced. At the forefront of the reform has been the priest of the local church, an inconspicuous yellow box with the trefoiled cross of the Coptic Church carefully painted on the door.

Singing and dancing have been a passion with Cairenes for centuries, and are forms at which they excel. The thrall of some Egyptian singers over their fellow-citizens is a thing of legend – though I have never been lucky enough to see one of the great performers *in situ*. In his *Manners and Customs of the Modern Egyptians* of 1837 the English Arabic scholar Edward William Lane wrote with unrestrained admiration of the professional women singers, or *awalim*. 'I have heard the most celebrated Awalim in Cairo, and have been more charmed with their songs than with the best performances of the A'lateeyeh [male singers], and more so, I think I may truly add, than with any other music that I have ever enjoyed.'

Modern singers have been attended by the wildest adulation. Umm Kulthum, a combination of Eva Turner, Elaine Page and Garbo, had fervent followers from all walks of life. Her funeral was said to have been followed by ten million mourners. A visit from the most celebrated Egyptian singer of the day to Libya persuaded the young Captain Qadaffi and his brother officers to postpone their coup for six months.

Egypt is also the centre of television productions for the Arab community, shown at peak times from Marrakesh to Baghdad. In the age of television, Cairo is the great entertainer, as well as great teacher, of the Arab world.

I was chatting to a friendly taxi driver on the way to the Pyramids. 'You a journalist?' he enquired. 'Radio, TV? BBC? Well BBC, NBC, ABC, CBC, I drive them all – I work for all BCs.' We were going to look at the damage done to hotels and luxury residences by troops of the militia police, conscripts so poor that they were not even provided with boot laces. They had broken out of their barracks, on learning their national service was to be extended. The Holiday Inn was gutted by fire and tourists robbed of cash and trinkets. The rioting went on for a couple of days and then subsided; but for a brief moment Egyptians feared it was the explosion they had always dreaded, remembering the food riots against Sadat in 1977 and the rebellion of Muslim militants after his assassination in 1981. And indeed I often heard Cairenes speak of the tension and frustration in the air as part of Egypt's political inheritance.

The public face of politics since 1954 has been largely the story of three presidents – Nasser, the liberator and visionary, Sadat the friend of the West, and Mubarak the caretaker who came to stay.

Nasser remains a giant presence in Egyptian life, a figure of endless debate and analysis. Though a British-trained career army officer, he was a politician first and foremost – but of a visionary rather than a practical bent. His great achievements were independence in 1952 and the success of Egypt in the Suez Crisis in 1956. Nothing else worked quite as well. He introduced a socialist regime which became increasingly oppressive. Based on his Arab Socialist Union, it was virtually a one-party state backed by extraordinary police powers, phone-tapping, informers and an atmosphere of official suspicion. Egypt looked to Moscow for moral, and material military support. The Soviet Union also backed the president's most elaborate development project, the Aswan High Dam. This not only turned out to be expensive, and late – it was only finished in 1970, the year of Nasser's death – but it failed to live up to expectations. It changed the relationship of the Nile to Upper Egypt forever. The Inundation no longer occurred, invaluable silt was washed away, and the 1.2 million acres of new farmland did not materialise.

Nasser's dream of an independent, united Arab world hardly fared any better. Union with Syria in the United Arab Republic lasted barely three years; the Egyptian general sent to Damascus to command the combined army was sent packing with his Algerian mistress in their night clothes.

Syria and Egypt came together again in 1967 for what was to prove Nasser's biggest setback – the Six Days' War against Israel. Within the first hours almost the entire Egyptian Air Force was destroyed on the ground. The Israelis grabbed Sinai and occupied the Canal, closing Egypt's biggest revenue-earner for eight years to come. Defeat was total, and Nasser resigned – only to be recalled to power within hours by popular acclaim. But it was the end of the pan-Arab dream, and the beginning of real economic difficulties. The strain on the president was enormous, hastening his death from a massive heart attack in the autumn of 1970. For Egyptians he was a prophet of Arab independence, and a genuinely popular leader, as his funeral cortege of an estimated four million suggests. For the West he was a dictator in thrall to Moscow.

Support for Nasser's political philosophy underwent a revival in the late Eighties under a band of secular-minded intellectuals, writers and politicians. Mohammed Shanawi, a columnist of the leading daily *Al-Ahram*, told me with pride that he had been jailed after the riots of 1977 for trying to reconstitute a Nasserite party. For him Nasser was the man who forged the distinctive Arab identity of modern Egypt. 'It was Arab rather than Muslim – we have more in common with the Christians of Syria and Lebanon with the Muslims of the Indian sub-continent.' This nationalism was blunted by the 1967 defeat, which led to a 'disintegration of the Arab world and a revival of Islam'. Sadat's mistake was to buy off religious opposition, 'not realising that he would be the first they would aim at.' Islam was no solution for Egypt, Shanawi claimed, and Egypt would reject a theocratic regime like Iran. He considered Sadat's ploys as 'escapism', whereas Nasser was always prepared to confront difficulties.

After 1967 Arab preoccupations centred on the Palestinian issue and the Occupied Territories. But when Sadat launched his mission to Israel in 1978, 'he confused non-belligerency with peace. In fact Sadat narrowed Egypt's options in foreign policy by the day.'

Of all the Free Officers who engineered the 1951 coup, Anwar Sadat was the man least expected to succeed. But he was a survivor, and when Nasser died he was the only one of the original circle still available. He was anxious to prove himself as a realist, as opposed to Nasser the Arab visionary. He cut the links with the Russians in 1972, and turned slowly to the West. Close links were established with Washington, who supplied military advice and equipment as well as food aid. In 1975 he launched his controversial 'Open Door,' programme to liberate the economy on free-market lines – a policy that was responsible for huge distortions to the economy, according to the opposition. A group of entrepreneurs, including the president's brother, were said to have made themselves extremely rich by bending the system. Egypt became a net importer of food on a large scale for the first time, and when the IMF recommended cutting subsidies, severe and widespread rioting ensued.

Later that year Sadat tried to divert attention from domestic woes by his dramatic journey to Jerusalem to secure a lasting peace with Israel. Despite the euphoria in the West, Egyptians always had their reservations. Old Nasserites like Mohammed Heikal, Nasser's friend and the editor of *Al-Ahram*, claimed that Sadat had not thought out his moves at all, and wanted a piece of theatre that would win the approval of the Americans. Men like Heikal believed that Sadat had needlessly cut Egypt out of the Arab political hinterland as Israel under Begin had no intention of fulfilling the spirit the Camp David Accords forged by President Carter nor conceding anything resembling a state for the Palestinians. For Sadat it was the approach of Nemesis.

At home he quarrelled with the secular opposition and with the leaders of both the Muslim and Copt communities. He became increasingly isolated, and in September 1981 he ordered the arrest of 1500 prominent public figures, Mohammed Heikal and the Coptic Bishops among them. A few weeks later, at a parade to commemorate the Egyptian army's successful storming of the Suez Canal in the 1973 war with Israel – an event which had done much to establish Sadat's reputation – he was murdered by a young lieutenant, who halted his troop carrier in front of the saluting base and coolly opened fire.

To his critics Sadat was a flawed figure – vain, lazy and prone to live in a fantasy world. He pretended to be a man of the country, of the *fellahin*, making much of his rural roots when visiting his rest house at Mamourah, usually with his half-English wife Jihan, of whom he was inordinately proud. He was frequently filmed at Friday prayers. He manipulated the media, and adored appearing on television. Finally, his critics claim, he not only tolerated corruption all about him, but concealed it by introducing the 'Shame Law,' which played on the Egyptians' natural reserve about parading the less dignified aspects of their society.

Going against the religious and secular tenets of society, leading children astray, broadcasting or publishing slanderous material against the state at home or abroad, forming illegal organisations, all incurred dire penalties and consequences. It was a catch-all to prevent dirty linen from being washed in public.

Dr Mustapha Khalil served both Nasser and Sadat, and was prime minister during the overtures to Israel in 1977. The two men were very different, he told me in his cool office in one of the big banks. 'Nasser never was a dictator – he offered something new for Arab nationalism, for the old nationalist party, the Wafd, had run its course. Sadat was far more pragmatic. His whole strategy was the "battle for peace", with Israel.' The word he used to describe Sadat was 'malleable' and in this there was a touch of the pejorative.

Looking to the future, he thought the population explosion a bigger problem for Egypt than militant Islam. Family planning was vital – it had a poor record – and the age of marriage had to be raised to at least seventeen or eighteen. As for Islamic fundamentalism, 'most Egyptians see religion as a moral and ethical institution – they are not fanatical and so tend to be tolerant. The extremists are living in an imaginary world and they want to make things as they were 1400 years ago.'

As for President Mubarak, he was 'a different man for different conditions'. Despite difficulties with his opponents, Mubarak has proved an agile president. In the 1990 crisis caused by the Iraqi invasion of Kuwait he showed that he had learned from the mistakes of both Sadat and Nasser. He knew he had to avoid a military confrontation he could not handle, and warned Saddam Hussein to do the same. He also endeavoured not to lose contact with Egypt's allies in the Arab community of nations. He had witnessed Egyptian's expulsion from the Arab League in 1978. The League's headquarters had moved to Tunis, but Mubarak managed to bring it back to Cairo after ten years.

The sun was setting over the Nile and the candles for Ramadan were being kindled when I went to see Mohammed Sayid Ahmed, a leading left-wing thinker. The defeat of 1967, he said, 'shifted the epicentre of the Arab world to the Gulf and away from the Mediterranean'; it also meant the beginning of what he called 'the search for certainty in religion'. Like Dr Khalil, the former prime minister, he was not afraid of the fanatics, but he saw them as a symptom rather than a cause, and a symptom of something highly noxious. 'What is most dangerous is not their religious colouring – but the degree of frustration. They have been extremely violent and out of control.' He cited the explosion of Muslim student gangs at Aysut after the murder of Sadat – anarchy had reigned for days, and the students had beheaded a Copt police officer – and the young soldier who had shot dead Israeli tourists at a check point in the Sinai Desert.

The murder of Anwar Sadat had implications for the entire Arab and Muslim world. It also had a peculiarly Egyptian aspect, which reaches back to the Pharaohs.

The plotters were descendants of the militant Muslim Brethren founded by Hasan al-Banna in Ismailia in 1928. The message had come to them via a famous Pakistani Brother Abu el A'ala Mawdudi, who had in turn inspired the populist preacher Sayyid Qutb. Qutb was hanged after the riots in Egypt of 1977, but not before he had helped to promote the militant student councils of the Jamiat Islamiya movement.

They maintained that Islam would only be successful through direct action rather than political agitation. It had to aim directly at the seat of power, and to work underground. Militant units were called *anquds* or bunches of grapes – one grape might be plucked, but the bunch would survive. The key figure in the *anqud* of Lieutenant Khaled el-Islambouli, the future assassin of Sadat, was an electrician Abdel Salam Faraj.

At his trial Islambouli said he had killed Sadat because he had embraced Islam falsely and betrayed it by making peace with the Jews. Faraj had issued Islambouli with a *fatwa* or holy order to murder Sadat. Once he had been ordered to take part in the parade the lieutenant knew there could be no going back, as the *fatwa* could not be withdrawn or broken.

The violence, premeditation, and lack of repentance of the conspirators astonished many Egyptians. It was, perhaps, a sign of things to come. Militant Muslims, and Sunni Muslims of Egypt and North Africa at that, were increasingly prominent on the campuses and in the big cities – the men with beards and flowing robes, the women with scarves and smart ankle-length coats.

For many of these Muslims Islambouli was an instrument of justice. Sadat's funeral was held in strictest security, with a suitable sprinkling of foreign dignitaries in attendance; there were none of the adoring millions who had seen Nasser to his grave. For those Egyptians who feared and prayed for the future, the cry of the young Lieutenant after he had fired at Sadat had an ominous ring: 'I am Khalid al-Islambouli, I have killed the Pharaoh, and I do not fear death.'

One morning I was looking down from the Pyramids towards Cairo when the air suddenly exploded with sound. The barrage of noise was almost visible. It was the noonday call to prayer for the first day of the month of fast, Ramadan. The calls wailed and fluted, growled and boomed – the volume depending on minaret's amplification system as well as the vocal powers of the *muezzin*.

The message was beautifully simple: God is great, and his word through his Prophet Mohamed should be heeded ever more faithfully. That first Friday of Ramadan preachers in Cairo laid about the seductive material- ism of the West in fire-brand sermons. The Islamic revolution was at hand, one apprehensive journalist assured me, though I learned later that the Friday sermon, the *khutba*, often carries a strong political message.

The Islamic movement has been growing at the rate of 16 per cent a year, according to Leila ey al Arab, a Cairo banker. She finished her studies in 1968 and went into finance – learning the profession at the multinational Citibank in Cairo. From there she had helped set up two Arab investment banks, the Delta Bank and the Cairo end of the Byblos Bank of Lebanon. Her conversation was sharp and eloquent, but still more striking was the cut of her figure – if that is the right word in the circumstances.

Her face was framed entirely by a silk scarf, matching a long, high- buttoned coat that reached to her ankles. On her feet were a smart pair of brown shoes, which looked far from cheap. She had been converted some three or four years before we met but, as she explained, 'the seed has always been within me'. Now she was working on the principles of Islamic bank- ing, writing a book and acting as an Islamic banking consultant.

Egypt's defeat of 1967 had been an overwhelming experience for her and her generation. 'We went through a deep depression, we lost interest in ourselves. It was only after the 1973 war that we could again say "I am proud to be an Egyptian."' The aftermath of 1967 brought the first of the 'personal problems' which were to draw her to the Islamic Move- ment, as she called it; her father and her brother – a naval officer – were imprisoned in the crackdown and national paranoia that followed the defeat by the Israelis.

Now she was prepared to be cautiously optimistic. Population was the biggest problem facing Egypt, but it was all a matter of good management, such as the utilisation of the desert. And answer did not lie with Western aid, particularly from America, which gave 'beautiful assets but rotten management'. Westerners were too narrow and technical to their approach to Egypt.

Her views on the economy reflected the spiritual crisis which had drawn her to the Islamic cult, the *tariqa*, symbolised by her dress. With two growing children and a husband who stayed at home, she had 'lived more like a male in a female body. I felt I could not be a proper career woman. Islam touches every aspect of my life. Because of my personal problems I knew I could always go to the Supreme Power. I found that Islam gave women many rights, rights which many Muslims then contrive to take away.'

The experience of conversion was summed up by the word 'relief'. 'It was a spiritual relief to be obeying an order,' not least in the manner of her dress. 'I am dressed like this as a direct order from God in the Koran. It was a great relief when I started to dress like this. You get to like yourself and your body – it's yours. Why expose it to everyone?'

Her attitude to the modern world was highly flexible, however. She had no inhibitions in shaking hands with a non-Muslim, which is vehemently forbidden in the sisterhoods of the Shi'ites in Lebanon. Nor was she concerned about the Sharia, the Islamic code of law. 'Rebribution is only one side of it, working on the basis that prevention is better than cure. But the law does believe in treating everyone fairly.'

Unlike Leila ey al Arab, Professor Magdi Wahba, a leading figure on the Consultative Council of the Coptic community, was pessimistic. He had just retired from teaching English literature at Cairo University, and was completing an English-Arabic dictionary. He spoke the English of the Oxford of his education, but his general dislike of the English for what they had done to Egypt was ill-disguised.

'We are in the twilight of secularism in Egypt now,' he mused when we met in his apartment. 'Islam is tolerant in itself, but now it faces it the moment of identity. It is difficult being non-Muslim in a Muslim country. The crisis is going to deepen; I know I will have to come to terms with it, rather than go into exile.'

The professor's misgivings were not private phobias, but were shared by the more sophisticated Copts. A Coptic doctor who had applied for a commissioin in the British Army Medical Corps at this time gave as his reason that 'there is no chance for the Christians in Egypt in the future'.

First among equals of the Copts is Pope Shenouda III, the Patriarch. Even without his splendid black habit with its flowery embroidery Pope Shenouda would be a commanding figure. A witty man with a distinct glint of mischief in his eye he loves to talk about his church and his people. He is a natural communicator, which he attributes to his work as a journalist and pamphleteer – as the politicians were to learn to their cost. Like the militant Muslims, the Copts had experienced a strong revival after the Six Days' War. Monasteries that had been half empty suddenly filled with new postulants and novices. In this atmosphere the new Patriach was in his element. At least once a week he would hold 'conversations' at the Patriarchate – sermons followed by open discussions. Sometimes up to 10,000 people crowded the compound of the church to hear him talk on all aspects of spiritual life in Egypt. Many in the audience were Muslims, curious to hear such a famous public orator.

These gatherings worried Sadat – they were beyond his control, try as he might to control the Coptic church through state subsidies for its new buildings. Shenouda was arrested, banned and sent into exile in the old monastic centre of Wadi Natroun in the western desert.

The siting of a new church provoked severe rioting in the al-Zawiyya al-Hamra district of Cairo in January 1981, and may have been one of the main causes of Sadat's crackdown on intellectuals and suspected opponents in September that year, a few weeks before his own murder.

The Copts claim that they were converted by St Mark when on a mission to Alexandria, which makes them one of the oldest of all Christian communities. It used to be said that the Copts were roughly one in ten of the population of Egypt, but this may be slightly less now.

Late one afternoon I went to see the Coptic Pope at the Patriarchate of St Mark's – a new-fangled establishment with a little too much concrete and pine panelling. I was ushered into his presence by a young monk who stooped and leered like a figure from Eisenstein's *Ivan the Terrible*. The Pope was all affability, while excusing himself for his bad English, which was punctitiously accurate.

First he wanted to explain the nature of Monophysitism – the Coptic view of the nature of Christ. Its key was the word 'logos', from the opening of the St John's Gospel: 'In the beginning was the Word, and the Word was with God, and the Word was God.' 'The two natures are completely united in a mysterious unity, not divinity nor humanity alone,' he explained. This led to a clash with the Church in Constantinople, who appointed new patriarchs to Alexandria after the Council of Chalcedon of 451 had decided against Monophysitis.

'Now we are beginning to move away from the fifth century and becoming far closer – the Copts and the Greek Orthodox, for instance – in our Christology. But I hope we may leave Greek theology in favour of a simple language to express our faith today.'

Co-operation with Muslims at the individual level was all to the good, but 'with the extremists there are big problems'. He saw himself as his community's protector, among them and not above them, a pastor with his flock – very much like a bishop of the Orthodox world. The fact that more Copts were turning to religion, more churches were being built, more priests and bishops ordained and elected was, perhaps, indicative of the Copts' increasing sense of beleaguerment.

Bestowed with the Pope's blessing, a commemorative felt-tip pen and a small leather cross from Wadi Natroun, I left for an encounter with a religious community of a very different kind. Not far from the Al-Azhar University they were preparing for a *zikar*, at the Al-Husayn Mosque. *Zikars* are dancing, chanting ceremonies, led by a cantor specially chosen for his voice to celebrate and offer adoration to a saint. The Al-Husayn Mosque is famous for its *zikars*, which have been held there for centuries.

Though of little architectural distinction the mosque contains one of the most significant shrines in all Islam – a sarcophagus believed to contain the head of Hussein the son of Ali, the fourth Caliph and the son-in-law of the Prophet. Together they are the most venerated figures of the Shi'ite sect, next to the Prophet himself. Ali was slain by his father's enemies at the battle of Karbala in Mesopotamia in 680 AD. His head was taken first to Askalon, and then in 1153 conveyed to Cairo in a green silk bag.

Since then the mosque has been a place of pilgrimage for Shi'ites, from Persia and Sudan – and for the performance of *zikars* by devout *fellahin* from the Delta.

Generally non-Muslims are not allowed to attend, but an obliging student doctor called Ali got permission for me to do so from one of the authorities. He spoke colourful, fractured English – and the more fractured his expressions, the more evident his fervour for Islam and the saint. The ceremony started with prayers, the men and boys of the congregation kneeling heads down in long rows. Then the responses began, slowly verbal exchanges, with little movement. Next came a chant and a response, accompanied by a slight swaying of the hips, a lurch forward onto one foot.

Gradually the chanting and movement gathered pace and the cries grew louder. Hands were clapped, torsos jerked and feet stomped. Male voices, from the piping treble of the boys to the bass rumble of the adults, filled the air. After much fervent chanting and swaying, the cantor ordered a break, and during an interval Dr Ali led me into a shuffling queue to honour the sarcophagus. Worshippers groaned and swooned in ecstacy, kissing, hugging and stroking the brass tops and balustrades round the said in a trance. Ali was among the most fervid.

The sense of ecstatic devotion is part of the spiritual path – *tariqa* associated with Sufi cults. Sufism emphasises loving God, growing closer to feel at one with Him. The stress laid on the mystical, private devotion differentiates Sufi cults from the more political organisations of the Islamic revival like the Brotherhood and the Jamiat Islamiya which emphasise the authority and command of God through the Koran rather than devotion. However, it seems that even the *tariqa* cults have been taking a more political complexion.

After the adoration of the shrine, Ali joined the *zikar* in its final and most abandoned stage. By now the chanting seemed almost primeval. The men were swaying and thrusting out their hips in an almost erotic display, while uttering loud grunts. And then, in one final release of energy and ecstacy, the celebration came to a sudden stop.

Outside, under the starlight, Sudanese dancers whirled and cavorted to the rhythms of a small drum and a reed pipe – rituals of mystery and magic from the farthest reaches of the Nile.

Exactly the same scenes had been witnessed by Edward William Lane on a visit to the Al-Husayn Mosque in the 1830s. 'The darweeshes [as he called the worshippers] who formed the large ring now commenced their zikr, exclaiming over and over again, "Allah!" and at each exclamation bowing the head and body, and taking a step to the right, so that the whole ring moved rapidly round.'

Unlike Lane, I did not see the 'darweeshes' whirl, but what I did see was an Islamic fervour affecting Cairenes of every station – and one that might swell to overwhelming proportions.

Twelve: The Crescent and the Mountain – Syria and Lebanon

i Syria

At the airport they had not put out the welcome mat. In the past Damascus had been one of the great ports of the desert, a caravanserai on the pilgrim routes south to the holy cities of Mecca and Medina, and to Aqaba and the Red Sea. Welcome and hospitality had been extended without question to pilgrims and merchants, but now things were different. Foreigners arriving in the new Damascus require visas.

In this I had been victim of my trade. Journalists faced longish waits for the visas enabling them to work in Syria – among the most enclosed and enigmatic of the countries on the Mediterranean. In March 1986 the authorities proved particularly unforthcoming. I had planned to travel from Syria into Lebanon, and could not wait until the summer. I decided to chance it.

At the airport guardpost I breezily assured the officers in rusty French that I had applied for a visa in London (true) and had been told that it would be waiting for me at the airport customs office (elastically true). I was saved by the durability of Ottoman bureaucracy. For nearly two hours the guards shuffled through hand-written files full of applications, visa slips and rejections, before eventually waving me through with, 'You want to travel to Syria – you take tourist visa, go.' I was in, but at a price. I was there as a tourist, not as a travelling writer, and certainly not as someone entitled to work.

Next day the man from the Interior Ministry told me I had broken an unwritten rule. 'You say you are writing a book? But we know you are a journalist. You mean journalists like you write books? That makes things difficult.' He then explained that, as a journalist, my application would have to be passed by at least five agencies or police and intelligence services, and somewhere along the line I had failed the test. No, I would not be allowed to meet any officials but was free to tour the country. He was as good as his word. An arrangement to meet the new Minister of Culture was cancelled at the hour of the appointment.

In their suspicion of the Western world, the Syrians know whom they like and like whom they know abroad. Journalists are invited, and often paid for, on the strict understanding they stick to the rules of the game. Their wariness reflects the tough, impenetrable nature of the regime of President Hafez al-Assad.

'In its make-up, Syria is one of the least Arab of the great Arab countries of today,' mused a journalist friend during my stay in Damascus. He was from the Greek Orthodox minority, and Syria is a mosaic of sects, tribes and peoples, including Bedouin, Kurds, Druze, Alawites, Circassians, Armenians and Jews. Before the First World War it had been part of the Ottoman Empire, whose grip on the provinces of Damascus, Tripoli, Beirut and Jordan had become progressively looser. As the Ottoman armies were driven back by Allenby, Damascus became the prize of Colonel T. E. Lawrence's Arab Revolt, though in fact Allenby's Australian troops reached and occupied Damascus before Lawrence's Arabs. The Emir Faisal of Hejaz established his capital there, though his kingdom turned out to be built on political sand. Faisal was tipped out by force in 1920 by the French, to whom the League of Nations awarded Syria as a mandate.

The French were deeply unpopular, and rioting and revolt broke out in 1925. They lost their hold in the Second World War when a Free French force backed by the British wrested Damascus from the Vichy powers. In 1945 Syria at last gained its independence.

The first years were chaotic, but in 1954 a new party emerged with a new slogan for the Arab world. Ba'athism – meaning 'Resurrection' – was the creation of two teachers, Michel Aflaq, a Greek Orthodox, and Salah Bitar, a Sunni Muslim, who had transferred their base from Lebanon to Damascus. Ba'athism stood for pan-Arab socialism – the unity of the Arab nation, the abolition of landlords and colonial controls, all summed up in the slogan 'Unity, Freedom and Socialism'.

The purity of Aflaq's message collided with Nasserism when Syria combined with Egypt in the United Arab Republic from 1958 to 1961. Two years later a coup produced the first Ba'athist government. The civil services and the armed forces were purged, and the government was dominated by Ba'athist military officers. Aflaq and his civilian supporters fled to Iraq where the Ba'athists had briefly won power in 1963, only to lose it and regain it in 1968. Aflaq died in Iraq in the 1980s – Bitar had been murdered in Paris – but by then Ba'athism had been submerged in the ruthless dictatorship and personality cult of Saddam Hussein.

In 1970 Syria fell to a bloodless coup led by General Hafez al-Assad, whose tightly-knit corps of Alawite officers dominated the army and air force. Regarded as heretics even by most Shi'ites, the Alawites are a sect within a sect, making up some 12 per cent of the Syrian population. Their homeland is in the hills overlooking the Mediterranean, running south of the port of Latakia. Under Assad they have dominated party, state, the armed forces, and internal security, often with uncompromising toughness. In the late 1980s Amnesty International claimed that some thirty forms of torture were in regular use in Syrian jails; in 1990 Middle East Watch, an American human rights group, estimated that the regime had been responsible for killing and torturing at least 10,000 citizens.

Assad himself was an extraordinary survivor, personally and politically. Before he took power Syria had suffered twenty-three coups since independence, three of them in one year. At home he survived attempts on his life, terrorist attacks and a full-scale revolt by Islamic fundamentalists. Abroad his troops and air force faced Israel twice, in 1973 and 1982, and were defeated with honour. But if dictatorships like that of Iraq are 'one bullet' regimes, in which an assassin's careful aim can trigger a revolution – Assad's Syria became a 'one heart attack' regime. In 1983 he apparently suffered a severe heart ailment, from which he made a slow and difficult recovery but despite his physical frailty Assad epitomised Syria's strength in the Arab world. If you could not make war against Israel without Egypt, King Abdullah of Jordan once said, you could not make peace without Syria.

Syria has had to face a daily drama of war and peace in its own backyard, in Lebanon. Romantics like to suggest that Lebanon is part of 'Greater Syria', a notion officially rejected by Assad's hard-headed counsellors. But Syria claims a special interest in Lebanon, a sensitive barrier of mountain and valley between Damascus and the Mediterranean. The prime irritant in relations with the West has been the Palestinians. As a senior partner in the community of Arab peoples, Syria is keenly aware of the plight of the Palestinians, on whose behalf she has had to go to war with Israel on four occasions. But tolerance and support do not stretch to all Palestinians, least of all those of Yasser Arafat's Fatah and the PLO.

When civil war engulfed Lebanon in 1975, much of the blame was put on the Fatah group. A year later Syria sent an expeditionary force to keep the peace, complete with its own cadre of Palestinians – the Palestinian Liberation Army, or PLA – claiming that they had been invited in by their allies in Lebanon. Eleven years later they repeated the manoeuvre, sinking deeper into the Lebanese quagmire. After savage fighting between the clients of the Shi'ite militias and guerrillas in the Palestinian camps, more than 7000 ground troops were sent into West Beirut for the first time. Within two years the Syrians had more than 40,000 men stationed in Lebanon with little prospect of withdrawal – a huge drain on manpower and funds.

Damascus played host to its own Palestinian clientele – the radicals who came to be known as the 'rejectionists'. They rejected any peace treaty or recognition of Israel, any underhand deals with the West and, initially at least, Yasser Arafat and PLO diplomacy. Some were clients of Assad, like the group called Saiqa. Others were provided with free board and lodging, like Nayef Hawatmi's DFLP (Democratic Front for the Liberation of Palestine) or Dr George Habash's Marxist PFLP (Popular Front for the Liberation of Palestine). Dr George was credited by the Israelis and Western agencies as the grand old man of Palestinian terrorism, and his group was said to be behind the first phase of hijackings, bombings and shootings in the late 1960s and early 1970s.

An offshoot of the PFLP, and PFLP General Command, also with offices in Syria, was rumoured to have been behind the blowing up of a Pan Am 747 airliner over Lockerbie in Scotland in December 1988. Its leader, Ahmad Jabril, an expert in delayed-action bombs, had served as a captain in the Syrian army.

Syria had been quarantined by the West for its support of the radicals. The Americans posted it high on the list of countries sponsoring terrorism, and the British took an even tougher line. In April 1986 a Jordanian, Nazar Hindawi, was arrested after his pregnant girlfriend had been discovered at London airport trying to take a ten-pound bomb, concealed by Hindawi in the false bottom of her case, aboard an El Al airliner bound for Tel Aviv. Only days before the Americans had attacked Libya, and this was evidently a reprisal. The girl was judged an innocent dupe, but on her arrest Hindawi fled to the Syrian ambassador in London. After the trial the ambassador was expelled and diplomatic ties cut.

But Syria slid slowly back into American favour. The moment of grace was when President Assad agreed to despatch far from token ground forces to back the alliance in Saudi Arabia against Saddam Hussein after Iraq's smash-and-grab raid on Kuwait in August 1990. Damascus needed Washington, not least because the friendship of Moscow under Gorbachev, preoccupied with the disintegration of his own political world, was now virtually worthless. Washington needed Damascus, too, for help against Iraq, and for dealing with the captors of Western hostages in Lebanon. Mrs Thatcher was more reluctant; she remembered Hindawi and Lockerbie. Her successor, John Major, relented and restored diplomatic links at the end of 1990.

President Assad's policy on Iraq was in part a very personal matter. His enmity with Saddam Hussein, and with Yasser Arafat, was deep, bitter and unswerving. In 1961 Saddam Hussein had been briefly a member of the Cairo Circle of Ba'athists in exile in Egypt, and had incurred the abiding suspicion of the Syrians. Assad believed Saddam to be a betrayer of the cause when the Ba'ath movement split and intellectuals like Aflaq took refuge in Baghdad. He neither forgave nor forgot. Throughout the Iran–Iraq War from 1980 to 1988 Syria was the only major Arab power to side consistently with Iran. It got little in return – some cheap oil for which it could not pay, and an annual gift of one million tons of fuel for the armed forces.

'Syria feels caught beween its two great Arab neighbours, Egypt and Iraq, the lands of the Pharaohs and the Assyrians, with their deep traditions,' mused a Christian journalist friend. Conditioning Syria's strategic choices, and its economic plight, are conditioned by one overwhelming fact of geography – the Fertile Crescent, that arc of verdant plain and hill stretching from ancient Mesopotamia, the estuaries of the Tigris and Euphrates in Iraq, through south-east Turkey and down Syria's coastland to Lebanon and Israel, the thin binding of abundance round the wastes of Syrian desert. Its broad swathes of green are studded with great cities and fortresses – Baghdad, Mosul, Dyarbakir, Aleppo, Hamah, Homs, Damascus. It was the genius of Salah al-Din – Saladin – to unite these centres and, as nearly as any man could, to unite the eastern world of the Arabs from Cairo to Baghdad. On the seaward flank of the crescent the crusaders, Saladin's foes, built their castles to guard the corridor by the sea to the Holy Land.

Only a third of Syria, in the Fertile Crescent and its fringes, is cultivated. What land there is has to support an increasingly youthful population. Between 1946 and 1986 the population had tripled to around 10.5 million, and by the end of the century the figure is expected to double again. Most Syrians live within sixty miles of the coast; more than half are city-dwellers who only a generation before had lived in villages. By 1990 well over half Syria's citizens were under fifteen, and had scarcely begun to multiply.

Those in work and with regular pay, however meagre, were expected to sustain large extended families. In the mid-1980s a junior officer in the army was reckoned to be keeping at least twelve adults on his salary, which was at the mercy of the fluctuating economy. The principal cash crop for export, cotton, diminished steadily in importance, accounting for under 10 per cent of all earnings by the mid-1980s. A big windfall was the discovery of substantial oil deposits near Dayr az Zawr in south-west Syria in 1984. Within five years the Omar field alone was producing well over 100 barrels of crude a day and Syria was potentially self-sufficient in oil and petroleum. The output of was tiny compared with that of Saudi Arabia, and in 1990 production had to be severely curtailed owing to problems of water contamination during extraction.

The harsh realities of daily life, the toughness of the regime, the vivid mosaic of religious and ethnic minorities, are classic ingredients of social tension and unrest. One afternoon I dropped into the hotel room of a friendly journalist in Damascus who was on a brief tour organised by the regime. Suddenly our conversation was punctuated by a sharp thud. 'That's a bomb, or an ammunition dump, or something,' I said. From the window I could see black smoke over a distant suburb of sand-coloured houses. 'I don't think it's anything important,' said my friend. 'You always hear bangs in Damascus – they never amount to anything.'

It did amount to something – and turned out to be one of my most curious and disturbing experiences as a wandering journalist. Within hours we learned that there had been a serious explosion. But we could get no details or official confirmation. Taxis and hire cars were not allowed to go near the area. The traditional skills of the journalist were useless, and the news blackout was total and uncompromising.

Some days later the official version began to emerge. A bomb had blown up a bus as it passed under a bridge in the afternoon rush hour. Some 60 people had been killed and about 100 injured. The television news reader making the announcement firmly put the blame on Iraqi subversion. And there on the screen was a bewildered young Arab who said that he had driven a truck packed with explosives across the desert from Baghdad. How he evaded border patrols and detection by security guards before detonating his lorry bomb at precisely the right moment, he did not explain, nor did he say who his accomplices were.

Exactly a month later further explosions took place in five different cities, and later that month a series of devices exploded on trains, buses and in public places, killing some 149 people. Pro-Iraqi or not, the bombs were probably the work of the hard-line religious opposition, the grumbling appendix of Assad's Syria.

Official recognition of my presence in Damascus may have been denied, but private hospitality was forthcoming. Somebody who was prepared to talk officially about Syria was Dr Afif Banassi, Director of the National Museum. 'Syria is a very old country – the name goes back to the sixth century BC,' he assured me briskly. Ancient Assyria stretched from the Euphrates to the coast. And of course the Phoenicians have given the Mediterranean people a common physiognomy, faces seen in their former colonies today – Tunis, Italy and Sicily, and Marseille. But the Mediterranean wasn't a very sure means of commerce for the Arabs. It was called Al Bahir, the wide or middle sea, because it was in the middle of so many Arab countries but even so the caravan routes overland were more reliable paths for trade. Now things are different. With Syria's new policy of becoming a tourist country, the Mediterranean has become more important. After all, our coast is not a bad advertisement.'

Despite its plain exterior, the museum itself is among the finest in the Levant. Bronze bulls and dogs have been rescued from Ugarit, where one of the oldest alphabets was discovered in 1933; they lie among pharaonic sphinxes, ornamental horses, the funeral monuments of Palmyra from about 200 AD, and records from Ur two thousand years before Christ. My eye was captured by the text of a treaty from the eighth century BC elaborately inscribed in the languages of the two parties.

Across the ages Syria and Damascus have been the victims of treaties and deals as well as wars. In 1076 Damascus was seized by the Seljuk Turks; in the middle of the thirteenth century the Mongols arrived, sacked the city and went away again, and in 1260 Syria became under the rule of the Egyptian Mamluks; Timur the Lame – Tamburlaine – and his Mongols returned to sack Damascus in 1401.

In 1516 Damascus fell to the Ottomans, and it remained part of their empire for four centuries. This did not prevent a fair amount of rearrangement by the tenants. The most significant sub-let was in 1830, when Mohammed Ali took Syria into what was virtually his independent kingdom of Egypt. Under him the foundations of modern Syria and Damascus were laid. Schools and factories were built, the cotton industry boosted, and railways extended Beirut, Haifa and Medina in the Hejaz. This made the city the natural choice for the Ottoman-German military headquarters in First World War, as they strove to prevent the British under Allenby advancing into Palestine.

One of the most significant diplomatic deals of the period was the Sykes-Picot Treaty of 1916 – a vivid testament to the meddlesome nature of European imperial policy in the Middle East. Cooked up between Sir Mark Sykes and Georges Picot, it aimed to carve up the eastern Ottoman Empire after the defeat of Turkey – with Persia and Mesopotamia going to the British, parts of Syria, the Lebanese coast and southern Turkey to the French and the Italians, and the north-east lands of the Causcasus to the Russians. Between the French and British zones would be two areas of French and British 'influence', including Palestine. The Sykes-Picot Treaty, with its secret clauses, was never implemented as such, but an extraordinary feature of it has survived; the line drawn by the French and English agents between the two spheres of influence is now the frontier between Syria and Jordan; and it is as straight and undeviating as a geometer's abstract design.

Best museum of all is old Damascus itself, with its souks and alleys, stalls and narrow streets. Even the Hejaz railway station is an ornate affair of wrought iron rococo from the last days of the Ottoman Empire. Old Damascus is one of the most pleasing capitals of the Levant in which to wander. As so often with repressive regimes, the visitor feels quite safe – the residents are pleasantly hospitable, or just ignore the foreigner. The souk has one of the famous antique markets of the Middle East, its cavernous shops are crammed with falconers' bells and drums, antique firearms, swords, samovars from the north, turquoise jewels, and Armenian rings and bangles in gold.

Some of the best shops are run by prominent families from the Jewish community, now some 5000 strong. The Jews rub along quite happily with their Christian and Muslim neighbours. From time to time Israel questions whether the Jews are free to leave Syria – with their property, of course. Several of their shops have world-wide reputations – one family does a good proportion of its business through showrooms in Kensington.

The covered market is flanked by a series of well-preserved columns and arches, which once guarded the forum of Roman Damascus but now look over a permanent car-boot sale – at the far end of which are the massive walls of the Omayyad mosque. The site was originally a pagan temple, later adapted by the Romans as a citadel and by the Byzantines, who built what may well have been the most magnificent Byzantine church in the Levant. The first caliphs of the Omayyad dynasty ordered its conversion to a mosque, but required no drastic structural alterations. In the first century of Islam the Omayyads proved remarkably tolerant of their Christian neighbours, and had none of the aggressive intolerance of the Abassid dynasty, who succeeded them in about 750 AD and transferred the caliphate to Baghdad.

The scale and proportions of the mosque suggest its kinship with the Church of the Nativity in Bethlehem, the Holy Sepulchre in Jerusalem and Hagia Sofia itself. Like them, it has had unwelcome guests. It was pillaged by the Mongols in 1260, and by Tamburlaine's army a century and a half later; but the greatest disaster was the fire of 1896, which destroyed nearly all the original Byzantine mosaics on the façade.

Its most striking quality was the sense of informal prayer and private meditation which filled the place. Nobody seemed disturbed by my walking round the colonnade of the great courtyard watching those at prayer, indeed, one or two of the worshippers quietly bid me welcome.

A street or two away from the Omayyad Mosque, in leafy seclusion, stands a small sanctuary which, though little advertised, attracts a steady stream of visitors paying their respects. In a twilight of candles, in the traditional green-covered catafalque of Islam, lie the earthly remains of Salah al-Din, the hero of the Arab world, who died in Damascus in 1193. Salah al-Din, the captor of Jerusalem, was half Kurdish, but for the Arabs he is their greatest military genius, who nearly made them one nation.

Close by a street weaves and undulates under the shadow of the old houses crowding in on either side. In this modest setting, it is claimed, the destiny of Christianity was cast, for it is said to be the street called Strait, where the newly-converted St Paul lodged after he had been blinded by a great light on the road to Damascus.

Since there was no welcoming light on the road to officialdom in Damascus, and the Palestinian rejectionist groups were rejecting casual callers, I decided to leave town and travel the Fertile Crescent to the Mediterranean shore. My visa said I was a tourist, so a tourist I would be.

The usual system is to hire a taxi, strike a deal and bargain all the way to journey's end. Herds of taxis gather round most of the big hotels like camels at an oasis. Many of the drivers fit that well-known phrase of 'being known to the police', indeed, I suspect that a number *are* police, associates of the Mukhabarat intelligence or their paid informants. My friend Tony the Orthodox journalist had tried his best to get me a French-speaking driver but instead I got someone who had only approximate French tourist-speak.

Nor did he know anything of the history of his country – or if he did, he kept his secret well.

The first call, a few dozen miles north of Damascus, was at a village called Ma'aloula, tucked into an outcrop of the anti-Lebanon mountains. Layers of sandstone houses were pinned to the rocks – among them several churches. Every Christmas articles about the village appear in the holiday editions of the European and American press, because this is one of the very few places where the people still speak a form of Aramaic, the language of Jesus of Nazareth. Once the language of all Syria and beyond, it is now little more than a dialect. The two main churches are rivals – Greek Catholic and Greek Orthodox – but provide a round of worship, prayer and votive candles for the desultory stream of pilgrims and sightseers. Behind the escarpment hides a convent, on the site of which an early female saint had been martyred. But according to the red spray-paint on the rocks nearby, it was not the meek that would inherit the earth, but proclaimed 'Manchester United Football Club Rules OK'.

At the crossroads by Homs we took a sharp turn into the desert, a dreary mud-brown waste dotted with spiky tufts of green. A Bedouin family, a camel and some absent-minded dogs and goats huddled round their tent, a simple black cloth slung over poles, the only shelter between the sea of sand and the steel grey dome of sky. It began to rain, a sullen, half-hearted drizzle which dissolved into steamy mist. The only features in the monotonous landscape were dunes and hillocks of sand, pimples erupting on the horizon. As the cloud cleared, aircraft glinted like sardines in the thin blue, swooping and soaring in simulated bombing raids across the desert wastes – MiG23 fighter-bombers, the eagles of Assad's air force.

Palmyra, the crossroads of the Syrian desert, is no ordinary oasis. The great ruins come fully into view as the road cuts through a barrier of dunes. To the south loom the sand-coloured blocks of the Temple of Bel, with its walls and huge gatehouse; to the north stretches the Roman city, endowed by Hadrian, the tourist emperor. From the nearest hill-top an Omayyad castle casts a watchful gaze.

Palmyra is the place of caravans. Here the overland routes from the Red Sea and the Gulf met the roads to the northern Mediterranean, and the Silk Road to the east. The fruits of the Mediterranean were exchanged for the silks, spices and jewels of the Orient. Here tribes congregated and became nations, and civilisations converged. The temples and theatres are fashioned in the styles of ancient Greece and Rome, inscriptions abound in ancient Aramaic, altars and statues invoke the deities of Babylon, of the early Hebrews, and of the old pagan civilisation of the Arabs.

Palmyra marks the outer edge of the Mediterranean world, where the lands of the olive, pomegranate, fig and grape merge into the desert – a frontier is marked by a profusion of decorative grapes and pomegranate seeds on the outer walls of the ruins and in the banqueting hall of the temple. They hang in almost neurotic abundance, as if their sculptors lived in fear of famine.

Such a strategic oasis was bound to become an important shrine, not least because it provided life-giving sustenance to passing caravans, slaking the thirst and stuffing the bellies of man and beast alike. Running water was always close to divinity, and Palmyra became a meeting place for pagan gods and goddesses. To begin with at least, worship focused on the sun, as it did at Heliopolis or at Baalbek. The top god at Palmyra was Bel, or Baal, a multiple deity who appears in shrines and temples all over this part of Syria and the Mediterranean coast.

The most remarkable of the Palmyra Bels was Malak-Bel. The Arabs seem to have translated him into She'a-alqum, 'the good and bountiful god who does not drink wine' and 'protects the people and accompanies them' – in other words, the god of the caravan. Malak-Bel was the lord of the magnificent temple which dominates Palmyra and its plain. Its vast banqueting hall and yard and the massive weight of the fortified gatehouse seem the epitome of permanence, yet its ornaments and inscriptions are powerful prayers for the protection of the caravan and the renewal of the fruits of the earth. In one relief the appeal is quite explicit where above a frieze of vines laden with grapes a procession of men plod wearily across the desert, leading their camels and horses.

The carvings of grapes and pomegranates, the egg and dart patterns, and the reel and bead decoration on the mammoth lintel of the temple gate are all in the classical Graeco-Roman style, which is not surprising, for much of what remains is late-Roman, from the brief period when Palmyra was the mistress of the Roman East, and a kingdom in its own right. Its period of glory began when the desert kingdom of Petra to the south was defeated and perished in 105 AD. Either the Emperor Septimius or his son Caracalla gave it privileges which made it the equal of the great Italian cities under the *Ius Italica*, or the law of privilege.

The Romans needed Palmyra as a buffer against the Parthians to the east. The Palmyrenes were aware of their strategic importance, but then became too independent. In the middle of the third century AD the desert kingdom was ruled by the remarkable Queen Zenobia. Calling herself 'Augusta', she began to mint her own coinage, from which she omitted the head of the real 'Augustus', the Emperor Aurelian. In the end the Emperor marched on Palmyra but deciding clemency was the best policy, executed only a few leading citizens and spared the rest. No sooner had he turned his back than the Palmyrenes rose again. Moving swiftly across Asia Minor, Aurelian took them by surprise, and massacred them in the autumn of 273 AD. Palmyra, the 'pearl of the desert', never regained its glory. Its reputation lived on with the fearsome Palmyrene archers, who were despatched to patrol the north of Britain.

In the evening the stones of the Roman streets and theatres turn from rose pink and orange to yellow. As the sun sank beyond the Omayyad castle, I walked the streets of the city endowed by Hadrian and Septim-

ius. By a pile of stones beyond the northern walls a shepherd was round-
ing up his shaggy black goats, whose aroma made up in intensity what
it lacked in fragrance. With the driver-guide's assistance we had a three-
way exchange of views on the weather in pidgin Palmyrene. We were
the only humanity in that astonishing desert scene. All day hardly a
foreign visitor had been sighted, and at the hotel a melancholy concierge
told me that the policy of the new touristic Syria had yet to reach
Palmyra. 'Politics is very bad for tourism,' he suggested. 'Even two sentences from our President are enough to keep them away for a very long
time.'

Recently the name of Palmyra has achieved a dubious fame in connection with the bloodiest episode of President Assad's rule, the suppression
and subsequent massacre of the Muslim Brotherhood in Hamah in February 1982 – a story that began with an attempt on the president's life in
June 1980. He had been waiting to welcome the President of Mali to
Damascus when Muslim Brothers are said to have fired shots and thrown
two grenades at him. A bodyguard smothered one of the grenades, while
the President kicked away the other.

Assad took his revenge in Palmyra. Squads of troops from the Defence
Companies, the regime's iron guard commanded by the president's
younger brother Rifaat, were despatched to the top security jail in
Tadmor, the biblical name for Palmyra, where they killed all the Muslim
Brotherhood prisoners they could find. Both Amnesty International and
Middle East Watch claim that at least 500, and possibly 1000 died.

The Brotherhood was not cowed, however, and continued their
attacks throughout the Fertile Crescent in 1981, with more than 200
killed in fighting in Hamah in April. The regime accused the Brothers
of setting off a bomb in Damascus in November, which killed more than
60 and injured 150. The score would be settled at Hamah, which since
the days of the French mandate had been a haven for dissidents of all
stripes, from freemasons and socialists to reactionary feudal landlords. It
also had a reputation for piety, and when the message of the Muslim
Brotherhood reached Syria from Egypt in 1930, Hamah became one of
its main centres. Assad had decided to crush the Brotherhood in its
stronghold.

But when 500 soldiers of Rifaat's Defence Companies moved against
Hamah in February 1982, they appear to have been taken completely by
surprise. Until then the security forces had been faced by well-organised
guerrilla tactics, including ambushes, kidnaps and hit-and-run attacks;
now they faced a full-scale insurrection. Banners appeared proclaiming
the 'Free Islamic Republic of Hamah'. After the first wave of troops and

police had been driven back, Rifaat ordered up the 47th Armoured Brigade, later joined by the 21st Mechanised Brigade. About 1000 Muslim militants faced nearly 30,000 soldiers. The Syrian army used area bombardments by tank, artillery and rockets, flattening apartment blocks and devastating the old quarters. In three weeks thousands died in the fighting and the ensuing 'mopping-up' operation. Numbers are impossible to establish. No reporter got into the town that month, and much of the subsequent information comes from the travellers' tales of refugees, and the speculation of diplomats. The Brotherhood later published their own fairly restrained account in Egypt.

The regime's estimates of the numbers killed are the lowest – one or two thousand. After exhaustive investigations, Amnesty and Middle East Watch gave a cautious estimate of about 10,000. The damage to the fabric of the city was still visible years later; for Syria and its military regime the Hamah chapter became one that refused to close.

From Palmyra we cut back across the desert to Hamah – much to the reluctance of the driver, whose performance became more muted than ever. The place seemed shut in on itself. Once poets had extolled the beauties of the gardens running down to the Orontes, the creak and gurgle of the huge water-wheels or *norias* churning in lazy harmony; its narrow streets and markets were once adorned by some of Syria's finest Turkish houses, mysterious with heavy casemates, shutters and balconies. My abiding impression was of hastily flattened areas, like bomb sites. As we drove gingerly into the city the silence was tangible. The mosque of Nur al-Din, Salah al-Din's uncle, was nowhere to be seen and is no longer advertised. In the main street the men and women were like sleep-walkers, gazing distractedly into space. A woman strode by, her head entirely masked by a black veil drawn tightly into her collar – the badge of the ultra-observant Muslim. Her face was completely closed to the world; just as her city, the once fair Hamah, seemed to be hiding behind the shutters of its sorrow.

I had caught a faint intimation of Hamah's lost delights on a brief stop in the neighbouring city of Homs, some thirty miles to the south. Homs is more industrial than Hamah, and has a purposeful, tough appearance; but it was Friday, the day of prayer, and before the Great Mosque we encountered a joyous scene. In the cool, aqueous green light of the prayer hall, the congregation was engaged in private worship or listening to the Friday sermon. Bedouin women clothed in gorgeous green dresses emerged from the chapels with their small families. They were country people, with sharp faces, brocaded caps and bangles of gold coins, copies of English sovereigns, in their hair. As they laid our their picnics on the grass in front of the mosque, they made final preparations for what was evidently the highlight of the week or the month. And then, with a quick, graceful movement, they removed their sumptuous over-dresses, revealing their work garments underneath. Flowing skirts of red and emerald silk were deftly packed away, as though they were so much tentage to be stowed before a journey across the desert.

The plain of rich farmland north of Hamah is overlooked from a hilly spur by the village and encampment of Qalaat Shaizar. Known to the ancient Egyptians and called Caesarea by the Romans, it is today the quintessential crumbling ruin. But Shaizar recalls one of the most engaging of all those associated with the Crusades. Its lord in the twelfth century was one Usamah Ibn-Munqidh who, in accordance with the chivalrous norms of his day, wrote his memoirs – translated into English as *The Memoirs of an Arab-Syrian Gentleman and Warrior in the Time of the Crusades* – and dedicated them to his commander, Saladin. Usamah was a charming snob, and knew he was superior in arms, in the chase and in manners to the often eccentric and unkempt Latin Christian knights who were his neighbours, whom he regarded with mild affection. His memoirs are full of tall tales about hunting in the plains round Aleppo and Shaizar. He admired his father's prowess with hawk and hound, and gives a vivid portrait of tackling lions, cheetahs and leopards in the fields about his beloved Shaizar.

The walls of the castle follow the line of the hill as it makes a dog-leg round a deep valley gouged by the river. On an early spring day it is a place of unhurried tranquillity, impregnable on its steep hillside. Both the castle and the village were shattered by an earthquake in 1157. By then Usamah held a high position in Saladin's court, and as a teacher of rhetoric at the Academy in Damascus. For reasons not fully explained, he fell from grace in his old age; rumour had it that he was too close to the Shi'ite tribes for Saladin's orthodox Sunni outlook.

Down by the bridge over the Orontes, the women of Shaizar were beating their washing on the river banks – a ritual unaltered since Usamah's day. Farther along the road, at Qalaat el Moudiq, we encountered another unchanging scene that can change little. Donkeys and mules were being loaded with sacks of flour at a mill, supervised and whipped on by an energetic Bedouin mother in a long dress of dark damson. They may not have been slaves any longer, but the women were doing all the work. At Moudiq the walls and courtyards of the castle had been breached by a fair-sized town, spilling down the hillside.

In the fields beyond the castle-town a line of columns, grooved like twisted barley sugar in a sea of waving wheat, marks the old Roman city

of Apamée. It is thought to have been one of the principal shrines for
the worship of Adonis, the dying man-god whose cult imbued these
hills. It then became the home of the early Maronites, now the leading
Christian community of Lebanon, who hold a particular belief in the
dying man and God in the nature of Christ. The combination of human
sacrifice and divine mission seem inherent in Maronites' role in Lebanon's bitter and bloody destiny.

The most impressive reminder of Saladin's power is the citadel which
dominates the old town at Aleppo – the northernmost point of our
journey through the Fertile Crescent. It is a solid cube of granite,
secure behind a triple barbican and an exaggeratedly deep glacis or
banked lower wall. The coffered and finely tooled timber ceilings of its
chambers and halls hang like canopies of heavy cloth, freshly gilded
for the meetings of the local command which are still held in the
castle.

Aleppo is hardly an Arab city at all, with its Kurds and Armenians,
it looks towards Anatolia and Asia. The town has a weary, dilapidated
appearance. Baron's Hotel – famous for its anglophile proprietor, host
to T. E. Lawrence, Agatha Christie and every representative of *The
Times*, real or imaginary, to pass that way – seems at its last gasp. Near
the citadel a huge space covered with broken concrete and rubble suggests
that a bout drastic town planning is on its way. The souk seems to be
sliding into desuetude and decay. In a house of many balconies, women
sew frenetically, men weld and madly hammer. An Armenian provides
a meal of many small dishes, delicious in its simplicity and the warmth
of the hospitality. In ten years the population of Aleppo had doubled to
two and a half million. Like so much in Syria, it is adrift on the surging
tide of demography.

From Aleppo we headed for the Mediterranean coast. The road winds
through deep hillsides and farmlands and orchards of rich red soil, now
carpeted by the first cherry blossom of spring. The villages area a delight,
but the coast itself is something of a disappointment. The ports of Tartus
and Latakia, which once sheltered the fleets of Rome, the merchants of
Venice and the mercenary transports of the Crusaders, are now modern
industrial cities, dulled by the conformity of container transport technology. They provide Syria with commercial lifelines and their prosperity
is evident in the burgeoning suburbs of utility apartment blocks.

Skirting Latakia, we saw a half-completed concrete bowl – the stadium
which was to be the centre piece of the Mediterranean Games that
autumn, another item in Syria's touristic offensive. A few miles farther

on, the small town of Ras Shamra holds one of the real surprises and puzzles of the Mediterranean story.

In 1929 a French archaeologist, Claude Schaeffer, began a series of digs, which are still incomplete, in the fields beyond the secondary school. At Ugarit, as the Ras Shamra site is now known, he found not one city but four, laid out on top of the other, the first dating from around 7000 BC, and the last destroyed by the ravagings of the Sea Peoples in about 1200 BC.

Wonderful pottery and jewellery were discovered, evidence that a highly sophisticated kingdom flourished here at a time when Phoenician cities like Tyre and Byblos, farther to the south, were in their first bloom. The kings of Ugarit traded with the Mycenaeans of Crete, the Egyptian Pharaohs, and the empire of the Hittites. A fragment of porcelain shows a hawk-faced goddess, with a wild head-dress and improvised skirt in coarse matting, her torso and face an odd mixture of Indian and Aegean. She is Astarte-Asherah, the buxom goddess of fertility, the female counterpart of Adonis, whose namesakes beguiled the worshippers at Palmyra and Carthage. But once again Bel, in partnership now with Dagon as the deities of spring and autumn, appears to have been the chief god in Ugarit – the largest of the temples so far uncovered is his.

The tour of the site was conducted by Mr Abd'El-Hak, a chatty and very friendly Palestinian. He began by explaining in his idiosyncratic but accurate English the genius of the royal builders of the last kingdom at Ugarit. They worked to a rule of seven, using no mortar between the stones, but shaving and shaping the blocks of stone so they locked like a jigsaw puzzle. But the greatest technical achievement, he suggested, was the plumbing. Running water was carried in stone pipes, which ran parallel to the drainage channels or, as he put it, 'the sewage canal'.

Fresh water was drawn from 150 wells in the city, which kept the surrounding fields irrigated long after the kings and merchants and marauders had departed. The fields of Ugarit glisten now with thick grass, aniseed clumps, star flowers, poppies and cowslips; purple, crimson and white blossoms stud the carpet of heavy green, while pale blooms of cyclamen warily test the daylight from behind the stones of a 'sewage canal'.

Conclusive proof of the power of the kings of Ugarit was found in the library off the entrance vestibule to the palace complex. In it were the remains of a diplomatic archive; and with them was our first complete record of an alphabet. The Ugarit alphabet remains something of a mystery. It stands on its own, since the Phoenicians of Tyre and Byblos are conjectured to have derived their semitic alphabet from eleswhere.

In the Ugarit library the characters of the consonants are tabulated on small clay discs or cylinders for the instruction of the royal clerks and scribes. All the characters are formations of consonants – the vowels are missing, and have to be supplied by the reader.

As I paid for and pocketed a few of the reproduction clay discs – they make the most pleasing of all Mediterranean souvenirs – Mr Abd'El-Hak told me his story, an eloquent lament of the Palestinian exile. He and his family had been forced to leave their homes in Haifa in 1949, the year after Israel achieved independence, but 'I would go back to Haifa tomorrow if I could'. I have encountered a few who expressed so lucidly the agony and despair of the Palestinian diaspora. As a parting gesture he offered me a huge bunch of aniseed – 'the symbol of Palestine and the name of this place, Shamra means aniseed, give it to my friends in Damascus' – before locking me in a firm embrace and showering kisses on both my cheeks.

One of the most puzzling aspects of Ugarit is why it should be regarded as a sideshow to the Phoenicians. According to M. Gabriel Saadé, 'They were Canaanites, not Phoenicians – that name was given them by the conquering imperialist Greeks,' and so they have been shunned by main-stream archaeologists. Monsieur Saadé had been educated by the French during the mandate, and his French was mellifluously perfect. His library in Latakia was his pride and joy, his passion and defence against an increasingly alien world.

The jewel of his collection was his bibliography of Western travellers on the coasts of the Levant from the earliest times, in which he had listed more than 2000 works. His love of all things French made his unrivalled favourite the sagacious Comte de Volney, who published his *Travels through Syria and Egypt* in 1787.

In a chapter entitled 'Of the Manners and Characters of the Inhabitants of Syria', the count observes dryly that 'In such a country, where the subject is perpetually watched by a despoiling government, he must assume a serious countenance for the same reason that he wears ragged clothes, and makes a public parade of eating cheese and olives . . .' He might have been writing for today.

The road from the coast to Qardaha in the hills follows the count's prescriptions against self-advertisement, though as a new double-lane highway generously topped with tarmacadam, it would not appear in any of the itineraries in M. Saadé's library. The road is the only remarkable feature of the town, where the houses are camouflaged with vines and the blossom of almond, apple and cherry in the spring. This is the country of the Alawites, most private of Muslim sects, and Qardaha is the birthplace of their most famous modern son, Hafez al-Assad. As befits both the man and his regime, Qardaha refuses to acknowledge presidential patronage in the form of vulgar statues or empty palaces. The streets themselves are the image of the new Syria – they brim to overflowing with children in their regulation school smocks and sashes.

Of all the visitors to this coast catalogued in M. Saadé's library the most showy must have been the Latin Crusaders. They came, they saw, they built. The best of what they built still stands in the string of castles and forts that stretches from Dalmatia and the Peloponnese to Acre, Asqelon and Jerusalem itself. The finest of all the keeps to guard the way to the Holy Land is Krak des Chevaliers, on Syria's southern border. I had long been prepared to be disappointed by Krak. The French authorities during the Syrian mandate, or so I had been told, had fallen for the Disneyland school of restoration, like Evans' busy reworking of Knossos or the fussy resurrection of medieval Carcassonne, leaving little to the imagination. At Krak they had even poured hundreds of cubic tons of concrete into the courtyards and towers to keep them standing. They had expelled the village encamped inside the walls, which had become instead a rambling shanty town, slithering down the hill below the main rampart.

And yet, for all its heavy-handed restoration, Krak remains a mystery. What was it really for? Was it a garrison, a watchtower, or some grand hunting palace for one of Usamah's like-minded Christian neighbours? Though well furnished with bed-chambers, chapels and cellarage, its plumbing and stabling are too restricted for all but the smallest armies. Most probably it was an outpost, the Alamo of one of the orders of martial monks on one of Christendom's most strategic frontiers.

The magic of the place is its position. It is like a great white ship, soaring above the green hills and ploughed fields of gleaming red soil. It seems unreal, suspended between heaven and earth as it looks south into another land of unreality – Lebanon.

ii Unhistoric Journey

The road from Damascus to Beirut is not one of the great highways of history – indeed much of it is less than a hundred years old. Most of the traffic – the caravans, the pilgrims, the invading armies – took the north-south route by the mountains of Lebanon and Mount Hermon, down the valley of Bekaa and along the coastal plain. Only when Beirut became a cultural and commercial centre in the middle of the last century did a major road across the mountains to Damascus become a necessity. Works began in 1860, a year which had seen 11,000 Christians killed in a mountain war with the Druze tribesmen, and was improved by French military engineers in the 1930s. The road across the mountains and the Bekaa is still one of the great journeys of the Mediterranean world.

The journey from Damascus should take under three hours, but much depends on the state of hostilities round the Lebanese capital and the number of roadblocks on the way. During the heaviest bombardments from the mountains the roads from the sea are choked with refugees, and it can take the best part of a day to reach to the Syrian border.

A new generation of highwaymen and footpads present a further hazard. By mid-1986 the kidnapping craze in Beirut had become less discriminating than ever before, and freelance militias and gangs hungry for publicity and money would grab anyone worth a ransom. Many journalist friends, especially those with young families, had fled to Cyprus and Cairo. Some noisy exceptions remained, parading their bravura or foolhardiness.

By the spring of 1986, the Associated Press Bureau chief Terry Anderson had been held for a year, and Michel Seurat, the French writer and expert on the Middle East had been hideously murdered in captivity. A year or so before Malcolm Kerr, the saintly President of the American University Beirut, still one of the greatest centres of liberal education of the Levant, had been shot dead on his campus. The Beirut that had been the intellectual centre of the eastern Mediterranean for more than half a century was becoming little more than a mirage.

I decided to cadge a lift from a Lebanese who only spoke Arabic, so we had to converse in sign language. It was one of those limpid days of early spring, when the air was so thin that it hardly existed. The snowy cap of Hermon seemed only a few miles down the road – as it always does, whether viewed from Damascus, Galilee or South Lebanon. As we chugged towards the crossing-point, the six-lane highway, built for tanks rather than mortals, was empty apart from the occasional military convoy crawling with a snail's reluctance towards Lebanon. In the fields a pair of diminutive donkeys laboured to break the hard ochre soil with primitive scratch ploughs.

At the first frontier we underwent a delicate balancing act with my two passports. In one I was leaving Syria as tourist, while the other allowed me to enter Lebanon as a journalist. The Syrian customs guards were as baffled as they had been at the airport two weeks before, but this time the driver sorted things out; the Syrians were glad to see the back of me. The border post on the Lebanese side was like a carnival, in which every other person was out to buy or sell something including a band of students from the American University of Beirut, waving bundles of bank notes and attempting some fast currency deals.

The road now crammed with all kinds of traffic – carts, large Fifties' American sedans, the ubiquitous Toyota truck. By the verges the stalls were full of spring vegetables and fruit, and the orchards were fountains of pale pink and white blossom. In the distance the minaret at Anjaar peered round a hillside; but of more immediate interest was the new Anjaar that had developed along the roadside, an almost entirely Armenian village which had become Beirut's biggest out-of-town department store. Many of the capital's television sets, washing-machines, freezers are said to be bought at Anjaar's discount houses, where the Armenians once more show their colours as one of the great trading notions in exile. The Armenians of Lebanon, some 120,000 strong in Beirut alone, are wealthier than their compatriots in Turkey, Soviet Armenia and Jerusalem, and are allied to the powerful and rich Armenian community in America, largely based in California.

From Anjaar the road crosses the floor of the Bekaa valley, the fertile corridor that runs south towards Tyre and the border with Israel. To the north, barely a dozen miles away, lay Baalbek with its Crusader castle and the majestic ruins of Heliopolis, the city and temples of the sun – and, of course, of Baal. I bitterly regretted not being able to visit Baalbek, but it was off limits for most Westerners, especially those with 'journalist' in their passports. The Crusader castle was the base for more than 1200 Revolutionary Guards despatched by Ayatollah Khomeini to help their Shi'ite brethren in Lebanon in 1982 – possibly the first Persian military expedition to the Mediterranean since the great campaigns of the early seventh century, just before the rise of Mohammed.

The Iranians promoted the rise of Hezbollah, 'the party of God'. It was better organised and more tightly-knit than its larger rival in the Shi'ite community, the Lebanese nationalist group, Amal. Like the militants of Egypt, it appears to employ an underground cell system, using a range of cover names – variants of 'Islamic Jihad' or the 'Struggle for the Oppressed of the World' – under which it raised kidnapping to an instrument of international politics. The hostages were a weapon against the West and its clients in the region, and a means of furthering Hezbollah's dream of establishing an Islamic regime on the Khomeini model in Lebanon.

We stopped for coffee, and the driver indicated I should stay in the car. The small fields of the Bekaa looked under-managed and unkempt, but in a muddy wadi a dozen large articulated lorries were parked side by side, loaded with cargos of what looked like brown and gold straw. This was the main cash crop – hashish for markets in Jordan, the Gulf and beyond.

We passed the neatly dug pits of Syrian anti-aircraft batteries and started to climb towards the Shouf, the main mountain chain of Lebanon. Roadblocks manned by Syrian soldiers in regulation fatigues gave way to roadblocks manned by youths in no identifiable uniform, this was militia country. Between the umbrella pines and the olive groves the snow-capped Mount Hermon shone like a beacon. Banners in the villages proclaimed this to be the land of the Druze, or rather the militia of the Progressive Socialist Party (PSP). Most bore the twin portraits of its leader, Walid Jumblat, and his father, Kemal, murdered in 1977 – possibly by the Syrians, for showing an excess of Lebanese independence. Both looked astonishingly youthful and hairy.

The Druze are the most mysterious of Muslim sects, and many Muslims regard them heretics who hardly follow Islam at all. They follow the teachings of the Fatimid Kalif Al-Hakim, who rose to power in Cairo in the eleventh century. Their cult is quite esoteric, its full secrets vouchsafed only to its priests – splendid bearded figures with red and white turbans and black knee-breeches, who are believed to have done more than their share of fighting in the recent troubles. The Druze hold Jerusalem as their holy city as much as Mecca; less emphasis is placed on the figure of the Prophet than in other sects. The Druze are mountain people, blue-eyed and frequently very tall. They tend to strike bargains with the regime in power, for they are small in number – about 350,000 in Lebanon. In Israel, where they have a tenacious toehold round the Golan Heights, they provide border battalions for the Defence Forces; another important community lives in the mountain borders of Syria round Jabal-Druze, where they also contrive to live with the powers that be.

Beyond the crest of the mountains the scars of war became more frequent. Spacious villas have broken doors and windows and roofs punched in. By the time we reached Allay, on the high western ridge of the Shouf, every building had been smashed by shellfire, some destroyed utterly. Every pump in a petrol station was broken, twisted and burnt. The story is the same at Bamdun and Souk al Garb, both raked by artillery duels and mortars in the Shouf War of 1983 when the Druze repulsed the Maronite Christians, driving families from homes held for centuries round Allay on the mountains and at Damur on the coast.

Beirut now appeared, a monument of devastation, basking in the haze along the curving line of its beaches, the corniche and the port. Below us the main highway into town past the presidential palace was closed; it is in Maronite country, and on the wrong side of the tracks for the purpose of our journey. We turned down a mountain track, clogged with cars and lorries in single file, and then hit the coast.

Just outside the city two small harbours cut into the shoreline, symbols of Lebanon's unofficial economy, by which many of its people now survive. Little more than smugglers' coves, they were the bond-free ports of the Druze and Amal militia.

The road passes up towards the airport, both infamous landmarks in the civil war which has been running since 1975. This has been a prime site for kidnaps. A ragged mound of earth and masonry on the seaward perimeter marks the spot where 241 American Marines of the incongruously named Multinational peace-keeping Force (MNF) were killed when a Shi'ite suicide-bomber crashed his truck full of explosives into their compound in October 1983.

Most melancholy is the distant prospect of the Palestinian refugee camps behind their makeshift bastions of mud and concrete at Bourj al-Bourajni, and closer to town at Sabra and Chatila. I had seen them before in late 1983, a year after the Maronite militia had massacred hundreds of men, women and children under arc lights thoughtfully left burning by the Israeli army – a gruesome and ill-aimed revenge for the assassination of their warlord, Bashir Gemayel, ten days before he was due to assume his country's presidency. A year later they were still sad, silent places, despite the comfort and understanding of Italian troops, the most practical and intelligent of the four contingents despatched with the MNF. But the Italians went away, and the Palestinians were to see yet more terrible fighting about their camps, the worst at Bourj al-Bourajni in 1987.

The destruction of Beirut does not really strike home until you get right inside the city. Its sheer mindlessness takes the breath away. An apartment block here, half a street there, houses are reduced to stumps and shops to gutted caves, while youths barely in their teens tote guns and rocket launchers in sentry posts made of burnt-out cars and old bedding, or on balconies turned into sandbagged crows' nests.

iii Human Mosaic: Lebanon

Beirut has become its own metaphor, a self-parody even. The catalogue of mayhem, death and destruction over the past two decades is almost incomprehensible. Without a hint of irony, the PLO Chairman Yasser Arafat said in 1984 that 'If things go on as they are, Lebanon will become another Balkans.' To which the Italian novelist Umberto Eco replied, 'This is a distortion of language and reality. With the passing of every two popes, the odd archduke might have been murdered, but the Balkans at the turn of the century were paradise on earth compared with Lebanon today.'

The urge to destroy has been staggering. Beirut was one of the finest commercial ports on the Levantine coast; it is now a ruin, an echoing charnel house inhabited by rats. What the Lebanese and their Palestinian lodgers could not do to create misery for themselves was made up for by the Israelis' full-scale invasion in 1982, and by the occupation of swathes of the countryside and much of Beirut by the Syrian army. Both were infected by Lebanon's peculiar ability to turn victory into defeat.

The violence could sometimes be ludicrous and pitiful. In the spring of 1986 the height of recognition for any new militia setting up in West Beirut was to be allowed free food from the Commodore Hotel. One evening the lights in the main hall of the hotel went out. We were told that a new Lebanese Ba'athist splinter group had threatened to lay siege to the place because they had been refused food from the kitchens. After a minute or so of silence the street outside was raked by a sustained volley of automatic weapons. 'They've shot the cook,' yelled a bellboy. More than a hundred shots had been fired, one of which had grazed the thigh of the chef in the Commodore's chinese restaurant. 'Perhaps they didn't like his chop suey,' commented a hard-bitten agency reporter as they dragged the wounded man to hospital.

In trying to understand the tangled web of Lebanon and its history, the outsider has to contend with two particular areas of confusion. The first is that the history and politics of Lebanon and its seventeen acknowledged minorities are so rich and convoluted, a chinese box of vendetta, rivalry, esoteric religion and tribal custom, that it is impossible to digest the whole story. The second is that Beirut has become the capital of the most narcissistic journalism. Correspondents write about Lebanon with unique possessiveness, as if it is exclusively their story which only they understand. In the tradition of William Howard Russell of *The Times*, first of the war reporters, they become the heroes of their own despatches.

The Beirut bores of the Eighties were the successors to the Vietnam junkies of the Sixties and Seventies.

The Lebanese of the cities are among the most Mediterranean of Mediterranean people – friendly, argumentative, shrewd, inventive and, at worst, bitterly vengeful. Their story is a characteristic Mediterranean muddle because every community is a minority, part of a mosaic of tribes, sects, families and nations. Outsiders have tried to exploit these tribal minorities drawn by greed and the wealth of the coastal cities, and of Beirut in particular.

To interpret the mosaic is, as the Italians say, to walk on mirrors. It requires expert assistance, and in my case it came from Kamal Salibi, of the American University Beirut, one of the most distinguished historians of the modern Middle East. He had lived the recent history of Lebanon as much as anyone – indeed, the printer carrying proofs of one of his books about the civil war had been shot dead by a sniper when he was crossing the green line between the warring factions of East and West Beirut. Salibi was a Lebanese Protestant by upbringing, which gave him an open and impartial attitude to all the main Muslim and Christian sects whom he taught in his university classes.

I had met him first in late 1983 – a time of dour festivity, with trashy streamers and plastic Santa Claus and Christmas trees doubling up as cedars of Lebanon hung between the lamps round Hamra Street. The night I arrived Shi'ite activists bombed a liquor store and delicatessen; it was said their protection money had not been paid on time. Round East Beirut huge placards displayed the portrait of Bashir Gemayel, the lost leader of the Maronites, who would return to redeem his people, like King Baldwin IX of Flanders or King Arthur. The death and resurrection and redemption of political and religious leaders was a theme close to Professor Salibi's heart.

When, two years later, he answered the door of his apartment overlooking the corniche and the sea, it was as if he had met only the day before. I asked him if he would tell me about the Lebanese mosaic, how it began and what its effects was. It was a tall order, but he began, almost without hesitation, one of the most brilliant discources on the Arab world and the Levant I have heard.

Kamal Salibi has written that

In the final analysis, history is not merely a search for knowledge. It is also a search for understanding; and the house of understanding has many mansions. As the mere story of the past, history can only have an antiquarian value, and as such can be left to the scholars. To be socially meaningful and useful, it has to be given relevant dimensions.

This is his creed. That he chose his metaphor from those words of the Bible ('In my Father's house are many mansions: if it were not so, I would have told you. I go to prepare a place for you') which open the Protestant funeral service can be no coincidence.

I have added to Kamal Salibi's discourse a rough chronology of events, culled from his and others writings. This is my work, and not his – a necessary safety warning, for in Lebanon as in so much of the Middle East, how history is interpreted can be the cause of war.

'The mosaic probably always existed,' he began, 'and it has not changed much since the rise of Christianity and the coming of Islam. Syria in general is broken into mountains, in the pockets of which live different tribes. Tribalism in the region is endemic. When the tribes divide into different religious sects, they are responding to politics.'

Tribalism is the key to his vision of Lebanon. Tribes have moved about the mountains and plains of Lebanon and Syria but have hardly changed their ethnic complexion in the last thousand years. 'In the fourth century AD there was a big reshuffle, with old and new tribes merging. Since then there has been no reshuffling of the pack – the tribes merely break into sects or, in the case of the Christians, into churches and communions' – of which there are nearly a dozen now in Lebanon.

Each tribe has produced its own myth, the most potent of which has been promoted by the Maronite Christians, who regard Mount Lebanon as their sacred mountain. They are the largest Christian community, and have dominated the state since it became independent in 1943. They claim unique status as Christian Arabs in a predominantly Muslim world. But, Salibi suggests, Maronites are not as exceptional, nor the Muslim Arabs as united, as either party likes to imagine. They are tribes, whose politics and religious beliefs vary according to the accidents of history and geography.

The Maronites have worked hard at nation-building, at the idea that a Lebanese nation has roots deep in the past, and that they are the custodians of the legacy. In the beginning, or very near to it, was the civilisation of Phoenicia, of Tyre, Sidon and Byblos. The Crusades brought the Maronites, who had migrated from Syria centuries before, into contact with the Church of Rome – a link that has been maintained ever since. (Maronite archers, incidentally, had a ferocious reputation in the Crusading armies.)

The big break came when Lebanon fell under Ottoman rule in 1516. The Maronites like to point to two local rulers who, they claim, became virtual monarchs of Lebanon. Fakhr al-Din Maan was the Druze lord of the Shouf, but came to rule most of what is Lebanon today. He made alliances with the Grand Duke of Tuscany, who wanted to buy Lebanese silk; his secret conversion to Christianity caused the Maronites to claim him as their own. His dynasty was succeeded by the Shihab, a prominent Sunni family of whom a part converted to Christianity. The most powerful of the Shihab lords was the last of the line, the Emir Bashir II; he threw in his lot with the Egyptian viceroy, the Albanian-Greek Mohammed Ali, who had appropriated Lebanon and Syria in the early nineteenth century, reinvigorating the silk and cotton businesses with his whirlwind modernisation programme. When Mohammed Ali withdrew from Lebanon in 1840, Bashir Shihab II fell with him.

Despite the claims that are made on their behalf, Fakhr al-Din and Bashir both remained vassals of the Ottoman Sultans, lords of the Ottoman *vilayets* of Lebanon, Beirut, Tripoli and the mountains. Under the Ottomans the warlords of the mountains dispensed their own justice, made their own deals, and fought their own feuds and wars. Their way of doing business was very like those of the mafia clans of Sicily, Corsica, Crete and southern Italy, and the mafia mentality is one of the most enduring features of Lebanon today in all parts of the community. As in Sicily, it depends on clan loyalty and blood ties, and a system of justice and retribution which is beyond the official authority.

In the sixteenth century, according to Salibi, the Druze communities in the mountains conducted their affairs very much like the Sicilian mafias. Secret courts supported those condemned in Ottoman courts, and demanded revenge; in 1711 the Shihab family defeated a rival clan in battle, and then divided with them the taxes collected by the Ottomans. In the eighteenth century most of Lebanon was in the grip of three clans – the Sunni Shihabs, the Druze Jumblats, and the Maronite Khazins.

The 1860s saw a major change. The reformed Ottoman sultanate of the Tanzimat tried to assert tighter controls. Beirut was expanding, and growing rich on cotton, silk and banking. A new wave of foreign interference began. For centuries ambassadors and consuls had roamed the eastern Mediterranean, meddling and exercising influence, but the consuls of the Great Powers in the mid-nineteenth century operated on a different scale, very often on their own initiatives. They dealt directly with the sects and the tribes, against the day when Ottoman power would finally disappear. For the sake of an old alliance, the French adopted the Maronites; the Russians adopted the Orthodox, so that amongst Beirut Orthodox families first names like Olga and Basil are not uncommon; and during the Shouf war in 1859–60 the British were adopted as protector by the Druze, a link which was to hold good throughout the civil war (Walid Jumblat has kept a well-appointed retreat in the West End of London). But the Druze offered only a small toehold for the British, who tried to persuade Orthodox Christians, and a few Maronites and Catholics, to convert to Protestantism.

American and British Protestant missionaries established a series of schools and, in 1866, the Syrian Protestant College, later renamed the American University Beirut. AUB still stands, only closing during the severest bombardments and disruptions of the civil war. A year or so after our conversation the risk of being shot or kidnapped on the campus were sufficiently serious for Kamal Salibi to beat a retreat to Amman for a few months. The AUB was part of the process whereby Beirut flourished as the centre of printing and publishing for the Arab world and the Middle East rivalling and usually surpassing Cairo in the annual output of new publications, and as a place in which foreign proconsuls, and spies, could learn Arabic among Arabs.

The French connection proved crucial for the Maronites, helping them to achieve their goal of an independent Lebanon, which would be largely run by them. Literary works celebrated notions of nationhood based on Phoenicia and the lands of the Cedars of Lebanon in the Old Testament; while the link with France had been established in the reign of Louis XIV, when Versailles appointed the Maronite Khazin family to be the French consuls in Beirut.

With the retreat and destruction of the Turkish armies in the First World War, the ties between France and the Maronites grew stronger; and the Maronites got their reward when France was granted a mandate over 'Greater Lebanon' at the Treaty of San Remo in 1920. In the Constitution of 1926 the Maronites, as the largest minority, were awarded the most important offices, and the Sunnis the second choices – an arrangement that continued when Lebanon was given its independence in 1943 after a wrangle between British-backed Lebanese and De Gaulle's Free French, following the earlier removal of the Vichy French authorities. The National Pact was an unwritten agreement, but it was the keystone to the new state – in theory it still held good throughout the civil war, though in the 1980s most ministers were conspicuous by their absence from their offices. The Pact held that the President should be a Christian (the first was an Orthodox, though his successors were all Maronite) and the Prime Minister a Sunni, with the Druze being awarded ministries in the cabinet. Only as an afterthought, in 1946, were the Shi'ites guaranteed the presidency of the parliament by right.

During the Fifties and Sixties the new state flourished. Its strength, and its Achilles' heel, was Beirut. It became the playground of the Middle East, the Christian coasts of East Beirut and Jounieh rivalling the Lido in Venice or the French Riviera. Playboys could ski on the slopes of Mount Lebanon in the morning, water-ski off the Corniche in the afternoon, and gamble the night away in the casinos. West Beirut spawned art galleries, cinemas and theatres. Friends who were students at AUB in the Sixties speak of its intellectual vigour and artistic freedom with misty eyes. It was an era of liberalism, and it was intensely secular.

In the cliché of the time, Lebanon was the 'Switzerland of the Middle East'. To compare a country with Switzerland seems like an invitation to disaster. Uruguay in the late Sixties was 'the Switzerland of South America', and like Lebanon its fame was based on banking, a fast buck, fun and gambling; it too was torn apart by terrorism, kidnapping and civil war.

But cosmopolitan and sophisticated as Beirut was, there was always, according to Salibi, 'a clash between the civic values of the city and the tribalism of the mountains'. In the end the mountain, with its clan loyalties and vendettas, proved stronger than the city, particularly when things started to go wrong.

An early warning of trouble came in 1958, as Camille Chamoun was coming to the end of his presidency. The whiff of civil war was in the air, with sporadic fighting in the city and the mountains. Chamoun was concerned about what the marriage between Syria and Nasser's Egypt in the United Arab Republic could mean for Lebanon. He accepted American gifts and friendship, but wanted security as well. When, in July, 1700 US Marines landed on the beaches in Beirut in what an onlooker described as 'the most unopposed landing in the history of amphibious warfare', they were handed ice-creams by girls in bikinis. But when the Marines returned twenty-five years later they faced a very different reception.

The flaws in the National Pact were evident even before the civil war finally erupted in 1975, according to Salibi. The French and the Maronites had concocted 'a state in which greater numbers had a vested interest outside or against the state than in it or for it.' The Pact was essentially a deal between the Maronites and the urban orthodox Sunni Muslims, on the assumption that these were the two biggest and most influential communities. It was a large assumption, because the last full census had been taken in 1932, so that all recent figures are guesses, or what the politicians and sociologists like to call 'projections'. In 1990 the statistical guides and international handbooks 'projected' Lebanon's population as about three million; in fact they hadn't the faintest idea, and were probably wildly inaccurate.

The Pact ignored the rate of growth among the Shi'ites – the 1932 census had described them as the third largest of the major divisions. However, the Shi'ites are the fastest growing of the sects and by the mid-1980s it was evident they were even more numerous than the Maronites. But the Maronites refused to accept this. When I put it to ex-President Chamoun in late 1983 – he was by then a formidably combative eighty-four – he told me that 'This is an assumption of which there is no proof. It is simply not true.' But the Shi'ites on the move from the countryside of south Lebanon and the Bekaa to swell the slums of south Beirut, their resentment and sense of injustice the most combustible ingredients in the exploding cocktail of the civil war.

As the state began to show the strain in the Sixties and Seventies, Lebanon became more its old tribal self, and the good-time playboy veneer of 'the Switzerland of the Middle East' became ever thinner. Private armies and militias grew in strength; the state tried tough tactics with its secret police apparatus, the Deuxième Bureau. It was the slow unravelling of a dream, of the nation that never was, but which the Maronites and their French allies had tried so hard to create.

The civil war brought different circles of conflict into play, like concentric ripples from a rock cast into a pond. The inner ripple was the fight between the Lebanese tribes themselves; next came the aggressive new lodgers, the Palestinians; beyond them were neighbours interested in keeping Lebanon quiet, Israel and Syria; finally, in the outer ring, the overseas powers and superpowers – France, the European Community, the USA and the Soviet Union.

The civil war began over the Palestinians in Lebanon – but whether they were catalyst or cause is still a matter of some debate. The Palestinians had lost their land for the second time in a generation when Israel took the West Bank, Jerusalem and Gaza in the 1967 Six Days' War. Their new liberation movement searched for a home. In 1970, after a month of bitter fighting ('Black September') in Amman, their forces were expelled from Jordan and they came to Lebanon – whose government had, after all, signed the Cairo Declaration of 1969 supporting the recovery of a Palestinian homeland.

For the Christian politicians and militia leaders, the Palestinians soon became the cuckoo in the nest. With their own militia, their own finances, their own army of guerrillas, they were effectively a state within a state. They were noisy cuckoos, too, throwing their weight around and attracting attention. From their southern bases they struck Israel with rocket attacks and hit-and-run raids across the border. Syria saw the Palestinians as a threat to the stability of their borders and their own clients and interests in Lebanon.

Fighting flared up after the murder of three Christian militia-men in Beirut. The Christians retaliated by ambushing a bus carrying Palestinians in the Ain el-Roumaneh district of Beirut on 13 April 1975, killing 27 passengers. Historians take this as the starting point of the war, which seemed at last to be drawing to a close in the autumn of 1990.

Earlier in 1975, in Sidon, the Lebanese army had fired on a crowd of demonstrating fishermen, killing the Sunni mayor, Marouf Saad. In the fighting that followed five soldiers and eleven civilians died. The incident made it clear that the Lebanese army was not impartial, that it was a tool of the Christian president and part of Lebanese tribal warfare. The Muslims would arm their own militias, like the Sunni guerrillas under Saeb Salem in Sidon, allying with the radicals of the Palestinian Rejectionist Front – who were beyond the control even of Arafat and the PLO.

The fighting caused alarm in neighbouring countries. Fearing that radical allies of the PLO would take Lebanon beyond their control, Damascus sent in its army under the guise of an international Arab Deterrent Force (ADF) in 1976, occupying the Bekaaa and parts of the mountains. Syria also began to arm militias who would toe the Damascus line – principally the Shi'ite militia, Amal. Those who displayed too much independence paid for it. The Druze leader, Kemal Jumblat, was ambushed and murdered on his way back to his mountain fastness in the Shouf in 1977. Despite the occasional gesture, Syrians have yet to withdraw from Lebanon. In 1986 they sent thousands of soldiers to 'pacify' West Beirut, and in 1990 they went into East Beirut with Lebanese army units to squash the rebellion of the renegade Maronite general Michel Aoun, with terrible reprisals.

Israel, too, decided on direct military action. Israeli settlements north of Galilee were coming under increasingly accurate fire from the Palestinians in southern Lebanon. Following a Palestinian attack in March 1978 on a bus near Haifa, in which thirty civilians died, armoured forces advanced to clear the country between the border and the Litani River. They, too, did not go away. In Beirut they allied themselves with the Christians and their militias – and in particular with the Phalange, later called the Lebanese Forces, of the Gemayel clan, which were to challenge then seize the apparatus of the Maronite state. In the south they created their own militia, the South Lebanese Army (SLA) under a renegade Christian officer who had been cashiered from the legitimate Lebanese army, Major Sa'ad Haddad. The SLA grew to be an integral part of Israeli strategic policy.

In 1982 Menachem Begin's Likud government decided to settle the Lebanon border question for good. How much Begin himself knew about the real objectives of the 'Peace for Galilee' campaign is not clear. It was planned by the hawkish Defence Minister, Ariel Sharon, a hero of the 1973 War, and the Chief of Staff of the armed forces, Lt-General Rafael Eitan, as a large-scale security operation to clear the Palestinians out of south Lebanon. In phrase of the day, the operation would 'stop the rockets raining on Kiryat Shmonah' – one of the northernmost settlements of Galilee.

An excuse was provided by the attempted assassination of the Israeli ambassador to London by members of Abu Nidal's Fatah Revolutionary Council, one of the most self-willed and violent of all Palestinian groups. Once the tanks had rolled north of the Litani River, it was clear this was no limited security operation but a full-scale invasion – only its planners had overlooked telling the Israeli cabinet the full details. The Israelis swept aside most of the Palestinian opposition, relying on firepower where it was needed. Sidon suffered massive bombardment from the air and ground, and many civilian lives were lost. Beirut was bombed from the air, with much of the wreckage still visible years later. Syrian air defence missile batteries in the Bekaa were knocked out in little more than a day.

If one includes the war of attrition between 1967 and 1973, this was, in effect, the fifth Arab-Israeli War, and its outcome was to be more equivocal. For the Israelis the problem was to hold on to its gains, populated as they were by enemy supporters and fickle allies. Israeli forces were to take as many years pulling back from Beirut to south of the Litani as they did weeks in getting there, losing as many men in the process from guerrilla attacks and suicide bombers as they had in the initial attack. As a victory 'Peace for Galilee' was less than total and it bred an increasingly bitter and brutalised army.

In Beirut the Israelis pinned their hopes on the Gemayel clan. The patriarch of the family was Pierre Gemayel, who had been so impressed by the Nazi spectacle at the Berlin Olympics in 1936 that he dressed and drilled his Phalange militia accordingly. At first he was a figure of fun, but in the 1970s his militia, also known as the Katai'b Party, was galvanised into an effective force by his younger son, Bashir. He bought or liquidated his enemies, directed the murder of Tony Franjieh, the son and heir of the most powerful family in Tripoli, and smashed the rival Tiger militia of the Chamoun clan. In the summer of 1982 he was elected President of Lebanon by Parliament, in the belief that he was the only Maronite tough enough to save the country.

Ten days before he was due to be sworn in as President, Bashir Gemayel was killed by a car bomb outside the Phalange party head-quarters in East Beirut. Amin Gemayel, his brother, was hurriedly chosen in his place. But the Phalange militiamen mourned their lost leader, and swore revenge.

In the cease-fire arrangements that summer the Palestinian 'fighters', as Arafat's rag-tag army in Lebanon was called, had been allowed to leave Beirut for foreign parts under international supervision. Maronite militiamen were convinced that Palestinian guerrillas had remained in Beirut and had been responsible for Bashir's death. In fact it is still far from clear who murdered their leader. A suspect was caught, but he was not sure who exactly had paid him and supplied the explosives.

One day in September Phalange guerrillas slipped into Sabra and Chatila, a poky shanty town of crumbling concrete boxes – standard housing for a Palestinian refugee camp – on a wedge of ground not far from the smarter boulevards of West Beirut. They butchered, knifed, machine-gunned and disembowelled every Palestinian man, woman and child in sight. Hundreds died, and it took nearly a day for the news to leak out. In charge of the death squads were two militia thugs, Samir Geagea and Eli Hobeikir, who later came to blows over Syria's involve-ment in a peace plan for Lebanon.

They had done their horrible work under the noses of the Israelis, who held a command post on a patch of high ground overlooking the camps. There was an outcry in Israel itself, forcing the eventual resig-nation of the Defence Minister, Ariel Sharon. It was initially claimed that the Israelis could have stopped the killing, but journalists on the spot produced evidence that the Israelis had let the militia thugs through to the camps.

For the Israelis it was a critical moment, when it became apparent that victory was less than complete, and that the tides of Lebanon were against them. As they withdrew to the south, they discovered that my enemy's enemy is only sometimes my friend and that the Palestinians' new enemy, the Shi'ite militias of Amal and Hezbollah, was also theirs.

As the Israelis started to pull back, the Americans and their allies of the Multinational Force – the French, the Italians and the British – came in to keep the peace and try to put the Lebanese state and army together again. In November 1983, they too became targets of the new enemy when a truck packed with explosives crashed into the compound of the US marine base by the airport, killing 241 soldiers, many in their bunks. Nearer town another bomb went off at the French barracks killing 59 paratroopers. Both suicide attacks had been organised by Shi'ite militias. A few months later the allies left and went their separate ways.

Once again, the principal victims were the Palestinian civilians in the refugee camps. Over the years their 'fighters' had incurred the wrath of the Maronites, the Israelis and the Shi'ite Amal militia. In 1976 the Tal Zataar camp, where 30,000 Palestinian and Shi'ite refugees lived in utmost squalor, was taken after a 53-day siege and torn asunder by members of the Chamoun Tigers and the Gemayel Phalange. Survivors, among them doctors and medical orderlies, were put up against walls and shot. Miraculously, in the 1982 Sabra and Chatila Massacre several hundred fled or hid and survived, but in 1986 and 1987 the largest of the Beirut camps, Bourj al-Bourajni, came under siege and bombardment from the Shi'ite Amal militia, who feared that the 'fighters' had returned to steal their turf in the southern suburbs of Beirut. The camp was on the edge of starvation, as relief convoys with food were turned back. Women ran the gauntlet of mortar and machine-gun fire to get water and the barest necessities from beyond the walls; inside a small and dedicated medical team, Britons and Canadians among them, did what they could to comfort the dying and mend terribly mangled bodies with ever diminishing supplies of drugs and instruments. Eventually the Syrians forced their clients in Amal to life the siege.

Farther south the big camps at Sidon and Tyre, Ein el Hilweh and Mieh Mieh, were subject to intermittent Israeli air attacks, reprisals for terrorist operations inside Israel itself. Unfortunately, reprisals fall on the innocent and guilty alike.

The 1980s saw era of the rise of the Shi'ite militias, Amal and Hezbollah, in the southern suburbs of Beirut. Kamal Salibi points to two strands in their development: an eternal sense of injustice and privation, and an adherence to a charismatic leadership which goes back to the family of the Prophet. Both Hezbollah and Amal were inspired by Bakr Sadr's Shi'ite school at Najaf in Iraq in the 1970s, where the Ayatollah Khomeini had taken refuge from 1963 until 1978, when he moved briefly to Paris before returning to Tehran. Bakr Sadr himself was to be hanged by Saddam Hussein for directing militant Shi'ites against the state in 1980.

Ayatollah Bakr Sadr's cousin was the partly Lebanese Imam Musa Sadr, who returned to southern Lebanon in the early Seventies to organise the Movement of the Deprived. This marked the beginning of Amal, an acronym which conveniently spelt the Arabic word for 'hope'. As the rural Shi'ites were forced to migrate from the country of the Bekaa and the south into Beirut itself, Amal became more active, and in the winter of 1983 their militias began to appear on the streets. By then the Imam Musa Sadr was no longer with them, most probably killed on a visit to Libya in 1978.

Amal demand a better and fairer deal for the Shi'ites in Lebanon. They are essentially nationalists, whereas Hezbollah ('the Party of God') is internationalist – 'They believe in carrying Islamic revolution all the way to Jerusalem,' says Salibi. Both are grass roots organisations – 'only in the case of Hezbollah the grass is thicker,' comments Salibi, implying they are the tougher and more durable party. Hezbollah's spiritual guide in Beirut has been the smoothly-spoken Sheikh Mohammed Hussein Fadlallah, another of Ayatollah Bakr Sadr's students.

Just as Assad's Syria became the armourer of Amal, the driving force behind Hezbollah has been Khomeini's Iran. Tehran's toughest Interior Minister, the cleric Ali Akbar Mohtashemi, appears to have been the link. The core of the activists were two families, the Mugnya and the Hamedi, who had been involved in Hezbollah's precursor, a group of militants called al Dawa al-Islamiya ('the Call of Islam'), founded in Iraq in 1968.

The Shi'ite groups brought new skills to the old techniques of kidnap, hijack and suicide car-bombs. Hezbollah were especially deadly. They kidnapped foreigners as a means of settling scores with the West, and car-bombed and rocketed those they regarded as invaders, such as the Multinational Force and the Israelis. Inevitably, Amal and Hezbollah clashed. In 1987 they fought in the suburbs of Beirut, and for years they have struggled for control of the villages of south Lebanon.

Both Amal and Hezbollah, explains Kamal Salibi, reveal the essence of Shi'ite belief. The Shi'ites make up about 15 per cent of the world's Islamic community, known as the *umma* – the deprived, the urban poor of Mesopotamia, Iran, Lebanon and the Afghanistan, who believe they have been wronged through the centuries. Theirs is an esoteric faith with a particular view of history understood only by them, and this allows them to dissemble, to conceal the truth from the enemy outsider.

Their founder, Ali, was a kinsman and son-in-law of the Prophet, and Shi'a means the party or following of Ali – whereas Sunni comes from the notion of *Sunna*, or 'path' based on the corpus of law and teachings from the sayings of the Prophet and his immediate circle, and the Koran. The Shi'a believe that Ali was cheated of the succession to the Prophet by the first three Caliphs. Although he was the fourth Caliph, he was murdered, and his son and successor Hussein was martyred at the battle of Karbala. Martyrdom, suffering and the expectation of retribution are fundamental Shi'ite beliefs. Pilgrimage to Karbala in Iraq is the major event of the Shi'ites of Najaf, and 'Ashura', the day of Ali's death, is marked by flagellants beating themselves raw with chains. Ali and Hussein were followed by a succession of Imams, 'God's representative on earth' and regarded as near-deities by extreme Shi'ite sects like the Alawites.

Some Shi'as the 'Severners' or Ismailis, of whom the Aga Khan is the principal leader today believe in the succession down to the seventh Imam, Isma'il ibn Ja'far; whereas 'Twelver' Shi'ites (Imami) believe in the succession down to Muhammad al Muntazzar, the twelfth Imam, who disappeared in 940 AD. The Twelvers believe he will return to earth as the saviour or *mahdi* at the end of the world. 'Until then, in the absence of the Imam,' observes Salibi, 'all state authority is illegitimate. There has never been a legitimate state since, but there are degrees of injustice. Some injustice is relative and tolerable, but some injustice is severe and must be fought to the death. Shi'ites are deeply attached to this view, and it is why they are prepared to blow themselves up when they attack the enemy.'

Lebanese Shi'ites are powerfully drawn to the idea of the vanished Imam who will return as their saviour. They, too have their own vanished leader in the Imam Musa Sadr who disappeared in Libya, and many believe his destiny is to return as rescuer. The martyr reborn is a potent belief shared by others in Lebanon, including the Maronites – who, Salibi observes, from the land in which of the worshippers of Adonis, the dying man-god reborn each spring, was worshipped.

The conflicts of Lebanon are not a sideshow. The term 'lebanisation' has entered the international vocabulary, signifying a mafia state in which militias and clans run their own operations for their own ends, ignoring the central power. Lebanon threatens to become the first mafia state, but not the last. The power of mafias and militias is growing throughout the Mediterranean.

Towards the end of our conversation Kamal Salibi offered a short explanation for the rise of fanatical religion in Lebanon and the Middle East: eschatology – doctrines of death and judgment, heaven and hell – has 'driven out all sense of ethics in religion'. The violent need to find identity in vengeance and salvation drives out all notions of tolerance and decency to humanity beyond the clan or tribe.

The Mountain

Above the bay by east Beirut and the port of Junieh the land rises lazily through hills clad with umbrella pines before soaring to the heights of Mount Lebanon. This the heart of Maronite country. Mount Lebanon is their refuge, their holy mountain. In the higher plateaus spring sparse clumps of cedars, symbols of eternal strength and the fairness of the land. It is to them that the beauty of the beloved is to be compared in the *Song of Songs*: 'His countenance is as Lebanon, excellent as the cedars.'

Some have called this region 'Marounistan', an enclave which could become a separate Christian statelet if the rest of Lebanon were to collapse into anarchy. Here too live the guardians of the Maronite soul. After an introductory phone call from Kamal Salibi I was invited to visit one of the most powerful Maronite clerics, credited with the most astute political brain of those in holy orders – Father Boulos Naaman, Father General and Secretary to the Lebanese Maronite Order.

Father Naaman enjoyed a close relationship to the Gemayel family – he had conducted the funeral rites for the murdered Bashir Gemayel – and was virtually the private chaplain to the Phalange and the Lebanese forces militia. He had been a political counsellor as well as spiritual guide to Bashir, and tried to play the same role to President Amin Gemayel when he succeeded Bashir. I wanted to see Father Naaman because of his formidable reputation as a power behind the throne – he was believed to have been the brains behind the Maronite-Israeli alliance. More than any gun-toting warlord or militia leader, he could take me to the heart of Maronite survival in modern Lebanon.

Arranging to see him was a complicated business. After crossing the green line between West and East Beirut, by now a snipers' playground, we were to go to the gates of the Patriarchate at Bkerké where Father Naaman's driver would meet me in his black Mercedes and take me to his offices in a priory farther along the hillside.

I was accompanied by Abed, a Sunni Muslim who drove for one of the broadcasting companies I was then working for. He was to be philosopher, guide and friend for the next ten days. He was a born survivor, with a generous spirit and a wonderfully oblique sense of humour.

Crossing the green line, we were both struck how busy and undamaged most of East Beirut seemed compared with the shambles and ruination of the West. Within three years East Beirut was to be as wrecked as the West in the marathon artillery duels between the Syrians and the Christians, and between rival Christians groups.

The ecclesiastical Mercedes was at the rendezvous on the dot and, with the sun a weak golden glow somewhere in the region of Cyprus, we hurtled down the mountain road to meet the monks.

I was greeted by Father Antoine at the door of what looked like a down-at-heel secondary school. It was in fact the headquarters of the Maronite Order, part seminary, part school and part dormitory for refugees. The hall was a waiting room to the ante-chambers of the great, where weeping mothers came to seek help, search for lost sons or find shelter and food. Father Naaman had urgent business with a brisk militia leader, kitted out in camouflage fatigues, thick-soled boots and woollen puttees, and then with a woman whose fears for her missing son had brought her to the point of collapse.

Father Antoine explained that the Maronite Order was the biggest of the religious communities on the Mountain and numbered about 500. Recruiting was good, and about a dozen applied to become novices each year. Numbers were very important to Father Antoine, as they are to nearly all Maronites. He said there were some eight million Maronites in the world, about one million of them in Lebanon – or at least, in the absence of a proper census, this was his 'projection'.

I was then ushered into the presence of Father Naaman, a thickset giant wearing a heavy pectoral cross – a talisman of his power and of the Maronite church militant. He offered a gruff, suspicious greeting; everything he told me reflected a brilliant mind locked into a permanent state of intellectual siege warfare, defending the Maronites, their mountain, and their Lebanon.

He began by explaining the origins of his church, on which he is the leading expert, with the Council of Chalcedon in 451 AD. Like the Copts, the Maronites took a particular view of Christ's nature, but unlike the Copts this did result in separation from the rest of the Church. But the Muslim invasions meant that 'geographical links with Rome were cut; we closed in on ourselves and retreated to our mountain' – this said with heavy emphasis, lest obvious parallels with the present be overlooked. Despite their close ties with Rome and France, the Maronites would always be Maronites, 'deeply attached to our autonomy and independence'.

The foundations of modern Lebanon had been laid down by the Maronites in partnership with the Druze – when they were not fighting each other. This equilibrium had been upset by the arrival of the Palestinians and the increasing 'Islamicisation' of Lebanon. By 1973 the Palestinians were quite evidently 'a state within a state'.

This had led to the arrival of the Syrians, ostensibly to defend the

Christians; but by 1977 they had begun the process of 'a complete Syrianisation' of Lebanon. This had come to obsess him, and was what the Maronites resistance particularly objected to. Matters had been further complicated by the arrival of the Israelis, with whom the Maronites were locked in a difficult alliance. 'But we never lost patience. We had the faith and the will to resist under the Turks – and the Syrians aren't the Turks.'

The most recent and difficult change, he added, almost as an afterthought, was fundamentalism – *integrisme*, as he called it with peculiar venom. His fear and loathing of the west and south of the city were almost physical; by staying at the Commodore Hotel I was well down the path of treachery.

Would Lebanon now disintegrate into separate Muslim and Christian cantons, a true parody of the Swiss Confederation on the Mediterranean? 'The National Pact of 1943 is at an end,' he rumbled, 'but not the Lebanese State. What we must seek is federalisation, decentralisation in its widest sense. That could even embrace Hezbollah.'

Although the Father and his allies in the militias seemed prepared to fight to the last, many Maronites had had enough of images of blood and sacrifice, and were leaving. Ecclesiastical property was being sold so that rich families could build havens in Cyprus, Paris or London, and even farther afield. Maronites were leaving Mount Lebanon, but Father Naaman was not disturbed. 'They will come back when we call,' he claimed.

The interview grew still more difficult as the sun sank into the sea behind the pines. The Father wanted to know the hidden political purpose behind my questions. 'Go back to West Beirut and your friends there, and don't come back,' he suddenly snapped.

Boulos Naaman and his supporters continued their anti-Syrian crusade in the years after our meeting, a remorseless trail of murder, ambush and artillery and rocket cannonade. The veteran Sunni Prime Minister, Rashid Karami, was blown up in his army helicopter in 1987; the militias divided over a Syrian peace plan and then fought each other. In his last days in office President Amin Gemayel, the family friend of Father Naaman and the monks, swore in the Lebanese army commander, General Michel Aoun, as acting president to defend the cause of a free Lebanon led by Christians against the Syrians. In October 1990, after eleven months of fighting which had destroyed much of East Beirut, Aoun was driven out of the presidential palace at Baabda in a single morning's cannonade. His forces surrendered and many were butchered by the Syrians, supported by Christian Lebanese who had once served the general. The civil war between the Christians cost thousands of lives.

A building close to Father Naaman's offices provided a small vignette of the years of civil war. A spartan set of dormitories, little more than a barracks, was the permanent home of some 800 refugee orphans – the Order then had over 2000 under its care, and within a couple of years would have twice as many. Most had come from villages of the Shouf smashed in the war with the Druze. The boys slept in one room – 300 of them, thin with close-shaved heads and hollow colourless cheeks. The boys were under the care of two older orphan girls who cooked and mended for them, and helped their lessons; the beds were stacked to the ceiling and jammed against every inch of wall.

Since it was dark, Father Naaman said I should not risk crossing to West Beirut in the dark, and that I should spend the night in Jounieh. Jounieh itself seemed subdued, though the lights were burning in some of the bars and nightspots, relics of the hedonist heaven of the coast. I thought I was the only guest in the hotel, but at breakfast I was flanked by seven Sicilians who discussed deals in their loud rasping dialect. I slunk away, not wishing to seem over-interested in their nefarious business, clearly an important component of the Christian enclave's unofficial economy.

Heading back towards the capital, the road crosses a small river, little more than stream – the Nahr el Kelb or Dog River. In the vines and bushes on either side are some twenty stones inscribed with the names of the powers and armies that have brought war and conquest to this place of coast for three and half thousand years. Among the earliest is Ramasses II of Egypt, shown sacrificing prisoners to his gods. Another, in ancient Babylonian, celebrates the victory of Nebuchadnezzar II, who destroyed the temple of Solomon and led the Israelites into captivity. Others record the armies of Alexander the Great and the Emperor Marcus Aurelius Caracalla; more recent stones mark Allenby's conquest of Palestine in 1918, the French capture of Damascus in 1920, and the 'liberation' of Lebanon by the Free French in 1941.

'We don't have leaders – our leader is a house,' a young Druze once told Kamal Salibi. 'When the Druze talk about their ruling house,' the professor explained, 'they mean just that – not a ruling dynasty or family, but a place, Mukhtara.' Mukhtara sits in the Shouf mountains south-west of Beirut, in the heart of Druze country. The chiefs of the Lebanese and Syrian Druze have been the Jumblat and the Arslan families, the principal tenants of Mukhtara; Walid Jumblat, the present chief, is decended from both. The house has had as turbulent a history as the families. In the last century the gambling debts of its occupants caused it to fall into disrepair, and it had to be rescued by Protestant missionaries, who used it as a school.

The Druze occupy the second mountain kingdom of Lebanon, a high-land canton that could survive in isolation like the Christian enclave of 'Marounistan'. Unlike the Maronites, the Druze make no claim to a majority stake in Lebanon – they know they are a minority, and quite a small one. Their game is survival, to maintaining an influential voice among the many in a united, tolerant, secular Lebanese state.

They are hill tribesmen, blue-eyed, much given to outrageous beards, with an eccentricity born of the religion by which they are identified. They combine wild romanticism and adherence to one of the strangest faiths of the Middle East with political shrewdness. They enjoy their reputation as experts in mountain warfare; they excel in the use of artillery, a notoriously difficult skill in such uneven terrain as the Shouf.

Their religion is based on the cult of Al-Hakim, the most celebrated and eccentric of the Fatimid Caliphs of Cairo. He was brilliant, precocious and unpredictable. He succeeded his father as a minor in 997 AD, but three years later took full authority after personally killing his tutor and guardian – so setting the pattern for the rest of his reign, which ended in 1021. He became less and less interested in the norms of Islam, ignoring the pilgrimage or Hajj, and even eating in the mosque during Ramadan. He smashed the Church of the holy Sepulchre in Jerusalem and banned alcohol, the eating of scaled fish and watercress, the playing of chess and the killing of dogs. Eventually he not only accepted the divinity of the Shi'ite Imams, but held that he himself was divine – a notion that was spread by a Persian missionary among the tribes of the Syrian mountains, so laying the foundations of the Druze religion.

He met his end walking in the Moqqattam hills outside Cairo. Some say he was murdered on orders from his sister, who knew she was next on the executioner's list. But for the Druze he 'disappeared', and will return as the redeemer at the end of the world.

The religion itself is esoteric, obscure to lay Druze and understood only by the *sheikhs* or clerics. It holds strictly to monotheism, the belief in one God, and while respecting the Koran believes that the ultimate revelation was to Al-Hakim, and not to Mohammed.

The Druze have lived by their own rules for nearly a thousand years. Their community councils and their private economy have run in parallel to whoever claimed authority in Beirut. Their parallel power, with its esoteric clan loyalties and religion, is that of a Lebanese mountain mafia. Their sense of family and of blood ties, and their equivocal attitude to the state, are characteristic of mafia societies. It is also an exclusive community. Since the early days proselytising has been forbidden – you are born a Druze, not made one.

On a brilliant Sunday in late March we drove up to Mukhtara. The valleys and ridges of the Shouf were as green as the hills of Tuscany, the roadside brilliant with poppies and lilac. Distant snow gleamed on Mount Hermon. In the village of el Kamal the *sheikhs* walked bow-legged on their black breeches, snow-white turbans with red crowns framing their grizzled features. A huge cross on the convent wall dominated the homely minaret of the little mosque. This was one of the last Christian villages in this part of the Shouf, and the birthplace of Camille Chamoun.

The house at Mukhtara has the domestic lines of a Scottish hunting lodge. A broad driveway sets off a homely exterior of wide windows and curling wrought-iron stairs, with just a dash of Art Nouveau about them. While a retainer was explaining that Walid Jumblat was not at home, I was buttonholed by a Druze student at the American University, who told me that 'Jumblat understands that there must be one Lebanon – he and Assad really understand the Middle East. If you start dividing Lebanon, the process will go on to infinity.'

Back down the road, the summer palace of Sheikh Bashir Shehab II – the virtually independent ruler who was overthrown in 1840 – was given over to a display of the life and achievements of Kemal Jumblat, Walid's father and founder of the Progressive Socialist Party (PSP), the Druze militia. In the courtyard stood a row of Russian T-34 tanks, the workhorses of the Red Army in the Second World War but now the heavy cavalry of the Druze. Inside documents and photographs revealed Jumblat – vegetarian, socialist and visionary – in the guise of world leader, hob-nobbing with Nehru, Nasser, Qadaffi, Dr George Habash, Arafat and Assad. His typically Druze display of idiosyncratic independence cost him his life in March 1977, ambushed by Syrian-paid gunmen on his way back to Mukhtara.

Though I was not to meet Walid Jumblat, I met his adviser Marawan Hamadi, who had served as a minister in the early 1980s. A brilliant journalist who had edited the French language paper *L'Orient du Jour*, Marawan was the brains of the PSP and the Druze's leading tactical thinker. His manner was as engaging as his talk was scintillating. In his smart leather jacket, he seemed more a product of Paris or New York, but was steeped in Druze logic. We met one afternoon in his study in the offices of the Greek Orthodox-owned daily *An Nahar*, close to the green line.

His family, Marawan declared, embodied the Lebanese mosaic. His father was Druze, his mother Catholic, and now he had a Sunni wife and an Orthodox brother-in-law. 'Once nobody talked about religion. Then belonging to one group or another became a badge of safe conduct. Now religion divides cousins. It really started in 1975 with the civil war. A few years earlier two children were interviewed by French TV. They were asked what religion they were, and they said "We don't know, we'll have to ask Mummy." Now it's on the tip of the tongue; it's a matter of survival.'

Though religion threatened to divide Lebanon, its fragmentation was unthinkable: 'This country will stay united or disappear completely. The Middle East cannot afford a divided Lebanon, because it will lead to a more divided Middle East. To provide a laager in each country for Christians, Sunnis and Shi'as would mean the end of Syria, Iraq and Jordan.'

The links between the Christians and the Druze had been the backbone of Lebanon and of Lebanese independence. The trouble started when the Maronites wanted their own confessional state. 'When Maronitisim became a political plan, we fought them very hard in the 1820s, 1840, 1860, and the 1980s. What foiled the plan for a Christian state was not the death of Bashir Gemayel but our victory in the Shouf war.'

Not that he was for Arab unity at all costs. It was all too easy to misunderstand or ridicule the Druze position – which was above all secular or *laique*, and opposed to religious fundamentalism or *integrisme*. The Druze community was spared such tendencies, since 'a *sheikh* cannot be a political leader.' The Druze could never be a majority, but 'we can be honest and secular in explaining the humanitarian socialist politics of Kemal Jumblat.'

He then gave a breath-taking justification of the power and conduct of the warrior house of Jumblat, which represented 'feudal strength at the service of the modern community, the seventeenth century at the service of the twenty-first.' In the end, Lebanon would have to choose between progressive, democratic ideals or 'the flight into Islam and fundamentalism. So far we have been saved from that by the mosaic of six major communities and seventeen minor ones. If that had been the case in Iran, fundamentalism wouldn't have taken over.'

The City: Beirut

Navigating the green line was one of Abed's greatest skills. He could use it to gauge the political climate of the city, and how much fighting was likely in the next hour or so. Returning from East Beirut one morning,

Abed stopped to pick up leaflets and newspapers from the militiamen at the checkpoint. 'You can tell who's running the show, who's on top, by checking these. Today it looks as if Hezbollah is gaining.'

Driving itinerant journalists around was a part-time activity for Abed, who also had a small shirt business in one of the suburbs. He and his family had more than lived the troubles of the city. A cousin had been blown up while chauffeuring the German ambassador; a brother had been killed ferrying film down the road from Damascus to Amman; he himself had been savagely beaten by Syrian troops when he took some journalists to overlook their positions by the Cedars of Lebanon in the mountains.

He and Sunnis like him had helped to make the city of Beirut, and contributed more than their share to its former reputation for generosity of spirit, hospitality and entrepreneurial skill. In the last century it had grown from a town of 10,000 in 1830 to a city of more than 100,000 by 1900. By then most of the population were Sunni Muslim or Greek Orthodox; the Maronites were still mostly rural peasantry living on the mountain, numbering under 30,000 in Beirut, as late as 1932.

Abed and his family and friends were extraordinarily devoted to those whom they had in charge. They had known many of the kidnap victims very well, including Terry Anderson of the Associated Press and Michel Seurat, the French Arabist. They sized me up immediately as an innocent abroad. They would tick me off for lacking a sense of security, like a jury marking off ice-dancers for merit and artistic content. 'That very foolish, Mr Bob,' Big Hajj would growl, 'things not good at the moment. Hezbollah getting active. Take care.' Hajj would confer about my movements with the girls in the office, who, God knows, had enough worries of their own. Several crossed the green line to get to work, listening avidly to the radios of the Christian militias to hear if there was any shelling near their homes or down by the shore road.

One afternoon I set out to buy some flowers for the girls in the office. I wanted to stroll about half a mile towards the Corniche, but Abed insisted on coming with me 'just to keep watch' – a gesture rather than a practical security measure on his part, to show that I was his friend and he was mine; a small touch of real Beiruti hospitality.

On the way back we paused by a huge shop stacked with Persian and Turkish rugs, and run by an acquaintance of his. We asked him how business was. 'Not good, yes, very bad,' he said. 'I can go for a bit, maybe months. But if it goes on like this, I'll have to close and leave before next year.' Quite how Beirut had continued to do business after fifteen years of civil war defies the normal laws of economics. The Rue Hamra has suffered, shops have been closed and the boutiques have gone. The

Commodore Hotel's days came to an end in a ferocious bombardment a year or so after my visit, and the site was sold for 'redevelopment' – Beirut jargon for a militia takeover, no doubt. But books are still printed to supply universities from Cairo to Casablanca; canned fruit, sauces, juices and ketchups are still processed and exported from south Lebanon. What is the secret of Lebanon's mercantile stamina?

Just below the promenade, beyond the western tip of the Corniche, the Summerlands Hotel complex crouches a few yards above the beach. It was developed for the Lebanese leisure boom of the 1970s, and opened for business just as the civil war was getting under way. Though damaged by a car bomb within three years of opening, and then bombarded by the Israelis during their advance on the city, it was still doing a roaring trade in weddings and parties, and as an informal meeting place for political bosses and militia chiefs. It has been a haven of liberty; when the American Television journalist Charles Glass broke free from his kidnappers after sixty days' captivity in 1987, it was his first refuge.

When I met Khaled Saab, the manager and co-owner of Summerlands, in 1986 he did not think the Lebanese economy had much time before it collapsed. 'The whole Arab economy is going backwards, as if they were prepared to face another one hundred years of war with the West.' This spelt disaster for Lebanon, which 'has always invested in professional people. We travel, know how to deal with other countries. For the Arab world we have provided the universities, the clinics, the shopping and the best cuisine. Our business is the hospitality business – that is our asset, our equivalent of Gulf petroleum.' Now he saw all this being thrown away in war and feuding.

His hotel employed 450 staff; these included 40 security guards, a small militia, whereas in normal times he would not need six. When the hotel was car-bombed the repairs cost 11 million Lebanese pounds, or about $2 million; while 'the Israeli invasion brought total destruction of one part, and that cost 37 million pounds.'

Mr Saab said about six months peace was needed in which the Lebanese economy could benefit from some sophisticated and systematic planning and repairs. It was not to be. During my stay convoys carrying pay to the army and police were being held up and hijacked regularly. In the business heart of the former Switzerland of the Middle East, anarchy stalked the streets.

During our drives across town Abed and I would endlessly discuss who was up and who was down in the militia world. 'Murabitoon, Murabitoon, where are you now?' he would shout, gesticulating alarmingly with both hands off the steering-wheel of his large sedan. He was calling to mind the Sunni militia, little more than commercial gangsters with a smattering of Nasserite politics, who had marauded the streets of West Beirut in the late Seventies. Now they were nowhere to be seen, but like Adonis they would make a comeback. They began to resurface with the Muslim Brotherhood a year or so after I'd left.

Some guerrilla and terrorist groups operating in the Beirut jungle remained obscure due to lack of success or serious analysis by the international news organisations. One of the most curious and potent of these originated among the Armenian community, the third largest Christian grouping after the Maronites and the Greek Orthodox. The Armenian Secret Army for the Liberation of Armenia (ASALA) was certainly born in Beirut, though it received political support from Armenians in Paris and money from America, while Dr George Habash's Popular Front for the Liberation of Palestine had a hand in its training and organisation. ASALA's trade was assassination, its targets Turkish officials and diplomats. The first victim, in 1975, was the Turkish ambassador to Paris. In under ten years they succeeded in killing and wounding some 40 Turkish officials, and quite a number of innocent bystanders.

It was assumed that ASALA had broken up after 1983, but it merely seems to have gone dormant. In May 1986 four prominent Armenians living in West Beirut were murdered. Only about 5,000 Armenians then lived in West Beirut; the bulk of the community, some 120,000, resided in the East. The men were well-known professionals, including a doctor and a lawyer. Nobody understood the motive for the killings, for the Armenians had studiously steered clear of intercommunal fighting. The Archbishop sent a delegation across to the East, who demanded – and got – an apology from the leading Muslim militias.

That was the version that appeared in the international media, but it is only the middle of the story. Neither its beginning nor its end were picked up by reporters, not even by the vociferous correspondent of the London *Times*, yet they cast an interesting light on the Armenian underground networks. Apparently the Armenian Archbishop had pledged humanitarian support for the beleaguered Maronite community of East Beirut; the Shi'ites had taken this to mean political support, hence the murders as a warning. The Archbishop sent his delegation to assure the Shi'ite militias he was not about to dive into the political cauldron – and to serve notice that in the event of further bloodshed, the culprits and their associates would be found and dealt with. This part was endorsed by ASALA; and there were no more killings of Armenians in West Beirut.

Most of my discussions with Abed dwelt on the role of the pro-Iranian Hezbollah. At the time a whole host of similarly named organisations had sprung up, like 'Islamic Jihad' and 'Movement for the Liberation of the Oppressed of the World'. 'Who are they? Are they the same? Are they friends of enemies of Hezbollah?' Abed demanded, almost rhetorically.

I said I thought they were roughly the same people. Groups like the IRA and the Red Brigades used different labels for a different kind of operation, particularly if something went wrong and the mainstream gang did not want to admit it.

'Excellent, Mr Bob, excellent.' Abed banged his steering wheel. 'I agree, I agree.' And so it turned out to be with Hezbollah, a hydra of many names if not of many heads.

But the real debate was whether for the purposes of my investigation we should seek out the Hezbollah. Its spiritual guide, though surely not its political or operational leader, was Sheikh Mohammed Hussein Fadlallah – an urbane and articulate man, judging by his performances on Lebanese television. We knew he received journalists for interviews; the problem was that you had to go to his mosque to make an appointment for the following day, and the risk of who might see you entering the neighbourhood. Only a week before a French television crew who had lingered too long had been kidnapped; news had just trickled through of the horrible torture and murder of Michel Seurat. We decided to give the Sheikh a miss this time, rather lamely convincing ourselves that the would only repeat his television message that he condemned kidnapping on spiritual grounds – not that his followers seemed to agree.

It proved almost as hard to get into the headquarters of their rivals, Amal, which was uncomfortably close to the green line and to the Iranian Embassy, whence Hezbollah received ideological support and one or two direct orders. At the gate of the apartment block I was given a perfunctory body search by miltiamen. 'You journalist? You carry gun? You not carry gun? You journalist crazy!'

The salon of Mr Nabi Berri, the Amal leader, was crowded with supplicants, the more privileged of them sucking cups of tea. Two young activists explained the origins of Amal as the Resistance of the Deprived. One, Mohammed, said he 'worked from the Koran only'. He was particularly proud of his cousin, Bilal Fakes, a 'martyr' who had blown himself up in a Mercedes in the middle of an Israeli tank patrol in south Lebanon, injuring sixteen soldiers. In March 1986 Amal was riding high, holding its own against Hezbollah in Beirut and the south of the country, though short of funds and arms from Syria. In June 1985 Hezbollah had hijacked a TWA 737 airliner from Cairo to Athens and brought it to Beirut, where they killed a young US Navy diver, Robert Stethen, throwing his body onto the tarmac. It took Amal to negotiate the release of the sixty-nine hostages on board in exchange for Shi'ites being held by the Israelis. Hezbollah would not forgive their hijack being hijacked.

I was ushered into the crowded office of the smartly suited Mr Berri who looked like the district attorney called in to run a wild life park. He is a lawyer, born in Sierra Leone and trained in Paris; many of his family now live in Detroit, and he himself possesses a 'green card' allowing him to work in America. When Amal's founder, Musa Sadr, disappeared in Libya in 1978, Nabi Berri became Amal's leader after a brief hiatus.

First he wanted to explain the meaning of the acronym AMAL so I should not mistake the reasons for its foundation. 'Afouz Mehoud Lebanon – the Army of the Lebanese Deprived. Imam Musa Sadr began the movement in 1974 in south Lebanon because he feared an Israeli invasion. When Israel did come in 1978 we were still found very weak, and there had been no resistance until now.' Amal aims to defend the deprived, maintain the integrity and unity of Lebanon against foreign interference, act with Arab allies and, above all, defend south Lebanon. It was totally opposed to Hezbollah's programme of an Islamic Republic. 'I am against it in the same degree as I am against a separate Christian Republic here. I am against a divided Lebanon, against any idea of splitting it up into different cantons for different sects. I just want equality and justice between the communities, equality between the citizens. The National Pact will have to be redrawn, and of course the Christians stand to lose more than the others.'

Mr Berri was a Lebanese nationalist, whereas Hezbollah was an Islamic internationalist movement. He was following the path laid down by Amal's charismatic founder Musa Sadr, the vanished Imam. Nabi Berri showed himself a true Shi'ite in his belief that the Imam might still return. 'There is no proof that he died in Libya; we have had some indications lately that he might be alive and in prison. What wonderful hospitality!'

The priority for the Shi'ites was to secure South Lebanon. The Palestinians, he said, were 'a big problem' for Lebanon and should never have been allowed to set up there on their own. It needed the effort of the entire Arab world to resolve the Israeli-Palestinian issue.

As for Lebanon, he confessed that 'I cannot imagine any future without a change of regime. When we finish in the south, we will fight the regime of the Christians and their musketeers here. If the law of numbers prevailed, we Shi'ites would have the presidency, the majority in parliament and the command of the army.

Outside the apartment block the guards had just exchanged fire with a rival neighbourhood militia. The only casualty was an old woman out shopping, who had been hit in the leg. As we drove past the Iranian Embassy, festooned in the national colours of green, white, black and red, we heard a loud 'pop' somewhere in the vicinity of our right ears. 'Sniper!' shouted Abed, laughing as he trod on the gas and we surged towards the Corniche.

Waters of Tyre

To the ancients the expression 'navigating Tyrean waters' meant courting serious disaster – a testimony to the trickiness of its currents, and the nautical skills of the Phoenicians of Tyre, the most independent of their race. But when Abed and I set out from Beirut to visit the southern port, we did not think we were courting anything very much. We had arranged to visit Amal in the south, and the spokesman of the United Nations cease-fire authority.

Passing the airport we encountered roadblocks by the unofficial ports of Amal and the Druze, each bearing portraits of their leaders, Berri and Jumblat. 'J and B,' Abed gurgled, 'J and B – that's the future of this country – Jumblat and Berri, just like the whisky.' In case I failed to get the joke, he pointed out that that Justerini and Brooks was the Beirutis' favourite tipple.

From the J and B free ports, we passed a long tableau of destruction. The Christian town of Damour had been a pile of empty masonry since the Druze attacked in 1977 and drove the people away; Sidon was all scars and gaps, the roads pitted with craters and shell-holes, while on the beach a small freighter lolled over like dead whale.

From the road the Palestinian refugee camps of Ein el Hilweh and Mieh Mieh looked like prisoner-of-war cages – in stark contrast with the sparkling green countryside around. The hills of south Lebanon are the fairest of all the Levant, like a picture from a child's book of Bible stories, gentler and more inviting than the harsher, broken folds of land in Israel and Palestine to the south. Vines in thick clumps, lemons, oranges and olive trees made the place seem the gift of nature and of God in some first Eden.

We stopped first call at Nabatieh, looking across the line of hills that run to the border. Abed wanted to check the lie of the land with Amal, to find out whether the Israelis or the South Lebanese Army were about, and to make sure that we could get into Tyre. Before us, looking south, was a sea of shimmering fertility. To the east rose Mount Hermon, and the Crusader castle at Beaufort, now occupied by the Israelis. Once it had been the best preserved of these fortresses in Lebanon, but the Israelis and their adversaries had reduced it to little more than a strategic stump.

We returned to the coastal road and crossed the Litani River into Tyre. The vegetation grew still lusher, with thick plantations of tobacco, sweet corn and bananas, shaded by eucalyptus and lilacs. The road was jammed with traffic – old limousines, trucks carrying produce from the growers, including hashish, and one or two militia lorries with anti-aircraft guns on the back. The procession was made slower by roadblocks, official and unofficial – most the latter belonging to local gangs marking out their territory. At the outskirts of Tyre we stopped at the UN guardpost not far from one of the refugee camps, Burj el-Shemali, but we were forbidden from going anywhere near the beleaguered camp.

Tyre turned out to be a provincial port where most of the business revolved around the sale of fruit, vegetables and other produce. In the harbour a few local fishing craft were alongside the quay, overlooked by a row of low Turkish houses. Sea-going commerce had been killed years ago by the first Arab-Israeli wars. Lounging outside one of the cafés we found the genial frame of Mr Timor Goksal, the official UN spokesman. As a Turk he was given free passage by Israelis and Arabs alike.

He was in expansive mood. 'It's one of the most peaceful periods I've known. Look at the amount of building here, it's a real sign of faith in life. There's a convergence of interests: the Israelis, the south Lebanese and the UN force all want peace. Amal here is indigenous – it's not imported. They only organise resistance where the Israelis are. Hezbollah is different, they want to liberate Jerusalem.' The notion that Amal would keep the peace on their home turf in south Lebanon made sense, but events were to prove otherwise. The appeal of Hezbollah in the villages was growing by the week, and was to develop into open clashes with Amal as well as with the Israelis.

On one subject the cheerful Mr Goksal could not lighten the gloom. The antiquities of ancient Tyre were in a poor state, and those that could be removed had been taken away by successive marauding armies. Much of the old port was decayed beyond recovery, and new houses had been built over many of the archaeological sites. Yet Tyre had been the commercial powerhouse of the Phoenician world, the home of the purple

dye industry from which they took their name. Along these coasts bred
the murex, the mollusc which exudes the dark ink from which the dye
was made. Tyre was built at the same time as the Temple of Hercules,
according to Herodotus, in about 2750 BC; it is known from more
reliable sources that, with its neighbours, Ugarit, Sidon and Byblos, it
paid tribute to the Pharaohs up to the time of Ramasses II in the thirteenth century BC. When the King of Askalon captured Sidon, the local
population sought refuge in Tyre, which became the leading Phoenician
city. Eventually it put down colonies in Africa, Carthage among them,
and trading beyond the Mediterranean on the Atlantic coast of Africa
and even in Britain. Hiram I of Tyre allied himself to the Jewish king
David and his son Solomon, for whom he provided cedars of Lebanon
and fine craftsmen for the building of the First Temple in Jerusalem in
about 1011 BC. Later a princess of Tyre, Jezabel, brought tribulations
upon King Ahab.

Defeat by the Assyrians and the challenge of the former colony of Carth-
age led to a reversal of Tyre's fortunes. Sidon became the leader of the
Phoenician federation; the old port was destroyed by Nebuchadnezzar II of
Babylon, who also destroyed Solomon's Temple. In its place an even fairer
Tyre arose, whose splendour is elegiacally celebrated by Ezekiel in the Old
Testament: 'O Tyrus thou hast said, I am of perfect beauty/Thy borders are
in the midst of the seas, thy builders have perfected thy beauty.' The prophet then gives a remarkably precise list of the wares and wealth of the
traders at Tyre: silver, tin, iron and lead, slaves ('the persons of men') and
vessels of brass; horses, horsemen and mules; emeralds, purple, embroidered work and fine linen, coral and agate; wheat, honey, oil, balm cloth
for chariots; lambs and rams and goats of Arabia. In the end we shall fail,
says Ezekiel, and the lamentation will go up 'What city is like Tyrus, like
the destroyed in the midst of the sea?' It seems not far removed from what
has happened to Old Tyre today.

Tyre was to fight on well after Ezekiel's day. It resisted assault by
Alexander the Great for seven months in 332 BC; from the successors
of Alexander, the Seleucids, it passed into the hands of the Romans,
and in 1124 it was taken, again after another long siege, by the Crusaders.
A new cathedral was built to replace an old Byzantine church, and in
1173 the greatest historian of the Crusades, known to this day as William
of Tyre, was consecrated bishop. Tyre hung on as a Christian stronghold
for more than a hundred years after Saladin and only surrendered after
the fall of Acre in 1291. Since then the old city and its ruins have been
used extensively as a quarry for building materials.

In the sixteenth century the Emir Fakhr ed-Din Maan tried to rebuild the old city, but was thwarted. Lately the cause had been taken up again by Maha Khalil Chalabi, from one of the leading Shi'ite families of the area. She has tried to persuade UNESCO and other international organisations to rescue what is left of the antiquities, and to set up a heritage scheme for youth in that part of south Lebanon. 'The city is unique,' she says. 'It saw eight of the great Mediterranean civilisations from the Phoenicians to the Ottomans. It had the first two-chamber parliament. It gave the world the alphabet, the skills of navigation, the purple dye industry, philosophy, mathematics. But we have had only twenty years of serious archaeology since 1952.'

The dilemma facing her birthplace is one that is growing throughout the Mediterranean. More and more historical sites are being lost to archaeology. Some are simply closed to visitors as a result of political or military circumstance, such as the great temples of Bacchus and Jupiter at Baalbek, the crusader castle of Beaufort and Tyre itself. Soon they could be places to be read about but never visited by students.

A small terrace with the remains of houses, a temple and burial ground, give a hint of what ancient Tyre might have been like. Its position above the sea, and the few columns left standing, give it a striking resemblance to the site at Carthage. And, as at Carthage, nearly all that can be seen is very late, and Roman. The remnant of Roman Tyre in which the locals most delight is the huge hippodrome, on open land near the big Palestinian camp of Rashidieh. It is a place of Cecil B. De Mille Hollywood vulgarity, in which eight chariots could race side by side and its most notable recent achievement, as no Tyrean will fail to tell you, was to provide the set for the chariot duel in *Ben Hur*. Forget about Alexander the Great or William of Tyre, the immortal Charlton Heston had trod these paved tracks! It was Mrs Chalabi's heart's desire to stage chariot races in the arena once again.

Despite serving as quarry and builder's yard for generations, the stadium is in reasonable repair. At one end complete rows of stone seating are in place, while huge arches mark the stabling for the animals and the higher levels of stand – behind which I found some lurid posters of the real militias, Amal and Hezbollah, spelling out what they would do to enemies, infidels and the Israelis.

I was still absorbing their message when I came across a group of teenage girls in white scarves and long blue coats, sitting in a circle under sprays of glowing yellow laburnam, engaged in what appeared part prayer-meeting, part picnic. Their leader explained that they were 'soeurs Islamiques' – and root-and-branch Amal supporters.

They explained that they had taken the veil at the age of nine. They were very fascinated by my camera, for their order forbids photography under the old Islamic rubric against reproducing the human image. When I told them that I would soon be seeing Nabi Berri, Amal's leader, they were gravely impressed and asked me to convey their greetings, good wishes, and loyalty. The girls were neither solemn nor censorious, but giggled shyly throughout. They were very curious about what I was going and what I thought about their country and their cause. In their weakness for dialogue and argument, they were true Mediterraneans.

At the end, without thinking, I held out my hand in a gesture of fare-well. The chief interlocutor went bright red under her scarf and said, 'Oh no, monsieur, we may not touch you. We must not shake your hand.' And she smiled and touched the front of her coat in traditional Islamic greeting. 'Au revoir, come and see us again,' her entourage chorused.

By then Abed was not entirely sure he would ever see me again, particu-larly after he had caught sight of six men armed with assault rifles and pis-tols descending into the hippodrome. By the time I reached him, his round face was glistening with sweat, his whole frame in an advanced state of agitation: 'You OK?' he shouted, 'I thought you really gone, Mr Bob, really gone this time. You stay with me.' Back in Beirut, I recorded the lowest marks ever for security and personal safety from Big Hajj, Little Hajj, Lilian and the girls of the office. I was more worried about Abed than myself, for I had touched the core of his sense of honour, obligation and friendship.

Getting out of Beirut and Lebanon proved more complicated than getting in. After consulting my bosses in London, Lillian our charming office manager, insisted that we should take two cars to run the gauntlet of Hezbollah in the last mile or so to the airport. (The technique did not prove effective a fortnight later for the journalist John McCarthy who was seized on this piece of road and who was to spend nearly 2000 days incaptivity.) So we all set off, Abed and I in front, Hajj and several of the others in the back-up vehicle behind. We skirted the camps at Sabra and Chatila, which seemed almost empty.

Once on the straight piece of road running parallel to the main highway by the coast, we gunned the cars for the final dash. I slid down in my seat so that my red hair would not be too conspicuous in the afternoon sun.

Once in the airport lounge, I said a sad goodbye to Abed, the best of West Beirut company. Of all my travelling companions round the Mediterranean that I am unlikely to see again, I think most about him and wonder at his ability to beat the odds in the Russian roulette of Lebanon today.

Thirteen: Promise and Predicament – Israel and Palestine

i The Grapes of Hebron

NEAR Hebron, Abraham brought his herds and flocks and pitched his tent beneath the Oak of Mamre. In the plains of Mamre he walked and spoke with God, receiving the promise, 'Unto thy seed have I given this land, from the river of Egypt unto the great river, the river of Euphrates.' Since then Hebron has become a city sacred to Jew, Christian and Muslim alike, for it is where Abraham and his son and grandson are buried. He was the first of the Patriarchs, who walked with God, and his grandson Jacob gave his name to the house of Israel.

Hebron today is a mantle of houses clinging to the rough screes of the Judaean Hills east of the Dead Sea. It is of distinctly Arab appearance, and from the distance it appears to slumber, just as it did under the Ottomans, but on closer examination the roof-tops round the souk are defaced by barbed wire barriers, police warning notices and sandbagged observation posts with the Israeli flag fluttering above. The markets and stalls close frequently as part of the protest in the Palestinians' Intifada or 'shaking'. These alleys have seen knifing and stone-throwing – and barrages of Israeli tear gas in retaliation.

One of the principal towns of the West Bank, Hebron was under the jurisdiction of the Hashemite Kingdom of Jordan until 1967, when it was seized by Israeli forces during the Six Days' War. Now Hebron and its surroundings, forms part of the Occupied Territories administered by Israel. They are not part of Israel proper, for they have not been formally annexed. For the Arabs, this means administration without proper representation; for the Israelis, the Arab militants are a security threat to themselves and to their state.

The fact that the Israelis are in Hebron is a sign of the Jews' success in establishing a state in the land of Israel. It is also an eloquent token of their biggest political dilemma: how to live with the Arab neighbours both inside Israel's borders and beyond them. The two communities have grated on each other since well before the State of Israel was born in 1948. In January 1988, two months after the Intifada began, I wandered through the souk at Hebron. It was closed. Shutters were bolted and barred for one of the protracted protest strikes ordered through leaflets and fly-posters by the shadowy leadership of the 'uprising'. I asked one trader in the modern Palestinian uniform of sneakers, tight jeans and a checked red and white *kifir* on his head, how long he could stay closed for. 'For about six months,' was his unhesitating, precise reply. 'That was how long my father kept the market closed in the Arab revolt against the British in 1936.'

Some Arabists say Israel might be on better terms with its neighbours when it finally joins the Middle East, and becomes more like an Arab country. Israel has begun to look more Middle Eastern, with its growing population of Sephardim, or oriental Jews; but the success of Israel seems to belong to another world from the Middle East, and to another sea than the Mediterranean. Its achievements are astonishing by any standards. From being a struggling statelet with under three-quarters of a million inhabitants in 1948, it now boasts a grand population of 4,250,000 in Israel proper in a country with a thriving industry and infrastructure and a gross national product of over $40 billion. It also possesses the only fully working democracy in the immediate neighbourhood, and in the non-European Mediterranean. Detractors like to claim that it could not have worked without outside help – principally from the United States, in return for being 'America's permanent aircraft carrier in the Middle East'. However, although American aid has been a vital ingredient in the Israeli economy, by 1990 it was about $3 billion, well under a tenth of GNP.

The point of difference between Israel and any other state on earth is in its Jewishness. For the Arab opposition, who refuse to endow it with the dignity of nationhood, it is 'the Zionist entity', or 'the Jewish entity'. But it is not a state which officially denies other religions; Christians and Muslims are allowed their own confessional courts and community councils. But as the British Mandate in Palestine began to lose control, the Jews in their settlements showed themselves far better prepared to build a state than their Arab neighbours in the villages. At independence the majority of the Jews in the new Israel were of European origin, more skilled than their Arab foes in the military arts. Many had the experience of resistance to the progroms of Eastern Europe, and later Nazi occupation, while others had served in the Allied forces in the war against Hitler, some in the Jewish Brigade of the British Army. Israel's survival was to be put to the test in no fewer than five Arab-Israeli wars from 1948 to the invasion of Lebanon in 1982; since then its troops have been deployed against the internal unrest of the Intifada, a form of opposition less susceptible to military remedy.

For decades the Arab-Israeli conflict has been synonymous with the Middle East crisis in the vocabulary of the world's politicians and diplomats. Other issues have tried to displace it, such as the OPEC oil price war of 1973, the Gulf War and Saddam Hussein's escapade in Kuwait, but the clash of Arab and Jew, Israeli and Palestinian, has never dropped from view.

At the heart of the conflict is that the need for security and fulfilment of one side seems to imply destruction and disaster for the other. A Jewish state – the fulfilment of a destiny pledged to Moses and King David – with secure borders, involves diaspora and displacement for Palestinian Arabs.

The instinct for survival runs deep in the Israeli character. Any discussion of Israel, its creation and destiny, has to consider the religion of Judaism, the repeated dispersal of the Jewish people, across the face of the earth, Zionism, anti-semitism, and the Nazi Holocaust. Nobody can claim to be impartial about the Arab-Israeli conflict.

The Jewish faith, Judaism, must be one of the most esoteric of the great universal religions. It is based on the belief that the Jews are God's chosen people, the tribes to whom He has made His promise of salvation. In their religion the Jews have given the rest of the world an extraordinary gift. God's promise to Abraham and Jacob, through Moses and King David, that their descendants were to be His chosen did not come without obligation. The chosen had to carry out their part of the contract, and conduct themselves in a manner fitting to their privileged status. Backsliding leads to destruction and punishment. The whole tangled story is wonderfully told in the Old Testament which, together with the classical culture of Greece and Rome, is the basis of all modern history and historiography, the way the civilised world looks and understands itself. 'Look at the story of King David,' said a Jewish friend, 'the whole story is laid before you in all its ghastly detail.'

Not far from Hebron, at the brook called Eshcol, Moses sent his spies into the Promised Land after he had lead the Israelities out of captivity in Egypt. They found the land populated with giants, but fair and flowing with milk and honey. As proof of its abundance, they cut a bunch of grapes to take back to Moses. 'And they came to the brook of Eshcol, and cut down from thence a branch with one cluster of grapes, and they bear it between two upon a staff; and they brought of the pomegranates and of the figs.' An enormous bunch of grapes on a staff has come to symbolise the land, and is the badge of the Israeli Tourist Office. (*Al Quds* – the Grapes – in the name of Jerusalim in Arabic.)

The tombs of the Patriarchs are housed in the Haram, the dominant landmark of old Hebron. Its wall was built by the Crusaders, but the shrine itself is a large mosque graced by two minarets. By its side run two steep stone stairways, evidence of the discrimination against the Jews and other infidels under the Ottoman authorities. As Baedeker's *Guide to Historical Palestine* of 1912 puts it,

'Unbelievers' may ascend to the seventh step of the flight on the south side. Beside the fifth step is a large stone with a hole in it, which the Jews believe extends down to the tomb. On Fridays the Jews lament here as they do at the Place of Wailing in Jerusalem – no Europeans, except a few of high rank, have been admitted to the interior of the Haram.

No such bar now stands in the way. In the main mosque are the two catafalques of Isaac and Rebecca, while those of Abraham and Sarah and Jacob and Leah are in side chapels. Across the courtyard an Israeli soldier was kneeling in prayer in a chapel reopened as a synagogue, while his comrades kept a wary eye from a sandbagged observation post.

To the north of Hebron concrete houses crawl up the hillside. This is the Jewish settlement of Kiryat Arba, the outward and visible sign to its inhabitants that this the land promised them in the Bible. They use the ancient names of Judaea and Samaria for them, but to the Arabs they are the Occupied Territories. Between 1968 and 1990 some 80 or 90 settlements were built by Israeli pioneers in the West Bank, and some 16 in Gaza. By the end of 1990 the number of West Bank settlers was thought to be approaching 100,000. The first such settlement was at Kiryat Arba, named after the burial place of Abraham's wife Sarah.

'That's our settlement, an abuse against humanity as bad as Treblinka,' cackled Eliakim Ha'ezni, one of the founders of Kiryat Araba. With a group of activists he had occupied the Park Hotel in Hebron during Pentecost in 1968, only leaving on the understanding that they could build on the hills outside the city. A lawyer by training, he was born in Kiel in Germany. In Israel he became one of the founders of the Tehiya (Zionist-revival) Party, a secular party on the right of the political spectrum, and eventually sat for it in the Knesset, the parliament in Jerusalem. In his mid-sixties he was little sparrow of a man, darting and gesticulating as he discoursed in his high-pitched voice; his energy bordered on the neurotic. He and his party firmly believe that Israel should stretch from the Mediterranean to the Jordan Valley, all under the same administration.

Hand-in-hand with his firm political belief was a deep love of the cultures, peoples and religions of the Middle East; much of his work was helping Arabs with their leases and land claims. His fizz and fire came from the trauma of escaping the Holocaust. 'This gives me my energy, my petrol as it were,' he confessed. 'Many of the *sabras* [Israelis born in Israel] just don't have it.' He had arrived in Palestine in 1938 with his mother, father and sister, but his grandmother did not escape from Germany – 'she went to her death carrying our picture.' Hebron was to become particularly important to him in his new life, 'It was my spiritual homeland, the one thing I could hang on to for self-respect.'

Eliakim frequently returned again to the historical argument that the Jews had been settled in Hebron when Jerusalem 'was neutral territory, the land of the Jebusites, before David and Solomon made it their capital.' He was immensely proud that he had helped to house 5000 Jewish settlers at Kiryat Arba, and some 500 families in Hebron. Nor did he see this as a threat to the Arab population. 'We are ready to co-operate with the Arabs, if they co-operate with us. The Jews have always had a presence here.'

I first met Eliakim in 1986. I next saw him early in 1988, when the Intifada had begun and Israel was facing its fortieth anniversary. His conversation was still as lively as a cricket, but it had a more sombre message. He was worried that Israelis had expected too much of their country. 'Zionism is not about utopia,' he explained. 'This was not to be a land exclusively of prophets and saints. We need a country of our own, a normal state neither better nor worse than others, a country that others will look upon with blind indifference.'

He was clearly upset by the Intifada, and particularly concered about the plight of the Arabs in the overcrowded squalor of Gaza. He wanted the Jewish labour organisation Histradut to press for proper wages and social security rights for the Arabs there. 'You can't let them go on waving the flag of an empty stomach. You have to drown the cats in cream.' He believed the crisis in Gaza was symptomatic of a profound change in the Arab community since 1948 – the shift from a rural village society to an urban one. He feared that, in the upheavals, Islamic extremism would come to the fore; 'Judaea and Samaria must not be thrown into the jaws of the tiger – it won't be sated once it scents blood.'

For all its apocalyptic overtones, Eliakim's words seemed mild compared with the torrent of verbiage I received from a young settler of Californian origin when I visited an education centre near the synagogue in Kiryat Arba. Yigal Kutai had studied in Los Angeles before deciding to make his *aliyah* or migration to Israel. He had been inspired by his readings of the Old Testament. 'I felt there were historical reasons for this being my land. The moment you learn about history you feel 5000 years old.' He seemed puzzled when I suggested that he was talking about matters of faith rather than of reason.

On the subject of his Palestinian neighbours, he was prepared to be generous, as his religion taught him. 'This is my land, they are my guests. We have a tradition for being hospitable.' But as to the Palestinian desire to be a nation and to have their own state, 'I don't believe we have to give it to them . . . they only really want to push Israel into the Mediterranean.'

Such attitudes were not uncommon among the Gush Emonim (Block of the Faithful), the organisation in the vanguard of the settler movement. Their faith in their destiny is unswerving. They see themselves as a pioneering band, prepared to fight for their beliefs. Many settlements are like stockades, with barriers and barbed wire fences. The settlers have formed vigilante militias and carry guns. Attitudes have hardened towards the Arabs.

For over twenty years the Israeli authorities have practised a twilight policy towards the Occupied Territories: they were neither annexed fully, nor were their Arab people allowed full local self-determination. One of the principal reasons for not letting these lands go was practical rather than ideological or religious – they were needed to provide a secure frontier against Arab enemies to the east, Syria, Jordan and Iraq.

The line of the River Jordan from the Dead Sea to Galilee makes a vivid natural frontier. The valley is below sea level, and the heights of the Samarian Hills above give a broad panorama well into Jordan itself. The sun dances and flashes off the irrigation sprays and the plastic sheetings of the tomato plantations on the floor of the plain – many of which are run by Palestinians, who constitute over 65 per cent of Jordan's population. It has been suggested that Jordan should become the Palestinian state, but this would solve neither Israel's need for security nor the refugees' dream of recovering their old homes inside Israel. In the meantime the Israelis are vigilant along the wire fences of the frontier. At night the lights of their jeeps and half tracks are glow-worms crawling through the dense growths of the river wadi as they search for guerrillas coming across the wire.

One blazing day in May I travelled the river frontier into Upper Galilee and on to the Golan Heights, the plateau which marks the frontier and battleground with Syria. Since this was a military zone, I was escorted

by an amiable reserve officer called Danny. In real life he was an executive with the Jewish Agency, the organisation responsible for immigrants.
He was friendly and hospitable, a man happy with his life. I offered to
buy him a coffee near Galilee. As we left the car, he reached for his Uzi
submachine-gun. I told him not to bother on my account. 'It's not for
you,' he said, 'it's for my own protection. You're a foreigner, a guest
here. I am in occupied territory.'

Round the shore of the lake the successors of St Peter were carefully
casting their nets in the shallows. I was surprised by the small scale of
the landscape. The Golan Heights themselves are shallow ridges, rising
by easy stages to a crest, with the eternal beacon of Mount Hermon
gleaming white in the background. Here Israeli and Syrian tanks had
pounded each other in advance and counter-thrust. In October 1973, in
the first few hours of the Yom Kippur offensive, the Syrians actually
broke through the Israeli emplacements, reaching into the valley until
they were halted, bewildered by the speed of their success and embar-
rassed by their lack of fuel and ammunition. The Israelis then took days
to slog their way back to the high ground, first taken and held in 1967.
At one point the ridge is marked by clumps of trees at regular intervals.
'Each was a gun emplacement or forming-up point for tanks,' Danny
said. 'We knew because our spies in Damascus told us.' The trees looked
ominously close.

A rough farm track led up the plateau itself, to meadows of lush grass,
clumps of clover and exuberant purple thistle flowers. Below us in the
heat haze, festooned with barbed wire, lay Quneitra, the strategic town
guarding the heights. The Syrians and Israelis had agreed to pull back
from here under an accord signed in 1974, which both parties observed
to the letter. Below Quneitra, obscured in the mist of the plain, lay
Damascus, only some forty miles away.

Deep ruts cross-hatched with the imprint of tank tracks led to the
tangle of wire and lookouts which marked the frontier. A herd of lazy
cows looked on, casually guarded by a Druze shepherd. Nearing the fence
we were stopped by a UN contingent of Austrian soldiers, healthy and
fresh-faced as a recruiting poster. They scrounged a few cigarettes, said
everything was peaceful, told us not to go into Quneitra for fear of mines,
and waved us on our way. Before the next clump of tents and wire stood
a small Israeli soldier with a goatee beard and a do-it-yourself uniform.

'Hello, pleased to meet you!' he said in a thick Cockney accent. His
name was Geoffrey, and had been born and bred in Stamford Hill in
London before coming to Israel in the late 1940s. He laughed. When
he saw me eyeing the three rows of campaign ribbons in his old tunic.

'Pretty good for a pacifist, eh? They keep on sending me back for my military service, though I'm getting on now. It's the only way I can get a peaceful holiday. Tell the folks back home that you've met a Londoner still guarding one of the last outposts of Empire.'

Descending the slope of the Golan to the north we passed fields full of gun-pits and infantry trenches and the detritus of war. Under the trees squadrons of tanks dozed like buffalos, waiting for a call to action. The valley itself is replete with well organised farms, laid out like little ranches complete with horseshoe arches and waggon-wheel decorations on the gates. A number are old kibbutzim, the collective communities which enshrined the utopian ideals of the early Jewish pioneers – though all are protected by walls and lookout towers, like little forts.

One of the ranches houses the Galilee Winery, well known throughout Israel for its fine light vintages. By now we were close to the line of advance into Lebanon. From the ruins of the old castle of the Assassins at Banyas one can see as far as the forward defence line on the Litani River well inside Lebanon itself. Israel's northern frontier is on a tiny scale – in the space of only a few miles, a matter of minutes for tanks or armoured infantry, the lines of advance from Syria, Lebanon and Jordan intersect and run together.

'Upper Galilee is now the bread basket of Israel,' said Danny as we looked at newly cultivated fields of wheat, 'but before 1958 it was mostly a swamp.' He was quietly hinting at one of the most powerful strategic reasons for Israel wanting to hang on to the West Bank territories – fresh water, that most prized commodity of the Mediterranean and the Middle East. Danny reckoned that a good 65 per cent of Israel's territory was desert and barren rock, unyielding of any crops except other than the barest pickings for the nomad sheep of the Bedouins. One of the most important sources of water in the east of the country was the Yarmuk River, a bone of contention between Israel and Jordan since their birth.

By 1990 the growth in Jewish settlements and Arab villages on the West Bank, and the growing demands the cities and suburbs of the coastal plain were placing heavy demands on the natural water sources in the Occupied Territories. An ancient spring near Jericho, which had run the year round since Neolithic times, dried up completely in the summer months; and in August the Ministry of Agriculture placed an advertisement in the daily press explaining that over 60 per cent of Israel's water depended on sources in the West Bank and Israelis should think again about suggestions that the Territories should in any way be under the control of their Palestinian residents. The advertisement concluded that 'It is important to realize that the claim to continued

Israeli control over Judaea and Samaria is not based on extremist fanaticism or religious mysticism but on a rational, healthy and reasonable survival instinct.'

In the olive groves and orchards of the hills round Tulkarm the artesian wells are rich prizes. Tulkarm has one of the largest Palestinian refugee camps in the entire West Bank, with some 12,000 occupants, and it is one of the most strategically sensitive. It lies a few hundred yards from the green line – the frontier of the Israeli State from 1948. Since the eruption of the Intifada, the camp has enhanced its reputation for militancy.

The camp had been placed under a curfew by the Israeli military authorities more often than any other in the West Bank, and its children received fewer days of schooling. Curfew moreover means curfew. Under the curfew, soldiers seal the entrances to the camp; nobody is allowed to leave the house, nor to go on the roof. In just under three years, 21 people were killed, including a 60-year-old and a three-month-old-baby, 1250 injured and 385 arrested; 225 houses were wrecked and three demolished under a military court order.

'When the battles are on the whole house shakes,' explains Attil, a heavily pregnant woman in a yellow print dress. She and her husband, Abdel-Karim, occupy three rooms in a yellow painted concrete box, which they share with several relations. Abdel-Karim used to work in a car repair shop in Tel Aviv until he was 'expelled'. Now he struggles to run his own paint spray and repair business.

'I don't like the children to go out in case the soldiers start firing down the streets when there is trouble. But it makes them nervous to stay in all day,' Attil told me. She used to be a kindergarten teacher, but now earns up to 100 shekels (about $45) a month supervising sewing classes and the like. 'We expect the world to look on us a nation. I have three children now, another is on the way. I would like six children, so three could be martyrs and I could keep three for myself.' But how her husband would earn a living might be open to doubt. Abdel-Karim had just had his green identity card stamped by a military patrol, which means he will not be able to work outside his village and the camp. 'They grabbed me and beat me up in front of my wife,' he said.

A variation on this kind of treatment is the punitive tax raid. An Israeli civil servant, backed by a hefty military escort, descends on a suspected tax defaulter to exact the tax and a thumping fine. If he continues to resist, his property is sequestered and his shop often sealed.

At Tulkarm I wondered if the military authorities were deliberately depriving the Palestinians of education. Mohamed Akel, the Acting Director of Social Services for UNRWA (the UN agency for the refugees) in the camp, said he thought not as a conscious policy, nevertheless opportunities for learning were being curtailed for Palestinians of all ages.

Just outside Ramallah, the Arab town closest to Jerusalem to the north, a curve in the road reveals the high wire and concrete walls of a military compound. Among the Palestinians this is known as the Bir Zeit extension dormitory, because so many teachers from Bir Zeit university have been held there in 'administrative detention' – in other words, internment without trial. Bir Zeit is known to have the most lively campus on the West Bank, rivalled only by Nablus, home of another of the six Palestinian universities of the Occupied Territories.

The campus itself is a model of modern architecture and landscaping, blending beautifully with the russet-coloured hills and built largely with funds from Kuwait and Saudi Arabia. (The academic foundation dates from the early 1920s.) In good years more than 2500 students would enrol one of the four faculties of engineering, medicine, arts and commerce. Most of those who qualify know they will have little chance of practising in anything connected to their chosen discipline. Even the doctors can only hope to get a job in the Gulf or in a Palestinian institution on the West Bank itself. Since the first stage of the campus was completed in 1983, the university has hardly had a semester that has not been disrupted or curtailed by the Israeli authorities.

I was invited to visit the campus in the summer of 1986 when the pressure was on for final exams. My host was Albert Aghazarian, 'Director, Public Relations and Lecturer Middle East History', as his visiting card put it. Albert has the nose of a hawk and the wild eyes of Sir Henry Irving hamming it up in *Macbeth*. A graduate of the American University in Beirut, he speaks eight languages and argues volubly in them all, a briar pipe describing wide arcs of fire in his right hand. Though he is Armenian, and an Armenian Catholic at that, he is the ultimate pro-Palestinian spokesman.

Albert has endeavoured to keep the Bir Zeit flag flying throughout, to make sure the world understands the Palestinians' educational needs and privations. During the closure he organised seminars and classes, and set up administrative offices in private houses throughout the Ramallah district.

Emerging into the sunlight from one classroom block, we saw a group of young men at prayer. 'Ah yes, the religious groups,' Albert remarked. 'They are growing. Now they want a second room for their meetings. Big change could be on the way.'

One of Albert's colleagues was Dr Salim Tamari, one of the most eminent social scientists of this part of the Arab world. Human statistics are highly volatile both in Israel proper and in the Occupied Territories. They seem to change every five minutes, and their interpretation provokes endless argument and debate. In this area Dr Tamari's authority is internationally respected, not least in Israel itself. Demography contains vital clues to the future of Israel and its relationship with the West Bank Arabs. In 1986 the Jewish population of Israel proper was about 4.2 million, the number of Arabs in the West Bank and Gaza was nearing 1.4 million, and there were around 100,000 Arabs, Druze and others who had accepted full Israeli citizenship. By 1990 the Jewish population was over 4.5 million and the total Arab population more than 1.8 million.

The Palestinian Arabs of the West bank, Salim explained, were still predominantly rural peasants in 1986, and only a quarter were genuine town-dwellers. Fifteen per cent lived in refugee camps. In Gaza nearly half the Palestinian population of 600,000 was living in camps. Their birth-rate was high even by Third World standards and roughly 52 per cent of all Palestinians under occupation were under the age of fourteen.

The crisis of sheer numbers was aggravated by economic difficulties. Half the West Bank was engaged in agriculture, but others worked abroad, in the Gulf or in Israel itself. 'They are willing to take the shit jobs – the dirty work the Jews don't want,' he observed. More worrying still was the plight of university students. Most graduates had to take unsuitable temporary work, and over 15,000 Palestinian graduates had no job at all. He was also concerned about the continuous restriction of their civil liberties during their studies. 'All forms of political expression are banned here,' he explained, for Bir Zeit had a reputation as the PLO academy among Israelis. 'The exception is journalism, but even so half the Jerusalem press is banned here. For instance, the weekly English language edition of *Al Fajr* (The Dawn) is not allowed. The law is such a monster in this respect. And even with unbanned books there are problems in obtaining import licences to get them here.' He feared that the campus itself was becoming 'a dead area culturally and for normal political activity'. Even in 1986, well before the Intifada, he thought that more than one third of the students over the past ten years had been detained without trial for more than one month. At Nablus he suspected the proportion was higher.

According to Dr Tamari's calculations the faster birth-rate of the Palestinians meant their numbers would exceed those of the Israelis in the first quarter of the next century. Jewish immigration into Israel had slowed in the early 1980s, and many Ashkenazim (Jews of European origin) were leaving. This had persuaded some Palestinian activists, notabley George Habash of the Popular Front for the Liberation of Palestine, that the Palestinians could breed their way to victory. As Arab numbers rose the Jewish State or 'Zionist Entity' would become less Jewish. But dishing Zionism by demography was to become a highly dubious ploy. It would contribute exponentially to the misery of the Palestinians – more numbers meaning greater privation, frustration and poverty – and it was a game that two could play. The picture was altered radically in favour of the Jewish population when immigrants began pouring in once more from Russia by the hundred thousand. In 1990 more than a quarter of a million arrived. In under a decade from 1990 Israel expected to receive more than three million new citizens from Eastern Europe and the Soviet Union.

ii The Land of Israel

The fields along the Mediterranean coast and inland from Tel Aviv are planted and harvested with the intensity of a small garden. This is Israel's garden, where every inch of ground appears to have been cajoled into making something grow – giving life to the well-worn cliché about 'making the desert bloom'. Jostling with the fields are the sprawling suburbs of Tel Aviv, Yafo (old Jaffa) and Haifa to the north, and Ashdod to the south. Some of the first Jewish settlements of modern times, Petah Tikva, Ramla, Yehouda and Lod are virtually one continuous metropolis. Over two-thirds of Israel's productive industries, from the building of main battle tanks to the processing of orange juice and tomato ketchup, is packed into this chunk of land, some 25 miles by 15, between Tel Aviv and Haifa. Some say it is why Israel is so vulnerable to aerial attack by its Arab enemies.

Such hectic activity is evidence of Israel's pioneer spirit, now fast turning into a new form of Mediterranean enterprise culture. It is also the realisation of a 2000-year-old dream, for this is *Eretz Israel*, the true, historic Israel pledged first to Abraham and then to his heirs. Yet a century ago much of this was semi-desert, lightly cultivated by Arab villagers and grazed by the flocks and herds of the wandering Bedouin. Fewer than 100,000 Jews lived in the entire Ottoman Empire, and immigration from Europe had only just begun.

That the pledge to Abraham was realised is largely due to an idea born at the end of the nineteenth century. Zionism had a simple message – that the Jews should have a national homeland. The modern term Zionism was largely the conception of a wealthy Austrian Jew, Theodor Herzl. The rise of romanticism and nationalism aggravated fresh bouts of anti-semitism, culminating in the court martial of a Jewish officer in the French army, Alfred Dreyfus, on trumped up charges of spying. Hertzl began to press for a homeland in Palestine. In 1897 he organised the First Congress of the Zionist Movement in Basel, and a year later he met Kaiser Wilhelm II of Germany in Jerusalem and petitioned him to help Jews go to Palestine.

Herzl's view was a secular one, that all Jews should eventually have the right to return to the country of their ancestors. Other homelands had been proposed, including even Uganda. Herzl himself was rather a latecomer to the idea. A group known as the 'practical Zionists' began leaving Russia for Palestine in the 1880s. The Tsar Alexander III headed the most overtly anti-semitic regime in Europe, and his decrees restricting the Jewish community had ushered in a wave of pogroms. The influx of some 25,000 Russian Jews between 1882 and 1903 was to be known as the first *aliyah*. By 1948 more than 580,000 Jews had arrived from abroad.

Modern Zionism had diverse origins and was to take diverse paths. As Herzl's movement shifted from dream to reality, divergent goals and tactics appeared. Some ultra-orthodox did not believe in it at all; Messianic Jews, and followers of the Hasidim – the ultra conservative 'pious' movement that originated in eighteenth-century Poland – still ignore the state of Israel, and refuse to serve in its forces. They believe that Jews should conduct themselves righteously to hasten the coming of the Messiah, an end to which the secular authority of modern Israel is irrelevant.

To trace the development of Zionism I turned to Professor Josef Nedava, a historian at the Hebrew University in Jerusalem. The professor was a firm believer in the Gush Emonim and their claim that *Eretz Israel* should stretch from the Mediterranean to the Jordan. 'It's a very long-running affair,' he began. 'It begins with the crushing of the two Jewish revolts by the Romans in 70 AD and 135 AD, and it simply involves the hope of a return home. In the diaspora Jews had to be ready to move on – which is why the rabbi traditionally slept with his staff beside him. Jews always prayed for rain and dew in Palestine, and not in the place where they were. They felt they were always living extra-territorially.'

The Jews lived under the threat of perpetual dispersal and discrimination. Their desperation is symbolised by their last stand against the

Romans in 72 AD at Herod the Great's fortress overlooking the Dead Sea at Massada, where rather than surrender they committed collective suicide. Massada is one of the most potent national shrines of modern Israel. With the triumph of Christianity, discrimination was based on the popular belief that the Jews had denied and murdered him, Christ who was one of their own. To this was linked a monstrous fabrication called the 'blood lie', according to which the Jews took the blood of the Christian first-borns for their rituals. This was still current in the last century.

Some of the worst European pogroms occurred during the Crusades, as rabble-rousing preachers suggested that infidels at home should be killed as well as those in the Holy Land. Some of the worst occurred in Rhineland cities such as Mainz and Trier, where the Jews had enjoyed the protection of the bishops; and the large Jewish quarter in York was burned to the ground. A most virulent campaign was that launched by the Catholic Ferdinand and Isabella of Spain in 1492.

The decisive step of persuading a great power to help the Jews achieve their homeland was not achieved by Herzl but his successor as head of the Zionist Federation, Chaim Weizmann. Chaim Weizmann was born in poverty in Russia, but when he was appointed a lecturer in chemistry at Manchester University, he took British nationality. He cultivated the friendship of Herbert Samuel, the first practising Jew to become a cabinet minister in Britain, and the editor of the *Manchester Guardian*, C. P. Scott. Weizmann was a born negotiator, a man of charm and humanity, and one of the greatest of Jewish statesmen. He became Israel's first President in 1948.

The material he had to work with seemed unpromising. But Weizmann enjoyed the friendship of Lloyd George and Winston Churchill and used all his powers of persuasion to put the case for the Jews. He told one British civil servant, 'I am not romantic, except that Jews must always be romantic, for them reality is too terrible.' In November 1917, a month before General Allenby captured Jerusalem, the Foreign Secretary, Arthur Balfour, sent a communiqué to Lord Rothschild as head of the British Jewish community, largely on Weizmann's instigation.

The text of the Balfour Declaration is brief to the point of bluntness. Its importance lay as much in what it did not say. 'His Majesty's Government,' ran the second paragraph,

> view with favour the establishment in Palestine of a national home for the Jewish people, and will use their best endeavours to facilitate the achievement of this object, it being clearly understood that nothing shall be done which

may prejudice the civil and religious rights of existing non-Jewish communities in Palestine or the rights and political status enjoyed by Jews in any other country.

In other words it was not offering a state, nor any form of self-government, to the Jews of Palestine, nor even a right to unlimited immigration. All this took place at the same time as Colonel T. E. Lawrence's Arab Revolt. The year before, 1916, had seen the Sykes-Picot agreement to carve up the Ottoman Levant between France and Britain, while in letters written between 1915 and 1916 Sir Henry McMahon, the British High Commissioner in Cairo, had promised the Emir Husain, Sherif of Mecca, 'that Great Britain is prepared to recognize and support the independence of the Arabs in all the regions within the limits demanded by the Sherif of Mecca.' In return the Arabs would help the British against the Ottoman-German armies in Palestine.

This fearful muddle and conflict of interests was not resolved by the award of the mandate over Palestine to Britain by the League of Nations in 1922. The imperial sun was past its zenith for the British and they could hardly hope to satisfy both the Arabs and the Jews. Characteristically, they tried to have it both ways and ended up satisfying neither party.

At this stage two other founders of modern Israel became of crucial importance – Vladimir Jabotinsky, a particular hero of Professor Nedava, and David Ben-Gurion, who was to become the new state's first prime minister in 1948. Vladimir Jabotinsky was a Russian Jew who, like Herzl, had spent much of his early life as a journalist. His legacy to Israel was largely military, together with an uncompromising view of the boundaries of the new state. Like Herzl, he had a strong romantic streak, and frequently he has been called the d'Annunzio of Zionism.

In 1917 he organised a force of 5000 men into the Jewish Legion to assist Allenby in Palestine – Professor Nedava claims his men were in the field before Lawrence had organised his Arab irregulars. After the First World War Jabotinsky helped the *Yishuv* – the Jewish community already in Palestine – to organise the defence of their settlements behind the Haganah, which after 1948 grew into the Israeli Defence Force, the modern Israeli army.

Jabotinsky's impatience with British controls on Jewish immigration caused him to break with the more moderate Zionist leadership. In 1925 his opposition faction became the Union of Zionist-Revisionists; this developed into the Herut Party which, as the centrepiece of the Likud bloc, enjoyed an unbroken run in government for more than ten years after 1977. Jabotinsky died in 1940, but the first Likud coalitions were led by one of his most ardent disciples, Menachem Begin. 'Herzl worked by infiltration, but Jabotinsky wanted a colonising regime; he felt you had to flood the land with Jewish immigrants to get what you want,' comments Professor Nedava. In 1931 Jabotinsky and the Revisionists decided to form their own underground force, the Irgun Zvai Leumi (IZL), to liberate Palestine for the Jews – though according to Professor Nedava, Jabotinsky 'had no intention of expelling the local population'.

It soon became apparent that British policies in the mandate were failing. Both the Arabs and the Jews were restive, eyeing each other with suspicion and raiding each other's settlements and villages. The Arabs also had national aspirations, and these burst out in 1936 in the Arab Revolt, a series of riots, raids and protests that were to crackle and splutter for another three years. Two British generals, Harold Alexander and Bernard Montgomery, were charged with dealing with the insurrection. A Commission of Inquiry headed by Lord Peel proposed partition of the land between Arabs and Jews, which was enshrined in the most significant of a series of British White Papers in May 1939. 'It was a death blow to Zionism,' commented Professor Nedava, 'because it restricted Jewish immigration to only 75,000 over the next five years.' It looked as if the Jews would only be given a slice of a state, instead of the longed-for homeland.

But the entire political landscape was to be changed by the Holocaust. In 1942 a Zionist meeting at Biltmore in the United States decided to go all out to achieve a Jewish state.

One of those who escaped the Holocaust, in an amazing story of personal bravery and survival – he was one of the few not to be broken by interrogation from the Soviet secret police, the NKVD – was Menachem Begin, the disciple of Vladimir Jabotinsky. Begin hailed from Brest-Litovsk where all but a very few of the Jews were wiped out, including most of his family. Although he had visited before, he arrived to stay in Palestine in 1942 as a private soldier in General Anders' Polish army, which had been allowed out of Soviet Russia via Iran.

Begin and his future deputy prime minister, Yitzhak Shamir, began to organise a terror campaign to get the British out. Shamir belonged to the Lohamei Herut Yisrael (LHI), otherwise known as the Stern Gang after its founder. The Stern Gang believed in assassination, and in 1944 shot dead Lord Moyne, the British minister for the Middle East. Begin worked on a broader canvas; in his most famous operation he directed the blowing up of a wing of the King David Hotel in Jerusalem in July 1946, killing 28 Britons, 41 Arabs and 17 Jews. He was also involved in the hanging of two British sergeants as a reprisal for the execution of two of his men; one of the sergeants turned out to be Jewish.

Even towards the end of the War and after, the British tried to restrict the number of Jews coming to Palestine. Their rule in the dying years of the mandate was marked by incompetence through weariness. In 1947 they handed over the whole issue of Palestine's future to the fledgling United Nations; and the UN resolved to partition Palestine.

The Zionists prepared to fight, and were threatened by the armies of Egypt, Syria, Lebanon and Jordan. The Arab legion of Jordan succeeded in taking the Old City of Jerusalem and overrunning Jewish settlements to the east. But Arab resistance groups in the villages were no match for the Haganah, now some 80,000 strong, and the IZL with its 10,000 gunmen. The Jews had far greater supplies of ammunition, much of it 'liberated' from the British. Arabs were ejected from Haifa and Jaffa and the surrounding countryside. In April 1948, at the village of Deir Yassin near Jerusalem, Begin's forces murdered more than 200 Arabs, causing panic and a mass exodus from the surrounding communities. Later that year Begin's IZL were fired on by the Haganah as they tried to get guns ashore from a freighter. In the hour of victory, the Jews seemed on the brink of civil war.

Begin averted the crisis by warning his men against 'fratricidal warfare'. Eventually all units were to be absorbed into the Israeli Defence Force – but not before the Stern Gang had carried out its most infamous assassination in Jerusalem in September 1948. The victim was Count Folke Bernardotte, the UN's special commissioner, who was trying to negotiate the return of Arab refugees displaced by the fighting.

If Begin provided the rough tactics which hurried the departure of the British, David Ben-Gurion was the real political architect of the new state. Ben-Gurion had also been born in Poland, but had come to Palestine in 1906. He was one of the founders of the Histradut, the organisation of labour unions, and the Mapai, which was to be Israel's Labour Party. In 1935 he became the Chairman of the Palestine Zionist Executive and the Jewish Agency Executive: in other words, he was the head of the Jews in Palestine, the *Yishuv*.

Ben-Gurion was a tough pragmatist, who would work with the British if need be. He could also stand up to the excesses of Begin and Shamir. When Britain went to war with Germany, he wanted the Jews of Palestine to help, despite his opposition to Britain's proposals to partition Palestine outlined in the 1939 White Paper. 'We must fight the war as if there were no White Paper,' he proclaimed, 'and fight the White Paper as if there were no war.' His offer to form Jewish units was opposed by many British commanders, but the Jews had a strong advocate in Winston Churchill; that Jewish units should fight the Nazis appealed to his sense of poetic justice. Eventually a Jewish Brigade of four battalions was formed under the British, fighting with distinction when finally committed to battle in Italy. The training they received was to stand them in good stead against the Arabs.

Ben-Gurion served twice as prime minister. But his sharp tongue and somewhat cantankerous approach made him impatient with his party and his colleagues, and he was to form two parties of his own before giving up politics for good in 1970. He was an ardent supporter of the kibbutz movement, encouraging young people to build pioneering communes in the Negev desert.

For all his respect for Ben-Gurion, Professor Nedava was a firm adherent of Jabotinsky and Begin. He favoured the occupation of Judaea, Samaria and Gaza, and opposed the Camp David Accords signed between Begin and Sadat in 1978 because it meant Israel's withdrawl from Sinai. His biggest worry was Arab terrorism, which would become increasingly violent as the extremists became trapped in their own fantasy world. 'Even before Zionism, Arabs and Jews did not get on well together. Maimonides [the great medieval Jewish sage from Cordoba] was persecuted by the Arabs.'

The story of Israel is intimately linked with its prowess in arms. The Israel Defence Force and the Israeli Air Force are two of the most revered institutions of the state. Young officers take an oath of allegiance at the Wailing Wall, the most sacred site in Old Jerusalem. The forces have been bloodied in five wars since 1948, and each has been seen as a struggle for survival. Israeli forces established a reputation for skill in tank warfare in the desert, and air combat against the numerical odds.

According to Ben-Gurion, Israel's forces would always need a 'qualitative edge' in equipment and training over their surrounding Arab enemies; their own ingenuity and the generosity of America would have to see to this. Under Ben-Gurion Israel started its own nuclear programme, with its own plutonium enrichment plant at the Dimona complex in the Negev Desert. Israel became the first nuclear power of the Middle East.

Israel kept the tactical edge by the use of the pre-emptive or surprise attack. By getting their blow in first, Israeli aircraft managed to destroy most of the Egyptian air force on the ground in the opening hours of the Six Days' War in June 1967. Surprise bombing and commando raids were mounted in Lebanon in the 1970s. In 1976 a commando force flew a round trip of 2,500 miles to rescue hostages being held by Palestinian hijackers at Entebbe airport in Uganda. Without warning, in 1981,

Israeli jets bombed the Osirak reactor in Iraq, where they believed nuclear weapons were being developed. The operation took only a few hours and the pilots were back at base well before lunch. The Americans were furious because the Israelis had used the latest F-15 and F-16 strike aircraft before they had become fully operational in the US Air Force.

But the Israelis were not to be put off from launching long-range attacks by air and sea against their enemies. In October 1985 their jets bombed Yasser Arafat's new PLO headquarters near Tunis, killing fifty; and in the spring of 1988, Israeli commandos landed near Tunis to assassinate the PLO operational commander, Halil al-Wazir, codenamed Abu Jihad, at his seaside bungalow.

Such tactics were backed by a biblical conviction that Israeli forces were the 'sword of the Lord'. The use of arms is seen as part of a process of purification – a notion severely tested by the rough policing tactics used by the army in dealing with Palestinian protesters in the Intifada.

Such firmness of purpose reflects a deep-seated insecurity about Israel's strategic borders. Although its frontiers as defined in 1949 received general recognition, the new borders established in the 1967 and 1973 wars did not. UN Resolution 242 in November 1967 said that Israel should withdraw from the territories occupied that June, and this was reaffirmed in Resolution 338 in October 1973. '242 and 338' have become the texts of the Palestinian cause as much as any Koranic text about a Holy War or Jihad. The only former Arab foe to offer a formal peace treaty was Egypt under Sadat. Ironically, it was to be agreed in 1977 by the former disciple of Jabotinsky, Menachem Begin, who had just become the Likud Prime Minister. Despite Sadat's dramatic flight to plead peace before the Knesset in Jerusalem, most Egyptians and many Israelis accepted the accord only grudgingly.

General Meir Zorea and his family embody the fighting and pioneering spirit of the new Israeli state. Half his career has been spent in the Israeli Defence Force, half cultivating and managing the kibbutz which has been his home. Of his four sons, one was killed in an aerial battle over Sinai in 1967, and another died leading Israeli tanks on the Golan Heights in 1973. His eldest son has been head of the Military Intelligence Corps.

I went to see him in his apartment in the Ma'agan Mikha'el kibbutz, south of Haifa – a place which looked more like an agri-business factory than a pioneers' ranch. Typically, the sixty-three-year-old general had to take leave from the irrigation equipment factory attached to the kibbutz to make our appointment. The old officer was a formidable but genial figure who seemed to have no doubts about anything.

He was of Ukrainian Jewish stock, but had been born in Romania. After leaving school he was involved in the kibbutz movement, but in 1942 he enlisted in the British army. His attitude to the British was ambivalent. 'We always had two loyalties – to the Allies and then to the Haganah.' He felt that the British had betrayed their mandate in Palestine because 'by definition it was given to the British to establish a Jewish national home.' He found absurd the idea that some Jew immigrants were 'illegal', and did what he could to get Jews into Palestine. Eventually he was discharged from the Jewish Brigade with the rank of captain, after being awarded the Military Cross for his daring operations behind enemy lines in Italy in 1945.

By the end of 1947 he was training men for the fight for independence, putting into practice all he had learned in Italy. He acquired a reputation for integrity and fearlessness, and commanded his own battalion of the Haganah in 1948. After independence he set up an officer training school and the Israeli Staff College, including exchanges with the military academies of the former enemy, Britain. He dabbled in politics, but found it too corrupt, and devoted himself instead to cultivating the kibbutz. In 1962 he became head of Israel's Land Authority, taking a characteristically fundamentalist approach, 'Land in Israel cannot be sold, for the Torah [the law of Moses] states all the land belongs to God. So it can be leased but not bought.'

I was curious how he managed to instil discipline into his soldiers. Israel is famous for its egalitarian traditions, and the army is a citizen army, with only 30,000 regulars in a force of over 140,000. Men have to serve at least three years full-time national service, and women two years, and males have to be available for at least one month's reserve duty each year up to the age of fifty-four. It is a colossal drain on the economy, the equivalent of more than a quarter of the national product, and some consider it a major contribution to Israel's recent hyperinflation.

'Discipline is a problem within the Jewish world,' he said. 'A Jew doesn't have an intermediary between him and God. The rabbi has a duty to explain what the Torah says, but not to tell the people what to do. We are a people chosen by God, not to give us more rights, but to make us do the right things, a matter of duty rather than privileges. Every Jew sees himself as a king, a son of David, so no one tells him what to do. How can you command a platoon of kings? Only if the platoon accepts the commander.'

Service in the army was a sacred duty. He believed Israel had an absolute right to maintain its control over the West Bank of the Jordan, and should be prepared to fight again to do so. The Jewish people were unique in their 4,000 years of history, he believed, though as a socialist he did not consider one being was better than another.

On the way to lunch he gave me a brief tour of the kibbutz, a 1500-acre estate supporting 1500 people, a third of them as full members of the community. It had workshops, processing and packing plants, a factory making irrigation machinery and another making metal-processing equipment. The older houses were graced with little gardens and small patios. Focal points were the meeting halls and the huge canteen, a mixture of airport lounge and campus refectory. We queued for trays at the entrance. Ahead of us a young woman soldier balanced her tray while she slung her bag over one shoulder and her Uzi submachine-gun over the other.

That day I journeyed north to Akko, or Acre, the last bastion of the Crusading kingdom which fell in 1291. The huge ramparts and sea walls of Richard Coeur de Lion's Acre still stand, encircling a small fishing port. In the old town stands a handsome mosque and old Crusading stables. The citadel is an Israeli national monument; the British detained some prominent Jewish activists in it, and some were hanged on terrorist charges. From the balconies of the houses nearby hung gaudily coloured Arab blankets – a dash of brightness against the drab surroundings of broken streets, heaps of rubbish and pools of stagnant water. Arab communities like this must have huddled in the centre of cities like Haifa and Jaffa over half a century ago. But this was now an Arab ghetto. In the land of the chosen, these Arabs in Acre were the unchosen.

I had gone north to Haifa to meet Professor Ozer Schild, a former vice chancellor of the university there. He was a quiet, reflective academic, in sharp contrast to the blustery style of General Zorea. The professor had come from his native Denmark in the 1950s and had worked for the Israeli government as an adviser. He had then moved to America before being invited to return to Haifa University.

His main area of interest was the relationship between the Ashkenazim and the Sephardim. The Sephardim had been outbreeding the Ashkenazim and contributed to the victory of the conservative Likud bloc over the Labour alliance in 1977 which had carried Menachem Begin to power – though Begin himself, as a Pole, was very Askenazim and not well disposed to some of the manners and beliefs of the oriental Sephardim. Professor Schild suspected intermarriage between the two groups was growing, though he thought this would not mean a return to the secular pioneering socialism of Labour as Israel's youth was becoming steadily more conservative and more orthodox in religion.

But it was on the question of the balance of population between the Israelis and the Palestinians that he was to prove prophetic. He believed that Jewish immigration to Israel was steadily declining, and that Israelis were leaving to receive further education and take jobs abroad. The Law of Return, introduced by Ben-Gurion in 1951, had resulted in a wave of immigration; Jews had come from Morocco and Tunisia, and more than 160,000 left Algeria when it achieved independence from the French. But recently the number of new arrivals had slowed to a trickle.

Like Salim Tamari, the sociologist at Bir Zeit, he believed that the Arab population, excluding that of Gaza, would match the Israeli Jews by the middle of the next century. If Gaza was included, it would happen even sooner. He was worried about the future viability of Israel. He could see little chance of avoiding another war over Israel's boundaries and the West Bank would have to be held as a strategic buffer to Haifa and Tel Aviv. 'But if I put myself in the shoes of a Palestinian my perception would be this: I have been ejected from home, by force of arms and money. But it is my land. Why should I reconcile myself to this?'

Reason told him that the outlook was bleak. 'If there is no major Jewish immigration in the next few decades Zionism will fail. But the Jews have always looked for miracles in their history, and we have to pray for one now.'

The miracle of further immigration was to occur, but not in the way the professor could have predicted in 1986. Even as we spoke that summer matters were on the turn in Gorbachev's Russia. Within four years his authorities were to process exit visas for nearly a third of the Soviet Union's three million Jews likely to want to leave. In 1990 more than 200,000 immigrants were expected, and within the next five years the Jewish Agency expected a total of two million Soviet Jews. This would bring the Jewish population up to about seven million by the end of the century, while the total Arab population, including the Occupied Territories, would be somewhere in the region of two and half million.

But the miracle had its drawbacks. The new arrivals needed to be housed, fed, given jobs and instructed in Hebrew. Some adults had to be circumcised and given religious instruction, for they had been forbidden to practise of their religion in the Soviet Union. It was to be a colossal strain on Israel's resources, not least because America, her staunchest ally, only gave cheap housing loans (of about $400 million in 1990) if the new arrivals were not settled on the West Bank – though after six months an immigrant became a citizen, and could choose where to live. In the short term it meant extra pressure on East Jerusalem, which Israel had annexed after the Six Days' War, and where more than 140,000 Jews were living in concrete bastions on hills that had once been part of Jordan.

The Russian arrivals provided an answer to the Palestinians' tactic of trying to beat Zionism by demography. But the numbers game would prove tricky for both Arabs and Jews alike.

The clash feared and foreshadowed by Professor Schild was not to be an attack from the outside. The revolt came from within the Arab communities of the West Bank, East Jerusalem and Gaza when, in the winter of 1987, rage and frustration at twenty years of military adminis-tration without real representation boiled over. It was called the Intifada – the shaking.

iii   Intifada

It was a remarkably good aim. The stone burst through the back window of the car, clipped my jaw, and showered the driver with glass and blood. We were in the middle of Gaza City on a strike day, and in the wrong vehicle, despite the fact that the taxi bore the number plates of Arab East Jerusalem. Welcome to the uprising, the Intifada, the slingshot marksman was saying. The *shebab* (the lads), as footsoldiers and messen-gers of the revolt, had spoken.

Superficial as it was, my injury provided a passport to the main hospital in downtown Gaza, where the Israeli military guard were trying desper-ately to keep out all foreign journalists. As we drove up to the barrier, an Israeli conscript jigged in front of the car in a frenzy of fear and rage, shoving us out of the way. My Palestinian friend explained that I had been injured, shoving me through the gate while the Israelis shouted that I was needed for questioning. She hurriedly entered my name in the hospital register as 'Robert Mohammed Fox,' and no doubt I am still on their books under that name.

In the clinic nurses and doctors surged round apologising for my mis-hap, for which they felt personally responsible. A doctor who had quali-fied in Cairo laboriously stitched the wound, apologising again for the lack of adequate materials. The whole hospital was always short of essen-tial instruments, medicines and drugs, and matters had been made a hundred times worse by the Intifada, now well into its second month.

That evening, I managed to slip back into the hospital for a ward round with one of the doctors. The rooms and corridors were scenes of indescribable squalor and filth. Blood and faeces choked the meagre sanitation facilities, and the bathrooms looked as if they had not been cleaned for a month. The place was like an abattoir. Young and old, male and female, lay on beds and makeshift bunks with lacerated stomachs, wounds from bullets and anti-riot rounds, smashed thighs, arms and shoulders. Not all the seemingly indiscriminate damage had been caused by the security forces, but according to those present a large part of it had.

Ahmed Iasigi, the doctor in charge, seemed on the point of despair. He had to work twenty hours a day in different shifts just to keep the wards going. He was worried about losing his job. He had been deprived of his livelihood before. After graduating in medicine and surgery at Cairo and Alexandria, he had been prevented by the Israelis from practising for one year in Gaza, and had been ordered not to travel for seven years.

That bleak January day I was witnessing both the symptom and the causes of the Intifada. It had been triggered off in Gaza on 8 December when an Israeli truck collided outside Gaza City with a Palestinian car, killing all four occupants. The Palestinians claimed the driver of the truck was an Israeli soldier, who had been allowed to go free instead of being charged with manslaughter. Different factions point to other incidents, including a bomb explosion at the Jaffa Gate in the Old City of Jerusalem. Signs of trouble had been appearing since midsummer; tension had been building up inside the detention camps and in Gaza's main jail. The autumn saw a series of strikes in schools, and increasing demands for civil rights. Frustration, the commonest commodity in Gaza, hung in the air.

The frustration is implicit in what the Gaza Strip has become since the Israelis took it from Egypt in the Six Days' War in 1967 – one of the most crowded spots on earth, and the most desolate habitation of humanity on the Mediterranean shore. Gaza was never a great centre for the Jews, and in ancient days it was the home of the Philistines. Appropriately enough, it is where the blinded Samson immolated himself and his enemies. In Ottoman times it was a centre of the cotton industry, giving its name to 'gauze'; the port prospered, its architecture that of a well-to-do provincial town in Lower Egypt, with elegant ochre-coloured houses with shady verandas and balconies. Ottoman Gaza was evoked for me by one of the last mayors of Gaza, Rashad al-Shawa, whose reception room, with its heavy brocades and settees and dark wooden chairs, had a touch of the late Ottoman era. He recalled the Ottoman regime as one of benign neglect – which suited the Shawa family fine, as they owned about a quarter of southern Palestine.

Everything changed in 1948. As a result of the war of independence the Gaza Strip received about a quarter of a million refugees. Its own administration was given to Egypt, who lost it temporarily during the 1956 War, and for good after the Six Days' War. Ben-Gurion believed that Israel should have nothing to do with it, allegedly saying that Gaza had as much to do with Israel as the other side of the moon. By 1990 the Strip was inhabited by nearly half a million Palestinians calling themselves refugees, two-thirds of whom still lived in refugee camps. The total population of the Gaza was nudging 700,000, including a few thousand Jews, whose settlements looked like fortified holiday camps, the beach furniture and bathings huts decorated with barbed wire, search-lights and machine-guns nests.

The Gaza Strip itself is a patchwork of grey refugee camps, and yellow-ing townships, interrupted by patches of green farmland and market garden. Getting into it is like crossing a no-man's-land into another country. The Israelis restrict access to four main crossing-points, each generously marked out by barriers, barbed wire and armed sentries. Meas-uring 40 kilometres by 8, it has more than 16,000 inhabitants to every square kilometre. The administration is largely Israeli, through their military courts, and permission to work and travel outside the Strip was rigorously supervised even before the Intifada. Under the peace accords with Egypt in 1979, Gaza was supposed to enjoy its own 'local autonomy', though this was never defined, let alone implemented. Work became even scarcer as the population in the camps swelled. By the mid-1980s, 45,000 Palestinians from Gaza (and a further 75,000 from the West Bank) sought jobs each day in Israel proper, many without legal permits. Knots of Palestinians gathered on the Tel Aviv road as building sub-contractors picked the cheap labour they required for the day or week. They were labouring in an alien land, a new race of helots according to one Israeli critic.

Gaza City was deluged by a torrential downpour blowing in from the Mediterranean as I toured the camps and the town that January day in 1988. Part of the main street had become a lake, lapping round a clump of forlorn palms. Most Palestinians I met combined desperation with a frantic elation that at last something was moving in the Strip. The *shebab* carried messages, organised street meetings, and threw the odd stone at passing Israeli jeeps or unfamiliar cars. Neighbourhood committees formed to deal with every conceivable activity.

In those first heady weeks it was still not absolutely clear who was in charge. Demonstrations, protests and strikes were ordered by night-letter and pamphlet, the first of which had been issued two days after the incident at the roundabout in December. At that stage, at least, most of the tactical decisions were being taken inside the Occupied Territories. Arafat's Fatah and the PLO had been caught unawares, and would take some time to establish their authority through the United Command councils. Religious militants from Islamic Jihad, and the offshoot of the Muslim Brethren, Hamas, had stolen a march on them and mosques had become information exchanges, command posts and field hospitals for many of the protesters.

The Israelis had also been taken by surprise, and took some time to realise that this was no passing phenomenon. The Defence Minister, Yitzhak Rabin, declined to cut short a tour abroad. After a few weeks he said that soldiers should beat protesters and rioters, since breaking bones was better than taking lives. When this policy drew unfavourable international comment, the soldiers went back to shooting. By the time the Intifada passed its thousandth day in September 1990, more than 600 Palestinians had been shot dead, and 6 Israeli soldiers and 13 settlers had died; more than 1500 had been wounded. In late September 1990 a reserve soldier returning to duty in Gaza City was beaten to death and his car set alight after he had taken a wrong turning; dozens of houses and business premises were demolished by the Israeli forces in reprisals.

The Intifada spread throughout the Occupied Territories in a few days, in each place taking a different form under different leadership. Nablus saw violent rioting and stone-throwing; strike-bound Ramallah and Bethlehem mounted continuous civil rights protests; villages like Dura in the hills of Hebron closed their roads to outside traffic.

At the house of a Red Crescent worker in Gaza, I was treated to a diatribe by Yusira al Barbara, a founder member of the Palestinian Women's Union. We had met before, when she had lost no time in telling me that the iniquities of the British had caused many of the woes of the Palestinians. She had grown up in Jerusalem under the mandate, and then studied at Cairo University where she became the first woman graduate from the Palestinian community. A tiny figure with silver hair in a tight bun, she said that she had endeavoured over the years to better the lot of Palestinian women with courses on domestic science, literacy and health and hygiene. But under Israeli military administration she had suffered interminable bureaucratic harassment. Four times she had been hauled before the courts, once for having a drawing of the Palestinian flag in her office, and on another occasion for holding classes in

English and sewing without a permit. She was particularly anxious about those women whose men had been dragged off to jail. She had just seen one whose house had been wrecked; the men in the family had been arrested, and she had been left with eight children under the age of ten to look after. She was upset at international indifference to the plight of the Palestinians, principally in Arab countries like Egypt and Syria. This, she foresaw, would lead to an increase in violence, but 'we will not suffer alone. In the end the whole world will suffer with us, as it did with Samson Agonistes. If every young Palestinian person here is driven to the violence of an Abu Nidal, it is the fault of the world.'

Her old campaigning colleague, Dr Haider Abdul Shafi, said he had seen uprisings in Gaza before – 'but this one involves all sections of the population,' he added. His organisation, the Red Crescent, could provide three dental and three antenatal clinics, but they were poorly funded. Other institutions such as the Sun Day Care Centre and the Blood Bank provided simple social facilities and a form of community politics, since all party activity was banned.

Dr Shafi had a sober, unromantic view of the future of the Israelis and the Palestinians of the Occupied Territories. They were tied by simple facts of geography and economics, and the 1.7 million Palestinians provided a large and essential market for Israeli goods. 'From my point of view it is inevitable that Palestinians and Jews will live in this part of the world. They must find out about each other, discover each other's view and find a way to peace. The Israelis are living in the past. In their enthusiasm for the Zionist programme they have locked themselves in an enclosed compartment. They cannot see beyond.'

From the house of the Red Crescent officers I was taken by the United Nations agency in change, UNRWA, on a clandestine tour of Jabalia, largest of the Gaza refugee camps. With a population of over 50,000, it had been the scene of the heaviest action in the early days of the uprising. In one house, the wreckage of furniture and personal effects had been laid out like a shrine – a pile of broken mirrors, ornaments, vases of plastic flowers, gutted radios and torn photographs. I saw battered ribs and cheekbones, bruised eyes, broken arms and legs. I was told, soberly and quietly, of chases in the street, arbitrary beatings, and the smashing open of homes in the middle of the night.

Once a week families put on their best to visit the barrier by the detention camp in Gaza known as Ansar 2. Women visiting their sons and husbands wear white kerchiefs and scarves, and black shawls and over-tunics decorated with embroidered flowers – the badge of the Palestinian nation. Mothers chase frantically for news of their sons, hoping to get a precious permission to visit, or – rarest of luxuries – to hear that he is to be discharged. 'They have no blankets in there for this cold weather,' one told me. 'They are treated like animals; this is no ordinary prison,' said another. A prison designed for 800 now holds 1700, its numbers swelled by midnight round-ups by the dreaded agents of the internal security, the Shinbet.

In Ansar and the other detention camps, like Atlit near Caesarea where hundreds of Shi'ites from Lebanon have been caged, the Israelis appear to have made a tactical blunder. Far from breaking the will of those detained, such institutions often galvanise it. Ansar 2, on the evidence of those who had been there, had become an academy for Palestinian activists.

Keeping up with the law administered by the Israelis was a nightmare, according to Shar Habed of the Gaza Bar Association. He had been trained in Egypt, 'but you come across things here that you will never hear about in universities.' He had been denied access to the records of clients in Ansar 2, he claimed; such documentation as he could acquire came from their families. There was no right of habeas corpus, and a suspect could be detained indefinitely without trial. Military courts worked like conveyor belts; sometimes he and his partner had to defend 60 cases without seeing the files the day before. Day and night the arrests continued. Conditions were deemed so impossible that all 330 lawyers in the Bar Association declared a boycott of the courts ten days after the Intifada began. Not that it would make much difference. 'Between 1967 and 1987, I calculate that only about twenty people have been found not guilty in the military courts, out of approximately 25,000 brought before them.'

I had previously visited Gaza and the camps in a moment of near tranquillity in the summer of 1986, the year before the outbreak of the Intifada. The older Palestinians were cocooned in their own melancholy. They identified themselves with the old villages and family homes they had fled in 1948 and 1949. More conspicuous were the flocks of small children swarming over the wastelands by the sea and through the alleys of the camp. The average Palestinian family in Gaza, according to the UN Works and Relief Agency, had between five and six children, many of whom had only one parent, and no visible means of support.

Such desolation seems almost intrinsic to the story of the Palestinians. Though they are within the Arab fold, some have claimed that part of their ancestry at least is non-semitic. This distinction has less to do with the shapes of noses than with the shapes of alphabets and language. The Assyrians, Babylonians, Phoenicians, the Jews and Arabs are all deemed semitic because they subscribed to the shape of lettering and writing which have come to us from Tyre and Ugarit; this broadly is the semitic alphabet. The Philistines, the early ancestors of the Palestinians in Gaza, are believed to have very different origins, though what they were precisely is largely an academic guess.

The 1912 Baedeker *Guide to Historic Palestine* thinks it has a clue, though no final answer. On the history of Gaza it states:

> In the country of Peleshet, i.e. the low plain between Carmel and the frontier of Egypt, we find in historical times the 'pelishtim,' or Philistines, a nation which did not belong to the Semitic race. Their invasion was from the sea about 1100 BC, when they took possession of the coast with its originally Canaanitish towns. Their origin is unknown.

It goes on to link them with Crete, and praises their prowess at arms, with javelins, archery and chariots. Here is a strong hint that they were relatives of the Peoples of the Sea, the men with horned helmets and hats of feathers who feature the sea battle on Ramasses III's mausoleum at Madinet Habu near Luxor, and are commemorated in the stone monuments of Filitosa in Corsica. Their champion was Goliath, the victim of David's sling-shot – a weapon that was enjoying a revival in the hands of the *shebab*.

In the Twenties and Thirties new champions of the Palestinians began to emerge. Their communities, some 850 villages in Ottoman and British mandate Palestine, were run by a dozen or so large clans, who owned most of the land. In the Haifa region Sheikh Izz al-Din al-Qassam based a guerilla band on his Young Men's Muslim Association. He staged one or two daring raids, but was killed when his band was surrounded in the hills near Jenin in 1935. He became a martyr of the Palestinian cause, whose legacy was to be remembered by Islamic militants in the Intifada.

The most powerful clan were the al-Husseini, whose head was Hajj Amin al-Husseini, Grand Mufti of Jerusalem and head of the Supreme Muslim Council. He fought the Jews, he fought the British, he fought the moderates in the Palestinian community. In 1937 he began to side with the Axis powers and was forced into exile. Defeat in the war of independence meant the end of his dream of his returning to an independent and free Palestine.

The Mufti's nephew, Abdul Khadr al-Husseini, died heroically in 1948 at Kastel, one of the few set-piece battles in the Israeli war of independence in which Palestinian irregulars managed to mount a full-scale military operation; while a distant cousin was to become the most famous

Palestinian politician in exile. His name was Yasser Arafat, and some of his formative years were spent in Gaza. Though a great showman and publicist, he has hardly ever acknowledged the al-Husseini connection.

Arafat's politics were formed by Israel's victory in 1948–49; by what the Arabs call 'al-Nakba' – the catastrophe. Between half a million and 800,000 refugees went into exile – many of them to refugee camps, where their families are still, mourning a distant home which they remember dimly or have never seen at all. Today about a million live in camps in Syria, Jordan, Lebanon and Israel, and a further million and half live abroad.

The Flying Dutchman of international diplomacy, Yasser Arafat claims that he was born in East Jerusalem, in a house near the Wailing Wall destroyed by the Israelis after the Six Days' War. Others say he was born in Gaza or Cairo. The son of a wealthy merchant in Gaza, his interest in politics emerged when he was a student in Cairo. In 1959, in Kuwait, a group of students headed by Arafat founded a new Party called Fatah. It had a single aim: the liberation of Palestine. Later other groups were founded with parallel aims, such as the Popular Front for the Liberation of Palestine, which had a more orthodox Marxist platform, and in 1964 the Palestine Liberation Organisation was founded under Nasser's protection. In 1968 the PLO was reorganised round Fatah, and Arafat became its chairman. It had an army of sorts, and a nominal air force, and received funds from Saudi Arabia and the Gulf Emirates, principally Kuwait.

Arafat's career seems a perpetual game of snakes and ladders, lurching between violence and diplomacy. The late Sixties saw a spate of plane hijackings and bombings by Fatah and its rivals. Driven from Jordan by the Bedouin forces of King Hussein in the 'black September' of 1970, Arafat's fighters set up in Lebanon, with their own police, factories and customs. They kidnapped and murdered Israeli athletes at the Munich Olympics in 1972; in 1974 the Arab League summit in Rabat proclaimed the PLO 'the sole legitimate representative of the Palestinian people'.

The following year saw the beginning of serious trouble in Lebanon. Arafat's fighters left Beirut in 1982; he set up a new headquarters in Tunis, only to be bombed by Israeli planes within two years. But his rhetoric could turn defeat into victory and his genius was to keep enough of the Palestinian cause together for enough of the time.

Fatah had more support in the Occupied Territories than any other group, but the Israelis would not negotiate unless he renounced terrorism. But if he was prepared to do so, other militants such as Abu Nidal, Ahmad Jabril, George Habash and Abul Abbas and their following were not. In 1988 Arafat publicly renounced terrorism and recognised the existence of Israel; and the Palestinian National Council declared the Palestinian government in exile, with the PLO at its head and Yasser Arafat as its first president. But still the Israeli government would not talk to him, and would only accept exploratory discussions with intermediaries of Palestinians not of the PLO.

Meanwhile the Intifada had burst into the open, in a manner which seemed to catch Chairman Arafat unawares. By late 1990 the *shebab* had found a new liberator for the Palestinian Arabs, Saddam Hussein of Iraq.

In September 1990, a month after Saddam Hussein's tanks had invaded Kuwait, our car was stopped south of Gaza City by a band of impromptu traffic cops. They wore black hoods and masks, and carried heavy meat cleavers. Another knot of vigilantes were spelling out with paint spray on a wall the message, 'The struggle in the Gulf is the fight against the American Crusader.'

These were the militants of the Islamic group Hamas which had been making steady ground since the Intifada broke out. Fatah was still the larger organisation and was the heart of the Unified Command, but in Gaza Hamas was gaining fast.

Hamas was disciplined and coherent, with an autonomous local leadership and an uncompromising message. The PLO and Fatah, on the other hand, were large and faction-ridden, their leader far away. Although Arafat had acknowledged the existence of Israel he then, true to form, endorsed Saddam Hussein's seizure of Kuwait, temporising by advocating a peaceful 'Arab solution'. This was no good for the *shebab*, who knew exactly what solution they wanted from their new hero, Saddam Hussein, whom they saw as Saladin come again. One Hamas supporter told me that Saddam would soon liberate Gaza and the West Bank.

The conflict between Fatah and the Islamic militants had been simmering for several years before it came into the open in 1990. In 1983 the battleground had been the Islamic University in Gaza, where more than 800 were injured in rioting and fighting. To begin with the militant Islamic force was Islamic Jihad, whose politics were modelled on Khomeini's programme for a wholly Islamic state even though most of its Palestinian supporters were Sunni. There is some evidence that the Israelis encouraged the religious groups as a way of reducing the hold of Arafat and Fatah.

Islamic Jihad continued to be influential, but was overtaken by Hamas, which had been founded in Gaza in 1986 by Sheikh Ahmed Yassin, a blind and half-crippled cleric with close links to the Ikhwan, the Muslim

Brotherhood. At first it was secret, but with the Intifada it began to issue some of the first calls to action. Once again it is possible that the Israelis allowed it to flourish in the early days to oppose Fatah.

One of Sheikh Yassin's first assistants was Dr Abd al Aziz al-Rantisi, a paediatrician who had led the final revolt against Fatah in the Islamic University, and had helped to found Hamas. When I met him in September 1990 he had just been released from thirty months of administrative detention and jail where he had shared a cell with Sheikh Yassin. We met in his home on the edge of the refugee camp at Raffah. The atmosphere was almost genteel as we sipped mint tea and made small talk on his chintz-covered furniture; yet only a few days earlier, just up the road in Raffah, Hamas *shebab* had beaten a woman to death for 'subversive prostitution'.

A round-faced man with close-clipped curly black hair, he wore a sports shirt, neatly pressed trousers, and a tie. He insisted on using Arabic, though his English was as good as his interpreter's. Saddam's confrontation with America, he said, 'had raised the people's morale here, and gives them hope they will return to their land.' He was not worried that Saddam previously had been hostile to Islam, for others had repented and become champions of the faith. He reserved some of his bitterest criticism for Fatah and the PLO. They had desecrated a mosque, kidnapped an Imam and attacked Hamas *shebab* 'while they were doing their duty against the Israeli occupation'. But the fundamental split with Fatah was on policy: 'Fatah wants recognition of the state of Israel, Hamas refuses it. Palestine is an Islamic land – nothing more.'

One of his supporters told me later that, 'if the PLO adopted Islam, it would be the beginning of the end for Israel.' Israel's policy of encouraging Islamic groups in the early Eighties now seems extraordinarily short-sighted, since it gave the Palestinian nationalists an even greater pool of support in the Arab and Muslim world to draw on.

Protests like the Intifada seem to develop their own dynamic. By the end of 1990 secular and religious militants in the Occupied Territories were talking more of resorting to arms to break the cycle of frustration that had gripped the Palestinians as the Intifada showed signs of waning; and that would provoke a retaliation from the Israelis, and further losses and privation.

As I left Gaza that September afternoon I came across some eight- and nine-year-old school children, in regulation government pinafores, hurling stones at a patrol of Israeli soldiers in a command post on an old apartment block. In keeping with the new low-profile policies ordered by the Defence Minister, Moshe Arens, they did not retaliate but laughed and joked with the children. The Intifada had become a game.

But it would not always be so. In early October 1990, on the Temple Mount, a holy site for Muslim, Jew and Christian, some twenty-one Palestinians were shot and killed and many more injured after sustained rioting and stone-throwing by the Wailing Wall. It was the bloodiest incident of the three years of protest and upheaval.

Once more the focus had turned to Jerusalem, the city of hope and despair for all who follow the three great religions of the Book.

iv Jerusalem

One Friday, at dusk, I approached the Wailing Wall in the Old City of Jerusalem. On the western wall of the Temple of Herod, destroyed by the Romans, Jews in prayer-shawls raised a steady murmur of prayer. As darkness fell, a clear, musical cry of 'Allah al Akbar', 'God is great' – the summons to prayer at the end of the day – burst from the minaret of the Al Aqsa Mosque. All down the valley minarets echoed the same cry, as if engaged in conversation. Looking skywards, I saw silhouetted against the roofs of the Jewish Quarter armed men with rifles and submachine-guns, keeping a wary eye on the Jews praying at the Wall.

Rising early next morning in the dark, the minarets were again chattering to each other; in the distance a peal of bells rang out at the Orthodox Patriarchate and at the Russian churches. It was their Christmas Day.

Jerusalem is the holy city of Jew, Muslim and Christian. For Jews it is Zion's City, where the Ark of the Covenant was carried up into the Temple of Solomon. For thousands of years the Jews of the diaspora yearned to return. 'If I forget thee, O Jerusalem, let my right hand forget her cunning,' wrote the Psalmist in exile in Babylon; 'Next year in Jerusalem,' was a favourite prayer of Jews for centuries. For Christians it was the highest object of earthly pilgrimage, the place where Christ had died for the sins of the world. And Muslims believe that, on the Temple Mount, the Prophet Mohammed was elevated into heaven on a white horse.

All three religions have dominated the city at different times. For four hundred years it languished under Ottoman rule, until General Allenby captured the citadel in 1917. In 1948 the city divided between the Israelis in the west and Jordan in the east. The Israelis built their parliament, the Knesset, on the western slopes; near it they raised the memorial of Yad

Vashem, recalling the six million Jews who died in the Nazi Holocaust.

In 1967 Israeli paratroops captured the eastern part, including the Old City, from Jordan's Arab Legion. The city was declared united once again, and the capital of Israel. But the annexation of East Jerusalem received no international recognition. The marriage of the two halves of the city has been frequently uneasy with rioting and violence during the Intifada.

Apart from the gleaming cupola of the Dome of the Rock, Jerusalem the Golden has given way to Jerusalem the Concrete. The city is surrounded by suburbs, like the concentric defences of a fortress, most built on land which belonged to Jordan before 1967. By the end of 1990 some 150,000 Jews were living in the suburbs of East Jerusalem, out of a total of about three-quarters of a million. The Israelis were trying to take and hold the city by numbers.

In the early nineteenth century Jerusalem was a sleepy and down-at-heel Ottoman provincial city. Travellers were put off by the squalor and stench of the Old City, within the Ottoman walls. The Jewish Quarter was near the slaughter-houses and the refuse-dump, by the appropriately named Dung Gate. A squeamish Karl Marx described his visit there in 1854:

> Nothing equals the misery and sufferings of the Jews at Jerusalem inhabiting the most filthy quarter of the town . . . where the synagogues are situated – the constant subject of Mussulman oppression and intolerance, insulted by the Greeks, persecuted by the Latins and living only upon the scanty alms transmitted by their European brethren.

A few years later Edward Lear struck the same note: 'physically Jerusalem is the foulest and odiousest place on earth.'

But help was at hand from Europe. This was the era of Protestant missionaries, of biblical scholars and archaeologists, of Jewish philanthropists, and organised travel. All were to have a vital role in rebuilding Jerusalem. In 1839 a young diplomat called William Tanner Young was appointed vice-consul, and became the first British representative in the city since the Crusades. He was to champion the Jews against the cruelties of Ottoman policing, and he encouraged missionaries, archaeologists and philanthropists to come. Other European powers, principally Russia and France, began to take an interest, and the row between them over the Holy Places helped to trigger the Crimean War. Christian missionaries brought schooling and hospitals. American missionaries founded their own colony, which served as a school and hospital until after the First

World War; today it is the American Colony Hotel, still owned by one of the founding families of the original community.

A relation of the American Colony dynasty was Gertrude Bell, the archaeologist and luminary of the British Palestine Exploration Fund; and with the archaeologists came the first modern commercial tour operators. Thomas Cook had a tented city outside the walls of the Old City, for the only place inside clean enough to stay was the Armenian convent, where the monks were criticised for being sleek and over-fed.

Of all the guests invited from England by Vice-Consul Young, the most celebrated was Sir Moses Montefiore, one of the greatest philanthropists Jerusalem was ever to see. A former Sheriff of the City of London, he had been knighted by Queen Victoria in the first year of her reign. He was President of the Board of Deputies of British Jews from 1838 to 1874, and he lived to see his hundredth birthday. In 1839 he made the first of five visits to Jerusalem, each time bringing funds and new projects – including a doctor – for the impoverished Jews there. He set up model manufacturing and farming projects, and built a windmill and artisans' cottages, which are still kept up as his memorial.

His greatest service in his first trips was to publicise the plight of the Jewish population of Palestine and their shameful treatment by the Ottomans. Vice-Consul Young's servant, a Jewish boy from Salonika, had been branded in the face and beaten till his flesh was in shreds. In 1840 an Italian friar and his Muslim servant disappeared in Damascus. The authorities rounded up seven Jews and accused them of murdering the two to obtain blood for their Passover ceremonies. The prisoners were tortured and their children arrested. Their case was raised by France and Britain with the Sultan in Istanbul. The prisoners were released, but some did not survive.

In 1840 an attempt was made to kill Queen Victoria and Prince Albert. When the news reached Jerusalem, the handful of British subjects sent a loyal address congratulating them on their survival. The leaders of both the Ashkenazim and Sephardim communities, possibly still under the influence of Montefiore's visit the year before, added their greeting and congratulation in Hebrew. Queen Victoria was seen as the friend of the Jews, and that year her Foreign Secretary, Lord Palmerston, had written to his ambassador in Istanbul that 'there was a strong notion among the Jews in Europe . . . that the Time is approaching when their Nation is to return to Palestine.' After the loyal address, Palmerston went one better, writing to the Sultan himself that he should make space for rich Jews and benefactors in the Ottoman dominions.

Travellers, philanthropists, consuls and scholars slowly established links between the Jews of Jerusalem and Europe and America. They were the harbingers of Zionism. By 1891 40,000 Jews were living in the city, as the first modern *aliyah* from Russia had already begun.

Israel's capture of East Jerusalem in 1967 has been traumatic for its Arab residents, according to George Hintlian, one of the shrewdest observers of local society. George is the Secretary to the Armenian Convent, a job held his father before him after fleeing Turkey. George is a natural gentleman, a scholar of the Old City, belonging to perhaps the oldest Christian community there. Like his friend Albert Aghazarian he speaks eight languages well, but prefers 'discussion' in English, the language of his studies in Beirut and the favourite tongue of his father. George is a genuine Mediterranean friend, generous, companionable, interested in ideas and a waster of many hours in the coffee shop or on strolls round the city, engaged in mildly conspiratorial chat.

According to George, the Arabs in East Jerusalem had to learn to work to a European or Western timetable, he said, instead of doing something only when it was necessary. The whole tradition of the long siesta was under threat now that they were expected to work to schedule in offices. They discovered Western commodities, and joined the video age, took a new, much less inhibited view of sex. 'No wonder they had so many heart attacks,' George comments.

But the traffic was not all one way. The rise of the Sephardim in Israeli society, and the switch of government from Labour to Begin's Likud in 1977, had produced subtle changes. Many institutions were becoming more eastern, more Mediterranean or Levantine in their approach. State offices employed twice as many officials as before, and did their business in twice the time and half as efficiently. It was all a matter of patronage with relations, friends and hangers-on much in evidence – much as they would be in Palermo or Piraeus.

If Jerusalem is the seat of Zion as reconstituted in the modern state of Israel, the nature and direction of that state is matter of hot debate. For insiders and outsiders, its identity remains a puzzle. Where does it fit in the Middle East? Does it belong to the Mediterranean or is it, as some critics maintain, a Northern European or North American island surrounded by a sea of Arabs?

In the summer of 1986 I asked a number of prominent figures in Jerusalem to give their views of Israel and its relations with the Arab neighbours. Two years later, as the state approached its 40th anniversary, I asked them if their views had changed. None gave exactly the same answer, but their mood was a good deal more sombre, for the Intifada was just getting into its stride.

Abba Eban was one of Israel's longest-serving Foreign Ministers, most notably in Mrs Golda Meir's administrations. Born in South Africa, he was educated in England and became Professor of Oriental Languages at Cambridge at a young age. He served with the British Army in the Second World War, and joined the Jewish Agency in 1946. He was a devoted follower of Chaim Weizmann, whom he quotes liberally in his conversation. One of his proudest moments was when he spoke success-fully for Israel's admission to the UN. His speech is beautifully con-sidered, ornamented with brilliant aphorisms, and his voice honks like a melodious if adenoidal clarinet.

He had no doubt that Israel was part of the Mediterranean. 'It means contact with the liberal values of the European Enlightenment. It stands for reason and the tradition of science – remember Weizmann was a scientist – and the non-Jewish element in our culture. Zionism is not a matter of Jewish piety.' The division by continents, the invention of Herodotus, he felt to be needlessly artificial. Israel's origins were in the old Judaic, Hellenistic, and Roman cultures.

The most urgent issue for Israel now was security. Israelis had been the victims of their spectacular victory in the Six Days' War. 'It was a poisoned chalice,' he explained, because it made peace impossible. The 1973 Yom Kippur War, on the other hand, was a more near-run thing, and did eventually lead to a peace settlement with Egypt. He was worried about the absence of a sustained policy towards the Occupied Territories, and was firmly against any proposal to annexe them.

I met Mr Eban again early in 1988. He thought the 40th anniversary would not be an occasion for joyful celebration. He described the predica-ment of the Palestinians in the territories as 'grotesque' as they were an occupied people with no representation, totally hostile to those who ruled them. He was against the tough physical tactics being deployed by his erstwhile colleague Mr Yitzhak Rabin, the Defence Minister. He did not care that a recent opinion poll had shown 69 per cent of Israelis to be in favour of such methods. 'That does not matter – 69 per cent of the Children of Israel were in favour of the Golden Calf of Aaron and against Moses and the Ten Commandments.'

Abba Eban told me that problems raised by the Intifada would have to be resolved within months, and not years. He was over-optimistic. Two years later it was still in full spate, and the new man in charge of security as Minister of Defence was Moshe Arens. A neat figure behind his large bureau, he seemed more like the senior executive of a powerful American business corporation than a minister – and was in fact a gradu-ate of the California Institute of Technology. A convinced member of

Menachem Begin's Likud bloc, his politics were driven by the memory of the Holocaust, and the need for maximum strategic security, and for Israel to remain firmly in the Western camp.

'I suppose you could say I am one of the original wandering Jews – my family came from Lithuania and Latvia originally,' he told me when we first met in 1986. He was briefly conscripted in the US forces, but by 1946 was working underground for Begin's Irgun in North Africa. 'It was three years after the Holocaust had been revealed, and I realised that this was the crucial hour of the Jewish People. I felt that British passivity had connived at the destruction of Jewry.'

The same hard-headed approach was to serve him after he entered politics in 1971. He insisted that Israel should keep all the strategic frontiers it had gained in successive wars, resigning as a minister rather than serve in a cabinet which had agreed to hand back Sinai in the peace agreement with Egypt of 1979. Three years later he was back as Defence Minister after Ariel Sharon was sacked following the official inquiry into the massacres at Sabra and Chatila. He was to serve as both Foreign Minister and Defence Minister in 1990, and began to be seen as a future prime minister and leader of Likud.

Moshe Arens believes that Israel is an island of Western culture in the Middle East, but that the Arabs would become increasingly westernised in their outlook and economies. Like Abba Eban, he did not think that militant Islam would present a big problem – reflecting, perhaps, their education in America and Britain rather than recent developments in the Levant.

A very different perspective on Israel and the Mediterranean was offered by another member of the Likud party, Eliahu Ben-Elissar. The descendant of an eminent Jewish family from Baghdad, he was Israel's first ambassador to Egypt after 1977. 'Of course Israel related to the Mediterranean and its heritage before the diaspora. But now I have some difficulty in defining us as a Mediterranean nation. Anyway, what is the Mediterranean today?' He found it hard to think of himself as related to a chattering Catalan or a conspiratorial Cretan. While he believed that the central Mediterranean, Italy and Greece, had made great contributions to civilisation, he felt as a Jew from Baghdad that the word 'Levantine' was always pejorative.

With his magnificent thick black beard Mr Ben-Elissar looks like an ancient patriarch, an intellectual warrior sure in his convictions. The first of these was that Israel was there to stay. He rejected any comparison with the Latin Crusader state, which barely lasted a hundred years in the twelfth century. 'We are not like the Crusaders because we are linked with the soil here, and unlike them we have real independence.' But like the Crusading knights he believed in strong defences. Israel must keep the Occupied Territories; it could offer local autonomy to the Arabs, but must reserve all control over defence and foreign policy.

The growing numbers and influence of Sephardic Jews like Eliahu Ben-Elissar helped propel Menachem Begin's Likud bloc to power in 1977. With the influx of Soviet Jewry, the balance was tilted once more towards the Ashkenazim; but unlike their predecessors from Russia, who backed Labour, the new arrivals have sided firmly with Likud and with even more extreme nationalists.

The orthodox religious parties were steadily growing in voice and numbers. After the November 1988 elections eighteen orthodox rabbis took seats in the Knesset; and in 1990 the third largest party in parliament, Shas, or the Sephardic Torah Guardians, became Lukud's principal coalition partner. Tortuous negotiations went on for weeks that summer to form the new government. At one point a crucial decision had to be taken by the leader of the strict Lubavitcher movement of the ultra-orthodox Hasidim sect, who lived in New York. As in the Arab communities, religion and politics were moving ever closer.

A member of an old Sephardim family, Meron Benvenisti has been a first-hand witness to the most dramatic days in Jerusalem's recent history, when he saw the Old City and East Jerusalem fall to Israeli soldiers in 1967. Later Teddy Kollek, the dynamic mayor of Jerusalem, appointed him deputy mayor, with special responsibility for East Jerusalem and for relations with the Arab community. As a local-born or *sabra*, he knew Arabic well. Three uncles from the Salonika ghetto perished in Auschwitz. The family had been set on its travels by the expulsion of the Jews from Spain in 1492. Some settled in Livorno in Italy, while the rest moved on to Salonika, whence his father had migrated in 1913. Meron once said that he felt the ejection of the family from Spain as sharply as if it was yesterday. He is a keen historian, with a penchant for the castles and architecture of the Crusades.

After four years he resigned from his post as deputy mayor to begin a careful study of the Occupied Territories which published invaluable and detailed statistical information. In time funds from the Ford Foundation dried up, and it proved impossible to continue after the Intifada broke out. Benvenisti himself became steeped in melancholia. 'I had hoped to make people aware of the cost what was going on,' he confesses, 'but the whole thing was futile. Historical forces were stronger than any of us, and we were moving inexorably to a situation I abhor.'

The victory of 1967, he explained, had posed Israel with 'the cruel dilemma'. He believed that 'Israel could not be the same Israel from the seventh day of the Six Days' war, and the change was more important and irreversible than the creation of the state of Israel itself. It meant that the Jewish state envisaged in 1948 could be no more.' He thought Zionism was becoming introspective, turning inwards to prepare its defences. He was particularly concerned about the abuse of civil rights in the Occupied Territories, and compared the plight of the Arabs to that of the Catholics in Northern Ireland – the subject of his doctoral thesis at Harvard.

When we met again in 1988, his mood of melancholy had slid into numb despair. He was appalled at the crude savagery on the streets of the West Bank and Gaza. He said he saw no grounds for optimism. He believed part of the Likud bloc, principally those led by Ariel Sharon, wanted to export the Palestinian problem physically by annexing the Occupied Territories and pushing as many Palestinians out as refugees; others, like Abba Eban, wanted to export the problem intellectually by saying the political rights and demands of the Palestinians should be the responsibility of Jordan. Neither was a solution. A year or so later, I heard Meron Benvenisti had retired altogether from public life.

The sense of sadness and loss had also struck his father, Dr Benvenisti told me in our meeting in 1986, but for a different reason. The old man, now well in his nineties, had just finished a dictionary showing the relationship between ancient Hebrew and the Ladino tongue – which had a framework of medieval Castilian but was depicted in Hebrew characters. By the time the book was completed, a task of many years, he realised Ladino, once the glory of Mediterranean Jewry, was virtually dead. 'He was pained by the end of Ladino,' said Meron, 'for my father it had been destroyed by modern Hebrew and the rise of secular Zionism.' The birth of the state of Israel was matched by a corresponding flight of Jews from the old centres and ghettos round the southern and eastern shores of the Mediterranean.

As an enthusiast of the architecture and artefacts of the Crusading era, Meron Benvenisti was also worried by what was being done to history in Israel, particularly the history that did not belong to the Jews. He had been particularly struck by the reaction to the discovery of the bones of a Jewish warrior of the Second Revolt against the Romans in 132 AD. 'They gave him a full military funeral. It was done in such a way as if it was to erase nearly 2000 years of diaspora. As if nothing had happened in the intervening years.'

The great clan of the al-Husseini have lived in Jerusalem for 600 years

– during most of which time the ancestors of most of those now living in West Jerusalem, and the politicians who take their seats in the Knesset, were scattered across the world. Today the clan is led by Faisal al-Husseini, the most persuasive of secular voice of the Arabs of the Occupied Territories. A tall, well-set man, with a high forehead, straight nose and subtle mouth, he sees himself as a militant, a soldier turned politician and an intellectual guide. His father was the Palestinians' military hero of the First Arab-Israeli War, Abdul Khadr al-Husseini, who died in the set-piece defence of Kastel on the heights above Jerusalem in 1948, and his fame is as great among Israeli soldiers of the time as among Arabs. His great-uncle was Hajj Amin al-Husseini, the Grand Mufti of Jerusalem and head of the militant Arab nationalist movement against the British mandate and the Jews, which led him to side with the Axis – a view his great-nephew totally discards.

Faisal is the man most likely to deliver an arrangement for Palestinian autonomy in the Occupied Territories, though he would prefer full statehood; he has the necessary charm, skill and force of personality. Many leading Israelis know this, though they are reluctant to admit it. A few talk to him direct, but in the past ten years or so he has spent more time under detention without trial, under house arrest, or in jail, than in freedom and his Fatah links make him a subversive. But in the traditions of the family he has become a counsellor and a guide to his community taking a seat on the *waqf*, the council of advisers for the Al Aqsa Mosque and the Haram Al-Sharif, the Noble Sanctuary, which also encloses the Dome of the Rock.

After some hesitation he agreed to see me in 1986. He was still under administrative detention in his house, and not allowed out at night, and it was the first time he had consented to be interviewed by a foreign journalist in years. He was formal, distant and polite – after all, I was from Britain, the enemy of his family for generations.

He had been born in 1940 in Baghdad, where the family had moved following the upheavals of the Arab Revolt of 1936–39. Part of his education was in Saudi Arabia and Egypt, and in 1964 he returned to Jerusalem. The year after he went to Syria and was trained as an officer in the Palestine Liberation Army in Aleppo. But then came the defeat of the Six Days' War, and Faisal chose a new course. 'I decided my duty was here under occupation, rather than as part of an army outside.'

His aim now was straightforward: recognition of Palestinian civil rights, and a state alongside Israel. In his tacit recognition of Israel, he seemed prepared to strike a braver and more conciliatory line than many of his old comrades in arms in Fatah. 'They will now have to give our people their rights, or Israel will have a dark future. The first step is to create a Palestinian state in the Gaza Strip and the West Bank – a Palestinian secular state fully achieved by peaceful means.'

The second stage was for the United States to support UN resolutions urging a peaceful settlement to the Arab-Israeli conflict, and not just those urging a return to the pre-1967 boundaries. The Israelis tend to reject most UN decisions as the work of their enemies, who can form an overwhelming majority with their supporters from the Third World, and they consider anyone associated with the PLO and Fatah to be tainted by terrorism. Faisal al-Husseini, on the other hand, has campaigned for a peaceful solution, though he believes time does not favour such an approach. The younger generation were becoming increasingly militant, and wanted complete independence.

I next saw Faisal in the autumn of 1990. The crisis in the Gulf had disturbed him. He did not think the seizure of Kuwait was right, and it had deflected attention from the Intifada. But if Saddam was to be condemned for Kuwait, then Israel should also be for holding on to the Occupied Territories. 'You cannot recommend war as the solution for one dispute, and peaceful dialogue for the other.' The peace camp in the Palestinian community was now beleaguered. 'We are in a jungle where Israel is the tiger. So you must find another tiger to limit the movements of the Israeli tiger – but not because you are in love with tigers.' He saw the new Likud coalition with the religious parties as more belligerent. His recent attempts at a dialogue between the Israeli peace movement and Palestinian intellectuals had been given a severe jolt by the Gulf crisis, and Arafat's open endorsement of Saddam. But he would stick to the belief that peaceful negotiation is the only reasonable course.

Our conversation was cut short so his aides could spirit him away before police surveillance became too intrusive. A fortnight later Faisal was again in administrative detention. He had been arrested two hours after the riots on the Temple Mount in which some twenty-one Palestinians were killed and more than 150 Palestinians and Israelis injured – he had gone there to discharge his duties as a member of the council of the mosque, the *waqf*. The Israelis said the incident had been provoked deliberately by Palestinians stoning worshippers at the Wailing Wall on the Jewish feast of Tabernacles. Palestinians were stirred up by the rumour that a group called the Temple Mount Faithful were going to make another attempt to place near the Al Aqsa a foundation stone for a Third Temple, from which they were banned by court order on a previous occasion. Once more the Old City of Jerusalem was becoming battleground of the Intifada.

'The problem is that the Israelis wanted a land without people, and the Palestinians are a people without a land,' was how Albert Aghazarian had described the causes of the Intifada. 'Now the invisible Palestinian has stood up.' Albert's home must have been one of the most beautiful apartments in the Christian and Armenian Quarters of the Old City. It seemed to be carved into the very walls of the place, with deep rooms and shadowy alcoves, snug in winter and mercifully cool in summer. From the roof the view was spectacular – domes, spires and minarets. But Albert had recently decided to take an apartment in the Armenian Convent. The Old City was a changed and less friendly place.

As one walks across its roofs and down the broad alleys carved like sewers through the souk, Old Jerusalem is a remarkably difficult city to read. Pilgrim and tourist routes to the Via Dolorosa, the Temple Mount and the Western Wall are well signposted, but whether a particular building is Roman, Jewish, Crusader or Ottoman is far from clear. The Holy Sepulchre, the site of Christ's Passion, is a giant nest of architectural egg-boxes locked together like a child's three-dimensional puzzle. The disputes between its various custodians, Franciscan, Greek Orthodox, Armenian, Copt and Ethiopian, are notorious. Some monuments seem only lightly anchored to their foundations – the church of the Byzantine Empress Helen seems to have moved several metres over the centuries according to accounts by different chroniclers. The same fate has overtaken some of the walls of the Roman city, as far as Albert could make out.

His biggest worry was the slow erosion of the Christian and Muslim Quarters in the Old City. In ten years the Christian population had dropped from 14,000 to 8,000. Jewish activists were acquiring more property throughout the Old City; archaeological digs were severely curtailed on the grounds that they could impinge on a sacred Jewish site. Groups of students were acquiring rooms and apartments for *yeshiva*, Hebrew religious schools – part of a plan to make Old Jerusalem increasingly Jewish, according to their opponents.

Matters came to head in a test case over a property claimed by the Greek Orthodox Patriarchate. Jewish activists said they had acquired the lease legitimately from an Armenian through an offshore company in Panama. It was a typically tangled tale of Old Jerusalem, where most communities are in dispute with another over something. The case of St John's Hospice, as run-down an establishment as you could hope to find, dragged on for weeks. At one point the Israeli court said the Greek Orthodox Patriarch was unfit to plead his cause because he did not have a valid Israeli work permit.

In the byways and courtyards of the Old City you can stray into vanished worlds. One of the largest, oldest, and most colourful is the Armenian Convent of St James, which has existed for a millenium and a half at least. It covers more than twenty-five acres, a series of courts, chapels, dormitories and apartments. Long balconies are festooned with purple wisteria and bright geraniums; yards of friendly uneven stone are gently stroked by trails of acacia. In the museum the photographs of one of the nineteenth-century Partriarchs are proudly displayed; he was in fact one of the pioneers of the camera in Jerusalem. Benefits of modern invention were rare in those days, and conditions were far from salubrious. In the archive, George Hintlian, the Community's Secretary, found the record of eleven marriages celebrated in the Cathedral in 1869. Within a year nine of the brides had died in childbirth. 'They didn't understand anything about controlling excess fluid in the body, principally albumen, let alone manage to control it,' he explained.

The library holds precious manuscripts from the medieval kingdom of Cilicia in Asia Minor. Glorious gospel illuminations and marginalia of the time of St Gregory the Illuminator and his successors who depicted birds and beasts, saints and martyrs in deep and sumptuous blues, subtle browns and reds, and the perennial dark greens. The tradition was to enrich the craft of ceramic and pottery, and contribute to the glory of Iznik tiling of the Ottomans. The manuscripts have brought the Convent its spot of bother, too. A few years ago some of them fetched up for auction at Sotheby's in London. They had been smuggled out by an unscrupulous cleric, and it took some neat detective work by the administration to get them back.

Old hurts, and the sense of lost nationhood, lurk in the shadows. The youth clubs still follow the banners of the three political parties at the time of the Armenian nationalist movement of 1891, and schoolchildren chant and stamp to the anthems of the Dashnaks, the most militantly romantic of the parties. On the walls of the club, the library and the corridors are recurring views of Ararat, the sacred mountain.

One morning George invited me into the chapel where an old servant of the community, who had died in his eighties, had been laid out in his coffin. The man, said George, had been a refugee when the Turks expelled the Armenians from their villages in 1915, in what the Armenians refer to as 'the massacres'. The symbol of Turkish persecution is an essential part of the Armenians' identity, referred to constantly in their literature, Turkish journalists who have visited the convent with trepidation, have implied it is a tale that is little more than an excuse for terrorism.

Today there are just over 2000 Armenians in the Convent community, which is a village in itself. It is one of the oldest Christian institutions in the Middle East – the first Armenians came to Jerusalem in the armies of the later Roman Empire, conscripts of Byzantium. Other churches in Jerusalem have rituals older even that the Christian Gospel.

One chilly evening in September I followed a procession to a roof near the Holy Sepulchre, where the Ethopians were celebrating the festival of Maskal – the discovery of the True Cross by St Helen. It began with some splendid chanting by the Archbishop – a bearded figure in sumptuous red robes and a tiara, seated on a chair beneath the fronds of an acacia tree – and his priests, monks and bishops, their rich baritone rumblings punctuated with shrill ululations from the congregation. The principals leaned on thin prayer sticks, ebony canes with silver rams' horn tops. As the chanting became urgent and more rhythmical, the chorus started shaking finely-tooled metal rattles – the *cistras*, sounded by the Israelites at the dedication of the Ark of the Covenant. Finally a deep leather drum signalled a processional dance in a broad circle round the yard. As the dancers wove their way round the yard, a priest lit three braziers of wood on a wall – the symbol of the equinox, a pagan ritual like bonfires at Easter, bringing Ethiopia the promise of the season of rain, and new fertility.

From a high window above, a group of Egyptian Copts looked on. Once they had bombarded the Ethiopians with rocks because they believed they had taken Coptic territory in the Holy Sepulchre.

The coincidences and crossings of history are among the great gifts and joys of the Mediterranean and the Middle East. But for many today shared traditions and cultures are anathema. Parties, sects, and nations increasingly see the past, their past, as exclusive, as a licence not to conform to the norms of good behaviour. History is no longer the great dialogue invented by Herodotus and the authors of the Books of Moses. It can be suspended in the interest of a particular cause, for private justification. One the greatest inventions of the Mediterranean, the universal endeavour to record and understand its peoples – all peoples – and their past, has become debased into propaganda and self-promotion. Peoples whose culture, heritage and faith are rooted in the same lands are left with little more than mutual intolerance. Nowhere is this dilemma more acutely etched than in the conflict between the Muslims and the Jews, the Arabs and the Israelis.

'Whatever you do, don't predict,' said George Hintlian one day. 'It's not your job. Who can say what the future holds for the Palestinians or the Armenians. Will the Palestinians become the Armenians of the Arab world – a people destined to be without a state? Who can say what the future is for Israel? It is all too complicated and uncertain to guess.' On several of our walks George took me to a simple house with a courtyard full of junk, a modest enough abode, a stone's throw (if that is the appropriate expression in the days of Intifada) from the Damascus Gate. In one of the rooms a mosaic floor is laid out like a carpet. It shows a tree, its branches laden with fowls of the air and fruit of the earth – pomegranates, grapes, cherries, peacocks, songbirds in cages, and eagles. In the iconographic code of the sixty century AD they symbolise the Passion of Christ, and His redemption of the world. At its head is a simple inscription in Armenian characters: 'This is in memory for the salvation of all Armenians whose name the Lord knows.' It is the memorial to the unknown soldiers scattered through the empire of Justinian and his heirs.

Promise and salvation for one people and one faith often mean diaspora and despair for another; the law of perpetual motion of the people of the Inner Sea.

Fourteen: Painting the Bridge – An Open Conclusion

In his mosaic portrait in San Vitale in Ravenna the Emperor Justinian appears an almost homely figure. He looks startled, as if he has just been disturbed from an afternoon siesta, with a hint of five o'clock shadow about his chin. The Empress Theodora, stone-faced and haughty, is a much tougher proposition; her stare would brook no opposition. The bleary and bewildered Justinian is hardly the icon of a hate-figure; he seems too private and withdrawn for that. The image belies the fact that he became a monster to many of his subjects, not least after the slaughter of 30,000 in the Hippodrome of Constantinople in the Nika riots of 532 AD.

The demon figure whose image became familiar in every household in the Mediterranean and beyond in 1990 was that of Saddam Hussein, Life President of Ba'athist Iraq, and by his own confession the Nebuchadnezzar of the new Babylon. His invasion and seizure of Kuwait on 2 August 1990 came as a profound shock to the international community. It should not have had this effect because Saddam had given ample notice that he would play the role of Macbeth of Mesopotamia, capable of violent and bloody action and with megalomaniac claims to dominate the family of Arab peoples. In his twenty years of running his regime in Baghdad, he had killed leading Shi'ite clerics, massacred the Kurds, carried war to Iran for eight fruitless years, causing the death and maiming of more than a million people. He had built up an army of more than a million men out of a population of eighteen million, and armed it with 5,500 tanks, a force bigger than NATO's European allies could assemble. In the year before his smash and grab seizure of Kuwait he had become almost carelessly provocative. He hanged a British-based journalist, resisting all appeals for mercy, was caught smuggling parts for nuclear weapons and missiles from California, and was revealed to be assembling huge machines and tubes for a so-called 'super gun'. The gun project infuriated his powerful neighbour, Turkey, whom he provoked further in a row about the headwaters of the Euphrates. Behind the posturing were signs of increasing desperation as the war with Iran had left Baghdad in debt to the rough extent of $100 billion. Each time the price of oil dropped by a dollar per barrel Iraq lost a billion dollars of export earnings. Saddam accused Arab neighbours in the Gulf, Kuwait particularly, of deliberately undermining the world oil price system by exceeding production quotas laid down by OPEC. He told the Kuwaitis that he regarded their actions as equivalent to waging war, and he would reply in kind. They ignored this rhetoric. Too late they realised that the chest-beating was not bluff.

Saddam's move into Kuwait meant a renewal of the ancient clash between Mesopotamia, the land of the Tigris and Euphrates, and Egypt, the land of the Nile. Furthermore it shifted and broadened the focus of the Middle East crisis from the Arab-Israeli conflict and the plight of the Palestinians. The full consequences for the eastern Mediterranean, and the Inner Sea as a whole, are yet to be seen.

The changes for the peoples of the Inner Sea at the end of the decade of the 1980s, during which most of the travels in this book were undertaken, have been sudden and dramatic. A few were foreseen, but some were quite unexpected, not least in their seismic scale. No book like this can claim completeness. It is rather like repairing or painting a grand bridge like the Golden Gate or the Forth rail bridge – no sooner do you reach the end than you need to start all over again. Conclusions have to be tentative – after all it is not, nor should it be, in the job description of a reporter to be a prophet. Having made these disclaimers, I have to admit that, as I witnessed its changes in my travels, my perception of the Mediterranean altered sharply.

It might be diverting and illuminating to list some developments in the Inner Sea since my journeys described in this book. They might give a clue as to what might be about to come.

The Kuwait crisis took British land forces once more east of Suez to the Gulf and the Kurdish lands in northern Iraq – a strategem London had renounced in 1967. It pitted Syria, a Ba'athist regime, against another in the Arab world, Iraq, and it brought Syria into alliance with America. This was not enough, however, to earn the Damascus regime most-favoured-nation status with Washington, nor did the State Department remove it from the list of those it considered sponsors of international terrorism. During the actual war in the Gulf Israel was attacked by the Scud missiles of Saddam's Iraq, and for the first time did not retaliate against Arab aggression.

Elsewhere in the Middle East, an agreement was patched up at Taif in Saudi Arabia to end the civil war in Lebanon. It worked better than any could have dared hope at the time. The green line that partitioned Beirut was dismantled, Christian, Druze and Amal Shi'ite militias agreed to lay down arms and withdraw from the capital.

In 1990 the three countries of the Maghreb became more Islamic in their politics – and this was foreshadowed in my travels. Tunisia unexpectedly cracked down and detained some members of the Islamic Tendency, echoing the authoritarian ways of Bourguiba's despotism. Algiria, too, in 1991 took heavy measures against IFS fundamentalists.

In 1990 Constantine Karamanlis, born a subject of the Ottoman Empire, was re-elected President of Greece, but with diminished powers from his previous incumbency. He was eighty-four. In Turkey a few months before, in October 1989, Turgut Ozal assumed the presidency, and became the most dominant civilian figure in the modern Turkish Republic since Kemal Ataturk.

In the former provinces of the Ottomans in the Balkans, the Federation of Yugoslavia became unstitched and torn by civil war – a process I found well begun when I passed down the Dalmatian coast in the spring of 1985. Albania, too, was caught in the wind of *glasnost*, and suffered the bout of rioting and killing which spread throughout eastern Europe as the gospel of Marx and Lenin withered on the ideological vine. Albania became a multi-party state but somehow the Communists, who, for convenience took to flying the colours of nationalism to conceal past misdemeanour, managed to cling on to power.

Two other important developments caught my eye at the beginning of 1991. They were unrelated to the storm caused by Saddam and Iraq, though it was while reporting that crisis that I heard of them. I was standing by some British Challenger tanks in the wastes of the Saudi and Iraqi desert when I heard on my short-wave radio that Michele Greco, once alleged to be the Boss of Bosses, and the 'Pope' of the Sicilian Mafia, had been released from jail and was allowed to return to his estates near Corleone. The appeal court had failed to meet the deadline to hear his appeal against the sentences for murder and extortion given him three years previously in the 'maxi-trial' of Palermo. As President Cossiga, the titular head of the Italian judiciary, had hinted, substantial parts of the law in Italy and Sicily were in thrall to the Mafia underworld. The parallel power of criminal clans and syndicates, which I had encountered more than a few times in my travels, shows every sign of growing in influence and political muscle.

When I called at the UN's regional centre for oil pollution in Malta in 1986, the scientists were drawing quiet comfort from the fact that the Mediterranean had seen as yet no major oil pollution from a shipping accident on the scale of the *Torrey Canyon*, and the *Amoco Cadiz* in the Atlantic. Nor by 1990 had it seen anything to match the grounding of the *Exxon Valdez* in Alaska the previous March – the worse ecological disaster to date caused by a tanker wreck. Perhaps I should have forgotten about the scientist's claim, and should not have mentioned it. In April 1991 the 109,000-ton tanker *Cypriot Haven* caught fire, exploded and sank in the Gulf of Genoa with a cargo of almost 100,000 tonnes of crude aboard. It was feared worse disaster threatened than that caused by the *Exxon Valdez* because of the shallow and constricted formation of the western basin of the Inner Sea. But luck was on the side of the vigorous rescue and salvage operation organised by the Italians. As the hulk settled on the seabed, most of the remaining cargo, more than 40,000 tonnes of crude, began to coagulate into a solid lump – making it easy to extract and dispose of. The whole episode was a warning that it is likely to be only a matter of time before a serious tanker accident does occur, as the Mediterranean remains one of the busiest of the world's waterways.

The crisis provoked by Saddam in the Gulf made the autumn of 1990 a bad time for prediction and prophecy, though it did not deter politicians and journalists the world over from offering their prognostications. Some saw the impending conflict in the gory hues of the apocalypse. The appearance of American, French and British forces in Saudi Arabia, the land of the two Holy Mosques of Islam, was described as a return of the Crusaders, and the allies were told by their enemies to expect the same fate as the short-lived Latin Kingdom of Jerusalem in the twelfth century – a clear case of history subverted by fantasy. The scribblers and sages of Washington and Whitehall should have heeded the advice of my Armenian friend George Hintlian, who declared in the autumn of 1990 that he could hardly predict what would happen in Jerusalem next week, let alone in the next decade.

Yet it was during my sojourn in Jerusalem in September 1990 that I was given the most interesting prognosis for future conflicts in and about the Inner Sea and the Levant. As the F-16 Falcon fighter-bombers of the Israeli Air Force whined and boomed across the bare landscape of the plateau of Judea and Samaria and the Jordan Valley, I took the road to Mount Scopus and the Hebrew University to meet Martin van Creveld, Professor of Military History. As a writer on all aspects of military affairs he has won opprobrium as much as honour in his land of adoption, Israel.

When we met, he said he thought full-scale war between the American and Saudi allies and Saddam was probable. 'Listen to the jets, they are more active over the Jordan than ever today – till a week ago they were quiet.' But he wondered whether the American action might leave the Middle East in as serious a mess, or worse, than before. After all, he argued, the threat of Saddam to the oilfields of Saudi Arabia had already been contained, and perhaps the best course now was to use boycott and sanctions to squeeze the economy of Iraq and the Ba'athist regime in Baghdad, which was now bankrupt.

Martin van Creveld's argument was no mere thing of the moment, but the results of research for a new book in which he suggests that the very nature of war and warfare is changing fundamentally, and in a way that advanced industrialised nations will find hard to control. He believes, he told me, that the superpowers and their wealthier allies, like Britain and France, are beginning to lack the social, political, and economic wherewithal to go to war, especially against nations and armed forces of the first rank. If this is so, then the leading international powers will not be able to resort automatically to arms or the projection of military power to support their foreign policy.

Some critics have countered that the 'Desert Storm' campaign disproves the theory. But in many ways the six weeks of bombing and hundred hours of land advance into Kuwait proves Martin van Creveld's contention. It was an attack by a First World power on a Third World power, and then the Third World power hardly fought at all. Saddam did not use his air force, and much of his front line forces pulled back from Kuwait and southern Iraq before the allied tanks arrived. Ever the master of paranoia, he kept his best tanks and helicopter gunships and the chemical weapons to be turned on his own people, the Shi'ites in the south and the Kurds in the north.

Wars, according to van Creveld, will be waged less by governments and armies supported by the people (the 'trinity' of constituents of modern warfare depicted by the Prussian strategist von Clausewitz), and will be waged more by the people *among* the people. The most important social development in warfare in the Second World War, according to von Creveld's thesis, is the innovation of the guerrilla or resistance army, which operates as a law unto itself and outside the direct, formal control of government. In the Middle East particularly, van Creveld conjectures, we might see the rise of a new breed of warlord, a contemporary version of the Italian *condottiero* of the late Middle Ages. The process had already begun in Lebanon which was largely run by militias. In Israel itself, he said, each of the major Jewish settlements of the West Bank now had its own armed militia beyond the control of government, the state police and army.

Some would like to dismiss these as the views of a crank, but I find they coincide in two vital respects with my conclusions about changes in the Mediterranean in the last years of this century. The conflicts in the Mediterranean in the 1970s stemmed largely from the ideological clash of the Cold War and the immediate post-colonial experience in the area. The Eighties saw the turn of the religious fanatics and extremists, the assassins of Anwar Sadat, the rise of Hizbollah in Lebanon and Hamas in Gaza and the West Bank. The frictions in the Mediterranean neighbourhood of the 1990s are likely to be generated by the sheer weight of numbers, the growth and movement of populations.

The expansion of mafia and clan organisms, parallel powers beyond the grasp of public authority and state, and the burgeoning populations of the eastern and southern shores, make the rise of the new militias and warlords the more likely. It is not now just the multiplication and breeding in itself that is the significant human feature of the Mediterranean, but the movement of peoples across it.

In the late spring of 1991 I stood on a mountain pass between Iraq and Turkey. Through the pouring rain families of Kurds, driven northward by Saddam's helicopter gunships a few weeks before, were making the long and weary walk home. The flight of the Kurds, some three million of them surging towards Iran and Turkey, had been one of the biggest refugee migrations in history. Historically and geographically the Kurds are an inconvenient people. Over the centuries they have been jammed into the mountains by invaders and raiders, the forgers of the great empires of the Hittites, the Persians, the Greeks, Romans and Ottomans. The Kurds themselves like to say they are the descendants of the ancient Medes, and they have no friends now but the mountains. On that mountain plateau I met a boy who had the aquiline profile of a warrior in a frieze of ancient Assyria.

In that solemn procession the women and girls were most prominent, as many of the men had gone to join the councils of war of the Pesh Merga guerrillas or to reconnoitre their homes in the valley to see if it was safe to return. Girls of ten, carrying younger sisters on their backs, splashed barefoot through the mountain mud. Of the mothers, nearly every one was pregnant or carried an infant at the breast. The gaudy, billowing bodices and dresses were the visible signs of a huge population explosion. According to official statistics the Kurds number roughly twenty-five million, spread across the borders of Turkey, Iraq, Iran, Syria and the Soviet Union. In Turkey they were until recently referred to as 'mountain Turks' and official use of the Kurdish language was restricted, though during the Gulf crisis this was relaxed. The official Turkish estimate of their Kurdish population is roughly ten million, though it may well be more, and nearly a fifth of the total population of Turkey today.

From the shores of the Mediterranean round Mersin and Adana to Turkey's mountain borders to the east with Iran, the fields are dotted with the brilliant headscarves and dresses of the Kurdish women and the bright sashes and turbans of the Kurdish men.

As the people of the Asian and African shores of the Inner Sea have multiplied, they have begun to move. The shift from south to north and east to west became dramatically visible in the closing years of the Eighties. Africans began to ply the streets of Athens, Barcelona, Milan, Genoa, Rome, for work or selling cheap clothes and accessories. Italy has become in a few years a country of immigration, whereas it had always been one of emigration. In the Foreign Ministry in Rome the official in charge of immigration policy now occupies the offices of the Councillor for Emigration, who in 1913 alone supervised the departure of 800,000 Italians to seek a new life abroad. In Italy racial conflict has arisen with the new arrivals from the Maghreb and West Africa in the most unlikely places, such as Florence and Piombino, the port for the ferry to Elba. Marseille has always had quarters more Arab than European, and now the same is happening in whole suburbs of Paris. Clermont-Ferrand, home of one of the big Renault motor works, and even provincial Narbonne, have seen strife between the migrants and older residents.

The presence of migrants and visitors from the south in the cities of the northern Mediterranean and beyond in Europe is likely to increase. As populations in the south and east grow, in many parts of the north they are shrinking, and in some imploding. The native populace of mainland Greece, northern Italy, southern France and much of northern Spain in the early 1990s is contracting. The census of 1991 recorded that Italy had more residents over the age of sixty than under twenty. On the European littoral of the Inner Sea, only Albania was growing, and that with an unsteady surge of population explosion. Farther north Britain appeared the exception in showing signs of growth, possibly because of the vigorous migrant communities from the Caribbean and Asia; for the first time in the UK the census of 1991 included questions about ethnic origin.

For years the city of Parma in the Plain of Emilia has regularly headed the Italian statistics of the city with the highest quality of life. It is a community proud of its status as an international power in the eighteenth century under the Farnese dukes. The cobbled streets and squares are still those described by Stendhal, and once frequented by the young Verdi. Prosperity comes from cheese and ham as finely textured and matured as the wines of Bordeaux and Burgundy, and from the biggest spaghetti and yoghurt-making factories in Europe. In 1990 the city and province had more jobs on offer than people to fill them. This is the cloud on the horizon for the future. Fewer Parmigiani are being born each year. By 1990 the average family had one or two children under twelve, and many couples were putting off having children until they were in their thirties. On the demographic trend of 1990 a municipality of 175,000 was likely to be reduced by the year 2050 to 35,000, the population of a large village.

Yet I cannot believe the spirit of Parma is doomed. Each evening in the summer the youth celebrate the beauty and wonder of their city. They descend on the Piazza Garibaldi with its huge clock on the ochre walls gilded by the sinking sun, and take coffee and ice cream, cool drinks and pistachio nuts at the bars and cafés. They flit and glide on bicycles through the arches and alleys, like young swallows in spring. You can cross the old city in five minutes by bike, and Parma has more bikes than the whole of Amsterdam. The favourite home-grown model is the Wanda, a dignified sit-up-and-beg machine which first wheeled these streets before the First World War. Parmigiani are content, a little smug even, to be themselves, secure in their own world of gentle culture and gossip. If this seems insubstantial, it can be set down in print in the *Gazzetta di Parma*, circulation a steady 50,000 plus – the oldest daily newspaper in Europe and the most profitable provincial daily in all Italy.

'I think you can say we really are a bit too provincial – we get caught up in our sense of *parmigianitá*,' declares Andrea Borri, who first represented the city in the Chamber of Deputies in Rome in 1976. His family has lived in Parma since the fourteenth century, and in the old centre a small street bears the name of a noble ancestor. The local brand of self-satisfaction and chauvinism has on occasion driven him to distraction, confessed Andrea Borri, 'but I think it conceals the source of our strength. The size and scale of the city and the community means we live life in a human dimension (*una dimensione umana*).' Life in the 'human dimension' should be the epigraph of success of the Mediterranean world ancient and modern.

With the movement of peoples from the southern shores into the north, and the need for their work and skills there, the Mediterranean is now becoming an integral part of Europe itself. No longer can it be dismissed as Europe's inconvenient annexe, part of the precarious passage to India, or the sun patio for occasional and casual use by northern hedonists and tourists. The new Mediterraneans and Mediterranean ways are firmly with us.

Index